Although the Restoration of Charles II in 1660 ended the Puritans' predominance, it did not terminate their activity in parliamentary politics or their adherence to parliamentarian constitutional conceptions. Nor did it end moderate Puritan hopes that the Church of England might be modified sufficiently to make it fully acceptable. Since this did not happen at the Restoration, most moderate Puritans became Dissenters and resorted to earlier practices of occasional and partial conformity. This made it possible for them to sit in Parliament, and approximately one hundred Presbyterians and Congregationalists did so at some time during the years 1661-1689. The more extreme Puritans who remained rigid in their dissent and therefore legally restricted in their political activity were nevertheless active on the hustings and in lobbying, petitioning, and pamphleteering.

The primary focus of this book is upon the politics of the moderate Dissenters who sat in ᴵᵘᵗᶦᵒⁿ, and from the Restoration to the Revolution of 1688 they worked to obtain a government essentially consistent with conceptions expressed by moderate Puritan parliamentarians in the 1640's.

\* \* \* \*

"This is a substantial work, which will be indispensable to those seeking a full understanding of the religious and political history of the generation following the Restoration of Charles II. . . . The tone is judicious throughout . . . [and] the work shows a knowledge of Restoration England that is both wide and deep. . . . The style is lucid and fluent. . . . This is a sophisticated work of real value."

William L. Sachse
Professor of History
The University of Wisconsin

"The surprising conclusion that emerges . . . is the degree of impact made by the Presbyterian bloc—far out of proportion to its numbers. . . . [This] study is painstaking in the research, solid in the narrative and conclusions. It is a valuable addition to the painfully meager list of works on the politico-religious history of the later Stuarts."

Robert Walcott
Professor of History
The College of Wooster

*Dissent and*
*Parliamentary Politics*
*in England,*
*1661–1689*

Charles II and the Parliamentarians
An explanation of this print appears on page vi

# Dissent and Parliamentary Politics in England, *1661–1689*

A STUDY IN THE PERPETUATION
AND TEMPERING OF PARLIAMENTARIANISM

DOUGLAS R. LACEY

RUTGERS UNIVERSITY PRESS
*New Brunswick, New Jersey*

Copyright © 1969 by Rutgers University,
the State University of New Jersey
Library of Congress Catalogue Card Number:
75-75678
SBN: 8135-0594-1

Manufactured in the United States of America
by Quinn & Boden Company, Inc.,
Rahway, New Jersey

*To M.M.L.*

# A NOTE ON THE FRONTISPIECE

The frontispiece is a composite print of Parliament, combining separate drawings of the House of Lords and the House of Commons. The original version was made in 1640 and depicted Charles I—identifiable by his characteristic beard—seated on the throne before the Lords. That same year the future Charles II first encountered the parliamentarians and Puritans in the two Houses, for at the opening of the Short Parliament on April 13, he took his seat to the right of the throne as Prince of Wales at the age of ten, and he was also there for the opening ceremonies of the Long Parliament on November 3. The version of the print reproduced here is an altered one made after 1660 by an artist who found it convenient merely to change the head of the King. Although not a very good likeness, it is now clearly Charles II without a beard who sits on the throne, and at the same time he is also still seated alongside as the Prince just as in 1640. The restored King is obviously pleased. Only in his memory were there as many parliamentarians and Puritans before him as here depicted. Yet neither Charles nor his brother James II was to be free of them, for as Dissenters they continued to confront the Crown with their parliamentarianism during the three decades ending with the Revolution of 1688.

The altered print was discovered by J. A. Gere, Deputy Keeper of Prints and Drawings, the British Museum. A reproduction of the original version may be found in *The Past We Share: An Illustrated History of the British and American Peoples,* edited by Peter Quennell and Alan Hodge (London, 1960), p. 94.

## ACKNOWLEDGMENTS

For stimulating an early interest in the development of representative and responsible government in England, I have long been indebted to the late Professors R. L. Schuyler and J. B. Brebner of Columbia University, each of whom was generous in his friendly encouragement. Of the many who have been of help only Professor R. W. Greaves has seen this work develop from its early stages during a year at the Institute of Historical Research, University of London. His lively questioning, wise counseling, and long interest have been deeply appreciated. Dr. Richard Schlatter, Provost of Rutgers University, and Professor Charles F. Mullett of the University of Missouri have also been of much influence. Each of them has given invaluable advice and support, for which I express my gratitude.

Of those who have read considerable portions of the manuscript and offered most helpful comments and suggestions I am particularly indebted to Professor R. K. Webb of Columbia University, Professor Sidney A. Burrell of Boston University, Professor David Underdown of Brown University, Professor Raymond T. Stearns of the University of Illinois, and Professor Gerald R. Cragg of Andover Newton Theological School. In helping with biographical problems concerning the members of Parliament, Professor B. D. Henning of Yale University has been very generous, and I am most grateful to him for his friendly assistance.

Others whose research has been in related fields have also been of much help, and I should particularly like to acknowledge the value of information received from Dr. Henry Horwitz of the University of Iowa, Dr. Arthur G. Smith of Chatham College,

Dr. W. A. Hayden Schilling of the College of Wooster, and Dr. Mary Whittaker Helms, formerly of Bryn Mawr College. In addition I thank Professor Charles R. Michaud of the United States Naval Academy for his help with the fine points of seventeenth-century French.

Librarians and their staffs everywhere have been most cooperative, but I must express special appreciation to the Rev. Roger Thomas, former Librarian of the Dr. Williams's Library in London, and to his assistants, as well as to the staffs of the Folger Library and the Library of Congress.

For permitting use of manuscripts in their possession I am grateful to the Duke of Portland, the Duke of Devonshire and the Trustees of the Chatsworth Settlement, and Lord Brabourne. The initial research for this book was made possible by a Rockefeller Foundation Postwar Fellowship in the Humanities, and its completion was facilitated by a grant from the United States Naval Academy Research Council.

To the late Professor Joe Patterson Smith of Illinois College I shall always be deeply grateful for arousing my interest in British history and for a long friendship and continued encouragement. Finally, for the year and more of exacting work involved in deciphering a seventeenth-century system of shorthand used in one of the major manuscript sources I shall be forever thankful to my father, the late Dean Raymond H. Lacey, Illinois College.

D. R. L.

## NOTE ON DATES AND STYLE

Dates are given according to the Old Style or Julian calendar, but the beginning of the year is considered to have been January 1 rather than March 25. Letters and dispatches written by foreign ambassadors in England or by persons on the Continent bear the date the writer gave them, which is in accordance with the New Style or Gregorian calendar. When it is either necessary or convenient in order to follow the chronology, dates are given according to both calendars or with the abbreviations N.S. or O.S. in order to make clear the calendar being used.

Contractions and unusual abbreviations or forms have been eliminated within English quotations, and spelling has been modernized in accordance with the American usage except in titles of published works.

# CONTENTS

*Introduction*

The Restoration seemed to bring complete catastrophe to the Puritans. But they survived and became resurgent. As Dissenters from the restored Anglican Church they faced prosecution for religious nonconformity which was almost always imminent and frequently was stringent. Yet many continued to worship together, and at times they enjoyed periods of governmental indifference or permissiveness when the laws were relatively unenforced or completely suspended. Similarly, they were deprived of almost all political power by the elections and legislation of 1661. However, those who followed the tradition of moderate Puritanism and conformed partially and occasionally to the Established Church were able to remain active in the political life of the nation, while those who were strict Nonconformists found other ways in which to become politically effective.

The parliamentarian conceptions of government to which the more moderate Puritans adhered during the Civil Wars continued to have strong appeal at the Restoration. As a result of this traditional parliamentarianism and also as a consequence of the tempering effect of their experiences between the Restoration and the Revolution of 1688, the main current of the Dissenters' politics shifted away from Leveller and Cromwellian channels and returned to that of the earlier parliamentarians who had submitted the Nineteen Propositions to Charles I in 1642, and who sought his acceptance of the more moderate Isle of Wight Proposals in 1648.[1] In many respects the majority of Dissenters became more conservative in their tactics and aims than the original parliamentarians. Rather than use revolutionary action, most Restoration Dissenters turned to parliamentary politics in their efforts to limit the powers and control the actions of the King.

And the limitations which Dissenters worked to obtain during the period 1661–1689 were in general even more restricted in scope than the Isle of Wight proposals.

But the Restoration experiences were not always moderating in effect. They also demonstrated that some of the Leveller ideas could be of much value. Thus many Dissenters became strong advocates of the principle that basic individual rights should be guaranteed by fundamental constitutional law, and also there were those who advocated a broader representative base for the House of Commons. They therefore sought a government in which Parliament would have a preponderance of power, but in which the power of both King and Parliament would be limited by fundamental law. In brief, they became advocates of "regulated mixed monarchy," or to use modern terminology, of limited or constitutional monarchy.

The focus of this book is primarily upon the politics of the moderate Dissenters who sat in Parliament. At the same time much attention is given to the activity of all Dissenters in parliamentary elections and to the pressure they exerted through petitioning, lobbying, and pamphleteering. Because of the constitutional implications and the political consequences there is a close examination of the sharply divided Nonconformist response to the major efforts to displace the King by force in the Rye House Plot of 1683 and The Monmouth Rebellion of 1685. Also of high significance were the Dissenters' conflicting reactions when Charles II and then James II sought their political support, and to this end granted indulgences allowing them freedom of public worship. In each of the instances when some Dissenters resorted to insurrection or when the King used his prerogative in order to grant relief and gain support, the impact upon the Dissenters was not only deeply divisive, but also the issues raised became pivotal in the parliamentary politics of the nation, most notably so in 1687–1688 as a result of James II's efforts to win Nonconformist assistance.

Since the number of Presbyterians and Congregationalists sitting in Parliament was always small, the political effectiveness of the Dissenters depended to a considerable degree upon the support which they gave to sympathetic Anglican candidates on the hustings, and thereafter upon the extent to which these moderate Anglicans and the Dissenters in Parliament cooperated with each other. It has always been recognized that Dissenters gave support to Anglican political leaders who were moderate in their religious views. But it has not been as generally accepted that along with the similarity in political and constitutional views which existed among moderate Dissenters and moderate Anglicans there also existed an affinity in religious outlook and aims. There were moderate Anglican political leaders who had been conservative Puritans prior to 1660, and they along with other low churchmen and latitudinarian divines were interested in obtaining a broadened Established Church. Moreover, they cooperated with the large number of moderate Puritans who could not fully accept the Restoration requirements for conformity and who also hoped and worked for a more inclusive Church.

Comprehension and conformity to any degree were abhorrent to the strict Nonconformists of strong sectarian traditions, for they desired separation from the Established Church and toleration of their own churches. Although they supported moderate Dissenters and Anglicans on the hustings, they invariably split with them when the alternative seemed to be either comprehension or toleration. Thus just as there had been major divisions among the Puritans upon religious as well as political issues prior to the Restoration, a similar divisiveness continued to exist among Dissenters thereafter. Moreover, this split became more pronounced and of decisive importance during some of the most critical junctures between the Restoration and the Revolution of 1688.

Usually it was upon the occasions when the Nonconformist ranks were most divided that moderate Dissenters and Anglicans became most closely allied in policy and action. Yet no matter how close this politico-religious affinity became, these Dissenters were not Anglicans. They shared with all Nonconformists the experience of religious exclusion and of not having a church within which they were able to worship with legal freedom. Although they could generally avoid disqualification from political office, they suffered the insecurity and privations resulting from the many penal laws directed against religious nonconformity. Thus even under the conditions most conducive to a working alliance between moderate Dissenters and Anglicans there was always a fundamental uneasiness and a lack of complete confidence. And during the periods when Nonconformists were under particular suspicion and unusually strict enforcement of the penal laws, there was an estrangement which undermined the common efforts of the moderates in both religious groups.

Under such duress Dissenters were more than ever aware of their need for constitutional changes which would alter the settlement made at the Restoration, when they failed to gain the ends they had sought. They remained convinced that a government essentially consistent with conceptions of the Puritan parliamentarians was their best hope. Fundamentally agreed as they were upon this constitutional goal, the Dissenters sought its attainment from the opening of the Cavalier Parliament in 1661 to the end of the Convention Parliament of 1689.

*Dissent and
Parliamentary Politics
In England,*
*1661–1689*

# CHAPTER I

## *The Disintegration of Puritan Power, 1659–1661*

After nearly two decades of the Civil Wars and Oliver Cromwell's ascendancy, Puritan political power and religious predominance rapidly came to an end. The process of disintegration was most extensive during the year of kaleidoscopic political change which followed Richard Cromwell's failure in the spring of 1659, and among the major sources of this momentous development were the intensified religious differences and political rivalries which divided the Presbyterians, Independents,[1] Baptists, and Quakers. Old hopes and ambitions were stirred by the opportunities that were created in the political vacuum following the collapse of the Protectorate, and thus the zealous and divisive partisanship which had been so evident at the end of the 1640's once again became prevalent.

The various religious and political convictions which had given strong motivation to Puritan moderates and extremists in their efforts to obtain power, and which by dividing them contributed to their political failure, were nevertheless the enduring heritage of this English Revolution. The whole period since 1640 had been richly productive of political ideas and constitutional plans, but never were there more proposals made in such a short span of time than during the year of anarchy between the end of the Protectorate in May, 1659, and the Restoration of the Monarchy in May, 1660. Their very number suggests a greater divergency than there was. In essence the Baptists, the Quakers, the Independents or Congregationalists, and the Presbyterians wanted one of two different forms of government prior to the Restoration. Most of those belonging to the first three religious groups continued to favor a republic in which individual rights and liberties would be guaranteed by fundamental law.[2] In addition there were some among these groups who seemed to believe that government should be based upon the principle of popular sovereignty; but there were very few who were actually democratic in their position, since almost all of them believed that only Godly men could be given the right to vote.[3] In contrast to the views of Baptists, Quakers, and Congregationalists, most of the Presbyterians looked to the establishment of a monarchy in which the authority and actions of the King would not only be constitutionally limited but also effectively controlled by the House of Lords and a House of Commons that was representative of property owners.

Those advocating the more radical proposals were in the ascendancy until the end of 1659, but as they lost control of the developing situation during the winter they began to retire into political passivity and at the same time retreat from their radical views. These developments became much more pronounced at the time of the Restoration in May and during the remainder of 1660, and as a result an ever-increasing number of Congregationalists, Baptists, and Quakers abandoned their republicanism and began to become advocates of constitutional monarchy.[4] However, during most of the critical year prior to the restoration of Charles II, the Presbyterians were the only Puritans who worked for a "regulated mixed monarchy."

After Richard Cromwell's withdrawal and the restoration of the Rump of the Long Parliament in May, 1659, Presbyterians quickly became aware of the possibility of restoring Charles II and the monarchy; and it was hoped that in return for Presbyterian support of his efforts to regain the throne, Charles would accept limitations upon his powers as King and agree to the establishment of Presbyterianism instead of Anglicanism. The terms most generally approved by Presbyterians until the spring of 1660 were those contained in the Articles of the Isle of Wight Treaty, or Newport Treaty, which Charles I had partially accepted before the Presbyterian and royalist members were ejected from the Long Parliament by Colonel Pride's Purge in December, 1648. Among the major proposals presented by the Presbyterian Commissioners from Parliament at Newport was that Parliament have the right of nominating all great officers, councillors, and judges for twenty years, and also that it have the power of controlling the military and naval forces for the same period. In addition the Commissioners sought the power for Parliament to raise money for public uses and to have such acts "bind all subjects" even though the King did not consent. Finally, the religious settlement was to be Presbyterian in character, and the King was to take the Covenant.[5]

Following the failure of the Presbyterian and royalist insurrection named after the Presbyterian Sir George Booth,[6] which occurred in August, 1659, the next important efforts to restore the monarchy were concentrated upon negotiations. Those with the King and his agents during the late autumn were fruitless, and Presbyterian leaders were also unsuccessful in winning support from General George Monck, whose army in Scotland was the only military force through which Presbyterian hopes might be realized. These failures, along with the rapid pace of developments during December and January, 1660, weakened Presbyterian support for the Isle of Wight terms, and there were leaders who proposed more moderate limitations to the King's agents and to General Monck as he proceeded with his army toward London.[7]

After February 21 when the General used his power to restore the members of the House of Commons who had not sat since their ejection by Colonel Pride, the Presbyterians who then predominated seemed to have gained a solid opportunity to bring about the conditional restoration of the King. However, during the one month that the House of Commons of the Long Parliament was to sit, there were far more immediate and demanding problems which were extremely time-consuming, and in addition the Presbyterians became more divided concerning the constitutional terms upon which they thought the monarchy should be restored. Most crucial of the immediate problems were those attendant upon the acquisition of power from the Rump and the Army under General John Lambert, and upon the necessity of asserting authority in the country after nearly a year of anarchic conditions. For example, the creation of a new militia loyal to the restored Parliament was of the utmost importance and difficulty, and this problem was not finally disposed of until four days before dissolution of Parliament, when the Militia Act was finally passed.[8] As a result other matters were delayed, such as consideration of fundamental changes in the form of government and passage of religious bills for settling the ministry. On the day following passage of the Militia Act, the House indicated its disapproval of a government without a King and a House of Lords.

It was especially concerned that the Upper House was not yet restored; and three days later, just before the Commons passed the Act for Dissolution of the Long Parliament, an amendment was added stating that its "single actions" were not intended in the least to infringe upon the right of the House of Peers to be a part of Parliament.[9] However, the far more involved and sensitive problem of whether Charles should be restored was never acted upon in an official manner.

Believing their work incomplete and controlling Parliament as they did, the Presbyterians were reluctant to bring about the dissolution they had promised at the time they were seated by Monck, and he was told by three leading Presbyterian ministers whom he had summoned that the "Presbyterian interest he had espoused, was much concerned in keeping up this house, and settling the government on terms." [10] Undoubtedly the ministers were thinking primarily of their hope to gain Charles II's acceptance of Presbyterianism as the established religion, for the actions of the Commons which looked toward this end had indicated that concerning the religious settlement there was essential agreement among the Presbyterian members.[11] But regarding the constitutional limitations which should be placed on the royal prerogative, Presbyterian members were increasingly divided. Speeches given by William Prynne, the leading propagandist for a restored monarchy, as well as by others at the end of Parliament on March 16 made it clear to all that some Presbyterians were such strong supporters of a restoration of the King that they were little if at all concerned about terms.[12] Also affecting the position of some were the pressures during late February and early March when a growing number of Presbyterian members promised their influence to Charles II, and at the same time indicated their interest in obtaining appointments to offices or expiation for their actions during the previous two decades.[13]

The most important Presbyterian leader to shift his position concerning terms was Arthur Annesley, who in the autumn of 1659 had written a pamphlet defending the Isle of Wight limitations as the basis for the King's restoration. However, after he became President of the new Council of State established by the Long Parliament in February, Annesley succumbed to the enticements of Charles himself and his representative Viscount Mordaunt. As a result, by March 8 Annesley was giving Mordaunt information concerning the Council's actions in return for which the King's agent recommended Annesley's Irish interests be given special consideration.[14]

There were a good number of others who made such a shift in position; however, at the same time, the King's chief adviser Sir Edward Hyde was told of other Presbyterian leaders who sought hard terms, and he was warned that "some who have made the King believe they will do great matters for him . . . are the most violent in this design [of hard terms], and express a great bitterness against the King's party. . . ."[15] Likewise evident from a later derisive comment from Mordaunt, those Presbyterians who corresponded with the King or who seemed to satisfy his informants as to their intentions were not necessarily so enthusiastic for the King's restoration that they wanted him placed in power without conditions.[16] Nevertheless, Presbyterians were clearly divided on the issue by the end of the Long Parliament; and even had time been found for the Commons to take action, this divisiveness would have seriously weakened efforts to obtain limitations. Moreover, the rapidly growing enthusiasm throughout the country for recalling the King was increasing the strength of those who wanted an unconditional restoration.

A major difficulty that faced the Presbyterians and a few other moderate Puritans who were seeking so-called hard terms was that their most influential leaders were peers—the Earls of Manchester and Northumberland and Lord Wharton [17]—and they did not have their normal position of political power until the House of Lords was reconvened when the new Convention Parliament met on April 25. Most important, these leaders were not members of the Council of State which was given the powers of government during the six weeks between the Long Parliament and the Convention Parliament. Nevertheless, during this period they assumed leadership of efforts to obtain a conditional restoration and worked through a half dozen or more Council members. With a sense of extreme urgency they resolved "they should immediately send propositions to the King . . . and so engage his Majesty . . . , before the new Parliament meet," for they were convinced that if they waited until that time they would fail because "the King will have so many friends in it, and the whole country [will be] violent for him."[18] The propositions which most of them still had in mind appear to have been the Isle of Wight terms, although some of them may have joined those desiring stronger and different limitations, including the abolition of the royal veto and establishment of permanent parliamentary control over the disposition of "money, commissions, appointments, and the choice of [the King's] Council." [19]

As the results of the parliamentary elections came in during the first half of April, their predictions were fulfilled. In the face of alarming losses in the House of Commons and their failure to send propositions to Charles II as planned, the leaders of the group seeking the more moderate limitations adopted a stratagem to maintain control of the House of Lords by seating only those peers who were in the House in 1648 and by excluding both the old cavalier peers who were still alive and the heirs of those who had died. By the time Parliament met, a good number of prominent Presbyterians and other moderate Puritans either belonged to or supported this group, which was frequently called the Suffolk House or Presbyterian Junto, and in the House of Lords presumably all of the ten Puritan lords who sat in the morning of the first day were ready to follow the plan which would have made them and others of their kind a "noble rump." [20] However, counter measures had already been taken. Under pressure from Mordaunt, Annesley had very reluctantly yielded to the request that he join the Suffolk House group in order to learn its secrets; and apparently in part because of being forewarned through this channel, the young royalist peers were able to seize an opportunity to take their seats in spite of the plans to prevent this action. [21]

Although this was a most serious setback, the Presbyterian leaders appear to have gone ahead with efforts to gain and retain control over the militia and to limit the King's powers of appointing major officials. As Parliament convened, Annesley had warned Mordaunt of these intentions, and the messages sent by the House of Lords to the Commons between April 27 and May 2 concerning the militia and the appointment of Manchester to be a Commissioner of the Great Seal completely convinced this royal agent that the Suffolk House Peers were endeavoring to invade the King's authority over the executive and change the government. [22] When reporting this to Hyde on May 4, Mordaunt was unusually perturbed, not only because of these efforts, but also because at least one of these lords was behind attacks upon Hyde, and finally because there had been reports from other royal agents that some of these very peers were zealous supporters of the King. On the contrary, he warned Hyde, "whoever tells you either Northumberland or Manchester or Saye, or Wharton will be made the King's, I am well assured he understands them not, or abuses you." [23]

In brief, it seems that at the opening of Parliament the leaders of the Suffolk House group realized that it was necessary to concentrate upon the most vital of the Isle of Wight terms rather than to work for the adoption of the whole set of proposals; and after the young royalist peers began to take their seats, leading Presbyterian and other moderate Puritan peers acted quickly during the meetings of April 27 through May 2 in an attempt to retain control over the sources of power in the militia and the important offices of state, in order to counter their loss of power in both Houses. [24] They were unable to act after that time, but there were those in the Commons who still thought some kind of restraint might be placed upon the power of the restored King; and they had a few supporters, such as Sir Walter Earle who went so far as to move "that the great officers of the nation ought to be chosen by parliament, and confirmed by the King. . . ." [25]

Some Presbyterians and other moderate Puritans continued to work until about mid-May for a treaty containing very moderate terms, while others sought enactment of bills for the King to sign which could have included such hard terms as Earle's proposal, but which usually would have provided only a very mild limitation or two. Among the prominent moderate Presbyterian political leaders who may have come to support the enactment of bills was Denzil Holles, who had been one of the Parliamentary Commissioners at the Isle of Wight in 1648. Although reported to be one of the Suffolk House group still favoring these terms on April 19, he could not have contributed much if anything to their support in the Council of State since he had already confessed that he was uninterested in his position as a member. [26] In addition, he as well as others became "more moderate" on terms as a result of General Lambert's attempted military coup and the specter of republican and sectarian resurgence which it raised. Nevertheless, the fact that on April 26 he called for an examination of the qualifications of the House of Commons members suggests that he might have hoped to expel the more than one hundred royal-

ists elected contrary to the Long Parliament's instruction and thus
to increase Presbyterian power. At the same time there was
also some suggestion that he had joined those who rejected the
idea of a formal treaty with the King in favor of the immediate
passage of bills to be presented to him embodying very mild
limitations. This was the procedure formally proposed by the
Presbyterian Sir William Morice in his Commons speech of May 1
concerning the King's message to the House and the Declaration
of Breda, and presumably he had the backing of General Monck.
In any event Holles along with Morice and Monck were appointed to a committee of seven which was to draft a letter of
thanks to the King.[27] It is now known that if Monck did support
such a move, he shifted his position within the next week and
joined with those Presbyterians who still hoped to obtain a treaty
which would call for very moderate concessions from the King,
and it is possible Holles could also have followed Monck's lead.[28]

By the end of the second week in May efforts to obtain a
treaty, even with mild terms, and attempts to secure bills containing new limitations upon the royal prerogative were abandoned.
But there were those who desired to have the traditional rights
and privileges of Parliament maintained and who believed that
there should be statutory confirmation of such fundamental constitutional documents as Magna Charta and the Petition of Right.
Thus on May 23 a Bill was introduced to affirm the limitations
upon the crown contained in these and other constitutional documents, and in the legislative history of this Bill, William Prynne
was very prominent.[29] However, there was no hope of passing it
and obtaining the signature of the King prior to his coronation;
and even had there been time to do so, the Bill did not embody
the kind of limitations for which many Presbyterians and a few
other moderate Puritans had worked.

By the middle of May complete failure faced the Presbyterians
who had sought to use their brief period of ascendancy in the
spring of 1660 to establish a constitutional monarchy, and they
were "greatly cast down."[30] Defeated though they were, their
efforts and proposals had demonstrated there was a strong conviction that new limitations and restraints should be placed upon
the power of the King. At the same time, however, the history
of their attempts to do so makes clear that they were disastrously
divided in their proposals and efforts, seriously weakened by defection, and without strong leadership in the House of Commons.

In addition the Anglican royalists had control in the House of Lords, and in the Commons they had sufficient power to gain their ends. Confronted by such a situation those Presbyterians who had opposed an unconditional restoration were compelled to give way. Apprehensive though many were, they could only join in welcoming Charles back to England and the throne on May 25.

This struggle for power during the preceding year, as each of the major Puritan groups had tried to obtain control and achieve the political and religious settlement which it desired, had a more lasting effect than was evident at the time of each failure. The older enmities, which had been revived and strengthened, and also such quietism as had developed out of defeat made cooperation among the Puritan groups impossible. Moreover, these attitudes became strongest in the spring of 1660, just at the juncture when a pooling of strength offered the only possibility of imposing some degree of constitutional restraint upon a restored King's political and religious power.

As in the past the Quakers and Baptists were particularly embittered against Presbyterianism and its leaders. George Whitehead contended that "Presbyterian government would have been as tyrannical as Episcopal," while the feelings of some Baptists are evident in a pamphlet published by the subsequently well-known Baptist printer Francis Smith in which he described Prynne as an "engine of mischief, and confusion, who is a spirit of a fiery exhalation, as constant in affirming a bad cause, as suffering for a good one." [31] According to George Fox's interpretation, the powers that had been persecuting Friends prior to this time "at last fell a biting and devouring one another until they was [*sic*] consumed one of another," and then "God overthrew them and turned them upside down and brought the King over them." Affirming a completely quietist position, Fox denied that Quakers "met together to bring in King Charles," and stated that they "did not concern themselves with the outward powers," a position which was echoed in the Quaker pamphlets of the day. [32] As for the Baptists, those who had placed their hopes in Lambert's uprising were stunned into silence and at least temporary inactivity. In general, Baptists were already of the same basic disposition as the Quakers, and when the King was restored each group affirmed its loyalty and declared that there should be no plots or insurrections against the government. [33]

Since the Quakers and most Baptists had withdrawn from active intervention in politics, while the Presbyterians and Congregationalists were the only non-Anglican Protestant groups having an appreciable number of members in Parliament, the relationship between the latter two was of much consequence. Heightening this importance were two other factors, the first being the King's willingness, expressed in the Declaration of Breda, to accept a parliamentary act concerning the religious settlement as well as parliamentary advice upon other matters, and the second being the hope that if Presbyterians and Congregationalists combined their strength they might be able to control the House of Commons.[34] With hopes that such a coalition might be effective, Lord Wharton made use of both his Independent or Congregationalist origins and his more recent Presbyterian connections in an attempt to establish some sort of parliamentary organization.[35] Unfortunately, however, events during April and May had only intensified previous strong feelings of rivalry and enmity between the political and ministerial leaders of these two religious groups.[36]

Nevertheless, relations between the Presbyterian and Congregationalist political leaders who sat in the House of Commons were to become temporarily more cordial during the summer as Anglican efforts to regain ecclesiastical power became evident. Cooperation between these political groups first appeared when Presbyterian and Congregationalist ministers then holding church livings realized that the return of the Anglicans was going to deprive many of their positions, and it became temporarily effective during the debates of August and early September over amendments to Prynne's Bill for Establishing Ministers Settled in Ecclesiastical Livings.[37] As a result the Bill was enacted, and not only the large majority of Presbyterian but also a considerable number of Congregationalist ministers were confirmed in the possession of the livings they currently held, the only religious disability or test that was established being public denial that infant baptism was efficacious.[38]

However, such solidarity as developed among Presbyterian and Congregationalist political leaders during the enactment of this Bill was to be destroyed in the attempts to move toward a broader religious settlement during the remainder of the year. First there were the embittered feelings created by the renewed negotiations between the Court and the moderate Presbyterians in September, and also by the resulting Royal Declaration Concerning Ecclesi-

astical Affairs of October 25, known as the Worcester House
Declaration. Moderate Presbyterians were surprised and enthusiastic to find that the concessions granted by the King would
probably permit their comprehension within the Established
Church.[39] But both the rigid Presbyterian and the Congregationalists were most dissatisfied, for their conceptions of church organization and government would not allow any compromise with
Episcopacy. Moreover there was no provision for toleration of
those who did not accept this more inclusive Established Church,
an omission which was the work of Richard Baxter.[40] As a result
there was a wider division within Presbyterian ranks, but most
important politically was the resurgence of rivalry between moderate Presbyterians and most Congregationalists.

The Presbyterians in the House of Commons, who were moderates for the most part, made a concerted drive to obtain the
greater security of having the Declaration enacted into law. As a
result there was a momentous battle that reached its climax in
the division of November 28. Although it was not very likely that
complete support from the Congregationalists would have resulted in victory, the failure of some of them to join the Presbyterian members certainly precluded passage of the Bill.[41] Moreover, it was symptomatic of the divisiveness and fundamental
political ineffectuality that had existed during most of the Convention Parliament, and even more during the year and a half
between the death of Oliver Cromwell and the return of Charles
to the throne. Such cooperation as did develop had come too late
and had been too faltering. The success of September, 1660,
proved to be very temporary, and never again were the Presbyterians in the House of Commons to lead even a coalition to victory against real Anglican opposition.

In the meantime a constitutional defeat was also clearly evident
in the House of Lords, for it had become obvious that the Bill
for the confirmation of the privileges of Parliament, of Magna
Charta, and other fundamental law, was to die in committee.
After passing its second reading on July 4, there had been no further action. However, Puritan support of the Bill was revealed
when the Presbyterians and Congregationalists were at their
strongest during early September, for it was then that the Commons officially reminded the Lords of the unpassed Bill three
times during a single week in an attempt to obtain action. There

was one other reminder sent two days before the Presbyterian defeat of November 28, but when the Lower House sent a message concerning three "undispatched" Bills to the Lords on November 30, there was no mention of the one Bill which represented an effort to clarify the constitutional relationship between the restored monarchy and Parliament while at the same time emphasizing the few fundamental limitations upon royal authority which did exist.[42]

The end of the Convention Parliament thus brought the defeat of this initially successful attempt to obtain a constitutional settlement which would have embodied some modicum of the Puritan plans and ideas of the preceding two decades. In addition, the religious settlement which would have fulfilled most moderate Puritans' hopes was also defeated. Ominous though these failures were in themselves, they were even more so when viewed from a purely political point of view, for Presbyterians and Congregationalists had been defeated in their traditional stronghold in national politics—the House of Commons—as well as in the House of Lords. Moreover, in a growing number of cases neither the Statute for Confirming and Restoring Ministers nor the King's Declaration were proving to be sufficient protection for Puritan ministers who declined to read the Common Prayer. Vindictive Anglican justices viewed the Puritans who were confirmed in their livings as imposters and turned to the old religious statutes in their determination to reinstate an orthodox Anglican clergy, and except in isolated cases the King and Chancellor Hyde did nothing to restrain the magistrates.[43]

Such evidence that a ground swell of opinion was running toward high-prerogative monarchy and strict Anglicanism indicated that Puritans were faced not only by a most decisive battle in the coming parliamentary elections, but also by the prospect that the Established Church would be one of uncompromising and intolerant Anglicanism. At the same time, they were in no condition to withstand the aggressiveness of Anglican royalists. Not only were they divided politically and religiously; they also had been weakened by defection and inaction during 1660. In actuality Puritan power had largely disintegrated, although this was not fully apparent until the following year.

Ahead lay defeat and three decades of duress.

CHAPTER II

*The Gradations and Criteria of Dissent*

There was too wide a variety and too great an intensity of religious belief prevalent in England at the Restoration for Anglican leaders to realize their hopes of attaining religious uniformity. Instead, the new Act of Uniformity and the first Conventicle
Act completed the transformation of Puritanism into Dissent.[1]
And just as there previously had been a great diversity of belief
and practice among Puritans, likewise many gradations of Dissent
appeared among those who refused to conform completely to the
restored Anglican Church. As a result, even though the new laws
seemed to have created a great gulf between those who conformed and those who did not, the distinctions between Anglicans and Dissenters were frequently so fine that it has always
been difficult to establish the distinguishing characteristics of
Dissent and to lay down a realistic line of demarcation.[2]

After decades of hoping to reform or change the Established
Church to suit their views, devout and moderate Puritans could
not suddenly accept the very ceremonies, practices, and hierarchy
they had sought to eliminate or modify. Consequently they felt
compelled to become Dissenters along with the more extreme
Puritans who were Sectarian, Separatist, or Independent in tradition. Yet unlike these Puritans who had always wanted to remain
outside the Anglican Church and enjoy toleration, this was not the
status the moderate Puritans had wanted. Their attitude did not
change when they became Dissenters. In their dissent they therefore did not become complete Nonconformists. Instead they
adopted the practice of occasional or partial conformity. Very
shortly after the Restoration, therefore, terms such as "conformable Nonconformist" came into existence to describe those who
conformed in varying degrees.[3] But the most revealing description

of this sector of the religious spectrum lying between uncompromising Dissent and complete Anglicanism was the title of a work written later by John Cheyney—*The Conforming Non-conformist and the Non-conforming Conformist.* "The title of my book is the image of my mind," [4] wrote Cheyney, and there were many others who could have said the same.

Those of Sectarian and Separatist traditions remained as they had been, decisive in their position. Most adamant in their Nonconformity were Quakers, and the strength of their feelings is seen not only in the writings of their leaders but in the actions of the rank and file. One illuminating incident occurred shortly after the Restoration in which a Quaker named William Watcher posted on the "Steeple-House door" in Cranbrook, Kent, this warning: "You that are called Presbyterians, if you join with [Anglicans] to read or hear read the Common-Prayer-Book in way of worship, then will you be found hypocrits and dissemblers, as well as the Episcopal men and women were in joining you and your worship. . . ." [5] Almost as inflexible in their position during the first two decades after the Restoration were the Baptists.[6] However, in the 1680's the Government's stringent enforcement of the laws against Nonconformity finally had some of the desired effect, and in September, 1686, the Presbyterian journalist Roger Morrice reported that the Baptists were "extraordinarily divided amongst themselves; those that go to the [Established] Church are most heinously censured by those that do not, and they think it such a crime in them that they are not willing to hold communion with them," while those who do not conform occasionally "are censured as severely by those that go to the Church. . . ." [7]

In line with their Independent traditions, most Congregationalists also remained strictly Nonconformist in their position.[8] However, they too were divided on the matter of occasional and partial conformity, and this division appears to have come considerably earlier than in the case of the Baptists. An older custom of attending the Established Church to hear the sermon but not to participate in the Common Prayer or Sacraments, which some Congregationalists had followed prior to the Civil Wars, appears to have been revived to some degree after 1662; and within the next decade this practice seems to have become the source of a major division.[9] According to one of the Anglican informants of Secretary of State Sir Joseph Williamson, observance of this custom in Yarmouth had so aroused the Congregationalist minister William Bridge that he threatened his members with excommunication if they were to hear the Anglican clergyman.[16] In spite of such opposition the practice continued, undoubtedly stimulated by the enforcement of the Second Conventicle Act between 1670 and the issuance of the Declaration of Indulgence of 1672.[11] Moreover, Congregationalists did not confine their conformity to mere attendance. A long pamphlet which Dr. John Owen published in 1672 seems to indicate that by that time there were those who were maintaining that they "should occasionally join with parish assemblies . . . in all their worship and sacred administrations," for Owen took great pains to refute this contention.[12] Indeed in this work and another written subsequently he argued against "any conformity to worship not of Divine institution," and in his mind this would have precluded attendance at the Established Church.[13]

The first Congregationalist minister of any prominence to defend the practice of attending the Established Church after the Restoration was Philip Nye, who contended about 1667 that it was not only lawful but even a duty to hear Anglican ministers.[14] However, he held to the old limitations set by John Robinson and maintained it was not lawful to join in the Common Prayer or to receive the Sacrament.[15] A decade and a half later when Nye's eldest son Henry republished the works of Robinson and his father on this problem, he did his best to find statements in the writings of these and other ministers which would support the position of Congregationalists who wished to participate in the Anglican liturgy. Although he was not successful in discovering any ministers who had written that Congregationalists might take Communion, he did emphasize that "the practice of some of them in receiving the Sacrament according to the manner of the Church of England, does evince, that all of them do not deny the lawfulness of it, but that they may sometimes communicate there, though ordinarily they do [so] with their own particular Churches. . . ."[16] The young Nye was probably correct about the increasing number of Congregationalists who were becoming occasional communicants, but he does not seem to have received the support of any leading Congregational publicist in his contention that the practice should be sanctioned. Stephen Lobb, one of the prominent younger ministers, even opposed this position and argued that "the true Dissenter, who is a thorough Nonconformist . . . cannot hold Communion with the Parish Churches in the liturgic worship as by law required," and added that if Dissenters "could conscientiously hold Communion . . . occasionally, it would be their duty to do so constantly." [17] The very tone of his chapter on this matter would seem to indicate that he was much concerned because Congregationalists were beginning to change in attitude and practice. However, it is undoubtedly true that most Congregationalists disapproved of occasional conformity, as did the majority of Thomas Jolly's church in 1678 when they admonished some of their church members who had been maintaining occasional communion with the Church of England. [18]

The attitudes and practices that came to prevail among Presbyterians were different. Traditionally desirous of reforming or altering the Established Church, occasional or partial conformity was much more acceptable to many of them than strict nonconformity. After the Restoration it was therefore natural that clergymen and laymen of this disposition communicated with the Anglican Church to some degree, just as Presbyterians had done in earlier Stuart and Elizabethan times. Although there were those whose rigid Presbyterian views would not allow them to conform to the restored Anglican Church in any respect, their numbers and influence declined with the impact of developments that came in the years following the Restoration. As Parliamentary regulations and repressive legislation became effective, and as the pressures of public opinion mounted, more and more of the Presbyterians turned to the practice of occasional and partial conformity. Thus by about 1673 one observer noted that Presbyterian "pastors and people . . . generally frequent the Church and the service of it," but he added that some were for three-fourths conformity, some for one-half, some for one-fourth, and a few for none at all. [19] It becomes evident, therefore, that a description of the growth and the gradations of this practice among the Dissenters becomes in the main a discussion of the extent to which Presbyterians adopted it, and of the degree to which they conformed. Yet at the same time it must be remembered that there were some Congregationalists and later a few Baptists, particularly the laymen, who followed the same course.

Among the first of the Puritan laymen to feel the compulsion to conform on occasion were those political leaders who were members of the House of Lords or who had been elected to sit in the House of Commons in the spring of 1661, for by mid-May each House had ordered its members to receive the Sacrament according to the rites of the Church of England, the Lords together in the Abbey Church at Westminster, and the Commons as a body at St. Margarets.[20] Although there were efforts to defeat this resolution, and although about one-third of the Presbyterian-Congregationalist group of members in the Commons either refused to attend or to follow the prescribed Sacramental procedure, in the end all but one of them did comply with the requirement even though obviously with reluctance and undoubtedly with reservations.[21] Thus did these members bend to the exigencies of the day, and occasional conformity as practiced by Puritans for political purposes have its beginnings.

By the end of the year local politicians in the boroughs felt a similar pressure to conform occasionally, for the Corporation Act went into effect on December 24, requiring municipal office holders to take Anglican Communion within the year prior to being elected or chosen.[22] Very different were the requirements with which Puritan ministers had to comply if they wished to hold a benefice in the Established Church. Constant and complete conformity to strict Anglicanism was imposed by the new Act of Uniformity, and as a result the vast majority of those who were still incumbents chose ejection on St. Bartholomew's Day, August 24, 1662.[23] This was a wrenching experience not only for the ministers but also for those moderate Puritan laymen who had until this time found some degree of conformity acceptable because of the presence and the Puritan practices of their old ministers within the Church. The experience was particularly traumatic for the great number of both ministers and laymen who held Presbyterian views. By law they had been made Separatists, yet almost all of them desired to remain within the Established Church. Thus there were ministers who made such resolutions as those of Henry Newcome and others in Lancashire and decided "to stick close to the public ordinances and not to separate. . . ."[24] The varying degrees of lay conformity to which many ministers turned was the only alternative for those who could not completely accept the terms of the Act of Uniformity, but who on the other hand did not desire to leave the Church entirely. And the laymen who still desired to follow the tradition of their moderate Puritan predecessors who had belonged to the Church of England in pre-Laudian days found reassurance in the example of their ministers.

At the same time since these occasional conformists could not fully accept the Anglican Church as it had been restored, they therefore attended Presbyterian as well as Anglican services. Their dilemma became acute in 1663 when it became evident that the Conventicle Bill would be enacted, and as a result there was a serious attempt to amend the proposed Bill so as to exempt from its penalties those who did "frequent the service at the Church, and receive the Sacrament thrice every year." [25] Not only would this amendment have given legal sanction to occasional conformity; it would also have tacitly acknowledged that those willing to conform to this degree could thereafter attend conventicles conducted by ejected ministers who were willing to practice lay conformity to the same extent. Passage of this provision would undoubtedly have brought a much wider adoption of occasional conformity, but even without this inducement the practice became increasingly prevalent during the Restoration period.

The "conformable Nonconformists" included ministers advocating many graduations of partial conformity. Fortunately these clergymen were very articulate about their positions and usually described in some detail the extent to which they would go in conforming to the Established Church. Fortunately too, there are more complete records as to their religious practices than in the case of the laymen. By tracing the degrees to which these ministers would accept the doctrines, rituals, and government of the Established Church it is possible to discover a realistic line of demarcation between Nonconformity and Conformity, and in the end the description of these more important graduations reveals the criteria of Dissent.

There were a large number of Presbyterian ministers who held views and adopted practices like those of the Congregationalist Philip Nye, good examples being Adam Martindale, Zachary Crofton and Joseph Eccleshall, for they approved of attendance at the Parish Church but would not participate in the Common Prayer or the Sacrament.[26] Of those who would go one step further, there is an excellent example in Philip Henry. He was a regular attender of Anglican services for thirty years after St. Bartholomew's Day, and unlike Crofton and Eccleshall he appears to have participated in the Common Prayer; however, he drew the line at receiving the Sacrament. "It grieves me to turn my back on the Lord's Supper," he wrote at Easter in 1663, and explained that the basic reason was because he was "not free to kneel." [27] There were others who had such scruples, but in some instances they were allowed to receive Communion while sitting, undoubtedly the best known being the case of William Prynne who refused to kneel when the two Houses of Parliament were receiving the Sacrament together at St. Margaret's Church in Westminster on May 13, 1661.[28] However, there were those who were willing to take the Sacrament kneeling on occasion, even though they preferred not to do so, and of these the most famous was Richard Baxter. "Had I my choice, I would receive the Lord's Supper sitting," he wrote, "but where I have not, I will use the gesture which the Church uses." [29]

Before considering the other respects in which Dissenters did or did not conform, it should be emphasized that the major remaining considerations which prevented acceptance of the Established Church were of direct concern to ministers. However, laymen were also highly agitated by the requirements and reasons that compelled ministers to remain Nonconformist clergymen even though they were "lay conformists" to one degree or another. The major obstructions to ministerial conformity were the clauses in the Act of Uniformity which required that Episcopal ordination be received if it had not been previously, and that there be subscription with "unfeigned assent and consent" to all of the Thirty-nine Articles, and to the use of all the prayers, rites, ceremonies, forms, and orders prescribed in the Book of Common Prayer.[30]

For moderate Puritans the requirement that they accept all of the Articles was a decisive blow. The Elizabethan Act of Uniformity had required subscription and assent only to those Articles which concerned the "confession of the true Christian faith and the doctrine of the Sacraments"; and as Sir Edward Harley later pointed out, the Church had considered that "this was sufficient for any minister even though ordained in other form than prescribed. . . ." [31] Evidence of the excisive impact of this requirement upon those who had been moderate Puritans is

revealed throughout the next three decades in parliamentary
proposals to have it removed or modified, beginning with one to
amend the new Bill of Uniformity during its passage so that
ministers without Anglican ordination could retain their livings
if they subscribed to the doctrinal Articles as enjoined by the
Elizabethan statute.[32]

As can be inferred from the willingness of many to accept the
statements in the Articles concerning the "true Christian faith
and the doctrine of the Sacraments," strictly theological considerations were not as frequently the sources of disaffection among
moderate Dissenters as were many matters of ritual, ceremony,
and Church government. Throughout the whole Restoration period there was constant objection by both laymen and ministers
to particular matters of ceremony and ritual, notably to the use
of the cross at baptism and to the wearing of the surplice.[33] Thus
the prescribed use of the Book of Common Prayer with all of its
prayers, rites, ceremonies, forms, and orders was a major obstacle,
one of the most important objections being that *ex tempore* prayer
was eliminated. However, there were many ministers as well as
laymen who accepted much that was prescribed in the Book of
Common Prayer, just as they accepted most of the Thirty-nine
Articles. Not only did they attend Church and join in the Communion, but the ministers would also read the ordinary service.
These ministers and their followers who came closest to complete
conformity were at the same time the most strongly opposed to
the requirement that they swear their assent and consent to everything contained in the Thirty-nine Articles and the Book of Common Prayer, and it was not only the requirement of complete
acceptance that was objectionable. In addition, the Declaration
which the Act of Uniformity required ministers to take was in
effect an oath that they would not seek to change the "liturgy
established by law," so that they would have been unable to work
for changes to make it more acceptable.[34]

Finally, there were the objections to the Episcopacy and the
Anglican Church government generally. Some of these can be
detected in the refusal to accept ordination by a bishop and in
the objections to the imposition of the Assent and the part of the
Declaration already discussed concerning the liturgy. Resistance
to the Church hierarchy and government is also very apparent in

the objection to the oath or promise of canonical obedience which was to be taken at ordination and in which candidates were to affirm they would "reverently obey" those in charge of the government over them.[35] But the issue of Church government was most pointedly raised by the part of the Declaration in the Act of Uniformity which required a minister to swear that there lay no obligation upon him or any other person "from the oath commonly called the Solemn League and Covenant to endeavor any change or alteration of government either in Church or State. . . ."[36] Although there was obviously a political and constitutional aspect to this Declaration, it was the religious restriction which weighed most heavily with Presbyterian ministers.

Of the Nonconformist ministers who could not become Anglican clergymen because they refused to fulfill one or more of these requirements, the case of the Presbyterian John Humfrey, who devoted much effort to seeking a union of all Protestants, is particularly revealing. Although he had accepted Anglican ordination prior to passage of the Act of Uniformity, he later recanted because he found some of the impositions of this Act unacceptable. He did not wish to be compelled to use the Liturgy as it was then established, even though he was willing to read the Common Prayer in ordinary daily service. Similarly, he objected very much to swearing that no obligation lay upon him or any other person from the Oath of the Solemn League and Covenant "to endeavor any change or alterations of government either in Church or State," for even though he had not taken the Covenant, he believed this Declaration in the Act of Uniformity should be altered to allow legal or constitutional efforts of reformation in the Church and State. Also he seems to have objected to the oath of canonical obedience, and he had a few exceptions to the Thirty-nine Articles.[37] As a result of this refusal to accept the terms of the Act, he was ejected from the vicarage of Frame Selwood; and he organized and preached in an illegal Nonconformist church in London during the Restoration period.[38] Nevertheless this is what he wrote concerning his religious practice in 1678:

I am one that has ordinarily gone to my Parish Church, not only joining in the public prayers, but receiving the Sacrament there, and never yet elsewhere, though I am a Nonconformist: So, if I shall conform (that is, so far as I can, which does but fix me so much more firm in that wherein I con-

form not), I intend not but to be the same man still, as to the keeping in
with my brethren, and to do as I did; which is to be sometimes with them,
and for the most part with the parochial congregation.[39]

The few Baptists, the more numerous Congregationalists, and
the large number of Presbyterians who advocated and practiced
some degree of conformity were described by many terms during
the years 1661–1689, the most general in its implications being
*partial Conformists*.[40] Of those implying a greater degree of conformity there were several, including Baxter's term *reconcilers*
and the phrase *conformable Nonconformists* which was used by
some ministers in 1663.[41] In the spring of 1673, at a time when
there were efforts to obtain comprehension within the Church,
Baxter also described those of this sector of the religious spectrum
as *Episcopal Nonconformists*.[42] Except for the fact that they were
no longer able to work within the Established Church to obtain
desired reforms as they had been before 1662, the term *Puritan*
used in its more restrictive sense would have been the best with
which to describe the position of these moderate Dissenters. Indeed older members of this group frequently used the phrase *old*
or *former Puritan*. However, because of the very fact that both
the Presbyterians and Anglicans who used the term *Puritan* qualified it so frequently, either by the adjective *old* or in some other
manner, it was clear that the word *Puritan* alone was no longer
adequate or accurate. The reason is clear. When such Presbyterians as Roger Morrice and Sir Henry Ashurst used the term *old
Puritan* they meant the Presbyterians and possibly a few of the
Congregationalists who had been excluded from the Church.[43]
Moreover, Morrice believed that within the Establishment there
was another variety of Puritan, for in 1686 he described the Anglican clergymen who opposed James II's ecclesiastical policy and
orders as the "Puritan clergy." [44] Although he believed such moderate Nonconformists and Anglicans all favored "Reformed Religion," and although he longed for comprehension within the
Established Church, both he and others of his disposition believed
there was a definite distinction between those whom they regarded as old or Presbyterian Puritans and those considered Puritan Low Churchmen.[45]

Efforts to locate the line of demarcation between these two
groups became more numerous as the practice of occasional con-

formity became more common, and the more common it became, the more apparent it was that occasional and partial conformists were not regarded as Anglicans. This is evident in a statement written by an unknown Anglican who described Dissenters as "not only such [persons] as never come to Church but such as come sometimes and go more frequently to Conventicles, whereof there are great numbers as ill-affected as those who frequent the Conventicles only. . . ." Continuing, he noted that Baxter and others allow "their people to keep partial and occasional communion, whence to qualify for offices, they will receive the Holy Sacrament at the Church in the morning and go in the afternoon to Conventicles," and in this practice he could find "no true sign of loyalty or love to the Church." [46] Church officials made similar complaints, the Bishop of Sarum reporting to the Archbishop of Canterbury in 1681 that there had been in his city a "Conventicle of persons pretending themselves friends of our Church [that] partakes of the public service and Sacraments," but that afterwards resorts to "an exercise of a Presbyterian. . . ." [47]

On legal grounds Dissent was not determined by the relative frequency with which Conventicles and Anglican services were attended. If a person attended any Nonconformist service at all, he became a Dissenter according to the law. This was clearly the intent of the men who passed both of the Restoration Conventicles Acts.[48] Moreover, the conviction that occasional conformity did not make one an Anglican, and the fact that any attendance at Nonconformist services did mark one as a Dissenter was also evident in the manner in which the Acts were enforced, particularly during the periods of strict enforcement. Although moderate Dissenters may have wished otherwise, occasional conformity did not give those who practiced it legal immunity if they were found at a Conventicle. A notable example of this was an instance of March, 1675, in which a Nonconformist meeting attended by a number of well-known occasional conformists, including Lord Wharton, Lady Bedford and others, was broken up and fines for Nonconformity were levied.[49] A decade later Morrice wrote that officials "prosecute all meetings and Conventicles, though they be made up of such as go ordinarily to Church (and Sacrament too) . . . ," and he also noted that these people had been going to Conventicles only on week days and out[side] of Church hours on Sunday.[50]

Those charged with the enforcement of the law were not only correct in their interpretation of it, but also in their conviction that occasional conformists had not in their own minds ceased to be Dissenters. The validity of this judgment is demonstrated by two men who regularly attended both Anglican and Nonconformist services and who were very candid in statements about their religious practices and their religious beliefs. One was the diarist Ralph Thoresby and another was the journalist and ejected minister Roger Morrice. Although Thoresby felt compelled to begin attending the Parish Church regularly as a result of his apprehension and indictment for being present at a Nonconformist meeting, which he was in the habit of attending, he did not thereafter cease going to Nonconformist services, and he continued to call himself a Protestant Dissenter.[51] Morrice, who also attended the Established Church, likewise leaves no doubt that he was a Dissenter;[52] and in addition he makes it very clear that the vast majority of those Nonconformists who did attend the Anglican services also continued to think of themselves as did Thoresby and he. When the Declaration of Indulgence was issued by James II after six years of rigorous enforcement of the laws against Nonconformity, Morrice wrote that upon his own "certain knowledge some of the most serious Churchmen" were concerned about the losses their congregations would suffer. He agreed that attendance in the churches of the moderate Anglican clergymen would be the most diminished, for, he wrote, "it is the Dissenters that filled their congregations";[53] and since the Indulgence would allow them, they would return to their own meetings. There is no doubt that the same development also took place when Charles II issued his Declaration of Indulgence 1672, but there were not as many occasional conformists at that time as there were after the strict enforcement of the laws during the mid-1670's and from 1681 to 1686. Nevertheless, there is convincing evidence that at the time of the earlier Indulgence those who had been occasional conformists actually considered themselves to be Dissenters, and it is to be found in the fact that all of the prominent Nonconformist ministers who had become occasional conformists took out licenses to preach under the Indulgence and that their reformed congregations included large numbers of those who had followed their practices of occasional conformity.[54]

Close though many partial and occasional conformists came to

complete compliance, it is evident that to a considerable degree
this was the result of legal compulsion or fear of reprisals, and
therefore when this pressure was removed the underlying Nonconformity again became apparent. Furthermore, it is evident that
a person who attended either public or private Nonconformist
services should be regarded as a Dissenter, even though he may
have attended the Church of England with some regularity and
may have received Communion according to its rites. Certainly
if this outward occasional and partial conformity had brought
complete religious satisfaction, there then would have been no
desire to turn either to public or private services conducted by
Nonconformist ministers.

To be sure, these occasional and partial conformists were not
the complete and scrupulous Dissenters whom Nye called the true
Dissenters and whom Morrice described as the "old cankered
sturdy Sectaries" or the "censorious sort of Dissenters that condemn others for complying in anything in Church and State." [55]
They recognized that in complying to varying degrees they were
more in the tradition of the old Puritans who sought to reform
the Church rather than separate from it, and they thought of
themselves as trying to "steer between these two extremes" of
Sectarianism and Anglicanism.[56] As it has been seen, there were a
few Baptists and some Congregationalists to be found among the
partial and occasional conformists, but the greatest number were
of Presbyterian background. Since so many of those calling themselves Presbyterians did become occasional conformists, the term
*Presbyterian* was commonly used to describe those who came
closest to conformity. Thus Sir Joseph Williamson was informed
in 1667 that the Common Council at Great Yarmouth was com-
posed of two parties, "Episcopal, and Presbyterians, who call
themselves moderate Episcopals"; and twenty years later when
describing the political situation at York, the Duke of Newcastle
reported that "there is of the Church of England and of the
Presbyterians that will be *called* of the Church, forty for one, to
the Nonconformist. . . ." [57] Although these comments are of interest because the writers recognized the proximity of the Presbyterians to the Church of England, their real significance is found
in the fact that at the same time the distinctions between these
two religious positions is clearly recognized. It should also be
emphasized that frequently those who came closest to conforming

were most adamant in adhering to Nonconformist views and practices, good examples being Thoresby, Morrice, Baxter, and Humfrey. To repeat, Humfrey had written, ". . . I shall conform . . . so far as I can, which does but fix me so much more firm in that wherein I conform not. . . ." [58]

In summary, it may be said that even though the line of demarcation between Anglicans and Dissenters is often difficult to discern, nevertheless it did exist. After the Restoration Act of Uniformity and the Conventicle Acts, old Puritan practices of partially conforming and accepting the Established Church were not sufficient to establish a person's Anglicanism. In law and in the judgment of the officials of both Church and State, as well as in the conviction of Dissenters themselves, those who attended Nonconformist services or objected to Episcopalian government, or to Anglican ceremonies or doctrines, had clearly demonstrated their dissent from the Church of England.

# CHAPTER III

## The Impact of Defeat, 1661–1668: Parliamentary Politics and the Constitutional Settlement

Although two decades of Puritan political supremacy had come to an end with the Restoration of Charles II, this momentous development was obscured at the time because political power was so nearly balanced in the Convention Parliament. At the beginning of 1661 it would have been difficult to foretell with any certainty whether the impetus of the complex developments that had brought the Restoration would add to the strength of the Anglican royalists in the coming elections, or whether there would be a resurgence of Puritan power. Presbyterians and Congregationalists still had hopes of regaining control of the House of Commons, and the Anglican royalists feared they might lose the small majority that they had managed to muster in the Convention Parliament.

In this atmosphere of tense feeling, heightened by the Venner Plot of January, the parliamentary elections were held.[1] None of them had more dramatic impact than that in London, for the highest hopes and the worst fears were realized. All four of the new members were Presbyterians or Congregationalists, and it was evident this success was due to the efforts of the Baptists and probably the Quakers, as well as to those of the Presbyterians and Congregationalists. Surprising though the appearance of this Puritan coalition seemed after all the political strife and division among them in the past, both necessity and interest had in recent months become powerful motivations for the formation of an "anti-Episcopal" party. Regardless of political and religious views that may have divided them, all Puritan purchasers of Church lands desired to have Parliament confirm the legality of their possession. In addition they were all concerned by the fact that during the preceding months old religious statutes were being used to enforce strict conformity in spite of the Act for Confirming and Restoring Ministers and the King's Worcester House Declaration of the previous autumn.[2]

Elated and eager to bring continued success in subsequent elections, the London Puritans and their allies swelled the mails with letters of encouragement to their friends in the country. Worried government officials retaliated by intercepting many of these letters and making arrests, but such tactics were not necessary.[3] When the elections were over it was all too evident that royalist fears and Puritan hopes had been delusions, for only a handful of Presbyterians and Congregationalists had been returned.

It is more than usually difficult to determine the religious position of the members of Parliament in 1661 because the pressures during this period of rapid political and religious transition were both changing and obscuring the views and practices of many men, particularly of those in public life. There were many who saw the advantages of becoming Anglicans, while there were many others who were highly reluctant to give any indication of their real positions. Previous estimates that there were between fifty and sixty Presbyterian and Congregationalist members elected to the House of Commons appear to have been slightly high, probably because too much emphasis was placed upon the members' religious affiliations prior to 1660.[4] Using the criteria which have already been described and considering evidence of religious views and practices after 1660 to be of primary weight, it has been possible to identify thirty-seven members elected to the House of Commons in 1661 who may be considered Presbyterians or Congregationalists.[5] Unquestionably there were others who also belonged to this group, possibly as many as a dozen.[6] However, this handful of between thirty-seven and a possible maximum of fifty in a House of 507 members was hopelessly outnumbered, and as the elections had progressed it became obvious that the Presbyterian and Congregationalist members would have to rely upon the help of others if they hoped to have any effectiveness at all.

Undoubtedly it was this realization that led Lord Wharton to take the lead in compiling a list of 125 friends and twenty-one additional moderates, and it is indicative of the rapidly shifting

views of many political leaders at this juncture that he included
a good number who proved to be neither friends nor moderates,
while at the same time he did not list a considerable number who
were supporters of the Dissenters. It is of particular interest that
of the thirty-seven known members who may be considered Presbyterians or Congregationalists, Wharton and his associates listed
only nineteen and did not mention the others even among the
names of friends. Notable among these omissions were leaders
of such prominence as John Swynfen, Hugh Boscawen, and more
understandably, William Prynne.[7] In addition the list does not
include others who had been Puritans before 1661 and who remained moderate or friendly even though they conformed not
long thereafter.[8] Nevertheless, in spite of miscalculations it appears that Wharton was about right in estimating the total
strength of the Presbyterians and Congregationalists when aug-
mented by their friends. Thus on a question that was primarily
religious, the proposal to have the Solemn League and Covenant
burned by the common hangman, they managed to muster 103
votes in the early days of the Cavalier Parliament. But encouraging though this might seem, they had to face the fact that they
and their friends were outvoted more than two to one.[9]

At the opening of this Parliament's first session there were also
ominous indications of the spirit of retaliation felt by the preponderance of Anglican royalists. The combination of this spirit
and the political weakness of the Presbyterians and Congregationalists could only mean that an era had ended and that the
scope of the calamity facing them was only partially evident.
Although Clarendon, the Lord Chancellor, was to prove himself
relatively temperate in his own attitude toward the more moderate Puritans, at least on critical occasions during the next few
years, in his opening speech to Parliament he called for the "utmost severity" to be used against the "seditious preachers . . .
who . . . by repeating the very expressions, and teaching the
very doctrine they set on foot in the year 1640, sufficiently declare they have no mind that twenty years should put an end to
the miseries we have undergone. . . ." Continuing, he could only
have given additional stimulus to those who were already vindictive in mood, for he maintained that if they "did not provide
for the thorough quenching of these firebrands; then King, Lords,

and Commons shall be their meanest subjects, and the whole
kingdom kindled into one general flame." [10]

Alarming though this was, there was a much more distressing
and immediate personal problem which faced each Presbyterian
and Congregationalist member of Parliament as a result of the
Order of the House of Lords that peers receive the Sacrament
according to the rites of the Church of England in the Abbey
Church at Westminster, and the Resolution of the House of Commons requiring all members to attend St. Margaret's Church in
Westminster on May 26 for the same purpose.[11] The four members from London apparently argued that they were "freely
chosen to serve in Parliament, and it is not a vote in Parliament
[that] can thrust them out." [12] When Sir Ralph Ashton desired
permission to state "why he could not . . . with a good conscience receive the Communion, as he was enjoined . . . ," others
of his disposition attempted to have a debate upon the Resolution
of the House, but they were voted down.[13] As the well-known
Nonconformist diarist Philip Henry noted, this was a resolution
"at which many stumble. . . ." [14] However, by early July there
were only seven known Presbyterians or Congregationalists who
had not received the Sacrament, and although the records are
incomplete, apparently all of these except Ashton and William
Love complied within a short period of time.[15] At the same time,
it should be emphasized that the Presbyterian and Congregationalist members who desired to obtain certificates that they had
received the Sacrament, as they had been directed, could still
find a large number of clergymen of their own Puritan religious
feeling within the Church. Occasional conformity did not become
truly difficult or impossible for the conscientious Dissenter until
the following year when these moderate Puritan clergymen were
ejected from the Church because they could not accept the terms
of the new Act of Uniformity.

Two vital questions faced the drastically weakened and highly
suspected Presbyterians and Congregationalists who sat in Parliament. What political tactics should they pursue? And to what
degree would they be able or willing to continue their efforts to
follow the parliamentarian tradition as the various bills of constitutional import were considered?

The initial reaction of these members became partially evident
in the debates upon religious and constitutional issues during

May and June. The large Cavalier-Anglican majority invariably compelled the Presbyterian-Congregationalist group to retreat, and as one member of the House wrote on May 16, "The Presbyterian is so inconsiderable in the House that the more prudent men of that party are silent."[16] Nevertheless, there is evidence that the minority did not give way without some determined rear-guard actions. Certainly William Prynne was not one of the "more prudent men" who remained silent, and as might be expected he was probably the most important of the leaders in the efforts to delay, to modify, and even to obstruct parliamentary action.

As already indicated, one of the earliest of the stands made by the Presbyterians and their supporters came when the Cavaliers urged the burning of the Covenant. Prynne was active in this debate which was prolonged for five hours.[17] However, such efforts could be no more than a delaying action, and when the Common's resolution reached the Lords some of the leading Presbyterian peers were absent, undoubtedly because of the hopelessness of the situation.[18] This was a disillusioning defeat to the Presbyterians, for as one of their pamphleteers of the day was quick to contend, support had been won for the Restoration of the King when it had been pointed out to "many considerable citizens and others" that in accordance with the Solemn League and Covenant they were engaged to restore the King.[19] At the same time, and quite possibly in part because of this defeat, Prynne was bitterly attacking the bishops in the Commons. Quite understandably his attack only increased the vindictiveness of the extreme Anglicans, who, according to a report Samuel Pepys heard, therefore brought in the bill to restore the bishops to the House of Lords sooner than planned.[20]

Among the major bills brought into the House of Commons during May there were three which raised important constitutional issues and which were to have particular effect upon those who were to remain Dissenters in the years to come; these were the Bill for the Safety and Preservation of the King, the Bill Against Tumultuous Petitioning, and the first Militia Bill.[21] Important though they were, there is evidence that members of the Presbyterian-Congregationalist group sought to modify some of the more objectionable clauses of only one of these Bills, William Love and Sir William Thompson making several objec-

tions against clauses in the Bill for the King's Safety.[22] Although
the lack of evidence concerning the response of this group to
the other two Bills does not mean that Presbyterian and Congregationalist opposition had disappeared, it does indicate that there
was much less activity; for any noticeable opposition would have
evoked comment from contemporary observers as it had in other
cases. Certainly Presbyterians and Congregationalists had reason
to be less aggressive, for these two Bills did not clear both
Houses until the middle of July, and by this time the opposition
had been defeated in its bold and resolute fight against the
Corporation Act. The Bill for the Safety of the King, on the
other hand, had passed its third reading by May 28,[23] before
the opposition had been worn down and discredited. Moreover,
neither of the other Bills had as direct a bearing upon religious
matters as did that concerning the safety of the King, for not
only did the Act for the Safety of the King declare the Solemn
League and Covenant an unlawful oath and unlawfully imposed,
it also made any person liable to the penalty of a praemunire for
maintaining "that there lies any obligation upon him or any other
person from any oath, covenant, or engagement whatsoever to endeavor a change of government either in Church or State. . . ."[24]

Just as the Presbyterians and Congregationalists in Parliament
seem to have been relatively inactive in the debates on these
Bills, so was the reaction of their religious colleagues throughout
the country also largely unexpressed. However, the Presbyterian
minister Henry Newcome recorded diary entries which show that
he was as much disturbed by the Act Against Tumultuous Petitioning as by that for the Safety of the King, and that he thought
both were likely "to prove a great snare to the ministers."[25] As
for the Militia Act, the only strong condemnation which has been
discovered was also written in a private journal, but many years
later. In 1679 as he looked back upon this Act, the ejected minister Roger Morrice wrote in a shorthand passage, which he left
untranscribed, that the Cavalier Parliament had "violated the
fundamental laws of the Kingdom and had assisted arbitrary
power and infringed law . . . by declaring the militia to be in
the power of the King solely which never Parliament before had
done. . . ."[26]

Although the Presbyterian-Congregationalist wing of the opposition was concerned when religious matters were involved, the

record of these men in fighting the Corporation Bill proved that they were most aggressive when the source of their political power and their constitutional principles were under attack. The counter-attack by the opposition in the Commons against this measure was not only strong, it became almost obstructive,[27] and the Presbyterians and Congregationalists were in the vanguard with Prynne as their leader. The most successful of the determined stands by the opposition was the first, which came on the second-reading division of June 20. The vote in this critical test was 185 to 136.[28] Defeated though they were, Prynne and his colleagues did not cease in their efforts, although as yet there was not the degree of religious and political motivation that there later was when the requirement of the sacramental test was added to the Bill by the House of Lords. After unsuccessful attempts to obtain favorable amendments [29] there was a decisive opportunity for a show of strength when the engrossed Bill was brought in. This time the opposition strength was cut to seventy-seven votes, almost half as many as in the division on the second reading; and it is significant both that the vote was much nearer the number of known Presbyterian and Congregationalist members, and also that the two opposition tellers were Presbyterians— William Prynne and Sir Ralph Ashton. On the other side the vote was 182, only three less than that on the second reading, and undoubtedly it was mainly this decisive and ominous defeat which led Prynne to make his next and desperate move—a published appeal to the House of Lords in an anonymous broadside.[30]

Prynne's indictment of the Bill was succinct and impressive. For the most part his attack was directed at the procedure for enforcing its provisions, and it was clearly an appeal to the Lords for their support. He pointed out that the commissioners who were given this task were being given powers greater than those "ever granted to any sort of judges, justices or commissioners in former ages," for they would be able to deprive commoners of their franchises and freeholds without any legal trial or due process of law, and they could just as summarily displace the greatest peers who held offices in boroughs and corporations. The commissioners were to take no oath of office, and they did not have to establish rules of law by which to operate; thus there would be no right of calling witnesses or having counsel. Most impor-

tant, there was "no appeal provided in the Act . . . as is usual
in all cases of dis-franchisement, other judgments and decrees
made by commissioners and all inferior courts of justice." Prynne
considered such arbitrary and irresponsible procedures contrary
to Magna Charta and the principles of English law, and he maintained the Bill would establish a dangerous precedent. Moreover,
he found enactment of the Bill "altogether needless . . . since
all magistrates, officers and members of corporations, formerly
ejected for their loyalty [to the King] are already restored, or
may be . . . upon request." It was not only the danger of the
arbitrary power but also the punitive potentialities that concerned Prynne, and it should be recalled that he was writing
before the sacramental test had been added to the Bill. The
whole tone of his attack indicates his great concern that fundamental legal rights be maintained because they were indispensable bulwarks protecting the nobility, the gentry and all freemen
against the arbitrary actions of governmental authorities.[31]

It was immediately suspected that Prynne was the author of
the bold broadside, and a committee of the House of Commons
which included no known Presbyterian or Congregationalist was
established to investigate. Within a few days he confessed and
was censured by the House.[32] The proud Prynne's manner when
he begged the pardon of the House "with tears in his eyes" and
"very submissively" was significant, and this was not missed at
the time. One Cavalier hastened to write his wife that this was
something Prynne "never could be brought to do before . . . by
any means imaginable," and that it was "contrary to what everybody expected from his temper." Indeed, he concluded, "this we
esteem I assure you a conquest worthy to be bragged of. . . ."[33]

The decisive defeat of the Presbyterian-Congregationalist group
in the division on the third reading of the Corporation Bill on
July 5, was unquestionably due in part to the stunning speed
with which the Bill of Religious Uniformity passed through the
House at this time; for after it was brought in on July 3, it passed
the third reading within a week without a single division. In
addition, pressure was being placed upon the Presbyterian and
Congregationalist members who had not yet received the Sacrament as the House had ordered.[34] As a result of these developments and Prynne's submission on July 15, the Presbyterian core
of the opposition was not only distracted and defeated; it was

also demoralized by the dire implications of the Bill of Uniformity. Unquestionably this helps to explain the apparent lack of efforts by the Presbyterian members of the House of Lords to fight the even more drastic proposals which emerged from the Lords' committee on the Corporation Bill.[35] Although the parliamentary recess which began at the end of July gave the embattled opposition some reprieve, there was no concerted effort to modify the Corporation Bill when it came up afterwards. Even more indicative is the absence of any evidence that the Presbyterian Lords took any steps to oppose the sacramental test which had recently been added. In the Commons there was likewise no effort to modify this direct and crucial attack upon Nonconformist political strength in the boroughs.[36]

Nevertheless, the Presbyterian-Congregationalist group had not given up, and even though they could not be effective they continued to exert such pressure as they could and to let their views be known. During the remaining winter and spring months of this session there were two bills of major constitutional importance which concerned these members, and in both instances they took steps which would have protected their interests and at the same time liberalized the bills. While the Second Militia Bill was under consideration, the Presbyterians and Congregationalists made two attempts to gain special provisions for London. The Presbyterian John Fowke was their main spokesman for the proviso "concerning ordering and disposing of forces in London." Unfortunately, he made several statements which the House regarded as "factious and dangerous," and when he failed to satisfy the House by his explanation he was "severely reprehended at the Bar." [37] In spite of this and the defeat of the proviso, a second attempt was made that day to have it passed.[38] Of even more interest was the attempt made to amend the Bill to License and Control Printing, which came on the same day that the King passed the Act of Uniformity. Obviously concerned about the stringent restraints in this Bill, the Nonconformists backed a proviso "concerning reprinting books" which probably would have placed few if any restrictions upon this type of publishing. The political and religious implications of their motion are obvious, and it is not surprising that the Anglican royalists defeated this measure by a three to one vote.[39]

Although the Presbyterians and Congregationalists fought these two Bills which in effect abolished freedom of the press and confirmed the King's control over the Government's police power, there were not the repeated attacks against them that there had been against the Corporation Bill early in the preceding summer. This is not surprising. Prynne had ceased to function as a leader, and other Presbyterian and Congregationalist members who were outspoken in defense of their political and religious views were also receiving retaliatory treatment, and even losing their seats in the House. The similarity between the cases of Prynne and John Fowke is already evident.[40] In addition, the Presbyterians lost two other leaders who were vulnerable because their elections were being contested. Sir Ralph Ashton's election was voided in February, and Sir James Langham's in April, just a month after he had been a teller in support of Fowke's amendment to the Militia Bill. In Langham's case the House even voted to make an exception to its standing rule in order to accept a petition against his election after the time lapse usually allowed.[41] In the face of such retaliatory measures the efforts of those Nonconformists who attempted to amend the Licensing Bill on the last day of the session is remarkable. However, this was the last instance for many years in which members of the Presbyterian-Congregationalist group in the House of Commons were prominent as leaders in efforts to restrict the Crown's constitutional powers.

When Parliament considered the next measure concerning fundamental powers of this sort, which was the Bill to Amend the Triennial Act of 1641, the religious situation had crystallized, the Act of Uniformity having been passed by the King on the same day as the Licensing Act.[42] Moreover, during the two-year period that the Triennial Bill was under consideration, the reaction against the Presbyterians, Congregationalists, Baptists and Quakers became ever more extreme. In the autumn of 1663 the Northern Plot occurred, convincing extreme Anglicans and Government authorities that Conventicles were hotbeds of treason, and in the subsequent investigations such Presbyterian leaders in Parliament as Lord Wharton and Colonel John Birch were accused of involvement.[43] Finally, the first Conventicle Bill was also in its final stages of enactment, and it was the most severe of all the measures directed at Dissenters.[44]

Weakened in leadership and numbers, and under duress as

they were, it is not surprising that the Presbyterian and Congregationalist representatives in Parliament were divided and that none of them took a leading part in opposing the new Triennial Bill, which was designed to undo the work of the parliamentarians and Puritans of 1641, and in effect to increase the power of the King and decrease that of Parliament.[45] "Above all expectations," William Prynne even favored passage of the new Bill and damned the Bill of 1641 "most desperately." In addition John Swynfen contended that "no coercion ought to be on the King or his government other than his oath and honor," and thus he joined Prynne in support of the new Bill.[46] Although there were Presbyterian and Congregationalist members who did oppose the Bill, this time they were the followers in the opposition. Those who led the attack were such men as John Vaughan, later Chief Justice of the Common Pleas, Sir Richard Temple, and Sir Thomas Meres, all of whom were prominent members of the group soon to be called the "country party," and all of whom appear to have been moderate Anglicans sympathizing with Dissenters or seeking their support.[47] Samuel Pepys, who had been kept informed by a member of the House of Commons, wrote on the day of the Bill's final passage that "the discontented Presbyters, and the faction of the House will be highly displeased with [it]; but it was carried clearly against them in the House." [48] There is evidence also that Dissenters in the country were "mad against King and Church, since repeal of the old Triennial Act," and that others in the future, such as Roger Morrice, were to hold that one "effectual means for the advancing of arbitrary power" had been this new Triennial Act that "took away the Statute for Triennial Parliaments, and left them arbitrary at the King's will to call any or none . . ." [49]

Although in 1664 most Dissenters appear to have opposed abolition of the automatic provisions of the Triennial Act, four years later when Temple brought in a Bill which would have restored these provisions there was no evidence of active support from any of the Presbyterians or Congregationalists in the Commons.[50] However, Temple's Bill was withdrawn about an hour after its introduction, and any response to it of either a positive or negative character was related to the political maneuvers and the alignments at the outset of 1668. Deeply involved in these machinations was Temple himself. He had been one of the leading

anti-Clarendonians supporting the impeachment of the Lord
Chancellor during the previous months, and he had been associated with George Villiers, the Second Duke of Buckingham, who
was the instigator of the impeachment. Although Temple had
high political hopes for himself and others of the anti-Claren-
donian group in the Commons, they were not yet in office. It
therefore appears that the introduction of the new Triennial Bill
early on February 18, 1668, might have been an attempt to use
this sensitive matter of royal prerogative in order to gain the
bargaining power with which to obtain a more lucrative position
from the King. At the same time, and for similar reasons, it appears that Temple thought the introduction of such a measure
would win support within the Commons where he was hoping
to crush the Clarendonians by welding his group with the Presbyterian-Congregationalist group and also with those members
best termed the country gentlemen.[51]

The Presbyterians and the Congregationalists were not the only
members from whom Temple anticipated support that was not
forthcoming, as his hasty withdrawal of the measure indicated.
Whether notified of his surprise maneuver in advance or not, the
Presbyterian and Congregationalist members would have had
mixed reactions to the attempt. Although introduction of Court-
backed measures for comprehension and toleration had been
blocked at the very opening of Parliament on February 6, Presbyterian and Congregationalist members would have been reluctant to jeopardize any hopes for religious relief through parliamentary action. They could have done this either by strong and
overt support of the new Triennial Bill, which would have antagonized the Court, or by refusing to give any support at all to
Temple's Bill and thereby losing such support as they might have
had for religious relief from the anti-Clarendonians. In the end,
however, they may well have been reluctant to speak out because
of the tactics of Temple and all of "that gang"—as John Milward
termed them—which must have been obvious and objectionable.
Nearly all these men had been among the most aggressive proponents of the impeachment proceedings against Clarendon during
October and November, 1667, just a few months earlier,[52] and
it appears that during the impeachment crisis the Presbyterians
and Congregationalists came to distrust the general leadership
of these men in the Lower House, as well as of Buckingham.

It has long been recognized that the Presbyterians and Congregationalists in Parliament were not among those who instigated or gave strong backing to the proceedings against Clarendon. As Baxter pointed out, it was notable that they "were most moderate in his cause, and many for him." [53] As soon as Parliament took up the dismissal of Clarendon after convening in October, 1667, the Presbyterian members were opposed to any measures of an extreme or unjust nature. Sir John Maynard and Colonel Birch were among those opposed to thanking the King for his dismissal of Clarendon because this would seem to be "precondemning him before any crime was laid to his charge." [54] Similarly Prynne opposed having him secured, and he maintained, "that before any impeachment be sent up against him, . . . witnesses should be examined, and . . . the House might be satisfied of the proofs of those things that were laid to his charge." [55] Maynard was also a strong supporter of this procedure and emphasized that "where life is concerned you ought to have a moral certainty of the thing, and every one be able to say upon this proof: In my conscience this man is guilty. Common fame is no ground to condemn a man, when matter of fact is not clear. To say an evil is done, therefore this man has done it, is strange in morality, and even more in logic." [56] When the charges were brought into the House no Presbyterian or Congregationalist offered to prove or affirm any of them; and after it was moved that it be specified whether he would be impeached for treason or misdemeanor upon each charge, the Presbyterians who spoke were strong opponents of impeachment for treason upon several of the accusations. In the great debate on treason of November 9–11, Maynard, Prynne, and Birch opposed impeaching him for treason on the first charge, which stated that he had "designed a standing army to be raised, to govern the kingdom thereby . . . ," and it was voted down. Prynne and Sir Edward Harley opposed impeachment for treason upon the Article concerning the sale of Dunkirk, and as a result there was no decision made. Finally Maynard, Birch, and Prynne questioned impeachment for treason upon the Article charging Clarendon had betrayed the King's secret counsels to his enemies because there was only one witness, and they doubted whether he was English.[57]

After the House of Commons finally made a general charge of treason in the impeachment submitted to the House of Lords on November 12, and the Lords refused to commit the Chancellor for this reason as the House of Commons desired, John Swynfen came into prominence during the ensuing dispute as one of the managers of conferences between the Houses. He was a most vigorous supporter of the Commons' wishes and rights, while at the same time in the House of Lords the Presbyterians Holles and Anglesey emerged as two of the leading proponents of the Lords' point of view. Although they differed on this issue, all of them made it evident they were concerned that Clarendon be given a legal and fair trial. There being no specific charges backed by sufficient evidence, Swynfen thought that the only way to obtain a trial in "the legal way" by impeachment was to proceed on the basis of the general charge, for the alternative being considered by Buckingham and the King, as Swynfen may have known, was a trial before a special court of twenty-four peers appointed by Charles with the intent of obtaining a conviction.[58] However, Holles and Anglesey believed that there were no judicially acceptable precedents for an imprisonment; and both were, as always, quick to defend the Lords' judicial powers because they thought they saw an attempted invasion by the Commons.[59] After Clarendon fled from England on the night of November 29, it was Swynfen who finally moved the House of Commons resolve that the Lords' failure to secure Clarendon on a general impeachment was an obstruction to public justice of a dangerous consequence.[60]

When the Lords accepted the flight as a confession of guilt and passed the Bill for Banishing and Disenabling Clarendon, there was a significant reaction among Presbyterian leaders. Holles was one of the Lords who registered a formal protest,[61] while Swynfen was one of the leaders opposed to the Bill's passage in the Lower House. In a major speech Swynfen attacked it because it shifted the procedure from a "judicial way to a legislative way," and he pointed out that if the Bill passed Clarendon could "say justly, he is condemned without hearing one witness, [which is] against the law of nature and nations." Continuing, he emphasized that "the legislative power of Parliament is great, . . . having no bound but the integrity and justice of Parliaments," and he warned that "if reason of state be a motive of Parliament to banish one man, so it may be for many. . . ."[62] Prynne supported this same basic argument by contending that it was legally wrong and unjust for Parliament to take this action against a man without hearing him, and also speaking against the measure was Sir Walter Yonge.[63]

The unusually strong Presbyterian attack upon the Bill of Banishment raises a question as to the reason. In this instance as throughout the whole crisis it is clear that these members were much concerned that any trial or punishment be both legal and just. It is also true that Anglesey and some of the Presbyterian members of Parliament who were more favorable to Clarendon may well have fallen back upon pleas for justice because of their concern for the Chancellor and their recognition of his efforts prior to 1664 to temper Anglican repression of Nonconformity, rather than because of a concern for the canons of justice themselves. But any gratitude for Clarendon's earlier attitude toward the moderate Dissenters would have been much reduced because the Chancellor's position changed, and in 1665 he had urged Parliament to take strong measures against the Dissenters.[64] Even though appreciation of his earlier efforts may have influenced some of the Dissenters' political leaders to a degree, their primary aim seems to have been that Clarendon be given a just and legally defensible trial and that constitutional processes be followed.[65] Both in this concern and in the fear of an irresponsible use of power, the moderate Presbyterians displayed the natural desire of a minority to prevent the government from acting in an arbitrary manner.

Another reason for the reaction of the Presbyterian and Congregationalist members to the impeachment proceedings was that they disliked and distrusted those who sought to ruin Clarendon by any means possible.[66] Moreover, the failure of Buckingham, Seymour, Temple and their group to command a following among the Dissenters in Parliament was later considered by Temple to be one of the important reasons for the "ill success" of the anti-Clarendonians in the session of 1667–1668. Small in number though the "Presbyterians" were—about forty according to Temple's estimate—he considered them "perfectly united, sedulous, and generally men of parts. . . ." When their support was gained along with those whom he called the "less active country gentlemen," he believed it would then be possible to carry the House.[67]

Buckingham's obvious effort to win Nonconformist support by backing toleration early in 1668 had been partially inspired by an appreciation of the value of the Dissenters' support, both in Parliament and in the country at large. However, his religious views were not orthodox and his personal life was not of the sort that would win Nonconformist approval. Particularly ill-timed was his duel in January with George Talbot, the Earl of Shrewsbury, which resulted in the Earl's death in March; but even more objectionable was Buckingham's open continuance of his liaison with the Countess of Shrewsbury. Thus his support of toleration for the Dissenters did not bring him the response that it might have.[68] Not only at this time but later as well, Buckingham does not seem to have been as successful as either some of his contemporaries or later historians have thought in winning Nonconformist followers. Two years after Clarendon's impeachment a list of those whom Buckingham might engage as his followers included only the names of Swynfen and Sir John Stapely, but in the spring of 1668 even these two men were among four Presbyterians included in a list of the Duke of Ormonde's followers, the other two being Sir Richard Ingoldsby and Colonel Richard Norton.[69]

Another reason Buckingham may not have appealed to the Dissenters as much as he might have was that he did not appear to share their great concern with matters of trade and taxation, which along with the religious question were of much importance to them, particularly during 1667 when they along with others became increasingly aroused by policies or measures affecting public funds and trade. In addition, they were among those members much alarmed over miscarriages of the second Dutch War, and in debates on all of these matters they supported and even led attempts to encroach upon the royal prerogative or restrain the King's actions. After members of the Lower House became disturbed about expenditure of the extraordinary supply which had been granted in order to carry on the Dutch War, the Presbyterian leaders became active in support of the Bill for examining and taking accounts of public monies; and in the end they were given positions of leadership in steering the Bill through the House.[70] However, the Bill failed in the spring, and it was not until the fall session after the impact of the Dutch fleet's devastating attack upon the Medway in June, 1667, that sufficient support developed for this measure which embodied the principle of inspection of accounts.[71]

The expenditure of funds and the naval defeat also brought threat of a traditional maneuver designed to restrain the King— a demand for redress of grievances before a grant of supply. Colonel Birch was one of the leaders in this attack, opposing a motion to consider the King's supply until it was perfected; and he therefore moved "that the two great miscarriages—the first was the mis-spending the great sums of money that have been raised, the other [was] the not securing the river Medway— should be looked into and examined." [72] Economic reasons again appear to explain the Dissenters' position, and this time they were of a more specific nature, namely opposition to various excise proposals which would directly affect the commercial interests. For example on March 31, the day following Birch's motion about considering grievances instead of supply, a proposal to levy a tax on the retailers of wine was debated, and it was "very much opposed by the Dissenters." [73] Further indicating the temper of the Dissenters on these matters was Birch's statement of April 1, that he "would have it treason to pay or receive any money upon the wines at the Custom-house, after more than the sum granted be raised." [74]

Concerned though Presbyterian and Congregationalist members were over such economic problems and their constitutional implications, it is evident that even upon these questions they did not assume the same position of leadership which they had occupied in 1661 in the fight against the Corporation Act. In the intervening years they had not only lost their political strength in the boroughs as a result of this Act, but they had also suffered from reprisals and some loss in numbers in the House of Commons. At the same time the Act of Uniformity and the Conventicle Act had had their drastic effects. Given such developments it is remarkable that they continued any opposition efforts at all, and it is not surprising that as time passed they became ready to follow the leadership offered by moderate Anglicans.

Although they became less aggressive and persistent in their parliamentary counter-attacks during the early years of the Cavalier Parliament, it is clear that they did take steps to modify such measures as the Second Militia Act and to liberalize the Licensing Act, and that except for Prynne and Swynfen they opposed the Triennial Act of 1664. Furthermore it appears that Nonconformist ministers and laymen found these Acts objectionable on political and constitutional grounds. Concern that just and legally defensible impeachment proceedings be followed and the fear of an irresponsible use of power also indicate the understandable desires of a minority to have a government in which prescribed legal procedures and constitutional limitations would restrain arbitrary actions by those in power.

Deprived of political predominance and prosecuted though they were for their religious and political views, there was still overt Nonconformist support for a "regulated mixed monarchy," particularly among the Presbyterians and Congregationalists who sat in Parliament.

CHAPTER IV

*The Impact of Uniformity, 1661–1673: Political*
*and Constitutional Aspects of the Religious Settlement*

The efforts to discover a settlement of the religious problem in
1660 had ended unsatisfactorily for all concerned. The basic
reason for the impasse was that no one religious group was sufficiently in possession of power to impose its will, but after the
parliamentary elections in the spring of 1661 it became clear that
at last Anglican leaders would be able to obtain the religious
settlement they desired. The newly elected Cavalier members
were in no mood to accept the spirit of tolerance and concession
found in the King's Worcester House Declaration of the previous
autumn, but its opening paragraph contained a statement of the
problem more as they saw it. The King had said:

How much the peace of the State is concerned in the peace of the Church,
and how difficult a thing it is to preserve order and government in civil,
while there is no order or government in ecclesiastical affairs, is evident to
the world; and this little part of the world, our own dominions, has had so
late experience of it, that we may very well acquiesce in the conclusion,
without enlarging ourself in discourse upon it. . . .[1]

Here is described the political aspect of the religious problem
that was to plague the Dissenters in the coming decades, for
staunch Anglicans believed religious order could only be obtained by uniformity and conformity. No Dissenters were to be
more constantly aware of this and more constantly confronted
by the problem than those who sat in Parliament and attempted
to temper the legislative blows that were to follow, nor than the
Nonconformist ministers who sought in various ways to obtain
the right to worship as they wished. Although their efforts were
rarely successful, they were of significance because they reveal

much concerning the political activities and constitutional ideas of the Dissenters.

With the collapse of the efforts of the Savoy Conference,[2] moderate Puritans found themselves confronting the prospect of the same basic status that Congregationalists, Baptists, and Quakers had long since known by choice, for they too were to become Separatists. Actually there were more ominous and decisive signs of their coming ejection from the Church even before the Savoy Conference ended on July 25, 1661, for within a week early in that month the Bill of Uniformity had been brought into the House of Commons, passed without a division, and sent to the Lords.[3] Moreover, after the next session of Parliament opened in November the Anglican leaders in the Commons again demonstrated their mood and their power. When a move was made to retain moderate Puritan ministers in the livings they then held by passing a Bill to Confirm the Convention Parliament's Act for Settling Ministers, the Anglican members were able to destroy the intent of the Bill by a series of amendments, although not without overcoming some determined opposition.[4] The situation was desperate, but there was to be one source of hope. When the Bill came to a test in the House of Lords at the beginning of 1662, the King's adherence to a policy of comprehension was clearly demonstrated. Even when faced by a threat from Anglicans in the Commons that they would withhold votes for additional revenue, Charles affirmed his intention to fulfill his promise made at Breda, and on the floor Clarendon was finally successful in his efforts to substitute a Bill which would in fact have completely confirmed the original Act.[5] Although the Commons refused to accept the Lords' Bill, the immediate threat to Puritan ministers then holding benefices had been defeated. Furthermore there now seemed to be a possibility that something might be done to temper the drastic impact which the Bill for Uniformity would have if accepted by the Lords as it passed the Commons, for Presbyterian peers had good reason to believe they would have the continued support of the Court.

The extent to which Puritans would have liked to change the Bill of Uniformity is best gauged by the proposals found among Lord Wharton's parliamentary papers. Included among the considerable number of draft amendments were proposals to establish both comprehension and toleration, either directly by the

terms of the Bill, or indirectly by giving the King parliamentary
sanction to use the royal prerogative to attain these ends. Presbyterian hopes for comprehension were best represented in a
proposed amendment which stated that nothing in the Act of
Uniformity should invalidate concessions which the King had
made in the Worcester House Declaration.[6] Even with Court
pressure, this was unquestionably a broader comprehension than
the Lords would have accepted, and perhaps it was for this
reason that the amendment which Clarendon introduced at the
King's direction would have been much less inclusive, authorizing the King to grant dispensations to ministers who had held
benefices since May 29, 1660, so that they would not have to
wear a surplice or sign with the cross at baptism.[7] Puritans of
Separatist traditions who sought toleration had also drawn up a
proposal which went too far for it to be adopted, for even though
it required assent to the Thirty-nine Articles concerning the confession of the "true Christian faith," it would have allowed public
meetings in such a place as was made known to the diocesan
and permitted exemptions from penalties for not attending the
Parish Church and for not "administering or receiving the Sacraments . . . or not observing the ceremonies . . ." of the Anglican Church.[8] Three other draft amendments among Wharton's
papers would have given parliamentary recognition to the royal
dispensing power, two of them going as far as to state that nothing in the Act should prejudice the King's supreme power and
authority in ecclesiastical affairs. However, there was no possibility of their acceptance, for each envisioned the existence and
toleration of meetings even more removed from Anglicanism, one
stating that all those professing the Apostles Creed and acknowledging the Old and New Testament to be the revealed word of
God would be allowed to exercise their religion.[9]

Lord Wharton's Independent or Congregationalist background
and his Presbyterian connections had obviously made him the
focal point of Puritan efforts to obtain changes in the Bill for
Uniformity, but his influence in the House of Lords was very
limited. Moreover, the Presbyterian-Congregationalist peers were
far too small in number, as was clearly evident when Anglesey
and Delamer were the only ones of their leaders who were placed
on the committee of thirty-two to which the Bill was referred.[10]
By April when Clarendon introduced a proposal to delete the

Bill's reference to the Solemn League and Covenant, even the Court's strong influence was not sufficient to overcome the weakness of the Puritan lords, and the motion was defeated. In the end there was only one other amendment adopted in committee that was of significance to them, beside the one providing for dispensations for not wearing the surplice or signing the cross, and it would have authorized the King to provide each minister deprived of his preferment under the Act with a grant of one fifth of its profits for the remainder of his lifetime.[11]

Modest though they were, the two modifications passed in committee would have given considerable freedom to the King to ease the impact of uniformity. A good number of Presbyterian ministers would have been able to remain in the Established Church, and some compensation would have been available for the Presbyterians and Congregationalists who were ejected. As a result many began to say that "the Lord's House is the House of Lords," [12] but such hopes as the two amendments created were premature. The House of Commons was still intent upon uniformity and strict conformity, and there was a vindictiveness prevalent against the Puritans as well as growing dissatisfaction with Court policy regarding religion. As a result both amendments were killed by the Lower House. The intransigence of the staunch Anglican members was too much even for the King to resist, and thus the Bill which he felt compelled to pass on May 19, 1662, marked the failure not merely of the Puritans but also of the Court.[13]

Thereafter the only manner in which to temper the Act before it went into effect was for the King to take prerogative action, even though Parliament had refused to give its sanction, and either grant a general indulgence or suspension of the Act or issue dispensations to individual ministers. Moved by indications of growing discontent among the existing and the prospective Dissenters and concerned by indications that Clarendon's political effectiveness was in question, both the King and the Lord Chancellor became increasingly receptive to the idea of resorting to the royal prerogative. Responding to a petition of June 2, presented by a group of Presbyterians to Clarendon, in which they asked for his assistance in obtaining a "grace of toleration" from the King, the Lord Chancellor gave his support to the idea of suspending the Act for three months; but this proposal was dropped when it met opposition from both the bishops and the lawyers who were consulted on June 10.[14]

As the summer months passed tension increased, and there was growing fear that there might be serious strife as the Act went into effect on St. Bartholomew's Day, August 24. The King therefore tried another maneuver. Following royal instructions, Clarendon and the Duke of Albemarle told Dr. Thomas Manton, Dr. William Bates, Edmund Calamy, and a few other Presbyterian ministers on August 20 that if they would petition the King, he would grant a limited number of individual dispensations.[15] This was the first instance in which the Court was to confront Dissenters with the proffer of an indulgence, and it was particularly tempting since it came just as ejection was imminent and seemed inevitable. "Past all expectations," the Presbyterian minister Henry Newcome described the offer, as he wrote in his diary on Saturday night, the eve of St. Bartholomew's Day. "God still puts off the blow," he added, "and one would think by his dealings that he did not intend they should harm us." [16] Newcome also made it clear that the offer had a divisive effect. To petition the King to dispense with an Act of Parliament would conflict with constitutional principles that Puritans had espoused during the preceding decades. There were those who stoutly opposed requesting the King to use the royal prerogative, and their parliamentarian views were reflected not only in the belief that "the House of Commons are like to call them to the bar for petitioning against an Act of Parliament," but also in the hope that "the next session of Parliament will relieve us all." [17] On the other hand there were strong supporters of the Court's proposed dispensations, and among them may have been Calamy who at the end of 1662 had developed the idea that "God has hitherto saved England by way of prerogative . . . ," instead of condemning her for sins for which other nations have been destroyed.[18] "Weighty matters lie on us," Newcome wrote after one obviously heated meeting of ministers, prayerfully adding, "the Lord make us unanimous." The next day after "tough debates" from noon until night, it was decided to petition.[19] Although the text of the petition was no more specific than to request the King to "take such effectual course whereby we may be continued in our stations to teach the people obedience to God," [20] it was clear that the twenty ministers who signed it had decided to accept relief by an exercise of royal prerogative when relief through Parliament was not to be had. In the end, however, they were not put to the test, for the Court abandoned its plans when it met compelling opposition led by the Bishop of London, Gilbert Sheldon, while the proposal was being considered by the Privy Council on August 28.[21]

In the meantime "Black Sunday" had passed, and the ministers who had anticipated a royal dispensation to relieve the impact of ejection suffered a second blow when they learned that there would be none. But unknown to the Nonconformist ministers the King had not abandoned hope of exercising his prerogative to grant them relief. Nor did he consult them during the next months regarding his plans, which were announced in the Declaration favoring toleration issued on December 26.[22] For those with parliamentarian views his plans did not have the constitutional objections of the last proposal, for he planned to persuade Parliament to sanction the use of an indulgence to grant toleration to all those not conforming to the Church, Catholics included.[23] Toleration was exactly what Congregationalists had wanted; and although there was a reluctance among them to see the Catholics included, Philip Nye and the King in the end gained strong support for the plan.[24] However, Presbyterians were much opposed to the King's offer, mainly because Catholics would be included, but also because most Presbyterians desired comprehension and not toleration. Thus the addresses of thanks that the Court sought by sending Nye to see Baxter on January 2, 1663, were not forthcoming, and when Parliament convened in February several "angry Presbyters of the House [of Commons] supposing Popery to be the game would not come up. . . ."[25] Charles was fully aware of Presbyterian desires, and sending for Calamy, Bates, and Manton he gave them "full assurance that a Bill should be brought into the House which would introduce most of them into their places again."[26] Thus the Court measure introduced on February 23 would have made such comprehension possible by giving the King parliamentary sanction to use his dispensing power, with the restrictions that he could not remove the requirements concerning use of the Book of Common Prayer and subscription to the doctrinal Articles. In addition he could have granted toleration, but he could not extend it to

Catholics. Finally, religious qualifications for officeholding, meaning those in the Corporation Act, were to remain in effect.[27]

Any possibility that relief might come through this Bill soon disappeared, for it was dropped in committee.[28] But far more ominous, the House of Commons turned to the Conventicle Bill. Strenuous efforts were made to have it amended so that it would be less severe in its effects than its promoters had designed it to be, and of the amendments offered in the House of Commons the most significant was the one which would have been "on the behalf of such as do frequent the service at the Church, and receive the Sacrament thrice every year." [29] Since those who came to Church and took the Sacrament as stipulated would otherwise have been permitted to worship publicly as they pleased, a limited religious toleration would have been allowed. But the effect of the amendment would have been political as well as religious. All those political leaders who had already become occasional conformists in order to comply either with the Corporation Act or the orders of the Houses of Parliament requiring them to receive the Sacrament in the Anglican Church would have been most reassured by such legal sanction of this practice. Furthermore, other moderate Dissenters would undoubtedly have followed their example if occasional conformity had been legalized, and thus their political strength in borough and Parliament might have increased somewhat. Moderate Anglicans were interested and gave support, for in division the amendment had eighty-nine supporters in a thin House, there being only ninety-four opposed. There were three other attempts to make the bill less severe on June 30, the day of its third reading, one of which was "on the behalf of such as were aiding and assisting to the Duke of Albemarle, and the Earl of Sandwich, in restoring his Majesty." But all were unsuccessful, and zealous Anglicans carried the day by passing the Bill 125 to 61.[30]

During the year that elapsed before the Lords passed the Conventicle Bill there was little real possibility of tempering its provisions. However the Presbyterian peers did find one opportunity to work for retention of an amendment providing for greater legal security to those who wished to continue worshipping in private non-Anglican services, since it would have prevented the search of their houses by all officers except the Lord Lieutenant of the County and would have permitted those who were found guilty to be tried only by their peers. Although the Earl of Anglesey, Lord Wharton, and the other peers who maintained private Nonconformist chaplains, would not have violated the Act unless five or more persons over sixteen from outside their households attended their services, still they could have been more certain of their privacy and security had this amendment been included in the Bill.[31] As the provisions stood, forcible search without a warrant could be used, and in effect it could be based upon rumor and hearsay that a Conventicle was being held. Furthermore, it was provided that the "oath of witnesses or notorious evidence" that the law had been violated was to be recorded, and the "record so made . . . shall to all intents and purposes be in law taken and adjudged to be a full and perfect conviction." [32]

Hopeless as the situation was, the amendments which the Presbyterians and Congregationalists backed make it evident that they did not cease struggling to obtain some legal sanction for the manner in which they wished to worship, and also that they were concerned about any political effects which the new law might have. Not only did they fail in efforts to modify the Bill, but with its passage any possibility of alleviation through comprehension or toleration was to disappear for nearly four years.

In the meantime the last of the four Acts constituting the Restoration religious settlement was passed. The significance of the Five Mile Act was political and constitutional in character as well as religious, for Nonconformist ministers were to swear that they would "not at any time endeavor any alteration of government in Church or State" if they wished to stay within five miles of any borough sending burgesses to Parliament, or any place where they had held a Church preferment after the Act of Oblivion or preached to an unlawful assembly.[33] Lord Wharton's papers make it clear that he and others were greatly concerned and that efforts were made to modify the Bill. Wharton himself made a speech prior to the vote of October 30, on the question that it be recommitted upon the oath, which he and others wanted altered so that only endeavors to alter the government "tumultuously and seditiously" would be prohibited, but those which were peaceful and in accordance with existing law would be allowed. In addition he did not want ministers imprisoned without a trial by jury, and he emphasized that many would be committed who had been instrumental in the Restoration and who were orthodox in religion, believing in the Thirty-nine Articles except for those on ceremonies and discipline.[34] The most important result of the Act was that it forced a large number of Nonconformist ministers to choose between abandoning homes, friends, and such economic security as they might still have had on the one hand, or forswearing their traditional role as religious and political reformers on the other. At least fifty took the oath, and it is thought that the total number doing so must have been greater. But this was a relatively small percentage of the approximately 1600 who had been ejected and remained Nonconformists. Since there were a large number of ministers who risked violation of the Act, it appears that the vast majority of Nonconformist ministers demonstrated the nature and intensity of their religious and political convictions.[35]

Now that the basic Restoration religious settlement was completed and the extreme Anglicans in the Parliament and the country were predominant in their power, there was not much point in attempting any basic modification or change in the *status quo*. However, by 1667 the intensity of the fear and dislike of Dissenters was to some degree obscured and perhaps diminished by the violent feeling against Catholics, who were widely blamed for the great London fire of 1666. Moreover, there were the momentous political changes which came as a result of the dismissal and impeachment of Clarendon at the end of the year. In the fluid situation which developed, Nonconformist backing throughout the country and the political support of the Presbyterian-Congregationalist group in Parliament was worth seeking both for their own sakes and also because the political leader who could claim them would probably be more certain of winning the approval of the King, for Charles also saw that his religious policy which had failed in 1662–1663 might be successful in the changed circumstances. Finally, within the Church itself developments associated with Clarendon's dismissal and impeachment appear to have encouraged those who were favorably disposed toward the Nonconformists to speak out for toleration and latitude, as did Edward Reynolds, the former Presbyterian who had become Bishop of Norwich at the Restoration, when he delivered a sermon to the House of Lords on November

7, 1666.[36] Thus there were good reasons for the Dissenters' growing hopes that relief would come.

Efforts to develop parliamentary and Court support for comprehension and toleration began with the publication of a number of anonymous pamphlets by ministers in 1667, notably the Presbyterians John Humfrey and John Corbet, and the Congregationalist Dr. John Owen. Humfrey, who ardently desired comprehension himself, completed his first pamphlet in June, and he advocated that the Church come to "an Act of Accommodation between the Conformists and Nonconformists that are sober in their principles, and indulgence toward others . . . ," a position Corbet also supported, while Owen wrote several pamphlets urging toleration.[37] Although Owen had much more important political connections than either of the Presbyterian clergymen, Humfrey in particular and Corbet to a lesser degree were at this juncture more influential than the veteran Congregationalist. On the title page of his *Proposition* Humfrey had announced that it was "Tendered to the Consideration of His Majesty and the Parliament Against the Tenth of October," when it met; and according to the information Calamy had later, "it took with many, and the King himself seemed pleased with it." In addition it brought an answer from a chaplain to the Archbishop of Canterbury, to which Humfrey replied.[38]

The connection between the efforts of the ministers and the next development is unknown, but prior to the autumn session a Bill that would have resulted in broad comprehension, presumably including some Congregationalists, was prepared in its final form by Sir Robert Atkins, a Judge of the Common Pleas, which Colonel John Birch was to introduce. The Bill was clearly too liberal for firm Anglicans, and it lacked sufficient political backing. Sensing this when he rose to offer it Birch did so only "faintly and despairing of success sat down"; and since he did not subsequently succeed in overcoming his reluctance, the measure was never formally introduced.[39]

Of far more promise were the next moves which began in January, 1668, for there was a much broader base of support, including the King and important leaders in the State and Church as well as Manton, Bates, Baxter, and later Owen. Two of the key figures were Sir Orlando Bridgeman, Lord Keeper of the Great Seal, and Dr. John Wilkins, whose moderate Anglicanism had been presaged by his marriage to Cromwell's sister prior to the Restoration. By the end of the year Bridgeman had approached Manton through Sir John Baber, and between January 4 and 12, after Wilkins had consulted with five bishops and had been closeted with the King for a two-hour period, he met with Manton, Bates and Baxter for the first time. The proposals which he offered were the basis of discussions which began at this time, and during this series of conferences the problem of comprehension was separated from the question of toleration. Manton, Bates, and Baxter, being primarily interested in comprehension, continued negotiations with Wilkins concerning this problem; and in the end their efforts resulted in a Bill which was drafted by Sir Matthew Hale, later Lord Chief-Justice of the King's Bench. Meanwhile, the Wilkins proposals concerning toleration were turned over to Owen who prepared his own "Bill of Indulgence for Sectaries." [40] Of the two measures, that for comprehension was of most significance since it was the product of concessions made by Anglican and Presbyterian clergymen. Thus instead of requiring reordination of a Presbyterian who had been ordained during the Interregnum, a bishop was to lay his hand upon the minister's head and bestow legal authority to preach and administer the Sacraments. Also the subscription of the Act of Uniformity was to be much modified. Profession and approval of the Church's doctrine, worship, and government was to be required, and no other doctrines were to be brought in or the peace of the Church disturbed. The usual objectionable ceremonies and the wearing of the surplice were to be optional, and some changes in the liturgy and the Book of Common Prayer were either specified or to be forthcoming. [41]

Moderate though this draft bill was, conservative bishops and faithful sons of the Church were unalterably opposed to such concessions. Overly enthusiastic and ingenuous, it was Wilkins himself who triggered the campaign opened by Church leaders against the measure, for relying on friendship he told Seth Ward, Bishop of Salisbury, all the plans and gave him a copy of the proposed Bill for Comprehension even though he knew Ward was a strong supporter of Gilbert Sheldon, the Archbishop of Canterbury. [42] If the terms themselves were not cause for undue alarm, the strong Court support given to the measure certainly was. Sheldon was immediately informed and went into action.

Within a few days a pamphlet appeared attacking the Bill clause
by clause, and at the same time more practical political maneuvers were planned. During the interim prior to the opening of
Parliament ecclesiastical favors were found for relatives and
friends of the members, and staunch Churchmen received the
word that the Bill would "be brought in and countenanced by
very great persons." [43] Decisive action would be needed at the
outset to prevent any surprise moves by those favoring comprehension and toleration and to forestall the increased support
which would develop as a result of the King's speech calling for
such measures. Thus as soon as Parliament met on February 6,
following the Christmas adjournment, the Commons voted
against considering any new business until the House was called
over a week later, when Anglican squires would have returned
from the long holiday period in full force. At the same time both
Sheldon and Ward attacked comprehension in the House of
Lords with a freedom they would not have had after the King
spoke. Moreover, Anglican leaders kept the initiative as well as
the control, and four days later the Commons voted that the
King be petitioned to issue proclamations "to restrain the dis-
orderly and tumultuous meeting of Dissenters . . . and . . . to
put the laws in execution against Conventicles. . . ." [44]

   Although there were several long and intense debates in which
Dissenters and their friends in the House vigorously sought to
have some measure of relief adopted which would be consistent
with the King's desire that Parliament find some way to unite his
subjects in matters of religion, all these attempts failed. [45] Indeed
they only stirred steadfast Anglicans to take more extreme steps
and introduce a new Conventicle Bill. [46] Thus were the hopes of
Dissenters destroyed, and they had good reason to feel embittered. Anglican political leaders who had backed efforts to obtain
relief prior to the meeting of Parliament, such as Bridgeman and
Buckingham, had been ineffectual or inactive; and Bridgeman
was even considered to have turned against Dissenters. [47] In addition Anglican Churchmen in the Commons had successfully ob-
structed the King's religious policy once again. The future seemed
ominous and there was deep discouragement even among those
Dissenters whose expectations had been more realistic, as those
of Thomas Gilbert had been, for he had written Lord Wharton
as the session opened that he was dubious about obtaining com-

prehension and toleration. His highest hope was "that they will not revive the Act against Conventicles," and that perhaps the Five Mile Act would be repealed.[48]

There was every prospect that the new Conventicle Bill would be passed and that it would be more severe. Thus each step of the Bill's passage through the two Houses during the next two years was marked by an intense struggle in which the Dissenters and their friends among moderate Anglicans constantly sought to delay and temper the Bill, while the more zealous Anglican members tried to drive it through as introduced in order to prevent a gap between the time the original Conventicle Act would expire and the time that a new one would go into effect.[49] In only one important way were the Nonconformists and "those that affect the Presbyterians"[50] successful during this two-year struggle. Attempts to rush the Bill through both Houses in the spring of 1668 failed when the House of Lords took no action beyond a first reading, and this meant that the opposition had defeated the last chance Anglican-Cavalier members were given to prevent a lapse between the two Acts.[51]

Although the Presbyterian members wanted a long adjournment, and Richard Hampden was even so outspoken as to suggest that he saw "no inconvenience in dissolving this Parliament," actually their desires had nothing to do with the long recess.[52] The King needed this time to undertake a thorough consideration of his fundamental policies in an attempt to free himself of parliamentary restraints, particularly those placed on him by the necessity of seeking parliamentary financial grants which even when secured had been inadequate. There seemed to be three possibilities: (1) to get along on existing income and not call Parliament into session; (2) to summon a new Parliament which it was thought would have a sufficient number of amenable Dissenters in addition to the Court supporters to make it possible to obtain large grants in return for a royal indulgence establishing toleration; or, (3) to continue with the existing Parliament.[53] But there was also another way in which Charles might obtain additional revenue and solve some of his political problems. If he could find an ally with sufficient power so that the Dutch could be defeated, there then would be a large increase in English trade which would also bring an increase in the royal revenues. Not only did Louis XIV have the power but his policy also now looked toward defeat of the Dutch, and in addition the possibility that he would give a subsidy for assistance was not to be overlooked. By the end of 1668 Charles had made the decision to seek a French alliance, and soon thereafter the negotiations began which were to lead to the secret Treaty of Dover which was signed May 22, 1670.[54]

Meanwhile the immediate pressure of domestic affairs and a critical phase of the French negotiations not long after they had started led Charles to summon Parliament, and it was during this session beginning in February that the Conventicle Bill was finally enacted. The climax of the struggle came in February and March as Dissenters and their friends continued to oppose "the terrible Bill against Conventicles," as Andrew Marvell called it.[55] Even though it had passed the second or third reading in two previous sessions, Presbyterian and Congregationalist members of the Commons continued to speak out in debate and try maneuvers which might delay or modify the Bill.[56] But it was primarily in the Lords that the battle took place this time, the debates becoming so prolonged and of such consequence that Saturday and Sunday sessions were held, two formal protests were recorded, and seemingly unprecedented visits to the House were made by the King while the debate was in progress.[57] The main results of the opposition efforts in the Upper House were to obtain amendments throwing out the clause making Conventicles riots and to "soften" several others.[58] Once again, as in the case of the First Conventicle Act, the Lords tried to protect themselves against search of their houses by a justice of the peace, and Holles and Anglesey were active in supporting this drive; but in the end they were forced to bow to the Commons' objections.[59]

Even with the modifications they obtained, the Bill remained severe. Unlike the original Act of 1664 it empowered one rather than two justices of the peace to take action, and in addition a justice who knowingly failed to take action was to be fined £100. There was also a provision which granted one third of the fine collected to those who gave information leading to conviction, and this understandably gave immediate rise to the professional informer.[60] In addition to these provisions there were those of the original Act which allowed "notorious evidence and circumstance of the fact" to be used as proof of guilt, and which provided that the mere recording of the offense by the justice would be "taken and adjudged a full and perfect conviction." [61]

As Lord Wharton circumspectly pointed out, quite possibly in a speech during the debates on the Bill, "the exorbitant power given to a single justice of peace or town officer [is] greater than [that which] the judges and all the justices of peace in England together now have or ever had," for he will have the power of "disinheriting the subjects both lords and commons from their birthright as to trials by twelve men their peers, and convicting them of offenses for greater penalties, by certificate of one person [62] who may be unskilled and illiterate, and possibly in such an opportunity partial also. . . ." [63] Sir John Maynard also believed that there was "more power by this Bill in one justice of the peace, than in all judges," and he pointedly asked if the members of the Commons would trust a justice who would not be accountable and could "maliciously make a record, and punish whom he will." In such a case, he continued, "though the man be ever so innocent, [there would be] no remedy in the case." [64] In the end, however, it was the gifted Marvell who expressed the Nonconformist and moderate Anglican view of the Act in a single succinct phrase—"the quintessence of arbitrary malice." [65]

There was immediately an outburst of more extreme opinion from Nonconformist publicists, for they could hide behind the protection of anonymity. Of these attacks none was more trenchant and widely influential than that in which the writer summarized his argument in his title: *Some Seasonable and Serious Queries upon the Late Act against Conventicles, Tending to Discover How Much It is against the Express Word of God, the Positive Law of the Nation, the Law and Light of Nature and Principles of Prudence and Policy, and Therefore Adjudged by the Law of the Land to be Void and Null.*[66] The writer of a second pamphlet took a more exclusively secular approach, maintaining that the Conventicle Act was "directly against our fundamental laws" and therefore illegal. Going one step further than the other author, he affirmed that if such laws are made "the people are obliged . . . to disobey the laws . . . and to give obedience to Magna Charta. . . ." [67]

The prevalence of such a feeling in May and June of 1670 is clearly evident in the response which greeted *Some Seasonable and Serious Queries* and in the difficulties the Government encountered in enforcing the Act at the outset. On the day it went into effect, May 15, the pamphlet was distributed at largely attended Nonconformist meetings in London, which were held in violation of the Act. Even more alarming were the numerous reports that justices of the peace and other officials over the country were being sent copies of the pamphlet [68] in an effort to intimidate these officials; for after the author of the pamphlet had carefully gone into the argument that the Act violated the Great Charter, he pointedly asked if it were not dangerous for any one to enforce such an Act, and then he cited the cases of officials who in the past had been imprisoned or executed "for having perverted the due course of law, justice, and right. . . ." [69] Sir John Trevor, one of the Principal Secretaries of State, reported to Lord Arlington on May 23, that he considered the situation "to be very dangerous," and that he had heard the Lord Mayor tell the Duke of York that civil authority could not cope with the situation.[70]

Steps were taken including use of the militia, which brought the immediate crisis under control.[71] But these measures did not stop the circulation of the contentions contained in the two pamphlets. Throughout the next two decades the arguments and ideas presented by the two Nonconformist writers of these pamphlets were to be used in attack, upon the Act that were made by those facing prosecution under its terms. Even though they may have been of little efficacy, the appeals to such principles indicated a continuing belief that a government restrained by fundamental law was the best guarantor of personal liberty.[72]

In a different vein there were also attacks such as that of the Presbyterian John Hicks, who did not "charge it upon any of our legislators, that they have made . . . unjustifiable laws, to be as swords and spears," but blamed those who executed the laws illegally.[73] Yet in spite of such reluctance to place the blame upon Parliament, in the circumstances it was difficult for Nonconformists not to do this. It seemed quite impossible that relief could come from this particular Parliament through an act which would grant comprehension, or toleration, or which would give approval for a royal indulgence, and thus even as early as the beginning of June there were reports that Dissenters were hoping that the King would grant them dispensations or indulgences.[74]

Although Charles had decided six months earlier that eventually this was the step he would take,[75] two years of complicated developments intervened before the decision was made to take action. There were many considerations which contributed to the issuance of the Declaration of Indulgence, but the two most influential remained the King's fundamental aim to obtain an adequate revenue so that he would be free of Parliament and his more obvious desire to give some relief to his Catholic subjects. In signing the Secret Treaty of Dover on May 22 and in concluding the Anglo-French Alliance against the Dutch, Charles was on his way toward solving his financial and political problems. There remained the problems of concluding the *traité simulé* which could be presented to the whole Privy Council, to Parliament, and the country, and then there was the difficult task of winning Protestant England's support for the French Alliance and a war against the Protestant Dutch.

While negotiations for the *traité simulé* were underway in the autumn of 1670, Parliament was called into session, and Lord Clifford, the strong Catholic member of the Cabal, made a carefully planned effort to obtain funds, especially those needed to build up the fleet. Even though the Court was relatively successful this time, the Government's financial condition became so serious that the Stop of the Exchequer was ordered January 2, 1672.[76] Of even more concern to Charles and Clifford, recently appointed Lord Treasurer, was the strong anti-French and anti-Catholic feeling evident in the debates, and the prospect that in order to obtain supplies Charles would in the future have to accept such measures as the Bill designed to prevent Catholics from holding office, which passed the Commons and lapsed in the Lords because of prorogation.[77] Such distasteful concessions for inadequate financial grants would be too much to endure for too little. On the other hand the country was obviously not ready to accept a war against the Dutch with the French as their ally. However, it was believed that a propaganda campaign emphasizing the commercial advantages of a victory in such a war would win general support, while it was hoped that a Declaration of Indulgence would placate the Dissenters. In addition it was clear that an Indulgence would unify the King's leading ministers, since each one of the Cabal favored this step for one reason or another.[78]

Reassured by the report from the Earl of Shaftesbury's secretary, John Locke, who concluded that the King did have the legal right to suspend ecclesiastical laws, Charles and his ministers began their deliberations at the end of 1671.[79] Some brief consideration was given to the idea that comprehension as well as toleration might be granted, but since it appeared this would be too involved, the proposal was discarded. Consequently, efforts were made to persuade the Presbyterians desiring comprehension to accept the plan for toleration. It was at this juncture that Joseph Williamson, who was charged with this task, encountered the division which had been developing between two factions of Presbyterian ministers since the passage of the Five Mile Act and which had become much more prominent after the failure to obtain comprehension or toleration in 1667–68. The older group of men led by Manton, Bates and Baxter, and called the "Dons" by Williamson, wanted comprehension and were bitterly opposed to toleration of Catholics. It was therefore encouraging to the Court that the younger men, who were led by Samuel Annesley and described as the "Ducklings" by Williamson, not only adhered to the position of the Congregationalists, Quakers, and Baptists and desired toleration outside the Church, but also had been growing in number. Although the Dons resisted and were reluctant, it appears that most of them came to accept the idea of a grant of toleration rather than comprehension.[80] Thus the Nonconformists in general were favorably pre-disposed to the Declaration issued on March 15, 1672 which suspended the penal laws against Protestant Dissenters and Catholic Recusants and which allowed the Catholics to worship privately and the Dissenters publicly after they had obtained licenses.[81]

At the appearance of the Indulgence all Nonconformists—particularly the ministers and the members of Parliament—were faced with the necessity of making a decision which involved a crucial constitutional issue, whether they weighed this aspect of the situation or not. Disregarding the technical question of the King's legal right to suspend the penal laws, which it should be remembered was supported by John Locke, there was a more fundamental question for those who held parliamentarian views. Should they accept religious liberty which was granted by an act of prerogative that in effect abrogated statutory law? Acceptance of the freedom to worship which the Declaration granted seemed to indicate a tacit approval of the prerogative grant. As a result Dissenters were open to a pointed question which the Anglican clergyman Samuel Parker soon raised, asking: "Did not these men in the late wars take part with the Parliament, and now they submit to the King's Declaration against an Act of Parliament?" [82] The Presbyterian John Humfrey, acknowledging Parker's question, had a forthright answer. "Be it so," he wrote. "The Act of Parliament is against the command of God: the King permits what God bids. Who should the subject obey, but God and the King?" Explaining his position Humfrey adds that "though the magistrate has an authority over his subjects, in the matters of religion as well as civil matters, yet has he no authority for all that over the conscience of any." [83]

The Congregationalist minister Philip Nye agreed with this basic contention.[84] However, he put his argument in support of it in terms that were much more favorable to the king's prerogative. It appeared to Nye that Parliament was very prone to enact legislation which violated men's consciences, for the "most conscientious in that assembly . . . are not always the major part. . . ." Therefore, he contended that there is a "necessity of a power to review, judge, and dispense with such laws. . . ." Although he stated that he did not want to "derogate from Parliaments," he argued that the King, Lords, and Commons are not equal, but that the "King has the supremacy" and therefore may act concerning the penalties of the law by exempting, dispensing, and pardoning, "more especially in ecclesiastical matters." However, he did insist there were legal limits to the King's prerogative and that he could not dispense with laws when dispensation would be "destructive to the great ends of a commonwealth, common justice, the properties of men, *et cetera*." [85] Using a somewhat different line of argument, an unknown Nonconformist writer denied that in exercising the Christian liberty granted by the Declaration they were contributing to arbitrary government and encroachment upon their civil liberties. Critics who "will have us to let go our Christian liberty to preserve our civil right," were asked: "but supposing we refuse licenses, will that secure our civil rights? Nothing less! The law has taken them all from us. Fines, imprisonments, seizures, banishment . . . yes death itself is our hire by law. Indulgence defends us from these laws, and thereby continues our national privileges, so far is it from taking them away." [86]

Although the constitutional aspect of this question did cause discussion and concern among Presbyterian and Congregationalist ministers, the strictly contemporary evidence in their diaries and letters at the time the Declaration was issued makes it obvious that the overwhelming sense of relief and the intense desire to preach reduced all other considerations to secondary importance. A few days after the Declaration had been issued, Henry Newcome wrote that there were "many thoughts of heart" about it, but he resolved to apply for a license as soon as possible "both in conscience of my own duty to preach the Gospel, as also of this people's need of more help than I could afford them in my fullest liberty." When he found how to obtain a license, his "head was filled too much" to sleep at night; and in April he wrote: "I began to preach . . . to our great satisfaction and rejoicing." [87] Lewis Stukely, the Congregationalist minister who corresponded with Lord Wharton, was even more pointed, writing on May 11, that "if by . . . infringements of liberties civil we have the continuance of spiritual privileges," he would "better digest" any further troubles; and a few months later in another letter to Wharton he elatedly wrote, "the Lord bless the King for his Declaration, for thereby many souls have the last months been converted." [88]

The reaction of Baptists is difficult to document. However, it is clear that a very considerable number of Baptist ministers did not apply for licenses, apparently because they believed that the right to worship freely was inalienable, that it had been granted by God, and that no other authority had the power to make this grant. [89] These were not only the views of a large number of Baptists but also of the Quakers, who did not apply for any licenses at all. [90] To these Nonconformists the King's Indulgence therefore seemed superfluous and even presumptuous.

If most Nonconformist clergymen felt at the outset that the issue between the prerogative and Parliament was less important than other considerations, the laymen in Parliament were of a somewhat different disposition. In the debates which took place when Parliament was finally called into session a year after the Declaration was issued, they were not as active as usual, [91] but it is apparent that they desired the Houses to take some sort of parliamentary action that would either establish toleration or comprehension by a regular act of Parliament on the one hand, or that on the other hand would give parliamentary sanction to the King's Indulgence or temporarily suspend some of the penal laws by a statute. Although John Swynfen did not explicitly state an opinion concerning the King's action, he did hold that it was important to "preserve the true strength of the statute law," and therefore he moved for a committee to prepare a bill which would give parliamentary sanction to the Declaration so that it could be "turned into a law." [92] Apparently somewhat more favorable to the use of the dispensing power were two other old Presbyterian leaders, the Earl of Anglesey and Sir John Maynard. Even though the evidence appears contradictory in Anglesey's case, and the statements made by Maynard are partially inconclusive, it appears that both thought that the King had acted within his rights but that there was definite reason for concern because of the scope of the dispensation granted. Maynard did not believe the Commons should go so far as to say that the Declaration was illegal, but he did want the King to remove the Commons' fears in the business and asserted that "it is agreed on all hands, that the King cannot suspend so as to repeal; else why do we make any law?" However, he did not want to go into the question of whether this universal dispensation of penal laws constituted such a repeal of law.[93] As for Anglesey, it appears that he gave at least tacit approval to the Declaration when it was decided to issue it in 1672.[94] However, a year later it seems evident that he would have preferred a parliamentary sanction of the Declaration; for in a committee of the House of Lords which was to prepare a bill of advice to the King, he proposed that there be a parliamentary enactment which would in the future deprive the King of the right to suspend penal laws in ecclesiastical affairs, and which would have suspended for five years certain penal acts and required that all other ecclesiastical laws "be indispensably put in execution." [95]

All were agreed that relief should be granted; and when a Bill for the Ease of Protestant Dissenters was introduced and debated, there were further discussions of the constitutional issue. Swynfen reaffirmed his earlier stand, while Hugh Boscawen and William Love also indicated their distrust of the prerogative and their desire to see Parliament limit its use. Most of all they desired to have comprehension and toleration granted by an act of Parliament.[96] In the House of Lords Anglesey likewise worked for the passage of this Bill and continued to support parliamentary limitation of the use of the prerogative, while Lord Wharton, long eager to bring about an easing of the Dissenters' conditions, corresponded with Nonconformist ministers and received their suggestions concerning the Bill.[97] Leaders of these ministers also took action on their own. Baxter saw to it that some members of Parliament were acquainted with his ideas, and John Humfrey wrote *Comprehension Prompted,* for which he was called before the Privy Council because it allegedly contained "several clauses of a seditious and treasonable nature. . . ."[98] "Great expectations" were raised as the Bill successfully passed through all three readings in each House, but in the end it did not become a statute because the King terminated the session while there was still strong difference of opinion between the Houses over the amendments added by the Lords.[99]

Since Parliament had been successful in forcing the King to withdraw his Declaration of Indulgence, and since it had then failed to enact the Bill which would have granted some degree of comprehension and toleration, there was some feeling of resentment and discouragement among Nonconformists, as well as a tendency to look to the King once again for assistance.[100] However, there were other developments to be considered, and they had a more enduring influence upon the attitude of Nonconformists toward Parliament and the Monarchy. Of major importance was the enactment of the first Test Act, which was designed to eliminate Catholic office holders.[101] At the same time an effort to bar all Dissenters from sitting in the House of Commons was defeated.[102] Since the Nonconformist fear of Catholicism had been increased by the freedom given it under the Indulgence, and since it had become even more intense by 1673, the Test Act was regarded as a "rich mercy."[103] Also of influence were the facts that in the same session the Bill for the Ease of Protestant Dissenters did come so near to enactment, while at the same time the King failed to take any action which would grant relief to Nonconformists following the withdrawal of the Declaration. Finally, the growing misgivings about the expanding Dutch War and Catholic influences at Court also contributed to the subtle change in the attitude of Dissenters toward the Monarchy which began to be evident in the closing months of 1673.[104]

In this changing climate of opinion it is not surprising to find Nonconformist ministers once again turning to Parliament rather than the King. Thus during the session beginning in January, 1674, John Humfrey "again printed another sheet, and put it into the hands of many Parliament men" in an attempt to obtain a bill of comprehension and toleration. In addition, Richard Baxter had drawn up a proposal of his own called an "Healing Act" which he showed to Richard Hampden.[105] In time others also changed, one of the most striking being Oliver Heywood. At the time the licenses issued under the Declaration were finally withdrawn, he told his congregation that one of the reasons he would not continue to preach was that if the Nonconformists behave peaceably, Parliament "may restore our liberty by law." More significant, he indicated that he now gave consideration to the constitutional issue involved in the issuance of the Declaration, for he continued: "Their licenses not being according to the established laws of the land, but by the King's prerogative, it is by some feared they may prove of dangerous consequence, for if he may dispense with laws upon one account, he may also supersede upon another." [106]

In 1672, when confronted by a choice of accepting or rejecting a religious liberty that was not in accordance with the laws of the realm, most Nonconformist ministers and publicists seem to have reached the same decision as that of the twenty ministers in 1662 who decided to accept the King's proposal and petition for a dispensation from the Act of Uniformity. In 1672 the justification of those who accepted licenses was stated by Humfrey and Nye in the contention that even though the King's action in effect repealed parliamentary enactments, they could accept it on the grounds that "the King permits what God bids." The appeal to a higher law was consistent with the political tradition of Puritanism, but the appeal was being used to lend sanction to an exercise of royal prerogative that was in conflict with parliamentarian constitutional views. To be sure Nye, Humfrey, and those who agreed with them also maintained at the time of the Declaration that there were limitations to the King's prerogative, yet the fact remains that they were willing to justify a royal act which in effect repealed parliamentary statutes, thus they tacitly rejected the essence of a limited monarchy.

On the other hand it is clear that the instances in which the initiative came from the Government in 1662 and 1672 were exceptional, and that in all efforts to modify the religious settlement which were instigated by the Nonconformists during the decade, they sought to do so through parliamentary action and legislation. In 1673 this was the procedure to which the Nonconformist ministers returned, and they came to see more clearly the basic inconsistency between their position in 1672 and the parliamentarian conception of monarchy which they had previously espoused. However, it was not until the relative security of the years following the Popish Plot and the dissolution of the Cavalier Parliament that the King's action in 1672 was unequivocally condemned by Nonconformist ministers as "an invasion of laws." [107]

In the meantime Dissenters continued to believe that the Acts preventing them from worshiping as they chose were "against the command of God," and in addition they continued to assert that many of these Acts, notoriously the Conventicle Act of 1670, violated fundamental constitutional law. Acting upon these assumptions, the Presbyterian and Congregationalist members of Parliament had endeavored ever since the Restoration to obtain enactment of measures which would have given freedom of worship, and although some of them gave partial approval to the Indulgence, they were much quicker than their ministers to maintain that the prerogative must be limited and "the true strength of the statute law" maintained. To this task they dedicated themselves when Parliament met in 1673, as they had before.

The King's Indulgence of 1672 was a severe test of the Dissenters' parliamentarian political beliefs. Although many of them condoned the grant tacitly, only a few did so explicitly, and nearly all of these men changed their minds after reconsideration. All Dissenters would have preferred parliamentary authorization for any freedom of worship, and apart from those who wavered in 1672 they remained dedicated to the concept of a monarchy which would be effectively restrained by Parliament and in which basic legal rights and religious liberty would be insured by fundamental laws.

# CHAPTER V

## Political Resurgence and Parliamentarianism, 1674–1678

The suspicion and distrust aroused by the policies to which Charles II had resorted during the years 1670–1673 became increasingly evident during the parliamentary sessions of 1673. As has been seen, the Presbyterians and Congregationalists in Parliament supported the resulting attacks upon the royal Indulgence, the Dutch War, and the growing Catholic influence at Court. Not until the session at the beginning of 1674, however, did the full import of these policies bring a thorough attack upon Charles and his ministers. Always quick to sense the possible and the impossible in politics, the King realized that the forced withdrawal of the Indulgence and the enactment of the Test Act would bring to an end the attempts which he had made since the Restoration to obtain religious toleration and thereby to promote Catholicism. Because of these developments and the strong anti-French and pro-Dutch feeling that emerged in 1673, he began to shift to new ministers and policies. The dismissal of the Earl of Shaftesbury from the Lord Chancellorship in November, and the appointment of Sir Thomas Osborne to the Lord Treasurship in October, followed by an earldom eight months later, were portentous to all Dissenters, particularly to those in Parliament.

There was a somewhat more definite indication of the nature of the new royal policy in October, 1674, when the King had the Bishops and the new Earl of Danby convene in Conference at Lambeth in order to give him advice, for in this instance Nonconformist divines were not included or consulted as they had been in previous conferences of this nature during the reign.[1] In accordance with the advice submitted to the King in January, 1675, an Order in Council and a royal Declaration were issued in February requiring enforcement of the laws against Noncon-formists.[2] This time, rigorous religious prosecution was also to be accompanied by a frontal attack upon the Dissenters sitting in Parliament, for in the spring session Danby proposed a test which was designed to eliminate from the Houses of Parliament those who were not loyal Anglicans. Understandably, this new royal policy of repression and of alliance with the Anglican clergy and lay politicians brought a most vigorous reaction from Noncon-formists.

Both before and after the shift in royal policy in 1674, the opposition counterattack—had the same political and constitu-tional purposes, namely to restrain the King's actions and to limit his powers and in the opposition's activity the Dissenters in Parliament became increasingly outspoken and aggressive. Reli-gious motivations were powerful, particularly for the Dissenters, since their strongest desire was to obtain religious freedom for themselves, and at the same time they feared and fought the growth of Catholicism.

Presbyterian and Congregationalist members of Parliament had opposed most Court policies ever since the opening session of the Cavalier Parliament in 1661, but after they lost the capacity to lead opposition efforts themselves they had not discovered a leader who was politically effective and personally respected, and whose views on religious, constitutional, and economic issues were either congruous or congenial. However, beginning with the session of January–February, 1674, it appeared that this great need was to be filled by the Earl of Shaftesbury, the recently dismissed Lord Chancellor. Since the Restoration he had not made any pretence that he adhered to the Presbyterian views he previously had avowed, and there were good reasons for Non-conformists to think that his political opportunism of the 1660's had also led him to abandon his former Presbyterian associates as well. True, he favored toleration and played a role of some importance in drafting and defending the Declaration to this effect in 1662. However, he was at the same time intent upon winning the favor of the King, and in supporting the Declaration he actually differed with the Presbyterians who did not want to see Catholics granted toleration. Moreover, there is no evidence he openly opposed the three Acts which were of greatest conse-quence to Nonconformists, the Corporation Act, the Act of Uniformity, and the Conventicle Act; and there is conflicting evidence as to whether he actually opposed the Five Mile Act.[3] Thus it is understandable why Dissenters apparently did not welcome Shaftesbury's replacement of Sir Orlando Bridgeman as Lord Keeper of the Great Seal in November, 1672, and why on the other hand there was some surprise and apprehension that a statesman who had appeared friendly was being removed.[4] However, Shaftesbury was one of the strongest supporters of the new Declaration of Indulgence, and when he attained the position of Lord Keeper and Lord Chancellor as well, he quickly came to the defense of Dissenters by obtaining the discharge of several who were being held or prosecuted. But far more impressive were his efforts to obtain passage of the Bill for the Ease of Protestant Dissenters in the spring of 1673.[5] Also contributing to the support he came to command from Dissenters were the continuing personal friendships and business partnerships which he had with such prominent Presbyterian merchants and members of Parliament as Thomas Papillon and Sir Edward Harley, along with the newer connections and associations with such men as Richard Hampden and the Baptist merchant William Kiffen.[6] But undoubtedly of greater influence than any of these factors in winning the Dissenters was the fact that Shaftesbury was a most astute and effective political leader, and he saw that Nonconformist support would contribute to his success. He therefore lost no chance to win them to his side. However, such association or cooperation as developed between Dissenters and Shaftesbury's inchoate organization of early 1674 was probably far more the result of the fact that each had a similar reaction to the recent developments than to any calculated appeal made by Shaftesbury or any conscious response by Nonconformist members to his leadership.[7]

As Parliament convened in January, 1674, the political, religious, and economic situations had combined to produce a storm of opposition. Earlier apprehensions about the spread of Catholicism and the decline in trade as a result of the French Alliance and the Dutch War were only intensified by the prevailing rumors that secret agreements had been made with France.[8] Instead of considering the supplies which Charles maintained were necessary in order to obtain an honorable peace, opposition members of the House of Commons in a defiant mood turned to a discussion of grievances and launched an attack upon leading ministers of the Crown. The Presbyterian members were outspoken and active in both of these major moves. John Jones, who sat for London, was concerned about prices, the financial policies of the government, and the fact that in his forty-five years in London he "never knew that impudence in meetings that the Papists have now." [9] Swynfen was very disturbed because of the "sad effects" of the War in "blood, and treasure, and loss of trade," while Richard Hampden and Hugh Boscawen also found the war grievous and costly.[10] Of much more consequence was the implication by all three that the Commons should have been consulted before the War was started, since such views indicated a feeling that the King should exercise his prerogative of making war and peace only with the consent of Parliament. But the Presbyterians were not as forthright as Colonel John Birch, who from this session must be considered a moderate Anglican, for in speaking just after them he did not hesitate to state that "somebody advised this War against consent, and without Parliament." [11]

In the attack upon three of the King's past or present councillors, the Duke of Lauderdale, the Duke of Buckingham, and the Earl of Arlington, the Presbyterians were in general not of the more extreme group and seemed primarily concerned that the House "proceed by such rules as agree with justice." [12] The leaders Swynfen and Boscawen therefore opposed the summary way of removal by hearing charges, judging the ministers on the basis of "common fame," and then addressing the King for removal on such grounds. They held that in "this summary way . . . you go to the King with nothing but bare desire; if the King removes him not, it tends not to your end; if he does, upon bare desire, without cause shown, it is hard." [13] Both therefore defended the procedure of impeachment instead, "for then all evidence on both sides is heard," rules of justice would be followed, and the dignity of Parliament upheld. Other efforts to rush the proceedings were also opposed, and inadequate proof was scored.[14]

These arguments and efforts were most evident when the case of Arlington was debated. Although Boscawen did not want to "extenuate nor aggravate the charges," and Swynfen refused to "touch on the merits of the case," it was apparently evident in their votes, if not their speeches, that not only they but also Richard Hampden and William Love "and most all of their sentiments in religion, were for my Lord Arlington . . ."[15] On the other hand it appears that they were not favorably disposed toward Buckingham. Boscawen was careful to make it clear that he had "no kindness nor relation to the Duke," and in contending that they ought to proceed by rules of justice there was some implication that he supported the charges, for he was concerned that otherwise their "judgment will not be thought just, though it is so in truth. . . ." Moreover, William Love joined in the attack and proposed that Buckingham be asked, "who advised that the army should be appointed to draw up towards London, to awe this House, to make us vote what they please?"[16] Regarding Buckingham, Swynfen was also concerned that they be just in judging, for he felt that they were lacking the kind of judicial proof they had had in the Duke of Lauderdale's case. In pleading for the use of impeachment as the just procedure, he stated he did not think "removal from the King's presence [was] a light thing." To Secretary Coventry who had contended that the Duke's office [Master of the Horse] was a patent and a freehold, he directed a telling question. "Would you have freeholds taken away without proof?" To Swynfen this would be an "ill precedent," for whether the case be one of "Lords or whose it will, we have nothing but justice for our own preservation."[17]

With the King's announcement on February 11, that an honorable peace had been concluded with the Dutch, the opposition saw one of its major aims of the preceding months achieved.[18] Members opposed to recent Court policies then launched a drive to eliminate the dangers of Catholicism in England, to prevent the threat of a standing army, and to limit the powers of Charles II's successor as well as of Charles himself in some respects. Such measures were strongly supported by the leading Presbyterian spokesmen. In the debate upon the danger of a standing army Swynfen was not content to vote that the standing forces were merely a grievance, and he favored having the resolution call for disbanding the forces raised after a specified time, January, 1663, being designated in the House vote.[19] Of the bills designed to curtail the King's powers, the Presbyterians spoke in support of two. In the debates concerning the bill to establish tenure of judges upon the principle of *quam diu se bene gesserint* rather than the prevailing principle of *durante bene placito,* which was terminable upon the death of a King, Boscawen presented the Noncon-

formist point of view in arguing that the principle of tenure during good behavior should be adopted because it would make the
judges less arbitrary than they had been while holding office at
the pleasure of the King.[20] Also of much concern to all Dissenters
were two bills pertaining to the writ of habeas corpus,[21] and the
Presbyterian members reflected this concern in their efforts to
make the bills truly effective and in their opposition to the
maneuvers of those who sought to defeat them.[22]

In implying that Parliament should be consulted before War
was declared, in advocating effective and just procedures of re-
moving royal ministers, in making efforts to eliminate the danger
of a standing army, and finally in supporting attempts to limit
the Crown's control over judges and its power to arrest and detain
citizens, the Presbyterian leaders clearly indicated their parliamentarian political views and their opposition to the royal policies of the recent past. However, they were not as extreme in
position and only occasionally were they as outspoken as the
leaders of the Anglican wing of the opposition. Although the
attacks levelled by each wing of the opposition had few if any
long-range effects, they did contribute to the timely prorogation
on February 19, 1674.

By the time Parliament met again in the spring of 1675, the
fluid political situation of the previous year had jelled to a considerable degree. Danby had become the leading minister, and the
alliance between Charles and the High Church party became
evident in the orders of January which called for enforcement of
the laws against Nonconformists and Catholics. The beginnings
of the political organization which was to give Charles control of
Parliament had also been started by Danby in his reorganization
of the excise farm and in the addition of some members of Parliament as pensioners during 1674.[23] Among the opposition groups
a similar process of policy formulation and of organization had
begun taking place. Shaftesbury had emerged as the dominant
leader. He had made known that his major aim was to obtain a
new parliament, and he had cemented his relationship with some
of the key leaders in the Lords who with him were to carry on
the defensive tactics against Danby's Test Bill in the coming session of Parliament.[24]

As the April meeting of Parliament approached, the Crown's
enforcement of the laws against Nonconformists was undoubt-

edly contributing to the coalescence of opposition factions. A striking example was the arrest of the Presbyterian minister to whom Lord Wharton, Lady Bedford and others of position were listening on Sunday, March 4, for this could have only made Wharton and Bedford more intent upon following Shaftesbury's leadership in the forthcoming attack upon the new Court policy.[25]

Overshadowing all other matters in the spring session of 1675 was the famous battle in the House of Lords which was precipitated by Danby's drive to obtain passage of the Anglican or Non-resisting Test. Nonconformist ministers were well acquainted with this Test, for it was the same as that contained in the Five Mile Act, better known as the Oxford Oath, requiring them to declare that they would not "at any time endeavor any alteration of government either in Church or State," and that the taking of arms against the King or those commissioned by him was unlawful on any pretense. Likewise, Nonconformist politicians were most familiar with the latter clause, for this declaration was one of the requirements of the Corporation Act. The Bill which Danby proposed not only combined these two tests; it also extended them to members of both Houses of Parliament and all other office holders, and it stipulated that they were to take them before being seated or invested with authority.[26] Obviously designed to restrict political power to staunch Anglicans, the Bill raised furious opposition from Dissenters, moderate Anglicans, and Catholics. The most unrelenting of the Presbyterian lords in the ensuing defensive stand were Wharton and Delamer. In addition Lord Holles was also credited with an important part in the debates, although he was restricted by absences because of the gout; and another supporter of their efforts was the Earl of Bedford, who signed three of the four protests. Only the Earl of Anglesey failed to sign the protests, but it appears that he openly opposed the Bill and made at least one speech in which he warned the Bishops that they sat by an Act of that Parliament, and he therefore advised them to be cautious.[27]

Once the Bill passed the Lords, Dissenters in the House of Commons were apparently resigned to its success in their House.[28] However, where direct counterattack had failed an indirect one was to succeed. As has long been known, the dispute between the Houses precipitated by the case of *Shirley v. Fagg* was cleverly used if not fomented by Shaftesbury and the opposition in order to block consideration of the Test Bill and other Court measures, and even at the time Charles "had great reason to believe the difference between the two Houses to be a malicious coordinance to frustrate all his counsels and prevent any good success of this meeting." [29] To some degree, therefore, the efforts to defeat the Test Bill are found in the vigorous attack upon the Lords for maintaining that they had jurisdiction over a member of the Lower House in cases appealed from inferior courts. In this attack Swynfen was the most active of the Presbyterians in maintaining that there was no superior court in their privileges, as he put it; while Hampden and Maynard also entered into the debates, and Swynfen, Boscawen, and Maynard were representatives of the Commons in conferences between the Houses.[30] At the same time the Presbyterian lords vigorously defended the appellate jurisdiction of their House. Holles was particularly active and wrote a pamphlet in which he held that if there were to be no appeals to the House of Lords in cases involving members of the House of Commons, then there would be no means of redress under writs of error for a man who received unjust or erroneous judgments. This would be "an absolute failure of justice" and "a privilege of Parliament against the Parliament itself," argued Holles.[31]

Such contentions as those of Swynfen and Holles are clear indications that they and their colleagues believed there were issues involved in the dispute which were of importance in themselves. Indeed, whether their intent was to defeat a Bill which would have threatened their political lives and arrested constitutional development, or whether they wanted to protect the elected members of the Commons against an apparent threat to their independence from the hereditary lords and the conservative bishops, or whether they desired to preserve the right of appeal to all Englishmen alike, the particular purpose seems less important from the point of view of this study than the fact that in each instance it was consistent with parliamentarian constitutional traditions.[32]

The result of the opposition's sustained and adroit counterattack was that Danby's plans failed, and when it became obvious that neither supplies nor the Test Bill would be voted, the King prorogued Parliament on June 9 until the following October.[33] The issues at stake, the intensity of the struggle, and the evenness of the relative strength of Court and opposition parties during this spring meeting of Parliament had much increased the desire and need of the party leaders to obtain new adherents and to establish better discipline over those already in their ranks. Having failed to obtain either of two major objectives, Danby was particularly aggressive in his preparations for the fall session. The addition of new pensioners, the dispatch of letters to those who had been laggard in attendance and support during the previous session, and the collection of proxies from lords who would be absent were the major steps which he took in order to build up strength.[34]

Such activity appears to have had the predictable effect of producing greater activity among opposition leaders, and as a result more cohesion developed among opposition factions. By early autumn Danby's policies and the growing threat of his political organization had brought some of the Nonconformists to follow in the steps taken by some of the Anglican opposition leaders during the spring, and as a result a rapprochement was established between them and the Marquis de Ruvigny, the Ambassador of Louis XIV of France.[35] This relationship may have been in part an outgrowth of a similar rapprochement which apparently had its beginnings in meetings that reportedly took place between the Duke of York and Shaftesbury shortly after Parliament was prorogued in June.[36] During the summer Ruvigny contributed his efforts to the development of an alliance of Nonconformists and Recusants while he carried on independent negotiations with the Duke of York, with the opposition leaders, and with Nonconformists in Parliament.[37] Reporting specifically upon his talks with a small number of Presbyterian and Congregationalist members of the Commons, he wrote in September that they were beginning to respond to his overtures and wanted him to use his influence with Charles to obtain freedom of conscience. In return they reportedly were willing to propose nothing against France and to grant Charles adequate supplies. Ruvigny stated that there were six Nonconformist leaders who were acting in this manner; and he indicated further that of these six, one had often spoken about this plan to the Duke of York and another had talked in confidence to him.[38] Although Ruvigny may have made payments to some of those in this group of six, this does not seem very likely at this juncture, for he made no claims that any agreement had been reached, and no alliance developed.[39] Nevertheless, there remains no doubt concerning the means that a few of the Nonconformist leaders were willing to consider in order to obtain religious freedom.

The activity of Dissenters in Parliament during this autumn session continued to demonstrate their desire to establish parliamentary controls over the King's actions, a striking example being the strong support given by Love and Boscawen to a motion that the money which had been voted for building ships "be put into the Chamber of London, and not be issued out thence without an Order from the Lord Mayor, and Common Council, to be the more certainly applied to the use of the fleet." [40] Also directed to the same end were the determined efforts in the House of Lords to obtain dissolution of the Cavalier Parliament. The famous motion of November 20 to address the King for dissolution, which was "long and seriously debated," had the support of the Presbyterian Lords with one exception, and those who were present signed the protest which was entered after the motion was defeated by the close vote of 50–48.[41]

Not only in this vote, but also in other instances towards the close of this session and in the months thereafter, there were additional important indications of a growing alliance between the Dissenters and the leaders of the so-called country party—Shaftesbury and his lieutenant Buckingham—while these two leaders were most aggressive in seeking Nonconformist support. It was obviously with this purpose in mind that Buckingham made his speech of November 16 requesting permission to bring in a bill for the ease and security of all Protestant Dissenters, and its potential appeal can be seen in the reaction of Lord Wharton and the Nonconformist ministers with whom he corresponded.[42] Although prorogation within a week prevented any other action, Nonconformist approval of the attempted move was sought by publishing Buckingham's speech, and included with it was Shaftesbury's of November 20 in support of the motion to dissolve Parliament.[43] An even more telling effort to bring moderate Anglican laymen of the opposition together in close association with the Dissenters was made by Shaftesbury in the compilation and publication of another pamphlet that concerned the proceedings of the House of Commons in the recent session. After admonishing the "country gentlemen" to take the pains to recognize that the greatest enemy of English law and liberty was an encroaching prerogative, he asserted that the "only way . . . to restrain prerogative" is to "give liberty to dissenting Protestants . . . for these must and never can be otherwise (unless by accident, and by mistake) than friends to liberty"; while Anglican Prelates "neither are nor can be otherwise than creatures to prerogative, for all their promotions, dignities, and domination depends upon it." In addition to this argument and the contention that Nonconformists had demonstrated their willingness to live peaceably, Shaftesbury had a final reason why religious freedom should be granted, and it was an argument which would have particular appeal to the politically conscious "country gentlemen" whom he addressed. Nonconformists and Conformists should be treated alike by Parliament, neither being oppressed, he asserted, "for we were chosen by both, and with that intention that we should oppress neither." [44] In his anonymously published pamphlet Shaftesbury had presented an effective case that there was an integral relationship between the acquisition of political power, the limitation of the prerogative, and the granting of religious liberty to Protestant Dissenters.

As Shaftesbury continued to develop the opposition forces into an effective political organization during the following months, it is understandable that he received increased cooperation and assistance not only from old friends and business associates among Presbyterians sitting in Parliament but also from others of this group. Government officials and their informants who visited his London residence found him on various occasions in consultation with Sir Edward Harley, Thomas Papillon, and Sir Samuel Barnardiston, as well as Presbyterian political leaders in the City and such opposition leaders of Parliament as Sir Thomas Littleton and the Earl of Salisbury; and according to the report of one government informant who had called upon Shaftesbury, these meetings appear to have been held regularly, mostly on Sunday nights.[45]

The deep concern, if not alarm, which such political activities aroused in government circles explains why Shaftesbury was visited by Sir Joseph Williamson, one of the Principal Secretaries of State, in order to deliver the King's message and advice that "it were much better you were at home in the country . . . [than] busy up and down here in town. . . ." [46] Also indicative of continuing apprehension during 1676 was the fact that Williamson apparently had Lord Wharton's movements and activities watched, and as a result a most revealing report was made that a Mr. Murray who was frequently with him both in London and the country was also as often with Lord Shaftesbury.[47]

The increasing political importance of Dissent during this year, when two relatively well defined and organized political parties were emerging under the leadership of Shaftesbury and Danby, is apparent not only in the overtures which the opposition leaders made to the Dissenters, but also in those made by other political leaders. The first of such moves was the attempt made late in May, 1676, by the Duke of York and Arlington to gain Nonconformist cooperation in an effort to obtain dissolution of the Cavalier Parliament, in the hope that a degree of toleration might be obtained from a newly elected one. However, since Dissenters saw the possibility of gaining religious freedom without inclusion of the Catholics by working with Shaftesbury, York's plan had little appeal; and the negative response which he received left him "most dissatisfied with the Presbyterian Party. . . ."[48] In addition there was a second and more significant tribute to Nonconformist political importance in the step which Danby reportedly contemplated, and which he may have taken at the end of the year. Obviously much worried about the strength which Nonconformist support gave to the opposition, he supposedly planned an attempt to separate the Presbyterians from the other Dissenters by offering them permission to build churches outside the limits of the principal towns. But this scheme, too, would probably have proved abortive in view of Presbyterian distrust of both Danby and the bishops.[49]

When Parliament finally met in February, 1677, after the extended prorogation of fifteen months, Presbyterian and Congregationalist members of Parliament were once again supporters of measures designed to control the King, but just as in the past, they were not as extreme in their positions as some leaders of the opposition. The situation was considerably complicated by Shaftesbury's plan designed to obtain the dissolution of Parliament, for his attempt to maintain that Parliament had ceased to be a Parliament because the King had prorogued it for more than a year created division within the opposition ranks, particularly in the House of Lords.[50] Among the small group of five who actively supported Shaftesbury's plan were the two most important Presbyterian leaders, Wharton and Holles, although this support was not as complete as Shaftesbury could have desired.[51] Wharton spoke in the debate at the opening meeting of Parliament on February 15 and held that it was wrong to say that no laws hindered the King. However, it is clear that he had changed his mind to some degree, for he did not go as far as Shaftesbury. Instead he maintained that the prorogation was illegal, rather than holding that Parliament was dissolved.[52] At the outset Holles took Shaftesbury's position and vigorously defended the contention that Parliament was dissolved in an anonymous pamphlet which was to have been published before Parliament met, but which was stopped by the authorities.[53] But he apparently did not continue to give such whole-hearted support. Although he argued for the dissolution near the end of the debate on February 15, his remarks were brief and restrained, and he spoke "with great temper and moderation." [54] There are several explanations, one being that he was suffering from an attack of gout, as it was stated, and another is that perhaps he had come to doubt the wisdom of the move. In addition there is also a third reason, for as Daniel Finch suggested, Holles may have been fearful because of the "libelous pamphlet . . . being laid to his charge." [55] Early investigations by the authorities to discover the publishers and authors of the three pamphlets supporting Shaftesbury's contention that Parliament was dissolved, which were considered scandalous and seditious, had led to an order on February 9 for the arrest of Dr. Nicholas Cary, an ejected minister who was Holles' physician and who had been involved in the arrangements to publish his pamphlet "The Grand Question Concerning the Prorogation of this Parliament." Cary had already been interrogated by the Privy Council and by the King; and although he refused to state who the author was, he had said enough so that the King was quite certain it was Holles.[56] Subsequently, on February 16, the House of Lords appointed its committee to make its investigations to discover the authors and publishers of the three pamphlets. It is therefore very possible that Holles did not want to place himself in greater jeopardy by vigorous support of the contention in the House debates and the following division.

Although Holles and Wharton may have wavered in one way or another on this issue,[57] they were firm in their refusal to be cowed by the Government's retaliatory actions. Required to ask the pardon of the King and of the Lords from his place in the House, Wharton refused to do so. He thereby indicated the strength of his feeling that such a reprimand by the House was unjust and in addition that it "was against the privilege of freedom of speech necessary in Parliament. . . ." [58] As a result he was held in contempt of the House and confined to the Tower of London where he remained a year. [59] The threat of a more severe punishment faced Holles for his pamphleteering, because the pamphlet he wrote was voted to be seditious. During the investigations carried on by a committee of the House of Lords, Holles became more openly implicated. Hearing that his name "had been tossed there concerning a book" while he was absent, "he came thither offering that if any had ought to object against him he was there and ready to answer it in any Court of Judicature." His move was impressive. There was "a long silence and none replying, they called for the reading of a bill." [60] In the end no proceedings were instituted against him.

Meanwhile during the opening days in the House of Commons, Hampden, Boscawen, Swynfen, and Maynard all spoke in subsequent debates bearing on the matter of dissolution. Since the major confrontation in the Commons was actually upon the issue whether the House should debate the question before beginning with the order of business normally followed at the opening of a session, no one made specific expressions of opinion concerning the constitutional issue except Maynard, who bluntly stated that the prorogation had been legal. However, he would have held the debate since so many were in doubt. Hampden, Boscawen, and Swynfen likewise contended the issue should be debated first, and though not stating so, their speeches suggest that they were among the doubters of whom Maynard spoke. [61] Regardless of their position upon the constitutional question, all four clearly supported the opposition maneuver of debating the question before following the regular order of business. But, it was defeated, and Danby therefore triumphed in both Houses. [62]

During the remainder of the session there were two other important constitutional questions raised, and in each case they were directly or indirectly the result of a military development on the Continent—the highly successful spring offensive of the French which threatened the Netherlands. The first step taken by the Commons as a result of these successes was to pass an address requesting the King to strengthen himself with such "stricter alliances" as may secure the Kingdom and preserve the Spanish Netherlands.[63] Although none of the Presbyterian members of the House of Commons seems to have entered into the original debate on this Address, which infringed upon one of the most fundamental prerogative powers, they did support it. Thus when the Lords wished to amend the Address and assure the King of the necessary supplies in order to carry out the requested policy, some members of the Commons contended that this was an encroachment upon their power in money bills; but Hampden, Swynfen, and Maynard each argued that the Lords' concurrence in the proposed Address was more important than any quarrel over the money bill issue.[64] At the same time, however, these three members made it most clear that although they would in this instance ignore the constitutional issue concerning amendment of money bills, they were by no means willing to allow any encroachment upon the Commons' powers. This issue was raised in a far more pointed manner in April when the Lords amended a tax Bill, and at that time the leadership of Swynfen and Maynard in defending the Commons' right was recognized by their appointment as two of the managers of the ensuing conferences with the Lords.[65] In the end the Commons were successful, for the Lords agreed to leave out their amendments.[66]

As the session continued, the struggle between the King and Parliament became much more intense. Although he refused to answer the message sent by Parliament, Charles continued to press for supplies. The House of Commons was just as adamant, and among the members urging that they hold out was Boscawen, who was against acting on the most necessary bills until the King replied to their Address concerning alliances.[67] Finally there was the outright invasion of the King's prerogative in the Commons vote of May 23 to refuse any supply until the King entered an "offensive and defensive alliance with the States General and other alliances to prevent growth of French King's power. . . ." Boscawen served on the committee which drew up this Address, and although the Presbyterian members of the House did not take part in the subsequent debates, they voted for the measure.[68] Striking back, the King in his speech of May 28 sternly rebuked the Commons and refused to allow any invasion of his power of making war and peace, and with that he adjourned Parliament.[69]

With Shaftesbury, Buckingham, Wharton and Salisbury still in the Tower, continued development of an effective and cohesive opposition organization had been at least temporarily arrested. Prospects improved somewhat in early August when Buckingham gained the favor of the King and was released. In fact Danby became much alarmed. With Buckingham restored to royal favor and supported by the opposition, he constituted a threat to the position of great power which the Lord Treasurer then enjoyed. Consequently, Danby began to advance a proposal by which he could strengthen his own position at Court and increase parliamentary support for his policies of undermining Catholic and French power at home and abroad, namely that the Duke of York's daughter Mary marry William of Orange.[70] There were substantial advantages which could be gained by such a marriage, and within two months Charles had accepted the plan and the marriage took place on November 4.[71]

As intended, this development had a decisive effect upon the opposition's foreign connections, for the relations which had prevailed between William and the English opposition were undermined.[72] However, as the King had not anticipated, a closer rapprochement between the French and members of the opposition also began to develop. The marriage immediately aroused serious concern among the members of the opposition, and it may have been reflected in the noticeable increase in the number of opposition leaders and emissaries who visited Lord Shaftesbury in the Tower after the announcement on October 22 of the forthcoming event, and during the next two months. Many were Presbyterians, including Lord Delamer, who was the most frequent of the callers, as well as Lord Holles, Sir Samuel Barnardiston, and Sir James Langham.[73] A more pointed indication of opposition concern is found in a report of mid-November made by the French Ambassador, Paul Barrillon, that some of the opposition members of Parliament "seemed desirous of forming connections with France and were making advances to him. . . ."[74] In January, 1678, these advances were renewed, and with the conclusion of an alliance between England and Holland by the middle of the month and the failure of French negotiations to prevent the meeting of Parliament, Louis and Barrillon began an intensive drive to obtain support throughout the opposition ranks.[75] This decision was to be of much consequence to the Presbyterian members of Parliament, for it was at this juncture that along with other members of the opposition they formed a definite connection with the French which in the end led some of them to accept French funds. In order to facilitate the development of this political alliance Louis sent to England the son of his former ambassador, the Marquis de Ruvigny, who was particularly qualified to win over those of Puritan and Presbyterian views because he was a Huguenot and had connections with opposition leaders.[76] Arriving in mid-January apparently on a trip concerning family matters, but actually with secret instructions from Louis, he began negotiations with the Duke of Buckingham, Lord Russell, Lord Holles, and through them with Shaftesbury until he was released from the Tower on February 26.[77]

The parliamentary activities of the opposition members during the next six months take on their full meaning only when examined in the light of these negotiations and of the funds distributed by Barrillon. Since the true basis of this rapprochement is to be found in the fact that Louis XIV and the English opposition forces were very much in agreement upon the necessity of achieving a number of immediate objectives, it would appear that French pressure, promises, and bribery had little if any effect upon the positions which the Presbyterians in Parliament or many of the other members of the opposition took upon domestic issues. In order that he might detach Charles from his new connections with the Dutch and eliminate any possibility that English troops might be used against France, Louis sought to prevent the grant of any supplies, and in addition, to obtain the dissolution of the hostile Cavalier Parliament. By these means he also intended to weaken Danby's influence and gain control over Charles.[78] At the same time opposition leaders were primarily interested in obtaining the dissolution of Parliament, fully expecting a general election to give them control in a new Parliament; they likewise deeply feared the use to which Charles might put English troops, always being mindful that he could use them to eliminate the opposition and obstruct or destroy representative government. Suspicious and even embittered, they too desired to destroy Danby as a political leader, and more than ever they sought to acquire effective control over the Monarchy. Presbyterian members of Parliament along with other members

of the opposition had long supported such objectives. Therefore, except for the inconsistency of means and ends, cooperation with the French should not be regarded as desertion of
their fundamental political objectives, but as the expedient acceptance of additional means to obtain these objectives, unreliable and uncongenial though these means were. All this became
evident in the negotiations and agreements between Ruvigny and
the opposition leaders during the months after he arrived. Holles
and Russell in particular were concerned that English liberties
be protected, and they therefore constantly sought assurances
that Louis would not endeavor to make Charles "the absolute
master in his kingdom," or to "hurt their constitution." [79]

The substance of the agreements reached as a result of Ruvigny's negotiations was that since it would be unpopular and too
obvious to oppose war with France directly, the opposition would
therefore either refuse to grant supplies [80] or place such specific
conditions upon their expenditure as would be disagreeable to
the King. It was felt that this would make him turn to Louis XIV
for financial assistance, and then Louis was to "contribute his
endeavors to bring about dissolution of this Parliament as soon as
the time should appear favorable." [81]

When Parliament finally resumed its proceedings on January
28, 1678, the impasse which had developed between the King and
the House of Commons during the previous spring was still present. Charles, having now concluded a treaty of alliance with the
United Provinces, anticipated the grant of an ample supply. However, the opposition leaders were not to be satisfied unless they
saw the treaty, which the King refused to allow.[82] Thereupon
all these leaders, including the Presbyterians, endeavored to obstruct the grant of supply in a manner and upon grounds that
were entirely consistent with their past tactics and views. Having
failed to defeat a motion that the House resolve into a committee
of supply on February 4, opposition spokesmen sought either to
delay proceedings or to propose strict limitations upon the
amounts granted, as well as upon expenditure of funds.[83] In the
debates of February 5 and 6, Thomas Papillon, Boscawen and
Swynfen took an important part, arguing that they could not vote
supplies until they knew more about the treaties; Papillon therefore moved to know "whether these alliances have been made
pursuant to our Address," and Boscawen spoke in support of the

motion after Colonel Birch had amended it in order to be sure the treaties were designed to suppress the power of the French King.[84] Using a similar argument in debating navy supply the next day, Swynfen held that "the uncertainty we are under, of peace or war" led him to advocate a grant to the King of only "such a moderate sum as shall be thought fit to support his alliances." [85] This uncertainty was a much greater restraining factor when considering the grant for land forces because of the dread of a standing army. In a strong speech, Swynfen declared: "I am not for any army, for the King's and Kingdom's sake. I reflect not upon commander nor soldier, but I know it is incident to mankind to adorn his own province. When once it is raised, no man knows when it will be laid aside. . . . Before we certainly know what use it must be applied unto, you never yet raised a land army. . . . I would have you seriously consider what we do before war be declared." [86] When on February 18 it was finally agreed that the inadequate sum of one million pounds be raised "for enabling his Majesty to enter into an actual war against the French King," the Presbyterian members undoubtedly supported the vote although they did not speak in this particular day's debate.[87]

As the Duke of York observed in a letter to his new son-in-law, the Prince of Orange, "those who seemed to be most zealous for a war with France last session, are those who obstruct the most the giving a supply," and Charles was even more suspicious, telling Barrillon that he believed the ambassador was responsible.[88] Whether or not the Presbyterians supporting these obstructive moves were doing so in order to carry out agreements with Louis XIV's emissaries is of less importance than the fact that the moves were consistent with their own ultimate goals. They were sincerely desirous of controlling the King's foreign policies, of obtaining some restrictions upon his expenditure of funds, and of preventing the possibility of a standing army which probably would have given Charles the power he wished to have.

The apprehension of opposition leaders that Charles might capitalize upon the developing situation and make himself an absolute monarch became a definite fear during March and a real danger in their minds by April; and the growth of this feeling was largely the result of two related events, one on the military front abroad and one on the political front at home. When

French troops took Ghent and Ypres late in February and thereby placed the Spanish Netherlands at their mercy, a situation was created which Charles could use in either of two ways in order to gain financial independence and be rid of Parliament and the restraints placed upon his actions by that body. Charles sent English forces to the aid of the Netherlands as he was obligated by the Anglo-Dutch Treaty (but without declaring war), and he was therefore in a position to exact larger amounts from Louis in return for the dismissal of Parliament and the submission to French demands. This is exactly what happened in the negotiations which Charles had already resumed with Louis because of his belief that Danby would not be able to get a satisfactory supply bill.[89] At the same time he could use the war situation as a pretext for obtaining larger grants of supply from Parliament, and then having dismissed Parliament he could avoid going to war.

Holles and Russell were fearful of the manner in which the war situation could play into the hands of Charles and of the agreements he and Louis might make; and on March 14 they expressed to Ruvigny their fears that Louis would approve a declaration of war against France by Charles "only to give him an opportunity of obtaining money, and under a promise that, as soon as he had got the money he would conclude a peace." Ruvigny's reassurances and his offer of "considerable sums" to be given to those named by Russell in order to block any Parliamentary grant of money for war appears to have satisfied them that there was no "private understanding" between Louis and Charles "to hurt their constitution," and that Louis would not fail to work for the dissolution of Parliament. Satisfied though Holles may have been, Ruvigny found him more reserved than Russell, for as it was reported to Louis XIV, although Holles was "very glad of your Majesty's intentions," he thought it would be "a long time before your Majesty can be in a condition to give them satisfaction by getting the Parliament dissolved." In spite of some misgivings they both agreed to "work underhand" to prevent any additional grants for war and to obtain the addition to the bill granting one million pounds "such disagreeable conditions to the King of England, as they hoped would rather make him wish to re-unite himself with France than to consent to them." [90] Louis would then exact dissolution of Parliament as a condition.

The domestic political event which increased opposition fears and changed them into a sense of alarm and danger came a week later when this supply bill was passed by the King in spite of the "disagreeable conditions" attached that Holles and Russell thought would be too much for the King to accept. As they explained to Ruvigny within a day or so, this evidence of "avidity for money, and the desire of having troops on foot . . . redoubles their fears of the designs of the Court, with which they are much alarmed"; and even though they were at that minute persuaded that Louis and Charles did not act in concert, they were "still under apprehension lest the war should serve only to bring them under subjection." [91]

By the end of the Easter recess (March 26–April 11) opposition leaders were convinced that the situation was dangerous, and the maneuvers which they attempted demonstrates that their basic concern was both to protect their own political future and to preserve the existence of an opposition in order to prevent the King from becoming absolute master of England. In a high level conference with Barrillon, Russell and Holles were joined by Shaftesbury and Buckingham. Both their alarm and their stratagem were evident when, pointing to the levy of troops already underway, they argued that:

when there is a sufficient number on foot, the Court will attempt everything that is agreeable to its interest; that by arresting the principal persons, they will put it out of the power of the others to resist, or oppose themselves to the designs of the Court; that when England shall be subjected at home, the Court will carry on a foreign war with the greater facility, and the whole nation being in one way of thinking, the supplies of men and money for Flanders will be great; that nothing is more proper to prevent this, than to press the declaration of war, and oblige his Britannic Majesty to determine (i.e., come to a decision) before measures are taken to support it.[92]

Continuing, they betrayed their actual fears, which were either that Charles was going to use the troops at home instead of against Louis, there still being no declared war, or that if formal war began it would only be in accordance with an agreement with Louis to stop once adequate supplies were granted. This explains why they were in effect threatening to force an immediate and all-out war with France to which Charles would be committed by the terms of their grants of supply, unless Louis would declare that the state of uncertainty was not agreeable to him, and that he desired to know from Charles whether he was to have peace or war. In this way they believed they would be assured that Louis XIV "not only has no connection with the King of England to oppress them, but that [he] will not suffer him under the pretence of an imaginary war to find means to bring him into subjection." [93]

Such reasoning was the explanation for the strong backing which opposition Lords, including Holles and Wharton, had given prior to the recess to the House of Commons Address requesting immediate war on France; [94] and it explains the mood of the opposition leaders in both Houses during the remainder of the spring, particularly in debates on foreign affairs and on the disbanding of existing troops. As in the past, Swynfen, Boscawen, and Papillon were the Presbyterian speakers. In the debates during early May on the Anglo-Dutch Treaty of December 31, 1677, which the King finally submitted to the House of Commons for their consideration and advice, these spokesmen maintained that the Treaty was not the best that could be obtained, that it was not pursuant to the Addresses of the House, and that the army had been voted in order to wage an offensive war against France, but that it was not being so used. Boscawen therefore felt moved to "damn the treaty." [95] The Government made a surprise attempt to move for supplies early in the session of May 11, when the House was still thin. Wanting to know whether there would be peace or war, and charging that hitherto they had been treated like children, Boscawen refused his consent for "a penny of money till we are plainly dealt with." [96] When they failed to gain satisfaction from the King concerning the war or peace question, Boscawen and Swynfen were among the active opposition leaders who proceeded in efforts to force a showdown and who voted at the end of May that if the army was not used in war against Louis XIV the House would proceed immediately in a bill to disband it. [97] Likewise, when Danby made his last effort to obtain an adequate supply for the Crown in late June, Swynfen was again the Presbyterian spokesman who opposed the motion which was defeated without a division. [98]

This defeat was of much importance, for it put an end to

Danby's hope of gaining sufficient revenue from Parliament to maintain the Crown, and it had a lasting effect upon his stature as a political leader, even though he made strenuous efforts during the remainder of the year to discover a method of maintaining his position and the authority and independence of the Crown.[99] The growing power of the opposition was also convincingly demonstrated in Danby's defeat, but it was only a power to obstruct and it had been gained with the assistance of French efforts and funds. Both these facts were most evident when opposition leaders failed in their attempt to obtain leave to bring in a bill which would have distinguished Popish Recusants from other Dissenters so that the latter, particularly Quakers and Baptists, would not be prosecuted under the statutes directed against Catholics.[100] This effort was spearheaded by Sir Thomas Lee and Colonel Birch who had the support of Boscawen, Swynfen, and apparently Love. This was the kind of step that had to be taken so that opposition strength could be increased through Nonconformist support on the hustings instead of through French bribery behind the scenes.[101]

Anti-Catholicism, which in part explains Presbyterian support for this measure requested by Quakers and Baptists, not only united all Dissenters, but also the Anglican and the agnostic wings of the opposition as well.[102] As is well known, it was the great wave of hatred for Catholics which followed the charges made by Titus Oates and Ezerel Tonge in the early autumn of 1678 that did so much to bring cohesion to these opposition factions and which gave the leaders a cause with sufficient emotional appeal to win decisive electoral support throughout the country by the spring of 1679. In order to win the political power which they had so long sought, opposition leaders first had to keep alive and exploit the fear and hatred of Catholicism which Oates' charges of a Popish Plot had aroused. In addition they needed to undermine the defensive political strength which Danby still possessed and to obtain dissolution of the Cavalier Parliament.

The first of these tasks was achieved primarily through the vigorous Parliamentary investigation of the story of the Plot after Parliament met on October 21, and also by passage of the Second Test Act excluding all Catholics except the Duke of York from sitting in either House.[103] In each instance Dissenters in both

Houses gave their active support. Anglesey, Wharton, Holles, and Bedford all favored strong penalties in the Test Act; and in the Lords' committee for Plot examinations, Anglesey and Wharton were among the seven lay lords who presided as acting chairmen.[104] In the House of Commons Boscawen, Hampden, and Maynard were active, the first two being of extreme importance in the investigations because they were among the four members who played key parts in preventing the disclosure of the names of opposition members who had been recipients of French funds and could therefore have been implicated in the Plot.[105]

While taking these anti-Catholic steps, the opposition at the same time needed to retain their alliance with the French Ambassador in order to secure sufficient strength to strike successfully at Danby. This was not at all difficult since both parties to this alliance had continued to fear the English troops then in England and Flanders, and by early December they both had come to feel that Danby must be destroyed. From the Lord Treasurer's point of view the most dangerous of the attacks against him in Parliament were made by those who continued to denounce the Court's efforts to raise revenue and additional forces as attempts to enslave the country rather than to check France; [106] and still prominent among those making such attacks were Swynfen and Boscawen, while other Dissenters followed their lead.[107] As is well known, however, the fatal blow against Danby came as a result of Charles II's dismissal of Ralph Montagu from his post of Ambassador to the Court of Louis XIV. Embittered by this treatment, Montagu agreed to assist in the attack upon Danby in return for a large pension which was offered by Barrillon.[108] The evidence possessed by Montagu concerning the negotiations carried on by Charles and Danby with Louis XIV not only substantiated the fears and charges voiced by all opposition leaders concerning the real intent of recent Court policy, but it also gave grounds for Danby's impeachment; and having been severe critics of Danby's policies, Presbyterian leaders in Parliament were among those active in the impeachment proceedings which were immediately instigated.[109]

Endangered as he was by the prospect of this trial in which the two chief participants each knew far too much about his machinations with Louis XIV, Charles suddenly prorogued Parliament on December 30, 1678; and thereafter the King, James, and

Danby were each driven to consider the possibility of coming to terms with opposition leaders.[110] As a result, an opportunity was created for the opposition to obtain the King's agreement to dissolve Parliament; and thus it was that a few Presbyterian leaders played the key role in the negotiations which led to the end of the Cavalier Parliament. This was an event which they had long desired, Roger Morrice wrote, because this Parliament "had so violated the fundamental laws of the Kingdom and had assisted arbitrary power and infringed law and property and religion also." Specifically the charges were that Parliament had done all this by "declaring the militia to be in the power of the King solely," by granting the power of search without warrants to justices under the Conventicle Act, and by giving power to the justices to convict those charged with violating this law and thereby denying them the right of trial by jury.[111] According to Morrice,[112] formerly a chaplain to Lord Holles and one of the very few knowing about the negotiations, it was Sir John Baber who suggested to Holles that it would be possible to come to an agreement with Danby and the King for dissolution, and it was Baber who then approached Danby.[113] Holles was "quite [over]-whelmed with this pleasant news." However, he thought the possibility of gaining dissolution by negotiations with Danby and the King were "but golden dreams," and Morrice wrote that he did not change his mind until Danby himself "came one evening at night late in a sedan privately to give my Lord Holles a visit." [114] In the subsequent negotiations, Holles, Baber, and Sir Thomas Littleton [115] were at first successful, so Morrice states, in obtaining Danby's approval and the King's consent to the declaration they had drafted which contained several very significant provisions. In addition to promising that he would disband the army, dissolve the existing Parliament and summon a new one, the King was to declare his resolution not to have any Parliament "continue less than six months nor longer than three years." Finally, he was to announce that he would grant commissions to "certain persons of both Houses and others well affected," including nearly a dozen Presbyterians along with the other opposition leaders, who were to have full powers to examine and imprison any person involved in the Plot during the six weeks before the new Parliament met.[116]

It has been known that the King found it extremely difficult to come to a final decision, and on January 17 he had taken steps to announce a prorogation beyond February 4 in order to obtain time to consider the question of dissolution.[117] According to Morrice he twice agreed to dissolution on the terms which Holles sought, but each time he "recoiled and changed his mind." After the first concurrence Baber reported that he and Danby did not want to hurry the King into a decision "of such great concernment that was utterly irretrievable if once done" and they therefore "left it to him for further reflection." During the second period of reconsideration "his Majesty hunted for four days (which made them absolutely desperate) but on the fifth day (after his Majesty's last consent) at night which was on the 23d of January, Sir John came again to the Lord Holles and told him his Majesty had . . . heartily concurred and [it] would be done tomorrow by declaration and so it was, but not by such a declaration as his Majesty first approved of." [118] That night, it appears, Holles and his group fully expected the forthcoming Proclamation would be based on the one they had drafted which provided for the interim investigating commission and contained the commitment concerning the frequency and duration of future parliaments. Thus it was a shock and "to the inexpressible grief of all concerned," that they discovered the King had rejected these terms to which they thought he had agreed.[119]

Since in the end it was the King's independent action which brought dissolution, there is a question concerning the agreements or obligations remaining between Charles and Holles. Four days before the final proclamation was drawn up and issued, when the King left to go hunting, Holles told Barrillon that "if they form a new parliament and if they disband the army he hopes to be able to save the Earl of Danby but not the Lord Treasurer," and that "if he will give up his position they can find the way of not pushing any further the accusation brought against him." In addition the Presbyterians offered to "procure moneys in London . . . for the disbandment of the army, in case that the Court wants to carry [it] out in good faith and [if] they assemble a new parliament." [120] In his report to Louis XIV, Barrillon said nothing about the interim commission to investigate the Plot or the provision concerning the frequency and duration of parliaments, but Holles would have been aware that the French probably would not have viewed these terms favorably.

Surprised and dismayed though Holles and his associates were by the King's proclamation, one major goal had been attained in the dissolution of the Cavalier Parliament. Moreover it soon appeared that their other major aim of disbanding the army would be achieved, for within a week the French Ambassador reported that the Court had "definitely promised the complete disbanding of the troops and that it will be carried out before the session of Parliament"; and he also reported that "a few important patriots are in agreement with Holles to have money lent by the gold and silversmiths which would be enough to dismiss the troops. . . ." Within a few days the Duke of Monmouth, Captain-General of the Army, informed the Commissary General of the Musters that "whereas the regiments of foot and dragoons are forthwith to be disbanded," he was to take certain actions in order to prevent delay in the process.[121] Both parties therefore seem to have been proceeding in good faith regarding this part of any agreement, but Barrillon was overly optimistic in thinking that all of the troops would be disbanded so quickly, and in April Parliament was still attempting to raise the amount required to gain the complete disbanding which both the opposition and the French sought so intently.[122] Finally, as for any obligations regarding the treatment of Danby, they could only be carried out in the new Parliament. However, his failure to persuade the King to adhere to the original terms certainly raised some question concerning the support he would receive from the group with whom he had negotiated.

Regardless of the ultimate outcome there were several highly significant aspects to these negotiations. In the first place there was the attempt to obtain concessions from the King regarding the duration and frequency of parliaments. Ineffective though the King's published commitment to the principle of triennial parliaments would undoubtedly have been in practice, the fact that Holles and his associates sought such concessions is indicative of their continued desire to give Parliament a more effective role in the government and to restrain and diminish the power of the King. Also of much consequence was the increased stature that Holles and the Presbyterians had gained as a result of the negotiations. Both Shaftesbury and Buckingham had been bypassed and were ignorant of the proceedings, though Barrillon reported that they were happy to have what they had wanted.

But in commenting on the importance of the Presbyterians the Ambassador even went so far as to say that everybody saw clearly that the Presbyterians were going to be more influential than all the others.[123] Obviously this was an overstatement. Nevertheless their influence was to become much more consequential in Parliament.

At last all Dissenters had the opportunity of a general election before them, and they were determined to recover at least some of the parliamentary strength which they had so disastrously lost in the general election of 1661. Certainly the political experience of the Dissenters from 1661 to 1679 had indicated that in order to obtain relief they needed to elect members of Parliament who were of their own religious views, or were true friends who would remember them once elected. In addition it had become most evident that this was also the only way in which it might be possible to restrain the extreme Anglicans as well as the King and to obtain the religious and constitutional changes they desired.

# CHAPTER VI

## *Electioneering and Lobbying Activities, 1666–1681*

More than half a century of intense Puritan electioneering and political activity abruptly ceased during the first five years of the Cavalier Parliament. The impact of defeat in the parliamentary elections of 1661 and of the repressive legislation which followed had the desired effects upon the overwhelming majority of Dissenters throughout the country, and except for the few who were involved in the plots of these years, all were passive and quietist in attitude.

Among the Quakers and Baptists this quietism, which had appeared even before the Restoration, was merely reinforced by the violence of the plotters and the vehemence of Parliament. After the Venner plot of January, 1661, over 250 Baptists of most shades of opinion united in professing their "humble subjection and fidelity" to the King, and by 1665 even one of a millenary disposition such as William Sherwin was writing that it was the "bold presumption and scandalous wickedness of our latter times, for any, under pretence of Christ's Kingdom given to the Saints, to go about by the sword, or any other unlawful means, to divest magistrates and governors of their offices, to take that Kingdom before Christ give it to them to whom it will belong. . . ."[1] Likewise the Quakers, led by George Fox, declared their innocence and loyalty both at the time of the Venner plot and in 1663 after the plots of that year.[2]

The Quakers were also quick to seek relief from the Cavalier Parliament, petitioning and testifying before a committee of the House of Lords in May, 1661, for legislation which would allow them to avoid taking oaths and which would grant immunity from the enforcement of earlier statutes requiring attendance at services of the Church of England. When their attempts only backfired and led to introduction of a Bill directed against them, they immediately turned to active lobbying and to testifying against the Bill at the Bar of the House of Commons, although unsuccessfully. There were other early instances in which Nonconformists presented petitions, but they did not appear before the Houses as did the Quakers, and they soon abandoned these tactics when their uselessness became evident.[3] While the other Nonconformists then appear to have ceased all efforts to influence the Government for some time to come, the Quakers turned from Parliament to the King, and during the five years from 1661 to 1666 they relied primarily upon personal audiences or appeals to Charles. George Fox was particularly convinced that this procedure was the efficacious one. Because of the fact that the 700 Friends who, according to his estimate, were in prison at the Restoration were released by the King, and because Friends were permitted to see Charles in seeking Fox's own freedom at this time, the Quaker leader became convinced that the King was moderate and that Friends had "gotten a place in his heart." [4]

In some respects Presbyterian and Congregationalist leaders were even more favorably disposed toward the Monarchy and more submissive than Baptists and Quakers during these years, partly because they continued to hope for some measure of comprehension or toleration, but even more because of the general discouragement that had come with the great failures of the preceding two decades, and their inability during the last two years to salvage any of their major religious or political programs. When the opinions and actions of the Presbyterian and Congregationalist ministers are compared with those of the laymen, it is evident that at least in the beginning the religious leaders were more quietist than those of their beliefs who were active in politics. However, disillusionment and a degree of quietism or caution also infected these men of affairs as the passage of the early repressive laws revealed the consequences of the political defeat in the election of 1661, and as the drastic enforcement of the Corporation Act during the first several years seemed to indicate that the defeat had been a disaster from which it would not be possible to recover.[5]

The impact of all these developments was overwhelming, and it is therefore not surprising that it has been impossible to find any evidence of Dissenters who were active in any of the by-elections that returned sixty-four new members to Parliament before September, 1666.[6] However, this period of inactivity on the part of the politically-minded Dissenters throughout the country came to an end in the autumn of 1666, and during the next four years they made many efforts to exert pressure at elections. Among the first instances are two which were very unusual, for they are among a total of only three elections occurring between 1661 and 1679 in which known or probable Presbyterians were returned in a by-election without later having their election contested by a defeated candidate. The first two new members having this distinction were the Presbyterian Sir Philip Harcourt, who was returned from Boston, Lincolnshire, in October, 1666, and the probable Presbyterian Sir Walter Yonge, son of the Puritan diarist, who was returned for Clifton Dartmouth, the following January.[7] Nonconformist activity on the hustings at this time is also illustrated by the double return the following month of the Presbyterian Michael Harvey and the Anglican Sir John Coventry for the Borough of Weymouth. In this case the outcome was much more typical of the vast majority of contested elections involving Dissenters during the remaining years of the Cavalier Parliament. In the first place it was a double return; secondly, while the merits of the case were being determined Harvey's opponent was seated; and finally, when Harvey petitioned to be seated he was turned down.[8]

Unsuccessful though they usually were in their attempts to elect and seat candidates of their own religious position, Dissenters were not without political effectiveness on the hustings. During the remaining years of the Cavalier Parliament there were many moderate Anglicans who either sought or welcomed Nonconformist support in parliamentary elections, and who as members of the House of Commons generally proved to be favorable to the Dissenters' interests. During the first four years of renewed activity on the hustings there were three instances in which such candidates received Nonconformist assistance and were elected, and in the latter two of these cases the returns were uncontested.[9] However, in the first election there was evidence that the Corporation Act was violated by Dissenters, and this not only led to voiding the election but also appears to have prompted efforts to obtain remedial legislation.[10]

Efforts of the Court to enforce the Corporation Act are most indicative of the increased Nonconformist activity on the local level during these years; [11] but in spite of these attempts, reports of violations continued to grow more numerous until the second Conventicle Act went into effect in 1670.[12] Obviously of most concern to the Government and the Anglicans were the instances in which such violations of the Corporation Act had a direct effect upon the outcome of parliamentary elections, and it is very likely that it was the instances of this sort that brought the introduction of a bill which would not only have tightened enforcement of the Corporation Act, but which also would have prevented the election of candidates who did not have certificates that they had received the Sacrament within a certain number of months prior to election.[13] Undoubtedly because of other clauses which most members found more undesirable, the bill was laid aside after one reading, and the next year the Government once again tried by administrative means to tighten the enforcement of the existing law.[14]

In spite of the continued activity of Nonconformists on the local level, the results in parliamentary elections were most discouraging. Of three candidates from their own ranks who stood in 1669 and 1670 only Thomas Trenchard was elected and seated.[15] At Liverpool in October, 1670, Dissenters attempted to elect one of their number in the by-election, but the opposing candidate who received strong backing from the King was successful.[16] In another instance determined Nonconformist support of Sir Francis Rolle, who was possibly of their ranks, resulted in a contested election. Presbyterian members and their allies in the House continued to support him, but the other candidate was seated primarily on the grounds that some of the burgesses had not complied with the Corporation Act.[17]

In addition to the resurgence of efforts to gain entrance into the borough corporations and the House of Commons between 1666 and 1670, there were also attempts to influence Parliament by legitimate petitioning and by more aggressive activities that are better described as the tactics of pressure groups, or simply as lobbying. The Quakers and Congregationalists were most persistent in these activities, the Congregationalists using the more traditional of the two methods. The Presbyterians were somewhat less frequent petitioners, having a considerable number of their own members in Parliament through whom they could work,

while the Baptists as a group do not appear to have taken any
steps of this nature during these years.

Among the early instances in which Quakers and others attempted to win support by handing printed material purporting
to be petitions to the members as they were going into the House
of Commons, there was one which resulted in a vote "that no
printed briefs, papers or breviates, of any matter, be brought to
the doors, or given, or distributed, amongst the members of this
House." [18] Although it would appear from lack of other attempts
that this vote was effective in eliminating such lobbying tactics
for the time being, there was at least one other case in November,
1670, when "some scandalous libel [was] dispensed by women
in the hall and given to the members at the House door. . . ."
As a result there was a motion to further suppress the Quakers. [19]

The efforts of the Congregationalists and Presbyterians to influence legislation seem to have resulted from the hope of obtaining comprehension and toleration just after the first Conventicle
Act expired, and also from the justifiable fears which were
aroused by the introduction of the second Conventicle Act. Dr.
John Owen was the leader of the Congregationalist efforts, and
according to George Vernon, an Anglican clergyman, Owen was
very systematic and had the cooperation of many other Congregationalist ministers. Vernon wrote that Owen worked indus-
triously, inquiring "whether things went well as to his great
Diana, Liberty of Conscience? How His Majesty stood affected
to it? Whether he would connive at it, and the execution of laws
against it? Who were or could be made his friends at Court?
What bills were like to be put up in Parliament? [And] how that
assembly was united or divided." He listed eleven other divines
as "under-officers" and stated that Owen would inform them of
the disposition of affairs and that they would keep the Congregationalists throughout the Kingdom informed. [20] It is well known
that Owen had connections with influential political leaders at
Court and in Parliament, including Lord Wharton and the Earl
of Anglesey whom he visited frequently, as well as Sir John
Trevor, Secretary of State in the Cabal. [21] In general the efforts
of both the Congregationalists and Presbyterians followed the
more traditional patterns of petitioning, pamphleteering, [22] and
of personal contacts with the members of Parliament. More frequently such contacts were with those of their own religious

views, but this was not always the case. For example, John
Hackett, Bishop of Coventry and Linchfield, complained in a
letter to Archbishop Sheldon prior to the meeting of Parliament
in February, 1668, that the Nonconformists " 'labored much with
many members of this county and have gained Mr. Dyot our new
burgess unto them: for they wholly possess him and converse
with him.' " [23]

All of these early efforts between 1666 and 1670 to win support
from members of Parliament and to elect members who were
either of their own religious persuasion or who were friendly
came during a period when there was a growing relaxation in the
enforcement of the statutes directed against Nonconformity and
the lapse of the most effective of these laws. It is therefore certainly not surprising that when the new Conventicle Act was
enacted and vigorously enforced, activities of this nature seem
to have completely disappeared until 1673, and Dissenters turned
instead to the King for help.[24] However, when the relief granted
by the King through the Declaration of Indulgence proved to
be only temporary, the Dissenters looked once again to Parliament for enactment of a bill of comprehension and toleration.
In support of this measure they engaged in lobbying to some degree, and at the same time there were a few instances of political activity on the hustings.[25] Just as in the late 1660's however,
efforts in 1673 and 1674 to obtain this legislation failed, but there
was some success on the hustings in three instances. During the
first two months of 1673 the Presbyterian merchant Sir Samuel
Barnardiston was elected for Suffolk; and Thomas Papillon, another merchant whose religious views were similar, was elected
for Dover.[26] The third successful candidate was Philip Foley,
elected in November for Bewdley, who was well known for his
Presbyterianism and for the wealth founded upon the family's
iron manufacturing.[27] Nonconformists also became active once
again in supporting moderate Anglican candidates on the hustings, a notable case being in the election of Sir John Hobart as
member for Norfolk County in February, 1673.[28]

The failure to increase their strength to any appreciable degree was reflected in the proceedings of Parliament. Although the
Nonconformist members were even more active in the sessions
of 1673 and early 1674, their impotency was apparent in their
failure to obtain comprehension and toleration at a time when

their chances were probably better than ever before. This was cause for real concern, but there were developments that came on the heels of this failure which were truly alarming. Certainly the King's shift from a policy of seeking religious toleration to one of repression of Dissenters and alliance with the Anglican clergy was most threatening, and it had an impact upon Nonconformists all over the country as well as upon those in Parliament. This change in policy became particularly evident to the imprisoned George Fox and his associates, for they had obtained a release from the King only to have it stopped by the Lord Keeper. Fox was suspicious of this action, writing William Penn that "it is much [as] if the King has my release [so] that the Keeper should stop it," while one of the chief Quaker agents in this intercession was even more pointed and wrote Fox that he was sure he had not known any Friends "so betrayed in any business with the King" since he had become a Friend. By the following spring the Friends had shifted their tactics. Instead of working primarily through the King as they had been, they turned to Parliament, as did the other Nonconformist denominations. "All their hopes now are in the Parliament, . . . now [that] they say there is no trust in princes," wrote one of Secretary Williamson's informants about the Dissenters in Yarmouth.[29]

The stringent enforcement of the penal statutes directed against Nonconformity did not have the same effect upon Dissenters as in the past. They had become completely inactive politically in the first periods of repression during 1662–1666 and 1670–1672, but this time they became even more active in their efforts on the hustings and in their pressures upon the members of Parliament than they had recently been, and this activity was only a prelude to the outburst that came after the Popish Plot and during the Exclusion Parliaments. Among the reasons why the Dissenters reacted differently in 1674–1675 was that in this instance the repression was a royal policy, while during the earlier periods it had been much more the result of parliamentary desires and enactments, particularly the two Conventicle Acts. More important, however, there was now a more cohesive parliamentary opposition proffering its help, and there seemed to be a real hope of increasing its strength and gaining relief by electioneering, lobbying, and parliamentary maneuvering. Shaftesbury's reminder to his associates in 1675 that they were elected by Nonconformists as well as Conformists was not overlooked by Dissenters.[30]

Of the four Nonconformist denominations, the Friends were in the best position to carry on political activity, for by 1675 Fox and his associates had created an effective, centralized church organization with the discipline that makes for effective lobbying and electioneering.[31] It was natural that Quakers turned to lobbying first and primarily, and it was to be expected that this time their efforts would be systematic and sustained.[32] Lobbying resembled the tactics which they had been using in approaching the King and Crown officials as well as members of Parliament on earlier occasions, and it involved less active and complete participation in politics and was therefore more acceptable to a group which had been generally quietist in temperament for a decade and a half. Quaker determination to win parliamentary support in their efforts to obtain relief from the renewed repression was clearly evident when both Fox and Penn refused to leave London during the parliamentary sessions of 1675,[33] but it was not until the next meetings of Parliament in 1677 and 1678 that the lobbying machinery of the Friends was fully developed. In order to handle the tremendous amount of work involved in efforts to protect Quakers from the rigors of prosecution and to free those who were imprisoned, a fully developed national organization, known as the Meeting for Sufferings, had been established by 1677,[34] and in the spring of 1678 the London representatives appointed specific members from their group to visit the House of Commons as observers and agents or lobbyists. The number of men appointed varied from time to time in 1678, running from five to fifteen, and at first they seem to have been charged with carrying out specific tasks. After trying several arrangements to rotate this duty during 1678, they finally arrived at the system of designating ten men who were to be responsible for the first three days of each week and another group of ten which had the assignment during the last three days.[35]

In other respects as well, the Meeting for Sufferings carried on an operation which had the basic characteristics of a modern lobby or pressure group. Orders were sent from London to all the County Meetings for Sufferings which stated that Friends were to write their representatives in Parliament pleading for a redress of their sufferings and informing them of new cases, particularly during the adjournments of Parliament when the London Meeting lost contact with the members.[36]

In addition reports of cases were sent to London. To these summaries of the sufferings in the various counties would be added legal and other arguments against prosecution, and then these documents would be presented to the appropriate committees in Parliament.[37] More frequently, and undoubtedly more effectively, such petitions, reports, letters and the like would be presented to individual members of the parliamentary opposition. Although relations between Presbyterians in Parliament and the Quakers were not cordial, the Friends did present petitions and papers to such leaders as Lord Wharton and Sir Edward Harley during these crucial years; [38] but it is clear that they approached the Anglican wing of opposition much more frequently, including Shaftesbury and Halifax in the House of Lords and Sir Thomas Lee in the House of Commons, as well as many others.[39] Indicative of the effect such work could have was the occasion upon which Sir Thomas Lee opened a Commons' debate by stating that he had "met with some people in the Hall" who presented him with a list of the "sort of people convicted as Romish Recusants." [40] Thereupon the opposition took concerted steps to free the Quakers and Baptists [41] from prosecution under the statutes directed against the Catholics.

Although most of the Quaker lobbying and pressure tactics were concerned with cases in which they held that their legal and religious rights had been violated, and although they worked primarily upon political leaders, these were not their only purposes, nor were these the only people from whom they sought assistance. Pending legislation and committee actions which might affect them were also watched closely, not only by the Quaker observers but also by such persons as the writing clerks of Parliament who appear to have been paid by the Friends to perform this service.[42] Such operations were expensive, and in 1679 the central Quaker governing body, the Yearly Meeting, gave full authority to the Weekly Meeting for Sufferings in London to handle all costs and funds. In addition it recommended that Friends in their collections remember the expense which several London Friends have borne freely "in waiting and attending upon the King and Parliament, Council Board and other magistrates . . . about the national sufferings," and also the money they "constantly expended and paid to the clerks and other officers belonging to the Parliament, Council Board, and other Courts searching of . . . records and such like. . . ." [43]

Since the other Nonconformist denominations did not have the national executive and administrative organization or the discipline of the Society of Friends,[44] it was impossible for them to exert such concerted and consistent pressure. The lack of such an organization also helps to explain the fact that only fragmentary evidence is available concerning the lobbying activities of Baptists, Congregationalists, and Presbyterians, for they have no church records such as the full and systematically preserved ones of the Society of Friends. Of these three remaining Nonconformist groups, the Baptists needed to resort to pressure tactics far more than the Presbyterians and Congregationalists, for, with the possible exception of Sir John Eyles, they like the Quakers did not have any members in Parliament of their religious disposition.

Beginning in 1676 there was some indication that after a decade and a half Baptist indifference to political developments was beginning to give way as the result of renewed persecution and the hope that the political situation was such that some relief might be obtained.[45] However, the Baptists were apparently not as quick as the Quakers to translate this change of attitude into action, for the first Baptist petitioning or lobbying occurred on March 25, 1678, when William Kiffen and a fellow Particular Baptist "appeared at the Committee for the discrimination of Quakers etc. from Papists and gave in a book . . . in the behalf of the Anabaptist[s]. . . ." [46] Although Baptists engaged in such activity during the next three years, it seems most probable that those who did were acting as individuals rather than as representatives of a church organization. There were apparently no other appearances before Parliamentary committees or as lobbyists in the halls of the Houses; but there was a considerable amount of petitioning and other activity more related to electioneering. Rarely if ever is any mention of political activity found in the few surviving Baptist church records, practically all of which are those of individual churches, but this is also the case in local Quaker records. Although a good degree of quietism undoubtedly did persist, the absence of evidence did not necessarily mean that Baptists and Quakers did not discuss or act upon political matters at this level. It is probable that there was a reluctance to make a written record of any political discussions or actions that took place because of a fear that church records might be seized by government authorities and used in prosecutions.[47] For such reasons and also because of the vehement passions aroused by the Popish Plot and subsequent crises, individuals were much more apt to be spurred to spontaneous action rather than to wait for the slower and probably more restrained reaction of church groups.[48] Nevertheless, it is clear that the Baptist's efforts in this field of political action were insignificant when compared to those of the Quakers.

As in the past, the political problem facing the Presbyterians and Congregationalists was different from that facing the other Dissenters. Since there were a good many members of Parliament who were Presbyterian, and some who were Congregationalist in their religious views, there was not the need for the kind of organized lobbying which the Quakers perfected. Moreover, the failure of past drives to obtain comprehension and toleration undoubtedly left Presbyterian and Congregationalist leaders more skeptical about the efficacy of such tactics and more convinced that a change in the membership of the House of Commons was of far greater importance as a step toward achievement of their goals. Since many of the lay leaders of the more moderate Dissenting groups were themselves politically ambitious, it was only natural that they were more prominent in the electioneering that increased during the last three years of the Cavalier Parliament and reached a climax during the following three years of the Exclusion Parliaments. However, there was a general quickening in political awareness and a growing participation in politics by all Dissenters during this time. Certainly there is no more decisive an indication of this increased awareness than the decision made by Quaker leaders on May 3, 1675, which resulted in the directive that

Friends in the several Counties [were to] seriously consider together and be unanimous about giving their voice in election of Parliament men to appear or not appear therein as in the wisdom of God they see convenient and safe. That such moderate and indifferent men as they are free to give their voice for first be advised to sign to Friends this or the like engagement . . . 1. To be for a general liberty of conscience . . . 2. To endeavor to the utmost of his power to remove all oppressive and Popish laws that are for coercion or . . . persecutions about religion.[49]

This was a highly significant action, for in addition to giving official sanction to Quaker activity in elections, it also was one of the earliest attempts by voters belonging to a religious group to obtain a candidate's engagement to specific policies before committing themselves to vote for him.

Ministerial and lay leaders among the Presbyterians were also taking steps to increase their representation in Parliament. For example, the Presbyterian Thomas Gilbert, one of Lord Wharton's chaplains, was quick to seek out a Nonconformist candidate when he heard that there was a parliamentary seat to be filled at Abington.[50] At this same time many Presbyterian politicians were planning who would stand in a general election if the Cavalier Parliament were dissolved;[51] or they were busy in by-elections, hoping to gain some greater representation by this slower process. The most significant candidacy in these by-elections was that of the Nonconformist Thomas Moore of Haychurch, Dorset, who stood for burgess of Weymouth in October, 1675. Shaftesbury himself went to Weymouth in support of Moore, and the Nonconformists were reported "very confident of their strength. . . ." However, he was defeated.[52] Dissenters also supported at least five other candidates during the period 1675–1678. These included Thomas Vane, son of the famous Sir Henry Vane of the Civil War and Interregnum period, who stood at Durham in 1675 and won the election; second, John Rushworth, the possible Dissenter and well-known Civil War historian, who stood at Berwick in February, 1677; third, Captain Richard Huntington, "a partial conformist" who sought election at Yarmouth; fourth, Sir Robert Kemp, a Norfolk candidate for knight of the shire in April, 1675, who was not a Dissenter; and fifth, Sir Robert Cann, also not a Dissenter, who stood at Bristol in October, 1677.[53] Undoubtedly the Dissenters also were active on behalf of five additional candidates whose religious views were Nonconformist to varying degrees, although explicit evidence of such support has not been discovered. Of these candidates, Sir John Hewly, and Philip Foley who stood at York and Bewdley respectively, were Presbyterians; while Sir Walter Yonge (grandson of the Puritan diarist), Sir William Ellis of Nocton, and Thomas Reynell, who stood at Newport in Cornwall, and at Grantham and Ashburton respectively, were possibly Presbyterians.[54]

Increasingly energetic though the Dissenters were, the results were most disappointing to candidates of their own religious persuasion, for only one was elected, and he died before being seated.[55] Such a complete lack of success marks a definite shift in the trend of the immediately preceding years, but it is not difficult to explain. The election of Foley, Barnardiston, and Papillon in 1673 and the additional reports of Nonconformist activity prior to 1675 had been sufficient to cause some alarm and create the feeling that if Parliament were dissolved "the Presbyterian interest and the fanatics will carry it in most counties." [56] As reports of electioneering came in to government officials in increasing number during the next three years, and as Shaftesbury worked more vigorously to create a political machine, Danby and his followers came to fight by-elections much more strenuously.[57] Particularly illuminating was the election at Berwick in which John Rushworth was opposed by Danby's own son, who was under the required age for members. Finding that the voters favoring Rushworth were more numerous, Sir Richard Stote, who was the sheriff, decided upon a plan not to deliver the writ or appoint the election day and in addition to disallow most of Rushworth's votes. In a subsequent letter to Danby, Stote wrote that at the election "we found that many of them stood excommunicate for not repairing to divine service and not receiving the Sacrament, and . . . we did except against their votes as not legal." [58]

Although such tactics gave grounds for a petition to the House of Commons against the return, this maneuver was a hopeless one. Because of Danby's control of the House, every one of the nine attempts made by five of the seven defeated candidates during the years 1675–1678 was voted down or allowed to die, and in addition the government forces were able to unseat Philip Foley in March, 1677.[59] Nevertheless there were candidates elected to the House of Commons during the middle of the decade who were supported by and friendly to Dissenters, and even the veteran Quaker lobbyist George Whitehead was sufficiently impressed by the cumulative results to write later the exaggerated estimate that "some time before the . . . Parliament was dissolved many (or most) of our old adversaries and rigid persecutors" were replaced by new members "of better spirit and tempers," leaving the House so "changed that it appeared almost like a new one. . . ." [60] However, only a general election could bring any possibility of electing and seating a sufficient number of friendly members and Dissenters as to have any real effect upon major actions and decisions of the Commons.

When the Cavalier Parliament was finally dissolved and the general election was to become a reality, there was a great surge of hope and activity among Dissenters all over the country. It finally seemed that the political disaster of 1661 could be partially overcome, for the political and religious atmosphere prevailing after the disclosures of Titus Oates and the following events was in sharp contrast to that just following the Restoration. Now it was Catholicism far more than Puritanism which was feared and hated, and nothing could give rise to greater political expectations and activity. The impact of the dissolution of the Cavalier Parliament and the coming general election upon Nonconformists was vividly illustrated by the reaction of Thomas Jolly and his congregation. He wrote of the "dreadful and hopeful importance" which "drove us together . . . when we had a more full [church] meeting and a better opportunity than ordinary," and also of another meeting "soon after upon account the great business of elections for a new Parliament and our great danger not only from foreigners abroad but traitors at home." [61] To a considerable degree, Dissenters regarded the election campaign as a religious crusade. As one of them wrote to Increase Mather in Massachusetts, "the great work is to serve the Providence of God in choosing a Parliament . . . while our enemies pursue their design in burning the City, etc." [62]

Feeling that the most vital religious and political issues were involved in the political developments of the day, even those Dissenters recently inclined to be quietists in attitude could not remain indifferent to worldly affairs. Urging them to abandon this attitude was the influential General Baptist minister Thomas Grantham, who wrote a telling attack against the views that made Christians "insignificant ciphers in a commonwealth." He maintained that being Christian made men "fitted for every good work even in civil things," and that "it cannot be unlawful for any Christian who is capable to serve his country to bear office in common with other men . . . Nor is that objection which some make of any real force, viz. that the civil power in many nations is mingled with the authority of mystery Babylon. . . ." [63] Grantham was not alone in advocating these views. Certainly one of his strongest supporters and probably the Baptist's most vigorous political activist was his publisher, Francis Smith, another General Baptist minister who was to become far better known as a printer and as one of the most energetic and important campaigners there was during the next three elections and parliaments.

Likewise, within the Society of Friends any remaining traces of earlier passive attitudes seem to have almost completely disappeared during the next three years. Not only were their lobbying activities intensified,[64] but they also became much more active in electioneering. There were petitions such as that from the Quakers at York in March, 1679, in which they addressed their newly elected members of Parliament, stating: ". . . we have at this time made our appearance with the rest of our neighbours at this city, in order to elect persons to sit in Parliament as the representatives of this County, and you being now elected, we look upon it our duty to acquaint you with our grievances, desiring that you would endeavor to redress them." [65] Such a suggestion that members of the House of Commons should act in accordance with the wishes of those who elected them, or as delegates, was a manifestation of the new type of Quaker pressure; for the implication was that their support in future elections would depend upon whether the members acted in accordance with their desires. The next step in the development of such realistic political tactics came prior to the elections of members for the Oxford Parliament in the spring of 1681. Upon this occasion the Quaker leaders once again sent out a general letter to Friends, as in 1675. They stated their desire that all "who are in capacity . . . may appear, and make what good interest they can in the elections of Parliament men, for sober discrete and moderate men such as . . . are against persecution and popery, and that deport themselves tenderly towards our friends." [66] However, they did not believe such a general appeal was adequate to meet the needs of this crucial election. Additional letters were therefore sent to individual Quaker meetings urging the members to "give their voices and make what of interest they can in the behalf" of specific members of Parliament who in the last session had "concerned themselves in our behalf." Letters of this sort were sent to Northallerton, in support of Sir Gilbert Gerard and Sir Henry Calverley, and to Haverfordwest in support of Thomas Owen.[67]

Moreover, since the letter to Northallerton makes it clear that the Quaker leaders were sympathetic to the nascent petition campaign which was to be organized by opposition forces, and which lauded certain previous members of Parliament for their record and urged their re-election, it seems probable that if this campaign had not developed leading Friends would have sent more of their own letters in support of specific candidates.[68]

Direct evidence that Quakers carried out the desires of their London leaders came to light after Charles had dissolved his final Parliament and the official policy of the day had become one of retaliation. At Cirencester, for example, Justice James George struck back with "severe proceedings" against Quakers because they had voted for his opponents rather than him, and at Bristol there were similar prosecutions because Friends had "joined with Presbyterians to choose Parliament men." [69] In addition there were Quakers who actively compaigned for individual candidates and who worked to arouse Englishmen to the importance of the elections, the most prominent being William Penn. His unsuccessful efforts on behalf of the republican Algernon Sydney are well known and have been frequently described.[70] Perhaps more significant was the degree to which he worked with the Presbyterian Sir John Fagg in these efforts and also in behalf of the candidacy of Sir Charles Wolseley, a prominent Nonconformist.[71] Of greater impact than any of his electioneering, however, was a pamphlet in which the vital importance of the election was stressed in terms that would stir all Dissenters, for he emphasized their major religious and political grievances.[72]

Such changes in attitude and such extensions of previous political activity as were found among Quakers and Baptists during the elections of the Exclusion Parliaments were matched by similar manifestations on the part of Presbyterians and Congregationalists. The major new development among these more moderate Dissenters was that many ministers became active campaigners. Among them were Lord Wharton's old correspondent Samuel Hieron of Honiton, Devon, who was obviously pleased to report to Wharton that he "contributed towards" Sir Walter Yonge's elections.[73] A Congregationalist minister, Samuel Jeake, courageously supported steps taken by Dissenters at Rye in an attempt to gain control of the Corporation and elect a mayor and burgess, actions which subsequently led to several prosecutions including

Jeake's; and elsewhere others unmentioned by name contributed their efforts.[74] Presbyterian and Congregationalist ministers were able to make important contributions by calling on their politically powerful Nonconformist friends to give assistance on critical occasions,[75] and even by encouraging them to be candidates in spite of personal considerations, as Roger Morrice did John Swynfen in the summer of 1679.[76] They also contributed by participating in the meetings and possibly in the planning prior to or at the time of elections, and by keeping their political friends informed of all important political developments.[77]

Of the electioneering in which Nonconformists engaged during the years 1679–1681, none was more vigorous, more sustained, and more effective than that of the colorful and courageous Francis Smith, the zealous General Baptist printer, who played a most important part in the opposition's press campaign.[78] Nor did any of the other opposition election activities have such historical import as this press campaign, for this was the first instance in which an intensive and organized effort was made over the country to win the elections by calculated manipulation of public opinion. Although Shaftesbury and other political leaders were responsible for this campaign, and although their support undoubtedly made Smith more emboldened, nevertheless the very volume of the material he published and his roughhewn yet trenchant prose that appeared so frequently in these publications stamp much of the campaign as the product of his own energy and enterprise.[79] During 1681, his most prolific year, Smith is known to have published well over a dozen pamphlets, most of them during the two months of the elections; and in addition he published his famous bi-weekly news sheet, *Smith's Protestant Intelligence*, which played a major role in the Whig campaign tactics.[80] The obvious intent of this publication was to create the impression that the whole country was enthusiastically electing Whig candidates and that a landslide would be the result. One of the main techniques used to obtain this result was to publish the many election addresses which were deceptively represented as the voters' spontaneous expression of congratulation to the successful candidate in which they stated their desire that certain specific policies and legislation be supported in Parliament.[81] Since the addresses were actually inspired by Whig party leaders as a major part of the whole campaign, Smith played a vitally important role in publicizing them, not only in his news sheet but also in broadside form, and possibly in their final collected version as a pamphlet.[82] Because of his aggressive activity the Baptist printer suffered innumerable prosecutions and privations, for though Shaftesbury and others of his party may have acted as protectors of a sort, they were powerless outside of Parliament. In the end the intrepid printer was ruined, and in 1689 the Whites Alley General Baptist Church, "considering his necessitous condition . . . ordered that Brother Joseph Walker give him ten shillings." [83]

Important though all such electioneering was, it could be no more than peripheral to the campaigning of the candidates themselves. Of those seeking election to the three Exclusion Parliaments none could have worked with a greater sense of the decisive opportunity facing them than the Presbyterians and Congregationalists who either had sat or hoped to sit in Parliament, as is evidenced by the amount and urgency of their correspondence and consultations concerning plans and maneuvers. As could be expected, Lord Wharton was one of the most active and influential. His own papers as well as those of other political leaders and ministers indicate that he, John Swynfen, the Hampdens, the Foleys, Lord Paget, Lord Anglesey, Sir Francis Wilbraham and others corresponded and met at each others homes frequently at the time of the elections, and that they were particularly busy prior to the first election with the tasks of deciding who would stand where, with lining up supporters, and with the other problems confronting them as a result of the first general election since 1661.[84] Unfortunately, records of such activity for other counties are not as rich as they are for Buckinghamshire, Worcestershire, and Staffordshire, yet there are enough to indicate that Presbyterian political leaders were everywhere similarly energetic in their efforts.[85]

In addition to conferring and planning among themselves, Nonconformist candidates worked with Anglican politicians who were of the Whig disposition. For example, such Presbyterian leaders as Wharton, Hampden, and Swynfen worked closely with Shaftesbury, Buckingham, Sir Thomas Lee, Lord William Russell, and other opposition leaders of their stature, as well as prominent moderate Anglicans within the counties like Sir Ralph Verney. Of particular import, it would seem, were such presumably social occasions as a dinner at Shaftesbury's in the midst of the elections of February, 1679, concerning which Lady Russell wrote to her husband, telling him that Wharton had also been a guest. A week after this dinner Sir Edward Harley wrote Wharton a letter which also did not directly concern politics. However it had definite political significance, for in this answer to a letter from Wharton, Harley replied that he too was most happy to hear of "Shaftesbury's desire for Mr. [William] Taylor, your Lordship's chaplain, to succeed Mr. [Samuel] Birch in the same employ at Shilton . . . ," Oxfordshire, where the Presbyterian Birch had operated a very well-known school until his recent death.[86] Through such actions as this the confidence of Presbyterian leaders, lay and ministerial, was won, and they were brought into closer cooperation with the Anglican leaders of the emerging Whig party.

Politically, socially, and religiously, Presbyterian politicians had more in common with their moderate Anglican counterparts than they did with some of their fellow Nonconformists, and therefore they undoubtedly agreed with Shaftesbury's contention that candidates should be elected who were of some means and judgment and who would command the respect of the voters as well as support the Nonconformist policies.[87] Discriminating though these leaders may have been in their efforts to select candidates, they do not seem to have offended the rank and file Nonconformist voter, whether Presbyterian, Congregationalist, Baptist, or Quaker. In the Yorkshire election of July, 1679, for example, that staunch supporter of the Court and the Church, Sir John Reresby, reported with dismay that "the sectaries and fanatics" stood for Lord Fairfax, and that among them were his friends the cutlers of Sheffield,[88] undoubtedly including such men as John Barber, a "paring-knife maker," and Joseph Hancock, "a shearer," both of whom had previously been reported to be Congregationalist teachers in their own homes at Sheffield.[89] In Somerset it appears that the candidates were somewhat more aggressive than Lord Fairfax, for evidence indicates that William Strode, John Trenchard, and Sir William Waller probably campaigned vigorously among the serge makers in Taunton "and all adjacent fanatic places of trade." [90]

In all their electioneering, Nonconformist politicians not only proved to be aggressive and ingenious but also ready to resort to various types of pressure and tactics which were devious, though not uncommonly used in the politics of the day. One maneuver to multiply the number of Dissenters eligible to vote in County elections was the practice of splitting freeholds, and the evidence indicates that Dissenters began to do this as early as 1666, if not before.[91] Moreover, it appears that some purchases of land for this purpose may have been only apparent or temporary, for there was a report that the Nonconformists who were supporting Sir Samuel Barnardiston in 1673 did "really or under color purchase so much in Suffolk as may make them capable to be electors." [92] Economic pressure could also be used. Not only landowners but also shopkeepers, tradesmen, and employers appear to have used such tactics. Although not concerning a parliamentary election, an observation made to Secretary Williamson about the situation in Yarmouth indicated the kind of economic pressure that could be exerted in some boroughs where there was a sufficient number of thriving Nonconformist tradesmen. It was reported that "the factious here are so numerous and eminent in trade that the rest depend upon them, so that few dare appear for the King or Church's interest. . . ." [93] Another indication of the tactics and power of Nonconformists in boroughs during the crucial years of the Popish Plot and the Exclusion Parliaments is that they were sometimes able to restore those who had been turned out of the corporations by the commissioners for the enforcement of the Corporation Act, and that far more frequently they ignored the provisions of the Act applying to newly elected municipal officials or disregarded other laws.[94] In addition to these maneuvers and tactics, there were the ever-present entertainments and drinking.[95] Also there were some charges of outright bribery, and there is evidence that occasionally Nonconformists were implicated in either temporary creation of burgesses or temporary granting of the freedom of the corporation in order to increase the number of supporters in parliamentary elections, all of these practices being not uncommon.[96]

Nonconformists who were active in electioneering unquestionably condoned such practices, particularly the circumvention or violation of the Corporation Act, but there were those who found this difficult or distasteful to do. Many probably felt as did Samuel Hieron, who wrote Lord Wharton that he thought it "an intolerable mischief, if a pot of ale must make our Parliament men," but that he did not see what could be done "until there be some remedy provided in Parliament. . . ." [97] Bills designed to control election practices and expenses had been supported by Swynfen, Boscawen, and Maynard in the past; and during the Exclusion Parliaments, Presbyterian and Congregationalist members took a most prominent part in working for much more thorough parliamentary reform measures, but all of their efforts were unsuccessful.[98]

The intensive activity of the Nonconformists in the elections of 1679 and 1681 created concern and alarm. Prior to those of 1679 observers presumed the Presbyterian would "have the ascendant in most places," and maintained that "if the choice be not so well as it might be you will find the reason to be in the industry of the Nonconformists and the negligence of the true Protestants who will miss coming to the election, which the others will sure not to be tardy in." [99] Although the two general elections of 1679 were even more of a landslide for the opposition forces than had been anticipated, the greatest gain in numbers was not made by the Presbyterians but by the moderate Anglicans, who had been vigorously supported by the Dissenters.[100] The known Presbyterian and Congregationalist gains in number were small in comparison, yet striking when viewed in the perspective of the low totals of known Presbyterians and Congregationalists who had previously sat in Parliament. The significance of the gain is therefore seen more clearly in the percentage of increase that occurred. At the close of the Cavalier Parliament there were only twenty-five members presently known who may be regarded as Presbyterians or Congregationalists. The elections of February–March brought this total to forty-two, or a 68% increase, and by the time the second Exclusion Parliament met there was a total of fifty-two Presbyterian or Congregationalist members, or a 108% increase over the number sitting when the Cavalier Parliament was dissolved, but only a 23.8% increase over the number in the first Exclusion Parliament. Moreover, Dissenters had reached the apex, for the election to the last Exclusion Parliament of January–March, 1681, brought a 11.5% decline in the known Presbyterian-Congregationalist members.[101]

Impressive though the results were in 1679, the election of these members was only a means to an end. The vigor of the campaigning is indicative of the Nonconformists' intense desire to see the adoption of such policies and proposed laws as those publicized by William Penn and Francis Smith. Among those having the more immediate appeal were the demands for the repeal of the Corporation Act and the Elizabethan Conventicle Act, and for passage of measures which would prevent the "misery which would come if James or any other Papist ascended the throne." In addition, it was proposed that there be legislation to remove the "just fears because of great forces in this kingdom under the name of guards," to eliminate drunkenness and debauchery at elections, to continue thorough investigation of the Popish Plot and punishment of those involved, and to bring about detection and punishment of pensioners and evil counsellors. Not content with these measures, there were also a good number of more fundamental constitutional demands such as the guarantee of frequent or annual parliaments and full rights of petitioning, the enactment of legislation to control ministers in the future, the publication of parliamentary votes, and the refusal to grant any money supply until the country was effectively secured against arbitrary power.[102] Such were the ends for which the Nonconformists had been working, and it is primarily for this reason that their electioneering and lobbying should be regarded as an indication of their basic parliamentarianism.

CHAPTER VII

*Political Prominence and Parliamentarianism During
the Exclusion Parliaments, 1679–1681*

The meeting of the first Exclusion Parliament was an event of
great moment to Nonconformists, and none of them marked the
occasion more characteristically than Thomas Jolly. On March 6,
1679, he retired for prayer and meditation "on account of the new
Parliament to convene that day, not only on my own more private
account but the public also, and posterity." [1] It was a time of
thanksgiving as well as of solemnity, for there was a strong feeling that the opportunity long sought was now at hand. Roger
Morrice was particularly sensitive to the changed atmosphere,
and in his attendance at the "Parliament house" and in his full
journal entries concerning the transactions of the Lords and Commons there is evidence of his deep concern and of his hope that
there would be "a changing of the state of the late politics that
were of such an ill aspect and tendency." [2] Optimistic though each
wished to be, nearly twenty years of unrealized hopes had
schooled them to be cautious and realistic in their appraisals, and
it was in this vein that Jolly wrote to Increase Mather in Massachusetts. "Some more hopeful members are chosen into our new
Parliament," he informed the New Englander, "and (it seems)
as there might be some lifting up of the yoke. The danger is lest
the Parliament be too good to sit long." [3] The prospects could not
have been anticipated more accurately.

The temper of the new Parliament quickly became evident,
particularly in the House of Commons where the normally routine
procedure of choosing a Speaker erupted into a sharp but short
battle between the King and the House over the right of nomina-
tion. During the ensuing ten days of furious struggle, most Presbyterian members of the House were staunch defenders of the

Commons' claim of the right to select a candidate not previously approved by the Crown. Richard Hampden was particularly vigorous in advocating addresses to the King and in maintaining their right to elect a Speaker of their choice, while Sir John Hewley affirmed that "the Speaker is our servant," and then asked rhetorically, "is he to obey his master, or no?" [4] Although conciliatory views prevailed in the end, and a completely new candidate, Sir William Gregory, was agreed upon in a compromise, this solution left the constitutional issue unresolved. However, the Commons' right was not challenged thereafter. [5]

There were critical political matters which the opposition leadership was eager to consider, most particularly the complex of issues revolving around Danby, the Catholic peers in the Tower, and the Plot. Therefore Holles and his group were immediately faced by the question of what they would or could do about carrying out those terms of their agreement with the King and Danby to which they believed they were still bound. Although elated that there was a new parliament and that progress in disbanding the army continued, there was still an undercurrent of disappointment that Danby had not been able to persuade the King to adhere to the terms they originally had sought. [6] But far more important, Danby was still in office, and thus there had been no fulfillment of the condition upon which Holles had agreed to "find a way of not pushing any further the accusation brought against him." Not until March 13, a week after Parliament convened and the day it was prorogued over the speakership crisis, did the King finally request Danby's resignation. It is therefore understandable that when Danby was estimating the number of those who would support and oppose him about the time Parliament met, he had reason to list Holles and all of the other lords of the Presbyterian-Congregationalist group as "against me." [7] Moreover, it was at this juncture that the King made Danby objectionable grants which certainly had not been a part of the agreement with Holles, beginning with the pension of £5000 and the new title. "I suppose all [news]letters tell you that the Lord Treasurer has demitted," Morrice recorded March 16, "but it is not yet so, in fact directions are given to create him Marquis of Carmarthen." [8] Nor was it reassuring to learn on this same day, when the warrant for the pension was formally presented to the Council, that the King was granting Danby permission to delay his resignation another ten days so that he could "get the accounts of his administration in order. . . ." There had been exactly two months for such ordering of affairs since Holles told Barrillon of his agreement with the King, and thus the reaction of those in the Presbyterian leader's group could only be that "the Lord Treasurer does still hold his staff." [9]

On March 19 when the House of Lords debated the question whether or not the Cavalier Parliament's impeachment proceedings against the five Catholic lords in the Tower were legally valid in the new Parliament, Holles supported the affirmative, which was the position adopted by the Lords without division; and so "they have done their parts abundantly," was the reaction of his former chaplain.[10] Since Danby's impeachment was legally in the same category as those of the five lords, Holles' position and Morrice's comment could be regarded as indicating they did not consider there was yet any obligation to "find the way of not pushing any further the accusation" against Danby, or that Holles was not willing to act on the assumption that the resignation would in fact become effective a week hence. But it is more probable that he was primarily concerned with the question of the moment, which was to see that the Catholic lords were prosecuted; and this is certainly what Morrice was intent upon. Nevertheless, as a result of the House vote Danby was ordered to put in his answers to the impeachment in a week. With the explosive potential of actual impeachment proceedings once again facing him, Charles called the two Houses together on March 22 and made the announcement which ended any remaining possibility that Holles and his group would or could attempt "to find the way of not pushing the accusation" against Danby, for the King informed the Lords and Commons that the Lord Treasurer had been granted a royal pardon because he had only carried out royal commands. The opposition furor that had been raised over the mundane issue of the pension and title now became crusading fervor to defend constitutional principles essential to responsible government.[11] Not only was there convincing evidence to back the previous fears and charges of arbitrary government, but in addition the day before the Commons had heard the testimony of the adventurer William Bedloe who swore under oath that Danby "did offer him great rewards not without some menaces to fly away and not to prosecute." [12]

Immediately after hearing of the pardon, the Lords appointed a committee which was charged with preparing a Disabling Bill that would have prevented Danby from holding office, entering the King's presence, receiving grants from the Crown, or sitting in Parliament, and Holles was made one of the thirteen members.[13] Danby's resignation was still three days away, but even when it came Holles had not bargained for a resignation accompanied by a pardon from the King with all the implications of this exercise of prerogative. On the other hand, it appears he could not forget that two months earlier Danby had called upon him and had used his considerable influence with Charles to bring the dissolution which the Presbyterians wanted above all else, and even at this juncture it is probable that he wanted to be as lenient with Danby as possible, a desire which he is known to have expressed somewhat later. Certainly the pardon, the issues involved, and the temper of Parliament confronted Holles with a hopeless and difficult situation, and the thought of serving on a committee charged with striking the kind of blows he had originally wanted to parry must have been more than he could contemplate. The multiple shocks of that Saturday's events were too much for him, and he did not attend the House the first four days of the following week, during which time the Disabling Bill passed all readings.[14]

Danby surely thought that Holles was failing to abide by the terms of the agreement with the King when he absented himself while the Lords took this action against him.[15] But Holles would just as surely have maintained that the King had undermined the whole basis of the agreement by failing to adhere to the terms his group thought Charles had originally accepted, and far more by granting the pension and the pardon. In addition, though Danby's resignation then seemed assured, there had been the long delay before it finally took place on the second day of Holles' four-day absence. The effect of these developments upon the Presbyterian-Congregationalist group in Parliament and their friends was predictable. One of the reasons there had been as much initial disappointment within the Holles group over the King's failure to stick to the original terms had been the conviction that he had thereby "disobliged the Parliament and those few friends they had" and destroyed "the great aid . . . members might have received in carrying out the King's desires . . ." When it became apparent that the new Parliament was constituted of such "worthy members" there was additional reason to believe that much would have been accomplished if the original declaration had been issued and there had been a commission to investigate the Plot during the period between the two parliaments.[16] However, the pension, the pardon, and the late resignation caused an even deeper erosion of the support Holles might have had; and another factor that must be considered is that even normally he did not have the degree of parliamentary influence which usually has been attributed to him, mainly on the basis of Barrillon's overestimates.[17]

With two or three notable exceptions, the Presbyterian and Congregationalist members of the two Houses resembled Holles in at least one of their major responses to the various issues raised by Danby's case. Although members of the Commons did not necessarily absent themselves, they did withdraw to the background, and almost all of them remained silent during the first few weeks after the Speaker had been selected.[18] Whether the Lords of this group were more forward is not known, with one exception, but in any event Danby continued to consider Anglesey, Wharton, Paget, Bedford, and Delamer against him or at best unreliable, estimates which showed them to be slightly more opposed to him than he considered Holles to be on successive occasions. The only one of the group known to have taken a position favorable to Danby was Anglesey, who protested against the Lord's Disabling Bill; yet the grounds of his action are in part to be attributed to his concern for the rights of peers and in part perhaps to the fact that as Lord Privy Seal he could see himself in a situation resembling Danby's.[19]

The positions of the Presbyterian and Congregationalist peers are much clearer than those of the members of this group in the House of Commons, for the M.P.s' silence had some contradictory implications as well as inherent indecisiveness. Failure to object to the Commons Bill of Attainder would certainly seem to have demonstrated strong opposition to Danby and also to the terms of the agreement between Holles and the King. At the same time, because of the furor over the pension and the pardon there was an overwhelming demand for the measure which made opposition to it hopeless. Moreover, the Presbyterian and Congregationalist members, with the possible exception of Hampden, apparently did not speak in defense of attainder when this was the popular position to take, and thus they were presumably not on the attack. Alone, this negative indication would mean little, but there was a more positive one. The initial and generally prevalent silence concerning the royal pardon would seem to indicate a more favorable attitude toward Danby, particularly since this was the kind of issue upon which Presbyterian and Congregationalist members would normally have spoken out in vigorous protest; and judging by the constitutional objections these members raised a month later when Danby offered the King's pardon as a bar to impeachment, there were surely silent members who concurred with Sir John Maynard on March 22. Even though he was one of the King's Serjeants-at-law, he was highly concerned about the legality of the King's move and indicated his parliamentarian background and convictions in contending that it was "in the power of Parliament to take off that pardon. . . ." [20] But to oppose the royal pardon on such grounds did not mean that Maynard or those who agreed with him were unfavorable to Danby himself.

Such indecision and silence as still existed among the Presbyterians and Congregationalists in Parliament regarding the issues raised by Danby's case rapidly began to disappear in the latter part of April and early May, after Danby pleaded his royal pardon as a bar to impeachment on April 24.[21] The fundamental constitutional issue and the inherent threat to responsible government were thoroughly recognized by the Presbyterians along with others, and they made important contributions during the ensuing struggle against this threat. Danby's plea had only focused attention on the basic question concerning the legality of the pardon which had already been debated, and upon which Maynard and Sir William Ellis had stated their views. Once again these two Presbyterians were prominent, Ellis being the leading speaker on the issue.[22]

By the time of the major debates on the issue, which occurred on May 5 and 7, the impeachment proceedings against the five Catholic lords who were imprisoned in the Tower had also become involved, and it appears that this issue combined with a concern about Danby's plea explains why the Presbyterians were more aroused. Maynard, who was particularly sensitive to questions relating to Catholicism or to the Crown, took a much stronger position regarding Danby than he had before. By his plea, Maynard contended, Danby had charged his crime on the King, and for this, "he deserves as much punishment as he can do." Continuing, he indicated the religious ramifications and pointed out the fundamental constitutional issue.

. . . Not only the safety of the King, but the Commons' lives, and religion, and all, may be in danger by it! The five lords in the Tower may have such pardons, by the same reason, and what then becomes of all your liberties . . . Great persons, too great for the law, and who have done ills by virtue of an exorbitant power . . . by such pardon, may defeat all calling them to account. There is no *obstante* to the impeachment of the House of Commons in this pardon. . . . If this be a good pardon, Parliaments are to little purpose.[23]

Hampden, who spoke shortly afterwards, agreed about the consequences of such a pardon. He reminded the House that when Charles I gave his answer to the part of the Nineteen Propositions regarding his power of pardon, he stated " 'that a prince may not make use of his high and perpetual power to the hurt of those for whose good he has it, and make use of the name of public necessity, for the gain of his private favorites . . . to the detriment of his people.' " [24] Swynfen, Sir John Hewley, and Paul Foley were also highly concerned and urged quick and decisive action, Swynfen being the most active member of the House in the debate of May 7. Such participation in the debates was recognized in committee appointments, Hampden, Maynard, Foley, and Swynfen being selected to serve either on the one charged with preparing reasons why the House was of the opinion that the pardon was illegal, or on a second one to confer with the Lords concerning the trials of Danby and the five lords.[25]

One problem concerning these trials was crucial. The superficial question was whether or not the bishops had a right to participate in capital cases heard before the House of Lords in its judicial capacity, but it became a much more serious issue because of the fundamental question whether Danby's plea of the royal pardon would be allowed by the Lords as a bar to impeachment.

The real battle began when the Upper House passed a resolution "that the Lords Spiritual have a right to stay in Court in capital cases, till such time as judgment of death comes to be pronounced," a provision which would have allowed them to vote on the plea of pardon, though not "to proceed to the vote of guilty or not guilty." [26] The Lower House immediately replied with a resolution of its own, making clear the position that the Lords Spiritual ought not to have any vote in any proceeding concerning the impeachment trials of the lords in the Tower, and that Danby's trial should precede those of the five lords. When the House of Lords ignored these desires insofar as Danby was concerned, there were vehement reactions in the Commons because, as Hampden pointed out, the matter of the bishops being present "is more in relation to Lord Danby's pardon than anything else." Foley urged the Commons to be adamant, while Hampden echoed some of his earlier speeches and took up the theme of the opening speech of this debate, in which William Sacheverell charged that if the pardon be confirmed they would "make the King absolute," and have an "arbitrary government without law." [27]

The degree of Presbyterian and Congregationalist concern over this issue which was constitutionally critical and religiously inflammatory cannot be gauged by the debates alone. The members of this group in the Lower House also became very much involved in the committee work as the dispute between the two Houses came to a head. Meanwhile in the House of Lords Wharton, Paget, Bedford, and Delamer opposed allowing the bishops any vote on Danby,[28] while Holles was sufficiently aroused about the issue to return to the House from May 10 to 14 and also to examine the precedents and present his findings in a lengthy anonymous pamphlet published after Parliament had been prorogued. As a result of his study and of considering "all that has been said on the other side," he found no reason to change his opinion that they ought not to have the right to be judges in such cases.[29]

Even though the positions taken by leaders of the Presbyterian-Congregationalist group on Danby's use of the pardon and the question of the bishops' rights in capital cases might seem to indicate they had become vindictive toward Danby, particularly in Maynard's case, this was not necessarily true, for they were motivated primarily by the constitutional and religious issues. Thus, discussing the pardon, Hampden was careful to indicate that his concern was with the constitutional implications rather than with Danby himself, and this suggests that he might even have favored giving Danby some clemency or consideration.[30] However, there was no doubt by then about the views of Holles, who according to his former chaplain, said in the House of Lords "that if the Lord Treasurer (then under . . . impeachment of high treason) were not only guilty of all those crimes . . . he was accused of, but of greater, yet these common blessings that he had had the happiness and honor to be the chief agent in procuring from his Majesty did at least merit a pardon from the Kingdom," which certainly would have been more acceptable than the royal pardon. As a result of the dissolution of the Cavalier Parliament Danby had not only gained the good opinion of Holles, but also of his friends. "They openly showed their gratitude," Barrillon later reported, and at that time they would have been happy if he received a simple banishment.[31]

Although the cases of Danby and the five Lords were of more immediate importance to the Parliament and the nation, the transcendent problem during the remainder of the reign was whether or not James, Duke of York should be allowed to inherit the Crown of England upon his brother's death. The wave of anti-Catholicism which had followed Oates' disclosures of the previous autumn and which aroused a deep fear of England's fate under a Catholic monarch was even more evident in the spring debates of the first Exclusion Parliament.[32] In an extraordinary Sunday session on April 27, a debate was held, in spite of the efforts of the Court leaders to prevent it, upon the problem of "how to preserve the King's person from the attempts and conspiracies of the Papists," and it led up to a discussion of the real issue when Colonel Birch noted that the declaration of the succession by Parliament was no new thing. As a "half-way" measure he therefore proposed a bill be brought in providing that "at the fall of the King by any violent stroke (which God forbid) no person come to the Crown of England till [the King's death] . . . be examined." Secretary Coventry replied that they were sworn to the King's successor and "for the Parliament to nominate the King a successor, I say . . . is against law and the government."[33] This moved Boscawen to come "home to the point," as Lord Russell declared when the Cornish veteran sat down. "As to what is said by Secretary Coventry, of 'being sworn to the King's lawful successors,'" Boscawen replied, "what is so by Act of Parliament is lawful, and it is *praemunire* to say to the contrary . . . ," and he pointedly referred to the statute which acknowledged Elizabeth I to be Queen.[34] The House was not yet quite ready to consider a motion for a bill to exclude James, but in this debate the attack was shifted from a motion directed against Catholics in general to one pointed at James in particular. Playing major roles in this shift, in addition to Boscawen, were Swynfen who twice gave strong support, and Hampden who stated the motion in its final form, namely "that the Duke of York being a Papist, and the hopes of his coming such to the Crown, have given the greatest countenance and encouragement to the present conspiracies and designs of the Papists against the King, and the Protestant Religion." [35]

In another Sunday session two weeks later, it was once again Richard Hampden who was in the vanguard, for he was the first to back the momentous motion made by Sir Thomas Player that James "be excluded from the Crown of England." Although there were twenty speakers who rose to address the House, only five of them gave unequivocal support to it—Birch, Foley, Booth, and Boscawen in addition to Hampden. The Puritan and Presbyterian parliamentarian tradition in the Commons could hardly be better represented than by these five.[36] However, there was not complete unanimity among the Presbyterian leaders in the House regarding the wisdom and efficacy of exclusion as a means to eliminate the dangers of having a Catholic king. The venerable John Swynfen gave a long and partially contradictory speech in which his final contention was that laws could not do any good against a Popish successor since he would not abide by them and had foreign power available from France and Rome to assist him by invasion if necessary.[37] Such considerations did not concern Swynfen's younger and bolder friend Hampden, who presented revealing views of monarchy. He compared the Duke of York as presumptive heir of the Crown to an ordinary man who is about to inherit an estate, and pointed out that men who were likely to ruin their inheritances were disinherited daily. Disagreeing with those who believe "it is no matter how low the people are, if [the Prince's] . . . greatness be kept up," Hampden declared: "I think that a prince is made for the good of the people, and where there is a Popish prince that may succeed, I think we ought to secure ourselves against that succession." [38]

The comparison between the heir to the Crown and a man who is to inherit an estate conveyed more extreme implications than some other Presbyterian leaders would accept. The temper of

Boscawen's speech, for example, was more moderate and it would appear that his views were too. He maintained that the two Houses and the King had a right to determine the succession and wrongly believed that Charles would give his assent to such a bill, but at the same time he acknowledged the authority of the King and asserted his own essential belief in monarchy. "Would you have Parliaments make laws without a Prince?" he asked. "Or would you have the government in conservators' hands, such as we may confide in? That would look like a commonwealth, and I know no such great men that we can trust upon such an account; besides, they have no power, and will be insignificant." Even though Boscawen wanted to restrict the right of succession, his explicit defense of monarchy made his views seem more moderate in tone and opinion than Hampden's, and there is no question that his speech was the more persuasive both to the members of the House and to Englishmen in general who read it in its quickly published, but apparently different version.[39] As he concluded, the Cornish member called for the question, and after the supporters of exclusion were successful in carrying a division to bring in candles, their opponents gave way *nemine contradicente* to the motion for bringing in a bill "to disable the Duke of York to inherit the Imperial Crown of this Realm." The real test of support for this first Exclusion Bill came on May 21, when there took place the famous division on the question of committing it to a committee of the whole house which carried by 207 to 128.[40] A very large number of members were absent, presumably because of indecision, but this was not true of those in the Presbyterian-Congregationalist group. Of these forty-two members there were only three who may have absented themselves for this reason, while ill health accounted for a fourth. The remaining thirty-eight were present, and all of them voted in favor of the motion.[41] The Dissenters thus proved to be exceptionally united in their action and strongly in favor of excluding James from succession to the Crown.

While playing a very important supporting role in the efforts to assert that Parliament's right of impeachment could not be overridden by a royal pardon, and a leading role in the attempt to determine the succession to the throne, Presbyterian and Congregationalist members also worked for the passage of other measures which were indicative of their parliamentarian political views

and of their desire for reform. Although these politicians were by
no means guiltless of electioneering practices which were prevalent at the time, they had ethical reasons as well as compelling
practical ones which made them interested in election reform, and
there was certainly strong Nonconformist support for such measures. The membership of a committee to bring in legislation regulating election of members and the complexion of the committee
to which it was later committed indicate that Presbyterian and
Congregationalist members were leading proponents of this measure; for Hampden was chairman of both committees, and a considerable number of his Presbyterian colleagues served with him
on each.[42] This well-known measure lowered property qualifications and standardized those in the boroughs as well by providing
that all householders rated for poor relief who paid scot-and-lot
and had resided in the borough one year could vote. It also provided stringent penalties against bribery, including disability from
sitting in Parliament, a fine of £500, and disenfranchisement of
the borough in which the bribery occurred. It also would have
fined persons bribing a returning officer to make a false return
and voided the election in such case. Sheriffs, mayors, and bailiffs
were to be required to hold elections at the specified time and
place and not adjourn them. A final provision which was consistent
with a long-standing Nonconformist desire was the one stipulat-
ing that no future parliament was to continue for more than two
years.[43]

The Presbyterian members were also active in efforts to investigate the expenditure of secret service funds by Danby's agents,
Boscawen being a frequent speaker on this matter, while Love
and Swynfen gave their support.[44] They were likewise interested
in efforts to prevent such practices and the future presence of
"place men" in the Commons. In the Lower House Hampden was
charged with drawing up a bill providing "that when any member
of this House is preferred by the King to any office to place of
profit, a new writ shall immediately issue out for electing of a
member to serve in his stead," while in the Upper House Wharton, Paget, Delamer, and Bedford were members of the committee
to which a measure was referred that was designed to prevent the
Lord Treasurer or other officers from offering any gifts, grants,
leases of land, or pensions to any person.[45] This was the climax of

efforts begun in 1675 to prevent office-holders from sitting in the House; and since many opposition members would have been affected by these measures, they were not adopted.[46]

There were only two major issues upon which those desiring to limit the powers of the Crown could be said to have won clear-cut victories during this Parliament. By far the most important achievement was the passage of the Habeas Corpus Act. Presbyterian members in both houses were very prominent in the committee work and in the conferences resulting from the amendments to the Bill. Maynard headed the committee to which the Bill was committed upon its second reading, and its members included Hewley, Irby, Reynell, Trenchard, Thompson, Young, and Papillon, while Maynard and Hampden served on the committee appointed to consider the Lords' amendments.[47] In the Upper House Wharton played a prominent role. He served on the committee to consider the Commons' Bill, was the most frequently appointed manager of subsequent conferences with the House of Commons, and in company with Shaftesbury and Anglesey he drew up a brief to be presented at one of these conferences. In addition to Wharton's contributions in the conferences, those of Anglesey and Hampden were also important, for both of them served as managers and reported to their respective Houses afterwards.[48] Of all the Dissenters none could have desired the enactment of this Bill more than the Quakers, and the Meeting for Sufferings immediately sent one of their members to get a copy of the "Act for the Liberty of the Subject."[49]

In addition to this notable achievement to which the Presbyterian members made a substantial contribution, there was a final respect in which the King's powers were restricted by this Parliament. Negative though the restriction was in character, the failure to renew the Licensing Act of 1662 was of major significance, and there is evidence indicating that Nonconformist pressure and the efforts of Lord Wharton may have played a part.[50] During the next two years the effects of this failure were of much consequence, for as a result the first party press appeared. Even though Charles attempted to control the publishing activities of such news printers as Francis Smith and Benjamin Harris by falling back upon his prerogative, it proved to be impossible for the courts to enforce his proclamations ordering suppression of seditious pamphlets and of all newsbooks not properly licensed, because juries, sheriffs' offices, and the House of Commons were all dominated by those hostile to Charles.[51]

During this session the Presbyterians took a leading role in the opposition attack which had been extremely alarming to the Court. Not only did they constitute the most solid block of challengers of James' right to the Crown, but they also threatened Charles' possession of it by their drive to obtain an impeachment trial which would probably have brought disclosures of the real "Popish" plot—the conniving of Louis XIV and Charles—during the frenzy of the fabricated one. As a result prorogation came late in May and dissolution in the middle of July.[52]

To Nonconformists, on the other hand, the record of this Parliament had been very heartening and the promise even brighter. They therefore would have completely agreed with the stand taken by the Earl of Anglesey on the question of dissolution, for he opposed it vigorously not only in the Privy Council meetings between July 3 and July 10, but also in a most extraordinary "large discourse" with the King that took place at a quarter before seven on the morning of July 6 after he had been summoned to Windsor "very early." Likewise Anglesey's comment after the Council meeting on July 10, when the King announced that he was going to dissolve Parliament, reflected the feeling not only of the Presbyterians and Congregationalists in Parliament but of all Dissenters, for the King's decision left him with a "sad heart."[53]

Dissenters who were politically alert were quick to react. Roger Morrice learned of the decision the day the King announced it to the Council, and he hurriedly wrote a brief note to John Swynfen that conveyed the vital importance that the Dissenters accorded to this news and also to the coming elections. Reflecting the same feeling was William Penn's pamphlet *England's Great Interest in the Choice of this New Parliament,* which describes the situation as being unprecedented and one in which all was at stake.[54] If this was not at once apparent, the sudden serious illness of the King in August and the summoning of James back from his forced exile on the Continent added a sense of crisis to the elections, which were held between August 6 and October 14.[55] This feeling was particularly evident in London, from which Lord Wharton's Nonconformist chaplain William Taylor wrote him reports of the agitation which resulted because of a feeling that the Duke had come "with a purpose of stay[ing] as they had reason to imagine. . . ." [56]

Nonconformists throughout the country both contributed to and shared in the substantial victory which Shaftesbury and his political associates won in the elections. Just as in the past, the measure of the Dissenters' political influence was more to be found in the support they gave on the hustings to moderate Anglican candidates than in the success they had in electing men of their own religious views. Although the number of known Presbyterian and Congregationalist members increased from forty-two to fifty-two, Dissenters had more reason to be elated because a large number of their moderate Anglican friends had been elected. As a result Shaftesbury had a commanding majority. [57] For this reason they were totally unprepared for the long series of seven prorogations which Charles astutely used during the next year to gain time, hoping that the high tide of anti-Catholicism and Whig success might begin to recede. By December the Whig leaders in the House of Lords and the Presbyterian Peers were sufficiently aroused to petition the King for the meeting of Parliament. By all reports, Lord Wharton was "earliest in this advice." But according to Sir Robert Southwell's full account of the affair, the Nonconformist leader "withdrew himself . . . as advised thereunto by my Lord Anglesey . . . ," and he did not even sign the petition. [58] The full import of his change of mind becomes apparent only in the light of the actions of other prominent leaders at this juncture. The Earl of Bedford and Lord Holles did go so far as to sign the petition, but when the time came to present it to the King on Sunday, December 7 as he came from Chapel, neither of these Presbyterian peers were among the nine signers who were presented by Prince Rupert. Published Whig accounts stated that the legal prohibition against having more than ten persons on hand at the presentation of a petition was "supposed to be the reason why no greater number of the Lords were personally present." [59] But there were also other reasons and considerations in the cases of Bedford and Holles. Bedford "came purposely to bear them company [but] fell that morning ill," while Holles was one of the "moderate men" on the issue of succession to the throne who reportedly had been working on an expedient which they claimed the King would accept. [60] As for Bedford, his illness would seem sufficiently timely to suggest that he may have had some desire to take a more temperate position, as Wharton had, while Holles seems to have been on the defensive for having signed the petition and explained to Barrillon that he had done so "in order not to lose his credit with the people and in order to be in a better position, when the Parliament would assemble, to back the King of England in what was just and to prevent the excluding of the Duke of York and also prevent any other wild attempts." [61] The picture becomes clearer. Anglesey, Holles, and Bedford were previously more moderate than Wharton, but in this case Holles and Bedford became more involved and then may have wished to draw back, while Wharton joined Anglesey in the most temperate position. But Wharton was not the only Nonconformist leader who clearly pulled back at this juncture. Three days before, Southwell informed Ormonde that William Penn told him "he saw plainly so much extremity intended on this side as well as on that of . . . [the Duke of York] that he resolved to withdraw himself from all manner of meddling, since things to him appeared violent and irreconcilable." [62]

It is possible that Shaftesbury and at least some of the other lords who petitioned were considering plans that went much further than the petition itself. If they were, undoubtedly such plans revolved about the Duke of Monmouth, who had returned to England late in November without permission from the King and probably as the result of Shaftesbury's efforts. Anglesey should have been aware of any such plans, for on November 30 he wrote that he had a "long private discourse with the King in favor of the Duke of Monmouth wherein he was very open to me, [and] after dinner having the King's leave I went to the D. of Monmouth . . . ," a call which Monmouth returned the following evening after Richard Hampden and his family had spent the day with Anglesey at his invitation. [63] Any plans Shaftesbury had would undoubtedly have been more extreme than any Anglesey had in mind, and this could have been the reason for his advice to Wharton within the next few days. When all of these developments are considered together they seem to indicate that the Presbyterian peers and Penn were not willing to support the more extreme steps which Shaftesbury and some of his other followers may have been considering, and this is a development of major import.

Three days after the petition was presented, the King announced his second prorogation, and his decision caused great dismay throughout Nonconformist circles. Anglesey was at the Council meeting all day on December 10, and afterwards he recorded in his diary that "the King against the full advice of his Council declared that fatal and dismal resolution of prorogueing this Parliament until November. The Lord save England," he concluded. Oliver Heywood and two of his friends were also perturbed, for he wrote that at "our solemn monthly fast . . . , God graciously helped [us] . . . in the work, having had the day before the intelligence of the Parliament's prorogation. . . ." [64] Perplexed and distressed though these ministers were, their reactions were very moderate. However, they could not remain passive in such a situation, and as the months passed some of them became involved in the famous petition campaign promoted by the Whig leaders in an effort to force the King's hand by building up an irresistible popular demand for the meeting of Parliament.

During the earliest phases of this campaign, which began in December and which reached its first climax in January, such Dissenters as Francis Smith "went up and down getting hands to petitions for [the] sitting of the Parliament," and then he and Benjamin Harris would publish them. [65] The more conservative ministers and laymen were not as precipitous. However, Roger Morrice approved of the idea from the beginning, and in reporting the royal proclamation of December 11, 1679, he was careful to emphasize that it was "against seditious and factious petitions only and [that there was] not a word in it against peaceable and regular petitions which upon just and necessary occasions are only to be encouraged. . . ." [66] Such activity might seem entirely "peaceable and regular" to him and to such Presbyterian laymen as Sir Henry Ashurst, who was one of those that presented the London petition on January 13, 1680, and to Sir John Hewley, who presented that of York City. But the King regarded the petition campaign as an attempt to invade his prerogative. [67]

During the spring of 1680 Nonconformist laymen appear to have continued their support of the petition campaign, Ashurst and Papillon being very active in the London Common Council. Also their political leaders seem to have been in consultation with Whig leaders, for it was reported that there was a great meeting of "malcontent lords" at Lord Wharton's at which it was decided to hold weekly meetings in various places.[68] However, in June it was evident that the Presbyterian peers remained unwilling to participate in the more extreme steps which Shaftesbury, Lord Russell and others were ready to take. This time, moreover, Presbyterian members of the Lower House indicated disagreement with the Whig leadership, for only one of them joined Shaftesbury and the fourteen peers and commoners who went to Westminster Hall on June 26, to present an indictment of the Duke of York as a Popish Recusant to the Grand Jury then sitting in the Court of the Kings Bench.[69]

By the end of June there was a shift in royal policy, insofar as the Dissenters were concerned, and Charles turned to a group of leading Nonconformist ministers in an attempt to find help in the accomplishment of his purpose. According to Morrice, Secretary Jenkins wrote letters to Baxter, Owen, Thomas Jacombe, John Howe, John Griffeth, and Daniel Bull on July 15 and asked them to come speak with him that afternoon "about some matter of great consideration." Although it was reported they were summoned because they had been "busy promoting petitions," actually the King wanted their support in his attempt to placate Nonconformists and quiet the country "by declaring himself openly against the Catholics." [70] Instructions had already been delivered to the judges by the Lord Chancellor on July 1, before they left on the coming circuit, ordering them not to apply to the Protestant Dissenters the laws enacted against the Popish Recusants, but to enforce them strictly upon Catholics. In addition they were also informed that "for the satisfying [of] men's minds, and to prevent the seditious way of tumultuary petitioning, they should acquaint the justices of peace and gentlemen of the grand juries in their counties that it was his Majesty's firm resolution the Parliament should undoubtedly sit in November at [the] farthest." Finally, Morrice reported that they were ordered not "to provoke the extension of the law against those that were peaceable," and that they were told "some that did not come to hear Common Prayer had done and would do the King good service." Unquestionably this news was as welcome and as "signal and surprising" to all Dissenters as it was to Morrice.[71]

One of the leading proponents of this policy within the King's official family must have been the Earl of Anglesey, who as Lord Privy Seal subsequently used his influence to relieve Dissenters from prosecution, and who even went to the extreme of writing a letter admonishing the Mayor of Gloucester for enforcing the laws against Dissenters because Parliament might soon offer the King bills to repeal several laws against them. A few weeks before Parliament met in mid-October, Secretary Jenkins also wrote a revealing letter in which he sadly observed to the Bishop of Bath that although he did not dare determine whether the Catholic threat had been a good reason for relaxing the enforcement of the laws, "certainly the true season to suppress Sectaries has been long since lost," and he added that "they have put us now on the defensive." [72]

Such was the situation in the late summer and early autumn of 1680. Undoubtedly it helped to create the feeling of relaxation in Philip Henry's visit of a week with Lord and Lady Paget, where the Philip Foleys and John Swynfen also were house guests, and where he read a lot, including Rushworth's famous collections of Civil War material. Likewise it explains some of the hope which moved Thomas Jolly to interrupt an extended devotional period in order to call upon "a worthy member of Parliament" because, as he wrote, "I had something upon my heart that day to say . . . , which counsel he then approved of. . . ." [73]

When Parliament finally sat on October 26, 1680, it quickly became apparent that the major issues which would stir the Presbyterians to debate in this Parliament were to be those arising from the fear of arbitrary government, which in their minds had become a much more real and imminent threat as a cumulative result of the events of the preceding two years and the delay in the meeting of Parliament. The most current and pressing of these issues was the right of petition, which they believed had been threatened by the King's proclamation of the preceding December. Thus when Sir Gilbert Gerrard brought the question to the floor in one of the first debates, Hampden was not content merely to have a House resolution assert the right to petition the King for the calling and sitting of Parliament. He proposed to add that those who had petitioned should be thanked by the House, and at the same time a good number of Presbyterian and Congregationalist members were appointed to serve on the committee to inquire of all persons as had offended against the right of the subject to petition the King. [74]

Adamant though the Presbyterian members were upon the

right of petitioning, they were careful while debating this question to emphasize their conviction that there should be no division between the King and the people, and that all Protestants should be united in the face of the Catholic menace. After declaring in one of his speeches that the security of the nation depended upon the king's prerogative as well as the subject's liberty, Boscawen said he thought they ought to inform the King in an address that they "would go as far to support the Government as ever any House of Commons did," and among those backing him were Love and Hampden.[75] Hopes for such unity within England could not possibly have materialized at this time, for now that Charles' illnesses had made the prospect of a Catholic monarch seem far more imminent than in the spring of 1679, English Protestants were becoming even more bitterly divided than before upon the constitutional issue of the succession. Moreover, Boscawen and Hampden had already helped to make this one of the great divisive issues of a century filled with such, and again in this Parliament they were to be strong advocates of exclusion.

Consistent with their position on the succession of James, there was in the late summer an obvious strengthening of the relationship between the Dissenters' political leaders and Monmouth, particularly during the Duke's trip into Western England where he was entertained by such members of the Presbyterian-Congregationalist group in the House of Commons as William Strode, Edmund Prideaux, Sir Walter Young, and Michael Harvey. Also it is reflected in the glowing accounts given by Morrice about the gentry who waited upon Monmouth at Bath, where the Nonconformist chronicler was visiting, and in his description of the vast numbers who appeared in the Duke's support in Somerset, Essex, and back in London early in September.[76]

Monmouth was not the only possible ally for those opposed to James, and this was a matter to which Barrillon was extremely sensitive. Believing that the "party of the Presbyterians is still very strong," and that "nothing . . . can be more useful than to remain on good terms with it in order to make use of it as the opportunity arises," he remained particularly concerned about the Presbyterians' political alliances.[77] During the summer and fall of 1680, Louis XIV and his Ambassador were not at all certain which English political faction they should back in order best to serve French interests. Beginning in early July, the French had supported the Duke of Monmouth and those backing him, but by late September the Ambassador had been ordered to discontinue close connections with Charles' son. There was then a shift of French support to the Duke of York's supporters, which Barrillon had recommended earlier in the month because it was the weakest; but as a camouflage to this policy, he suggested in mid-November that Monmouth be given the impression that he had the French backing.[78]

Primarily concerned as always with his Continental plans, Louis wished to prevent the possible development of a confederation of England, Spain, the Empire, and the United Provinces. However, it was the Prince of Orange himself who loomed as the most dangerous threat to French policy as both exclusion and civil strife became increasingly possible during the fall and winter of 1680–1681, for not only was he "the principal author of all that has been proposed on the subject of alliances," but also he rather than Monmouth might well gain the crown of England. Barrillon therefore did all he possibly could to prevent William from gaining supporters, and he was much concerned about the relations between the Presbyterians and the Dutch ruler. "The only thing to be feared," he wrote Louis concerning them as political allies, "is that they favor the interests of the Prince of Orange and that they allow themselves to be deceived by promises made to them to be well treated when the government shall be in the hands of a Prince whose religion is more in conformity with theirs than with the Anglican Church." Although somewhat reassured because he believed the "more reasonable among them fear greatly . . . the domination of the Prince . . . , and well know that he would govern with more force" than Charles, Barrillon apparently did not want to take any chances.[79]

Most immediately important, Louis and his ambassador wanted to be certain Charles did not receive any funds from Parliament with which to support anti-French alliances. As a result, sometime during the autumn, or possibly the late summer, a select group of influential Presbyterian leaders were once again approached by the Ambassador or those working with him, including Sir John Baber, and by the end of the year, if not before, Richard Hampden, Hugh Boscawen, Paul Foley, and Sir Edward Harley were among those who accepted French funds.[80] Having even less reason to trust Charles with an army than previously, and undoubtedly fearing as a result of his two illnesses within the previous year that the army might soon be at the command of his Catholic heir, Presbyterian leaders were among those ready to accept money from Catholic France once again. Expediency was obviously their guide, and they accepted support where they found it, undoubtedly justifying their action on the grounds of their belief that the fate of England was in the balance.

Just as in the exclusion debates of 1679, this belief was once again most evident in the debates on the Exclusion Bill of 1680. At the same time, Presbyterian leaders in Parliament were still concerned that the Monarchy be preserved. To them it seemed the government could not survive if there were to be a Catholic king, and therefore they felt that a parliamentary change of the succession was absolutely essential. This line of argument was somewhat more evident in the debates of November, 1680, particularly in Boscawen's only major speech on the exclusion issue, in which he stated that he would not open his mouth against the Duke's succession if there were the least possibility of security otherwise. But this he did not see, for he was "afraid there can be no expedients offered in this case, that can be sufficient; unless such as may shake the throne as to all future kings." Arguing that self-preservation was no breach of Christianity and that it was natural for a government to preserve itself, he contended that an Exclusion Bill was essential since the preservation of England's government was at stake.

The obvious rebuttal to this argument was made by Secretary Jenkins two days later in his speech opposing the second reading of the Bill when he charged that it would "change the very essence and being of the Monarchy," and "reduce it to an elective monarchy." [81] By overstatement and emphasis upon what the ultimate implications of the Exclusion Bill might be, Jenkins had made his argument potent and dangerous to discuss; for there were few, if any, who would have supported an elective monarchy. But Hampden met the constitutional issue head on and declared that he could not "see the danger of reducing the government to be elective by it," for *though the succession of the crown has been formerly often changed by acts of Parliament; yet hitherto it has not made the crown elective. . . ."* He then returned to the argument Boscawen had presented, and contended that if the successor in an hereditary monarchy would destroy the Kingdom he did not know why he should not be excluded from the succession. "The Pope is your king if you have a Popish successor," he affirmed, and after playing effectively upon the fears of Catholicism he moved for the second reading, which carried.[82]

Although Grey records only three speeches by Presbyterian members during these two debates, both Boscawen and Hampden spoke as leading proponents at the end of each debate, and the other Presbyterian-Congregationalist members probably gave nearly unanimous support to this second Exclusion Bill as it passed rapidly through the three readings.[83] However, in the House of Lords members of the Presbyterian-Congregationalist group did not play a leading role in the dramatic events of November 15 that decided the fate of this Bill. In the momentous debate that day before the King and members of the House of Commons, who remained after delivering the Bill, the only Presbyterian peer speaking was Lord Paget. However, Wharton, Delamer, Paget, Bedford, and Anglesey all voted against the rejection of the Bill, and after the motion to reject it was carried by a vote of 63–30, Anglesey, Paget, Delamer, and Bedford signed the formal protest.[84]

When the Exclusion Bill had first been considered in this Parliament, Dissenters were elated, and their hopes had been further raised by the Bill's easy passage in the Commons.[85] The decisive defeat in the Lords was thus a blow to them. Nonconformist divines were discouraged and apprehensive. Presbyterian members of the Commons were stunned yet stubborn. The Presbyterian lords were undoubtedly equally dismayed, but some seem to have felt that alternative measures were worth trying, Anglesey and Bedford being members of the small committee of six appointed on November 16 to prepare the Bill for a Protestant Association which provided that when the King died all bishops, judges, members of Parliament and other officials were to take up arms until the meeting of Parliament.[86] The limitation of the powers of a Catholic successor appears to have been supported by Lord Wharton, and probably by the other Presbyterian lords as well. Among his parliamentary papers were drafts of the various proposals adopted by the House which stated that if James became King he would not be able to make ecclesiastical or military appointments or raise any forces without consent of

Parliament, and also that he would not have a veto power.[87] Presbyterian members of the Commons also favored an Association Bill; however, this measure was not designed to limit the powers of a Catholic monarch, but rather to make certain that he would be excluded from the throne. The attainment of this goal by an association to be formed at the death of Charles was too uncertain, and to the end they remained unshaken in their conviction that "nothing can be a compensation for our loss of the Bill against the Duke's succession." [88]

In the meantime there were religious and political grievances which also claimed the attention of the Presbyterian-Congregationalist group and those with whom they worked in Parliament. They came nearest to success in their efforts to repeal the old Elizabethan Act against Sectaries (usually referred to as "the Act of 35 Eliz."), and it should have been presented to the King for his assent.[89] However, the King was in no mood to relieve Dissenters of the threat which the severe penalties in the Act provided; for the Presbyterian members, whom he thought of as republicans, had exasperated him too much in the recent past, and in addition there was strong pressure from the bishops opposing repeal. Therefore he ordered the clerk of the Parliament not to present this Bill for signature, and by this means was able to dispose of the Bill without incurring the reaction that would have resulted from a legitimate veto.[90]

Partially as an outgrowth of Committee hearings on repeal of the Act of 35 Eliz. and also because of the rampant anti-Catholicism then prevailing, considerable progress was made with measures to distinguish Dissenters from Catholics and to prevent the misapplication of the old laws against Recusancy. William Love was most prominent in seeking a bill of relief in the Commons, and he also had sent Lord Wharton the draft of a similar measure. It was in the Lords rather than in the Commons that efforts were successful. Anglesey and Wharton played important roles in preliminary hearings as well as in the drafting and passage of a Bill for Distinguishing Protestant Dissenters from Popish Recusants, which would have pardoned those already prosecuted and prevented future cases of the same sort. But unfortunately prorogation and then dissolution stopped the Bill in the Commons.[91] Late in the year there were several bills introduced concerning the more fundamental religious and political issues of comprehension, toleration, and repeal of the Corporation Act, and which would have eliminated basic features of the Restoration settlement. The bill providing for comprehension and indulgence was supported in debate by Boscawen, Hampden, Paul Foley, Maynard, Birch, and Titus, as well as by others, who unlike these men were not and had not been Presbyterians.[92] However, among the Nonconformists as a whole, Morrice reported, "opinions about these bills are various," and it is evident that the traditional cleavage between moderate Dissent and strict Nonconformist appeared to some degree.[93] Dissenters would not have been divided concerning the second of these fundamental measures, for all of them would have welcomed the repeal of the Corporation Act. When it was moved by Sir Thomas Lee and seconded by Boscawen, Reynell, and Sir William Waller in the debate of December 24, it was hailed as "a very great thing," but those who were hopeful were soon disillusioned.[94]

The Presbyterian members of Parliament were also deeply concerned about many other fundamental political grievances during this Parliament, and they were among the leading supporters of actions and measures which would have curtailed the royal prerogative and increased the power of Parliament. One of the most pressing grievances concerned the recent actions of some judges, which Boscawen described in an early debate as "almost like Star Chamber sentences."[95] His desire that something be done was fulfilled on November 23, when the House investigated the discharging of the Middlesex Grand Jury by Lord Chief Justice Scroggs and Judge Thomas Jones before the end of the Term because the Government feared it would indict James for recusancy. After passing a resolution that such action by a judge was "arbitrary, illegal, destructive to public justice . . . and a means to subvert the fundamental laws of this Kingdom," a committee which included a half dozen Presbyterian members was appointed to examine the proceedings of the judges at Westminster Hall. During the debate on the resolution Love had urged the House to broaden the scope of the investigation, and continued Presbyterian pressure to do this was exerted by Paul Foley, Barnardiston, and Hampden, who moved and seconded the impeachment of Lord Chief Justice North.[96] Moreover, when the report of the Committee was made a month later, Hampden was one of the leading advocates for impeachment proceedings against Scroggs,

Jones, and also Sir Richard Weston, Baron of the Exchequer; and in the short debate before it was resolved to do so Boscawen took the same position.[97]

Since Hampden was a member of this investigating Committee, he was aware of the findings before the report was made and had already made an even more significant move to obtain a more enduring impartial administration of justice. It was evident that a basic cause of the trouble was the fact that the judges in England were completely dependent upon the King, and therefore he had proposed that they should have tenure *quamdiu se bene gesserint* instead of *durante bene placito*. Boscawen also spoke forcefully upon this proposal, which he had supported in 1674 as well. Both he and Hampden were obviously motivated by their great fear of a Catholic king, for each urged that this reform should be combined with the Exclusion Bill and a Protestant Association in order to eliminate all possibilities that James might gain possession of the Crown upon the death of Charles. As a result of past abuses and the fear of greater dangers in the future, therefore, the members of the House resolved that a bill be brought in to change the principle of tenure.[98]

The same considerations and fears led to the conclusion that there should also be a bill for the more "effectual securing of the meeting and sitting of frequent parliaments, as a means to prevent arbitrary power," and another one making it high treason to exact money from the people illegally. Certainly it was understandable that Nonconformists, who had long been advocates of frequent parliaments, hailed the resolution calling for the introduction of such bills.[99] Among other reform measures which received particularly strong support from the Presbyterian members of the Commons was a bill for the relief of the subject from arbitrary fines. It was entrusted to a committee headed by Paul Foley after he and Boscawen had defended it in the debate at its second reading, and on his committee were nine others of the Presbyterian group.[100] In addition, measures to regulate the election of members and to prevent "bribery and debauchery" were still considered of much importance by Presbyterian-Congregationalist members.[101] Also of significance was the continued adamancy of Hampden and Boscawen that the King would have to accept Exclusion and grant remedies for "miscarriages past and grievances present" before his financial needs would be satisfied.

The royal message on January 4, which repeated the King's refusal to accept Exclusion and which requested supplies, was once again a signal to these two Presbyterian leaders. They immediately rose to the question and spoke several times in the debates that resulted in the resolutions of January 7, 1681, reaffirming the Houses' refusal to grant supplies until the Exclusion Bill was passed. There could be only one outcome to such an impasse, and two days later the knock of the Black Rod came.[102]

The prorogation and then the dissolution of this Parliament was a blow to Nonconformists, for they had been elated by the "good tidings of the Parliament's undertakings" and "mightily applauded" the House of Commons for its "courage and counsels." Thomas Jolly retired for meditation and prayer "upon account of that sentence of death upon the hopeful proceedings of the Parliament . . . ," and Thomas Heywood felt that no effective resistance to an inundation of Popery and arbitrary government was left now that this "hopeful, useful, active Parliament" was dissolved.[103] However, as the election results for the new Parliament to meet at Oxford came in, hope revived somewhat, stimulated by the publicity Francis Smith and Benjamin Harris gave in their news sheets to the results and to the addresses which were presented to the successful candidates. Thus as the time for the meeting approached a feeling of great anticipation developed, and evidences of it are found in Smith's description of the ceremonies and celebrations given to the Whig and Nonconformist members of Parliament as they left for Oxford, as well as in the letters written by Thomas Gilbert, whom Lord Wharton had sent to Oxford to arrange quarters for himself and others.[104] In actuality there were six fewer of the known Presbyterian and Congregationalist members elected, but almost all other changes were considered for the better.[105]

Recognizing their reliance upon their political allies, Gilbert tried to arrange for Shaftesbury and Wharton to be lodged near each other. To Shaftesbury's agent, John Locke, Gilbert recommended that the Earl be lodged at the house of Dr. John Wallis, for as he wrote Wharton, this house was so near to the Nonconformist leader's quarters in Hart Hall "that you might have looked into, and called to one another out of each other's chambers; much more, dispatches by servants, and visit between yourselves, might upon all occasions have been . . . both speedy and easy;

which I apprehended would have been as grateful, as useful to both your Honors." [106]

Among the Presbyterian members of the new House of Commons who journeyed toward Oxford in the middle of March were the veteran leaders Boscawen, Hampden, Love, and Philip Foley, and they were joined by the venerable and highly respected John Swynfen whose presence had been missed in the debates of the previous Parliament. With a heightened sense of mission resulting from the elections, the election addresses, and the tension that led many members to come to Oxford armed, the Presbyterians and Congregationalists continued their efforts to obtain a monarchy in which Parliament and particularly the House of Commons would have a greater degree of power. One of the issues over which these members were most vehement during this short Parliament was why the Bill for the repeal of the Elizabethan Act Against Sectaries had not been presented for the King's assent at the end of the previous Parliament. As soon as this "miscarriage" was brought up, Hampden opened a frontal attack and proclaimed that he looked upon it as "a breach of the Constitution." Continuing, he acknowledged the Court's views of the Presbyterians and boldly turned the charge against them back at those responsible for the illegal "veto." "We are told that we are republicans and would change the Government," he said. "But [in the minds of those] such as are about to do so, it is a natural fear in them to be thought so, and they will cast it upon others." [107] Boscawen also attacked this "new way found out to frustrate Bills," while both he and Hampden moved for a conference with the Lords upon "the constitution of Parliament in passing of bills." [108]

The clerk of the Parliament, who did not submit the Bill for repealing the Act against Sectaries, was not the only person who was under fire for carrying out the King's commands, for the House once again brought up the impeachment of Danby, and Hampden was appointed chairman of a committee to inspect the Lords' Journals for action taken upon this issue in recent Parliaments. Impeachment charges were also the source of another highly important issue that arose when the Government forces in the House of Lords refused to receive the Commons impeachment of the informer Edward Fitzharris. [109] In the House of Lords, Wharton, Paget, and Bedford were among those who entered a formal protest against this action, and during the brief defiant debate in the Commons, Maynard charged that "in effect, they make us no Parliament."[110]

In addition to the leading or prominent parts taken by Presbyterian leaders in these matters, they were again outspoken in the debate on the Exclusion Bill and argued on Saturday, March 26, that it should be brought in and passed. John Swynfen assumed leadership of the Presbyterian group once more, and he was supported by Love, Hampden, and Boscawen, who was again the last speaker before the resolution to bring in the Bill passed.[111] Determined though the Presbyterians, Congregationalists, and other followers of Shaftesbury were in their efforts to obtain passage of an Exclusion Bill, developments had already occurred which were to make the efforts of the Parliament completely abortive. Several weeks before, the King had instigated negotiations with Louis XIV in order to obtain a subsidy which would enable him to dispense with Parliament, and on March 22, the day after the session began at Oxford, Barrillon reported to Louis the terms of the verbal treaty that he and Charles had finally concluded, which provided the essential funds.[112] Given this treaty and a Commons determined to pass the Exclusion Bill, the King's decision was inevitable. On Monday morning just after the Bill's second reading had been ordered for the next day, the knock of the Black Rod was heard, and when the Commons hurriedly assembled with the Lords they found to their great surprise that the King was dressed in his Crown and Robes, the regalia in which he declared the dissolution of Parliament.[113]

From the Nonconformist point of view, Thomas Jolly's premonition about the first Exclusion Parliament was even more appropriate as an epitaph for the last. It had been "too good to sit long."

CHAPTER VIII

*The Tactics of Desperation, 1681–1686*

The five years of political crises and strife which followed the Oxford Parliament were turbulent for all Englishmen, but they brought the Dissenters the most violent experiences and the most extreme change in status and power. After their relative security and political resurgence during the years of the Exclusion Parliaments, they were once again severely prosecuted under the penal laws and deprived of practically all local offices and sources of political power. The suppression became increasingly severe until it reached the extremes of the Bloody Assizes of 1685, and Nonconformist political power almost disappeared entirely in James II's Parliament of that year. Although there was only this one short Parliament during these years, other major developments such as the Rye House Plot and the Monmouth Rebellion had transcendent political and constitutional consequences for all Dissenters.

Since they became prime targets of Royal prosecution, the Nonconformists were once again subjected to the pressures they had felt during similar periods of Court policy during the earlier years of Charles II's reign. Many if not most of these pressures centered around the problem of deciding what should be done to bring more immediate relief as well as to attain long-range goals. Quietism was once again attractive, but political activism still had the strong appeal generated by political success during the years of the Exclusion Parliaments.

After the sudden and stunning political blow which Charles delivered by dissolving the Oxford Parliament, there were at first some isolated reflex actions reported among Whig and Nonconformist political leaders,[1] but there appear to have been no efforts of a more concerted and planned character until the late summer.

By then the visits which such leaders were making upon each other seem to have had definite relation to political activity. Some were apparently working through William of Orange, then visiting England, hoping to have the King call Parliament; and there are some indications that the Presbyterians and other Dissenters were active in drawing up lists of candidates and "making all the interest" they could in preparation for the next parliament.[2] Nor was this all. There were some exclusion leaders who "began to fear what would become of themselves, and saw no legal method of safety, but in the choice of a parliament before the ferment of the nation, raised by the terrors of the Popish Plot, was sunk, and their interest in the boroughs of the country ruined." As a result they reportedly "made very large propositions to the ministry of granting what money the King should desire, without either meddling with the Duke of York or any of the ministers in case the King should think fit . . . to call a parliament, and pass a general act of indemnity."[3]

Actually the continued struggle between Exclusionists and the Government was shifting to the courts and to London politics, and in these arenas Nonconformist support was a major source of strength. There were Dissenters who served on the so-called "ignoramus juries" that failed to give the indictments and convictions that the Government sought against both their own leaders as well as other Whigs, the most prominent of the latter being the case of Shaftesbury. When a grand jury, whose foreman was Sir Samuel Barnardiston, failed to return an indictment against the Whig leader in November, 1681, both ministers and politicians among the Dissenters were greatly cheered.[4] They likewise seemed to have had reason to feel successful in the Michaelmas election of Sir John Moore as Lord Mayor, for he had been a Dissenter and had persuaded Nonconformist ministers to obtain votes for him among their congregations;[5] but his role in the election of sheriffs the following June made it most evident that actually the Dissenters had helped put a man in office who would join their opponents. In the December elections of Common Councilmen, Dissenters and Whigs suffered additional losses; but they were not as serious as claimed at the time, for Court supporters made a net gain of only fifteen Councilmen and had important gains in only two wards.[6]

The considerable political strength which the Dissenters continued to possess in London and other cities and towns during the late summer and early autumn of 1681, and also the relative impunity with which they held conventicles only made officials of the Church and the Government all the more vigorous in the attack which they launched. "Our corporations and boroughs, who have so great a share in the government, are nurseries of faction, sedition and disloyalty," wrote the Bishop of Exeter to Archbishop Sancroft in August, "and we do humbly desire that all the laws regulating corporations particularly that . . . in restraining Nonconformists from entering in corporations, may be duly put in execution." [7] Although progress in enforcement was made during the autumn, it was not until the beginning of 1682 that results pleasing to officials appeared in outlying areas, while in London and the adjacent centers of Nonconformist strength the Government's success came more slowly. [8]

The political motivation of the attack on Dissenters was candidly expressed by Government officials. Quakers of Bristol and Gloucestershire were told that they had brought their prosecution upon themselves because they joined Presbyterians "to choose Parliament men," [9] while at Nottingham it was evident that the mayor and burgesses were actually bringing suit against the Nonconformist John Sherwin because of his "heading the Dissenters in all elections to oppose the interest of his Majesty and the majority of the town. . . ." [10] Political retaliation and religious antipathy were also the motives in the efforts to remove Dissenters holding positions in the King's household and in the Customs House, Navy Office, Excise Office and other Government offices. [11]

Although the measures taken against Dissenters were increasingly effective, the Government's efforts to prosecute Exclusionists in the courts during the winter and spring of 1681–1682 were still being thwarted by "ignoramus juries." Thus the Court supporters were determined to obtain sheriffs in London who would empanel juries more favorable to the Government prosecutions. In spite of the most determined campaign by Whigs and Nonconformists, two Tory sheriffs were finally selected. [12] An additional crucial political defeat was soon to follow, and in the process of delivering it Court supporters used legal maneuvers that were to bring additional losses for the Whigs and Nonconformists in other elections. In the Michaelmas election of London's Lord Mayor in 1682, the Dissenter Henry Cornish was defeated by the Tory Sir

Thomas Gold when the votes of Dissenters, including those of Quakers, were thrown out.[13] Along with other procedures which were used during the election, the King and his supporters insisted upon vigorous efforts in Church courts to obtain the excommunication of Nonconformists in order to have grounds for depriving them of their votes, and this tactic was shortly thereafter suggested to Secretary Jenkins as a means to prevent Dissenters from voting in Parliamentary as well as in local elections.[14]

There was to be a growing use of the civil and religious courts to strike at the power of such Nonconformists who might still hold local offices and to undermine or destroy the Dissenters' voting strength.[15] However, such efforts to purge corporations of Nonconformists did not necessarily eliminate the Dissenters who were occasional conformists, nor were the moderate Anglican sources of opposition strength affected. Moreover, they could not insure that members of Parliament would be elected in the future who would be favorable to the Court. Since nearly all of the major leaders of the opposition were of these two groups, it was of vital importance that the King find an effective means of attacking them and of establishing effective control over the corporations. These ends were to be accomplished in the concerted drive, begun in 1682, to revoke existing municipal charters and issue new ones in which the Crown would be granted the powers it desired.[16]

By the summer of 1682 the Court and Tory counterattack against Exclusionists and Nonconformists had resulted in many decisive successes in both the boroughs and the courts. However, the campaign in London still lagged, and in addition there still remained the one man of Presbyterian views who had held high office under Charles. Anglesey, the Lord Privy Seal, was already vulnerable because of his support of the Exclusion Bill, and his convictions regarding James remained so strong that in the spring he wrote in a memorandum intended for the King that it was the "perversion of the Duke of York . . . in point of religion" which was the "cause of all our mischiefs . . . and which, if not by wisdom antidoted, may raise a fire which will consume to the very foundations." Anglesey did not stop with forthright remarks concerning James in this memorandum, later published under the title *State of the Government and Kingdom*. Speaking to the King, he first called for a cessation of attacks upon members of the Exclusion Parliaments, and he included the pointed reminder that "though your Majesty is in his own person above the reach of the law . . . yet the *Law is your Master* and instructor on how to govern. . . ." Finally, he sought to undermine the status of his political enemies concerning whose activities the King himself had given Anglesey a warning, not without ominous undertones, just a fortnight earlier in a long private audience. "Your subjects," wrote Anglesey "assure themselves, . . . you will never attempt the enervating that law by which you are king . . . and that you will look upon any that shall propose or advise to the contrary, as . . . the worst and most dangerous enemies you and your Kingdom have." [17]

Within two months Anglesey's old rival and enemy the Duke of Ormonde began the open attack in the Privy Council resulting in the King's order that the Lord Privy Seal deliver the insignia of his office. For a man who had such pride in the stature the office had given him during the previous ten years, this was a humiliating defeat. However, some five years earlier when Anglesey once again had engaged a Nonconformist chaplain he had given the first indication that he would become increasingly independent of the Court. The course he took during the years of the Exclusion Parliaments and his political activity thereafter made it clear that he would no longer compromise his religious and political principles in order to keep the office, as he had to some degree when Danby was powerful during the middle of the previous decade. His sense of relief thus overcame his feeling of defeat as he returned home after delivering the Privy Seal on the evening of August 9. "The Lord be praised," he wrote in his diary that night; "I am now delivered of Court snares. . . ." [18]

The greatly increased effectiveness of the Government's attack explains the alarm and despair which spread among the Nonconformist leaders and the elation which grew at Court. Because he felt "the occasion extraordinary," Philip Henry left a very sick wife on July 23 so that he could take the trip to Boreatton and "discourse Lord Paget and Mr. Swinfen concerning public affairs," and he reported that "by them both I understand [there is] no hope but upwards." [19] In September a Court supporter found evidence that "the Saints begin to quake"; [20] and the continued success of the Court's various campaigns during the remainder of the year, particularly the flight of Shaftesbury to Holland and his death there on January 21, 1683, made the King most confident. In fact, Roger Morrice considered the King's statement to the Privy Council on February 23 to be "the greatest discovery that ever his Majesty made of himself and shows that he is resolved never to comply with Parliaments—and that he is free from all fears and apprehensions foreign and domestic, and that he concludes that he shall master all difficulties whatsoever." [21]

At this point Charles II still had one last major battle to win, and it was of critical importance to both sides. The City of London had refused to forfeit its charter, and the King was determined to force its surrender. Nothing better illustrates the intrenched and tenacious character of opposition political strength in London than the struggle which ensued in 1683. In spite of the judgment of the Court of the Kings Bench in June, which gave legal sanction to the Crown's *quo warranto* proceedings begun in February, and in spite of the interrogations and imprisonments during the summer that resulted from the disclosure of the Rye House Plot, the London Common Council refused to surrender the charter in September.[22] Active in the campaign against surrender were such Dissenters as the Baptist printer Francis Smith and Henry Ashurst, a Presbyterian and an occasional conformist. A pamphlet Smith published concluded by reminding its readers that Sir Edward Coke had said it would take a volume to treat of the liberties, franchises, and privileges of the City; and they were warned that "no less a volume would be necessary to describe the disorders, losses, distractions, mischiefs, and confusions, that must attend the destruction and death of so great a body politic." [23] All efforts were to no avail, and the momentous event Smith so vividly described took place in October. With the power of the Law Courts behind him, the King gained the complete control he had sought through a remodelling of the Corporation and the granting of a new charter.[24]

Faced by the continuing political and judicial triumphs of the King and his supporters, and also afflicted by increasingly relentless prosecution, Dissenters reacted in various ways. On the one hand there was a reappearance and spread of political quietism, and on the other a growing tendency to conform at least occasionally and to continue such political activity as was possible. In addition, partially because constitutional or legitimate political activity seemed to become either ineffective or impossible, some

Dissenters became involved in the Rye House Plot and a much larger number in the Monmouth Rising.

Among the Quakers, renewed caution if not quietism had become the official policy by the end of 1681. This was indicated by a letter which was issued to be read in all Monthly Meetings of London warning of "the hurt that may issue" to Friends "by the unprofitable talking of news in coffee houses, taverns, clubs, and ale houses . . . and particularly of matters relating to the government and magistracy (which we are bound in conscience to live peaceably under). . . ." In addition Friends were advised "not to use those reflecting, disgustful terms of distinction of *Whig* and *Tory* or any other . . . tending to provoke one neighbor against another. . . ." Soon thereafter Bristol Friends who were being apprehended were told by the officials that they "should have been quiet" instead of voting for members of Parliament. When George Whitehead and Gilbert Laity had an audience with the King in April, 1683, Whitehead agreed with this contention and told Charles that those Friends who had voted "are not in society with us, or we with them," while Laity added that they were "as much dissatisfied with such as have so done, as the King can be." [25]

In a plea to all Dissenters an anonymous writer, who may have been a Baptist, presented a justification for this quietist position. Although Christians might concern themselves in the State through petitioning and prayer, they must do so in a peaceful and not a disruptive manner. "We have enough to do . . . to work out our salvation," he contended, and even though the laws were hard on them and their civil rights invaded, they "ought to be quiet and silent" and leave such matters to the "judgment of the nation in the great Council of it. . . ." [26] There were also Presbyterians eager to profess their loyalty and political compliance, and they reminded the King that there were some of them still surviving who supported the Crown in the Second Civil War and stated that they would preserve his authority, government, interests, and prerogatives. [27]

Religious compliance in the form of occasional conformity also became more widespread. Government and Church officials received complaints that increased numbers of Dissenters were conforming occasionally and partially on Sunday mornings in order to qualify for offices and then attending Nonconformist services in the afternoons. It was reported that the continuance of the Nonconformist faction was "not owing so much to the professed Separatists as to others who go to church, take all the oaths and tests and crowd into public offices. . . ." It was therefore recommended that those holding government offices should present certificates that they lived "in the sole communion of the Church of England." [28]

Occasional conformity was not necessarily accompanied by political quietism. Indeed, as Roger Morrice emphasized with strong feeling in April, 1684, the quietists were usually the "Separatists" or the "censorious sort of Dissenters that condemns others for complying in anything in Church and State [and who] have absented themselves from all public places or courts where they were members for these two years last past or readily concurred to yield up all. . . ." [29] His contention is clear: some degree of compliance was essential in order to be politically effective.

That a considerable number of Dissenters agreed with Morrice is evident from the difficulties which the Court had experienced in its efforts to eliminate them from government offices and positions and local governments. However, with the attack upon municipal charters the occasional conformists in borough politics fought a losing battle, but even when the remodelling of the corporations was completed there were Exclusionists and Dissenters who had sat in Parliament against whom the Government did not have adequate grounds for prosecution. The disclosure in June, 1683, of a plan to assassinate the King and the Duke of York as they passed near the Rye House was to offer the Court a means of solving this problem. It now had the opportunity not only of a more general retaliation, but also of one that was quicker and more indiscriminate. Thus the political importance of the revelation of the Rye House Plot was that the Government was given grounds upon which to make an effective attack against the opposition members of the Exclusion Parliaments as it already had attacked their supporters or allies in the boroughs and government offices.

In July, 1682, when John Swynfen and Lord Paget told Philip Henry that concerning public affairs there was "no hope but upwards," these Presbyterian leaders clearly realized they faced an impasse because there was no longer any hope for a meeting of Parliament.[30] By this time leaders of the Anglican wing of the opposition were also well aware of this impasse, and critical de-

velopments took place. Lord Russell and the Earl of Essex came
to the conclusion that since the King was intent upon their
destruction they were no longer obligated as subjects not to resist
the King's authority. There followed the secret discussions of
resistance among Whig leaders during which plans were osten-
sibly made for a general rising throughout England, the so-called
insurrectionist part of the Rye House Plot; and as a preliminary
test of support it was arranged for Monmouth to make a formal
journey through Cheshire in the autumn.[31] Although a number
of the Presbyterian political leaders were willing to come to
meet the Duke in the course of his travels, this action in itself
did not mean they were ready to consider resistance.[32] But there
were two or three Presbyterians who did become much more
implicated, notably Lord Anglesey and John Hampden. Long a
friend and defendant of Monmouth, and recently dismissed from
office, Anglesey was susceptible. During the autumn Monmouth
frequently dined in Anglesey's home in Drury Lane, and other
guests included the Earl of Essex and Lord Howard of Escrick,
both of whom were deeply involved in the Rye House Plot. Din-
ners having such political implications were curtailed by Christmas festivities and a three-month attack of gout which kept
Anglesey in bed, but on May 29 Monmouth along with Bedford,
Macclesfield and others had a dinner with him which was later
reported to the authorities. It was therefore not surprising that
his house was searched and ransacked at midnight about a fortnight after the assassination plot was disclosed to the Government on June 12, 1683, but it was another six months before he
was examined by the Privy Council, where according to Roger
Morrice he was asked especially about "what private discourse
he had had with the . . . Duke." Although ready to tell the King
alone, "he did not think he was obliged to tell the Board what
private discourse he had . . . , for he had none that was any
way penal or criminal." The King did not speak with Anglesey
alone, for in this instance the evidence was completely lacking,
and the King apparently knew it. Thus the former Lord Privy
Seal was dismissed.[33]

Of the inner group accused of considering a general rising
throughout England, John Hampden was the only man who was
a Presbyterian, but in addition John Trenchard, who was possibly
a Presbyterian, was accused of having an important role.[34] Also

frequently mentioned along with these men when the Nonconformist coloration of the Plot is discussed is Lord William Russell, but though he had a Presbyterian background he had become an Anglican whose religious views were similar to those of
his chaplain Samuel Johnson and of his friend Bishop Burnet,
who was almost constantly with him in prison during the last
week of his life.[35]

Although there were only two Presbyterians accused of involvement in the insurrection plans, and the suspect Anglesey
who appears to have had some connection with this part of the
Rye House Plot, there were a larger number of Nonconformists
who were deeply implicated in the assassination plot. According
to the first information of June 12, the Baptist and former Cromwellian officer Captain Thomas Walcott was to lead the group
attacking the King's guards as they passed the Rye House owned
by Richard Rumbold, another Baptist and Cromwellian officer,
who was to lead the attack upon the King himself. Moreover, the
information was given by Josiah Keeling, who was also known
as an Anabaptist.[36] The evidence of Nonconformist involvement
was sufficient. With alacrity Tories, Churchmen, and Government
officials labeled the plot a "Presbyterian fanatic plot" and "the
damned plot . . . by Dissenters," or variants of each, while the
King gave official sanction to the view that the plot was an attack
on the Church of England by Nonconformists and Whigs.[37] It
did not matter to the Government that preparations had actually
not been made for the execution of the plan.[38]

Information about the assassination plot implicated the opposition leaders who had been planning for an uprising, and although
the connections were vague they were sufficient to enable the
Government to charge them with responsibility for both the
murder and insurrection proposals and to extend the attack to
Exclusionists in general.[39] As a result of the Crown's attack upon
both the Exclusionists and Nonconformists, all those Presbyterians and Congregationalists who had sat in Parliament were in
double jeopardy. The Government soon swung into action, and
its motivation was just as quickly evident. "Strange things are
said to be discovered concerning this new and I think sham plot,"
wrote John Burd in a letter from London to Taunton about a
fortnight after Keeling's first information. Obviously well informed concerning the Government's moves and well acquainted

with John Trenchard as well as others of the Presbyterian-Congregationalist group in Parliament, Burd's comments were revealing and portentous. Trenchard was apprehended at three in the morning that day, he reported, and "the Council ordered him pen, ink, and paper and desired him to be ingenious in confessing; the meaning I leave to you." Continuing, he added that "all the most considerable persons in most counties are sent for as being concerned in this sham plot . . . ," including William Strode, and Mr. Boscawen among others.[40] A considerable number of Presbyterian or Congregationalist members of Parliament were quickly considered suspects, and many of them had their homes searched and even ransacked for arms, including Philip and Thomas Foley, Major Richard Beake, John White, Sir William Ellis, Lord Paget, Thomas Papillon, and Edmund Prideaux, as well as Anglesey.[41] The results were revealing. At Major Beake's in Buckinghamshire there was "but one little sword." At John White's in Nottinghamshire it was reported some five dozen blunderbusses were found, but both Secretary Jenkins and the Duke of Newcastle were unable to obtain verification. The Earl of Lindsey, who searched for arms in Lincolnshire, stated that Sir William Ellis and others "deal much in blunderbusses," the evidence being that most of them had some. Ingenuously he added that "most of their arms are hid underground and so not to be discovered," but he did not doubt they intended to raise an insurrection. The source of this suspicion was actually not a matter of blunderbusses, as Lindsey made evident in noting that Ellis was a nephew of the Protector's solicitor of the same name, that he voted for the Exclusion Bill, and that he was a brother-in-law of John Hampden and was "head of all the Presbyterians in the County. . . ."[42] Few of those making the searches were as candid as the deputy lieutenants of the North Riding, who after going through several houses reported that "in spite of very diligent search the number [of arms] is so small that they are not much encouraged to make further noise in the matter."[43]

Because they were mentioned by the informers or because of their relations with those who had been involved in the plot, Sir Walter Yonge and Sir Robert Rich were under suspicion, but neither became involved themselves, and no charges were made.[44] Even against Hampden and Trenchard, who were accused of being either leading or important figures in the insurrectionist plot, the Government had been unable to make a case. Indeed it was having such difficulty that on October 31 the King told the Earl of Bedford while walking in the Park that Hampden, Trenchard and "all the prisoners in the Tower must be discharged for there was but one witness against them. . . ." [45] Accordingly, Trenchard was released along with others a month later; but in order to keep John Hampden confined, it is well known that the charge was changed from treason to misdemeanor, an admission of the Government's failure to obtain the required two witnesses for the former charge. However, by gaining Hampden's conviction in February, 1684, and by sentencing him with imprisonment until a £40,000 fine was paid, the Government did succeed in continuing his confinement until the capture of a second witness after the Monmouth Rebellion made it possible to try him for treason. [46]

Although the Crown was able to obtain conviction of only one of the Presbyterian-Congregationalist group in Parliament on the charges of direct involvement in the Rye House Plot, and only on the secondary charge of misdemeanor rather than treason, yet this was not the extent of its success. There were also successful legal prosecutions which were the indirect result of the plot, the most notable being the conviction of Sir Samuel Barnardiston in February, 1684, on the charge of misdemeanor because he wrote some private letters which contained allegedly "scandalous and seditious" reflections concerning the prosecutions of Lord William Russell, the Earl of Essex (who he said had been murdered) and Algernon Sidney. Sir Samuel, who had been foreman of the Grand Jury which refused to indict Shaftesbury in 1681, was sentenced to imprisonment until he paid a fine of £10,000, and this he refused to do for over a year. [47] In addition, Presbyterian or Congregationalist members of Parliament faced another type of legal procedure that could be used much more indiscriminately. At the assizes in the spring of 1684 grand juries presented Michael Harvey in Dorset and William Strode in Somerset as disaffected and required security for good behavior, and since they also refused they faced imprisonment. [48]

It becomes clear that the success of the attack upon Dissenters who had sat in Parliament cannot be measured by the number of convictions actually obtained against them. The nature of the charges, the quality of the evidence accepted, and the character of the sentences must be given equal if not greater weight if the true impact is to be understood. On all of these grounds the Dissenters who had been active in parliamentary politics and even in local government had ample reasons to feel that their personal freedom and their property were in jeopardy.

Vulnerable though the Dissenters' political leaders were, generally speaking it was not these partial and occasional conformists who suffered most severely, but rather the rigid Nonconformists. During the greatly intensified prosecution after the Rye House Plot, the Government continued to be motivated by a desire to eliminate Nonconformist support of the parliamentary opposition wherever it existed in the country; and in addition it was strongly believed that neither the Monarchy nor the Church would be safe until all Nonconformists and their conventicles were extirpated. As a result of the assassination plans of the former Cromwellians Walcott and Rumbold, old fears of republican Secretaries took on a reality they had not had for two decades, and they were heightened by information that the famous Cromwellian Dr. John Owen, as well as Stephen Lobb, Robert Ferguson, and other ministers had supported the plot. However, attempts to prosecute failed because of a lack of legal evidence, except in the case of Robert Ferguson, who was clearly an active participant and who escaped to Holland. In addition it appears that at Bristol the well-known ejected minister Dr. Ichabod Chauncy and the Baptist Dr. John Griffeth were members of a club which supported a rising. All the evidence that has since been discovered indicates that at the most there were only a few Nonconformist ministers involved in the Plot. It also appears that only a very small minority were aware of any efforts to instigate a rising and even fewer were willing to give as much as tacit support.[49] Supporting this view are comments which such ministers as Thomas Jolly and Henry Newcome confided to their diaries after the Plot became known. After they were accosted by several persons concerning the Nonconformists' involvement, Jolly wrote that they were opposed to rebelling against authority. Similarly, after hearing of Essex's suicide and Russell's death sentence, Newcome thought it saddest of all that these two leaders "should be so left of God as to be guilty of so horrid a conspiracy"; and he added, "they are happy that are innocent. . . ." He knew whereof he spoke, for ten days earlier Ferguson came to him "in disguise, flying upon the Plot." Not daring to betray the plotter since he knew that even if he did he would be hopelessly implicated, Newcome stated that he "only got him some direction for his way to Dunham, and he went from me quickly." [50]

Among Nonconformists generally there was very probably a division in opinion similar in proportions to that among their ministers. As usual the Society of Friends was quick to make an official statement, this time an "Address to the King" in which they declared themselves clear of all "hellish plots," and the evidence verifies their contention.[51] Other Nonconformist rebuttals included those of Thomas Jolly and Thomas Delaune, who both noted that most of those involved were Conformists and emphasized that it would not be just to consider all of them guilty for this reason. But regardless of evidence or logic, Dissenters were to retain the stigma, and those who were innocent among them were "to bear a share of the reproach" as Newcome had predicted they would in July, 1683.[52]

Another acute observer of that summer was Dr. Ichabod Chauncy, who wrote Increase Mather that the Plot was "like to prove the greatest advantage to our popish adversaries, that ever God's providence put into their hands." Foreseeing long-range political consequences, he thought it "probable, after some more leading men are taken off upon the account of it, a Parliament will be called (which will, in all likelihood be according to the mind of them that call [it]). . . ." [53] Insofar as he went, his predictions were correct; but he did not anticipate the duration or stringency of the coming prosecutions. "We are all in expectation of ruin," wrote a minister to his friend; yet he still had some hope and resilience, since he encouragingly added, "be not crushed." [54] A year later, however, it was all too obvious not only that a great many had been ruined, but also that they had been crushed.[55]

In October, 1684, it was reported to Sunderland that "in general all the Dissenters lie so under the lash of the penal statutes that it restrains them taking the liberty as formerly of discourse." Indeed, it was noted that "a great number of such as are outwardly good Church of England men . . . do at this juncture speak more plainly and resolutely against the government than the Dissenters." [56] Evidence that there was at this juncture some resurgence of Anglican opposition is to be found in the appearance of Halifax's *Character of a Trimmer* and in the Government-inspired attack which Roger L'Estrange directed against those of this disposition.[57] But even though there had been some development of moderate Anglican criticism by the time Charles II died on February 6, 1685, the way had been largely prepared for the kind of parliament Dr. Chauncy had predicted, and James II made more certain of the election results by his policies during the first six weeks of his reign.

The situation in which Dissenters found themselves at the time of the elections which started in March was revealed by Thomas Jolly, who wrote in his diary that "most of a night was spent by the church in prayer not only as to my own case, being bound to appear at the Assizes, but the case of many others in worse condition, that fetters might fall off and prison doors fly open . . . ; also it was on behalf of the new elections for the next Parliament." [58] Not only were Dissenters to be less effective because of the quietism, which had developed since the Oxford Parliament of 1681, but they were also to be severely handicapped in other ways. An unknown number who might have voted were undoubtedly in prison; others who had voted in the past would not be able to because of strict enforcement of the Corporation and Five Mile Acts. Finally, the changes regarding elections of burgesses made in nearly ninety borough charters since the last Parliament were unquestionably effective against Dissenters, particularly those who conformed occasionally and who were thus relatively immune from prosecution under the penal laws.[59] In addition there were other factors explaining the Court's success which did not involve Dissenters as directly. Opposition political leaders had been discredited, imprisoned, and executed. Or they had fled into exile or died. At the same time the King and Sunderland supplied a most aggressive and thorough leadership for those favoring the Court, and Anglican Church officials also took an active part.[60]

Nevertheless a good number of Presbyterian political leaders were active candidates, and there is evidence of Nonconformist support of these and others on the hustings. In Herefordshire Sir Edward Harley, his son Robert, and their associates were busy; but reports prior to the election indicated the defeat which was forthcoming. In Bridgewater, as soon as there was the first intimation that there would be a new Parliament, a "fanatic and servant" of Sir Francis Rolle's was busy visiting the "grand fanatics" in anticipation of the election.[61] Better known were the efforts of the Earl of Bedford to obtain the election of his son Edward at Tavistock. Even though he had suffered heavy blows personally and politically through the execution of his son Lord Russell and the change in the Tavistock charter, which deprived him of his previous control of the borough, his power in the County was considered sufficiently a threat to have brought the on-the-scene intervention of the Lord Chief Justice Jeffreys. Roger Morrice reported that the Lord Chief Justice forced the Mayor of Bedford to hold the election the day after the writ arrived instead of giving greater notice as was usual, his contention being "that the Earl of Bedford's interest was such, that otherwise he would choose whom he pleased." Jeffreys and the Earl of Aylesbury, the Lord Lieutenant, were also able to control the County election by their presence and pressure.[62] In Buckinghamshire, however, Richard Hampden was not only successful at Wendover, but he was also able to assist Thomas Wharton's election for the County in spite of the intervention of the Chief Justice and his sudden adjournment of the election from Aylesbury to Newport. On the other hand Hampden's support of Sir Roger Hill in the Agmondesham election failed to bring success.[63] Also unsuccessful in the face of Court-supported activity was Thomas Foley, who stood for Worcestershire.[64] This was not the extent of the efforts of the Dissenters in this election, for a number of others who had been of the Presbyterian-Congregationalist group in Parliament were candidates, including Hugh Boscawen, John Trenchard, Michael Harvey, William Strode, Sir John Stapely, and Sir William Ellis. None of these candidates were returned; and while all except one petitioned the House to be seated, not a single one of their cases was reported from the Committee on Elections to the House. Thus the overwhelming defeat of this group on the hustings was not altered.[65]

When Parliament assembled in May only Sir John Maynard, Richard Hampden, and Sir John Fagg were present in the Commons, and in addition there was one newcomer, Sir John Thompson.[66] The remark James II reportedly made that "there were not above forty members but such as he himself wished for" in the whole Parliament, must be recalled in order to view these results in perspective, for the comment is a reminder that the Anglican wing of the opposition also suffered a great loss.[67] Being so weakened in numbers, members of the opposition were largely unheard during the debates of the first session of this Parliament, and in a few instances they even were afraid to be seen. Lord Wharton, for example, after being present regularly for a fortnight following the opening of Parliament, suddenly ceased to attend.[68] Of those who had taken a prominent part with Wharton in the Exclusion Parliaments there was Richard Hampden, but although he did continue to attend he apparently did not speak.

Nevertheless there were a few of the Presbyterian-Congregationalist group who were not silent. On three occasions Anglesey entered protests against the action taken by the Lords, the first being a protest against the reversal of the first Exclusion Parliament's vote that impeachments be continued from one Parliament to another, and on the second occasion he dissented from the vote to reverse Lord Stafford's attainder. In both of these protests he was joined by two or more Whig Lords who were Anglicans. However, when the Bill for Monmouth's attainder passed on June 15, Anglesey alone opposed it because at that juncture, only two days after first word of Monmouth's landing at Lyme had reached Court, the evidence was too general he contended, and too much based on notoriety to warrant such severe punishment.[69] As for other legislation immediately following Monmouth's invasion, Sir John Maynard was somewhat more successful in the Commons. When the Bill for the Better Preservation of His Majesty's Person and Government was introduced, it contained a clause declaring it to be treason for any person merely to assert the legitimacy of Monmouth or of his title to the Crown. The veteran Sergeant-at-Law was vigorous in objecting to this clause which would have made words as well as acts the basis for charges of treason, holding that "words are often ill heard and ill understood," and that "it would lead to the punishment of innocence and the commission of perjury." Although he failed in his efforts to have overt acts alone the grounds for charges of treason, as they had been in English law, the Bill that passed the Commons after "many and long contests" included important amendments offered by a committee on which Maynard served, the major safeguard being that the information should be reported within forty-eight hours after the words were spoken. With the force of the Bill tempered, the Lords previously favoring it appear to have thought it not worth passing, and it died.[70]

In June and the following few months the imminent threat to the Government was the attack directed against the King by Monmouth and his followers. There was therefore a much greater concern that James be secure than that an innocent person might be found guilty of treason. However, by the opening of the second session of this Parliament in November a dramatic change was becoming evident. It now began to appear that the real threat to the Government and to the rights of Englishmen was the King himself. In his opening speech to Parliament he made known his desire to have a standing army for defense at home and abroad, and announced that no man was to take exception because there were Catholic officers in the army. The few intrepid members who had acted in opposition in the early summer were now joined by a majority of the Commons. Sir Thomas Clarges was one of three Anglicans who led the emerging opposition force and opposed both a standing army and raising the revenue needed for it. Among those of the Presbyterian-Congregationalist group Maynard once again was articulate. In a speech of November 12 he opposed the grant of supply for an army, being particularly concerned that the King was violating the Test Act; and he along with Richard Hampden served on the committee headed by Clarges which was directed to draw up an address requesting that the King do something to relieve apprehensions resulting from this violation of the law.[71]

This was the extent of Presbyterian-Congregationalist activity in this Parliament, which was shortly prorogued and was never to meet again. When it is viewed in the light of the contribution of the Anglican members who were opposed to the Court, it becomes evident that Anglesey and Maynard were almost alone in their efforts during the first session, while in the second session the Anglican members took the leadership and Presbyterian members gave support.

Nonconformist opposition to the new King and his policies was not expressed primarily in parliamentary activity during the first months of his reign. The recent intensive prosecution and the accession of an avowed Catholic, combined with the Court's election maneuvers and their results made many Nonconformists receptive to the idea that force should be used in order to make fundamental changes in the government. Not only was it felt that James II should be deposed and the Duke of Monmouth put in his place, but also that there should be important constitutional changes. Not since the Restoration had those who planned plots or insurrections drawn up a manifesto as reminiscent of the ones which appeared during the Civil Wars and the Interregnum. Written originally by the Presbyterian minister Robert Ferguson and submitted to Monmouth and others for revision before they sailed from Amsterdam, the Declaration was designed for use in winning support for the Rebellion after the Duke's forces landed in England. It was contended that it had been the glory of the English people in the past to have had a monarchy in which the ruler "stood so limited and restrained by the fundamental terms of the Constitution," that he could not hurt them without violation of his own oath and the rules and measures of the Government. However, it was charged that "all the boundaries of the government have of late been broken and nothing left unattempted, for turning our limited monarchy into an absolute tyranny." Specifically the King was attacked because of his Catholicism and his illegal appointment of Catholics to government positions, his collection of customs and the excise which was to have expired with Charles II's death, and finally because of the false returns and the "new illegal charters . . . depriving us of all expectation of succor in Parliament." Of more interest and importance were the legal and constitutional changes which were sought. Protestant Dissenters were to enjoy equal liberty with other Protestants. Parliaments were to be "annually chosen and held, and not prorogued, dissolved, or discontinued within the year, before petitions be first answered and grievances redressed." Judges were to hold their places *quam diu se bene gesserint,* and Parliament was to approve of those appointed. Both the Corporation and Militia Acts were to be repealed, and new laws were to be enacted providing that sheriffs were to be elected by the freeholders and that they were to have control over the militia. Finally there was to be new legislation to "prevent all military standing force, except what shall be raised and kept up by authority and consent of Parliament." [72]

Obviously the Declaration called for much which the Puritan Parliamentarians sought before the Restoration and which the Dissenters worked to attain thereafter. Furthermore, during the Parliaments of the Restoration there had been a growing support among the moderate Anglicans of the opposition for some of these proposals, such as those concerning the tenure of judges and the repeal of the Corporation Act. On others, such as complete religious toleration for Protestants and annual parliaments, those who rallied to Monmouth's program would have gone further than most moderate Dissenters and Anglicans who were members of the Parliamentary opposition, for the M.P.'s wanted comprehension with toleration, and triennial parliaments. Likewise, proposals to have sheriffs elected and in control of the militia were too extreme, while the declaration of war upon James II as a "murderer, Popish usurper, traitor and tyrant" [73] was outright revolution which no moderate could accept.

The Dissenters became sharply split, and the larger number of them refused to give their support or approval, not only before but also following Monmouth's arrival off Lyme on June 11. Most important the Duke failed to gain the support of any of the leading Presbyterian or Congregationalist members of Parliament, although he made particular efforts to obtain financial support from one of the Hampdens and Sir Samuel Barnardiston.[74] Of the lesser members, John Manley, a Cromwellian captain who was to be an M.P. in 1689, joined Monmouth on the Continent and served in the invasion force as a major. In addition there were four who were accused of involvement. One informer charged that Henry Henly, of Colway near Lyme, contributed £300, and that William Strode of Barrington gave both money and horses; however, there apparently was no evidence even for the charge of high misdemeanor, since neither was prosecuted.[75] In the case of John Trenchard the evidence is not only incomplete but also somewhat conflicting in implications. He reportedly promised 1500 men, but fled and escaped to France in order to avoid arrest. This would seem to imply he was involved, yet his escape occurred somewhat over a fortnight before Monmouth's landing at Lyme, and he did not join the Duke as he might have on the Continent.[76] To be sure, it could be contended that he had been sobered by the nearly successful attempt to arrest him, or that he knew too well the lack of support in England, either of which would have been sufficient reason for abandoning any association he might have had with Monmouth.

Even more complicated and inconclusive is the case of Edward

Prideaux. At first it would seem he was definitely involved. There were two informers, both prisoners who accused him of complicity; however, the man who charged that he gave £500 and some horses had already been condemned, and he decided to save his life by making this charge. The other man who made a charge against Prideaux is unknown. Presumably he was not a witness and his testimony would not even permit the Government to proceed on the basis of corroborative evidence as it had in Sidney's case; for although Prideaux was arrested after the testimony of these two men, and on a charge of high treason, the King later indicated that he would let Jeffreys dictate the terms of his release from the Tower without a trial. The enormous sum of £14,500 which the prisoner paid Jeffreys for his release without trial might at first seem to be an admission of guilt but there are two factors to be weighed in the balance.[77] In December Prideaux became seriously enough ill for the King to grant permission for his wife to be confined with her husband and for a physician and apothecary to come and go for him.[78] Poor health may have had some bearing on his decision to avoid the further imprisonment which would undoubtedly have resulted from a trial for misdemeanor. Furthermore, even an innocent man would have wished to avoid trial in the aftermath of the Monmouth Rebellion, when too frequently the acceptance of perjured testimony and hearsay as evidence made trial tantamount to conviction. Nevertheless, such contentions are no more proof of Prideaux's innocence than the payment to Jeffreys is proof of his guilt.

Except for Manley's participation and the partial or promised assistance which may have been given by Trenchard and Prideaux, it appears that no Presbyterian or Congregationalist who had been or was to be a member of Parliament gave support to the Monmouth Rebellion.[79] However, the political implications and consequences of Nonconformist involvement cannot be gauged merely by considering the degree of support given by the Dissenters' political leaders. Of equal if not greater political import were the reactions of Nonconformist ministers and laymen to the Rebellion and also the extent of their involvement in it.

Relatively few ministers are known to have become supporters of Monmouth, but unlike the Dissenters' political leaders most of the ministers who did become involved were actively engaged in the Rebellion itself. Particularly notable because of his role in the conspiracy from the very beginning was Robert Ferguson, a Presbyterian minister of Scotch origins who had been ejected from an English living in 1662 and who subsequently assisted Dr. John Owen in his Congregationalist Church.[80] He was the author of at least one anonymous pamphlet in defense of Monmouth's legitimate birth as the son of Charles II. Later he played a leading role in the efforts of the English refugees in the Low Countries to win Monmouth over to plans for a rebellion, and after their success in April he wrote the Declaration or political manifesto which has already been discussed.[81] Following the landing at Lyme another ejected minister is known to have joined the Rebellion, the Presbyterian John Hicks, while a third named Joseph Bennett found himself in difficulty for having preached a thanksgiving sermon for a supposed Monmouth victory.[82] Also known for having joined Monmouth with a half dozen or more of the members of his church was the Congregationalist minister Stephen Towgood, of Weycroft Chapel at Axminster, who after strict prosecution had been resumed in 1681 conducted services in various inconspicuous places including three months in a cave.[83]

How much indirect influence these few Presbyterian and Congregationalist ministers had upon those outside their immediate acquaintanceship is difficult to estimate. In any event, Dissenters of these persuasions who were looking for guidance or leadership from their ministers would have found that the vast majority did not give active support to the Rebellion, and it is probable that a great many if not most of these clergymen agreed with those of their number who condemned it in private. Of these there was Roger Morrice who was quick to describe Monmouth's Declaration as treasonable and to call his army the "rebel forces," while Adam Martindale stated that three years before he had written against Monmouth's claim to the throne and ever since had declared himself for "submission and obedience (in lawful things) to the King and his ministers, whatever his principles or practices be. . . ."[84] Philip Henry was also opposed to the Rebellion, for to those who visited him in prison and who "were big with the expectation of . . . Monmouth's success," he reportedly said: "I would not have you flatter yourselves with such hopes, for God will not do his work for us . . . by that man. . . ."[85] Such hopes as Henry's visitors had can also be detected in a most revealing diary entry made by Thomas Jolly. Apparently it was only with some difficulty that he was able to make his judgment prevail over his hopes for relief from persecution, for he wrote: "I had great exercise through the various reports of the Western commotion, yea, when the tydings came that Monmouth's army was dispersed and he taken, oh! how good it is to stay on the rock of ages and not on the broken reeds of Egypt." [86] Tempted though he may have been, he nevertheless did not give support. His experience and his decision were probably widely shared by Presbyterians and Congregationalists not in the Western Counties, as well as by a good number in this area. However, there is no doubt that Presbyterians as well as Congregationalists in the vicinity of the Rebellion did give active support.

Unlike these two branches of Dissenters, the Quakers reacted to the Rebellion with almost complete unanimity. Reflecting the strong resurgence of quietism which developed during the extremely severe prosecution which they had experienced since 1681, the Friends agreed that whatever their sufferings were they "must not expect deliverence by the arm of flesh. . . ." They were therefore "not to concern themselves in this war and all unanimously consented thereto." [87] George Fox and George Whitehead, as well as other leaders, were highly concerned to see that this policy was followed by all Quakers, Whitehead being the most actively involved. As a result of these steps there were only three or four members of the Society of Friends who are known to have joined Monmouth's forces; and because of the official warning not to do so, those who violated this agreed upon policy were then excluded from the Society. [88]

Although quietism had been strong among Baptists since the Restoration, they also had a tradition of political and military action which was a product of their previous history. Both were prevalent among those of this persuasion during the spring and early summer of 1685, but the compulsion to act seems to have been dominant among the Baptists in the Western Counties and probably was prevalent in other areas as well. Although not many ministers are known to have joined Monmouth's forces, there were the well known cases of Samuel Lark of Lyme, who became a captain of horse and was executed for his part, and also of John Griffeth the General Baptist. [89] Certainly of greater notoriety were the Baptist laymen Richard Rumbold, Abraham Holmes, and

Colonel Henry Danvers. All were Cromwellian soldiers with long careers in conspiracy which came to an end with the failure of the Rebellion, Rumbold and Holmes being executed and Danvers dying two years after he fled to the Continent.[90] However, a man like John Holloway, the tobacconist of Lyme and member of Samuel Lark's church, was probably much more typical of the majority of Baptists who joined the ranks of the insurgents.[91]

Whether the men who joined Monmouth were Presbyterians, Congregationalists, or Baptists, most of them were apparently motivated more by religious beliefs than by political or constitutional reasons, while economic considerations were probably of even less influence.[92] This was to be expected, for the prosecution of the previous four years had made the religious issue of most immediacy to all Dissenters other than some occasional conformists, while the concomitant political reprisals which the Crown effected through charter revisions and trials for treason or misdemeanor were more removed from the experience of most Nonconformists. However, those who joined or supported Monmouth usually included both religious and political reasons when explaining their position. The most representative was probably the entry in the church book of the Congregational Chapel at Axminster where it was recorded that Monmouth "gave forth his Declaration to restore liberty to the people of God, for the worship of God, to preserve the rights and privileges of the nation. . . . Now were the hearts of the people of God gladdened, and their hopes and expectation raised, that this man might be a deliverer for the nation, and the interest of Christ in it, who . . . were broken with the weight oppression. . . ."[93]

Dissenters who were politically more aware and sophisticated and who were recognized as political leaders in Parliament were not found among those following or favoring Monmouth, nor were the more responsible and moderate ministers and religious leaders. It appears, moreover, that the larger number of Nonconformists were more disposed to follow these leaders than to join those involved in the Rebellion. Nevertheless, support for the Monmouth Rebellion, unlike that for the Rye House Plot, came almost exclusively from the Nonconformists. Furthermore it was not merely a planned attack but an open, armed insurrection against the English King and government. The reprisals therefore fell almost completely upon the Nonconformists, and they were not only notoriously severe, but in important instances based upon questionable legal procedures and applications of the law. The most reliable investigations indicate that probably about 300 persons were executed following the Bloody Assizes presided over by Chief Justice Jeffreys. In addition about 800 were consigned to courtiers for transportation to the West Indies for a ten-year instead of the usual four-year period of servitude. Many others were whipped in a manner designed to endanger their lives; and finally there were the sums shared by Jeffreys and the King which were paid by prisoners to avoid trial, amounting to £10–15 for those who were poorer, but which went as high as the £14,500 in the case of Prideaux.[94]

The autumn and winter of 1685–1686 were bleak for Dissenters. Typical were the reactions of the minister Thomas Jolly and the political leader Sir Edward Harley, both of whom had weathered other storms of prosecution and were sensitive to their unpredictable dangers. Jolly retired for prayer because of the "darkness of . . . public and private concerns," while Harley wrote a most apprehensive letter to his son Robert in London telling him that he should hasten home and bring with him a younger brother.[95]

The Dissenters had faced desperate situations under Charles II, but never had the Court and Anglican leaders had such a convincing reason for stringent prosecution as after the Monmouth Rebellion, and never had Nonconformists greater reason to feel that it was hopeless to expect relief than they did following the Bloody Assizes. However, Nonconformity had reached the nadir. The decline which started in March of 1681 with the dissolution of the Oxford Parliament had come to an end.

CHAPTER IX

*The Impact of Enticement: James II and the*
*Divided Dissenters, 1686–1688*

With the coming of spring in 1686 there also came most unexpected signs that Dissenters could hope for relief from the King. Moreover, the grants of relief that James began making in a selective manner were continued throughout the year, and by that time it was apparent that they were the prelude to a complete reversal of the King's political tactics. Instead of continuing his previous alliance with the Church of England, he was about to seek Nonconformist support for his religious and political program. With this shift there began a new and critical period in the history of Nonconformity, and during the next few years Dissenters were to experience severe pressures of a new nature, as well as a dramatic change in their status and power.

From the time the King reversed his alliances until the autumn of 1688 it appeared that the Dissenters might hold sufficient power to tip the political balance either toward the Court and the Catholics on the one hand, or the Anglican leaders and William of Orange on the other. Thus in the developing political and constitutional struggle during most of the remainder of James II's reign they occupied a pivotal position, and as a result not only did their status improve but their new position also raised hopes of realizing long-sought religious and constitutional goals. At the same time, however, they were confronted with crucial problems concerning the means which should be used to obtain these aims. Although the problems were reminiscent of the issues faced when Charles II sought Nonconformist support in 1662 and 1672, this time they were much more complicated, for they were integrally related to the central political and constitutional crisis confronting the whole country.

As a result of the Dissenters' pivotal position and the critical character of these national issues, the pressures emanating from the other two politico-religious groups were most extreme, and the enticements offered were very appealing. The impact of all these forces upon Dissenters had various consequences, but above all it was divisive. Old differences and enmities reappeared among them and became virulent, particularly the split between the strict Nonconformists and the moderate Dissenters or old Puritans who were occasional and partial Conformists and who desired comprehension within a broadened Anglican Church. In addition, a pre-Revolutionary development of great political and constitutional importance took place. By the beginning of 1688 the old alliance between the political and religious leaders of the moderate Dissenters and the moderate Anglicans began to emerge once again and to become viable.

The new position of the Dissenters vis-à-vis both the Court and the Anglican leaders began to appear in the spring of 1686, and by late autumn it was clearly evident. The first step came on March 10 when the King issued his General Pardon and granted freedom to those in prison for Nonconformity, the greatest number of whom were Quakers.[1] In addition some royal orders and promises freeing Quakers from prosecution seem to have been issued in circular warrants and verbally in the presence of those appearing before the King with petitions during the spring and early summer, but the Friends received only very partial protection.[2] Nevertheless, they enjoyed a somewhat more favored position than did the other Nonconformists, as was indicated by the Dutch Ambassador's report that soldiers who were protecting the Catholic Chapel in Lime Street during Sunday worship in late May "disturbed a Presbyterian conventicle, and left undisturbed the Quakers who have obtained his Majesty's permission for that purpose. . . ." However, the Ambassador added that it was said the King would willingly grant such permission to all the Dissenters "if his affairs would admit of it."[3]

The King's reasons for restricting his dispensation were soon to disappear. By August it became both possible and desirable to extend religious liberty because of the politico-religious developments during the earlier summer months. In the first place Anglican resistance to Court policy was dramatically evident when the Bishop of London refused to follow orders and suspend

John Sharp, Rector of St. Giles-in-the-Fields, for preaching two sermons critical of Catholic dogma. When the King created the Ecclesiastical Commission in July and the Bishop was ordered to appear before it, there were Dissenters as well as his old friends urging him to make a resolute defense of himself; "indeed it was never known of late years that so universal an interest of Churchmen, Tories, Trimmers, and Dissenters did follow any one cause as now follow the Bishop's case," for "all think themselves struck at by it." [4] However, the cooperative mood resulting from this common threat was almost completely confined to the Bishop's case. Animosity continued to exist between the Dissenters and Anglicans because during the summer it was clear that the Anglican hierarchy was largely responsible for the continued severe prosecution of Dissenters, including even those conventicles and meetings "made up of such as go ordinarily to Church (and Sacrament too). . . ." [5]

The King appears to have been aware of the opportunity to win the occasional and partial Dissenters who were being prosecuted by the "hierarchists" at the very time that they were willing to give support to the Bishop of London. On August 2, 1686, Sir John Baber, continuing in his old role as the Court's contact with the Presbyterians, told his friend Roger Morrice that "it was his positive opinion there would be no coalition between the Church of England and the Church of Rome . . . and that the Court was in a great distress, finding the Church [of England] . . . uncompliant, and had therefore taken a great displeasure against it, and it should be made to feel the effects of it. . . ." Then came a crucial exploratory question. Morrice recorded that Baber wanted "to know whether if liberty and impunity would be granted by a law, we would in a body signify our thankful acceptance thereof." [6] There was no suggestion that Catholics would receive freedom to worship publicly, nor was anything said concerning repeal of the Test Acts. Most important was the fact that the religious liberty and freedom from punishment which was offered was to be established by parliamentary law rather than granted by royal prerogative. It seemed to Morrice that there were three courses open to the Dissenters of his disposition. If they joined with the Anglicans he believed that "they certainly will break all the measures of the Court. . . ." However, he thought that in delivering the Church from Catholic power the Dissenters would "expose themselves to the malice and persecution both of the Church and of the Court" and thus be utterly destroyed; for he apparently contended that the Church would turn all its efforts against the Dissenters as soon as it felt the Catholic threat had been overcome, while the Court would attack the Dissenters in the meantime for supporting the Anglicans. The second possible course was to sit still and "wait what providence will do in process of time for their deliverence." Finally, they could join with the Court, presumably on the basis of the proposals described by Baber. Obviously favoring this policy, he wrote that some Dissenters say that by cooperating with the Court they would be able to "establish such a liberty by a law as should give them unalterable liberty, the Court dissolving this Parliament and the Court and Dissenters joining in choosing another Parliament. . . ." [7]

In addition to the Court's attempt to sound out Presbyterian and moderate Nonconformist opinion and perhaps to win support through such offers as that suggested by Baber, the King also took steps in August to win Baptist approval. Just as in the case of the Quakers, he made use of his prerogative to stay legal proceedings in cases arising out of statutes against Nonconformity.[8] Finally, in an audience granted to grateful Baptists at the end of August the King reportedly stated that he "would not only give them liberty by his own authority for his life, but have it together with the same for the Papists confirmed by this or another Parliament if their friends would concur," to which they agreed and promised support on the hustings.[9] In brief, the King proposed the very policy of granting religious freedom to Catholics as well as Dissenters which he was to adopt formally and completely in his Declaration of Indulgence of the following spring. Moreover, this group of Baptist petitioners agreed to give the political support that James was to expect and demand after issuing his Declaration.

The split between the Court and the Anglican Church regarding treatment of the Dissenters was accompanied by the split developing among Dissenters over the reception they should give to the Court's overtures and policies. It appears that it was primarily the Quakers and Baptists who were receptive to the earlier royal dispensations and to the plans for a parliament that would remove the penal laws, and as a result they were criticized by many Presbyterians and Congregationalists who wanted nothing to do with "anything that may tend to bring in Popery." [10] However, even among the Baptists there appears to have been a very sharp division, primarily between those who attended Anglican services on occasion and those who would not do so. The strictly nonconforming Baptists who had been petitioners and addressers to the King were "heinously censured . . . by those that go to the Church, and also by some that do not," for some of this latter group had also refused to petition for relief or thank the King for that which he had granted.[11]

At the same time those moderate Dissenters who were occasional or partial Conformists and who did not petition for dispensations or "show their readiness to influence the Parliament, or to choose another" for the purposes he had in mind, suffered the great displeasure of the King. He reportedly was most offended with the Presbyterians and Congregationalists because they would not be "beholden to him for their liberty, but in opposition to him fall in with the Church that has used them so severely." Indeed there were those who became convinced during the latter part of 1686 that the Church took "advantage of his Majesty's displeasure to fall upon and utterly break into pieces all such Dissenters." [12] The attitudes and activities of Anglican justices, local officials, and clergymen were undoubtedly intensified by the rumors and fears that "some fanatics should be put into the Commission for the peace . . . ," for the Court's efforts to remodel local government became apparent during the last few months of the year and made the Church "extraordinarily afraid" that such appointments would be made.[13] Also contributing to Anglican alarm in November was the Court's establishment of a license office where for fifty shillings there could be purchased a family dispensation that would stop all legal proceedings for Nonconformity and that also granted permission for religious services. The Baptists were the primary applicants, while Presbyterians and Congregationalists made little use of the dispensations, probably because they did not want to give countenance to the Court's "assumed power of dispensing," as Morrice had described it. However, some of these Nonconformists took advantage of the situation and began meeting without licenses.[14]

Thus by the late autumn of 1686 the Dissenters had been confronted by most of the essential aspects of the critical situation that was to face them with full impact the following year. However, the pressures and enticements emanating from the Court were as yet relatively mild and uncoordinated, while on the opposite side the efforts of the more moderate Anglicans to win Nonconformist support were barely discernible. In addition, the constitutional issue had not been fully posed to the Dissenters.

There were dramatic changes when the King issued his first Declaration of Indulgence on April 4, 1687. The Dissenters were immediately under pressure from the Court to express their thanks in addresses to the King, and this in turn confronted them with the constitutional issue. Unlike the Indulgence issued by Charles II in 1672, this one made evident the King's intention to obtain parliamentary sanction of his suspension of the penal laws and the Test Act,[15] and thus the constitutional issue was not as decisively one of royal prerogative versus statute law as it had been in 1672. Nevertheless, issuance of the Indulgence was an exercise of royal prerogative; and just as in 1672, any address of thanks by Dissenters would seem to condone the King's action. In addition, the severe prosecution during the preceding five years, climaxed by that for which James himself was responsible following the Monmouth Rebellion, made the relief and freedom brought by the Indulgence much more irresistible in spite of misgivings concerning the King's motives and ends. Thus the Dissenters faced a more complicated and difficult situation than in 1672.

For those who opposed the King's action on constitutional grounds there were two courses of action possible. Either they could refuse to join in an address at all, or they could take care that it avoided an explicit acknowledgment of the dispensing power, while at the same time it emphasized their thanks for the King's intention to obtain parliamentary concurrence and expressed the hope that religious freedom would be made lasting by a statute. The Dissenters who opposed all forms of address were relatively few in number, and in some of these cases religious motives were more compelling than the constitutional issue. However, among these men were such influential leaders as Richard Baxter, and the Presbyterians Dr. Bates and John Howe, as well as the Congregationalist Richard Stretton (former chaplain to Lord Fairfax), and the Baptists William Kiffen and Joseph Stennett.[16] Most of the other responsible leaders of all Nonconformist denominations worked for addresses containing support for parliamentary concurrence. Of the London addresses, both those of the Presbyterian ministers and the Congregationalists expressed their desire that Parliament enact appropriate legislation,[17] while the addresses from both of the national organizations of the Quakers and Baptists called for legislative approval so "that all this may be confirmed unto the present and after ages by law." [18]

Although on a strictly numerical basis there were twice as many addresses that did not mention parliamentary concurrence, this must be weighed against the fact that specific acknowledgment of the royal prerogative cannot be found in any of the approximately eighty addresses emanating from Nonconformist sources and published in the London *Gazette*.[19] This failure to state approval of the royal dispensing power was impressive, for Nonconformists were under particular pressure from royal agents to do so because the King was most eager to obtain support of his prerogative act and not merely to be thanked for the relief which it brought.[20] Indeed, from the viewpoint of the constitutional issue, the overwhelming manner in which the Nonconformists refrained from giving this support was of more significance than the fact that a large number of addresses expressing relief did come from them. As has been known ever since the addresses were drawn up, they were to a considerable degree not spontaneous, but rather the product of official pressure.[21] In brief, therefore, those Nonconformists who did address the King bowed to the pressure to express their thanks for relief, but they were unwilling to give specific support to his prerogative.

In 1687, just as in 1672, Nonconformists in general welcomed the freedom to worship. Indeed, in view of the more stringent and prolonged prosecutions preceding the Indulgence granted by James, there was undoubtedly a more profound sense of gratitude and relief. However, since Catholics were also to be given the freedom of public worship, instead merely of private worship as in 1672, and since they were also to be allowed to hold governmental positions, the Dissenters were far more wary and uneasy than in the previous instance. Ralph Thoresby undoubtedly expressed the feeling of a vast number when he wrote of the Indulgence that "though we dreaded a snake in the grass, we accepted it with due thankfulness"; and he then noted that the first sermon in public worship was preached on the text "that whoever be the instruments, yet the supreme author of all good to his people, is God himself." [22] The "snake in the grass" was clearly the chief source of concern. And the need for the reminder that God was originator of all good probably arose more because the instrument of religious freedom was a Catholic than because he was an English King abrogating parliamentary law.

If the freedom to worship after long deprivation helps to explain the attitude of Thoresby and many other moderate Dissenters, then freedom from the many years of harsh prosecution helps to explain the contentions and actions of those strict Nonconformists who were so relieved that they almost completely overlooked both the Catholic and the constitutional questions. [23] The most famous Nonconformist who gave full support to the King was William Penn, but there were others, such as George Whitehead and the Congregationalist Stephen Lobb. The long years of prosecution, which had hit the Quakers most severely, were obviously an important factor in motivating their two leaders, yet neither this suffering nor previous association and friendly relations with James are sufficient to explain the degree to which Penn became involved. [24] The underlying reason is found in his long-held conviction that the attainment of complete religious liberty and the elimination of religious barriers to political activity and office holding were of transcendent importance. The King's similar convictions and his willingness to use his prerogative offered an opportunity of immense attraction to Penn. In addition colonial proprietorship created other exceedingly strong reasons for cooperation with the Court. Penn's gratitude to James for support in 1681, when he was seeking proprietary rights to Pennsylvania, is well known. More compelling than gratitude was the real possibility that the colony could be lost if the King were displeased or had other reasons to take action; and this was dramatically demonstrated in May, 1686, nearly a year before the first Declaration of Indulgence, when James ordered *quo warranto* proceedings against Pennsylvania and other proprietary colonies. Penn was quick to act, and within a week the King had countered the order for the writ against Pennsylvania. Successful though he was, Roger Morrice noted at the time that "it is like enough he will at latter end ensnare himself by his agency." [25] This he certainly did do, but this threat was only the most immediately compelling of the reasons for Penn's future involvement. [26]

Soon after James II's accession in 1685 the Quaker leaders were busy advocating an indulgence as well as a general pardon. Whitehead even obtained an audience with the King in May, 1685; and a year later, not long before the *quo warranto* writ was issued against Pennsylvania, Penn wrote a warm defense of Charles II's Declaration of Indulgence. Thus his basic position did not shift as a result of the legal proceedings planned by the Crown. During the summer of 1686 Penn travelled to the States General, perhaps as the King's unofficial emissary, and made an effort to gain William of Orange's support for granting religious and civil liberty to Catholics and Dissenters. William would not approve of repealing the Test Acts; however, he readily consented to a repeal of the penal laws and the establishment of religious liberty, but only if enacted by Parliament.[27] This was a most important qualification; and though Penn continued to advocate the use of an initial abrogation by royal prerogative, he also became a strong proponent of parliamentary repeal following a declaration of indulgence. Although he may not have been directly responsible for the clause in the King's Declaration regarding Parliament's concurrence, as has been claimed, he undoubtedly advocated its insertion.[28]

Shortly thereafter he published a plea for parliamentary action and a strong defense of his position on religious liberty, and he either wrote or inspired numerous other pamphlets reiterating his contentions later in the year.[29] However, in all of these works he wrote more of the merits or right of toleration and the need for a secure liberty than he did of the constitutional issue raised by the King's prerogative grant. If the Friends saw a danger in not having the Declaration sanctioned by an act of Parliament, it was, as Whitehead later wrote, because "we did not think our liberty secured to us thereby, any more than it was under the reign of his brother . . . but uncertain and precarious, as it was before, when we had only that King's specious promises and declarations. . . ."[30] Although it was more the permanency or security of religious liberty that was the primary concern of these Quaker leaders, nevertheless there was an oblique recognition of the danger involved in royal suspension of law, and a clear understanding of the value of rights based upon the action of the King, Lords, and Commons together, rather than of the King alone.

Even though a Dissenter did no more than take advantage of

James II's Declaration to worship as he wished, he made himself
vulnerable to the charge that he was giving tacit approval to a
royal act which in effect repealed statutory law, just as in 1672.
Once again, too, there was a defense reminiscent of the one
offered by John Humfrey at that time, for John Howe held that
the penal laws and Test Acts were not laws since God has not
given men authority to make laws against themselves, and Englishmen have not entrusted to their representatives their religion
and their consciences. "We are therefore injuriously reflected on,"
he contended, "when it is imputed to us, that we have by the use
of our liberty, acknowledged an illegal dispensing power." Moreover, he argued that in attending conventicles, just as they had
done when there was no Indulgence, they were being consistent
in their contention that the penal laws were no laws because they
violated the law of God.[31] In brief, he completely agreed with
Humfrey's earlier contention that the Acts of Parliament were
"against the command of God," but that "the King permits what
God bids."[32]

Nevertheless, the reactions of Dissenters in 1687 were different
than in 1672. As has been seen, there was evidence that their
religious leaders were reluctant to support James II's exercise of
the royal prerogative, and this time there were some ministers
who even attacked the King's prerogative grant. Although there
were also addresses of thanks for relief, they contained evidence
of an antipathy to such extensive use of royal power in that none
of them gave explicit support to the prerogative and about half
of them gave pointed endorsement to the statement in the Declaration concerning parliamentary concurrence. Finally, as Roger
Morrice pointed out, the large majority of Dissenters did not
participate in the addresses at all, even though there was pressure to do so.[33] As has also been seen, however, there were two
complications in 1687 that gave a religious motivation for Nonconformist actions and opinions that at first would seem to be
purely the product of parliamentarian constitutional views. First,
the demand for parliamentary concurrence was in many cases
more the outgrowth of a desire for a secure religious liberty than
of a concern for the inviolability of parliamentary law or a belief
that the prerogative had been misused. In addition this time
there was the certain knowledge that it was a Catholic King who
had dispensed with laws and that the "snake in the grass" was in

a real sense James himself. Thus for all those Dissenters who feared Catholicism, and this included a large majority, there was a strong religious motivation for adhering more closely to the traditional parliamentarian position.

The variety of positions taken by the Nonconformists in response to the King's Declaration and policy were accurately appraised at Court by Sunderland during the talks about the next Parliament which followed the King's order dissolving his first Parliament on July 2, 1687. First, there were the Dissenters "who would repeal all of the penal laws against religious worship, but maintain the disabilities for office and Parliament," or in other words, who would retain both the Test Act of 1673 and that of 1678; a second group would allow Catholics to hold governmental offices by repealing the first Test Act, but exclude them from Parliament by retaining the second Act; and a third group would have repealed both Test Acts and trusted to the Oaths of Allegiance and Supremacy to prevent Catholics from sitting in the Commons (though this had not been effective in the past), while permitting them in the Lords. In Sunderland's estimation "most of the fanatics" took the first position; [34] and since they wanted Catholics kept out of all offices, the Dissenters in this group adhered to the position farthest removed from that to which the King hoped to win them.

In spite of his concentrated efforts, James could only be certain of the support of Nonconformists who favored his position that both Test Acts should be repealed by Parliament. Thus in order to carry out royal policy it would be necessary to win additional Nonconformist support, hopefully from the group which wanted the Test Act of 1678 kept in effect, but it appeared that such support would be difficult or impossible to obtain in view of the King's determination to have Catholics eligible to sit in Parliament. It was therefore with some reason that Sunderland was most uneasy and fearful that in spite of the Court's best efforts it might in the end "prove impossible to work through the Dissenters at all." [35] However, at this juncture he would seem to have had less reason to be fearful about obtaining increased Nonconformist support than did the moderate Anglicans and those who favored William of Orange. Not only had the efforts of these Anglicans to win the Dissenters come as a reaction to the Court's efforts, but they had thus far been too tentative, too contradictory, and too spasmodic to remove the distrust and bitterness which prevailed between Anglicans and Nonconformists.

In 1686 Roger Morrice was told by a friend that any prospects of a coalition between Dissenters and the "sober part of the Church" were to be viewed with misgivings. The friend also contended that "if the Prince of Orange would come to the Crown probably he would keep on the laws that he finds upon the Protestant Dissenters, but would not make any new laws against them only, and most certain it is that he will fall in with that party that will most enlarge his power and prerogative, which the Church has always been most apt to do." [36] But in spite of the problems to be faced, Morrice became one of the strongest advocates of a coalition with the moderate Anglicans and a supporter of the Prince of Orange, and during the following two years his large acquaintanceship with both political and religious leaders among the moderate Dissenters and Anglicans placed him in a most advantageous position from which to observe and comment upon Anglican and Dutch efforts to win Nonconformist support, and also from which to exert some influence on very important occasions.

His dual role was clearly apparent during the mission of the Prince of Orange's envoy Everhard van Weede Dykveld in the spring of 1687, for some of the leaders with whom Dykveld made contact reported their conversations to Morrice, and one of them asked him for his opinion of Nonconformist sentiment. Morrice assured him that in case the King died the Dissenters "were universally fixed" for the succession of the Prince and Princess and that they "would inflexibly do all in their power to promote it against all others . . . ," adding that they "only hoped to be set upon equal terms with other subjects by a law." [37] At first Morrice and John Howe were given "all possible assurance" that the Prince would do this, and the Presbyterian leaders were highly impressed by Dykveld's statesmanship and the Prince's interest in them.[38] But Dr. Bates had a later interview with the Stadtholder's envoy in the new library of Dr. Thomas Tenison during which Dykveld stated that although "the Prince would give them some liberty by a law . . . it was his opinion that if ever the Prince came to the throne he would fall for all intents and purposes with the Prelatists. . . ." Understandably the two Dissenters found that the qualified liberty of which the envoy now spoke and the more candid statement of the Prince's probable position created a very different second impression; and Morrice concluded that it gave them "great reason to think he is a man of very much art and inconsistency." [39]

The Dykveld mission therefore did not have the degree of success among Dissenters which has sometimes been attributed to it.[40] Furthermore, old Nonconformist misgivings, criticisms, and doubts regarding the Prince and Princess were to some degree reinforced, including the fears expressed the previous September that the Prince would "fall in with that party that will most enlarge his power and prerogative, which the Church has been most apt to do." [41] Nevertheless, Dykveld may still have had some effect in encouraging and furthering the efforts of Anglicans to persuade Dissenters to come to an understanding with them and thus to deprive the Court of some of that Nonconformist support which it then had. Just before the Declaration of Indulgence was issued on April 4, Nonconformists were surprised by the amount of talk they heard that "sober Churchmen" were now willing to "coalesce with sober Dissenters," and during the next two months some Anglican clergymen went as far as to state in sermons that an understanding with the Nonconformists was for the interest of the Church, and they advised "relaxing and remitting those points of conformity and ceremony that had made the breach. . . ." [42] "It is plain to all mankind," wrote Morrice in a prescient passage, "that a coalition between the sober Conformists and Nonconformists is the only expedient that is within the reach of human prospect to save this nation, together with impunity to those that cannot come within that coalition or comprehension . . . , for this would carry with it the common genus and currents of this nation . . . , and the torrent of the Kingdom would run so strong this way that it would weigh down the Court [and] the King." [43]

Yet there were good reasons to fear that this coalition could not be achieved. Even in April, Dr. Thomas White, Bishop of Peterboro said there was "no danger at all of Popery, but only of the fanatics." [44] By the end of August moderate Dissenters were induced by many reasons to believe the "Hierarchists" were treating with the Court, and they also found that even the most moderate Anglican clergymen "utterly disclaimed not only all hopes but all endeavors after an accommodation with them." [45] Moreover, on the political front there was evidence of a continuing breech in the old alliance between moderate Dissenters and Anglicans, for John Swynfen told Philip Foley, Robert Harley, and others that the "Churchmen must not be trusted." [46] Thus when Halifax's *Letter to a Dissenter* appeared in late August or early September warning Nonconformists they should suspect the Catholics and asking if they would work with the Anglicans, there had been a resurgence of distrust of the Anglican leaders among the moderate Dissenters who most wanted the political and religious coalition Halifax recommended, and this development had occurred because after some approaches to them it then appeared that the Church leaders were reversing their policy. It is therefore not surprising that the effect which Halifax's pamphlet had upon those Dissenters most amenable to his argument was considerably deadened. Edmund Calamy, for example, later wrote that although the *Letter* "came out very seasonably, and was of use," and although Halifax's "cautions were regarded by the wisest part of them," yet there was "uncertainty with what design this application was made to them." In addition there were reasons for Dissenters to think that Halifax had little if any following among Churchmen and Tory leaders, and a few months later to state point blank that in the past Halifax had "most highly disobliged the Protestant Dissenters. . . ." [47]

The fears and doubts concerning Nonconformist support that haunted Sunderland in August, 1687, were not unlike those that moved Halifax to write his *Letter* during the same month. Moreover, it was at this time that the King was also making his progress to and from Bath while his agents were pressing Dissenters to offer addresses of thanks. Such anxiety and activity on both sides made the pressures upon the Dissenters much more intense, and the conflicting forces and admonitions tended to bring perplexity and indecision to some Nonconformists, while at the same time sharpening the divisions that already existed among them. The autumn months were particularly difficult for the moderate Dissenters who feared and opposed alignment with the Court and the Catholics, but who at the same time were apprehensive of a coalition with the Anglicans. The situation was made more pressing by the prospect of a new Parliament. [48]

The Presbyterians and Congregationalists who had previously been members of Parliament were particularly aware of the polit-

ical complexities and ramifications of the moderate Dissenters'
dilemma. As a group they continued to oppose repeal of the Test
Acts, but if they stood for election and refused to go along with
the King's program for repeal they would "expose themselves to
great displeasure," and lose the toleration they were enjoying, as
the Earl of Nottingham observed in a letter to the Prince of
Orange during early September. On the other hand, if they did
not seek election at all they would lose all possibility of influencing policy in matters of critical importance to them and the nation. Nottingham predicted that the Anglican members would
prevail because few Dissenters would stand, but John Swynfen
had already advised the Foleys and Harleys that "those that can
should get into the House" when he was also telling them that
"the Churchmen must not be trusted"; and although they preferred not to be too forward, they acted upon his advice during
the early autumn.[49]

The transcendent political and constitutional importance with
which these political leaders and their associates regarded the
situation facing the country brought Richard Hampden and John
Howe to Swynfen's Staffordshire home for discussions. Young
Robert Harley, who followed after them in early October, on one
of his several visits, reported to his father that the Parliamentary
veteran of nearly fifty years had the conviction that "none but
staunch men are to be trusted." Looking beyond the immediate
political problem, Swynfen viewed the broader perspectives for
the young man who was later to become a preeminent parliamentary leader. "The case is something like [16]60, when honest men
declined to stand," he contended; ". . . to lie still will betray the
interest of England. Every person is now valued according to his
interest and what he can do. The eyes abroad are on this scene
and will accordingly hereafter esteem men by their interest, and
it is to be feared that if the country be deserted now they will fix
their favor on others another time." [50] He was speaking not only
from bitter experience, but also with the knowledge that John
Howe brought from the audience granted to him by William of
Orange prior to his return to England in May.[51] To Swynfen it
seemed that the Dissenters must demonstrate their political
strength and leadership so that they would not lose the favor of
William of Orange and be impotent in the face of Anglican power
if and when he became King.

To other Dissenters the dangers sometimes seemed more apparent than the opportunities, and not all were as certain as Swynfen. Thomas Foley was of mixed reactions, and apparently there was a division of opinion among his associates and friends. He had decided to stand, and at a meeting of political leaders at the Michaelmas sessions in Worcestershire he was proposed as a candidate for knight of the shire by one who was the spokesman for many gentlemen of the County, but in the end he was rejected. Although relieved, he confessed that "if the people thought so to, I should still have a good call to sit . . . but my friends will not let me." With much feeling he wrote that he desired "to do as God would have me, begging my way may be plain before me," and added: "I think we never needed more wisdom from God than now. . . ." [52] Such were the crosscurrents of pressures and reactions which were only beginning to develop for Dissenters.

Opinion was divided upon the best political means to use at this juncture, but there was much agreement among moderate Dissenters upon their basic aims, and these had been long and strongly upheld by those of this group who had sat in Parliament. Many had hoped for comprehension, but failing this they along with other Dissenters wanted religious liberty established by an act of Parliament that would have the status of constitutional law and that would give Catholics only "bare liberty" to worship. More important, they would have Catholics "kept out of the legislative and executive part of the Government," and they were therefore opposed to repeal of either Test Act.[53] And finally, they did not believe the royal prerogative should be used to abrogate parliamentary law. Actually the strength and general prevalence of their convictions were not fully revealed until the next major move was announced by the King, and they then had much to do with the reaction of moderate Dissenters, particularly the Presbyterians. Most important, these convictions helped to bring greater agreement among the moderate Dissenters at that critical juncture, and also between themselves and the moderate Anglicans.

In late October the King promulgated the famous three questions asking deputy lieutenants and justices of the peace whether they would favor repeal of the penal laws and Test Acts if they should be chosen M.P.s, whether they would work for election of M.P.s who would support repeal, and whether they would support a royal declaration for liberty of conscience. As a result he created a crisis for both Dissenters and Anglicans that marked the beginning of a new phase in the developments that eventually led to the Revolution a year later. Dissenters who had previously been receptive to the King's policies came to have serious misgivings about his motives and ends, and even some of those who had given him strong support became hesitant and doubtful. The King's earlier moves to change officials in the corporations and the commission of the peace had been limited and had not sufficiently dramatized the fact that Dissenters were sharing royal favor and appointments with Catholics. However, the three questions and the accompanying directives to the Lord Lieutenants made it vividly clear that the King was beginning a vigorous and thorough campaign to obtain a parliament packed with members who before election would have committed themselves to the repeal of the penal laws and the Test Acts, and that he would replace local officials refusing to support such candidates by men who would do so. The full impact of this move was felt by the politically active Dissenters and Anglicans at all levels of government as they weighed the answers to be given when they appeared before the Lord Lieutenants. First reports of the replies given by the Dissenters during November indicated that there was a surprising amount of Nonconformist opposition to the removal of the tests and that this feeling was very strong and widespread among the moderate Dissenters, particularly those who conformed occasionally and thereby made themselves eligible for governmental positions in accord with the first Test Act. James Johnston, who had just been sent to England with Henry Sidney to assist him as a secret agent of William of Orange, and who quickly developed close relations with Penn, Sunderland, Halifax, John Hampden, and other key leaders, reported that the Court was extremely angry with the Dissenters and that the King "complained heavily of the Presbyterians" for their answers to the questions. To his certain knowledge, Johnston stated in an intelligence report, even "such of them as declare themselves for taking off the test etc. have promised their voices to men who have told them they will never consent to it." [54]

It seems probable that it was at this juncture that William Penn wrote an unpublished essay dated 1687 in which he took a completely different position regarding the Test Acts from that which he defended in his published pamphlets. Instead of holding that they should be repealed, Penn wrote that he thought it was "the true interest of all Dissenters . . . to keep up the test . . . ," and he even went so far as to state that he would "rather let the penal laws stand as they are than do anything that may tend towards repeal of the test." [55] However, it was still his hope that there could be repeal of the penal laws, and in November when it seemed highly unlikely that the King would have sufficient support for repeal of the Test Acts, Penn and the other Nonconformist royal favorite tried "to prevail with His Majesty to consent to taking off penal laws without the test," but James was adamant in his refusal.[56] Johnston found Penn "down a little" as a result of his failure; but of much greater importance was his report in the same letter that Penn's "own people tell him that the scene opens too fast on him." [57] In addition, a move probably inspired by the Court to check the decline in Nonconformist support only revealed other evidence of a rift between the Dissenters who had been cooperative and the Catholic leaders, for van Citters reported that each approved as little as the other of a conference which had been planned "to hit on some further expedients through which means to understand each other. . . ." [58]

While responsible leaders among the Quakers began to have doubts, and some of them along with other strict Nonconformists were moved to resist royal pressure for the first time, those Dissenters who had previously been most opposed to the King were both apprehensive and deeply mystified by his plans. "None of my acquaintance," wrote Morrice, "can yet comprehend any reason great enough to bottom so great a revolution upon as this is. To say their general design is to bring in Popery is to say nothing, for that is acknowledged; but the question is how these means can conduce to this end, that is to say how giving liberty to the Protestant Dissenters and letting them into the Government can answer to this end." These moderate Dissenters saw "nothing but inavoidable desolation and destruction" if the Court succeeded in its attempts either by a law "or such other new measures as they shall . . . think fit to take. . . ." But they believed this could be avoided if "it should please God to incline the Conformists to a good understanding with the Nonconformists so that by their interest and number they would easily weigh down all the extremes both Papists and Sectaries." [59]

By the end of November some of the moderate Dissenters and a few of the prominent Anglican clergymen became much concerned that they were not cooperating to meet the threat inherent in the King's moves.[60] As a result a revealing meeting was arranged by Dr. Nicholas Stratford between Dr. William Lloyd, the Bishop of St. Asaph, and Dr. Bates. These two leaders agreed upon "the absolute necessity of a good understanding or coalition," and recognized that its importance was evident in the Crown's absolute opposition to it. However, even in this atmosphere of agreement Dr. Bates stated that "considering how falsely they had been dealt with at first about [16]60, and how violently they had been dealt with afterwards, few of them escaping prisons and almost none of them distresses and fines, it was reasonable and proper for him to say only this, that now there could be only a concord in desire and affection." Cooperation Bates could envision, but not comprehension. And most important at the moment was cooperation in their endeavors to keep the Test Acts. The Bishop agreed, but unfortunately he too had a major complaint. He wanted Nonconformist meetings during Church hours to cease; quite predictably Bates declared this would be impossible.[61]

Though the two groups represented by these leaders could agree upon the Test Acts, the critical source of division between them at this juncture was the question of the penal laws. "The truth is," Johnston reported to the States General in mid-December, "Churchmen are for penal laws and there is no reasoning with such as pretend to speak in God's name," [62] an observation sufficiently true of the leaders on both sides to explain many of the past and present difficulties in the way of an Anglican-Nonconformist agreement. However, political developments were beginning to have their effect upon religious leaders. At the same time that Johnston was making his observation about churchmen, the Dean, Chapter and Church of Lichfield agreed among themselves that John Swynfen, recently endorsed as a parliamentary candidate by Lord Weymouth, was "the fittest man to serve them"; and that in the past they had been mistaken about him. Now they had information that he had been against Charles I's death, and that he had "carried in all Parliaments with great moderation and temper. . . ." [63] Having believed at the end of the previous summer that Churchmen must not be trusted, Swynfen may well have had some reservations about his new supporters, yet the fact re-

mains that moderate Anglicans had begun to make some significant approaches to Dissenters at the very end of 1687.

For some time there had been Court concern that such a rapprochement might develop, and leading Nonconformist supporters of the Court had already published pamphlets in an effort to
prevent such a development. Without question the most effective
argument to use in dissuading Dissenters was that old enemies
could not be trusted, and that the "King had never broke his word
[while] the Church has, and . . . in this very point of Indulgence." [64] However, on this matter, the Presbyterians were also
open to attack. In another pamphlet, supposedly by Penn, readers
were reminded that in 1672 the Dissenters sitting in Parliament
concurred in an address to Charles II requesting that he withdraw
the Declaration of Indulgence. By holding that these men were
"trying to play the same game over again" Penn played on deep-
seated fears of the strict Nonconformists who wanted complete
toleration rather than comprehension. Likewise effective was his
earlier warning to Anglicans that they would not want the Presbyterians in their chair, having "tasted enough of that regiment to
be once wise." [65]

Such arguments had strong appeal, but developments which
were to make the old enemies seek similar ends occurred rapidly
in December and January, and thus new arguments came to replace the old. The focal issue facing those desirous of a coalition
of moderate Anglicans and Dissenters was the question of the
penal laws, and moves made by the King and the Prince of Orange
were primarily responsible for the more rapid shift in politico-
religious alignments. Reports concerning reactions to the Court's
proposed actions, as well as to those actually taken, made the
King realize that it would be necessary to use more than arguments to prevent the development of such an opposition coalition.
Because of the failure to gain the initial support he sought from
moderate Dissenters and from all Anglicans in answer to the three
questions, the King was angry and reportedly considered such
drastic measures as withdrawing the benefits of his Indulgence
from Dissenters not favoring repeal of the Test Acts, and also
requiring clergymen to recognize his dispensing power in a Convocation of the Clergy under pain of losing their livings. However,
the rumors of these proposals which circulated among Presbyterians and Anglicans most interested in a coalition only made

them more convinced that not only must the Test Acts remain, but in addition the penal laws must be repealed; and others were attracted to this position.[66] At the same time such Presbyterian leaders as Richard and John Hampden were "much sollicited" by the Court, which made them "great offers" if they would engage themselves, but both refused to respond.[67]

Undoubtedly an important factor in explaining the measures James was reported to be considering, as well as the overtures made to the Hampdens and their response, was the advance knowledge they all had of an important move made by the Prince of Orange. Both the King and John Hampden had seen a manuscript copy of the famous letter authorized by William and written by Grand Pensionary Fagel in which it was announced that the Prince and Princess favored toleration and thought that Parliament should repeal the penal laws but not the Test Acts. Upon hearing this read to him the King said that they "made a great mistake if they took him to be such a fool as to separate the test and penal laws," while John Hampden welcomed the letter because he believed "it would intimidate the scoundrels among the Dissenters and encourage the right people and would cause them to like the Calvinistical Prince. . . ."[68] Even more reassuring to some of the London Presbyterian leaders was the presence of the Dutch agent James Johnston, who had shown Fagel's letter to John Hampden in early December and who may have been partially responsible for Morrice's somewhat earlier conviction that the Dutch would invade England if Catholicism were entirely successful in Church and State. If this were to happen, Morrice optimistically predicted, "great numbers from about London were very likely to go meet them when they land."[69]

Although Johnston was incorrect in believing that all of the Dissenters would greet Fagel's letter favorably if it were published, he was right in his conviction that "the generality of the Nation will be pleased with it."[70] Judging by the actions of the Court, the King and his advisers shared this opinion far more than they wished they did. First a report emanating from Court sources appeared in the newsletters erroneously stating that the Prince and Princess of Orange had declared they favored abrogation of the Test Acts as well as the penal laws; and then when William countered by authorizing the publication of an English translation of Fagel's *Letter,* Government authorities launched a vigorous campaign to seize all copies and deny its authenticity. These measures were temporarily very effective in prohibiting the circulation of the pamphlet, particularly outside of London, and they created more enduring skepticism concerning its origin.[71]

Nevertheless, the pamphlet or news of its contents gained sufficient currency in London to have an influence upon some of the Anglicans who had previously opposed removal of the penal laws and upon some of the Dissenters who had favored repeal of the Test Acts. True, there had been some previous indications that a few of the more staunch and unbending Nonconformists and Anglicans had been shifting from these views, but the published *Letter* gave the movement more strength. Although Anglicans of the sort whom Johnston described to Bishop Burnet as the "best kind of zealots" still would have preferred to retain the penal laws, and although they feared that Dissenters might take advantage of an improved status to retaliate for past treatment, they realized that the policy enunciated in the *Letter* would help win Dissenters who had been supporting the Court. They therefore were favorably inclined to a remedy that according to Johnston they otherwise would have regarded as a great evil.[72]

Contributing to the shift of position among Anglicans of this group were the continued reports of the King's hostility to the Church and the general fear of Catholicism.[73] In addition, during an autumn visit to England Dr. William Stanley, Anglican Chaplain to the Princess of Orange, had assured Anglican clergymen that the Prince would adhere to the Church of England. He described the Prince as "invincibly attached to the slightest bagatelle of the ceremonies of the Church," and he also created the impression that the Prince would uphold the penal laws. Although Stanley did much to win support for William among the zealots in the Church, moderate Anglicans were most disturbed, and when information concerning his statements reached the Dissenters it also had adverse results. Dr. Edward Fowler was especially critical of him and worked vigorously among the several thousand Dissenters in his Parish to correct the effect of the chaplain's statements. But there were other Anglican clergymen who continued to circulate Stanley's views.[74] Earlier attempts to create favorable impressions among the Dissenters concerning the religious views of the Prince and particularly of the Princess of Orange had largely failed because of the "high Prelatical" character of Stanley and her other chaplain, and thus his appearance on the scene prior to the publication of the English translation of Fagel's *Letter* only revived earlier impressions, and they were in turn re-inforced by the Court's denial of the authenticity of the *Letter*.[75] Consequently, when it was published in January the primary question among the moderate Dissenters, who were already of the same views presented in the pamphlet, was whether or not it was authentic; and many asked Johnston that they be assured that Fagel wrote it upon order of their Highnesses. Once they knew this, Johnston wrote Burnet, they would rely on it absolutely, for it was "all they could ask for during another reign, if there is no way then to get minds together," that is if a combination of com-prehension and toleration were not possible.[76]

Among the more strict Nonconformists the *Letter* had an im-portant impact even before they received final proof of its authen-ticity. There were those who had told Johnston that they had been so desirous of doing away with the penal laws that they were willing to pay the price of also having the Test Acts repealed. They assured him they had supported the King not because they trusted the Catholics, but because they thought there would be no other opportunity to obtain religious freedom; for these Non-conformists believed that the Church would give such strong support to the Prince and Princess as successors that they would have to continue the penal laws in case the Church so wished. However, since the *Letter* gave hope of penal law repeal under William and Mary, they would not "hurry to eliminate" these laws and thus pay the price of having the Test Acts repealed too.[77]

Although the potentially receptive Nonconformists were some-what restrained in their very first reactions to Fagel's *Letter,* and zealous Anglicans were rather reluctant to concede that the penal laws should be repealed, it was evident to van Citters toward the end of January that the Anglicans and Dissenters were "uniting more and more" against the plans of the immoderate Catholics and King and "admonishing each other to constancy, in which they were not a little encouraged by the declarations of their Highnesses, concerning the liberty of conscience and abolition of the penal laws. . . ."[78] Thomas Heywood concurred, and hearing that Church leaders had said the Dissenters must either stick with them on the questions of the penal laws and Test Acts or be undone, he exuberantly wrote, "yea tis verily thought this will be an occasion of a greater union amongst both parties then hath been: this is *Digitus dei. . . ."* [79]

At Court during January there was discouragement accompanied by great debates on future policy, as well as renewed efforts. Penn was much involved, and he discussed the developments in considerable detail with Johnston a number of times, on one occasion inviting the Dutch agent for dinner and continuing the conversation until 2:00 A.M. Although he recognized the obstacles at Court, including a "Superior Council which did everything," he was determined "that they should not make a fool of him." He staked his hopes upon convincing the King that he should summon a Parliament, and upon working with the Catholic moderates to persuade James that one step should be taken at a time, in other words that the penal laws should be repealed "while leaving the affair of the test aside," or at least that if the Test Acts were repealed there then should be a provision or an "expedient" that Catholics not sit in the House of Commons.[80] Deeply committed to these endeavors though he was, perhaps the possibility of another course crossed Penn's mind momentarily, for he asked Johnston whether the Prince of Orange was really a friend of the Dissenters. Doing his best to win Penn's support and dissuade him from persisting in his efforts at Court, Johnston assured him that if William ever came to England he would follow the policy stated in Fagel's *Letter.* The Dutch agent ardently wished Penn could extricate himself from a bad situation, for though he had good intentions "he was dealing with people who were weak or . . . acting in bad faith." Penn admitted this "with much regret," but believed he should continue his efforts, stating that if he failed he planned to go to Pennsylvania—his country in the Indies as Johnston called it. The Quaker leader believed that James "was the best man in the world but unfortunate." Then in a statement that does much to explain his relationship with the King and the Court, Penn declared: "I would like to prevent . . . by risking myself, that things should go to extremities." [81] Johnston believed that in general Penn was having this effect, for in appraising his influence the Dutch agent wrote:

[Penn] does good with one hand, and harm with the other; however, I believe that things will not go as well when he will no longer be mixed up in them. He placates His Majesty; he follows the plans of violent people, just as these people follow his; it is so much time gained. The truth is that the Papists have neither the heart nor the hands, without the Dissenters.[82]

According to Penn the King was highly perturbed over the effect that Fagel's *Letter* would have upon the Dissenters, saying that his "greatest enemies . . . were not in a position to do him such great harm considering his designs." [83] Partly from Penn and partly from another Court source Johnston also learned that the King had said that if William favored the Dissenters even a little bit he would have them all for him, since both their interest and inclination led them to support him, and since they liked the Prince and his family as much as they hated his own.[84] Believing that the Nonconformists' support was essential, James renewed efforts to win them to his position and to split them from the Anglicans by such maneuvers as having Lobb circulate information that "the Church had been with him, and had offered to take off the penal laws and the test from the Papists if they might be left on the Protestant Dissenters, but he would be true to his Declaration and not comply with them." The Hierarchists denied the overture "most peremptorily," and Morrice believed it probable that the proposition had been made only unofficially by a few Churchmen in the name of the Church.[85] This interpretation and the strong denial of those whom Morrice called the Hierarchists indicated a disposition on both sides to resist the efforts of those who would prevent the development of a coalition between moderates among the Dissenters and Anglicans.

In another move designed at the least to establish contact with moderate Dissenters and supporters of the Prince of Orange, the King summoned John Howe, and he was conducted to Court by Penn for a two-hour secret audience on at least one occasion. Johnston and London Presbyterian leaders were highly concerned, for Howe had been cooperating with the Dutch agent to some extent and had also been in correspondence with Burnet. Johnston had an investigation made by John Hampden whose advice he had sought previously and who performed special services for him at least from the time of this incident, apparently with the approval of the Dutch Government.[86] Confused at first and then angry, Howe pleaded in his defense that before he had left the States General in May, 1687, the Prince of Orange had advised him to see the King if he were invited to do so. Moreover, he had received the same advice when he had gone into the country for the express purpose of consulting with Richard Hampden, apparently after having received the King's invitation to come to Court—an overture which Hampden himself still refused to accept.[87] Whatever Howe's response had been at Court, the King and Penn failed in their effort.

Meanwhile Penn once again sought to persuade James to moderate his position, and early in February when Johnston had been with Penn, just after the latter had come from the King and Sunderland, he reported that the Quaker leader was "more full of hopes then ever he was that he will carry his business, I mean have the penal laws taken off and the test let alone [in] whole or in part; and for such parts of the test as shall be . . . taken off, equivalents shall be offered that all the nation will accept. . . ." Indeed Penn was "so full of hopes that he said he doubted not but before a year went over, the King and the Prince of Orange should live in a perfect good understanding." [88]

Penn's efforts to prevent extremities and to attain concord by seeking the adoption of a generally acceptable solution were characteristic of Quakerism. But the compelling considerations which led him to this course of action were more practical and immediate. The reaction to the King's policies and actions since November, 1687, made it clear that Court attempts to obtain Parliamentary repeal of the Test Acts would seriously jeopardize repeal of the penal laws and the establishment of religious toleration by parliamentary enactment. A fully legal and therefore more secure possession of the right to worship as they pleased was much more cherished by Quakers than a repeal of the religious tests for office holders and members of Parliament. Moreover, there was the much increased tension which had recently developed in the relations between the King and the Prince of Orange, initially because James was furious with William for having the English translation of Fagel's *Letter* published and circulated throughout the country in large quantities. This was, after all, a bold move to win the King's subjects to the view that the Test Acts should remain law, and thus a direct attack upon a most vital royal policy. The ensuing dispute between the two heads of state over the withdrawal of the six English regiments in the United Provinces therefore had ominous implications, and by early Feb-

ruary it was beginning to harden into the impasse that brought
them to the verge of war by the middle of March.[89] Thus Penn
had reason to feel highly apprehensive and to declare, as he had
to Johnston, that he hoped he could make it possible for the two
rulers to live in peace.

With religious toleration as well as both domestic and foreign
peace at stake it becomes more understandable why the Quaker
political leader had worked so vigorously since November to persuade the King to let the tests stand in whole or in part, even
though at the same time in his published—though anonymous—
pamphlets he was an advocate of complete repeal of the Test
Acts. This still remained his ultimate goal, and he had by no
means abandoned his hope that they would in the end be abolished.[90] In bowing to the exigencies of the moment he was being
realistic and seeking to attain his most important goals of religious
freedom and the conditions conducive to its survival at a time
when they were both in jeopardy. However, Penn was certainly
not realistic in hoping that James would actually alter his policy
regarding the Test Acts. William's propaganda thrust into James
II's realm had made him obdurate. Yet on occasion he was willing
to seem amenable to compromise, apparently thinking he could
gain some Nonconformist support as a result. Thus Johnston was
confident that the King had given Penn reason to feel optimistic,
but he had reason to doubt the King's willingness to change his
real position on the Test Acts. The Dutch agent had already been
told by Silius Titus, after this former Presbyterian had been summoned to Court late in January, that James had indicated he
wanted Catholics to be able to sit in the House of Commons. But
on the weekend of February 4, when Penn was so optimistic, Titus
reported to the Dutch agent that although the Court had been
considering propositions for equivalents or expedients in place of
the test, "now they are quite off that bottom that they call equivalents. . . ."[91] Johnston informed his government that he did not
know how to reconcile these reports, but he also implied that the
King was misleading Penn—and in this he was certainly correct.

This instance in which the King allowed it to be understood
that he might change his views on the Test Acts was not isolated.
A similar case occurred within the next fortnight when support
for leaving the Test Act of 1673 in force came from the "old Sectaries," who were members of the committee that had been sit-

ting in London to assist in the selection of persons fit to serve in corporations and on the commission of the peace.[92] With some audacity they informed the King they could not concur in letting Catholics into governmental offices. Although James did not make a formal reply, the two men who served as King's agents to the committee reported that he said he would "rest satisfied . . . taking off the penal laws and continuing on of the test." Moreover, the agents stated that the King had made his statement in "plain words [and] as they understood it with an intention that they should propagate it." [93] However, the back-stairs manner in which the King chose to circulate his statement stamped it as a stratagem rather than a change in policy. As such, its impact could only have been slight at best, even upon those who desired such a change. In addition the position taken by the "old Sectaries" on the committee charged with reorganizing corporations and the commission of the peace was another indication that some of the more strict Nonconformists were gravitating toward the views of Presbyterians and moderate Anglicans.

Thus moderate Dissenters remained uninfluenced by the confused and misdirected royal efforts during the first month or so of the year. However, the real test facing the King and his followers was whether or not their major policies could check the continuing development of an opposition coalition. The interrogations of the Lord Lieutenants which continued during the early months of the year were followed by the work of the royal agents who were sent into the counties in April to discover the "right" candidates for Parliament and the amount of support there would be for them in an election. The reports of both contained indications which from the Court's point of view were ominous. The conditional and evasive replies of most Anglicans to the three questions which are contained in the Lord Lieutenants' reports have long been recognized for what they were—clear evidence of resistance to Court pressure and policy. At the same time there was evidence that among the Nonconformists there was also resistance and opposition. "The Dissenters were divided," wrote Lord Granville concerning those in Cornwall: "some were positive [favoring repeal of the penal laws and the tests]; others [were] doubtful, desiring that the questions might be debated by a free parliament, and in case a reasonable expedient or equivalent could be found they were ready to serve his Majesty in all things, which was also the unanimous answer of those of the Church of England."[94] The pattern set by the earliest returns from Dissenters in November still persisted. Most Presbyterians and most of the occasional conformists among the other Nonconformist groups opposed repeal of the Test Acts, and they therefore usually gave conditional or sometimes negative answers to the three questions. On the other hand Quakers, and the strict Nonconformists among the Baptists and Congregationalists usually gave support to the King.[95] In fact the royal agents who were sent into eight counties searching for parliamentary candidates and political supporters reported that the members of these three Nonconformist groups were "unanimously agreed to elect such members of Parliament, as will abolish these tests and laws," while usually comment upon the Presbyterians is pointedly missing.[96]

However, both the statement that there was unanimous support among three Nonconformist groups and the implication that there was little or none from the Presbyterians must be qualified. The feeling that Penn had become too involved in supporting royal policies, which had been expressed by some Quakers at the end of 1687, had spread and become much stronger within the Society of Friends during the spring as he continued to assist in the King's campaign to gain a favorable Parliament.[97] Division developed within the Society over the matter of participating in electoral activities and of accepting offices. By June, 1688, the question had become a major issue and was discussed in the Yearly Meeting when Penn sought official approval and encouragement of political activity. George Fox was the leading spokesman in opposition to Penn, and he was successful in opposing the discussion itself as well as the adoption of any official position on the matter. However, quietism had by no means become dominant, for without any official statement it still would be possible for Quakers to participate in political activity, and there was some explicit official support for voting in elections.[98] Thus even among the Quakers, who as a group had probably been the strongest Nonconformist supporters of repealing the penal laws and the Test Acts, there was divided opinion as to how politically active and involved Friends should become in support of the King. Moreover, there were probably Quakers who along with Penn had modified their position concerning repeal of the Tests and believed that it was wise not to press for this goal at that juncture.

Opposition to repealing the tests had also spread to some extent among the Congregationalists and to a lesser degree among the Baptists, appealing particularly to those few who were occasional conformists.[99] Thus there was some division and lack of unanimity in support of the King's policies among all the more strict Nonconformist groups.

The problem concerning the Presbyterians and the relatively few Congregationalists who conformed occasionally is more complicated and politically far more important. Although the King's agents visiting the eight counties in the spring apparently did not find such men promising much support of royal policies, the fact that a good many were regarded by the agents as "right" candidates for the House of Commons would seem to indicate that more support was being given than had been promised. However, it should be emphasized that the agents also approved a considerable number of candidates who were Anglicans. This immediately suggests that their recommendation did not necessarily mean that a proposed candidate actually favored the King's program at the time, or that after election he would have supported repeal of the Test Acts as well as the penal laws.

It should not be surprising that the King's agents did recommend a considerable number of moderate Anglicans. In making their selection of candidates they relied heavily upon Nonconformist advice and approval, and for two decades Dissenters had been supporting selected moderate Anglicans on the hustings, while the Presbyterians and the few Congregationalists who sat in Parliament had worked with these Anglicans in opposition to the Court and in their efforts to obtain legislation giving Nonconformists religious freedom and the right to hold governmental offices. Moreover, during the most crucial and bitterly fought constitutional conflict throughout this whole period—the Exclusion Crisis—these two wings of the parliamentary opposition became well fused, and received overwhelming support from all segments of Nonconformity throughout the country. Although largely destroyed during the years 1682–1687, the coalition of moderate Dissenters and Anglicans was once again emerging in the spring of 1688, and nothing better demonstrates this than the fact that of the sixty candidates for Parliament who appear to have been proposed or backed by the Dissenters and also accepted by the King's agents in April as "right," there were twenty-six known to have been Anglicans and twenty known Presbyterians or Congregationalists.

But the resurgence of this coalition was not the only development which had ominous implications for those concerned with the King's policies. Among these two groups of candidates that his agents recommended in the spring there were twelve Anglicans and ten Presbyterians or Congregationalists who had been members of the House of Commons in May, 1679, and nine of the twelve Anglicans voted for the Exclusion Bill while all ten of the Presbyterian-Congregationalist group were Exclusionists (see Table 1).[100] In other words nearly one-third of these sixty candidates were old Exclusionists, and they were drawn almost equally from the Anglican and Presbyterian-Congregationalist wings of the parliamentary opposition which had faced Charles II. As a group these candidates along with the fourteen other Anglican candidates having Nonconformist backing would have resisted repeal of the Test Acts, and it is probable that most of the re-

TABLE 1

Parliamentary Candidates Supported by Nonconformists and Recommended or Accepted by the King's Agents in April, 1688

|  | Dissenters | Anglicans | Religion Undetermined | Totals |
|---|---|---|---|---|
| M.P.s in May, 1679 | 10 | 12 |  | 22 |
| Other M.P.s 1661–1689 | 3 | 11 | 1 | 15 |
| Not M.P.s 1661–1689 | 7 | 3 | 10 | 20 |
| Unidentified |  |  | 3 | 3 |
| Totals | 20[a] | 26[b] | 14 | 60 |

[a] Although the King's agents did not explicitly state that a good number of the Presbyterian-Congregationalist candidates were supported by Dissenters, it may be assumed that they did have the backing of either the moderate or the strict Nonconformists, though not always both.

[b] In the cases of seven Anglican candidates the King's agents did not explicitly state that they had Nonconformist backing, but there is indirect evidence that the Dissenters either proposed or gave support to these candidates.

maining fourteen whose religion is unknown would have taken the same position, thus the re-emerging parliamentary coalition of moderate Anglicans and moderate Dissenters would have constituted the opposition to Court policy.

There was one respect in which the developing coalition was weaker than it had been during the Exclusion Parliaments and therefore one source of hope for James. Because of the division among Dissenters over the repeal of the Test Acts, there was not the same general support throughout all groups of Nonconformists for moderate Anglican and Presbyterian or Congregationalist candidates as there had been during the reign of Charles II. In the spring of 1688, for example, there were instances in which the King's agents reported that the Presbyterians and moderate Churchmen were supporting the same candidate, while other Dissenters and the Catholics in the same place were backing a different candidate.[101] Divided though Nonconformists were, such alignments provide an additional indication that many candidates who had been reported "right" by the King's agents because they had Nonconformist support were in fact not in favor of repealing the Test Acts. Indeed this opposition to repeal of the Tests was probably the very reason why Anglican, Presbyterian, and Congregationalist candidates received support from moderate Dissenters.

An examination of the statements and actions of the Presbyterians and the few Congregationalist candidates approved by the King's agents in April reveals that their positions on the King's program and their tactics under questioning by the Lord Lieutenants were very similar to the Anglican candidates. For example, the Exclusionist and possible Presbyterian Thomas Reynell consented to the first two questions "provided the Protestant religion can be secured," and at the same time he reportedly made a speech against concurring with the King's wishes. Similarly, Ambrose Barnes would allow the Catholics no more than religious toleration. Nevertheless, the King himself intervened to give Barnes backing as a candidate, and his agents considered Reynell "right" in April, just as they did most of the Anglicans who gave similar answers if they were at the same time supported by the moderate Dissenters.[102]

In a separate category were the cases of several leading Presbyterian members of former Parliaments, and they were of much significance. Although John Swynfen was not recommended by the King's agents presumably because he was "superannuated," his prior record and particularly his outspoken views of the previous year made clear his opposition to the King's program, and this could well have been another important factor in the agents' decision.[103] Also not recommended were Sir John Maynard, Hugh Boscawen, and Richard Hampden. Regardless of the reasons for the agents' failure to recommend these former members, the King had obviously either failed to win or had not sought the support of the four most aggressive and influential political leaders among the moderate Dissenters who had sat in the House of Commons.

Early in March Sunderland had described the Court's problems with unusual candor in Cabinet Council. Since the Anglicans were utterly estranged, he pointed out, the Court's hopes rested upon the Dissenters who must therefore compose a majority in the new Parliament; and if the Dissenters became estranged then the whole kingdom would be united in opposition, and the Catholics would not be strong enough to form a counterbalance.[104] Most important, he recommended that the calling of Parliament be delayed until the autumn because there was inadequate support from the Dissenters at the time. It was after winning the King to his position that the special royal agents were appointed and sent into eight counties to look for parliamentary candidates, and as their reports were submitted Sunderland's astuteness and accuracy became most evident. It was clear that the King and his advisers were "not finding their expectations answered by the Dissenters," as both Halifax and the Dutch Ambassador reported to William.[105]

But this was not all. As has already been seen, the King's efforts to obtain control of local governments and Parliament through the Dissenters had brought developments which could only have caused much concern at Court. Even among the strict Nonconformists, from whom the King had received almost all of his support for repeal of the Tests, there had been some recent and highly significant cases of shifting to the position of the moderate Dissenters who regarded the Tests as most desirable safeguards, notable examples being the Nonconformist members of the very committee which was charged with reorganization of corporations and the commission of the peace. Most serious, however, was the increasing evidence that the King's major policies were not only failing to check the continuing development of an opposition coalition, but that they were actually contributing to the closer political cooperation between the moderates among the Dissenters and the Anglicans.

The King and his advisers could not have been fully aware of the extent to which these trends had developed, nor of the degree to which some Presbyterian and Congregationalist political leaders had gone in their opposition to royal policies. Nevertheless, they did realize that the policies that first began to emerge in the spring of 1686 had since then failed to win a sufficient number of adherents among the Nonconformists, and that this failure had occurred largely because of resistance among the moderate Dissenters. A new and major effort had to be made if they were to win Nonconformist support sufficient to their ends. It was quickly forthcoming, and concomitantly there came developments leading to momentous results in the history of the nation as well as of the Nonconformists.

# CHAPTER X

## Dissent and the Revolution, 1688–1689

During the spring of 1688 James II made two major moves in his renewed campaign to win Nonconformist support for his program, and the consequences were far-reaching. Instead of attracting moderate Dissenters and thus destroying the coalition which was just emerging with the moderate Anglicans, the King's Second Declaration of Indulgence and his following Order in Council confronted these two religious groups with a new crisis which only drove them closer together. As a result moderate Dissenters were presented with new and far more acceptable opportunities to attain their religious and political goals than those which James had offered them. In addition they found themselves in the mainstream of developments leading to the Revolution of 1688. But the same cannot be said of the Nonconformists who had previously supported the King and who found his new efforts sufficiently appealing to make them overlook the fears aroused by the birth of the Catholic heir to the throne in June.

Although the new Declaration of Indulgence issued April 27 was largely a restatement of the First Declaration, there was one most important difference between the two. Instead of a passing reference to an intention to have Parliament concur in his prerogative action, this time the King proclaimed: ". . . we have resolved to use our utmost endeavors to establish liberty of conscience on such just and equal foundations as will render it unalterable . . ."; and to this end he asked that such members of Parliament be chosen "as may do their parts to finish what we have begun. . . ." [1] A toleration established by parliamentary law had long been sought by Dissenters, particularly by the Presbyterian and Congregationalist members of Parliament, and it is possible that the King's new emphasis upon legislative action would have increased his Nonconformist support. However, any Court hopes that this would happen were largely destroyed by the sequence of events which began just one week later with the issuance of the Order in Council of May 4 directing that the Second Indulgence be read in all Anglican Churches.

Anglican clergymen and churchmen reacted to the Order with alarm, and during the many consultations and conferences which ultimately led to the Petition of the Seven Bishops on May 18, two highly important developments occurred.[2] When some apprehension was expressed that Nonconformists might be antagonized and driven to support the King if Anglican clergymen opposed the Declaration and refused to read it as directed, some of their representatives approached leading moderate Dissenters to discover what their reaction would be if the Anglican clergy did follow this course, but at the same time attacked the legality of the dispensing power. Dr. Edward Fowler, who seems to have taken the lead in these overtures, approached his friend Roger Morrice who first of all supplied him with a paper containing arguments why the Anglicans should not read the Declaration, a major one being that it was "most heinously criminal to publish the Prince's private will and pleasure against his legal and incontrovertible will," for the "dispensing power . . . overthrows the very Constitution of the Government." Morrice later reported that in answer to the "great inquiry" made by the Anglican clergymen they "received full satisfaction" that Dissenters "would be very well satisfied" with the refusal to read the Declaration if the Anglicans "would come up to a national temperament, and keep the Papists out of the Government, and concur to a due liberty to others; this gave them great encouragement and to it they very readily concurred."[3]

Whether or not there was some overstatement in Morrice's last description of the Anglican reaction, it is true the Church leaders' decision against reading the Declaration was not made until after they were assured of the moderate Dissenters' support in this course of action.[4] Moreover, the first draft of what was to become the Petition of the Seven Bishops was drawn up within a day or so, and it gave recognition to the Dissenters' desires for a new religious settlement by stating that the Anglican clergymen were "willing to come to such a temper as shall be thought fit when that matter shall be considered and settled in Parliament and

Convocation," which was the same phrasing used in the Petition presented to the King on May 18.[5] Thus instead of driving Dissenters and Anglicans apart as he had intended, James had given them reason to draw closer.[6] Indeed, as a result of the moderate Dissenters' willingness to support the Bishops in their refusal to read the Declaration, they found the Anglican leaders willing to commit themselves to a religious accommodation that looked toward comprehension and toleration. The cautious phrasing of the Petition indicated that it was more a commitment to consider such an accommodation than a promise to bring it into being. Nevertheless, a tacit agreement had been reached between the moderate Anglicans and Dissenters.[7]

Little did the Nonconformists participating in these efforts realize what Royal pressure they themselves were then to experience, partially in retaliation for "their misbehavior of holding afresh with the English Church," [8] but also because the King had counted on widespread Nonconformist support. Within the same week the Dutch agent James Johnston reported it had been decided at Court that the Dissenters should also be ordered to read the Declaration of Indulgence in their meetings, but to the surprise of the King and his advisers they encountered resistance. Some ministers were already prepared not to do so, and Johnston was "sure many of them will not. . . ." However, before the order was given Roger Morrice "used all means in his power to prevent such a command and did to his great satisfaction effectually prevent it." [9]

Now twice provoked by this same group of Presbyterian and Congregationalist ministers in London, the Court reacted. The Nonconformist leaders found themselves "pressed fervently to sign a congratulatory address to the King for . . . his Declaration," [10] and it was apparently the King himself who exerted this pressure through William Penn and Stephen Lobb. Although Penn had opposed the Order in Council and the imprisonment of the Bishops,[11] he and Lobb seem to have been the initiators of a crucial meeting of ministers in London on May 23 at John Howe's house. Most of those invited had promoted addresses of thanks in 1687, and it was hoped a new address could be obtained on this occasion. According to a later account, two of those present, presumably Penn and Lobb or possibly Sir John Baber, were "from the Court, and intimated that His Majesty waited in his closet, and would not stir hence until an account was brought of their proceedings." The proposal for an address was defeated, but it was not merely a refusal that Penn and Lobb or Baber had to report to the King. Among the reasons given for not addressing there was one that hinted at the understanding which had just been concluded with the Anglican clergy.[12]

Five days earlier Archbishop Sancroft had presented the Bishops' Petition against the Order in Council, and the King reacted with surprise and anger. He might well have responded in the same manner to the news brought by Penn and Lobb, for the actions of both the bishops and of these London ministers were closely related in origin and had high political import. Anglican and moderate Nonconformist leaders had been strengthened in resolve by the support they had given and received, and this was dramatically demonstrated when ten Nonconformist ministers visited the seven bishops in prison, a visit for which four of the ministers felt the ire of the King in audiences to which they were summoned.[13] The royal anger was understandable. Not only had the moderate Dissenters refused to give him the support he had previously sought, but they now were openly demonstrating that they had supported the Anglicans in their defiance of his authority. The implications were portentous.

At the same time, leaders of the Church of England also took steps which indicated their desire to create confidence in the rapprochement already accomplished, as well as to discover the terms necessary for a new religious settlement which would include both comprehension and toleration. While Archbishop Sancroft and the other bishops were still in prison, Dr. Sherlock invited John Howe to dinner and asked him what he thought Nonconformist ministers would do if they were offered preferments which should be made vacant. Completely taken by surprise, Howe replied that reactions would vary, but that he would not balk provided he could accept the terms.[14] After his release the Archbishop and the London clergy took steps to deal with the problem of terms, and by the middle of July consultations had reportedly been held with London Nonconformist ministers to discuss proposals that should be made to the next Parliament to broaden the Church and establish toleration for those who could not accept the terms of comprehension.[15]

Archbishop Sancroft's gratitude for Nonconformist support during the recent crisis involving the Bishops, and his desire to attain a religious accommodation can be seen in the articles he issued to all Bishops within his jurisdiction on July 16, recommending that they "have a very tender regard for our Brethern the Protestant Dissenters," and that they "visit them at their houses and receive them kindly at their own, and treat them fairly wherever they meet them, discoursing calmly and civilly. . . ." Yet Nonconformists would have been sensitive to the attitude which lay behind his desire that there should also be attempts at "persuading them (if it may be) to a full compliance with our Church, or at least that whereto we have already attained, we may all walk by the same rule, and mind the same thing." [16] Nevertheless, out of the crises following the Order in Council of May 4 and the petition, imprisonment, and trial of the seven bishops there had come cooperation and continuing efforts to discover concrete terms for a new religious settlement that would be acceptable to Nonconformists. Moreover, these efforts were being directed by the Archbishop of Canterbury himself. [17] But most important, they were contributing to the groundswell of opposition to the King.

The crises of the late spring and early summer that resulted from the King's maneuvers and the birth of his son on June 10 also had a most profound impact upon Nonconformist and Anglican political leaders. The Dutch agent Johnston, who continued to remain in touch with William Penn, wrote on June 13 that he had just then met with the Quaker leader who "said he is now fully satisfied that it is vain to endeavour to beget an understanding between our Court and [the Prince of Orange]." [18] Not only did Penn once again reveal how fundamental the hope of obtaining such an understanding had been in all of his efforts during the preceding year, but in acknowledging defeat of this hope he made clear the decisive effect of the events of the six weeks which culminated in the birth of the Catholic heir.

At the same time, there were political leaders among the Presbyterians and Congregationalists who had served in Parliament and realized, just as did some of the Anglican leaders, that the momentous opportunity which they awaited had now arrived. John Hampden, who had continued to work with the Dutch agent Johnston in order to maintain connections among Nonconformists and Whig political leaders, was particularly quick to sense the rapidly developing situation. By June 13 he had told Johnston that William's "compliments here . . . would be well considered," and a few days later the Dutch agent reported Hampden's careful analysis of the chances which a Dutch invasion of England would have of succeeding at that time. The Presbyterian leader thought that after three months it would be "in vain to expect any opportunity at all. . . ." On the other hand, it was not certain that the "present opportunity [would] be sufficient for the business." Not only was France "at hand" to offer assistance to James, but he thought the populace would be reluctant at the outset to join actively in a rising, and it was apparent he was thinking particularly of the rank and file of Nonconformists. Unfortunately, the Monmouth Rebellion and the drastic consequences of its failure were "yet fresh," and in addition the nation had been "corrupted," which was undoubtedly a reference to the King's tactics of wooing support. On the other hand, Hampden continued, "the Church of England is entire and numerous and may furnish hands enough. . . ." In his estimation, "all will depend on the first brush," and although he thought "the whole nation is alienated from the Government in their inclination," yet Englishmen "have lost both virtue and courage and will stand in need of some prosperous beginning to make them determine." In brief there were definite risks, yet Hampden was convinced "that the Prince had only this summer" to strike; and Sir Thomas Lee, who had been with Hampden a day or so before June 18 was of the same opinion.[19]

Even though there was reason to believe at this time that Nonconformists would be reluctant to give open support to an invading force at the outset, Johnston knew even before the birth of the heir that the Nonconformist leaders who supported the King did not have the following which was attributed to them, while moderate Dissenters who supported and sought the approval of William of Orange were far more numerous than they might seem to have been. In fact Dissenters complained to the Dutch agent because of reports from Holland that "the Prince and Princess are alienated from them because of the knavery of some [presumably such men as William Penn] that are tampering, or have tampered with both Courts," and they assured Johnston that they "disowned such men." In addition they explained that since at present they were "sheltered from the laws by this Court, decency obliges them not to seek an occasion to show their dislike"; but, they said, "whenever the Court puts them to a trial, it will appear that such men have no credit among them." At that very time some London ministers were already being put to a trial by the Court, and as Johnston wrote in this same intelligence report of May 23, they were making known that they would refuse to comply with the proposed order that Nonconformist ministers read the Declaration of Indulgence in their meetings. Moreover, it was during the same week that the small group of London Presbyterian and Congregationalist ministers refused to make an address of thanks even though the King exerted direct pressure, and thus they demonstrated that Nonconformists who were agents of the Court such as Penn, Lobb, and Sir John Baber, did indeed "have no credit among them." Also in view of the support these ministers had already given the seven bishops, Johnston had good reason to assure the Dutch authorities that "the Dissenters at present do all that is desired of them." [20]

Though many moderate Dissenters had been hesitant to show their opposition to the King and their support of William, they did have both religious and political leaders who were ready to do so. John Hampden, who had been working with Johnston since the beginning of the year, was among the earliest of all Englishmen to commit himself to William's cause, and he was undoubtedly the first Presbyterian or Congregationalist political leader of any prominence to take this step. By April the Earl of Danby and other staunch defenders of the Monarchy and the Church had made their critical decision to support William, and as they subsequently considered men of substantial ability and political influence who would support a movement against the King, they concluded there were about twenty leaders now considered to have been Presbyterians or Congregationalists who could be counted upon, including Richard Hampden, Hugh Boscawen, and Sir Edward Harley.[21] The disposition of these men to give such support was unquestionably strengthened by the events of May and June. Thus when Admiral Herbert set out on June 30, disguised as an ordinary seaman, to deliver the letter of invitation that the Prince of Orange had awaited before committing himself to an invasion of England, the Dutch leader had reason to believe that some Presbyterian and Congregationalist political leaders were already willing to give active assistance. Moreover, Johnston's reports had indicated that these men would in turn receive support from leading Presbyterian and Congregationalist ministers as well as their followers. Finally, there were indications that other Dissenters were sufficiently opposed to James so that they could be counted on not to oppose a move by William, while those Nonconformists who would give active support to the King were not of sufficient political power and probably not of sufficient number to be of real concern.

The other momentous event of June 30 had more immediate impact. With the acquittal of the Seven Bishops on that day and the tumultuous approval of this verdict, Sunderland realized that it was absolutely essential to conciliate the Dissenters.[22] Within a week the King made his first move and appointed three men to the Privy Council who were then considered to be Dissenters. But contrary to opinion then and since, this is a misconception. Sir Christopher Vane would seem to have been the most likely Nonconformist of the three, but no evidence has been found that he adhered to the religious position of his father. Of the other two, Silius Titus had abandoned his Presbyterian position twenty or more years before, and Sir John Trevor had moved so far from his family's traditional Presbyterian position that he considered John Tillotson a fanatic.[23] Obviously the appointment of men with such little standing among Presbyterians and Congregationalists could not possibly have had influence among the moderate Dissenters, whose support the King needed to win if he were to be successful.[24]

Even if these appointments had created the desired effect, Sunderland realized that far more was needed to win support from moderate Dissenters. Therefore in the Council meeting of July 6 he proposed that the King shift his policy regarding repeal of the penal laws and Test Acts by agreeing that the Test Act of 1673 should be left in effect so that Catholics would be prohibited from holding governmental offices except by individual dispensations from the King, and he also wanted the old oaths of allegiance and supremacy left in effect so that Catholics would be excluded from the House of Commons. Such a shift in policy would make Nonconformists feel more secure than they would if both Test Acts were repealed, he contended, and thus the King would obtain the additional support he desperately needed. However, Englishmen who wished to have Catholics excluded from governmental offices and the House of Commons could not have been much reassured by these proposals. They were well aware that the Test Act of 1678 had been passed because the oaths had not been sufficiently effective in barring Catholics from Parliament, and they could not trust James to exercise restraint in granting the dispensations which would allow Catholics to hold governmental positions. Moreover, after the events of May and June the moderate Dissenters from whom James needed to win support were more than ever opposed to having Catholics sit in Parliament or hold office. Thus even if the King had accepted Sunderland's proposal on July 6 instead of waiting seven weeks to do so, and even if he had at that time published the "Expedient," it would not have been sufficiently reassuring to Dissenters.[25] Once again, therefore, the King and his advisers failed in their efforts to win the Nonconformist backing they sought.

Meanwhile, some leaders of the moderate Dissenters began to anticipate the coming success of the Prince of Orange. More important, some of them began to give overt support to his cause. As early as the beginning of August, Sir Edward Harley and his sons Robert and Edward were working to organize support for William, as was revealed after the two young men dined with Lord Chandos and Robert wrote his father the highly revealing report that Chandos "will adhere to the Prince's interest and steer as Sir E[dward] will desire." [26] There were probably relatively few Presbyterians or Congregationalists in England who either previously or subsequently were M.P.s and who had gone as far as the Harleys and John Hampden. But there were two of parliamentary political stature who were preparing to come over with William—John Manley who had been a captain under Cromwell and a major under Monmouth in 1685, and Sir William Waller, a possible Presbyterian who had been implicated in the Rye House Plot and who had been in Holland since then.[27] By the beginning of September there were undoubtedly a considerable number who would have completely agreed with Roger Morrice. After some initial apprehension over the first news of preparations in the Dutch fleet, the Presbyterian journalist was cheered by news of William's visit to the German Princes and his reported statements that in order to check Catholic power he "was not unwilling to make an expedition into England, if they would advise him thereunto, and give him their assistance." This proposal and his Continental policies were "glorious purposes" to the London Dissenter who had so long been opposed to James and his policies.[28]

Six weeks earlier the King had once again dispatched his agents into the country to sound out Nonconformist opinion and willingness to support candidates favorable to the Court's policies, and when their reports were submitted in early September they contained the optimistic assertion that the Dissenters over England were "firm to their resolutions [to support royal policies] and not shaken by any endeavors that have been used to the contrary." The King and Sunderland remained convinced that the estimate was accurate but they should have examined the reports more closely, for the agents' judgment had been influenced by the Court's pressure to discover supporters in that increasingly desperate situation.[29] Thus their claims or implications that such Presbyterians or Congregationalists as Richard Hampden, Sir Richard Norton, Sir Walter Yonge, Sir John Gell, and Sir Samuel Barnardiston no longer opposed the King's policies, as they had earlier in 1688, and now favored repeal of the Test Acts must be considered very unreliable.[30] Noting on September 8 that the King remained "firmly persuaded he shall carry his point by the Parliament," and that Sunderland agreed, Morrice was perplexed. Though he undoubtedly knew of the agents' inquiries, he apparently could not conceive that their reports would lead to this conclusion. In any event, he wrote, "whoever gives them such information I know not, but it is certain they are misinformed, and have no reason at all to be of that persuasion." [31]

Within a fortnight this appears to have been recognized at Court. On the night of September 21 after a meeting of the Privy Council, van Citters quickly sent off a secret dispatch informing William that, "the King being disappointed in all his measures, seems now again enclined to embrace those of the English Church, seeing that Dissenters are too powerless or too unwilling to procure him a favorable Parliament. . . ." [32] Moreover, Sunderland tacitly recognized the lack of Nonconformist support, for in the letters he had already sent to Lord Lieutenants and others in order to obtain backing for a large number of candidates, he recommended only two Presbyterians who were members prior to 1689, Sir Samuel Barnardiston and Sir John Gell, and in neither case was there any indication other than the unreliable September reports of the King's agents that these men would have supported the King.[33]

Knowledge that the King had again made overtures to the Anglicans came near the end of September at the very time it finally became known for certain that the Dutch were going to invade England. Nonconformist ministers were disturbed and fearful, particularly those in outlying areas who, like most Englishmen, were unaware of many recent developments, and they undoubtedly would have agreed with Oliver Heywood in Yorkshire that nobody could believe the Prince of Orange was coming against James II when the King announced it on September 28. Not knowing what it meant, they were "the more startled" and saw themselves "in the mouth of danger." [34] There were others who were too fearful during early October, and it appears that their apprehension was the result of their partial knowledge of the situation and also of the high stakes involved. First, there was concern as a result of the King's decision to seek Anglican-Tory support, because the Nonconformists were "not very certain" what the outcome would be. It appeared at first that some Anglican leaders had agreed to support the Court and that it was "very likely, even certain they will obtain a Tory Parliament," a prognosis which was based on the Court's replacement of Nonconformists by Anglicans and Tories in the commission of peace and the previously remodeled corporations. On the other hand Nonconformist leaders in London accepted the fact that William "had been encouraged, and invited by the leading persons of the hierarchical party in Church and State, in the Army and in the Fleet," and they also believed that the King would not win Anglican support for "introducing Popery." [35] For this reason, apprehension concerning Anglican intentions probably subsided to some degree during October, but at the same time the prospect of the Dutch invasion heightened anxiety because of the unknown consequences, particularly because of the fear that the whole pattern of the Monmouth Rebellion and the Bloody Assizes might be repeated. Thus on October 8, Thomas Newcome noted in his diary that some of his friends were "less concerned and afraid" than he, but that for him "things are dark, and in great confusion." [36]

In a move that compounded the confusion, the King called leading Nonconformist ministers before him on three different days in mid-October. Among them were Dr. Bates, John Howe, and George Griffiths who had shown their opposition to the King the previous May at the time of the Petition of the Seven Bishops and when the King exerted pressure to obtain an address of thanks. Once again he sought their support, exhorting them to keep to his party and assuring them that the Queen was the mother of the Prince of Wales, to which it was replied: "the nation knows not so much." Although they agreed to pray for the King and to remain "in a peaceable and dutiful obedience," they made no other commitments.[37]

As William approached the shores of England, Nonconformists viewed his arrival with a mixture of disbelief and anxiety, but some also seem to have had an underlying hope which was usually apparent only after the fear of dire consequences decreased. Newcome, who had found things "dark and in great confusion" in mid-October, greeted the news of the Prince's landing at Torbay on November 5 as an "astonishing providence," though confusion still prevailed.[38] Yet now that the time for commitment had come, the possible consequences of an unsuccessful rising were the more vivid, and there was at the very outset a widespread reluctance among all Englishmen to take decisive steps. Some of the Devonshire religious leaders were under most immediate pressure, and the well known initial refusal of the Anglican clergy in Exeter to receive Bishop Burnet, along with the efforts of the Nonconformist ministers to avoid Robert Ferguson, both of whom came over with the Prince, were indicative of the reaction of those who were first forced to face the critical issue. The doctrines of passive obedience and non-resistance were compulsive on the one hand, and the specters of Monmouth's Rebellion and the Bloody Assizes evoked by the return of Ferguson were at least temporarily traumatic on the other.[39]

The Dissenters' initial reactions to the landing were of a wide variety. On the one hand there was the elation of Newcome and the fulfilled anticipation of Morrice, while on the other there were reports of continued Quaker support for James. Between these two reactions there was the noncommittal and bewildered mood of Thoresby who wrote: "we underlings knew not what to make of these affairs." Likewise perplexed, yet in this case also approving, was Thomas Jolly who found the landing "strange to us who were altogether unacquainted with the thing and with the grounds of it, yet we might hope that such men had good grounds for what they did and we must needs wish well to them as Protestants." [40] During the first ten days after the landing those Dissenters who were most favorable to William were much concerned. Newcome and his followers had a day of prayer because of the "sad occasion of the confusion in the nation," while Morrice observed that "most wise men . . . dread the thought of a war," not merely because of bloodshed and other evils but also "because the ends that those who begin a war design to themselves are seldom obtained, but often times that which is contrary thereunto, and dreaded by them, is brought to pass." [41]

By the middle of November the initial reluctance of many Englishmen to take action in support of William began to disappear, and it became possible to judge a man's position by what he did or did not do more than by what he said. [42] Already a few Dissenters had taken action, the most prominent being the Presbyterian Sir Edward Harley who sent his son Edward to London to buy arms for two troops of horse and to transmit intelligence, and after doing this he got out of the City and joined William at Salisbury. Others who were among the first to act were Thomas Dore, formerly mayor of Lymington, Hants, who offered and presumably attempted "to carry in a great number of horse with him upon the Prince's first appearance," while in Derbyshire Philip Prime raised a troop of Dissenters for the Earl of Devonshire's forces. Also a supporter was Sir Robert Pye, the Presbyterian Parliamentarian and brother-in-law of Richard Hampden who sat for Berkshire during the Interregnum, favored the Restoration, and who finally came out of political retirement to join William on his march to London. [43] Of the Presbyterians or Congregationalists who had served in Parliament after the Restoration, Sir Edward Harley assisted by his sons was one of two major leaders in Hereford, while Thomas Foley played a similarly prominent role in Worcestershire. Others are known to have joined the forces of the Prince or to have given financial assistance, including Philip Gell, Sir Walter Yonge, William Trenchard, Edward Russell, Paul Foley, John Bramen, Sir William Waller, and John Trenchard. [44]

Although a good number of the political leaders among the Dissenters were actively engaged by early December, Morrice reported that it had been noted there were not many Nonconformist ministers who had "actually come in," and in the same vein he stated at the end of the month that "great imputations are laid upon the Dissenters in that they did not more openly and publicly rise for, and serve the Prince of Orange in his great attempt for the redeeming of this Kingdom." [45] The ministers thought they had given "sufficient testimony of their affection," nevertheless the charge concerning them was largely true; while the "imputations" concerning the Dissenters in general serve as a reminder that there were a good number of Presbyterian and Congregationalist political leaders who were not heard from until after the King's flight on December 11. [46] However, it was the Baptists and Quakers who were most notably absent.

True, some Anglicans were willing to discredit the Nonconformist participants and contributions in any way that they could, and of particular interest was the Nonconformist assertion that "very many more of the Dissenters [would] have openly appeared, but not only the moderate [Anglican] clergymen, but many also about the Prince assured them their appearance would give great offence to the Hierarchy and induce them to oppose, or not to go on to assist the Prince in his purposes." [47] That this was a real possibility is clearly indicated by Reresby, who at the time of William's arrival in London on December 18 reported that the Prince "seemed to countenance Presbytery more than those of the Church of England, which startled the clergy." [48] In fact when the Bishop of London and his clergy met a day or so later to draw up an address to William, there were some so much disturbed that they were vehement in their demand that he be asked to preserve the Church of England. However, there were also clergymen who were receptive to the request of the Nonconformist ministers that the Bishop represent the divines of both persuasions, and they prevailed. As a result a most hurried meeting of sixteen Nonconformist ministers was held, and four representatives were selected to accompany about 100 Anglican clergymen when the Bishop made the presentation, at which time both he and the Prince took particular notice of their presence. [49] Feeling that this had not been an adequate expression of their gratitude, the Presbyterians and Congregationalists were introduced to William by the Earl of Devonshire, Lord Wharton and Lord Wiltshire on January 2, and with Howe as their spokesman they presented their own address, while the Baptists led by Kiffen did likewise.[50]

Meanwhile some of the Presbyterian and Congregationalist political leaders were among those active in the efforts being made in London to meet the exigencies created by the flight of the King and the presence of the Prince of Orange. Lord Wharton was among the Lords in and about London who met at the Guildhall as soon as James fled and unanimously offered to assist William by obtaining a Parliament, while in the London Common Council others such as Sir William Ashurst were leaders in the address of December 13.[51] Most important were the major roles played by Wharton, Maynard and Paget in the meetings of the Lords held on December 21, 22, and 24 at the summons of William. At the last meeting Wharton strongly opposed any consideration of the rights of the Prince of Wales. Paget "urged . . . that the King's withdrawing was a demise in law," and he therefore held that the Princess "might be declared Queen," according to Clarendon, while Morrice indicated that he also moved that the Prince be declared King.[52] Although Maynard had been called in as one of five legal counsels for the last two of the Lords' meetings, it was at the meeting of about 220 officials of London and members from Charles II's Parliaments, held two days later, that he played his more important role. Since the Lords were opposed to having the Prince and Princess assume the positions of King and Queen, he believed it would be best to avoid the issue at that time. However, as his former chaplain Roger Morrice reported after the meeting, "there were few men in the House . . . more desirous to come to it," or who were "more positive in their opinion . . . that it was not only the best course but the only course that could overcome difficulties and save both the Prince and us." [53]

For the moment, however, it was indeed more important to delay decision on this vital issue and to support the efforts of a committee which was charged with bringing in the address thanking the Prince for the preservation of England's religion, laws, and liberties, and also requesting him to assume the administration of government and to take steps to call a Convention. In view of his active support of William's cause during the previous year it was most appropriate that John Hampden was apparently made the chairman of this committee.[54]

At this juncture the financial needs of the government were of critical importance, and in a letter to the London Court of Aldermen on January 8, 1689, William proposed a six-month loan that the Aldermen immediately and unanimously approved. In the subscription to the loan Nonconformist support appears to have been particularly strong. "Upon strict observation," Morrice later reported, probably after examining the Posting Books, it appeared that of the nearly £190,000 subscribed all but about £37,000 was from Dissenters; and entries in the Posting Books record that of the London Dissenters who sat in Parliament at some time during the Restoration period, Sir William Ashurst subscribed £1000, William Love and Sir Henry Ashurst each £500, and Sir John Eyles £200.[55]

Having contributed to these important political and financial developments, Dissenters appear to have turned confidently and quietly to the business of electioneering. The elections were "contested fervently in very many places, but with great regularity and fairness, and with less violence and arbitrariness than has been known."[56] Thus Dissenters were in general satisfied even though the results were not as encouraging as they had hoped. In Lancaster, for example, Thomas Jolly wrote: "Though we were surprised and friends failed as to the election of knights for the county, yet did the Lord signally help me in that journey to Lancaster," where Sir Charles Hoghton "was chosen freely as possible" because of the Dissenters' support. In London the results were more gratifying. Although the only Presbyterian chosen was the veteran William Love, the other three members were Sir Patience Ward, Sir Robert Clayton, and Sir Thomas Pilkington, all of whom had proved themselves to be friends of the Dissenters. In all there were thirty members elected at the outset who may be considered Presbyterians or Congregationalists, on the basis of the information which has since been discovered, and three more were added by June 20.[57] This was still thirteen fewer than the number known to have been elected in 1681 and would seem to have been an important loss; but this time as well as before, Nonconformist hopes rested upon the considerable number of moderate Anglicans with whom a tacit political alliance had once again evolved as a result of the developments since the end of 1687. Nothing better reveals the outcome of the elections and the Nonconformist reaction to the newly elected Convention

Parliament than a moving and also prescient Nonconformist journal entry headed *SINE METU*—without fear:

I, Roger Morrice, was never at Westminster Hall, nor at the Parliament House since anno 1679 that the Second Westminster Parliament sat there, until Monday, February 4 [1689], nor have scarce ever walked one turn in that Hall without fear since anno 1662, until the day aforesaid when I walked with true liberty and freedom, and saw very many persons that I knew well of great worth and integrity, whom I was very glad to see there, and many others who were like to be instruments of much mischief.[58]

Not since the Convention Parliament of the Restoration had there been a comparable opportunity to create a new constitutional and religious settlement, and no Englishmen could have viewed the prospect with more anticipation than the Dissenters. For nearly three decades they had faced constant reminders of their failure at the Restoration, and in spite of all efforts to obtain any change in the settlement reached at that time, defeat had always been the result—even during the promising years of the Exclusion Parliaments. Finally in 1689 Dissenters along with their friends appeared to have gained a similar success on the hustings. Although there were many elected who "were like to be instruments of much mischief," there was now the prospect of having a King who was apparently favorable to many of the changes which the Dissenters and moderate Anglicans had previously sought, and the Anglican leaders had made at least a tacit commitment to comprehension and toleration. As a result of this happy conjunction there was considerable activity in planning for legislation.

Prospects of obtaining a satisfactory religious settlement seemed particularly bright, for not only was there the commitment of the Anglican leaders that had been first made the previous May, but also William favored repeal of the penal laws and he was of the Dutch Reformed Religion. Thus when Richard Baxter, Dr. Bates and John Howe conferred early in January to make preliminary plans, they thought in terms of all that they could desire. For their model they therefore turned back beyond the Worcester House agreement of 1660 and to the Uxbridge Treaty of 1645 in which they found "many particulars . . . fit to be offered. . . ."[59] Although their friend Morrice also wanted to be ready for any opportunity to meet with Anglican clergymen

and work for such a comprehension or Presbyterian reformation,
he had no illusions. Being well aware of the issues discussed and
many opinions expressed in the January meetings of the bishops
and other leading clergymen, he concluded with reason that
"there is likely to be none." [60] Actually this experienced observer
believed that the religious goal could best be obtained through
political means. If Parliament would allow Dissenters back
into the local offices in counties and corporations and thus back
"into the state . . . they will let the outed members into the
Church." [61]

Stimulated by the opportunity, Dissenters also drew up plans
for the whole constitutional settlement and also for many other
reforms, some of which they had long sought. Proposals later
found among Lord Wharton's papers were designed to limit the
constitutional powers of the King while increasing those of Parliament and giving greater political weight to the freeholder of some
property. The King's ministers, the members of the Privy Council, and some judges were to be approved by both Houses of
Parliament, and he was to lose much of the power to influence
the political composition of the House of Lords since newly
created peers were not to sit or vote without approval of both
Houses. Likewise, the power of the Crown to influence the composition of the Commons by creating new boroughs or by changing the representation of those in existence was eliminated, for
the former was to require parliamentary approval and all representation was to be based upon the amount of taxes paid by the
boroughs and counties. The requirements in the Test Act of 1673
concerning the Sacrament and the oaths of allegiance and supremacy were to be removed, but the transubstantiation test was to
be continued. Another basic change proposed was that freeholders were to "nominate" sheriffs, justices of the peace, and militia
officers "as they now choose coroners. . . ." And a final major
proposal was that consideration be given to the union of England
and Scotland as well as "the like with Holland." [62]

The Presbyterian minister John Humfrey was also spurred into
action by the hope of obtaining constitutional changes. He wrote
a brief anonymous pamphlet entitled *Advice Before It Be Too
Late: or, A Breviate for the Convention,* and copies were handed
to the members of the Convention Parliament.[63] Humfrey would
have gone considerably further than Wharton in restricting the

King's prerogative and augmenting the power of Parliament. In two respects, however, his proposals were somewhat similar, for he would have had Parliament have "the power of the militia, and choosing magistrates" such as judges and sheriffs, the latter probably amounting in practice to a right of passing upon appointees nominated by the Crown. Although he believed that by these changes Englishmen would be "fundamentally delivered" from the danger of oppression by any King either by force or injustice, there was still the problem of "the negative voice of the prince in his Parliament" which needed consideration according to Humfrey. Because of the "great evil" that would result from an obstinate King, he considered it would be better to give legislative power to the Lords and Commons alone, and in addition he would also have given the two Houses the power of calling and dissolving Parliaments.[64]

Both Wharton and Humfrey looked for changes which in general were consistent with those proposed previously by parliamentarians, but Humfrey was clearly the bolder. Indeed there was a Leveller coloration to his thinking. "Let us remember the state we are in," he wrote, "a state that puts the supreme power in the hands of the people, to place it as they will: and therefore to bound and limit it as they see fit . . . ; and if they do it not now, the ages to come will have occasion to blame them for ever." It seemed to him at that juncture that there was reason to hope that some means could be found to remove the difficulties and disputes that had prevailed between King and Parliament, for they had "the golden opportunity to bring a crown in one hand, with their terms or conditions in the other." [65] Thus did a leading Dissenter put the issue to those members of the Convention who received his *Breviate,* and in particular to the Presbyterians and Congregationalists and their friends. Although relatively few of them would have been receptive to the more extreme and impractical proposals, certainly all were fully aware of the "golden opportunity," and they quickly moved into action during the first week of the session.

During the crisis over the succession to the throne a number of those in the Presbyterian-Congregationalist group played leading roles, but Richard Hampden immediately became of major prominence. Against the wishes of some of his political allies who wanted his assistance in the first great Commons debate,[66] he was made chairman of the Grand Committee on the State of the Nation; and when he was later appointed manager for the Commons in two critical conferences of early February between the two Houses, it became evident that he would exercise a leadership in the House that would be rivaled by few others during the coming year.[67]

The speakers among the Presbyterians during the first days of crucial constitutional debates were Sir John Maynard, John Hampden, Hugh Boscawen, and Paul Foley. The venerable Sergeant-at-Law was a most vigorous and acute definer of the issues and defender of Parliament's right to determine the succession to the throne, not only on the floor of the House, but also in the most important conference between the Houses where he spoke twice as frequently as any other member and at the most heated moments of the debate. In the House he contended that "the question is not, whether we can depose the King; but, whether the King has not deposed himself." Holding that the English Government was "mixed [and] not monarchical and tyrannous" and that "it had its beginning from the people," he concluded that "there may be such a transgression in the Prince, that the people will be no more governed by him." Developing his position further in the first Conference with the Lords, Maynard maintained that when there is a breach of the constitution, "that will be an abdication, and that abdication will infer a vacancy." Furthermore, "declaring a vacancy, and the provision of a supply for it, can never make the crown elective," and referring to legal principle he contended that "no man can pretend to be King James' heir while he is living." Finally, he offered the ultimate rationale for declaring the abdication and vacancy: "If we look but into the law of nature (that is above all human laws) we have enough to justify us in what we are now doing, to provide for ourselves and the public weal in such an exigency as this." [68] Although Boscawen and Foley did not speak nearly as frequently nor develop their views as fully, they, together with Maynard were strong and articulate advocates of the abdication and vacancy.[69] Meanwhile in the House of Lords the embattled minority favoring these views struggled to prevail. Though records are fragmentary it is clear that Lord Wharton spoke in the debates, apparently holding on January 29 that the very fact that the administration of the government had been temporarily given to William was indicative of both the abdication and the remedy to it, while among those registering protests after key divisions were Bedford and Paget.[70]

The critical dispute which raged for ten days, and particularly the "fierceness and violence" of the debates in the Lords led many to fear that the Revolution would not "be now without blood," and that those opposed to the Commons' Resolution "would put it to a decision by the sword." Thus Morrice reported that the Lords' final acceptance on February 7 of the Commons' position on abdication and vacancy in return for deletion of any reference to a contract between King and people, was "a very joyful vote to all about the Parliament House," and to the people, who built bonfires and rang church bells all over the town that night and in the surrounding villages the next day.[71]

With this decision the "golden opportunity to bring a crown in one hand, with the terms or conditions in the other" had actually arrived. The Commons had already explored the problem in the famous two-day debate in the Grand Committee on the State of the Nation at the end of January, with Richard Hampden in the chair. At that time John Hampden and Boscawen were the most vigorous and explicit speakers from among the Presbyterian-Congregationalist ranks. Speaking in the parliamentarian tradition of his grandfather, the patriot of ship money fame, as well as of his father who was in the chair, the younger Hampden insisted that for the safety of the people it was not sufficient merely to fill the throne that was vacant. It was also "necessary to declare the Constitution and rule of the Government"; and as he was adamant in contending that steps be taken to do this before they adjourned the debate, he moved that they consider the vote of the Restoration Convention declaring the Government to be in King, Lords and Commons. Boscawen was more explicit and developed the argument that "arbitrary government was not only by the late King that is gone, but by his ministers, and farthered by extravagant Acts of the Long Parliament [of the Restoration]." In particular he had in mind the Corporation Act, the Militia Act, and the Triennial Act.[72] In the end, a committee was appointed to bring in the "general heads of such things as are absolutely necessary to be considered for the better securing the laws and liberties of the nation," and the proportion of committee members from the Presbyterian-Congregationalist group—eight of thirty nine—is indicative of their relative importance in the House debate as well as of their concern with this problem which Boscawen called "as great an affair as ever was before a House of Commons. . . ." [73]

Although little is known about the work of the members of this committee from which emerged the document that became the basis of the Declaration of Rights, there were two occasions when Richard Hampden and Hugh Boscawen played important roles in defending its work on the floor of the House. The whole conception of presenting terms along with the Crown was under attack on February 6 when the Lords voted that the Prince and Princess of Orange should be declared King and Queen, for enthusiastic members of the Commons then urged that the House proceed at once to join with the Lords in this declaration. Boscawen and Richard Hampden were quick to oppose such precipitous action, Hampden urging that they "consider well what must be for the benefit of all posterity. . . ." [74] Such arguments were persuasive. The committee thereafter appointed to amend the Lords' resolution was the famous one that drew up the final draft of the Declaration of Rights, and it was appropriate that among its twenty-one members were Richard Hampden, Boscawen, Maynard and Paul Foley.

The major issue that arose in the process of drawing up the Declaration was an important one to the Dissenters, since it involved the question whether many of the political and constitutional changes that they had sought should be asserted to be fundamental rights. Thus when it was debated whether the Declaration should contain such articles as were introductory of new laws as well as those declaratory of ancient rights, Hampden asked: "Is it not natural to present the Prince of Orange with what you are aggrieved with, and suffer under all the infringements of your rights?" [75] He supported inclusion of prepared articles asserting that there should be frequent meetings of Parliament, restriction of the royal power to terminate its sessions, repeal and re-enactment of laws governing the militia, freedom to worship publicly and the uniting of all Protestants in the public worship as far as may be attained, protection of corporations from *quo warranto* proceedings and tenure for judges on a basis of good behavior with removal by due course of law. He also sought judicial reforms to protect the individual, such as the prevention of exacting promises for the forfeiture of fines before conviction and security against excessive bail.[76] However, efforts to include these articles failed, and the Declaration of Rights which was tendered William and Mary with the Crown on February 13 contained only articles assertive of ancient rights. Although they were not as successful as they had hoped to be, it appears that members of the Presbyterian-Congregationalist group had at least sought to make full use of the "golden opportunity." Moreover, such leaders as the Hampdens and Boscawen had given substantial support to the principle that a statement of the limitations upon the prerogative should accompany the offer of the Crown.

Efforts to obtain the omitted constitutional changes and the other reforms were now to begin through the normal legislative procedures, and the outlook seemed promising. The developments of the first few weeks of the Convention were described by Sir Edward Harley and his son Robert as "a mercy to the nation" and "the providence of God," and the elder Harley therefore trusted that "all wicked counsels will be dissipated." [77] Hopes for legislative successes had been raised because several of their veteran leaders had gained a stature that gave them added weight and importance, and this was emphasized by the new King when his appointments to the Privy Council included Lord Wharton, the Earl of Bedford, Richard Hampden, and Hugh Boscawen.[78] But just as in every Parliament since 1661, the Dissenters' main source of strength lay in the moderate or latitudinarian Anglicans who favored comprehension of the moderate Dissenters and toleration for others. Since there was a considerable number of such Anglican members, the prospects for an acceptable and stabilizing religious settlement seemed good, and it likewise seemed possible that even those who did not accept the terms of comprehension might hope that Dissent from the Established Church would no longer be used as a deterrent to political activity and as a bar to office holding. However, it will be remembered that on February 4 Morrice had noted the presence of many in Parliament "who were like to be instruments of much mischief," and by the end of the month there were additional reasons for concern.

Such success as the moderate Dissenters and Anglicans had enjoyed to this point had come to endanger the religious and constitutional settlement that they sought. Indeed it had been sufficient to move Danby to inform the King that "he did all things to encourage Presbytery and to dishearten the Church of England, and that he would absolutely prejudice himself and [the] government by it." [79] William's recent selection of Danby himself to be Lord President of the Council and of Halifax to be Lord Privy Seal had clearly not eliminated such alleged partiality in the minds of those for whom Danby spoke, while on the other hand these very appointments seemed ominous to Dissenters. The selection of such leaders and the rejection of men like Lord Delamer and Sir Edward Harley led to fears that the "government should slip into the old channel. . . ." [80]

Real alarm and discouragement developed as additional evidence accumulated that those whom Morrice called Tories or Hierarchists were gaining key sources of power in the Government, the developments having the greatest impact being the appointment of the Earl of Nottingham to be Secretary of State on March 5 and disclosure of the Privy Council list of those proposed for the commission of the peace ten days later. Describing the reaction he observed to Nottingham's appointment, Morrice reported "the whole Kingdom . . . alarmed at his advancement to such a place where he must be privy to all the secret counsels . . . ," for he "has so consistently opposed the King ever since his coming. . . ." [81] This reaction can be explained in part by the Nonconformists' disappointment in the terms of the Comprehension Bill for which Nottingham was largely responsible, and which had become known to some of them a few days before the Earl's appointment. But the real source of the strong opposition to the King's choice lay in the implications of the appointment, for the new Secretary was an acknowledged spokesman for the "Church party." [82]

In the light of such indications that the lines were being drawn and that the position of the Presbyterian-Congregationalist group in Parliament was by no means as favorable as it first might have seemed, their leaders laid their plans. In a memorandum that was endorsed "to be discoursed with Mr. Hampden," Lord Wharton drew up a priority list of bills that may be regarded as the Dissenters' legislative calendar for the immediate future. First and most important would be the removal of the religious tests barring Protestant Dissenters from office. After noting that the test against transubstantiation and the oaths in the Test Act of 1678 were "judged to be a sufficient test for the members of each House in Parliament, which is the greatest trust in the nation under the King," he contended that there should be no other test "for any officer or place of inferior trust or required from any such person." In brief, legislation was to be sought that in effect would have repealed the sacramental test in both the Test Act of 1673 and the Corporation Act. Next they wanted to gain repeal of the Conventicle and Five Mile Acts in order to achieve some degree of religious freedom before attempting to obtain enactment of religious comprehension and toleration bills.[83]

In the past, proposals to remove the sacramental test had always evoked opposition from the Anglican political leaders regarding themselves as true defenders of the Church. True, there may have been some disposition to consider "expedients" during 1688, but now that James and the Catholic threat had disappeared there was once again no reason to seek Nonconformist support by considering such a relaxation. Fully aware of this and of the predominance of Anglicans among the King's recent appointees, Wharton and Hampden realized that it would take influence and pressure of the highest order to overcome Anglican opposition. This is exactly what they sought and obtained at the first opportunity to eliminate the sacramental test, which came during consideration of the Bill for Abrogating the Oaths of Supremacy and Allegiance. While this Bill was being debated in the Lords, Richard Hampden advised the King that he should deliver a speech from the throne in which he recommended to both Houses that the sacramental test be eliminated so that all Protestants could hold governmental offices. Without consulting his other Privy Councillors, William proceeded to do this on March 16 by saying that it was his hope that the Houses would "leave room for the admission of all Protestants that are willing and able to serve."[84] The Tory Anglicans' reaction was sudden and had a backlash. Morrice reported that:

Sir Robert Sawyer, Mr. [Heneage] Finch, Sir Thomas Clarges, Sir Christopher Musgrave, Sir Joseph Tredenham and a great many more, some say some scores in number, being very angry hereat met at the Devil Tavern . . . this night being Saturday the 16th and then appointed another meeting on Monday following, and there declared their resolution . . . that they would keep in that clause in the Act concerning the receiving of the Sacrament . . . and urge other parts of Conformity with great strictness, and that they would make a motion to have . . . Mr. Love, Mr. Papillon and all other members of the House of Commons removed . . . that would not conform thereunto.[85]

As Burnet wrote, there was not "any one thing upon which the Church party reckoned that their security depended more than this . . . ," and those of this conviction were convinced the King was "willing to sacrifice the Church to the Dissenters." [86] Thus they not only tried to hold the line, but they also wanted to strike back at Dissenters in the Commons. Not only was a devastating attack led by Nottingham, Danby, and Devonshire against amendments which would have either abolished the test or allowed those taking communion in any Protestant Church to hold office, but also Nottingham was prepared to bring in a bill that would have prohibited occasional conformists from holding office.[87] The outcome in the Lords was a blow to the Nonconformists, and although there was hope that there would not be the same result in the Commons, the vigorous activity of the Presbyterian-Congregationalist members was insufficient to overcome the adamant Anglican opposition.[88]

But it was the next defeat which had the most telling effect. At issue was a clause proposed for the Coronation Oath Bill requiring the King to swear to maintain the Protestant Religion as then established by law. Fearing that since William was soon to take the oath any possibility of comprehension would thereby be jeopardized, if not forestalled, John Hampden and those sympathetic to the hopes of moderate Dissenters fought unsuccessfully to obtain a modification allowing Kings and Queens, after they had taken the oath, to give assent to bills altering any form or ceremony, but not the doctrine of the Church.[89] Anglican observers agreed with Nonconformists concerning the results. Reresby found that the two victories for the Church of England "showed the strength of that interest in Parliament. . . ." And Morrice wrote: "I take it plainly to be the vertical point of this session and [it] gives a full demonstration that the [hierarchical or Tory] interest is predominent there as well as in other places, and will be to the end of the sessions in all points." [90] In brief, as young Edward Harley wrote his brother Robert, "Toryism is now in the ascendant."

More eloquent than these comments on either side was the urgency with which Robert Harley's two uncles, John Hampden and Paul Foley, along with his father-in-law, Thomas Foley, were already at work with Hugh Boscawen to obtain young Harley's election to the Tregony seat left vacant by the death of Hugh

Boscawen's brother Charles. Every vote was desperately needed in Parliament, and as soon as there was word of Robert's unanimous election Sir Edward wrote the son who was to have such a notable parliamentary career: "Your presence is expected here with all speed and must not be delayed." [91]

Moderate Dissenters now seemed to have a clear indication that all efforts to obtain their comprehension in the Established Church would fail, and they were much disappointed in the original House of Lords Comprehension Bill since it did not contain the "very great and large concessions," contained in the Bill of 1680. Nevertheless, there was still sufficient latitude to make the Bill of some attraction, and thus determined efforts to amend it were made with surprisingly close votes occurring until its passage in early April. However, Presbyterian and Congregationalist members of Parliament and Nonconformist office holders who could not have accepted its terms of comprehension found that they had another reason to oppose the Bill as it was passed, for in the end the Lords accepted an amendment offered by Nottingham that was designed to eliminate the Dissenters' practice of occasional conformity in order to qualify for office.[92] Meanwhile a far more liberal Commons Comprehension Bill was being drawn up by a committee whose chairman was John Hampden. Since it would have allowed an incumbent to have the Common Prayer read for him by a vicar and since it also accepted ministers who had been ordained in any Reformed Church, Anglican members of the Commons saw the gates of the Church being opened not only to a wide variety of English Dissenters, but also to Dutch and French Calvinists. In both alarm and disdain one staunch Churchman made a motion interpreted by the Speaker to mean that further consideration of the Bill be adjourned "till Doomsday." [93] In effect his wish was to be granted, for the Bill was sidetracked and killed as a result of a well known political arrangement made between some of the Whigs and Tories, apparently as a result of a Devil Tavern meeting on April 9, in which the Whig leaders agreed they would support a move to turn the problem over to the Church of England Convocation, in return for assurances from the Tories that they would support the previously introduced Bill for Indulgence granting limited religious toleration.[94]

Although this was presumably an arrangement sought by Anglican political leaders rather than by the clergymen, there is immediately a question concerning the commitment first made to moderate Dissenters at the time the bishops desired Nonconformist support in their resistance to James in May, 1688. Although a number of these leaders had spoken "very earnestly" in support of the Comprehension Bill in the recent Lords debates, Dissenters had reason to believe that the clergymen had become "narrow spirited," and even more to think that the commitment of 1688 would not be fulfilled.[95] However, at this stage it was the opposition of the Anglican political leaders which was responsible for the defeat of comprehension. In both the Houses there was unyielding resistance to letting the Dissenters have any share in the government, and there was a real fear that the Anglican character of the government service would be dangerously altered by the influx of Dissenters who would qualify for offices by accepting the terms of comprehension.[96]

It was not only their "malicious enemies" whom the Dissenters held responsible. More disheartening was the performance of their "weak friends." Indeed in an embittered mood Morrice charged on April 13 that at that juncture only enemies and friends of this nature would "bring in any Bill for the uniting, or giving impunity to Dissenters, because all wise men knew [the bills] would be prostituted and made ineffectual to their end, and were intended so to be by those cunning men that brought them in, or influenced others so to do. . . ." Burnet concurred. "Those who proposed this [Bill] acted very disingenuously," he wrote, for "they opposed it underhand and set on all their friends against it . . . ," while at the same time they sought to obtain a reputation for their "show of moderation."[97] Presbyterian ministers and political leaders were not alone in their deep disappointment and bitterness. They were joined by such Anglican leaders as Halifax and Burnet who saw that turning the problem over to Convocation would only "ruin the design of comprehension."[98] This was undoubtedly the intention of those who were parties to the Devil Tavern bargain, and it was most certainly the result.[99]

With the struggle for comprehension removed from Parliament and with moderate Dissenters facing the probability of continued exclusion from the Church, most of them found additional reasons to hope that toleration might now be established by parliamentary enactment. The Bill that Nottingham introduced on Febru-

ary 28 had still not passed the Lords; and during its consideration both in that House until its passage April 18, and then in the
Commons, the Presbyterian and Congregationalist members along
with their true moderate Anglican friends defeated efforts to restrict the scope and duration of the concessions and fought to
obtain an Act which would be generally satisfactory to Dissenters.[100] The outcome was by no means certain. Two days before
the final reading in the Commons the Presbyterian leaders and
their friends found the situation so doubtful that they took most
unusual steps. With Richard Hampden's knowledge, John Hampden and Sir Henry Ashurst went "into the City, and spoke privately to some citizens, telling them that his Majesty had present
use for £40,000, and they desired it might be borrowed only of
Dissenters, for they conceived his Majesty would resent [*sic*] it
very kindly, and it would turn to their advantage." [101] Morrice,
who made this report, did "not know the first spring of this no-
tion" at the time, but it became evident during the final debate
of May 17. Faced by an amendment to limit the duration of the
Indulgence to seven years, the moderate Anglican Sir Thomas
Littleton pointedly stated that the Dissenters might give the King
money, while Richard Hampden contended that they would be
true to the Government and in support of this contention he announced: "at this time, they are lending a considerable sum for
uses you will approve of, I am sure." With this the amendment
was rejected, and the Bill to be known as the Toleration Act was
passed.[102]

Nonconformists aware of the situation in Parliament were
amazed, Thomas Jolly stating we had "almost given up our hopes
thereof, the majority of Parliament being of such a complexion,"
while Morrice wrote: "I do not understand the mystery of it, nor
the true reason why the Lords Spiritual, and those Lords and
Commoners of their sentiments did pass that Bill." However, he
hinted that possibly it might be found in the political bargain
to accept indulgence in return for shifting the consideration of
comprehension to a Convocation when noting that "certain it is
the Devil Tavern Club did call for it and did promote the passing
of it," and he added that it was "as certain they do now heartily
repent they have past it . . . ," another conclusion with which
Burnet concurred.[103] But more moderate Anglicans had helped
carry the vote by pointing out that if Dissenters made ill use of

the indulgence "there will always be enough in this House to take it away," and in addition there were several who contended that Dissenters would be attracted to the Church by this policy of "tenderness" and that it would "increase daily." [104] Finally, the news that Littleton and Hampden presented concerning the Nonconformist's financial loan probably had effect, for the loan was undoubtedly in an amount and for uses which did have the members' approval.

Even though this was an Act of Indulgence and therefore did not repeal the penal laws, it gave the Nonconformists "great reason to be thankful, for it answers its end and gives them a due liberty with entire security . . . ," and John Howe was able to assure the King that the Act "did fit them well." [105] True though this was for the majority of Dissenters, many Presbyterians who still looked toward comprehension tended to speak of the Act as though it would have an effect only upon Nonconformists who would not have considered comprehension under any terms, and thus these Presbyterians seemed to regard it as only temporarily applicable to them.[106] However, contrary to their hopes and consistent with their fears, they were to retain their legal status outside the Church along with other Nonconformists. The religious settlement of the Revolution had been completed. Although the freedom granted to Dissenters was only partial and permissive in character, orthodox Protestant Nonconformists did have their long sought "public liberty established by law." [107] For the first time since the Restoration settlement, use of a permission to worship publicly could be enjoyed in the knowledge that it was consistent with parliamentarian traditions.

"When you write to any of our lawmakers," Philip Henry wrote his son Matthew after passage of the Toleration Act, "acknowledge their kindness and pains in procuring it with all thankfulness, but until the sacramental test be taken off," he pointedly added, "our business is not done." [108] Since Anglican political leaders continued to guard most jealously their legal monopoly of offices in the national political establishment during the struggle over the religious settlement of 1689, and since they had defeated the Comprehension Bill mainly because it would have allowed a segment of former Dissenters to hold such positions, it was obvious that there would be no repeal of the Test Act of 1673. Thus Nonconformists were to fail in obtaining one of their major political aims. However, there remained the critically important question concerning eligibility for offices in municipal corporations. If Dissenters were to attain a more equal status as well as other goals, they and their political allies needed to obtain repeal or modification of the sacramental requirement of the Corporation Act of 1661 and thereby the hope of increasing their parliamentary representation from the boroughs.

The outlook was not as bleak as it might have seemed. Although earlier support for repeal of the Corporation Act had eroded considerably, it was apparent even during the sharp encounters and the defeats of late March and early April that there was more support for eliminating the Corporation Act than for any tampering with the first Test Act, and this was undoubtedly because there were many Anglican political leaders who knew they could continue to count upon Nonconformist support in the elections of parliamentary corporations, just as they had in the past. Thus on the second reading of the Bill of Repeal on April 1, when the Tory Anglicans succeeded in passing an instruction to the Committee that no one should be admitted to any place of magistracy without having received the Sacrament during the preceding twelve months, members of the Presbyterian-Congregationalist group and their friends were still able to adjourn the debate by a division of 116–114.[109] By June the continuation of this parliamentary impasse had begun to build up pressure among those outside of Parliament who not only desired repeal of the sacramental test required by both the Corporation Act and the first Test Act, but who also sought restoration of the rights of corporations. When a petition to this effect was presented by the City of London, the Commons spent "two or three hours in fierce objections and wranglings" before it was accepted by a division of 174–147.[110] But such pressure was ineffectual. The majority favoring acceptance of the Petition could not be converted into one favoring the abolition of the sacramental test, even in corporations alone.

However, the Nonconformists and their allies did have enough strength on July 23 to defeat a Tory amendment to the Bill for Restoring Corporations that granted the power to elect officials only to those who were members of the corporations in 1675. As Morrice noted, this would have meant "very many would have had corporations filled up by those that were members in 1675 and 1676 when Toryism was at a great height." Then seizing upon their advantage in the House that day, they went on to pass a resolution that corporation elections should be by all those who were freemen in each corporation three months before any surrender under all types of seizures.[111] Morrice thought the Bill had been made "as good as it can be desired, and far better than anybody expected," apparently because occasional conformists would have been eligible to participate. However, it was still believed that because of other provisions the Bill would reduce the corporations to the status they possessed in 1675.[112] This was merely a preliminary skirmish, and the ending of the session on August 20 only brought a calm before the bitter battle which was to develop over reorganization of the corporations during the next session.

When Parliament was convened again in October, Roger Morrice noted that many believed it should instead have been dissolved because it had failed the King in so many respects, and indeed there had been some consideration and hope for such a step among his chief advisers.[113] However, in the estimation of the Nonconformist journalist, "wiser men are of another opinion because the Corporation Act is yet in being, and by virtue of it all the disaffected persons in the corporations in England [i.e. those whom he thought were opposed to the Revolution and the subsequent legislation], and indeed none else are mayor, bailiffs, and members of the companies and of the town halls, and they will certainly choose and return disaffected members [of Parliament] if there should be a new election." Therefore, "the Country party will offer and press the revising of the Corporation Bill. . . ."[114] Such charges and such determination to obtain a legal right to the sources of parliamentary power in the boroughs were to be matched by those on the other side in their efforts to keep their legal monopoly of that power. Thus the struggle over legislation affecting the corporations led to the climactic battle of the Convention Parliament.

The critical period began at the end of the year. On December 19 the Bill for Restoring Corporations was read a second time in this session and committed in a form that did not satisfy Dissenters and their allies, while it "seriously perturbed" such a leader as Nottingham who thought it would be "of very mischievous consequence, for it restores the Corporations as they were in the year 1660 and consequently readmits all sorts of Dissenters." [115] However, the sacramental test had not been eliminated, and thus the fourteen members of the Presbyterian-Congregationalist group on the Commons committee could not rest content. As the holidays neared there was a report that a clause would be added to remove the test, and this led a highly worried Nottingham to beseech staunch Anglican members of the House not to leave town during the Christmas recess of a week, and according to another Tory they did not do so until they found that the key clause in the Bill had been "settled in a harmless restitution to the state of 1675. . . ." [116] The incorporation of this provision was not the only blow to any hopes the Nonconformists and their allies may have had of regaining the legal right to hold municipal office, for any efforts there were to remove the sacramental test during the committee sessions also failed. As Morrice made clear, the Bill as reported to the House on January 2 would not only exclude Nonconformists from office, but in restoring the men who held office in 1675 it would also give political power to those who were regarded by the Dissenters as "the worst sort of men in the Kingdom generally, and many of them the givers up of charters . . ." under Charles II and James II. [117]

The combination of adding the 1675 clause concerning charters, while at the same time retaining the sacramental test, could not have made the Committee's work better calculated to evoke a counterattack in the House. It began with "the great proviso which was brought in by Mr. Sacheverell that those who had given up charters without a majority [in the corporation] should be incapable of holding any [municipal] office for seven years. . . ." But this amendment was regarded as insufficient, as Morrice made clear in continuing his account of the January 2 proceedings. Richard Hampden, "who was all along very fervent for this Bill," is identified by Morrice as the member who thereupon moved that "they who gave up charters might be liable to this penalty although they were [supported by] a majority . . ." in the surrender. [118] As a result "the other side were full of fury," but this was not the extent of the counterattack. There was also the motion, generally thought to have been made by the Anglican Whig Sir Robert Howard, that established the penalty for violating the seven-year restriction on office holding as a £500 fine and incapacitation for any governmental office for life. Although maneuvers and countermaneuvers continued into the evening, "the other side" was not successful, and Sacheverell's proviso as amended by Hampden and Howard was adopted 133–68.[119] Thus the provisions of the reported Bill that in effect eliminated Nonconformists from municipal offices were countered by clauses designed to exclude a specific group of Anglican politicians. Vindictiveness had been compounded.

As is well known, the victory could not be sustained when the engrossed Bill was read in a full House on January 10, after a much larger number of Tory Anglicans had returned with haste from holiday festivities. Realizing that a House of nearly 400 would be of a much different disposition, Sacheverell sought to save the clause by introducing a "moderating rider," and then in embittered debates and many divisions the battle raged again. Presbyterian members were prominent in their efforts. Hampden wanted to know if the House would restore men who had betrayed the corporations and let them do it again; Foley asserted that by revoking charters "it was endeavored, the last two reigns, to pack a Parliament to subvert all our Constitutions"; and Maynard warned that "if there be no penalties [for surrendering the charters], you had better like what King Charles and King James did," adding that "if those surrenders stand, they may make what Parliament they will at Court. . . ." But the "other side" had the majority, and on the final division the whole Sacheverell clause was thrown out, and the Church party thus maintained the legal basis of their political power in the corporations and Parliament.[120]

Even had the clause survived there would have been eventual defeat, for the King told the Lord Privy Seal that he would not have the Bill pass. Moreover, added Halifax, the King "seemed to be weary of Parliament." On too many critical matters the Whigs had thwarted the King, and most recently some who were strong supporters of an amended Corporation Bill "had sent him word, that if he interposed or meddled in it, they would not finish the money bills." [121] In addition after their defeat in attempting to amend the Corporation Bill they had refused to proceed with the Indemnity Bill, and they opposed William's plans to conduct the Irish campaign in person. Such obstruction had a predictable result. There was renewed Tory pressure for dissolution, and with good reason the King ended the work of the Convention on January 27.[122]

In the year that had passed since the Convention had begun its efforts to establish a new constitutional and religious settlement following the Revolution, there had been major disappointments for the Dissenters. The "golden opportunity to bring a crown in one hand, with terms or conditions in the other" had not been used to the degree that John Humfrey, Hugh Boscawen, Richard Hampden, John Hampden and others had desired, nor was this failure redeemed by subsequent efforts to obtain major political and constitutional changes through legislation. Likewise the religious settlement that such leaders sought had not been realized, since efforts to obtain comprehension had failed. As Morrice had noted when he walked in the Parliament House during the early weeks of the Convention, he not only saw "very many persons . . . of great worth and integrity," but also "many others who were like to be of much mischief." [123] From the Nonconformist point of view it had been the latter who in the end prevailed.

Yet all Dissenters realized they had made greater gains in the one year of this Convention Parliament than in all the years since the Restoration. There was a Bill of Rights asserting many of the principles for which they had worked. But most important there was finally a parliamentary enactment permitting Trinitarian Dissenters to worship as they pleased.

*Conclusion*

The dissolution of the Convention Parliament of 1689 ended nearly three decades of parliamentary politics during which Presbyterian and Congregationalist members experienced extreme vicissitudes in their status and power. After their loss of effective political power at the beginning of the Cavalier Parliament, they gradually reasserted themselves in debate even though there was a continuing erosion of their strength in the House of Commons. In the Exclusion Parliaments there was a marked resurgence in the number of their members, and they shared leadership of the opposition with the moderate or latitudinarian Anglicans, though not in equal partnership. The same pattern was repeated during the violent changes of the next decade, for following the almost complete destruction of their political power after 1681 there was a considerable revival of Presbyterian-Congregationalist strength in the Convention Parliament of 1689, and their leaders held positions of power within the House of Commons that had not been attained since the Convention Parliament of 1660.

The influence of the moderate Dissenters in Parliament was unquestionably greater than their numbers or the frequency of their speeches would indicate, and this was true for a number of reasons. Presbyterian and Congregationalist members as a group were conscientious in attendance and active in committee work, in part because they were such a small minority. Moreover, they generally acted as a cohesive parliamentary group. To be sure there were differences of outlook among them, and until the death of Holles there was perhaps some division in such parliamentary leadership as did exist. There is little to indicate that Wharton and Holles consulted and acted together, but neither one seems to have made any concerted efforts to assume a position of dominant leadership over the Presbyterians and Congregationalists in Parliament, and they therefore should not be considered as rivals with political ambitions that divided the Presbyterians and Congregationalists in Parliament. Anglesey and Wharton did have contacts with each other, and it seems that the two were cooperative, particularly during the Exclusion Parliaments. By 1689 Richard Hampden had become the most influential Presbyterian leader, and it is known that he and Wharton worked together.

The generally prevailing political cohesiveness of the Presbyterian-Congregationalist group was the product not only of a common political background, but also of similar religious views and of the resulting social and family connections that had been established over the years. The letters, diaries, and family papers of Presbyterian and Congregationalist ministers and political leaders are filled with accounts of the many occasions upon which they met, visited, and dined with each other, and these records as well as others attest to the numerous marriages that took place among these families.

Their cohesiveness and conscientious parliamentary attendance help explain why Nonconformist political strength cannot be measured solely by the numbers of Presbyterians and Congregationalists in Parliament, but neither was the activity of these members the complete measure of Nonconformist political influence. Because of the strong support the Dissenters gave to a very considerable number of moderate Anglicans on the hustings, they had political allies who were always sensitive to their desires and problems. Finally, the Dissenters also exerted political influence by the pressure they brought to bear through their petitioning and lobbying activities, and also through the large number of broadsides, newssheets, pamphlets, and books which they wrote.

The Presbyterians were most effective in exerting political influence because of the considerable number and the prominence of their leaders who sat in Parliament. Also they were the most active of the Nonconformists in electioneering. Although the Congregationalists exerted some influence through the small number of their persuasion who sat in the Commons and because of their activity in electioneering, they were probably most influential through friendships and contacts with political leaders which such ministers as Dr. John Owen and Thomas Jolly maintained, notably with Lord Wharton, and also through the pamphlets which Owen and many others wrote. The Quakers' quietism kept them largely inactive except as petitioners in the 1660's, but after the King's change of policy in 1673–1674 they became very effective as lobbyists and as organized voters, and in addition they were prolific pamphleteers. The Baptists as a group were the least active politically, yet such individual members as Francis Smith made contributions of much influence and significance, and there is evidence that Baptists generally heeded Grantham's plea not to remain political ciphers at the time of Exclusion Parliament elections, and undoubtedly in 1689 as well.

The fear that involvement in secular affairs would distract one from Christian obligations and corrupt the person was a potent source of the quietism among the Baptists and Quakers. To some degree these feelings were also prevalent among Congregationalist and Presbyterian ministers, who were inclined to be quietist in attitude on occasion. However, these ministers seem to have been moved more by a sense of the danger and futility of political action when faced by such vindictiveness and adverse odds as prevailed in 1661–1662 and 1681–1686, or by a strong feeling of the flux of human affairs, as they were when they failed to obtain comprehension or toleration after enjoying the Indulgence of 1672. Revealing his reactions to the danger and futility, the Presbyterian minister Henry Newcome wrote in 1661: "But what sad times are these wherein men's liberties are just at the measure of some men's suspicion or confidence in them! How even must we carry [ourselves] and how warily in this world! How should this make us long for eternity! *Where the weary are at rest and the wicked cease from troubling.*" [1]

Although the combined impact of political defeat and religious uniformity in 1661–1662 were temporarily traumatic, the activities of Presbyterian and Congregationalist members of Parliament and the efforts of their Nonconformist supporters indicate that Dissenters once again began to be involved in English politics about 1666. They remained advocates of a monarchy in which the authority of the king would be constitutionally limited and in which his actions would be effectively controlled by a Parliament with a broader representative base, but there is no question that there was less open and vigorous support of parliamentary measures looking to these ends in the atmosphere of defeat and retaliation following the Restoration, and also between 1668 and

1673, when the more extreme Anglicans in Parliament were immediately responsible for the suppression of Dissenters. Because this suppression was primarily of parliamentary origin, they also came to find that their traditional parliamentarian views appeared somewhat less valid to them at certain times. The first severe test of these beliefs came when the King granted the Indulgence of 1672. Although Nonconformist ministers at first found the constitutional issue between prerogative and parliamentary power less compelling than the question of whether or not they would preach, most of them soon came to agree with the moderate Dissenters in Parliament, who contended throughout the three decades that there should be parliamentary enactments either granting toleration and comprehension or giving sanction to a royal indulgence.

From 1673 until the end of the Oxford Parliament of 1681, a combination of political, religious, and foreign developments made the Dissenters increasingly persistent and aggressive in efforts to restrain the King's actions and to limit his constitutional powers on the one hand, and to increase the powers of Parliament on the other. In debates, committee work, political maneuvers, and pamphleteering they worked to gain some degree of parliamentary control over the conduct of foreign affairs, to obtain some power over royal ministers and policy, to eliminate the dependence of judges upon the Crown, and to restrict its legal powers through such measures as the Habeas Corpus Bill. They also sought to undermine the Court's political power in the Commons by means of parliamentary reform measures. Particularly important were their efforts to curtail or eliminate the King's control over the frequency and duration of Parliaments, not only through parliamentary action, but also in their negotiations with the King regarding the dissolution of the Cavalier Parliament. Finally and most significant was their position upon the critical constitutional question of succession to the Crown of the Realm as it was raised by the Exclusion Bills. Among the most aggressive of the opposition leaders working for these Bills were Richard Hampden and Hugh Boscawen, who contended that it was necessary for Parliament to alter the succession in order to save the monarchy from destruction, and to this position the Presbyterian and Congregationalist members gave almost unanimous support.

Both the growth of the opposition's strength and the contributions that had been made toward the development of limited monarchy prior to 1681 seemed largely nullified during the following five years. Not only did Charles II emerge victorious from his struggle with Parliament, but the opposition forces became widely dispersed, deeply divided, and largely discredited as a result of royal policies and their own actions. Of these developments, the division in the ranks of the opposition had the most lasting consequences. Goaded by the Court's success and frustrated by their own failure, a small number of both Nonconformist and Anglican Whigs became involved in the Rye House Plot, but this resort to extremism was condemned by the much greater number of moderates associated with these two wings of the opposition. Even more divisive in effect was the larger Nonconformist participation in the Monmouth Rebellion. Although the constitutional changes advocated in Monmouth's Declaration contained many of the proposals and reforms that moderate Dissenters had sought to obtain since the Restoration, there were others that they considered too extreme. But the main source of the divisions which appeared was the fact that many Nonconformists resorted to military force and open insurrection, while these tactics were condemned by moderate Dissenters and also the Quakers. During the subsequent period of stringent prosecution, the bitterness already prevailing between Anglicans and Nonconformists increased to such a degree that the earlier understanding and cooperation between moderate Anglicans and moderate Dissenters was largely destroyed.

During 1686 the alignment of Nonconformists began to undergo a most important change as James shifted his policy and started to seek Nonconformist support. Most of the strict Nonconformists were strongly attracted by the dispensations that he granted and by the Indulgence and the promise of penal law and Test Act repeal that came in 1687. As a result, they ceased their opposition and began to support royal policy. The moderate Dissenters on the other hand, were extremely wary of the motives that led the King to abandon the Anglicans and seek Nonconformist support. Thus when he began the fully developed campaign to obtain control of local and national governmental bodies in the autumn of 1687, they refused to commit themselves to repeal of the Test Acts, and in addition they became increasingly receptive to both moderate Anglican and Dutch overtures during the winter of 1687–88.

Faced by the realization that he had not gained sufficient Nonconformist support, the King and his advisers renewed their efforts. But the second Declaration of Indulgence (April, 1688) did little if anything to win additional approval from the strict Nonconformists, while the Order that it be read in all Anglican Churches only drove leaders of the moderate Dissenters and the Church into a closer association and a tacit understanding concerning a new religious settlement that would embody comprehension and toleration. Meanwhile the old coalition of moderate Anglicans and Dissenters was not only re-emerging in the political maneuvering that occurred in the boroughs and counties, but also a few leaders from both wings of this coalition had begun to maintain contact or actually work with James Johnston, one of the Dutch secret agents in London. A most significant pre-revolutionary development occurred in mid-June when John Hampden and the former Presbyterian Sir Thomas Lee informed Johnston that in their opinion the time had come for the Prince of Orange to take action. During the crucial developments of the next six months a growing number of moderate Dissenters came to hope for Dutch intervention, though only a few are known to have actively worked in William's behalf prior to the news of late September that he was going to invade England. This time, unlike the occasions of Rye House Plot and the Monmouth Rebellion, it was the political leaders of the moderate wing of the Dissenters who turned to revolutionary action, and by the end of November a good number had joined William's forces.

In the meantime the strict Nonconformists, most of whom had continued to support the King until he seemingly abandoned them in late September, were left immobilized by the decisive changes taking place, as well as by their vivid memories of the Monmouth Rebellion and the Bloody Assizes. It was apparently not until December that they recovered themselves and gave support to William, and with this development Dissenters were once again generally united in purpose. As a result there were high hopes during the parliamentary elections of January and as the Convention assembled. The Nonconformists' political position seemed more advantageous than it had been throughout the whole Restoration period, and it appeared that at last they and the Anglican Whigs would be able to limit the power of the Crown, establish religious comprehension and toleration, eliminate the religious tests for Protestant officeholders, and assert other fundamental rights in the new constitutional settlement. Although they were more successful in their efforts to have the presentation of the Crown accompanied by constitutional conditions than they had been in 1660, the Declaration of Rights and later the Bill of Rights did not embody as many parliamentarian principles as they had advocated. Still their vigorous efforts were important in obtaining the assertion of those rights which were finally enumerated in these two documents, and in addition their activity was a major factor in the passage of the Toleration Act.

The contributions of the Dissenters to the Revolutionary settlement cannot be restricted to those made during 1688 and 1689. When the Revolutionary settlement is viewed in broader perspective and considered as an integral part of the political and constitutional development since the Restoration, it becomes apparent that the Dissenters had contributed much throughout this whole period that prepared the way for the final adoption of the Bill of Rights and the Act of Toleration. Moreover, they also made similar long-range contributions to the subsequent enactment of the other major measures considered to be part of the constitutional settlement following the Revolution of 1688. Thus the passage of the Triennial Bill of 1694 may to some degree be regarded as the result of past Nonconformist efforts to limit the Crown's power to determine the frequency and duration of parliaments, and the same may be said of the Act of Settlement, since it reduced the power of the King over judges, who were to sit *quamdiu se bene gesserint,* and since it also prohibited him from transacting affairs of state with Privy Councillors in secrecy or from protecting impeached ministers by royal pardons. These limitations had long been sought and supported by Dissenters, and it was therefore appropriate that the former Presbyterian Robert Harley introduced the Triennial Bill and played an important role in the passage of the Act of Settlement, as well as in other parliamentary successes in diminishing the Crown's control over the armed forces and foreign policy during the reign of William III.

It was when the Dissenters sought to free themselves from political and legal restrictions that they were least successful, for too many Anglicans were fearful of weakening their own political positions. Thus the Corporation and Test Acts remained in effect until the successes of the early nineteenth-century reform movement not only freed them of these political restrictions, but also resulted in parliamentary reforms similar to those they had sought.

The experiences of the Dissenters between 1661 and 1689 made many of them seek a more prominent role for the House of Commons, advocate a more popular suffrage, and emphasize the value of having rights established in fundamental constitutional law. Thus, particularly during the decade 1679–1689, they came to a partial acceptance of a few of the basic political ideas that were found in the old Leveller programs. However, even though there was this admixture from the more radical traditions of the Puritan revolutionists, the main tradition to which the Dissenters of the Restoration adhered was that stemming from the Nineteen Propositions and the Treaty of Newport. Furthermore, in most respects their parliamentarianism was even less extreme than that inherent in these documents of the Civil Wars.

The tempering effect that the Restoration experiences had upon the parliamentarian views of the moderate Dissenters was of enduring significance. In the first place it did much to make possible the working alliance between moderate Anglicans and moderate Dissenters that was the backbone of the opposition to the Court during the two decades of Charles II's Parliaments and again in 1688. In addition it was possible for them to contribute to the development of limited monarchy more empirically and effectively than did the parliamentarians of the Civil Wars who relied upon constitutional blueprints and an army.

During the decades between the Restoration and the Revolution of 1688, when the conceptions of parliamentarianism were under attack and the Nonconformists were being suppressed, they remained dedicated to these principles for various reasons. It would seem that most were moved by an intense belief in the rectitude of their religious and political principles. On the other hand, the form of government they envisioned would obviously have been to their advantage, and there was also a considerable degree of expediency in the religious and political temporizing during these years. At the same time, there was a real desire to be as effective as possible in the support of the religious and political ideas in which they so strongly believed, and some compliance in church and state was necessary for this reason. Whether motivated by dedication to their principles or by a desire for political and religious advantages, open avowal of their beliefs and active support of their interests generally called for a willingness to risk property, position, and personal freedom.

The more immediate importance of the Dissenters' parliamentary politics during the critical years 1661–1689 is that through their activity they made substantial contributions to the perpetuation and to the ultimate adoption of highly important constitutional ideas, many of which they had earlier helped to create. But the enduring significance of their efforts is that they contributed to the development of a form of government to which minorities and individuals turned during future centuries when they sought full recognition and protection of their interests and rights.

## Abbreviations

*Note:* All works were published in London unless otherwise indicated. Full information concerning manuscripts is given at the end of the Bibliographical Note on Manuscript Sources.

A.A.E. Archives des Affaires Étrangères, Quai d'Orsay.

Abernathy George R. Abernathy, Jr., *The English Presbyterians and the Stuart Restoration, 1648–1663, Transactions of the American Philosophical Society*, New Ser., Vol. 55, Pt. 2 (May, 1965).

Add. MSS British Museum Additional Manuscripts.

A.H.R. *American Historical Review.*

Al. Cant. *Alumni Cantabrigiensis*, eds. John Venn and John A. Venn (4 vols.; Cambridge, 1922–27).

Al. Oxon. *Alumni Oxoniensis, 1500–1714*, ed. Joseph Foster (5 vols.; 1813–20).

Baxter Richard Baxter, *Reliquiae Baxterianae: or Mr. Richard Baxter's Narrative of the Most Memorable Passages of his Life and Times*, transcribed by Matthew Sylvester (1696).

Beaven A. B. Beaven, *Aldermen of the City of London* (2 vols.; 1908–13).

Besse Joseph Besse, *Collection of the Sufferings of the People Called Quakers* (2 vols.; 1753).

B.H.S.T. *Baptist Historical Society, Transactions.*

B.I.H.R. *Bulletin of the Institute of Historical Research*, London.

B.M. British Museum.

| | |
|---|---|
| Bosher | Robert S. Bosher, *The Making of the Restoration Settlement: The Influence of the Laudians, 1649–1662* (1951). |
| Bramston | John Bramston, *Autobiography,* Camden Society Publications (1845). |
| Browning | *Thomas Osborne, Earl of Danby and Duke of Leeds, 1632–1712* (3 vols.; Glasgow, 1944–51). |
| Brunton and Pennington | D. Brunton and D. H. Pennington, *Members of the Long Parliament* (1954). |
| Burnet | Gilbert Burnet, *History of My Own Time,* ed. Osmund Airy (2 vols.; Oxford, 1897–1900). |
| Calamy, *Acct.* | Edmund Calamy, *An Abridgement of Mr. Baxters History of His Times: With an Account of the Ministers, Who Were Ejected after the Restoration, of King Charles II* (2 vols.; 2d ed.; 1713). |
| ———, *Cont.* | ———, *Continuation of the Account of the Ministers, . . . who were Ejected and Silenced after the Restoration in 1660, by or before the Act for Uniformity* (2 vols.; 1727). |
| C.Clar.S.P. | *Calendar of the Clarendon State Papers Preserved in the Bodleian Library,* ed. F. J. Routledge (4 vols.; Oxford, 1872–1932). |
| C.H.J. | *Cambridge Historical Journal* (since 1958 the *Historical Journal*). |
| C.J. | *Journals of the House of Commons.* |
| Clar.S.P. | *State Papers Collected by Edward, Earl of Clarendon,* ed. Thomas Monkhouse (3 vols.; Oxford, 1767–1786). |
| Coate | Mary Coate, *Cornwall in the Great Civil War and Interregnum, 1642–1660* (Oxford, 1933). |
| C.S.P.D. | *Calendar of State Papers, Domestic Series.* |
| C. Treas. Bks. | *Calendar of Treasury Books.* |
| Dalrymple | John Dalrymple, *Memoirs of Great Britain and Ireland* (3 vols.; 1773–78). |
| D.C.N.Q. | *Devon and Cornwall Notes and Queries.* |
| D.N.B. | *Dictionary of National Biography.* |

| | |
|---|---|
| Duckett | *Penal Laws and Test Act, Questions Touching Their Repeal Propounded in 1687–88 by James II,* ed. Sir George Duckett (2 vols.; 1882, 1883). |
| E.H.R. | *English Historical Review.* |
| Feiling | Keith Feiling, *A History of the Tory Party, 1640–1714* (Oxford, 1924). |
| Friends MSS | Friends Library, London, Manuscripts Collection. |
| G.E.C., *Bart.* | G. E. Cokayne, *Complete Baronetage* (6 vols.; Exeter, 1900–1909). |
| ———, *Peerage* | ———, *Complete Peerage,* ed. V. Gibbs (1910–1959). |
| Gordon | *Freedom after Ejection: A Review (1690–92) of Presbyterian and Congregational Nonconformity in England and Wales,* ed. Alexander Gordon (Manchester, 1917). |
| Henry | Philip Henry, *Diaries and Letters,* ed. Matthew Henry Lee (1882). |
| Heywood | *The Rev. Oliver Heywood, 1630–1702, His Autobiography, Diaries, Anecdote and Event Books,* ed. J. H. Turner (4 vols.; Brighouse, 1882–85). |
| H.M.C. | *Historical Manuscripts Commission Reports.* |
| H. of L. | House of Lords. |
| Hunter | Joseph Hunter, *The Rise of the Old Dissent, Exemplified in the Life of Oliver Heywood . . . 1630–1702* (1842). |
| Jolly | Thomas Jolly, *The Note Book of the Rev. Thomas Jolly A.D. 1671–1693; Extracts from the Church Book of Altham and Wymondhouse, A.D. 1649–1725,* Chetham Society Publications, New Ser., Vol. 33 (Manchester, 1895). |
| J.B.S. | *Journal of British Studies.* |
| J.E.H. | *Journal of Ecclesiastical History.* |
| J.F.H.S. | *Journal of the Friends Historical Society.* |
| J.M.H. | *Journal of Modern History.* |
| Keeler | Mary Keeler, *The Long Parliament, 1640–1641. A Biographical Study of Its Members* (Philadelphia, 1954). |

Kenyon             J. P. Kenyon, *Robert Spencer, Earl of Sunder-
                   land, 1641–1702* (1958).
LeNeve             *[Peter] LeNeve's Pedigrees of the Knights
                   Made by King Charles II, King James II,
                   King William III and . . . Queen Anne*, ed.
                   G. W. Marshall, Harleian Society Publica-
                   tions, Vol. 8 (1873).
L. J.              *Journals of the House of Lords.*
Martindale         *The Life of Adam Martindale Written by Him-
                   self*, ed. Rev. Richard Parkinson, Chetham
                   Society Publications, Vol. 4 (1845).
Marvell            *The Poems and Letters of Andrew Marvell*,
                   ed. H. M. Margoliouth (2d ed.; 2 vols.; Ox-
                   ford, 1952).
"Mather Papers"    *Collections of the Massachusetts Historical So-
                   ciety*, 4th Ser., Vol. VIII (Boston, 1868).
Matthews           *Calamy Revised: Being a Revision of Edmund
                   Calamy's Account of the Ministers and
                   Others Ejected and Silenced, 1660–2*, ed.
                   A. G. Matthews (Oxford, 1934).
Milward            *The Diary of John Milward, Esq. Member of
                   Parliament for Derbyshire (September, 1666
                   to May, 1668)*, ed. Caroline Robbins (Cam-
                   bridge, 1938).
Newcome, *Auto-*   *The Autobiography of Henry Newcome*, ed.
    *biog.*         Richard Parkinson, Chetham Society Publi-
                   cations #26 and 27 (Manchester, 1852).
———, *Diary*       *The Diary of Rev. Henry Newcome from Sept.
                   30, 1661 to Sept. 29, 1663*, ed. Thomas Hey-
                   wood, Chetham Society Publications (Man-
                   chester, 1849).
O.R.               *[Official] Return of the Names of Every Mem-
                   ber Returned to Serve in Each Parliament*,
                   Part I, 1213–1702. Accounts Papers, Session
                   of 1878.
Palmer             Samuel Palmer, *The Nonconformists Memorial*
                   (2d ed.; 3 vols.; 1802).
P.C.2              Privy Council Register.
P.C.C.             Prerogative Court of Canterbury Wills.

| | |
|---|---|
| Pepys | *The Diary of Samuel Pepys,* ed. H. B. Wheatley (10 vols.; 1893–99). |
| P.R.O.30/24 | Public Record Office, Papers of the Earl of Shaftesbury. |
| ———31/3 | ———, Bashet Transcripts. |
| Rawl. Ltrs. | Rawlinson Letters, Bodleian Library. |
| Reresby | *Memoirs of Sir John Reresby,* ed. Andrew Browning (Glasgow, 1936). |
| *R.H.S.T.* | *Royal Historical Society, Transactions.* |
| Sharpe | *Reginald R. Sharpe, London and the Kingdom* (3 vols.; 1894). |
| S.P. | State Papers, Public Record Office. |
| *Statutes* | *The Statutes of the Realm* (11 vols.; 1810–1828). |
| Sykes | Norman Sykes, *From Sheldon to Secker, Aspects of English Church History, 1660–1768* (Cambridge, 1959). |
| Thoresby | *Diary of Ralph Thoresby,* ed. Joseph Hunter (2 vols.; 1830). |
| Turner | *Original Records of Early Nonconformity under Persecution and Indulgence,* ed. G. Lyon Turner (3 vols.; 1911–14). |
| W.S.L. | William Salt Library, now part of the Staffordshire Record Office. |

# NOTES

## NOTE FOR THE INTRODUCTION

1 The authoritative study of the more radical tradition of the mid-century English Revolution has been written by Caroline Robbins, who found there were few Commonwealthmen during the period between the Restoration and the Revolution of 1688. *The Eighteenth-Century Commonwealthmen: Studies in the Transmission, Development and Circumstance of English Liberal Thought from the Restoration of Charles II until the War with the Thirteen Colonies* (Harvard University Press, Cambridge, 1959), Chapter II, particularly pp. 24–31.

## NOTES FOR CHAPTER I

1 The terms *Presbyterian* and *Independent* are used to describe religious rather than political positions. During the years 1659–1660 rigid Presbyterians once again saw the possibility of attaining the kind of true and exclusive Presbyterian Church which they had sought but failed to attain in 1645–1646. In addition there were also moderate Presbyterians who looked for a modified episcopacy and comprehension within a re-established and broadened Anglican Church. The Independents or Congregationalists continued to seek toleration. On the problem of religious and political Presbyterians and Independents during the Civil Wars and Interregnum see J. H. Hexter, "The Problem of the Presbyterian Independents," in *Reappraisals in History* ([Evanston], 1961), pp. 163–84 (a revised version of his article of the same title which appeared in the *A.H.R.*, XLIV (Oct., 1938); George Yule, *The Independents in the English Civil War* (New York, 1958), pp. 1–4, 29–46, 54–64, 77–82; and Hexter's review of Yule's book, *A.H.R.*, LXIV (Jan., 1959), pp. 362–63. David Underdown has written an incisive critical analysis of Yule's work in "The Independents Reconsidered," *J.B.S.*, III (May, 1964), 57–84, to which Yule has replied, "Independents and Revolutionaries," *J.B.S.*, VII (May, 1968), 1–38. Underdown's rejoinder will appear in the Nov., 1968, issue of the *J.B.S.* Also relevant to the

whole problem is Yule's "Some Problems in the History of the Presbyterians in the 17th Century," *Jour. Presby. Hist. Soc.* of England, XIII (1965), 4–13. The problem of terminology after 1661 is discussed in Chapter II.

2   Quaker views are expressed by Edward Burrough, *To the Parliament of the Commonwealth of England* (n.p.; 1659), pp. 2, 7. The continued republicanism of the Baptists and their desire for fundamental guarantees in "laws that cannot be altered, no not [even] by future representatives" were expressed by many. *A Word of Seasonable and Sound Counsell* (1659), proposal number ten; Jeremiah Ives, *Eighteen Questions Propounded* (1659), pp. 2, 6; *An Essay Toward Settlement upon a Sure Foundation* (n.p.; 1659), a broadside signed by prominent Baptists. The Congregationalists' position is found in Lewis du Moulin's *Proposals and Reasons Whereon Some of Them Are Grounded* (1659), pp. 1–3, 6, 7–32. On the republicanism of these sects in 1659 see also William C. Braithwaite, *The Beginnings of Quakerism,* ed. Henry J. Cadbury (2d ed.; 1955), pp. 457–62; Louise Fargo Brown, *The Political Activities of the Baptists and Fifth Monarchy Men in England During the Interregnum* (Washington, 1912), pp. 181–99; and Godfrey Davies, *The Restoration of Charles II, 1658–1660* (San Marino, Cal., 1955), pp. 88, 95–96, 175.

3   The most thoroughgoing democratic plan advanced by a Quaker was contained in a pamphlet undoubtedly written by Edward Billing, but it was too sweeping for the leading Friends. E. B., *A Mite of Affection, Manifested in 31 Proposals* (2d corrected impression; 1659), pp. 2, 6–7, 9–10; John L. Nickalls, "The Problem of Edward Byllynge," in *Children of Light,* ed. H. H. Brinton (New York, 1938), pp. 119–25. George Fox expressed the views of most Quakers in attacking property qualifications as the basis of suffrage, but in also holding that a parliament "chosen by most voices" is not "like to act for God and the good of his people. . . ." *A Few Plain Words to be Considered* (1659), pp. 1–3. For the Baptist and Congregationalist views of a similar nature see Peter Chamberlain, *Legislative Power Considered or Posed in Problems* (1659), pp. 2, 7, [8]; Ives, *Eighteen Questions,* pp. 2, 6; Dr. Williams's Library, Harmer MSS, No. 2, Entire Records of the Congregational Church at Great Yarmouth, transcribed by Joseph Davey, entry of Dec. 12, 1659, fol. 111; *The Clarke Papers,* ed. C. H. Firth (4 vols.; 1891–1901), IV, 121–24; John Browne, *History of Congregationalism and Memorials of the Churches in Norfolk and Suffolk* (1877), p. 265. The reasons which prevented

most Puritans from accepting democracy have been cogently analyzed by Leo F. Solt, *Saints in Arms: Puritanism and Democracy in Cromwell's Army* (Stanford, 1959), particularly pp. 3–5, 8, 66–72, 99–104.

4 Quaker leaders adopted a policy of neutralism and quietism by the end of 1659, *A Declaration from the People Called Quakers* (1659), p. 11; James F. Maclear, "Quakerism and the End of the Interregnum: A Chapter in the Domestication of Radical Puritanism," *Church History*, XIX (Dec., 1950), pp. 259–69. Baptist and Congregationalist views of a similar nature developed more slowly during the following months. Peter Row, *The Magistrates Power Vindicated, and the Abominableness of Resisting their Power Discovered* (n.p.; 1661), pp. 1, 2, 10, 13; Philip Nye, *A Sermon Preached to the Honourable Citizens of London, September 29, 1659* (1661), pp. 7–8. Both of these works were written in 1659 but were delayed in publication until the position advocated was more generally accepted.

5 There was a difference of interpretation regarding the financial proposal, which read in full that Parliament would have the power to raise money "to pay public debts, and for other public uses." In the account of the negotiations and royal concessions which Charles I wrote at the time for the future use of his son he stated that "we conceived it looked backwards only; and therefore we consented to the same for debts incurred and past." However, he added: "in another paper [presumably of parliamentary origin] it being declared it looked to the future as well as the time past, . . . we limited it to the space of two years. . . ." *S.P.Clar*, II, 439. For the proposals offered by the Commissioners from Parliament, see the diary of the negotiations kept by Nicholas Oudart, one of the King's attendants at Newport. *Desiderata Curiosa: or a Collection of Scarce and Curious Pieces Relating Chiefly to Matters of English History*, compiled by Francis Peck (2 vols.; corrected ed.; 1779), II, 387.

6 See Appendix II, for summaries of the evidence concerning the religious position of the members of Parliament who are called Presbyterians or Congregationalists in this study and who sat in one of the two Houses between 1661 and 1689. The summary for Booth appears under his later title of the Baron of Delamer. On Booth's Rising see Davies, *Restoration*, pp. 123–43; and Abernathy, pp. 31–32.

7 *Ibid.*, p. 37.

8 On the problem of the militia see *C.J.*, VII, 847–48, 857, 862–71, 873. The difficulties resulting from the possibility of army

interference are discussed by Davies, *Restoration*, pp. 298–300.

9   *Ibid.*, 880. The kind of government desired by the Commons is suggested in the resolution of March 13 to the effect that the engagement which they had earlier been required to take that they would be " 'faithful to the Commonwealth of England, as the same is now established, without a King, or House of Lords;' be discharged, and taken off the file." *Ibid.*, 872.

10  The ministers were Edmund Calamy, Simeon Ashe, and James Sharp. Letter of Sharp to Sir Joseph Douglas, one of Monck's Scottish associates, March 13. Robert Wodrow, *The History of the Sufferings of the Church of Scotland from the Restoration to the Revolution* (4 vols.; Glasgow, 1835), I, 11.

11  The Presbyterianism of the Commons in the full Long Parliament was demonstrated by its adoption of the Westminster Confession and the Solemn League and Covenant as the bases of the newly prevailing religious settlement. *C.J.*, VII, 858, 862; *C.S.P.D.*, *1659–1660*, pp. 392.

12  The strong royalist and traditional character of Prynne's constitutional views is emphasized by William M. Lamont, *Marginal Prynne* (1963), pp. 205–209. Two other Presbyterian members who were little if at all concerned about limitations upon the crown were Sir Harbottle Grimstone and Edward Stephens, as Abernathy notes, p. 43. Both Prynne and Grimstone moved away from Presbyterianism following the Restoration, but it appears doubtful that Prynne completely abandoned it for Anglicanism as did Grimstone. See Appendix II; *H.M.C.*, *Veralum*, pp. 65–72.

13  Abernathy, pp. 41–43, gives major emphasis to the desire many Presbyterians had for personal reward or safety. He also maintains that those who sought or made engagements with the King were disinterested in a conditional restoration, but this was not necessarily the case. For evidence and comment see Chapter I, notes 16 and 23 below. See also David Underdown, *Royalist Conspiracy in England, 1649–1660* (New Haven, 1960), pp. 308.

14  *England's Confusion*, p. 22; Abernathy, p. 42.

15  The source of this report was the sister of the Earl of Bedford, who was one of those in the Presbyterian Junto who were seeking hard terms. Henry Slingsby to Hyde, March 23. *S.P.Clar.*, III, 705; *C.Clar.S.P.*, IV, 614.

16  Mordaunt reported to Hyde on April 19 that William Pierrepoint, regardless of his letter of engagement, was one of the Presbyterians supporting the Isle of Wight terms and favoring a maneuver to block royalists from the House of Lords. On the same date Lady Mordaunt also reported that Lord Fairfax was an-

other of the group which supported this maneuver and settlement even though the agent had reported to Hyde through Lady Mordaunt that Fairfax had made an engagement to the King. *Ibid.*, pp. 592–93, 665–66. Abernathy has contended that Col. John Birch was another prominent Presbyterian who indicated his capitulation, but the report upon which this contention is based was written by Col. Edward Massey who within a month made another report about Birch that was very adverse, and as late as April 26 Mordaunt considered him one of the most violent in opposition. *Ibid.*, 573, 674; Massey to Hyde, March 16, *A Collection of the State Papers of John Thurloe*, ed. Thomas Birch (7 vols.; 1742), VII, 855; Abernathy, p. 42.

17 Lord Wharton had been a religious Independent, and his inclination in 1660 was probably still toward Independency or Congregationalism. However, he worked with the Presbyterians from the time of the Restoration, and thereafter he apparently became somewhat more Presbyterian in his religious inclinations. In 1660 his religious position is best described as that of a moderate Puritan. See Appendix II for a full discussion and the evidence of his religious views.

18 [S. Morland] to the King, March 19; *C.Clar.S.P.*, IV, 609; Slingsby to Hyde, March 23, *S.P.Clar.*, III, 705. Slingsby's informant was the sister of the Earl of Bedford, previously noted as one of the Presbyterian leaders involved. The Council members included William Pierrepoint, John Crewe, and Sir Gilbert Gerard.

19 S. Morland and R. C. to the King, March 19 and April 3; James Hassall to Hyde, March 23; and Mordaunt to Hyde, April 19, *C.Clar.S.P.*, IV, pp. 609, 616, 634, 665–66; Antoine de Bordeaux (French Ambassador in England) to Cardinal Mazarin, April 1, F. P. Guizot, *History of Richard Cromwell and the Restoration of Charles II*, trans. A. R. Scoble (2 vols.; 1856), II, 389; *A Collection of Original Letters and Papers, Concerning the Affairs of England, from the Year 1641 to 1660, Found among the Duke of Ormonde's Papers*, ed. Thomas Carte (2 vols.; 1739), II, 319–21; *S.P.Clar.*, III, 705, 713; Thurloe, *State Papers*, VII, 872–73.

20 The leaders supporting this plan were the Earls of Northumberland and Manchester. In addition to having the support of most of the surviving lords, which would have included Wharton and Saye, they had according to Mordaunt won support from Lord Fairfax, Sir Denzil Holles, Sir William Lewis, William Pierrepoint, Sir Gilbert Gerard, and Sir Anthony Ashley Cooper. *C.Clar.S.P.*, IV, 665–66.

21  In his letter to the King of April 24 Mordaunt acknowledged that Annesley was "hardly persuaded" to join the Suffolk cabal. Clarendon MSS 72, fol. 19. Monck is supposed to have agreed to the plan to seat only the 1648 peers, but according to older accounts he backed out on April 26, the day when the first young peers took their seats. However, Abernathy has pointed out that Monck was much displeased with the young lords, and he contends that the General was tricked by them just as the Presbyterians were. Abernathy, p. 56. *C.Clar.S.P.*, IV, 680. Dering MS Diary, fol. 2.

22  Mordaunt to the King, April 24–26, *C.Clar.S.P.*, IV, 674; *L.J.*, XI, 5, 10; Mordaunt to Hyde, May 4, *S.P.Clar.*, III, 738–39. For additional evidence that there were efforts to obtain control of the militia and the privy council for five years as well as to gain other so-called "hard" terms, see Henry Coventry's letter of May 4 to Hyde, Clarendon MSS, 72, fol. 180.

23  Mordaunt to Hyde, May 4, reprinted by Thomas H. Lister, *Life and Administration of Edward, First Earl of Clarendon* (3 vols.; 1837–1838), III, 99–100. It appears that Mordaunt was aware that the royalist agent Sir Philip Warwick had reported April 27 that the Earl of Southampton "moulds Northumberland and Saye, and they the rest, to send petitions not propositions, to the King," and that Barwick informed Hyde the same day that Northumberland had become "a great zealot for the King," and Saye "now is an old Caballist." Based on Annesley's reports to him, Mordaunt had already asserted in his letter of April 24–26 that Northumberland "was not to be made the King's"; and since he not only had Annesley's reports but also saw the Earl of Southampton daily himself, Mordaunt must be considered more reliable than Warwick, who appears to have been too willing to accept Southampton's claims, or than Barwick. Clarendon MSS, 72, fol. 50; *C.Clar.S.P.*, IV, 683. However, Mordaunt was incorrect concerning the course Manchester was to take. In May this Lord's interest in office became evident and eventually led to appointment as Lord Chamberlain. But at the same time he began moving away from Presbyterianism, and from 1661 there is insufficient evidence to warrant considering him a Presbyterian. Alderman Bunce to the King, April 24, *ibid.*, 673; Bordeaux to Mazarin, June 7, Guizot, *R. Cromwell*, II, 435; Davies, *Restoration*, p. 342.

24  The ten lords who first took their seats on the morning of April 25 were out-numbered by the time Manchester was nominated for the Great Seal on April 27, as well as when the Committee on the Militia was appointed on May 2. However, the fact that

the Militia Committee of twelve contained six of the lords who were present on the first day indicated that the Presbyterian peers had managed to maintain some degree of influence. *L.J.*, XI, 3–4, 5, 10. See also Dering, *Diary*, fol. 2. Concerning Presbyterian strength in the Commons, see n. 34 below.

25 Broderick to Hyde, May 13, *S.P.Clar.*, III, 748. Earle's motion which Broderick discussed with Annesley and Speaker Grimstone was probably made in the committee appointed on May 3 to consider the King's letter to the Commons as well as the Declaration of Breda and for preparing bills accordingly. Col. John Birch, who was a member of the committee, twice referred to the debate on the motion years later in parliamentary debates. Grey, II, 269 (Jan., 1674); III, 111 (May, 1675). Earle had been a leading Puritan in the Long Parliament. Keeler, pp. 165–66.

26 Mordaunt to Hyde, April 19, *C.Clar.S.P.*, IV, 665–66; Holles to his wife, April 5, Add. MSS, 32,679, fol. 60.

27 Mordaunt to the King, April 24–26, *C.Clar.S.P.*, IV, 674–75; Abernathy, pp. 55, 58; *C.J.*, VIII, 4. The other Presbyterians on the committee were Annesley and Sir William Lewis.

28 Abernathy, pp. 58–59.

29 *C.J.*, VIII, 42, 49, 80; *L.J.*, IX, 81; *H.M.C.*, *7th Rept. Pt. I, H. of L. MSS*, p. 113. The Bill did not pass the Commons until July 3, when Prynne who had been chairman of the committee on the Bill carried it to the House of Lords.

30 Bordeaux to Mazarin, May 11, Guizot, *R. Cromwell*, II, 420.

31 *The Copies of Several Letters, Which Were Delivered to the King, Being Written by Sundry Friends* (1660), p. 52; *A Reply to Mr. William Prinne* (1659 [1660 N. S.]), p. 2.

32 Fox, *Journal*, I, 343; *Copies of Several Letters*, pp. 1, 16; George Fox and Richard Hubberthorne, *An Answer to the Oath of Allegiance and Supremacy from the People (Called Quakers) A Copie of Which Was Given to the King by Them upon the 4 Day of the 5 Month, 1660* (1660), broadside.

33 Richard Hubberthorne, *Something That Lately Passed in Discourse Between the King and R. H.* (1660), p. 5; George Fox, *A Word in the Behalf of the King* (1660), p. 10; *Copies of Several Letters*, p. 16; Fox the Younger and Hubberthorne, *An Answer to the Oath of Allegiance*, broadside; A. C. Underwood, *A History of the English Baptists* (1947), pp. 89–91; Brown, *Political Activities of the Baptists*, p. 203. Baptists of all shades of opinion were much more outspoken upon this matter in their declarations after the Venner Plot of the following January. See *The Humble Apology of Some Commonly Called Anabaptists,*

*in Behalf of Themselves and Others of the Same Judgement with Them: With Their Protestation against the Late Wicked and Most Horrid Treasonable Insurrection and Rebellion Acted in the City of London; Together with an Apology Formerly Presented to the King's Excellent Majesty* (1660), pp. 6–10.

34 The conclusion first reached by Louise Fargo Brown that the Presbyterian members were somewhat outnumbered by the Anglicans has recently been verified and extensively amended in a careful analytical study of the Convention Parliament made by M. E. W. Helms, who found 36.2% of the members to be Presbyterian and 37.3% to be Anglican. However, the classification of each member according to religious views in this study has made it clear that the Independent (Congregationalist) minority of 5.5% and the additional 5.5% who are considered Independents or Presbyterians were not the only ones affecting the balance of power, as Brown had thought. The strength of both these minorities to one side of the Presbyterians was equalled by the 11.2% of the members on the other side who are classified as either Presbyterians or Anglicans. Helms has pointed out that the combined strength of the Presbyterians and Independents was 47.2%, but it should also be emphasized that included among the Presbyterians are 53 members, or 9% of the total House, who conformed after 1660. Judging by the known actions of many nominal Presbyterians after May, 1660, it would seem that many of the members who conformed after 1660 and many of those classified as Presbyterians or Anglicans probably voted with the Anglicans on occasions. In any event, the Anglicans and those Presbyterians inclined toward them made up 57.5% of the members (37.3% Anglican, 11.2% Presbyterian or Anglican, and 9% Conformists after 1660). Louise Fargo Brown, "Religious Factors in the Convention Parliament," *E.H.R.*, XXII (Jan., 1907), 63; M. E. W. Helms, "The Convention Parliament of 1660" (unpublished Ph.D. dissertation, Dept. of History, Bryn Mawr College), pp. 141–43, 164 (Table 17).

35 G. F. Trevallyn Jones, "The Composition and Leadership of the Presbyterian Party in the Convention," *E.H.R.* (April, 1964), vol. 79, pp. 310 ff.

36 Bosher, p. 117; Abernathy, pp. 61–62, 66.

37 Brown, *E.H.R.*, XXII, 58–59; Helms, "Convention . . . ," pp. 335–39; Abernathy, p. 72.

38 An Act for the Confirming and Restoring of Ministers, *Statutes*, V, 242–46.

39 E. W. Kirby, "The Reconcilers and the Restoration (1660–1662),"

*Essays in Modern English History in Honor of Wilbur Cortez Abbott* (Cambridge, Mass., 1941), pp. 61–65; Abernathy, pp. 74–77.

40 During the negotiations the Congregationalists and Baptists had petitioned for a promise of toleration, but when Clarendon suggested that "others also be permitted to meet for religious worship" if the public peace were not disturbed, Richard Baxter refused to accept the proposal, believing that toleration was being sought for Catholics. Baxter, Pt. II, pp. 276–79. See also Abernathy's account, p. 75.

41 This vote on the first reading was 157–183. Two contemporary observers reported that, as one of them put it, "some of the old commonwealth party joined with the Cavaliers." *C.J.*, VIII, 194; *H.M.C., 5th Rept. Sutherland MSS*, pp. 158, 196.

42 *L.J.*, XI, 82–83, 153, 156, 165, 192, 194–95.

43 Bosher, pp. 201–204; Matthews, p. xi; Abernathy, p. 78. For the best summary of the legal position of Nonconformists in 1660 see Charles F. Mullett, "The Legal Position of English Protestant Dissenters, 1660–1689," *Virginia Law Review*, XXII (March, 1936), 495–97.

NOTES FOR CHAPTER II

1 The impact of the Restoration religious settlement is discussed in Chapter IV.

2 Scholars from Edmund Calamy to those of the present have found it difficult in many instances to decide whether a person was an Anglican or a Dissenter, even when concerned with ministers who generally are classified with relative ease since Anglican clergymen had to take the various required oaths and subscriptions which became a matter of record and public knowledge. See for example Calamy's remarks concerning Mr. John Chandler, *Acct.*, II, 315. A. G. Matthews, the compiler of *Calamy Revised*, has stated in another of his works that the line dividing Conformists and Nonconformists is "often almost invisible." *Congregational Churches of Staffordshire, with Some Account of the Puritans, Presbyterians, Baptists and Quakers in the County During the 17th Century* (1924), pp. 44–45. See also Benjamin Nightingale, *The Ejected of Cumberland Westmorland, Their Predecessors and Successors* (2 vols.; Publications of the University of Manchester, Manchester, 1911), II, 1106–1109.

3 The phrase "conformable Nonconformists" was used by five anonymous ministers to describe themselves on the title page of

their pamphlet, *A Short Surveigh of the Grand Case of the Present Ministry* (n.p., 1663). At the end they stated that they prayed they might have religious peace, "though not conforming to the whole of the order of England's Church." p. 47.

4  Published in 1680. The quotation is from the Introduction, p. [2].

5  Besse, I, 293.

6  There was one minister who disagreed with the uncompromising position taken by the Baptists prior to about 1680. John Tombes became a lay-conformist at the Restoration, and in 1667 wrote that it was lawful both to attend service and take the Sacrament. *Theodulia, or a Just Defense of Hearing the Sermons and other Teaching of the Present Ministers of England* (1667), was dedicated to Clarendon, who had befriended Tombes after the latter had defended the supremacy of the King in civil and ecclesiastical affairs in three pamphlets: *A Serious Consideration of the Oath of Supremacy* [1660]; *A Supplement to the Serious Consideration* [1660]; and *Saints No Smiters; or Smiting the Civil Powers Not the Work of Saints* (1664). When it is added that Tombes favored Presbyterian church government, it becomes clear that he was hardly a representative Baptist minister.

7  Morrice MSS, P, 623.

8  See, for example, the comments concerning Congregationalists' practices made by William Hooke, one of Cromwell's old chaplains in his letter to an American colleague in February, 1663. "A Censored Letter," ed. A. G. Matthews, *C.H.S.T.*, IX (Sept., 1926), 270–71; see also Philip Henry's diary entry of April 23, 1663, p. 135.

9  The famous John Robinson (1576–1625) was one of the leading advocates of this practice. His defense is found in a pamphlet published posthumously in 1634 entitled *A Treatise of the Lawfulness of Hearing of the Ministers in the Church of England* [Amsterdam], pp. 3, 63–64.

10  *C.S.P.D., 1668–1669*, pp. 11, 159–60. Although the Minute Books of this Church have been preserved, unfortunately there was "a long silence" in the keeping of minutes after 1662. Harmer MSS, No. 2, Entire Records of the Congregational Church at Great Yarmouth (transcribed by Joseph Davey), fol. 122.

11  See Chapter II, pp. 26–27.

12  John Owen, "A Discourse Concerning Evangelical Love, Church Peace and Unity," *Works*, ed. Thomas Russell (28 vols.; 1826), XXI, 158.

13  "An Answer unto Two Questions: with Twelve Arguments Against Any Conformity to Worship Not of Divine Institution,"

*ibid.,* XXI, 519–36. This short work was found among Owen's papers at his death in 1683, and although Richard Baxter answered it in his *Catholick Communion Defended* (1684), it was not published until 1720.

14 Philip Nye, *A Case: Whether We May Lawfully Hear the Now-Conforming Ministers, Who Are Re-ordained, and Have Renounced the Covenant* (1677), pp. 4–6. Baxter implies that Nye wrote this pamphlet some five or six years before his death in 1672. *Reliquiae,* Pt. III, p. 19.

15 Nye, pp. 20–23.

16 *The Lawfulness of Hearing the Publick Ministers of the Church of England Proved,* comp. Henry Nye (1683), "Addenda" p. 39. See also Henry Nye's remarks in the preface "To the Reader." The main section of this compilation includes a reprint of his father's *A Case* and John Robinson's *A Treatise.* In the "Addenda" Henry Nye quotes briefly from Owen and others, and he adds his own comments.

17 Stephen Lobb, *The True Dissenter, or the Cause of Those that Are for Gathered Churches* (n.p., 1685), Preface, and p. 120. His position had also been stated in *The Harmony Between the Old and Present Non-Conformists Principles, In Relation to the Terms of Conformity, With Respect Both to the Clergie and the People* (1682).

18 Jolly, pp. 136–37. On Jolly's attitude see also Newcome, *Autobiog.,* II, 244.

19 Stowe MSS, 185, fol. 172.

20 *L.J.,* XI, 11, 15; *C.J.,* VIII, 247. Since there are no entries concerning the matter in the Lords' Journals after May 3 and 5, it appears that the Presbyterian lords complied with the order.

21 For the details see Chapter III, p. 32.

22 *Statutes,* V, 322–23.

23 A full discussion of the Act of Uniformity will be found in Chapter IV.

24 Newcome, *Diary,* p. 119.

25 *C.J.,* VIII, 513. The full title was "A Bill to Prevent and Suppress Seditious Conventicles." For a discussion of its provisions and its passage see Chapter IV, pp. 53–54.

26 Martindale, pp. 173, 180 n.; Calamy, *Acct.,* II, 23–24; *Cont.,* II, 777–78. Calamy states that after Eccleshall preached he would go with his congregation to the Anglican Church, but that they avoided the Common Prayer and the Sacrament.

27 Henry, pp. 134–35. See also his more lengthy explanation written in 1666, pp. 177–80.

28	See Chapter III, n. 14. Henry records in his diary one instance in which "many . . . tendered themselves sitting . . . and received," p. 166. See also Calamy, *Acct.*, II, 453–54.

29	*Christian Directory: or, a Summ of Practical Theologie, and Cases of Conscience* (1673), p. 859. Concerning Baxter's habits of occasional communion, see his statements in *Reliquiae*, Pt. I, Sec. 2, p. 437. Some of the Presbyterians conforming occasionally at York accepted the practice of kneeling. Thomas Comber to the Archbishop of Canterbury, Oct., 1689, Tanner MSS, 27, fol. 93.

30	*Statutes*, V, 367–69.

31	*Ibid.*, IV, 546–47; [Sir Edward Harley], *An Humble Essay toward the Settlement of Peace and Truth in the Church As a Certain Foundation of Lasting Union* (1681), pp. 24–25. For a discussion of Harley's religious views, see *infra*, Appendix II.

32	The proposal concerning the Act of Uniformity is in the papers of Lord Wharton, Carte MSS, 81, fol. 109. For examples of later Bills providing for modification of the subscription to the Thirty-nine Articles, see those of 1673 and 1680. *C.J.*, IX, 259; *H.M.C., Beaufort MSS*, pp. 101–102. There was most objection to Articles 36–38 and to the clause in Article 20 stating that "the Church has power to decree rites or ceremonies, and authority in controversies of faith. . . ." *Ibid.*, p. 101.

33	See the draft of a petition to the King from some Nonconformist ministers apparently in 1674, *H.M.C., Portland MSS*, VIII, 14; and also Sir Edward Harley's comments in *An Humble Essay*, p. 25. William Prynne was one who had strong feelings concerning such matters, as is apparent in the summary of his religious views, Appendix II

34	*Statutes*, V, 366.

35	The so-called oath of canonical obedience was contained in the Ordinal that was appended to the Act of Uniformity along with the Book of Common Prayer. *The Book of Common Prayer from the Original Manuscript Attached to the Act of Uniformity 1662, and Now Preserved in the House of Lords* (1892), p. 531.

36	*Statutes*, V, 366.

37	[John Humfrey], *The Healing Paper: or, a Catholic Receipt for Union between the Moderate Bishop and Sober Non-Conformist* (1678), pp. 5–8. For his efforts in 1667 and 1674 see Chapter IV, pp. 56–68.

38	Calamy, *Acct.*, II, 615–23; Matthews, pp. 284–85.

39	*Ibid.*, p. 17. Ten years earlier Humfrey had stated his position in another pamphlet entitled *A Defence of the Proposition: Or, Some Reasons Rendered Why the Nonconformist-Minister Who*

*Comes to His Parish Church and Common Prayer, Cannot Yet Yeeld to Other Things that Are Enjoyned, Without Some Moderation* (1668).

40  For examples of this usage in addition to those already cited, see *C.S.P.D., 1677–1678,* p. 559; *1682,* pp. 608–609.

41  Baxter, Pt. I, Sec. 2, p. 387; *Short Surveigh of the Grand Case . . . , By some Conformable Nonconformists.* Cheyney's *The Conforming Non-Conformist and the Non-Conforming Conformist* is a later variation.

42  Baxter, Pt. III, p. 100.

43  W.S.L. MSS, 254, Swynfen Ltrs. No. 15 (May, 1669); Sir Henry Ashurst's letter to Henry Newcome in 1668, in Hunter, pp. 200–201; Morrice MSS, Q, 237, 368, 562.

44  *Ibid.,* P, 557 (shorthand passage).

45  *Ibid.,* 556–57. The phrase "Puritan Low Churchmen" has been used by C. E. Whiting to describe the position of Sir Patience Ward, and it is an accurate description of the views of many others, a good example being Henry Booth, Second Lord Delamer. He was raised a Presbyterian and later conformed, but he believed that there was "too much idolatry" in some of the ceremonies and thought that the Bishops contended strongly for ceremonies "not to preserve the Church, but to support themselves. . . ." He wanted ceremonies "indifferent" because then there would be "many pious and able men who would conform. . . ." "Some Reasons against the Prosecuting of the Dissenters" (1682), and "Reasons for an Union Between the Church and the Dissenters," *Works of Henry Late Lord Delamer and Earl of Warrington* (1694), pp. 412, 414, 461. On Ward see C. E. Whiting, "Sir Patience Ward of Tanshelf, Lord Mayor of London," *Yorkshire Arch. Jour.,* XXXIV, Part 3 (1939), pp. 257–58, 268, 270–71; also his correspondence with Thomas Papillon in 1688, A. F. W. Papillon, *Memoirs of Thomas Papillon* (Reading, 1887), pp. 336–47

46  *C.S.P.D., 1682,* pp. 608–609.

47  Tanner MSS, 36, fol. 196.

48  The intent of the first Conventicle Act is particularly evident in the clause which declared the Elizabethan Conventicle Act (35 Eliz. cap. 1) was still in effect, for that Act provided that any person over sixteen convicted of being present at a conventicle had to conform within three months or they had to abjure the realm or be declared felons without benefit of clergy. Also of specific relevance was the refusal of the House of Commons to accept an amendment to the first Conventicle Bill which would

have given legal sanction to the practice of occasional conformity
by exempting from the penalties of the Act those who did "frequent the service of the Church and receive the Sacrament thrice
every year." *Statutes,* IV, Pt. II, pp. 841; V, 516.

49   See Chapter V, n. 25.

50   Morrice MSS, P, 574.

51   *Diary of Ralph Thoresby,* ed. Joseph Hunter (2 vols., 1830), I,
      169–72, 181, 186–87.

52   For Morrice's own position, see Chapter VIII, pp. 177–79.

53   Morrice MSS, Q, 90. Among the moderate Anglican clergymen
      with whom Morrice was very friendly were the following: Dr.
      Edward Fowler, the leader of the London clergy in their refusal
      to read James's Indulgence of April, 1688; Dr. Richard Kidder,
      who had been ejected in 1662, but who conformed by 1664; the
      Rev. John Strype, the ecclesiastical historian; and Dr. John
      Moore, later chaplain to William and Mary; all but Strype be-
      came bishops. Morrice, who was well-to-do, left a ring to each
      of these men at his death. *Ibid.,* 204, 254 (Fowler's name is in
      shorthand); P.C.C. 9 Hearne. The Anglican diarist Sir John
      Evelyn confirmed Morrice's observation concerning the effect of
      the Indulgence, noting that at Deptford on April 4, 1687, there
      was a large Nonconformist meeting while the Parish Church
      was "left exceeding thin." *The Diary of John Evelyn,* ed. E. S.
      de Beer (6 vols., Oxford, 1955), IV, 546–47.

54   Henry, Martindale, Baxter, Nye, Crofton, Eccleshall, and Hum-
      frey who have been the examples used to illustrate varying
      degrees of conformity, were all licensed in 1672–1673. Turner,
      II, 734 *passim.* A particularly significant instance of a reunion
      between a minister and congregation occurred at Warrington,
      Lancashire, in which the Nonconformity of the members was
      asserted after they were unable to obtain the service of both
      their parish clergyman and their Presbyterian minister. Francis
      Nicholson and Ernest Axon, "Robert Yates, Rector of Warring-
      ton," *Trans. Lancashire and Cheshire Antiquarian Society,* XXXII
      (1915), 213.

55   Morrice MSS, P, 430; Q, 237.

56   This was a distinction made by the Earl of Masserene in de-
      scribing the religious position of the Presbyterian minister John
      Howe in a letter to John Swynfen in 1676. W.S.L. MSS, 254,
      Swynfen Ltrs., No. 24.

57   *C.S.P.D., 1667–1668,* p. 88; S.P.31/IV/2, fol. 109. The word
      *called* has been italicized because it is evident Newcastle recog-
      nized that although it would be stated that the Presbyterians

were of the Church, actually they were not. Hopes of comprehension at this time (October, 1688) as in the past, tended to divorce many Presbyterians from the other Dissenters.

58 *Healing Paper,* p. 17

NOTES FOR CHAPTER III

1 On the political consequences of the Fifth Monarchist plot of January, 1661, see W. C. Abbott, "English Conspiracy and Dissent, 1660–1674 [Part] I," *A.H.R.,* XIV (April, 1909), 504; and Maurice Ashley, *John Wildman* (1947), pp. 164–65. On the plot itself, which was a desperate move made by a very small group in reaction to the execution of the Fifth Monarchist leader and of the regicide Major-General Henry Harrison, see Champlin Burrage, "Fifth Monarchy Insurrections," *E.H.R.,* XXV (Oct., 1910), 739–46; Max Beloff, *Public Order and Popular Disturbances,* 1660–1714 (Oxford, 1938), p. 35; P. G. Rogers, *The Fifth Monarchy Men* (1966), pp. 112–22.

2 *A Dialogue Between the Two Giants in Guildhall* (1661), pp. 4–5; *C.S.P.D., 1660–1661,* p. 542; The Diary of Col. Buller Reames, B. M. Egerton MSS, 2043, fols. 29–30; *The Oceana and Other Works of James Harrington,* ed. John Toland (1747), pp. xxxiv–xxxv; *C.J.,* VIII, 339–40, 342. There were also instances of cooperative effort elsewhere, *C.S.P.D., 1660–1661,* p. 542; *H.M.C., 5th Rept., Sutherland MSS,* p. 181.

3 *C.S.P.D., 1660–1661,* pp. 535–43. The Privy Council ordered the arrest of the Presbyterian minister Zachary Crofton and others after hearing several letters read. He was lodged in the tower "for matters of high treason" and not released until July, 1662. P.C.2/55/178, 202, 418; Matthews, pp. 144–45.

4 See David Masson, *Life of John Milton* (6 vols.; Cambridge, 1859–1880), VI, 158; Frank Bate, *Declaration of Indulgence, 1672: A Study in the Rise of Organized Dissent* (1908), p. 20; G. N. Clark, *The Later Stuarts, 1660–1714* (Corrected reprint, Oxford, 1940), p. 53. Among those frequently considered Presbyterians were those who rapidly shifted their views and actions to be in accord with the new situation following the Restoration. Two excellent examples were Sir Anthony Ashley Cooper, and Sir Richard Browne. Louise Fargo Brown, *The First Earl of Shaftesbury* (New York, 1933), pp. 100–103. As Lord Mayor, Browne began apprehending Nonconformists in the summer of 1661. *H.M.C., Le Fleming MSS,* p. 28; *C.S.P.D., 1661–1662,* p. 70.

5 Twenty-three of this number may be regarded as certain Presbyterians or Congregationalists, while nine were probably and another five were possibly of these religious positions. A general discussion of the sources used in this classification is found in Appendix I. For the names of the members see Appendix III, and for the summary of the evidence concerning the religious views of each M.P. see Appendix II. There were two cases in which Presbyterians were returned on double returns, and in each case the opponents were seated both temporarily and permanently. On these cases of Sir Thomas Barnardiston and Sir Samuel Luke, see *C.J.*, VIII, 253, 360; *O.R.*, I, 519 n., 529 n.

6 The most reliable contemporary estimate of the strength of parliamentary groups during the first decade of the Cavalier Parliament was that made by Richard Temple, and he thought there were about forty Presbyterians in the House in 1667–1668. This is twelve more than the number for whom evidence of Presbyterianism (or Congregationalism) has been discovered as of that date in this study, and it suggests that there were about a dozen more Dissenters sitting in 1661 than listed in Appendix III. Stowe MSS, 304, fol. 88. *Huntington Library Quar.*, XX (Feb., 1957), 136–44.

7 Carte MSS, 81, fols. 81–83. H. N. Mukerjee first hinted that there were some members of Wharton's lists who were not friends or moderates. "Elections for the Convention and Cavalier Parliaments," *Notes and Queries*, CLXVI (June 9, 1934), 421. The lists have been edited by G. F. T. Jones, *E.H.R.*, Vol. 79, pp. 350–54 (Documents III and IV).

8 Although Wharton includes Sir Harbottle Grimstone he omits such men as Sir John Trevor. For the previous Puritanism of these men see Keeler, pp. 199, 365; Helms, "Convention Parl., pp. 1095–96. On their subsequent friendly disposition see Burnet, II, 77; Baxter, I, 445; *C.S.P.D., 1670*, pp. 233–34; *1671*, p. 569.

9 The vote was 228–103. *C.J.*, VIII, 254. Abbott used this division along with others to support his contention that the opposition to the Anglican Cavaliers was double the fifty or so Presbyterians. He was wrong in seeming to imply that the additional votes were those of Dissenters, and he was unaware of Wharton's list, but he too was correct concerning the approximate strength of the opposition at that juncture. "The Long Parliament of Charles II," *E.H.R.*, XXI (Jan. and Apr., 1906), 27–29.

10 *L.J.*, XII, 242–43, 246–47. On Clarendon's position regarding the Dissenters, see n. 64 of this chapter.

11 *L.J.*, XII, 11, 15; *C.J.*, VIII, 247. The entries in the Lords' Jour-

nals are dated May 3 and 5, and there are no subsequent ones concerning this matter; the Commons' resolution was passed May 13.

12 *H.M.C., 5th Rept., Sutherland MSS*, p. 202.

13 *C.J.*, VIII, 258, May 22. It appears from the report on this matter of receiving the Sacrament made July 3, that Ashton "had the tacit dispensation" to abstain from carrying out the House's order. However, it seems significant that he was unseated February 4, 1662. *C.J.*, VIII, 289, 357.

14 Henry, p. 87. Some members asked for permission to go into the country at this time, as did Sir Anthony Irby, and the Sacrament issue may have been the reason. Undoubtedly others took the Sacrament with outward reservations, as did William Prynne and Hugh Boscawen when they refused to take the prescribed kneeling position for receiving the wine and bread. According to Col. Reames' diary entry of that day, Dr. Gunning refused the bread to Prynne, but Boscawen took it standing. B.M., Egerton MSS 2043, fol. 10; Pepys, II, 42–43; *H.M.C., 5th Rept. Sutherland MSS*, p. 160.

15 In the report given to the House all five members listed as having no reason for their failure were Presbyterians or Congregationalists; they were Richard Hampden, Henry Henley, William Love, John Ratcliffe, and Colonel Richard Norton. One of those listed as sick at the time, Sir William Thompson, was also of this group. The seventh was Sir Ralph Ashton who had been given a tacit dispensation by the House. *C.J.*, VIII, 289, 294–95, 444; and the note on each man in Appendix II.

16 *H.M.C., 5th Rept., Sutherland MSS*, p. 207.

17 *Ibid.*, pp. 160, 170; *C.J.*, VIII, 254.

18 When the House was called over both Wharton and Bedford were absent. *L.J.*, XI, 259–61.

19 *The Funeral of the Good Old Cause, or a Covenant of Both Houses of Parliament Against the Solemn League and Covenant* (1661). This purports to be a speech given in Parliament May 20.

20 Pepys, II, 46. Undoubtedly reiterating views expressed at this time, Prynne argued in a lecture of the following February that the Bishops should not sit in Parliament except "by reason of their temporal Baronies." Inner Temple MSS, 538.32, fol. 11, Reading of William Prynne at Gray's Inn, February 17, 1662, on the Petition of Right (1628); and Observations on the Right of Bishops to Sit in Parliament.

21 *Statutes*, pp. 304–306; 308–309.

22 *H.M.C. 5th Rept. Sutherland MSS*, p. 196. For part taken by

Sir John Maynard and John Swynfen regarding another matter in the Bill see *C.J.*, VIII, 255, 256, and *Notebook of Sir John Northcote*, ed. A. H. A. Hamilton (1877), p. 128.

23  *C.J.*, VIII, 256, 304; *L.J.*, XI, 263, 317.

24  *Statutes*, V, 305.

25  Newcome, *Diary*, p. 8.

26  Morrice MSS, P, 112. Morrice expresses a similar view in writing about this Act along with others in another, undated note. Morrice MSS, U, "Outline of First Sketch for the Politico-Ecclesiastical History of England," fol. 107.

27  This is the opinion of J. H. Sacret who has written a full account of the opposition efforts against this bill. However, not knowing the identity of most of the Presbyterian and Congregationalist members, he did not attempt to distinguish between the activities of this wing of the opposition and the efforts of the members who were either friendly to Puritans and Nonconformists or anxious to have their political support. "The Restoration Government and Municipal Corporations," *E.H.R.*, XLV (April, 1930), 248–51.

28  *C.J.*, VIII, 276.

29  *Ibid.*, pp. 282, 288. Two such amendments were introduced, one by Prynne which was voted down without a reading, and the other by the four Presbyterian and Congregationalist members from London providing that the Act would not apply to this great center of Puritan and Nonconformist strength. Defeated on this measure, these four members then refused to nominate commissioners to enforce the Act, and as a result a special clause concerning London was inserted which provided for their selection by the King.

30  *C.J.*, VIII, 291; *Summary Reasons, Humbly Tendered to the Most Honourable House of Peers, by Some Citizens and Members of London, and Other Cities, Boroughs, Corporations, and Ports, Against the New-intended Bill for Governing and Reforming Corporations* (n.p., 1661).

31  See the conclusion of *Summary Reasons*.

32  *C.J.*, VIII, 299, 301–302.

33  *H.M.C.*, *Beaufort MSS*, pp. 50–51; *C.J.*, VIII, 302; Lamont, *Prynne*, pp. 226–27.

34  *C.J.*, VIII, 288–89, 291, 294–96. The enactment of the Act of Uniformity is discussed fully in Chapter IV, pp. 48–50.

35  Lord Wharton along with three other Presbyterian lords served on this committee of thirty-five members, but only one or two documents which appear to concern this bill have been found

in his parliamentary papers, while in contrast there are a considerable number regarding the Uniformity Bill, including nearly a dozen possible amendments. *L.J.*, XI, 313; Carte MSS, 81, fols. 260, 587; *L.J.*, XI, 322; *C.J.*, VIII, 310–11, 313.

36 See *C.J.*, VIII, 336–38; *Statutes*, V, 321–23.

37 A motion to send Fowke to the Tower of London was defeated. *C.J.*, VIII, 386.

38 On the first attempt there was a division in which the Presbyterians Sir James Langham and Sir Thomas Lee were the tellers in favor of the measure. The "Noes" polled 116 votes; the number for the "Yeas" is not given in the Journals. *C.J.*, VIII, 386.

39 The division was 92–34. Mr. Boscawen, undoubtedly Hugh rather than Edward, was the only teller listed for those favoring the measure. *C.J.*, VIII, 434. On the problem of distinguishing between these two Presbyterian members see the information about them in Appendix II. The Bill was passed. *Statutes*, V, 428–33.

40 After Fowke's severe reprimand there is no record of any activity on his part; he died a month later on April 22, 1662. Beaven, I, 277.

41 *C.J.*, VIII, 357, 414. For additional data concerning Langham's case see the information about him in Appendix II. It is also significant that while these two Bills were under consideration Sir John Davie, Sir Edward Noseworthy, and Sir Thomas Barnardiston, three members of the Presbyterian-Congregationalist group, were denied seats in the Commons' final decision on their disputed elections. Davie was the only one actually sitting at the time. *C.J.*, VIII, 334; *O.R.*, I, 521 n.1 and n.2; 529 n.1.

42 *L.J.*, XI, 471–72, May 19, 1662. For its enactment and provisions see Chapters II and IV.

43 S.P.29/93/11, fol. 20. Confession of Captain Robert Atkinson, February (?) 1664. The Northern Plot was to have been a rising in many different places by old republicans and the extremists among the Dissenters, but it was foiled by the government. For differing interpretations as to its seriousness see Henry Gee, "The Derwentdale Plot of 1663," *R.H.S.T.*, Series III, Vol. 41 (1917), pp. 125–42, and Ashley, *Wildman*, pp. 192–95.

44 For an account of its enactment and its provisions, see Chapter IV, pp. 53–54.

45 Contemporary accounts of the debates of March 25, 26, and 28 do not include any speeches by Dissenters in opposition to the Bill. In addition there were three divisions in the Commons on the Bill, and in no instance were the tellers of the Presbyterian-Congregationalist group. *H.M.C., 7th Rept. Verney MSS*, pp. 484–

85; Pepys, IV, 87–88, 92; *C.J.*, VIII, 536, 538; *Statutes*, V, 54–57, 513.

46   The authoritative account of the repeal of the Act of 1641 is Caroline Robbins' "The Repeal of the Triennial Act in 1664," *Huntington Library Quar.*, XII (Feb., 1949), pp. 121–40; on Prynne's part see pp. 130, 136, 138. Swynfen's statement was recorded by Sir Henry Capell in his notes of the debate. Add. MSS, 35,865, fol. 213. See also Pepys, IV, 87–88; *H.M.C.*, *7th Rept.*, *Verney MSS*, p. 484; *C.J.*, VIII, 537.

47   Vaughan's feeling for Dissenters is evident in his attempt to amend the Bill in order to counteract the effect of the oath required of Dissenting ministers by the Five Mile Act; Lord Wharton regarded Temple and Meres as friends and moderates in 1661. Temple in particular may have been motivated by opportunistic considerations in his friendliness toward Dissenters. Burnet, I, 402; Carte MSS, 81, fols. 81–82; Godfrey Davies, "The Political Career of Sir Richard Temple (1634–1697) and Buckingham Politics," *The Huntington Library Quar.*, IV (Oct., 1940), 58. For their leadership of the opposition against repeal of the Triennial Act, see *C.S.P.D.*, *1661–1662*, p. 330; *H.M.C.*, *7th Rept.*, *Verney MSS*, p. 484; *C.J.*, VIII, 536, 538.

48   Pepys, IV, 92; *C.J.*, VIII, 538.

49   See reports dated April 12–17, 1664, *C.S.P.D.*, *1663–1664*, pp. 553, 556–57, 559; Morrice MSS, U, fol. 107.

50   Grey, I, 82–84; Milward, p. 190; *C.J.*, IX, 52.

51   D. T. Witcombe, *Charles II and the Cavalier House of Commons, 1663–1674* (Manchester, 1966), 78, 81.

52   Those of the "gang" whom Milward mentioned were Sir Thomas Littleton, Sir Robert Howard, Sir Robert Carr and Sir Robert Brooke. Milward, p. 190; Grey, I, 82–84. Of these men whom Milward and Grey report as strong supporters in the short debate on the Triennial Bill, all but Brooke were among Clarendon's prominent antagonists. Grey, I, 8, 15, *passim*, Milward, pp. 116, 118, 176.

53   Baxter, Pt. III, p. 20.

54   Milward, pp. 86, 328 (Appendix II, "Notes [on Debates of October and November] Attributed to Arthur Capel.") See also Lamont, *Prynne*, pp. 222–23.

55   This was his speech of October 26; see also that of November 6, Milward, pp. 101–102; Grey, I, 18.

56   Grey, I, 13–14 n.; *Proceedings in the House of Commons, Touching the Impeachment of Edward Late Earl of Clarendon, Lord*

*High-Chancellour of England, Anno 1667* (2nd ed.; n.p., 1700), p. 12.

57  *Proceedings . . . Touching the Impeachment,* pp. 21–26, 28, 36–38, 47, 49; Grey, I, 29–30, 33, 34; Milward, 112–16, 118–25, 336–37 (Appendix II, "Notes [on Debates of October and November, 1667] Attributed to Arthur Capel.").

58  Grey, I, 65–66; *Proceedings . . . Touching the Impeachment,* pp. 126–28; Clayton Roberts, *The Growth of Responsible Government in Stuart England* (Cambridge, 1966), p. 169 n.1.

59  *C.J.,* IX, 27; Milward, pp. 142–45, 148; Grey, I, 48–52; Lister, *Clarendon,* III, 474; *L.J.,* XII, 137, 144, 146, 149. Clarendon's chief enemies, the Dukes of Buckingham and Albemarle, took the opposite position and led twenty-seven other peers in protesting against the Lords' vote refusing to take him into custody. *Ibid.,* pp. 141–42. This action was in accord with an agreement the two Dukes concluded with the King to "push Chancellor Hyde wholly and to rigorously oppose the designs of those who would like to save him by means of the disagreement they have created between the two Houses concerning the general or specific accusations." French Ambassador Ruvigny to Louis XIV, Nov. 22–23/Dec. 2–3, P.R.O.31/3/117, fol. 168. It does not seem very likely that Swynfen worked for the commitment of Clarendon on general charges, and that Holles and Anglesey opposed this, more because they were deliberately planning to maintain a disagreement between the Houses in order to save Clarendon, as Ruvigny previously reported the King, Buckingham and Albemarle to believe. P.R.O.31/3/117, fol. 39. It also does not seem at all likely that Swynfen was working with Buckingham, since he immediately was opposed to Clarendon's banishment.

60  The motion passed in the affirmative. *C.J.,* IX, 29; *Proceedings . . . Touching the Impeachment,* pp. 95–98; 118–19; Milward, pp. 151, 155–56; Grey, I, 60–61.

61  *L.J.,* XII, 167.

62  Grey, I, 65; *Proceedings . . . Touching the Impeachment,* pp. 126–28.

63  The Bill passed the Lower House and was signed by the King on December 19. *C.J.,* IX, 40–42; *L.J.,* XII, 177, 179.

64  Clarendon's efforts to obtain a religious settlement more in line with the Dissenters' desires are described, Chapter IV, pp. 48 ff. First to note these efforts was Keith Feiling, while Abernathy has discovered new evidence and discussed the Chancellor's policy much more thoroughly. Feiling, "Clarendon and the Act of Uniformity, 1662–1663," *E.H.R.,* XLIV (April, 1929), 289–

91; Abernathy, pp. 75–77, 82–91; "Clarendon and the Declaration of Indulgence," *J.E.H.*, XI (1960), 55–73. Bosher contends that Clarendon's interest in a more lenient and comprehensive religious policy was always coincident with real or imagined Nonconformist threats to his ultimate aims, and that when these threats disappeared he returned to the policy of seeking uniformity. Witcombe has concluded that Clarendon shifted toward this policy by late 1663, and that by 1665 he sought severe measures against the Dissenters. This would seem to be indicated by his opening speech to Parliament. However, the tone of this 1665 speech is basically the same as that of his opening speech to the first session of the Cavalier Parliament in 1661. Whatever his motives, Clarendon's attitude and policy toward both the moderate Dissenters and the "fanatics" had gone through changes, and there is need for further investigation of them. Bosher, pp. 176, 198–99, 217–18; *L.J.*, XII, 246–47, 688–89; Witcombe, *Charles II and the Cavalier House,* pp. 36, 211; *supra*, pp. 31–32.

65 On August 27, Anglesey wrote Ormonde a letter which appeared to be a reflection of his own views as well as an account of developments. He reported that "many, out of zeal to justice and the King's service, interposed with his Majesty in his behalf, that at least he might be left to a fair trial. . . ." Lister, *Clarendon,* III, 469.

66. Clayton Roberts has attributed the Presbyterian attitude to the fact that they "were offended by the unscrupulous conduct of those who sought Clarendon's destruction," while at the same time they recognized him as an honorable opponent who, as Baxter believed, was the chief means of hindering rule of the army. "The Impeachment of the Earl of Clarendon," *C.H.J.*, XIII (1957), 6. Prynne's views were similar, Lamont, *Prynne*, 222–23.

67 Stowe MSS, 304, fols. 85, 88.

68 *L.J.*, XII, 184. Since any support of toleration was welcomed, Nonconformists were undoubtedly less extreme in their condemnation of Buckingham's personal life than they would otherwise have been. Nevertheless Prynne called for the confiscation of the estates of the duelists in a Commons' debate of March 18, 1668; while Baxter, who became involved in the move for comprehension and toleration, later wrote: "The man was of no religion, but notoriously and professedly lustful, and yet of greater wit, and parts, and sounder principles as to the interests of humanity and the common good than most lords in the court." Grey, I, 118; Milward, p. 230; Baxter, Pt. III, pp. 21–36 (second page so numbered).

69 For opinions of Buckingham's leadership of Dissenters, see *C.S.P.D., 1667–1668,* p. 259; Wilbur Cortez Abbott, "English Conspiracy and Dissent 1660–1681," *A.H.R.* (July, 1909), XIV, 710–11. Browning, I, 74; III, 33–44.

70 *C.J.,* VIII, 660–61, 670, 683.

71 A half dozen Presbyterians served on an early committee to consider the Bill of the previous session, and in October, 1667, Prynne was apparently made chairman of the committee of about fifty members appointed upon the second reading of the Bill, while William Love headed a smaller committee to bring in an amendment. *C.J.,* IX, 3, 9, 41. When the Commons debated the Naval catastrophe, the Presbyterians were unusually active, Prynne, Birch, Massey, Yonge, and Boscawen all speaking in the opposition's attack. Grey, I, 76–82; Milward, pp. 185–88.

72 Milward, pp. 239–40.

73 Milward added that the vintners "are fallen in with the Presbyterian party to avoid the present payment and indeed to throw out the bill and so to obstruct the raising this money." Milward, p. 240. Throughout February and March most Dissenters opposed the proposed excise on French and Spanish wines. Grey, I, 95, 101, 107; Milward, pp. 223–24.

74 Grey, I, 123.

NOTES FOR CHAPTER IV

1 *L.J.,* XI, 179.

2 Baxter, Pt. I, sec. 2, pp. 230 ff.; Edward Cardwell, *A History of Conferences and Other Proceedings Connected with the Revision of the Book of Common Prayer; from the Year 1558 to the Year 1690* (3rd ed.; Oxford, 1849), pp. 238–68; Bosher, pp. 120, 274–76; Kirby, "The Reconcilers and the Restoration (1660–1662)," *Essays . . . in Honor of Wilbur Cortez Abbott,* pp. 69–79.

3 *C.J.,* VIII, 288–89, 291, 296.

4 Egerton MSS, 2043, fols. 24, 27, 31, 32. *C.J.,* VIII, pp. 325–26, 330–34, 341; Abernathy, pp. 81–82.

5 *Ibid.,* p. 82.

6 Carte MSS, 81, fols. 121, 133.

7 *L.J.,* XI, 409; *H.M.C., 7th Rept., H. of L. MSS,* pp. 162–63.

8 Carte MSS, 81, fol. 113.

9 *Ibid.,* fols. 112, 120, 131.

10 *L.J.,* XI, 366.

11 The leading part played by the Presbyterian lords in backing this amendment was evident in the composition of the committee of

ten members directed to draw up the clause, for Anglesey was the chairman while Wharton and Holles served with him. *L.J.*, XI, 423–25; *H.M.C., 7th Rept., Pt. VI, H. of L. MSS*, p. 163.

12 *Correspondence of John Cosin, Lord Bishop of Durham*. Part II, Surtees Soc. Pub., Vol. 55 (1872), p. xviii n.

13 *C.J.*, VIII, 402; *L.J.*, XI, 471.

14 For the details see Abernathy, p. 85.

15 The chief contemporary evidence concerning the original overture is a letter to the Earl of Bedford's chaplain, John Thornton, from an unidentified correspondent with the initials "J.O." Rawl. Ltrs., 109, fol. 87. Keith Feiling was the first to give some account of the Court's maneuver in his article, "Clarendon and the Act of Uniformity, 1662–1663," *E.H.R.*, XLIV (April, 1929), 289–91. A complete account is given by Bosher, pp. 260–66, and Abernathy corrects one or two details, p. 85, particularly n. 46.

16 Newcome, *Diary*, pp. 113–14.

17 These were the views expressed by John Thornton's correspondent "J.O." Rawl. Ltrs., 109, fols. 83, 87.

18 *Eli Trembling for Fear of the Ark* (Oxford, 1663), p. 22. Similar views are implied by Newcome's belief that the Court's offer was a dispensation by God to put off the blow, *Diary*, pp. 113–14.

19 *Ibid.*, p. 115.

20 The text of the petition is found in Thomas Rugge, *Mercurius Politicus*, 1662–1672, Add. MSS, 10,117, fol. 45. It is also reprinted by Bosher, p. 261.

21 See Bosher, 261–64; and Abernathy, p. 85.

22 Letter of William Hooke, March 5, 1663, "Mather Papers," p. 207.

23 *Documentary Annals of the Reformed Church of England; Being a Collection of Injunctions, Declarations, Orders, Articles of Inquiry, from the Year 1546 to the Year 1716*, ed. Edward Cardwell (2 vols.; Oxford, 1844), II, pp. 311–20. On the origins of the Declaration see Abernathy, "Clarendon and the Declaration of Indulgence," *J.E.H.*, XI (April, 1960), pp. 66–67.

24 Baxter, Bk. I, Pt. 2, pp. 430, 433; Hooke letter of March 5, "Mather Papers," pp. 207–209. See also "A M[emorandum] of what the Independent Ministers Said to the King, Feb. 27, 1663," Sloane MSS, 4107, fols. 16–20.

25 Baxter, Pt. I, Sec. 2, pp. 429–30; Hooke letter of March 5, "Mather Papers," p. 207.

26 *Ibid.*, p. 208.

27 The full text of the Bill is reprinted by W. D. Christie, *A Life of Anthony Ashley Cooper, First Earl of Shaftesbury* (2 vols.; 1871), I, Appendix VI, pp. lxix–lxxxi.

28 *H.M.C., 7th Rept., App. H. of L. MSS,* pp. 167–68; *L.J.,* XI, 482, 491.

29 *C.J.,* VIII, 513.

30 *Ibid.,* pp. 513–14. D. T. Witcombe has discovered evidence that Sir John Holland and moderate Anglicans considered a move to temper the Act by drawing a distinction between peaceful Nonconformists and potential rebels. *Charles II and the Cavalier House,* p. 19 n.3.

31 In the series of conferences between the Houses, the Earl of Anglesey was one of the three original managers appointed for the House of Lords, and he reported to the House after four of the series of conferences held between May 12 and May 17, when the King passed the Bill. The amendment was apparently adopted in the Upper House May 11, and knowledge of its content is derived from the full report given by Pepys regarding one of these conferences which he attended. *L.J.,* XI, 613, 616–21; Pepys, IV, 131–32. Other clauses were also under consideration at this time, and Anglesey served on a small sub-committee of the whole House regarding them. House of Lords Record Office, Main Papers of 18 April–20 Aug., 1664, Papers of 13 May.

32 The clause concerning search read: "the justices of the peace . . . shall and may, with what aid, force, and assistance they shall think fit for the better execution of this act, after refusal or denial, enter into any house or any other place where they shall be informed any such conventicle as aforesaid is or shall be held. . . ." The Act appeared to provide that there could be no search of a peer's dwelling without a warrant from the King, actually it stated that this was not required if the search was conducted in the presence of a Lord Lieutenant or a deputy lieutenant or two justices. Lords were to be tried by their peers for the third and every offense thereafter. *Statutes,* V, 519, 520.

33 *Statutes,* V, 575.

34 Wharton himself kept notes on this debate which are found among his parliamentary papers wrongly endorsed as a debate in the House of Commons, there having been no vote on this question in the Commons on October 30. Carte MSS, 80, fols. 757–58; *C.J.,* VIII, 623; *L.J.,* XI, 697. Caroline Robbins has edited this manuscript in her account of "The Oxford Session of the Long Parliament of Charles II, 9–31 October, 1665," *B.I.H.R.,* XXI (May and November, 1948), pp. 222–23. For drafts of other amendments see Carte MSS, 81, fol. 260. Wharton was a member of the committee on the Bill, but since it received all three readings between October 26 and October 31, 1665, when the King

passed it, there was little time for modification; in fact there seems to have been only one short meeting of the Committee on the Bill which was held October 28. House of Lords Record Office, MS Minutes of Committees 13 Dec., 1664 to 10 April, 1671, p. 89. (The entry is wrongly dated October 21.) See also *L.J.*, XI, 695, 697–98, 701.

35 Matthews, pp. xxxviii–ix, lx.

36 *A Sermon Preached before the Peers, in the Abby Church at Westminster, November 7, 1666* (1666), pp. 7, 24–25, 28.

37 [John Humfrey], *A Proposition for the Safety and Happiness of the King and Kingdom both in Church and State* (2nd ed.; 1667), pp. 10, 67, 93. This pamphlet is usually attributed to David Jenkins, but Edmund Calamy, the biographer of ejected ministers, who corresponded with Humfrey concerning his views and works, states that Humfrey was the author. The McAlpin copy at Union Theological Seminary has the initials "J. H." penned on the title page in a contemporary hand. A second pamphlet entitled *The Defense of the Proposition* (1668) which the title page states is "By the Same Author" is usually and correctly attributed to Humfrey. Owen's pamphlets of 1667 were *Indulgence and Toleration Considered* and *A Peace-Offering in an Apology and Humble Plea for Indulgence and Liberty of Conscience.* John Corbet wrote *A Discourse of the Religion of England, Asserting that Reformed Christianity Settled in its due Latitude is the Stability and Advancement of this Kingdom* (1667).

38 Calamy, *Acct.*, II, 620–21. The Anglican answer to Humfrey written by Thomas Tompkins, but appearing anonymously, was *The Inconvenience of Toleration* (1667). Humfrey first replied to Tompkins in the second edition of his *Proposition* (1667), pp. 97 ff., and later he wrote a second pamphlet, *A Defense of the Proposition* (1668). Tompkins also replied to Corbet in his *Answer to a Discourse* (1667).

39 The Bill's clause allowing clergymen of the Established Church to obtain a deacon to read the Common Prayer for them if they so desired was designed to eliminate a major Congregationalist objection. Thomas Barlow, later Bishop of Chester, first drafted the clauses of this Bill, and all subsequent accounts of the Bill are based on the one which he compiled and which is in the Bodleian Library as a MS introduction to its copy of *Several Tracts Relating to the Great Acts for Comprehension* (1680). For the most recent discussions see Sykes, pp. 70–71; Walter G. Simon, "Comprehension in the Age of Charles II," *Church History*, XXXI (Dec., 1962), pp. 440–41; Roger Thomas, "Com-

prehension and Indulgence," *From Uniformity to Unity,* pp. 197–98.

40 The main contemporary sources are Thomas Barlow for the Anglicans and Baxter for the Nonconformists. The important part of Barlow's account is printed in Herbert Thorndike's *Theological Works* (10 vols.; Oxford, 1844–1856), V, pp. 301–308, and Baxter's is in *Reliquiae,* Pt. III, pp. 23–36. Recent full accounts are given by Simon, *Church History,* XXXI, pp. 442–43; Thomas, "Comprehension and Indulgence," *loc. cit.,* pp. 198–200; and Sykes, pp. 72–75. See also J. B. Williams, *Memoirs of the Life, Character, and Writings of Sir Matthew Hale* (1835), pp. 184–85.

41 The terms of Owen's Bill would have given the right of public worship for three years to those teachers and members of congregations who registered and paid a fee for their indulgence. They also were to pay tithes, but be free of all penalties for not attending the Established Church. As Thomas points out, the Bill did not exclude Catholics. Thorndike, V, 304–305; Sykes, pp. 74–75; Thomas, "Comprehension and Indulgence," *loc. cit.,* pp. 199–200.

42 The preceding and following information concerning Wilkins' indiscretion and the activity of Ward and Sheldon is drawn entirely from Simon, *Church History,* XXXI, p. 444 and notes.

43 Milward, p. 179.

44 *Ibid.,* p. 180.

45 See particularly the debates of March 4, 11, and April 8, Grey, I, 103–106, 110–14, 127–31; Milward, pp. 206, 214–22, 248–49.

46 *C.J.,* IX, 66, 71, 78, 90.

47 Baxter, III, 22. On Buckingham's ineffectuality see *supra,* pp. 43–44.

48 Rawl. Ltrs., 52, fol. 115. See also Henry Ashurst's letter to Henry Newcome, in Hunter, p. 201; and *A Few Sober Queries upon the Late Proclamation, for Enforcing the Laws against Conventicles, and the Late Vote of the House of Commons, for Renewing the Said Act for Three Years More* (1668), S.P.29/251/186, p. 3.

49 The Conventicle Act of 1664 was to remain in force three years from the end of the session in which it was passed by the King, plus one session thereafter. The three years was over on May 17, 1667, and the next session was prorogued March 1, 1669. *Statutes,* V, 520; *C.S.P.D., 1668–1669,* pp. 256–57.

50 This phrase is used by Milward to describe those who were not Dissenters but who spoke against the Conventicle Bill on April 28, and who unsuccessfully backed amendments offered "on purpose to clog the Bill that it might not pass in the House of Lords." During the preceding weeks such members included Andrew

Marvell, Sir Thomas Littleton, Sir Robert Carr, and Sir William Waller. Milward, pp. 225, 238, 282; Grey, I, 146.

51  *L.J.*, XII, 237; *H.M.C., 8th Rept., Pt. I, H. of L. MSS*, p. 126. The efforts in the House of Commons were partially successful, but the Bill passed the third reading on April 28 by a division of 144–78. No conclusive evidence has been discovered which would indicate the extent to which the Presbyterian lords were responsible for stopping the measure, but Wharton probably led an attack upon it. *C.J.*, IX, 90; Carte MSS, 81, fol. 305.

52  Milward, p. 300. Francis Buller moved on May 7, to petition the King "to give a longer time of adjournment than August." This motion was defeated. *Ibid.*, p. 298.

53  For a brief discussion of the situation see David Ogg, *England in the Reign of Charles II* (2 vols.; Oxford, 1934), I, 340–41.

54  Lee, *Cabal*, pp. 96–97, 101–103.

55  Marvel, II, 301.

56  Sir Edward Harley wrote his wife on February 11 that "the only thing that stays me in London is the Bill of Conventicles . . . I know you would not have me absent at that time." In the debate of March 9 three of the seven speakers noted by Grey were the Presbyterian members, Love, Birch, and Maynard. Love offered an amendment "that the teachers, taking the Oaths of Allegiance and Supremacy, and subscribing the 39 Articles, may, by the allowance of a justice of peace, teach, the doors being open, and at the time of divine service," which as Mr. Henry Coventry remarked, contradicted the Bill. The division on the third reading of 138–78 indicated that the strength of the opposition was at high level. *H.M.C., Portland MSS*, III, 320; *C.J.*, IX, 136; Grey, I, 228.

57  *L.J.*, XII, 317–318, 320–322, 324–26, 340.

58  Marvell, II, 134; *H.M.C., Portland MSS*, III, 323; *H.M.C., 8th Rept. Pt. I, H. of L. MSS*, p. 142.

59  Each of these lords took part as managers and Anglesey reported on all of the conferences between the Houses in which differences upon this matter as well as others were discussed, and Holles joined the protest recorded when the Lords voted to agree with the Commons concerning the matter of search. *L.J.*, XII, 333–40; Grey, I, 245–46, 263–64; *C.J.*, IX, 153–54.

60  For an account of the early activities of two such informers, both of whom had previously been involved in robbery, see *The Minute Book of the Monthly Meeting of the Society of Friends for the Upperside of Buckinghamshire, 1669–1690*, ed. R. S. Snell (Buckinghamshire Arch. Soc., Records Branch, vol. I; High Wy-

combe, [1938]), xiv, xv, 5, 6, 8. Although the Quaker charged with violating the Act was fined and imprisoned, he was eventually cleared and perjury suits against the informers were won.

61 *Statutes*, V, 648–51.

62 This statement was apparently written before the requirement of two witnesses was adopted in amendments and later embodied in the Act.

63 This is a rough draft, on the back of which are some sketchy notes in Lord Wharton's writing of the sort he frequently jotted down on such papers as were at hand, during the proceedings of the House. Carte MSS, 77, fol. 592. There is another copy of the same material in Carte MSS, 81, fol. 331 which is dated March 23, and is endorsed "for a friend."

64 Grey, I, 227–28.

65 Marvell, II, 301.

66 Published before the Act went into effect on May 15, 1670, presumably in London.

67 *The Englishman, or a Letter from a Universal Friend: . . . With Some Observations upon the Late Act Against Conventicles* (n.p., 1670), pp. 9–10.

68 *C.S.P.D., 1670*, pp. 233–34, report of Sir John Robinson to Sir Joseph Williamson. See also reports from local officials who were alarmed by this procedure and the contents of the pamphlet. *Ibid.*, pp. 219, 222, 230, 240, 290.

69 *Some Seasonable and Serious Queries*, p. 6. For the same argument see also *The Englishman, or A Letter from a Universal Friend*, p. 12.

70 *C.S.P.D., 1670*, 233–34.

71 On June 10, the King issued a proclamation ordering all the cashiered officers and soldiers of the "late usurped powers" to depart from London, Westminster, and Southwark before June 16, and not return before December 16. At the same Council meeting, the architect Christopher Wren, then Surveyor General of his Majesty's Works, was ordered to seize houses used for worship and to pull down the seats and pulpits and secure them in safe places. P.C.2/62/190, 193, 247, 344, 357, 361; *C.S.P.D., 1670*, pp. 236, 237, 239, 267; Dalrymple, II, 60.

72 Friends' MSS, Book of Cases, I (1661–1695), 16–17 (late 1676); see also Friends' MSS, Meeting for Sufferings, Minutes I (1675–1680), 101 (May, 1679). For published contentions of this sort see [Francis Bampfield], *A Just Appeal from the Lower Courts on Earth to the Highest Court in Heaven* (1683), p. 5; [Henry Care], *A Perfect Guide for Protestant Dissenters in Case of Pros-*

ecution upon *Any of the Penal Statutes, Made against Them*
(1682), p. 11 [John Howe], *The Case of the Protestant Dissenters
Represented and Argued* (1689), p. 2. In some of these cases
they argued that the Act had altered the fundamental laws of
the Kingdom more than they maintained that it was contrary to
them.

73   *A True and Faithful Narrative of the Unjust and Illegal Oppres-
sions of Many Christians* (1671), p. 4. See also the pamphlet
which John Owen published anonymously, "The Case of Present
Distresses on Non-Conformists, Examined in the Execution of an
Act, Entitled, An Act against Seditious Conventicles," *Works*,
XXI, 475–76, 479.

74   *C.S.P.D., 1670*, pp. 248, 255.

75   Lee, *Cabal*, p. 180.

76   *Ibid.*, pp. 144–47.

77   *C.J.*, IX, 210–11, 217; *H.M.C., 9th Rept. H. of L. MSS*, p. 2.

78   Lee, *Cabal*, pp. 186, 214–15.

79   Brown, *Shaftesbury*, p. 196; *C.S.P.D., 1671–1672*, pp. 562–63.

80   Thomas, "Comprehension and Indulgence," *From Uniformity to
Unity*, pp. 204–205, 208.

81   P.C.2/63/193–94 (entry of March 15); *C.S.P.D., 1671–1672*, p.
288.

82   Parker's question is posed in the preface which he wrote to
*Bishop Bramhall's Vindication of Himself and the Episcopal
Clergy from the Presbyterian Charge of Popery* (1672), and it is
quoted by John Humfrey, *The Authority of the Magistrate About
Religion, Discussed, in a Rebuke to the Prefacer of a Late Book
of Bishop Bramhalls* (1672), p. 28.

83   *Ibid.*, and p. 41. Another Presbyterian minister, Philip Henry,
wrote similarly in his diary entry of June 3: "Some think by accepting of . . . [licenses] we give the King a power above the
laws, so we do above such bad laws as that of Uniformity."
Henry, p. 253.

84   Nye wrote that "To laws ecclesiastical . . . made in Parliament,
we give only a conditional consent, that is, a consent to them so
far as they are agreeable to God's word, and concur with Gospel-
rules." If a law concerning religion raise a doubt or scruple, he
concluded, then "I sin if I submit." *The King's Authority in Dispensing with Ecclesiastical Laws, Asserted and Vindicated*
(1683), pp. 15–16. In the dedication of the 1687 edition, Henry
Nye states that his father wrote this pamphlet at the time of
Charles II's Declaration of 1672.

85   *Ibid.*, pp. 1–2, 12–14, 30. He emphasized that the severity of the

laws against Dissenters created a "necessity that some remedy be speedily applied." *Ibid.*, p. 55.

86 *Vindiciae Liberatatis Evangelii* (1672), pp. 24–25.

87 Newcome, *Autobiog.*, II, 199, 264.

88 Rawl. Ltrs., 50, fol. 72; 104, fol. 86. After the Declaration had been withdrawn Stukely wrote Wharton on August 2, 1673, that "it's almost insufferable to be thus unserviceable. . . ." *Ibid.*, 50, fol. 141. The Congregationalist Thomas Jolly was also thankful for the opportunity the Declaration gave him to work "for the good of souls." Jolly, p. 9. For additional Presbyterian opinions see Heywood, III, 107; Henry, pp. 251–52.

89 The conclusion of religious historians that a large number of Baptist ministers did not apply is based upon a comparison of the number who did apply, which was 210 or more, to the number of Baptist ministers there presumably were, which is thought to have been about 420. This latter figure is the estimate of William T. Whitley and is apparently based upon the parochial reports of 1669. Underwood, p. 102; William T. Whitley, *A History of British Baptists* (2d rev. ed.; 1932), pp. 123–25; Turner, III, 740.

90 W. C. Braithwaite, *The Second Period of Quakerism* (2d ed.; 1955), p. 82.

91 Burnet states that they "got great reputation by their silent deportment" in this session which began February 4, and ended March 29, 1673. II, 17.

92 Grey, II, 27.

93 *Ibid.*, p. 23. Maynard's position as one of the King's Sergeants-at-Law undoubtedly explains to some degree his indecisive position. In a debate of 1678 on a question which involved the prerogative and the rights of Parliament, he pointed out his dilemma, stating: "I am bound, as I am the King's Sergeant, by oath, to maintain the prerogative, and I am under another obligation here, as a member of this House, to maintain your privileges. . . ." *Ibid.*, V, 139.

94 Anglesey's tacit approval is suggested by the views he expressed in the Privy Council noted in his diary entry of March 15, 1672. His only objection was that "the Papists are put thereby into a better and less jealoused state than the Dissenting Protestants." Add. MSS, 40,860, fol. 25. Very conclusive, however, is the contention of an anonymous pamphlet which he seems to have written and which is entitled *The King's Right of Indulgence in Spiritual Matter, with the Equity Thereof Asserted* (1688).

95 This was offered on March 7, the day the Declaration was cancelled. *H.M.C., 9 Rept. Pt. II, H. of L. MSS*, p. 25.

96 Grey, II, 40, 46–48, 70, 168, 178–79. In the House of Lords the Catholic Lord Treasurer Clifford, apparently in Committee of the Whole House, proposed that the King should have the power, if he did not already, to suspend penal statutes in matters ecclesiastical out of time of Parliament. House of Lords Record Office, MS Minutes of Committees, 13 Feb. 1672 [O.S.]–19 Nov. 1685, entry of March 6, p. 16. See also entry of March 7.

97 *Ibid.* (March 7); *L.J.*, XII, 579. Rawl. Ltrs., 50, fols. 103, 106; 53, fol. 94; 104, fols. 87–88.

98 Baxter MSS, Ltrs., I, 70 (Anon. to Baxter, 26 April 1673); P.C. 2/63/404 (March 21, 1672/73); 64/4 (April 16, 1673).

99 Rawl. Ltrs., 53, fol. 94; *C.J.*, IX, 279–82; *L.J.*, XII, 576, 579, 584; Grey, II, 135–36.

100 Heywood, III, 153–54; Rawl. Ltrs., 50, fol. 141; 51, fol. 13.

101 *Statutes*, V, 782–85.

102 There was a motion to have the Committee on the Bill for the Ease of Dissenters instructed to include a clause to this effect. It was defeated on a division of 163 to 107. *C.J.*, IX, 266; Grey, II, 93–96; *The Parliamentary Diary of Sir Edward Dering, 1670–1673*, ed. Basil Duke Henning (New Haven, 1940), p. 135.

103 Heywood, III, 154. The fear of Catholicism in 1672 was one of the compelling reasons why many ministers accepted licenses to preach, see Baxter, Pt. III, pp. 99–101; Martindale, pp. 198–99. In early 1673 even John Milton came from his retirement and joined the attack upon Catholicism in his pamphlet "Of True Religion," *The Works of John Milton*, ed. Frank Allen Patterson (18 vols.; New York, 1931–1938), VI, 167, 171, 173–78.

104 On October 31, Boscawen spoke against granting further supply for the War, which he regarded as the source of "great grievances," and had been "waged against the advice of the whole body of the merchants." Some of the Nonconformist ministers were also disturbed over the War, for Lewis Stukely wrote Lord Wharton in December of his dread of the War's continuance "because of the consequences upon manufacturing." In addition the impending marriage of the Duke of York and the Catholic Princess of Modena caused concern. Grey, II, 190–91, 197, 211; Rawl. Ltrs., 51, fol. 23.

105 Baxter reprinted the sheet Humfrey circulated, Pt. III, p. 143, 147. Baxter states that Hampden told him his "Healing Act" would never pass, and his accounts of this measure, as well as of another which resulted from the efforts of the Earl of Orrery, are colored by the fact that nothing came of them. *Ibid.*, pp. 109, 140, 157.

106  Heywood, I, 304.
107  Morrice MSS, U, 159.

NOTES FOR CHAPTER V

1  *C.S.P.D., 1673–1675*, pp. 390, 549–51; Baxter, Pt. III, p. 153; Browning, I, 148.
2  P.C.2/64/372.
3  Brown, *Shaftesbury*, pp. 110–11, 119, 122; Abernathy, *J.E.H.*, XI, 66–67; Robbins, *B.I.H.R.*, XXI, 220.
4  Shaftesbury was given the position of Lord Chancellor as well as Keeper of the Great Seal. When Bridgeman, who held only the latter position, was elevated to this office in 1667, Nonconformists were pleased; and his subsequent efforts to obtain comprehension and toleration gave them continued reason to consider him a friend, even though there was some recrimination because the efforts failed. Thus when the change came, Samuel Hieron had reason to write Lord Wharton that he "was surprised at the cancelling of the Great Seal after so much seeming fitness . . . : But the tidings of Parliament's preparing a Bill [of Ease to Protestant Dissenters] gives hope again. . . ." *C.S.P.D., 1667*, p. 457; Baxter, Pt. III, pp. 23–24; Rawl. Ltrs. 50, fol. 103.
5  Lee, *Cabal*, pp. 186–87, 214. Calamy, *Acct.*, II, 456; Turner, III, 548; Brown, *Shaftesbury*, pp. 117, 210.
6  His association with Papillon began when the two were at Oxford together, and it continued during their membership in the Barebones Parliament and in later business ventures. Harley and Shaftesbury were engaged in a mining venture together. *Ibid.*, pp. 192–93. Hampden was an agent in a later business partnership, and since he was not as conscientious as Shaftesbury wanted him to be the effect could have been negative as well as positive; the evidence regarding Kiffen is only suggestive, indicating some transaction involving silks. P.R.O.30/24/VI, A, fols. 299, 314 (*verso*).
7  Available evidence indicates that Lord Holles was the only Presbyterian who had any direct and continuing contact with Shaftesbury in the House of Lords; reportedly it was at his house that Shaftesbury and others of the opposition met and as Ruvigny reported, "concerted matters to be brought forward by the Commons." P.R.O.31/3/130, fol. 283 (Feb. 1, 1674 N.S.). See also letters of Lord Conway some few days later, *Essex Papers*, eds. Osmund Airy and Clement E. Pike (2 vols.; Camden Soc. Pub. New Ser., XLVII, and Third Ser., XXIV; 1890, 1912), I, 168.

8  Charles acknowledged these rumors and offered to let a committee of both Houses see his treaties, planning to show only the
   fictitious treaty of December 31, 1670. *L.J.*, XII, 594–95.

9  Grey, II, 234.

10  *Ibid.*, pp. 348, 351, 352–53.

11  *Ibid.*, pp. 348, 351–54. See discussion of Birch's religious shift
    in Appendix II.

12  This was Swynfen's statement. Grey, II, 267.

13  *Ibid.*, p. 323; see also pp. 308, 320.

14  *Ibid.*, pp. 267, 320. See positions taken by Boscawen, *ibid.*, pp.
    243, 252.

15  Leicestershire Record Office, Finch MSS, Political Papers, #34,
    p. 12. I am indebted to Henry Horwitz for bringing to my atten-
    tion this evidence of the Dissenters' support of Arlington. He has
    identified the probable writer of the letter from which it is taken
    as Daniel Finch. It was the letter writer's opinion that the Dis-
    senters supported Arlington "as a favorer of them," for he had
    been told that the Earl had "conveyed pensions and very con-
    siderable sums of money of a long time to Dr. Owens and many
    excluded ministers; and this not of himself but he has been in-
    strumental in procuring these bounties to them." However, since
    there is no other known evidence, this reason for the support
    remains a matter of hearsay. Richard Baxter also commented
    upon the support Arlington received from members "who fa-
    voured the Nonconformists," and stated that those who were
    exasperated by the outcome "reported that they did it because
    he had furthered the Nonconformists licenses for tolerated
    preaching." Baxter, III, 108.

16  Grey, II, 252, 260. The Commons voted to petition the King to
    remove Buckingham from his employments and from the King's
    presence and councils forever; since he was angry with the Duke
    for appearing before the Commons without permission and for
    revealing Privy Council secrets, the King was happy to comply.
    The vote for removal of Arlington failed in the House, and
    though that against Lauderdale was passed unanimously the
    sudden prorogation on February 24, put an end to any other
    proceedings. *C.J.*, IX, 293, 296. See also Lee, *Cabal*, pp. 247–49.

17  Grey, II, 267. The only speech by a Dissenter which Grey re-
    cords regarding Lauderdale was Boscawen's in which he desired
    "that Lord Clarendon's Bill of banishment may not be a prece-
    dent," because, "that was done somewhat hastily." *Ibid.*, p. 243.

18  *L.J.*, XII, 622–23. (Treaty of Westminster.)

19  Grey, II, 399; *C.J.*, IX, 305.

20  Grey, II, 416. Until April, 1668, Charles had generally followed the principle of making appointments that were to continue during good behavior, as his father had declared he would do in 1641, but after that date he reverted to the general practice of appointing all judges during his good pleasure. A. F. Havighurst, "The Judiciary and Politics in the Reign of Charles II," *Law Quarterly Review,* LXVI (Jan., 1950), pp. 64–65.

21  In addition to that for the speedy relief of prisoners detained for criminal matters, there was also one to prevent the imprisonment of the subjects in illegal and secret places beyond the seas and out of the jurisdiction of courts. Each was passed by the House of Commons and sent to the Lords. They were eventually combined in the Habeas Corpus Act of 1678. *C.J.,* IX, 305, 313; *H.M.C., 9th Rept. Pt. II, H. of L. MSS,* p. 42.

22  See speeches of Maynard, Boscawen and Hampden in Grey, II, 389–90, 434. Each bill failed in the House of Lords because of prorogation on February 19. *Ibid.,* III, pp. 42, 46. *L.J.,* XII, 631, 648.

23  To the sixteen pensioners originally approved after the reorganization of 1674, seven more were added during the year. Of these twenty-three pensions, sixteen were given to members of Parliament. See discussion given by Browning, I, 169–70.

24  Shaftesbury's biographer L. F. Brown believes that these results were accomplished primarily by the Earl's letter to Lord Carlisle of February 3, 1675, which he asked Carlisle to pass on to the Lords Holles and Fauconbridge (not a Presbyterian). *Shaftesbury,* p. 227. It appears that Shaftesbury did not pass the letter to Lord Wharton, for the copy in his papers bears the endorsement "Supposed to be" from Shaftesbury, which suggests that Wharton did not obtain his copy until it was being circulated in the Coffee Houses. Carte MSS, 228, fol. 125.

25  A contemporary account states that Wharton and Lady Bedford and the rest of the congregation were apprehended along with the minister, and that members of the congregation paid their own fines. The minister this particular Sunday was the Presbyterian James Bedford, who was substituting for Dr. Manton since the latter heard that he was to be arrested under the Five Mile Act. According to Baxter, Wharton and others paid a £20 fine on James Bedford and a £40 fine on the place of meeting, which according to the Second Conventicle Act should have been £20. *H.M.C., Buccleuch MSS,* I, 321; Baxter, Pt. III, p. 156; Matthews, p. 44.

26  *H.M.C., 9th Rept. Pt. II, H. of L. MSS,* pp. 51–52.

27 *Essex Papers*, II, 1, 8; Marvell, II, 143; Baxter, Pt. III, p. 167; *L.J.*, XII, 668–669, 671, 677. Protests dated April 21, 26, 29, and May 4, "A Letter From a Person of Quality to His Friend in the Country, Giving an Account of the Debates and Resolutions in the House of Lords, in April and May, 1675," *Parliamentary History of England*, ed. W. Cobbett (36 vols.; 1806–20), IV, xlvi–l, lvii, lx, lxii, lxiv. This pamphlet is the chief source for the debates. It was apparently prepared under the supervision of Lord Shaftesbury. W. D. Christie, *A Life of Anthony Ashley Cooper, First Earl of Shaftesbury* (2 vols.; 1871), I, 207 n.; Burnet, II, 82; *H.M.C., 7th Rept., Verney MSS*, p. 492. Wharton's concern is also reflected by the fact that he took notes on the debates of the opening day. Carte MSS, 79, fols. 25–26.

28 See the letter intercepted by the Post Office which contains a comment reported to have been made by William Love, *C.S.P.D., 1675–1676*, p. 96.

29 It was noted that Fagg leapt from rags into new clothes with money "even to spare for lawyers," and though it was not known who supplied him it was also noted that Holles was "his great friend." Aiken Collection, Transcripts of Finch MSS, "Journal," p. 83.

30 Grey, III, 169–71, 184, 192–98, 271; *C.J.*, IX, 338–39.

31 *The Case Stated Concerning the Judicature of the House of Peers in the Point of Appeals* (1675), pp. 75–76. See also the protest of May 6, *L.J.*, XII, 680.

32 On the purely legal issue the Lords were in the right; and since in the future the Commons did not protest against appeals to the Lords of cases involving their members, the outcome of this dispute was a tacit recognition of the Lords' appellate jurisdiction. W. S. Holdsworth, *History of English Law* (13 vols.; 3rd ed. 1922–1952), I, 374–75.

33 *L.J.*, XII, 729.

34 Browning, I, 166, 170–72; III, 56–61.

35 Early in 1675 when it seemed that Danby, who was strongly anti-French, might be able to control the House of Commons, the Marquis de Ruvigny had begun to work upon Anglican opposition leaders and presumably distributed bribes to them in order to prevent control of the House by Danby. F. A. M. Mignet, *Négociations Relatives à la Succession d'Espagne sous Louis XIV* (4 vols.; Paris, 1835–1842), IV, 330–34; Clyde L. Grose, "Louis XIV's Financial Relations with Charles II and the English Parliament," *J.M.H.*, I (June, 1929), 184–87.

36 *Essex Papers* (1675–1677), [II], 32.

37  Ruvigny to Louis XIV, July 22, 1675, P.R.O.31/3/132, fols. 114–114A.

38  Letter dated September 19, 1675, quoted by Mignet, *Négociations,* IV, 365. Unfortunately, Ruvigny mentions no names and there is no known evidence, French or English, of this date which would indicate who the six were. Although some of the other French ambassadors of the Restoration period used the terms *Presbyterian* and *Independent* (*Congregationalist*) with less concern for their religious meaning than for their political implications, the Huguenot Ruvigny was probably more exact in his usage. It is therefore likely that those whom he called Presbyterian and Independent were of such persuasions, though he may have included those who were reputedly such, but who had changed in their religious feeling. The six involved in these talks may well have been some of those who accepted French payments in 1680. See Chapter VII, pp. 141–42.

39  There are no records of this date concerning the disbursements made by Ruvigny during these sessions. *Grose, J.M.H.,* I, 186.

40  Grey, III, 354, 358, 366. The motion was voted down by a vote of 171–160.

41  Wharton and Delamer, who were present, voted for the address and signed the protest. Holles was sick, but had given a proxy for the address. Absent, but favoring the measure was Bedford. Only Anglesey, undoubtedly because of his position as Lord Privy Seal, was against addressing the King. *Two Speeches. I. The Earl of Shaftesbury's Speech in the House of Lords the 20th of October, 1675. II. The D. of Buckingham's speech in the House of Lords the 16th of November, 1675* (Amsterdam, 1675), pp. 15–16; Carte MSS 72, fol. 293; *L.J.,* XIII, 33; Browning, III, 125. For intimations of a similar desire in the Commons, see *C.S.P.D., 1675–1676,* p. 323.

42  This Bill would have allowed two or more justices to license any place for worship under specific regulations which were laid down. *H.M.C., 9th Rept., Pt. II, H. of L. MSS,* p. 68; *C.S.P.D., 1675–1676,* p. 404. It is possible that Wharton was consulted concerning the bill which was submitted; there is a draft copy of it in his papers. Carte MSS, 77, fols. 595–96; Rawl. Ltrs., 51, fol. 62. A revealing appraisal of Buckingham's connections with the Nonconformists and the "country" M.P.s at this juncture will be found in Ruvigny's letter to Louis XIV of Nov. 21 (N.S.), P.R.O.31/3/132, fol. 118.

43  For the title and data concerning this pamphlet which Shaftesbury probably compiled, see *supra,* n. 41.

44 [Anthony Ashley Cooper], *A Letter from a Parliamentman to His Friend, Concerning the Proceedings of the House of Commons this Last Session, Begun the 13 of October, 1675* (n.p., 1675), pp. 3–6.

45 *C.S.P.D., 1675–1676*, pp. 559, 562–63.

46 Williamson's narrative of his visit made February 16, 1676, *C.S.P.D., 1675–1676*, p. 559.

47 *C.S.P.D., 1676–1677*, pp. 358–59; *1677–1678*, pp. 14–17, 29. The order was given Sir Philip Musgrave in October to watch and report on "L. W." The editor of the *Calendar* believes this was Lord Wharton.

48 *Essex Papers,* [II], 51.

49 Browning, I, 203; Letters of the French Ambassador, Honoré Courtin to Louis XIV, Jan. 21, and April 8, 1677 (N.S.), P.R.O. 31/3/135, fol. 13.

50 This argument was based upon a statute (4 Ed. III, cap. 14) which required that Parliaments should be held once a year. See Wharton's notes on Buckingham's speech, Carte MSS, 79, fol. 33.

51 The other lords were Buckingham and Salisbury. The only Presbyterian speaking in opposition to Shaftesbury was Anglesley. Carte MSS, 79, fols. 37–38, 42.

52 *Ibid.,* fols. 31–33, 37–38, 41–44. P.R.O.31/3/135, Courtin, to Louis XIV, March 1 and 4, 1677, fols. 36–37.

53 "The Grand Question Concerning the Prorogation of this Parliament for a Year and Three Months Stated and Discussed." Evidence and testimony in the subsequent investigations concerning the authors and publishers of this and two other pamphlets were to indicate that Holles was unquestionably the author of "The Grand Question." The other two pamphlets, which were published, have also been ascribed to Holles by authorities ever since, but there is little if any evidence at all that he was the writer. The records of the Privy Council investigations are contained in the reports of the subsequent ones made by a committee of the House of Lords after February 16. *H.M.C., 9th Rept., Pt. II, H. of L. MSS*, pp. 69–73.

54 Carte MSS, 79, fols. 32, 42. Aiken Collection, Transcripts of Daniel Finch's MSS, Political Papers 42, Letter to Sir John Finch, pp. 1–2.

55 *Ibid.,* Burnet's remark about the gout is in general verified by Holles' physician. Burnet, II, 117; *H.M.C., 9th Rept. Pt. II, H. of L. MSS*, p. 72. The contention that Holles came to doubt the wisdom of the move was advanced by Courtin as well as Finch. P.R.O.31/3/135, fol. 39.

56  Aiken Collection, Transcripts of Finch MSS, Political Papers 42, p. 5; *H.M.C., 9th Rept., Pt. III, H. of L. MSS,* p. 72; Courtin to Louis XIV, Mar. 22, P.R.O.31/3/135, fol. 57.

57  According to Danby's biographer, Shaftesbury himself had misgivings about his plan at the last moment and attempted to come to some agreement with Danby. Browning, I, 213 n.4.

58  Wharton may not have made the point concerning freedom of debate on the floor as did Shaftesbury and Halifax, but one of the accounts of the debate based upon his notes and probably drawn up by one of his amanuenses makes a statement on this issue, and it undoubtedly reflects Wharton's position. Carte MSS, 79, fol. 38.

59  Also imprisoned were Salisbury, Buckingham, and Shaftesbury. During this year Wharton suffered from ill health; and finally in February, 1678, he asked the pardon of the House "for having offended in what I said concerning the illegality of the late prorogation." Carte MSS, 79, fols. 35, 39, 60; *H.M.C., 9th Rept., Pt. II, H. of L. MSS,* p. 95; *C.S.P.D., 1676–1677,* pp. 555–56; *1677–1678,* p. 631 (records of the House of Lords proceedings against these lords, which were vacated from the Journal).

60  House of Lords Record Office, House Main Papers, 17–19, Feb. 1676/77, fols. 91–93; *H.M.C., 9th Rept., Pt. II, H. of L. MSS,* pp. 71–92, *L.J.,* XIII, 42–55, 64–65; *C.S.P.D., 1675–1676,* pp. 547; *Marvell,* II, 177–78.

61  Grey, IV, 66, 86–87, 90, 95.

62  A motion was made to proceed with the appointment of the standing committees, and in a division it passed 193–142. *C.J.,* IX, 384.

63  Grey, IV, 223–24; *C.J.,* IX, 396.

64  Grey, IV, 247–48, 252–53; *C.J.,* IX, 398, 401; *L.J.,* XIII, 68, 69, 71, 73–74.

65  Unfortunately Grey has no reports on the debates which took place during the days when this question was considered, April 12–16. *C.J.,* IX, 418, 422.

66  They still maintained their privilege to amend such bills, however, and the issue was not finally settled until 1678. *L.J.,* XIII, 118; *C.J.,* IX, 423. One of the most outspoken peers in upholding the Lords' claims was Holles, who wrote a pamphlet in which he stated that if the Lords did not have this power it would "shake the very foundation of Parliament, and utterly overthrow the being of their House. . . ." *The Case Stated of the Jurisdiction of the House of Lords in the Point of Impositions* (1676), p. 4. In another pamphlet the preceding year Holles had ac-

knowledged that the Lords did not have power to "propose the raising of moneys by way of tax or subsidy. . . ." *The Case Stated Concerning the Judicature of the House of Peers in the Point of Appeals,* p. 77.

67 Grey, IV, 343, 346; *C.J.,* IX, 418, 422–23; Egerton MSS, 3346 (Leeds), fol. 14.

68 *C.J.,* IX, 424, 425, 426. The vote was 182 to 142 on a maneuver to eliminate the phrase "offensive and defensive alliance with the United Provinces."

69 *Ibid.,* p. 426.

70 Browning, I, 249.

71 Mignet, *Négociations,* IV, 509–10.

72 K. H. D. Haley, *William of Orange and the English Opposition, 1672–1674* (Oxford, 1953), pp. 185–86; Mignet, *Négociations,* IV, 473–75.

73 List of persons who were allowed to have access to Shaftesbury, *C.S.P.D., 1677–1678,* pp. 267–69.

74 Dalrymple, II, 129.

75 P.R.O.31/3/138, fol. 37; Grose, *J.M.H.,* I, 193–194.

76 The younger Ruvigny was the cousin of the wife of William, Lord Russell, and both he and his wife had many Presbyterian contacts, including Lord Wharton. In December, 1675, when the elder Ruvigny was the French Ambassador he wrote Louis XIV: "Mon fils ne m'estant plus tant necessaire qu'il estroit pendant la tenue du Parlement. . . ." P.R.O.31/3/132, fol. 121; *Letters of Rachel, Lady Russell,* ed. Lord John Russell (2 vols.; 1853), I, 18, 163; Rawl. Ltrs., 109, fol. 106.

77 Mignet, *Négociations,* IV, 533–34; *H.M.C., Ormonde MSS, N.S.,* IV, 88.

78 Louis also instructed Barrillon to prevent anti-French moves in England by negotiating with Charles as well as the opposition. Louis to Barrillon, January 23/February 2, Mignet, *Négociations,* IV, 534; *Recueil des Instructions Données aux Ambassadeurs et Ministres de France depuis les Traités-de Westphalie jusqu'à la Révolution Française,* Tomes XXIV et XXV, *Angleterre* (1648–1690), ed. J. J. Jusserand (Paris, 1929), XXV, 258–59.

79 Barrillon's letters to Louis XIV concerning Ruvigny's negotiations with Russell, Holles, Buckingham, and Shaftesbury of March and April, P.R.O.31/3/138, fols. 132–33; 31/3/139, 157–58; Dalrymple, II, 131–39.

80 In the first agreement Holles, Russell and Buckingham "ont assuré M. de Ruvigny que le Parlement n'donneroit point d'ar-

gent." Barrillon to Louis XIV, February 14, 1678, P.R.O.31/3/138, fol. 79.

81  Barrillon's memorandum of Ruvigny's discussion with Russell and Holles, March 14, Dalrymple, II, 132–33.

82  Speech from the Throne, *L.J.*, XIII, 130–31; *C.J.*, IX, 431–32.

83  Danby's forces won, the division being 193–151. *Ibid.*

84  Grey, V, 91–93. The motion was defeated.

85  *Ibid.*, p. 110; *C.S.P.D., 1677–1678*, p. 644.

86  Grey, V, pp. 150–51.

87  Colonel Birch, with whom the Presbyterians had agreed throughout these debates, took a leading part, proposing the limitation that the funds be used for war with the French King. *Ibid.*, 162–79.

88  Dalrymple, II, 147; Mignet, *Négociations*, IV, 533.

89  Grose, *J.M.H.*, I, 195–96.

90  Barrillon's memorandum of Ruvigny's discussion with Russell and Holles, March 14, translated by Dalrymple, II, 132–33.

91  Barrillon to Louis XIV, March 24, P.R.O.31/3/138, fols. 132–33 as translated by Dalrymple, II, 135–36.

92  Barrillon to Louis XIV, April 11, P.R.O.31/3/138, fols. 157–58 as translated by Dalrymple, II, 138–39.

93  *Ibid.*

94  *H.M.C., Ormonde MSS*, N.S., IV, 416; *L.J.*, XIII, 184, 185, 191–94, 196; *C.J.*, IX, 454, 458–61.

95  Grey, V, 310–11, 326, 329; *C.J.*, IX, 474, 475; *C.S.P.D., 1678*, pp. 154, 158–60.

96  Grey, V, 382–83, 388–89; P.R.O.31/3/139, fol. 201, and 140, fol. 2.

97  It was Swynfen who moved for disbanding, while Hampden, Papillon and Irby were on the committee to draw up the bill. Sir Samuel Barnardiston and Richard Hampden were also supporters. The Bill was passed by the King July 15. Grey, VI, 12–14, 20–21, 34–35, 38–39, 85; *C.J.*, IX, 485, 493; *L.J.*, XIII, 288.

98  Grey, VI, 97–98; *C.J.*, IX, 499–500.

99  In Danby's subsequent consideration of alternative methods there is little doubt, according to his biographer, that for a short time in June he considered the possibility of using the army to maintain the royal authority and his own supremacy, and there is no doubt that the Duke of York favored such a scheme and that Charles gave it some consideration. Browning, II, 282.

100  After February, 1676, when the fear of Catholicism resulted in an Order in Council which required strict enforcement of the laws against Popish Recusants as well as against Dissenters, the

authorities enforced the severe Elizabethan and Jacobean laws directed against Catholics with much greater frequency against the Quakers and Baptists. According to these Acts persons over sixteen who did not attend the Established Church could be fined twenty pounds a month for non-attendance, or the King could seize and hold two-thirds of the guilty person's estate as long as he did not attend Church. Additional fines of £200 could be imposed after twelve months' absence from Church, and also fines of £20, £40, and £60 for the first, second, and third years in which the Sacrament was not received. *Statutes*, Vol. IV, Pt. I, pp. 657–58; Pt. II, pp. 771–72, 1071–77. For examples of such cases see, Friends' MSS, Meeting for Sufferings Minutes, II (1680–1683), 72; Friends' MSS, Book of Cases I (1661–1695), 78–80; Besse, I, 121–22.

101   The division on permission to bring in a bill was 100–67 in favor of refusal. Grey, V, 250, 252–55; *C.J.*, IX, 455–56, 506.

102   For an appraisal earlier in the year, see P.R.O.31/3/138, fol. 89.

103   *Statutes*, V, 894–96.

104   Carte MSS, 81, fol. 380; *H.M.C., 11th Rept., Pt. II, H. of L. MSS*, p. 1.

105   Grey, VI, 153–57; *C.J.*, IX, 523, 532, 533. Other prominent Presbyterians serving on various committees whose work concerned the Plot were Love, Papillon, Irby, Barnardiston, Waller, and Harley. *Ibid.*, 518, 520, 523.

106   Browning, I, 11, 300.

107   In a debate of November 27 concerning disbanding of the army, Swynfen and Boscawen each wanted immediate action, Boscawen referring to the Civil War when the army did not disband and did what they would. Papillon also spoke in a very apprehensive tone. Grey, VI, 282–84; *C.J.*, IX, 550–51.

108   P.R.O.31/3/141, fols. 25–27.

109   On the committee to draw up articles of impeachment were Hampden and Maynard; and in two separate divisions on December 21, when the articles were being voted upon, Barnardiston served as one of the tellers for those favoring impeachment. *C.J.*, IX, 560, 562. In the House of Lords the Presbyterians present (Wharton, Bedford, and Delamer) voted to have Danby committed to prison after he had been impeached by the Lower House. Carte MSS, 81, fol. 399; Browning, III, 129 n.

110   Browning, II, 311.

111   Morrice MSS, P, 112.

112   Morrice's account of these negotiations is contained in a long series of shorthand passages which he left untranscribed, un-

doubtedly because of the nature of the information they contained. *Ibid.*, 113–125. The previously known information concerning these negotiations is derived chiefly from the passages in the letters of Barrillon to Louis XIV on January 26, 30, and February 9 (January 16, 20 and 30 O.S.). Barrillon's source of knowledge was also Lord Holles, with whom he had private meetings and from whom he heard of "all the offers the Court was making them." However, it was Morrice who had more immediate and thorough knowledge of the developments as they occurred and who knew of additional concessions which Holles and the others sought. Bishop Burnet was the earliest source concerning the negotiations. A.A.É., Angeleterre, Vol. 133, fols. 171–72; Burnet, II, 187–88.

113 Morrice knew Baber well and wrote: "It is most clear (I can speak knowingly) that Sir John Baber has for many years been consistently and unalterably . . . for the dissolution of this Parliament, so that he was the first that served it to the Lord Denzil Holles . . . and told the Lord he would acquaint the Treasurer Danby with it and by him transact it with his Majesty. . . ." Morrice MSS, P, 113. True though this may have been, it is possible that Baber acted at Danby's suggestion. The previous autumn Barrillon twice reported that Danby hoped to win over the Presbyterians "at whatever price is necessary," and Baber would have been the man to make the approach. He had a Puritan background, and after he had been made a physician to the King in 1660 at the suggestion of Dr. Thomas Manton, he had been used by Charles in negotiations with the Dissenters. However, Baber was also being used and paid by Barrillon at that time in efforts to attain dissolution and the disbanding of the army. These were also major aims of Holles, with whom Barrillon had "established a closer liaison" through Baber. With his entrée at Court, his friendship with the Presbyterian leaders, and his connection with Barrillon, Baber was certainly in the position to make the move Morrice attributed to him, but his motivations were more complex than Morrice thought. P.R.O.31/3/141, fols. 12, 48, 55, 63, 96 (letters of Oct. 13, Nov. 14, Nov. 17, Nov. 24, and Dec. 22).

114 Morrice MSS, P, 113.

115 Differing with the previously accepted account, Morrice states that the negotiations were "carried on and transacted solely by his Majesty, the Lord Treasurer, the Lord Holles, Sir John Baber, and Sir Thomas Littleton, but Mr. Morrice was privy to it all along from the beginning to the end and no man else." This

statement was modified somewhat by a later shorthand entry in which he wrote that "very few if any" in addition to these six knew about these negotiations. Burnet's short paragraph, which has been the traditionally accepted account, states that Boscawen and Hampden as well as Holles and Littleton were involved in consultations with Danby. Morrice, who must be regarded the better source in this instance, eliminates Boscawen and Hampden as active participants in the negotiations; however, it is evident from his later entry that they could have known about them. *Ibid.,* pp. 114, 123; Burnet, II, 187.

116  A copy of this draft is given in shorthand by Morrice. There were thirty-nine commissioners named at the end of the draft declaration. Ten of those named were Presbyterians and the others were well-known opposition leaders; two names cannot be transcribed. Among the Presbyterians were: Wharton, Holles, Delamere, Anglesey, Bedford, William Love, John Jones, Sir John Maynard, Hugh Boscawen, and Richard Hampden. Morrice MSS, P, 118.

117  P.C.2/67/27; *C.S.P.D., 1679–1680,* pp. 37, 41; Barrillon to Louis XIV, Jan. 16/26, A.A.É. Angleterre, Vol. 133, fols. 121–22.

118  Morrice MSS, P, 113.

119  Morrice thought that the King "continued to consent to it [the draft declaration] until the night before the dissolution. . . ." Morrice MSS, P, 113. In one respect he was correct, for the first draft of the Proclamation that was issued was apparently not drawn up until the following day according to Daniel Finch, who on January 24 wrote in his diary that the King sent for Lord Chancellor Finch, his father, and the Attorney General and declared he was "peremptorily resolved to dissolve the Parliament and to avoid all importunities . . . he ordered Mr. Attorney to prepare a proclamation to that purpose against the time that the Council met in the afternoon that so his pleasure might be obeyed as soon as known. This was done. . . ." Aiken Collection, photostat of Daniel Finch's Diary, fol. 92; *C.S.P.D., 1679–1680,* p. 52.

120  Barrillon to Louis XIV, Jan. 20/30, 1679, A.A.É. Angleterre, Vol. 133, fols. 148–49. Barrillon's exact words in reporting the key statement which Holles made concerning Danby were "que s'il veut quitter sa charge, on peut trouver les moyens de ne pas pousser plus loin l'accusation intentée contre luy." Burnet's statement of the agreement on Danby was that Holles would "carry off his impeachment with a mild censure." *History,* II, 188.

121  Barrillon to Louis XIV, Jan. 30/Feb. 9, A.A.É. Angleterre, 133,

fols. 167–68; *C.S.P.D., 1678–1679*, pp. 87–88; Morrice MSS, P, 130, 152.

122 Grey, VII, 67–73, *passim.*

123 Barrillon to Louis XIV, Jan. 30/Feb. 9, A.A.É. Angleterre, Vol. 133, fol. 167. At the time Shaftesbury was carrying on two separate intrigues, one with Danby and the other with the Duke of York, hoping thereby to set them against each other. Browning, I, 312 n.2. Danby's brief account of the negotiations leading to the dissolution, which was written in a letter to Lord Treasurer Rochester six years later, introduces some contradictions. He says nothing of any approaches to either Holles or Shaftesbury, and he makes Monmouth the intermediary between leaders in the House of Commons and the King. Either lapses of memory or personal involvement would seem to be the most likely explanation of the major differences between his account and the information contained in letters and accounts written at the time of the negotiations. A copy of his letter to Rochester of Feb. 28, 1684/85 is in Alfred Morrison's collection of manuscripts. *Catalogue of the Collection . . . Formed between 1865 and 1882* (6 vols.), 1st Ser., III, 119–20.

## NOTES FOR CHAPTER VI

1 *The Humble Apology of Some Commonly Called Anabaptists,* p. 6; William Sherwin, ΠΡΟΔΡΟΜΟΣ: *The Fore-Runner of Christ's Peaceable Kingdom on Earth* (1665), p. 15.

2 *A Declaration from the Harmlesse and Innocent People of God, Called Quakers, Against All Plotters and Fighters in the World* (1660); Fox, *Journal*, II, 34–35.

3 House of Lords Record Office, MS Minutes of Committees, 19 May 1661–13 May 1664, p. 12; *L.J.*, XI, 267, 299, 306–307; *H.M.C., 5th Rept., Sutherland MSS*, p. 151; *C.J.*, VIII, 305; George Whitehead, *The Christian Progress of that Ancient Servant and Minister of Jesus Christ* (1725), pp. 261–62, 265–71; *H.M.C., 7th Rept. Pt. I, H. of L. MSS*, 144, 148.

4 At this juncture Fox wrote that Richard Hubberthorne, another prominent Friend, "was with the King and the King said none should molest us so [i.e., if] we lived peaceably." There is ample evidence that this estimate of the King's favor continued to prevail in 1666, and even until 1674, particularly in Fox's case. Fox, *Journal*, I, 371–73, 384–85; II, 101–102, 169, 298, 424; "Thirnbeck Manuscripts," *J.F.H.S.*, IX (April, 1912), 97.

5 *Henry*, p. 138; Newcome, *Autobiog.*, I, 119; Philip Nye, *Sermon*

Preached to the Honorable Citizens of London, September 29, 1659, pp. 7, 8. The dedication of this pamphlet is dated September, 1660. Concerning the early effects of the enforcement of the Corporation Act by the commissioners which it established, see J. H. Sacret, "The Restoration Government and Municipal Corporations," *E.H.R.*, XLV, 251 ff.

6   Wilbur C. Abbot estimated that sixty-four M.P.s were elected prior to 1666. "The Long Parliament of Charles II," *E.H.R.*, XXI (Jan. 1906), 37.

7   *O.R.*, I, 521, 524; *C.S.P.D.*, *1666–1667*, pp. 445–46, 470.

8   *C.J.*, VIII, 691; IX, 3, 23.

9   On April 4, 1668, Pepys wrote that he had been talking with the King and the Duke of York, among others, "about Quakers not swearing, and how they do swear in the business of a late election of a Knight of the Shire in Hartfordshire in behalf of one they have a mind to have. . . ." Though unidentified, there is no question that the new member was James, Viscount Cranborne, returned April 4; he was called to the Upper House Nov. 11, 1669, as the third Earl of Salisbury. Pepys, VII, 392; *O.R.*, I, 523. In the other case it was reported to Sir Joseph Williamson that Nonconformists supported Lord Hinchinbroke, who was returned for Dover, November 3, 1670; he also was called to the Upper House some two years later, as the Second Earl of Sandwich. S.P.29/280/33, fol. 41; *O.R.*, I, 532; G.E.C., *Peerage*, XI, 433.

10   The election of Sir John Austin who was returned for Winchelsea, October 4, 1666, was later voided. His opponent contended, first: that of "the persons that voted for Austin, which were nine, six of them were Quakers, or such as had not received the Sacrament within 22 months before the election, nor had taken oaths according to the Act. . . . Secondly (which was more insisted on) it was urged that the Mayor which had made the return had not received the sacrament of 12 months before the election, or before he was chosen mayor. And so by the Act of Regulating Corporations he was not a legal mayor, and so could not make a legal return." In a decisive vote (138–63) on January 10, 1667, the House voided the election on the grounds that the Mayor had not taken the Sacrament within a year prior to election. *O.R.*, I, 532; Milward, p. 60; *C.J.*, VIII, 672–74.

11   *C.S.P.D.*, *1666–1667*, 173; S.P.29/269/41, fol. 67.

12   The most fully reported cases in which Nonconformists regained positions in municipal governments were those of Yarmouth, Hull, Gloucester. *C.S.P.D.*, *1667–1668*, pp. 88, 145; *1668–1669*, pp. 10, 95 *passim*; *1670*, pp. 233 *passim*; *1671*, pp. 419 *passim*. Others in-

cluded Haverfordwest and Newcastle-under-Lyme. P.C.2/62/
196; T. Pape, *The Restoration Government and the Corporation
of Newcastle-under-Lyme* (Manchester University Press, 1940),
p. 24.

13  Milward, p. 65; *C.J.*, VIII, 678. The bill was introduced January
17, 1667, one week after the Winchelsea election case had been
voted upon.

14  *Ibid.* In September, 1668, the Privy Council ordered sheriffs and
Lord Lieutenants to check upon mayors and to watch for the read-
mission of officials who had been formerly removed under the
terms of the Act, the Council having had frequent reports of such
violations. P.C.2/61/42, 46.

15  His return was dated November 7, 1670, from Poole, Dorset. *O.R.*,
I, p. 522.

16  The Presbyterian Sir Charles Hoghton, who later served as a
member of the House for Lancashire, urged Edward Moore of
Liverpool to use his interest to secure the election of one of the
two sons of the Presbyterian Henry Ashurst of London, undoubtedly the elder one who was also named Henry and was a Presbyterian, as was his brother William. There were a few violations
of the Corporation Act in Liverpool during this period, which
would indicate some Nonconformist political activity in the Corporation. The King's powerful interference, which even antagonized local Anglican politicians, seems to indicate much royal
concern about the outcome. *H.M.C., Westmorland MSS*, pp. 117–
20; *City of Liverpool, Selections from the Municipal Archives and
Records, from the 13th to the 17th Century*, ed. James A. Picton
(Liverpool, 1883), pp. 245 ff.

17  Tellers favoring Rolle in the House division of December 9, 1669,
were the Presbyterian Henry Henley and Andrew Marvell. *C.J.*,
IX, 118.

18  Milward, p. 59; *C.J.*, IX, 29.

19  Dering, *Parl. Diary*, p. 4.

20  *A Letter to a Friend* (1670), p. 34.

21  Rawl. Ltrs. 51, fol. 121; 53, fols. 19, 53; Add. MSS, 40,860, fols.
6, 9, 28, 77; 18,730, fols. 20, 36, 85–86. The Countess of Anglesey
was a member of Dr. Owen's Church. See also the data concerning Wharton and Anglesey in Appendix II.

22  For pamphlets written by John Humfrey in 1667 which were circulated among members of Parliament and read by the King, see
*supra*, p. 56, n. 37. In 1670 Owen wrote "The State of the Kingdom with Respect to the Present Bill against Conventicles," a
pamphlet which ended with a petition to Parliament and was

probably the material on the Bill which was submitted by him to the House of Lords. *Works,* XXI, 465.

23 Tanner MSS, 45, fol. 278.

24 *C.S.P.D., 1670,* pp. 151–52; Baxter, Pt. III, p. 87.

25 For the lobbying activities of John Humfrey and Richard Baxter, see *supra,* pp. 56–57, 69.

26 Both were supported by Dissenters in the election, and this would appear in part to explain why there was a double return in the case of Barnardiston and the necessity for two petitions from Papillon to the House of Commons before he was seated in January, 1674. *C.S.P.D., 1672–1673,* pp. 510, 522, 597; *1673,* p. 38; *C.J.,* IX, 252, 294; *O.R.,* I, 528, 532.

27 Foley's opponent, Henry Herbert the zealous Whig who was later created Baron Herbert of Cherbury, filed a petition in which he complained of an "undue return," but no action was taken until March 10, 1677, when Foley was unseated on charges of bribery. *C.J.,* IX, 252, 293, 397; Morrice MSS, P, 53; Josiah Wedgewood, *Staffordshire Parliamentary History* (2 vols.; Collections for a History of Staffordshire, ed. by William Salt Arch. Society, 1920), Vol. II, Pt. I (1603–1715), p. 167; *O.R.,* I, 531, n.4. Some contemporary and also some more recent accounts mistakenly state that it was Thomas Foley who was unseated in March, 1677. *C.S.P.D., 1677–1678,* pp. 8, 11.

28 *C.S.P.D., 1672–1673,* p. 572. See also Tanner MSS, 36, fol. 230; 39, fols. 24, 174; *Domestick Intelligence,* #19, 9 Sept. 1679; Bate, p. 126; *O.R.,* I, 525.

29 "Letters to William Penn, from Worcester Prison," *J.F.H.S.,* VII (April, 1910), 73; Letter dated September 3, 1674, Fox, *Journal,* II, 302–304; Friends' MSS, Morning Meeting Book, I (1673–1692), 7; *C.S.P.D., 1675–1676,* p. 54.

30 *A Letter from a Parliamentman to his Friend,* p. 6.

31 Braithwaite, *Second Period,* pp. 275–85 has a discussion of this development.

32 A different reason is suggested by Ethyn Williams Kirby, who has pointed out that lobbying was akin to proselytizing and therefore more congenial to the Friends. "The Quakers' Efforts to Secure Civil and Religious Liberty, 1660–1696," *J.M.H.,* VII (Dec., 1955), 407.

33 Penn to Richard Baxter, August, 1675, Baxter MSS, Letters, II, fol. 303; Fox, *Journal,* II, 310.

34 Braithwaite, *Second Period,* p. 285.

35 This was the system used again in 1680. The problem at the time of the Oxford Parliament in 1681 was met by designating five

who were to go to Oxford, with three others to do so "as they have freedom." Friends' MSS, Meeting for Sufferings Minutes, I (1675–1680), 46, 49, 56, 71, 75, 92; II (1680–1683), 12, 32, 33.

36  Friends' MSS, Meeting for Sufferings Minutes, I (1675–1680), 90; Friends' MSS, Book of Cases, I (1661–1695), 41; Friends' MSS, Bristol MSS, I, Item 82.

37  Friends' MSS, Meeting for Sufferings Minutes, I (1675–1680), 53; Besse, I, 445–48.

38  Carte MSS, 77, fols. 602–604; *H.M.C., Portland MSS*, III, 367.

39  Some of the other members were the Earls of Bath and Yarmouth; the Marquis of Worcester, the Lords Brandon Gerard, Fairfax, and Radnor, Sir Baynham Throckmorton, Sir Robert Atkins, Henry Powle, and Leveson Gower. Friends' MSS, Meeting for Sufferings Minutes, I (1675–1680), 46, 64, 76, 95; II (1680–1683), 26, 34, 37, 101, 103, 122, 177, 198, 226.

40  Grey, V, 250, debate of March 16, 1678.

41  See *supra*, p. 93.

42  Friends' MSS, Meeting for Sufferings Minutes, I (1675–1680), 73.

43  Friends' MSS, Yearly Meeting Minutes, I (1668–1693), 70.

44  The General Baptists or "connexionalists," to use the term of A. G. Underwood, the most authoritative Baptist historian, had more of a central organization than the Particular or "independent" Baptists, or than did the Congregationalists or Presbyterians. The General Baptists held national or General Assemblies in 1672, 1678–1681, and 1686; the Particular Baptists did not hold such a meeting until 1689. Such national organization as the Presbyterians had prior to the Restoration quickly disappeared thereafter, leaving them in autonomous congregations as were the Congregationalists. *Minutes of the General Assembly of the General Baptist Churches in England, with Kindred Records*, ed. W. T. Whitley (2 vols.; Baptist Hist. Soc. Pub. (1909–1910), introduction pp. xxvi–xxxii, 22n.; Underwood, *English Baptists*, pp. 119, 129; Whitley, *A History of British Baptists*, pp. 87–92; Gordon, pp. 153–54; C. E. Whiting, *Studies in English Puritanism from the Restoration to the Revolution, 1660–1688* (Church History Society; 1931), p. 62.

45  Both the Particular and General Baptists first took steps to demonstrate greater unity with Presbyterians and Congregationalists by issuing new Confessions which approached the theological position of these two more than before, especially the Particular Baptist's which was based upon the Westminster Confession of 1648 and the Congregationalist revision of it in 1658. Underwood, *English Baptists*, pp. 104–105; Whitley, *British Baptists*, pp. 128–

29; *Baptist Confessions of Faith,* ed. William J. McGlothlin (Baptist Historical Society Publications; 1911), pp. 124–61, 216–17, 220–89.

46  Morrice MSS, P, 74. Kiffen, a merchant and a Baptist minister, had been member of Parliament for Middlesex from 1656 to 1658. *O.R.,* I, 504.

47  Typical of such entries as are found with political implications is the following of October 31, 1680, from the records of a Baptist church in Bristol: ". . . the church being apprehensive of the great designs and endeavors of men to undermine the interest of our Lord Jesus in these nations and the many dangers and judgments that were impending, did agree together to spend two or three hours every week in prayer, as many as could assemble together . . . And so the first of November we began, and in three hours six brethren prayed, and one spake." *The Records of a Church of Christ, Meeting in Broadmead, Bristol, 1640–1687,* ed. Edward B. Underhill (Hanserd Knollys Society Publications, No. 2; 1847), pp. 426–27. For examples of the non-political character of Baptist church books and Quaker local records see also: Add. MSS, 36,709, Bradburn and Sevenoaks Church Book (General Baptist), 1671–1802, fols. 14–15. *Records of the Churches of Christ, Gathered at Fenstanton, Warboys, and Hexham, 1644–1720,* ed. Edward P. Underhill (Hanserd Knollys Society Publications, No. 9; 1854), pp. 254–64; *The Church Books of Ford or Cuddington and Amersham in the County of Bucks,* ed. W. T. Whitley (Baptist Historical Society Publications; 1911); *The First Minute Book of the Gainsborough Monthly Meeting of the Society of Friends, 1669–1719,* ed. Harold Brace (2 vols.; Lincoln Record Society, Vols. 38, 39; Hereford, 1948), I (1669–1689), pp. 1–84; *Minute Book of the Monthly Meeting of the Society of Friends for the Upperside of Buckinghamshire, 1669–1690,* ed. B. P. Snell (Buckinghamshire Archeological Society, Records Branch, Vol. I; High Wycombe, 1938), pp. 1–92.

48  Even individual Quakers found they sometimes desired greater freedom of action so that they could cooperate with other Dissenters in petitioning members of Parliament, and when two Southwark Friends so requested in April, 1679, the London Meeting for Sufferings advised them that they might do as they wished. Friends' MSS, Meeting for Sufferings Minutes, I (1675–1680), 94.

49  Friends' MSS, Morning Meeting Book, I (1673–1692), 7.

50  Letter to Lord Wharton, April 5, 1675, Rawl. Ltrs. 51, fol. 52. As would be expected Nonconformist chaplains were somewhat more

politically conscious than other ministers, particularly when developments occurred which might affect their patron's political fortunes. See also Calamy, II, 283.

51  See for example the reported plans of such leaders in Herefordshire. *C.S.P.D., 1675–1676,* pp. 460–61.

52  *C.S.P.D., 1675–1676,* pp. 232, 245, 331, 355.

53  *Ibid.,* pp. 184–85; *1677–1678,* pp. 426, 531, 555–56, 559; *H.M.C., 6th Rept. Ingilby MSS,* pp. 371–72; *H.M.C., Duke of Leeds MSS,* p. 12; Browning, I, p. 206 n.5.

54  *C.J.,* IX, 354, 397, 444, 482, 486, 492–93; *C.S.P.D., 1675–1676,* p. 122; Marvell, II, 316–17.

55  This was Thomas Vane, who died of smallpox within a few days after being elected. John Willcock, *Sir Henry Vane, Statesman and Mystic, 1613–1662* (1913), p. 345. Newdigate Newsletters, L.C. 200, July 11, 1675.

56  Letter of Walter, Lord Aston to Secretary Williamson, April, 1675, *C.S.P.D., 1675–1676,* p. 87.

57  See Browning, I, p. 206.

58  *Ibid.,* p. 206 n.5. There had been earlier inquiries as to whether excommunicated persons and Nonconformists had the right to vote, and also complaints that they were voting, but there was no general use of this means to deprive Dissenters of the vote until the period of reaction and persecution following the Oxford Parliament of 1681. Stote himself thought that such tactics had been rarely if ever practised. S.P.29/280/33, fol. 41; *C.J.,* IX, 118, *C.S.P.D., 1670,* p. 506; *1682,* p. 571; Narcissus Luttrell, *Brief Historical Relation of State Affairs from September, 1678, to April, 1714* (6 vols.; Oxford, 1857), I, 242, 341. See Chapter VIII, p. 153, for its use in the London mayoralty election in 1682. Although no example of the use of excommunication against candidates themselves has been discovered, it was not overlooked as a possible deterrent, for there were some who said the Bishop of Chichester had "excommunicated a great fanatic because that town should not choose him parliament-man." Claydon House, Verney MSS, John Verney to Sir Ralph Verney, Aug. 7, 1679. For a discussion of the origin of the legal concept that "an excommunicated person cannot do any legal Act," as Bracton stated it, see Holdsworth, I, 631–32; also John Godolphon's *Repertorium Cannonicum, or an Abridgment of the Ecclesiastical Laws of this Realm Consistent with the Temporal* (1687), pp. 623–37; and *infra* Chapter VIII, n. 14.

59  The five petitioning were Hewley, Rushworth, Yonge, Ellis, and

Reynell. Only Hewley had no real grounds for complaint. *C.J.*, IX, 397, 400, 444, 482, 483, 485, 486, 492–93, 521, 532; *C.S.P.D.*, *1675–1676*, p. 122; Marvell, II, 316–17.

60 For example, Sir Robert Kemp and Sir Robert Cann, who as have been indicated were supported by Dissenters, were both elected. *O.R.*, I, 523, 525; Whitehead, *Christian Progress*, p. 490.

61 Jolly, p. 36.

62 "Mather Papers," p. 591.

63 *Christianismus Primitivus: or, The Ancient Christian Religion* (1678), Book III, pp. 51–52.

64 See Friends' MSS, Meeting for Sufferings Minutes, I (1675–1680), 90, 95; II (1680–1683), 26, 34, 37, 101, 103; Besse, I, 445–48; *H.M.C., Portland MSS,* III, 367.

65 Besse, II, 144. Specifically they wanted relief for those suffering from prosecution under the laws directed at Catholics, and also relief for those prosecuted because they worshipped according to the dictates of their conscience.

66 Letter from London Meeting for Sufferings, January 21, 1681, Friends' MSS, Book of Cases, I (1661–1695), 82.

67 *Ibid.*, pp. 81, 83–84. Gerard and Calverley were elected, but Owen was not. *O.R.*, I, 550.

68 Friends' MSS, Book of Cases, I (1661–1695), 81; *C.S.P.D.*, *1680–1681*, pp. 137–38.

69 Friends' MSS, Meeting for Sufferings Minutes, II (1680–1683), 103, 122; Bristol MSS, V, 142. Accounts given by Richard Davis and William Sewel, both prominent Friends and reliable sources, indicate that the Court felt that Quaker activity at Bristol had been of crucial importance. According to William Sewel, there was a proposition passed underhand at the time "that if Mr. Penn or Mr. Whitehead would undertake for the Quakers not to vote at elections of Parliament men, there should be no further persecution of them." *History of the Rise, Increase, and Progress of the Christian People Called Quakers* (n.p., 1725), pp. 652–53; *An Account of the Convincement Exercises, Services and Travels of that Ancient Servent of the Lord, Richard Davies* (1710), p. 222.

70 The best account is given by Mary M. Dunn, *William Penn, Politics and Conscience* (Princeton, 1967), pp. 34–37.

71 Letter of William Penn to Algernon Sydney, July 29, 1679, George W. Meadley, *Memoirs of Algernon Sydney* (1813), App. XII, pp. 336–37; *Diary of the Times of Charles II by Henry Sidney*, ed. R. W. Blencowe (2 vols.; 1843), I, 115.

72 The pamphlet is entitled *England's Great Interest in the Choice of This New Parliament; Dedicated to All Her Freeholders and*

*Electors* (n.p. [1679]). David Ogg suggests that Shaftesbury may also have had something to do with its composition. *England . . . Charles II*, II, 586 n.2. For a summary of its contents, see the end of this chapter, p. 120.

73   Rawl. Ltrs. 51, fols. 89, 91, 98; 53, fol. 97. Yonge was a possible Dissenter who sat for Honiton in each of the Exclusion Parliaments.

74   *C.S.P.D., 1679–1680*, p. 526; *1680–1681*, pp. 174, 210, 422; *H.M.C., Montagu MSS*, pp. 174–75.

75   In May, 1679, Samuel Hieron sent a plea to Lord Wharton and his son to "make an interest" for Richard Duke, Jr., Sir Walter Yonge's brother-in-law when it appeared he would lose the election. He was the successful candidate in the end. Rawl. Ltrs. 53, fol. 97; *O.R.*, I, 541.

76   Add. MSS, 29,910, fols. 119–20. See also *ibid.*, fol. 108.

77   At the time of the York elections in September, 1679, Oliver Heywood was a house guest at Sir John Hewley's and writes of dining with Lord Clifford, Sir Gilbert Gerard, and Sir John Brooke, all of whom sat in each of the three Exclusion Parliaments except Brooke, who was a member of the last two; he also notes in his diary the day after the election: "I preached in Sir John Hewley's chamber, God helped in duties with the family, none besides. . . ." Heywood, II, 104; *O.R.*, I, 539, 545, 550. Other ministers playing important roles were Hampden's chaplain John Nott and Roger Morrice. Add. MSS, 29,910, fols. 84–85, 108, 119–20.

78   The character of Smith's religious views are indicated in his work *Symptomes of Growth and Decay in Godliness in Eighty Signs of a Living and Dying Christian, With Causes of Decay and Remedies for Recovery* which was first printed in 1660, and published again in 1672 and 1673. Smith refers in the Postscript of this work to his preaching. It seems somewhat questionable whether he was the Francis Smith whom Calamy reports ejected from an uncertain place in Surrey, and who was licensed under the Indulgence of 1672 to preach at Croyden, Surrey, as is sometimes stated, for there was a Francis Smith who was buried at Farnham, Surrey, July 6, 1688, while the printer lived until 1691. However, there is no doubt that he was the "Frans. Smith bookseller at Temple Bar" who was reported in 1670 as teacher of a meeting in London, and who was licensed as a Baptist Teacher in Cornhill Street in 1672. Baptist historians disagree somewhat as to whether he started the well-known meeting at Glasshouse Alley, the best evidence being that he did not, although he may have been a member. A minute concerning him in the White's Alley General Baptist Church Book

March, 1689, indicates that he could have been a member of that Church at that date. *C.S.P.D., 1670,* p. 209; Turner, II, 988, 1017; "London Churches in 1682," ed. W. T. Whitley, *B.H.S.T.,* N.S., I (1922–1923), p. 85; E. A. Payne, "The Glasshouse Yard Minute Book, 1682–1740," *Baptist Quarterly,* VII (1934–35), p. 321; Guildhall Library MSS, White's Alley Church Book, 1681–1841 (4 vols.), I, fol. 38.

79 Smith dedicated one of his pamphlets to Shaftesbury, writing: "I having in many cases experienced your Lordship's kindness towards me and my family; I cannot . . . but make my thankful acknowledgments to your honor as any occasion offers itself; and therefore could not omit this duty at this time, when I am making public an abstract of my sufferings; in many of which I have been much helped through your Lordship's goodness. . . ." *An Account of the Injurious Proceedings of Sir George Jeffreys Knt., Late Recorder of London, Against Francis Smith, Bookseller, with His Arbitrary Carriage towards the Grand-Jury at Guildhall, Sept. 16, 1680* (1680), Dedication.

80 See W. T. Whitley, *A Baptist Bibliography* (2 vols.; 1916 and 1922), II, 205, *Smith's Protestant Intelligence: Domestick and Foreign,* February 1–April 14, 1681; twenty-two issues were published.

81 Dorothy M. George has described thoroughly the calculated character and the essentially new and revolutionary nature of this press campaign in which a vocal minority attempted "to create a public opinion, and then to present it as the demand of the nation . . . ," and she deals briefly with Smith's important role. "Elections and Electioneering, 1679–1681," *E.H.R.,* XLV (Oct., 1940), 552–78, particularly 568, 572–73, 575. See also J. R. Jones, *The First Whigs: The Politics of the Exclusion Crisis* (Oxford, 1961), pp. 166–72.

82 Smith began publishing the addresses in his news sheet on February 15. For those he published see *Smith's Protestant Intelligence,* Numbers 5, 6, 8–14. The two published as broadsides were: *A True Narrative of the Proceedings at the Guildhall, The Fourth of This Instant February, in Their Unanimous Election of Their Four Members to Serve in Parliament* (1680 [O. S.]); and *The Addresses of the Freeholders of the County of Middlesex* (1680 [O. S.]). The pamphlet was entitled, *Vox Patriae, or the Resentments and Indignation of the Freeborn Subjects of England against Popery, Arbitrary Government, The Duke of York and Any other Popish Successor, Being a True Collection of the Petitions and Addresses Lately Made by the Divers Counties, Cities and*

*Boroughs of This Realm to Their Representatives* (1681). The printer given as Francis Peters, but as George points out there was no publisher of this name known, and contemporary references imply that Smith was the printer. *E.H.R.*, XLV, 573.

Another famous printer, Benjamin Harris, also played a role in this press campaign. He had some Baptist connections, but there is no evidence in Nonconformist sources that he was a Baptist of standing such as there is for Smith. W. T. Whitley, *A Baptist Bibliography*, II, 205. An attempt to deny that he was a Baptist is found in issue Number 51, December, 1679, of his *Protestant (Domestick) Intelligence.*

83 Smith had claimed that he had not been fully compensated for printing which he had done several years prior at the request of both General and Particular Baptists. The Church minute states that the members "do not find ourselves concerned to reimburse him" on this account, yet they were moved by his plight to act. It appears that Smith may have approached other Churches in a similar manner. Guildhall Library MSS, White's Alley Church Book, I, fol. 38. His own listing of prosecutions to September, 1680, is found at the end of his pamphlet, *An Account of the Injurious Proceedings of Sir George Jeffreys*, pp. 17 ff. Subsequent ones are noted in the records and chronicles of the day. *C.S.P.D., 1680–1681*, pp. 137, 482, 554, 667; Morrice MSS, P, 295, 439; Luttrell, *Brief Relations*, I, 64, 75, 92, 109.

84 Carte MSS, 79, fols. 170–71, 175–76, 185. W.S.L. MSS, 478, Swynfen Ltrs. (Philip Foley to Swynfen, Feb. 4, 1678/1679); Add. MSS, 18,730, fol. 60; 29,910, fols. 33, 291; Henry, p. 292; Rawl. Ltrs. 53, fol. 97; *A Letter from a Freeholder of Buckinghamshire to a Friend in London Concerning the Election of the Knights of the Said County* (n.p., n.d.) signed at Aylesbury, August 23, 1679, pp. 1–4.

85 For examples, see the following sources concerning the activity of Sir John Hewley and Henry, Lord Fairfax in Yorkshire; Sir Edward Harley in Hereford; and William Strode and John Trenchard in Somerset; *H.M.C., Various MSS*, II, pp. 393–94; Thoresby, *Diary*, I, 28, 31, 79; Reresby, 188n., 190; Heywood, I, 348–49; *H.M.C., Portland MSS*, III, 363, 364, 369; VIII, 15; *C.S.P.D., 1680–1681*, pp. 514–15.

86 Buckingham to Wharton, Feb. 4, 1678/79, Carte MSS, 79, fol. 179; *C.S.P.D., 1679–1680*, p. 66; Claydon House, Verney MSS (Letters of Sir Ralph Verney Jan. 29, Feb. 2, 1678/79; Jan. 27, 1680/81; Thomas Wharton and Sir Richard Temple to Sir Ralph Verney Jan. 30, 1678/79 and Feb. 3, 1680/81 respectively);

*Letters of Rachel, Lady Russell,* I, 49; Rawl. Ltrs. 51, fol. 103; W.S.L. MSS, 478, Swynfen Ltrs. (Philip Foley to Swynfen, Feb. 4, 1678/79).

87  Lady Russell is the source of the frequently cited evidence concerning a report that letters between Shaftesbury and the Lord Marquis Winchester were intercepted, in all of which "they give their friends great caution not to choose fanatics, at which the King was much pleased, and said he had not heard so much good of them [in] a great while." *Letters of Rachel, Lady Russell,* I, 47. See also Brown, *Shaftesbury,* p. 255; and, E. Lipson, "The Elections to the Exclusion Parliaments, 1679–1681," *E.H.R.,* XXVIII (Jan., 1913), p. 73.

88  Reresby explained that in the past when the receivers of hearth money had levied this tax on the furnaces which these cutlers used for manufacture of "edge tools," he had intervened and gained relief from the taxation. Feeling that they were much obliged to him, he was understandably bitter that they did not vote for the candidate whom he had recommended as his friend. He concluded bluntly: "so much at this day did faction prevail above friendship. After this I concerned myself very little for the Sheffieldians." Reresby, pp. 104, 185, 187.

89  Episcopal Returns of 1669, Turner, II, 663.

90  This report of campaigning is dated October 15, 1681, and thus postdates the last Exclusion Parliament election, but the writer intimates that this kind of activity was not new. *C.S.P.D., 1680–1681,* pp. 514–15.

91  A bill for regulation of elections introduced in the House of Commons in January, 1667, provided no man shall "settle his land to several persons in such a manner as to gain by plurality of votes." This was clearly an Anglican sponsored Bill, since it also contained a clause which would require proof that those standing and voting had recently received the Sacrament according to the rites of the Church of England. Milward, p. 65; *C.J.,* VIII, 678. For evidence of later use of this tactic by Henry Henly, a Presbyterian M.P., and others, see *C.J.,* X, 141.

92  *C.S.P.D., 1670,* p. 519; *1672–1673,* p. 597.

93  *Ibid., 1675–1676,* pp. 184–85; *1670,* p. 519.

94  P.C.2/67/123; 68/439–40, 455; 69/25, 33; *C.S.P.D., 1677–1678,* pp. 536–37; *1678,* p. 131; *1679–1680,* pp. 312–13, 526–27, 534; *1680–1681,* pp. 174, 210, 505; *H.M.C., Rutland MSS,* II, 54; Morrice MSS, P, 339.

95  For examples, John Swynfen entertained modestly, while William Strode and John Hampden (with Thomas Wharton) did so on

a lavish scale. According to Sir Ralph Verney, Wharton's and Hampden's bills came to £800 each in the February, 1679 election of knights for Buckinghamshire, and Sir Ralph who supported them, considered this amount "very high," adding that "one inn (and that none of the chief) sets down 800 bottles of sack." Add. MSS, 29,910, fols. 86–87, 90; *C.S.P.D., 1680–1681*, pp. 514–15; Claydon House, Verney MSS, letters of Feb. 10 and 17, 1678/79 from Sir Ralph.

96    *Ibid., 1672–1673*, pp. 576–77, 587; *1675–1676*, p. 122; *1678*, p. 373; *C.J.*, IX, 397.

97    Feb. 10, 1679, Rawl. Ltrs. 51, fol. 91.

98    See House of Commons debates of Jan. 22, 1674, and Nov. 12, 1675; Grey, II, 333–34; IV, 2–3; *C.J.*, IX, 374; and Chapter VII, pp. 132, 146.

99    *H.M.C., Ormonde MSS*, N.S., IV, 311; *ibid., 7th Rept., Verney MSS*, pp. 385, 390. Other tributes to the effectiveness of Nonconformist electioneering are found in the design in some places to have voters swear that they had been at Church and received the Sacrament within the last year. *Domestick Intelligence*, No. 19, Sept. 9, 1679. See also, *Considerations offered to all the Corporations of England* (1681), pp. 1–2.

100   In addition to the sources already cited, see Morrice MSS, P, 122, 296–98, 300–301. In his illuminating accounts of these elections J. R. Jones discusses the activities of Holles, Wharton, Swynfen, the Hampdens, the Boscawens, and Sir John Hartopp. However, since he considers Holles and his friends to be "former Presbyterians" and does not discuss Nonconformist support of Whig leaders who were moderate Anglicans, the degree to which the Dissenters were active and successful is not clear. *The First Whigs*, pp. 10–11, 35–48, 92–106. See also, Browning, I, 315.

101   For complete data, see Appendix III.

102   These are the items which are found in *England's Great Interest in the Choice of This New Parliament*, the anonymous pamphlet attributed to Penn, in the two broadside editions of the London and Middlesex election addresses which Smith published, and also in the other addresses he published in his news sheet. *England's Great Interest*, pp. 1–2; *Address of the Freeholders of the County of Middlesex*, p. 1; *A True Narrative of the Proceedings at the Guildhall*, pp. 1–2; *Smith's Protestant Intelligence*, Nos. 5, 6, 8, 10–14. Although Shaftesbury may have had something to do with the composition of the pamphlet attributed to Penn, and undoubtedly did have a part in the campaign of addresses, it should be remembered that he was well aware of

the measures which Dissenters favored and that he desired to have their support.

NOTES FOR CHAPTER VII

1 Jolly, p. 36.
2 Morrice MSS, P, 113, 122, 137–94.
3 "Mather Papers," p. 325.
4 *Correspondence of the Family of Hatton being Chiefly Letters Addressed to Christopher First Viscount Hatton,* ed. Edward M. Thompson (2 vols.; Camden Society, New Series Nos. 22, 23; Westminster, 1878), I, 179–80. Grey, VI, 417, 433–35. Mainly because of his position as the King's Sergeant-at-Law, Sir John Maynard did not line up with the others of the Presbyterian group. *Ibid.,* pp. 422–23, 431–32.
5 *Ibid.,* VII, 1–4; *L.J.,* XIII, 461. On the whole question, see Joseph Redlich, *Procedure of the House of Commons,* Trans. by A. Ernest Steinthal (3 vols.; 1908), II, 156–58, 162–63. Of Gregory and his selection, Morrice wrote that he was "a very just and impartial gentleman," and added "God seems . . . to be multiplying mercies upon us."
6 On February 19 Morrice noted: "I think seven more regiments are disbanding or have been ordered to be." Morrice MSS, P, 130. The continuing disappointment over rejection of the draft declaration is found in his shorthand passages, *ibid.,* pp. 112–13, 120.
7 Browning, III, 140–43.
8 Morrice MSS, P, 140. This entry occurs between those of the 15th and the 17th; it is misdated the 18th. Browning concurs that Holles would not have assented to the pension and suggests that in its offer the Presbyterians "found at least a fair excuse for receding from their bargain with the Court. . . ." *Danby,* I, 321.
9 P.R.O.31/3/142, fol. 70 (Barrillon to Louis XIV, 17/27, March); Browning, I, 321; Morrice MSS, P, 142 (entry of March 17).
10 Carte MSS, 228, fol. 229 (Lord Wharton's rough notes of the debate); *L.J.,* XIII, 466; Morrice MSS, P, 142. Swynfen's remarks in the Commons seem to indicate a similar position, though he may have been thinking more specifically of Danby. Grey, VII, 6.
11 A lucid statement of the constitutional issue has been made by Clayton Roberts, *Growth of Responsible Government,* pp. 217–18.
12 Morrice MSS, P, 144.
13 *L.J.,* XIII, 471. Wharton was also a member.
14 *L.J.,* XIII, 474–84. Holles had attended the House every day

prior to March 24, when his four-day absence began. He returned the next four days, March 28 through April 1, when no particular business concerning Danby was before the House; but after the Common's Bill for Attainder passed the first reading on April 1 when Holles was recorded as present, and a debate was ordered in the Committee of the Whole House the next day, he reacted as before and absented himself. His health and age were apparently of some influence, for he did not return until May 10 after having been recorded as "not well, excused" when the House was called over the previous day. Although this seems a quick recovery, he was highly concerned with the issue being debated. Barrillon testified to Holles' lack of "health and strength" and reported that "his great age keeps him away from affairs." *L.J.*, XIII, 484–94, 561; A.A.É. Angleterre, Vol. 135, fol. 53.

15 Danby's successive appraisals of Holles as a supporter are relevant, since in his second list he considered the Presbyterian leader as "doubtful" and a later list noted his absence. Browning, III, 144–48.

16 Morrice MSS, P, 113, 122 (shorthand passages).

17 For examples of Barrillon's overestimate of the influence of both Holles and the "Presbyterian Party," see A.A.É. Angleterre, Vol. 135, fols. 53, 56; P.R.O.31/3/142, fol. 93; and *supra,* p. 98.

18 See Grey, VII, 19–30, 37–47, 60–62, 85–89; debates of March 22, 24, 27, and April 7.

19 Browning, III, 140–42; 144–51; *L.J.*, XIII, 476. Anglesey did not sign a protest registered on the reading. *Ibid.*, p. 481.

20 Grey, VII, 29. One reason for the silence of most other Presbyterian members on this debate may have been that the legal technicalities of the issue made it rather forbidding, but this would hardly be the complete explanation for their silence. Their inactivity becomes more evident in view of the frequency of Presbyterian speakers during these same days upon such matters as the Popish Plot and the importation of Irish cattle. *Ibid.*, pp. 41–42, 51–55, 99–101.

21 *L.J.*, XIII, 537–40.

22 Grey, VII, 133, 152–54, 157.

23 *Ibid.*, pp. 179–80. On May 24, Hampden echoes Maynard's statement concerning the five lords, and strong anti-Catholicism is also found in his speech of March 25, *ibid.*, p. 325.

24 *Ibid.*, p. 183.

25 *Ibid.*, pp. 170, 175, 199–203, 206; *C.J.*, IX, 612, 615, 619. Hampden was on both. For the work of the second of these committees, see *H.M.C., 11th Rept. Pt. II, H. of L. MSS*, 30–37.

26  *L.J.,* XIII, 570.

27  *C.J.,* IX, 623; Grey's report of Hampden's speech becomes some-
    what garbled. His key words were that if "the pardon be good,
    what can the nation bear?" *Ibid.,* 301–302.

28  This is evident in Wharton's own reports of the debate of May 6,
    during which he gave two speeches, and in his records of the
    divisions on the questions during the last day of the session, as
    well as in the formal protests against the majority views which
    were entered on the House Journal. Carte MSS, 81, fols. 551, 566,
    567, 569; *L.J.,* XIII, 594.

29  *A Letter of a Gentleman to His Friend, Shewing that the Bishops
    Are Not To Be Judges in Parliament in Cases Capital* (1679),
    pp. 118–19. According to the *Journal* of the House of Lords,
    Holles was sick and not present on either May 6, or May 27,
    which explains the absence of his name in Wharton's records.
    *L.J.,* XIII, 555, 561, 594.

30  His exact words were: "I respect not Danby in the matter, but
    the business of the pardon." Grey, VII, 302.

31  Morrice MSS, P, 125 (Shorthand passage); A.A.E., Vol. 135,
    fol. 57. This attitude toward Danby was stated more extremely
    in 1689 by Dr. John Howe, who wrote that "the noble Earl of
    Danby" procured the dissolution of the Cavalier Parliament "to
    his immortal honor." *The Case of the Protestant Dissenters*
    (1689), p. 2.

32  See debates of November 4, 1678. Grey, VI, 133–48.

33  Baxter, Pt. III, p. 186; Grey, VII, 144–46.

34  Grey, VII, 147; *Statutes,* IV, Pt. I, pp. 358–59.

35  Grey, VII, 150–51. The original motion had been to bring in a
    bill to banish all Catholics from London. *Ibid.,* p. 138.

36  *Ibid.,* pp. 240–60. Hampden, Foley, and Boscawen were of the
    existing Presbyterian group in the House; Birch had been a Pres-
    byterian during the Civil War, the Interregnum, and the first
    decade of the Restoration; and Henry Booth was the son of Sir
    George Booth, then Lord Delamer, famous leader of Booth's
    Rising 1659. Although raised in the Presbyterian tradition, Henry
    Booth is best described as a "Puritan Low Churchman." See
    *supra,* Chapter II, n. 45.

37  Grey, VII, 248–49.

38  *Ibid.,* p. 243.

39  *Ibid.,* pp. 258–59; *C.J.,* IX, 620. The published version of the
    speech entitled *A Speech in the House of Commons on Reading
    the Bill Against the Duke* (n.p., 1679) does not have much re-
    semblance to the report in Grey. One important difference is

that the published speech contains a statement that a Catholic King could control the House of Commons by purchasing votes in the "many small boroughs and towns who choose us, where there are but few voices." In the subtitle of a reply to this pamphlet it was described as a speech "pretended to be spoken" in the House, and because of the differences from Grey's report there seems some reason for this claim. However, Morrice, who knew Boscawen and who recorded the published version between the entries of May 27 and 28, seems to have accepted it as the one given, entitling it "A Speech Made by a Cornish Gent. in the House of Commons." *Fiat Justica et Ruat Coelum, Or, Somewhat Offer'd in Defense of the Imperial Crown of England, and Its Successor* (1679); Morrice MSS, P, 192–94; O. W. Furley, "The Whig Exclusionist: Pamphlet Literature in the Exclusion Campaign, 1679–81," *C.H.J.*, XIII (No. 1, 1957), p. 32.

40  *C.J.*, IX, 626. Morrice has the most complete division list. Morrice MSS, P, 238–40. It has been combined with another list and edited by Andrew Browning and Doreen J. Milne in "An Exclusion Bill Division List," *B.I.H.R.*, XXIII (Nov., 1950), 205–25.

41  The absentees, Maynard, John White, and Sir Richard Norton, apparently stayed away because of indecision; Col. John Fagg was given leave to go into the country for his health on April 17. *Ibid.*, p. 221. The support given to the Exclusion Bill by Presbyterian and Congregationalist members is particularly impressive in view of the discovery made by J. R. Jones that "there were more abstentions among those whom Shaftesbury had regarded as his supporters than among those he had classed as hostile," "Shaftesbury's 'Worthy Men': A Whig View of the Parliament of 1679." *B.I.H.R.* (Nov., 1957), XXX, 233.

42  On the drafting committee were Maynard, Ellis, Foley, and Reynell; and on the other one Hewley, Maynard, Boscawen, Love, Young, Foley, Papillon, Barnardiston, and Reynell served. *C.J.*, IX, 577, 585. Hampden also headed a committee to which there was committed a bill for the better attendance of members elected to serve in Parliament. Foley, Papillon, Reynell, and Love were members of this committee. *Ibid.*, p. 616. Wharton's deep concern about parliamentary reform can be seen in the draft of a bill concerning election practices found in his parliamentary papers of this debate. Carte MSS, 80, fol. 827.

43  *A Collection of Scarce and Valuable Tracts* [Chiefly from the Collection of John Somers] (4 vols.; 1748), Pt. I, Vol. I, pp. 63–66. See also Wharton's draft bill. Carte MSS, 80, fol. 827.

44  Grey, VII, 316, 317, 319–20, 323, 328. It may have been either

Boscawen or Swynfen to whom Morrice refers as the source of some of the information which he records upon this matter. Morrice MSS, P, 189.

45 *C.J.*, IX, 609. The Lords version declared them void and provided that the grantor would forfeit his office and be incapable of holding any other. *H.M.C., 11th Rept., Pt. II, H. of L. MSS*, p. 119; *L.J.*, XIII, 511.

46 Hampden's bill was not introduced as ordered and the Lords' bill died in committee. *C.J.*, IX, 609–10; *H.M.C., 11th Rept., Pt. II, H. of L. MSS*, pp. 119–20. Col. Birch is a good example of an opposition member who held an office (Auditor of the Excise) which would have made him ineligible for the House according to Hampden's bill. *C. Treas. Bks., 1660–1667*, p. 195.

47 The title reads "An Act for the Better Securing the Liberty of the Subject and for the Prevention of Imprisonments Beyond the Seas," *Statutes*, V, 935–38; *C.J.*, IX, 582, 611, 634.

48 *L.J.*, XIII, 528, 552, 561, 562, 584; *H.M.C., 11th Rept. Pt. II, H. of L. MSS*, pp. 132–36. Grey does not record any debates in the House of Commons upon the Habeas Corpus Bill.

49 Friends' MSS, Meeting for Sufferings Minutes I (1675–1680), 108.

50 Carte MSS, 77, fol. 616; Frederick Seaton Siebert, *Freedom of the Press in England, 1476–1776, The Rise and Decline of Government Controls* (Urbana, 1952), p. 298, n. 26.

51 *Tudor and Stuart Proclamations*, I, pp. 448, 450, No. 3699 (October 31, 1679); No. 3715 (May 12, 1680). The Government finally fought the activities of Smith, Harris, and others by having Roger L'Estrange publish *The Observator, in Question and Answer* (April 13, 1681–March 9, 1687; later published in collected form, 3 vols.; 1684–1687). See Siebert, *Freedom of the Press*, p. 299.

52 The near consternation which had seized James is evident in his letters to William of Orange between late May and early July, which exaggerated the strength of the Presbyterians in the Commons, and justified his fears that "measures will be taken which must ruin our family, and with it the Monarchy; for the republican party get ground every day, being backed by the Presbyterians." Dalrymple, II, 219, 221, 224; *L.J.*, XIII, 595.

53 Add. MSS, 18,730, fol. 57, diary entry of July 6. Roger Morrice's journal entry of July 9, tells of a report about the Council meeting at Hampton Court on July 3, in which dissolution was debated and after which an oath of secrecy was taken. Continuing, he stated that the following Monday one of the Council "came to my Lord Holles, and pressed him to go to the Council at

Hampden Court next morning, for there were great things debated there the last Council day, but no conclusion put to them which he could not tell his Lordship because they were under secrecy; said the Lord Holles, 'I can tell you that you debated there about the dissolution of this Parliament, I think the French Ambassador told me so and who were for it and who were against it . . . by name. Thus you keep the King's secrets.'" Morrice gives those who favored dissolution at this meeting as Halifax, Essex, Sunderland, Temple, and Lauderdale. Anglesey gives only the names of Halifax and Essex as favoring it, and he also states that Lord Chancellor Finch and the Lord Chamberlain argued against dissolution along with him at a conference on July 6. Holles attended the meetings of July 9 and July 10, and unquestionably he also opposed dissolution. Morrice MSS, P, 207; Add. MSS, 18,730, fol. 57; P.C.2/68/161, 164, 168.

54 Add. MSS, 29,910, fol. 108. Morrice's initials are distinctive. See his full signature at fol. 120; *England's Great Interest,* p. 1.

55 Personal considerations and perhaps a feeling that the Presbyterian interests would continue to be well represented in the Commons led John Swynfen to decide at first that he would not stand. Even though Richard Hampden, Lord Crewe, Lord Paget, Roger Morrice and others pleaded with him to change his mind, he did not do so until August, which suggests that the King's illness may possibly have been a factor. In the end he was defeated by one vote. Add. MSS, 29,910, fols. 117, 119–20, 130, 137, 149–50; 30,013, fols. 291–92; also Appendix II, information concerning Swynfen.

56 Carte MSS, 228, fol. 103, 105. John Verney paid tribute to the Dissenters' campaigning, reporting that "if the choice be not so well as it might be, you will find the reason in the industry of the Nonconformists. . . ." *H.M.C., 7th Rept. Verney MSS,* p. 475.

57 See Appendix III for the names of the Presbyterian and Congregationalist members. Election activities of the Dissenters are discussed *supra,* pp. 115, 117.

58 *H.M.C., Ormonde MSS,* N.S., IV, 565–66. *H.M.C., 7th Rept., Verney MSS,* p. 496. It should be noted, however, that Wharton was not reported present at a meeting of Shaftesbury and six of the petitioning lords held on November 26, after which it was said they intended to address the King for the certain sitting of Parliament at the time appointed. Newsletter dated December 2, *C.S.P.D., 1679–1680,* p. 296. Morrice gives in full the draft of the petition which "the lords intended to present" to the King,

"but several of them meeting together a little before and not hav-
ing the draft among them [they] presented that which is in print."
Morrice MSS, P, 244–45; *The Humble Address and Advice of
Several Peers of this Realm, for the Sitting of Parliament* (1679).

59  *Ibid.*, p. 2; Morrice MSS, P, 245. The Statute Against Tumultuous
Petitioning of 1661 permitted a maximum of twenty to sign and
ten to present a petition. There were seventeen signers of this
petition, and although Rupert was not among these seventeen,
it was presumably believed safest to count him as one of the ten
allowed to make the presentation. *Statutes*, V, 308.

60  *H.M.C., Ormonde MSS*, N.S., IV, 566–67. Barrillon verifies Southwell's report concerning Holles, stating that he wanted a Catholic king's powers limited, instead of exclusion. Letter to Louis
of Dec. 14 N.S., P.R.O.31/3/143, fol. 113.

61  Barrillon to Louis, Dec. 21 N.S., *ibid.*, fol. 129. A month later the
Ambassador reported that Holles and the other Presbyterians
"would like to see both sides restrain themselves within legitimate limits, and would be satisfied to see England governed
according to the laws which are established there." This was
much more the position of Holles, and is the final statement of
his views, for the following month he died after a long and active
career. *Ibid.*, Vol. 144, fol. 29.

62  Southwell used a code for the names of the Duke and Penn in
this letter. *H.M.C., Ormonde MSS*, N.S., IV, p. 565. Fulmer
Mood dates Penn's decision to cease following Shaftesbury's
leadership sometime in the late spring of 1680, and uses as evidence the Quaker's decision to petition for the grant of Pennsylvania, which he dates no later than June 1. However, Penn's
statement to Southwell indicates that his break with the Whig
leadership came some six months earlier, and his decision to look
for a solution of Quaker problems in Pennsylvania would seem
to have followed as a consequence, as Mood has suggested.
*J.F.H.S.*, XXXII, 6, 8.

63  Christie, *Shaftesbury*, II, 354; P.R.O.31/3/143, fols. 106; Add.
MSS, 18,730, fol. 63.

64  *Ibid.;* Heywood, II, 111–12; Morrice MSS, P, 242; Jolly, p. 39.

65  Smith admitted he had done this in answer to questions put by
the Lord Chancellor when he was interrogated before the King
in Council on December 18. He was confined to Newgate and
on December 19, was released upon a writ of habeas corpus
issued under the new Act. His account of these matters is found
in his pamphlet, *An Account of the Injurious Proceedings of Sir
George Jeffreys . . . against Francis Smith . . . Together with*

an *Abstract of the Very Many Former Losses, and Publick Sufferings Sustained by Him* . . . , pp. 20 ff. See also the reports of the interrogation, confinement, and release published by Harris in his *Domestick Intelligence*, No. 48 (Dec. 19, 1679), and No. 49 (Dec. 23, 1679).

66  Morrice MSS, P, 242.

67  Morrice MSS, P, 246; *The Humble Petition of the Right Honourable the Lord Mayor, Alderman, and Commons of the City of London, in Common Council Assembled, on the Thirteenth of January, 1680* (1680 [O.S.]). Hatton, *Corres.*, I, 215; *H.M.C., Ormonde MSS, N.S.*, IV, 574.

68  *C.S.P.D., 1680–1681*, pp. 279–80. Hatton, *Corres.*, I, 223–24.

69  *H.M.C., 7th Rept., Verney MSS*, p. 479; *H.M.C., Ormonde MSS, N.S.*, V, 340. The only person appearing whose religious views may have been Presbyterian was John Trenchard. Lord Wharton's eldest son, Thomas Wharton, was there; but it is well known that he rejected the Presbyterian views and outlook of his father, and it is probable that this reaction had already taken place. Morrice MSS, P, 262; *Memoirs of the Life of the Most Noble Thomas Late Marquess of Wharton; with His Speeches in Parliament, both in England and Ireland. To which is added, His Lordship's Character, by Sir Richard Steele* (1715), p. 16.

70  Morrice MSS, P, 264; *H.M.C., 7th Rept., Verney MSS*, p. 479; Barrillon to Louis XIV, July 15, 1680, P.R.O.31/3/146, fol. 234.

71  *Ibid.*; *H.M.C., Ormonde MSS, N.S.*, V, 342; Morrice MSS, P, 263.

72  *C.S.P.D., 1680–1681*, pp. 45–46.

73  Henry, p. 292; Jolly, p. 43. A similar mood is reflected in Morrice's note about his stay in Bath (July 26 to September 4) and his account of Monmouth's visit there and elsewhere in the West. Morrice MSS, P, 264–65.

74  Although they did not speak prior to the vote upon the matter, it is apparent from their later speeches that Boscawen and Love also favored it. Grey, VII, 369–71, 372, 374. The resolution was passed *nemine contradicente* as proposed, and the following were appointed: Irby, Love, Hartopp, Papillon, Reynell, Paul Foley, Hampden, John White, John Trenchard, and Philip Foley. *C.J.*, IX, 640–41, 657.

75  Grey, VII, 372–74, 376. It was voted on October 27 that an address be made, and the committee to draw it up included Hampden and Boscawen. *C.J.*, IX, 641.

76  "An Historical Account of the Heroick Life and Magnanimous Actions of the Most Illustrious Protestant Prince, James Duke of Monmouth (1683)," reprinted in *Historical and Biographical*

*Tracts,* ed. George Smeeton (2 vols.; 1820), II, 31–32; Morrice MSS, P, 264–65.

77  P.R.O.31/3/145, fol. 174.

78  Grose, *J.M.H.,* I, 200; P.R.O.31/3/146, fols. 237–38, 296–98, 317–21; 147, fols. 387–88.

79  P.R.O.31/3/145, fol. 174; 147, fol. 384. Barrillon was also pleased to learn through "Two accredited ministers" whom he had won over with the help of Baber, that William's habit of hunting every Sunday was considered by the Presbyterians to be "a very criminal act and quite opposed to the religion they profess." *Ibid.,* 146, fol. 305.

80  *Ibid.,* 146, fols. 241, 242, 305; 147, fol. 401. The expenditures report is printed in Dalrymple, II, 315–17. Hampden, Boscawen, and Sir John Baber received 500 guineas each, while Harley and Foley were each given 300 guineas. Others of note receiving 500 guineas were Titus and Sidney; Sacheverell and Shaftesbury's secretary Bennett received 300. Unfortunately, an earlier report of disbursements dated October 31, is apparently no longer extant. Grose, *J.M.H.,* I, 198, n. 103. Hampden's contribution appears to have been more extensive and valuable than those of the others, for on February 19, 1681, Barrillon reported that he gave the Presbyterian leader another 500 guineas which had been promised "in case the session of Parliament passed without giving anything to His Britannic Majesty to maintain the alliances against France. . . ." P.R.O.31/3/148, fol. 48.

81  [John Torbuck], *Collection of Parliamentary Debates in England* [1668–1741] (21 vols.; 1739–1742), I, 352; Grey, VII, 411–13, 419. Hampden, Boscawen, Foley, and Trenchard were appointed to the committee of eighteen to draft the bill after a favorable vote. *C.J.,* IX, 645.

82  [Torbuck], *Collection,* I, 356 (italics are in Torbuck); Grey, VII, 421.

83  Boscawen prefaced his speech with the remark that he had not spoken earlier because the question was being so well debated. The third speaker was Sir John Trenchard. There was a debate on the third reading in which Lord Wharton's son Goodwin Wharton made his maiden speech. *Ibid.,* 411, 413, 448–49.

84  Carte MSS, 77, fols. 649–51; 81, fols. 654, 668; *L.J.,* XIII, 665–66. The notes on the debate kept by Lord Wharton, as well as lists which he compiled of the Lords voting against rejection of the Bill attest to his concern over the issue. Even though he apparently did not speak himself or sign the formal protest, it appears that he used whatever influence he had in support of the meas-

ure, for Goodwin Wharton and Thomas Wharton, his two sons in the House of Commons both supported the Bill. Grey, VII, 448–49.

85 See for example the account of bonfires and bell ringing by Dissenters in Walsall, Staffordshire, and also Morrice's reports that the business was "the grandest ever debated in that House." *C.S.P.D., 1680–1681,* p. 555; Morrice MSS, P, 271.

86 Jolly, p. 43; Morrice MSS, P, 277; Grey, VIII, 4, 6–7, 14; *H.M.C., Portland MSS,* VIII, 16; *H.M.C., 11th Rept., Pt. II, H. of L. MSS,* pp. 210–11; *L.J.,* XIII, 672; *H.M.C., Ormonde MSS,* V, 488. This measure was similar to the Associations authorized by 27 Eliz. I, cap. 1, *Statutes,* Vol. IV, Pt. I, p. 704.

87 Carte MSS, 228, fol. 208; 81, fols. 658, 660. These provisions along with the one repealing James' exemption from the Test Act and another guaranteeing the meeting of Parliament upon Charles' death were later embodied in the Bill for Securing the Protestant Religion; *H.M.C., 11th Rept. Pt. II, H. of L. MSS,* pp. 220–22; *L.J.,* XIII, 684.

88 See speeches of Hampden, the Foleys, Trenchard, and Boscawen. Grey, VIII, 158–59, 168–70, 186–88, 266–67, 273, 280; *H.M.C., Beaufort MSS,* "Diary of Parliament," pp. 99–100, 110–12.

89 For the provisions of this Act see *supra,* Chapter II n.48. Its severe penalties brought the Act under fire, though they were hardly ever enforced. 35 Eliz. I, c.1, *Statutes,* IV, 841–43; Grey, VII, 424–25; *C.J.,* IX, 681; *L.J.,* XIII, 717–19; *H.M.C., 11th Rept., Pt. II, H. of L. MSS,* p. 214.

90 *H.M.C., Beaufort MSS,* p. 84; Burnet, II, 279; *H.M.C., Buckinghamshire, Lindsey MSS,* p. 425; Christie, *Shaftesbury,* II, Appendix VII, cxiv (letter of John Locke). Morrice reported on January 11 that most persons thought the failure to present it was an accident rather than a design. Morrice MSS, P, 292.

91 Led by Penn and Whitehead, the Quakers were particularly active in petitioning and testifying in Committee hearings. Crewe, Delamer and Bedford served on the committee to draw up the Bill. A draft in Anglesey's writing is in the House of Lords MSS, while Wharton's papers had drafts and amendments, one similar in substance to that proposed by William Love in the House of Commons. House of Lords Record Office, Committee minutes 13 Feb. 1672/73–19 Nov. 1685, pp. 374–76; Whitehead, *Christian Progress,* pp. 493, 495; *L.J.,* XIII, 654, 680, 693–94, 709 *passim; H.M.C., 11th Rept., Pt. II, H. of L. MSS,* pp. 201–205; Carte MSS, 77, fols. 565, 599, 620–21, 618; 81, fols. 650–51; *C.J.,* IX, 695–97; Grey, VII, 423; VIII, 216–18.

92 Morrice MSS, P, 287–88; *H.M.C., Beaufort MSS,* "Diary of Parliament," pp. 101–102; Grey, VIII, 201–205. Grey's report of this debate is very incomplete, giving the speeches of only four members. Morrice states that about nineteen spoke against the bill (listing five of them), and he gives the names of twelve who spoke for it. The "Diary of Parliament" in the Beaufort papers does not give as many speakers, but it does have a brief summary of what was said. The Bill for Uniting Protestants received its second reading on December 21, and on the committee then appointed were Boscawen, Hampden, Paul Foley, Maynard, Love, Thomas Foley, Sir William Waller and John White. Morrice states that it passed the committee; however, it was not reported to the House. *C.J.,* IX, 687; Morrice MSS, P, 288.

93 He added: "all that I have heard of who desire comprehension, desire indulgence also for others, though multitudes desire indulgence that most fervently oppose comprehension . . ." *Ibid.,* 288. See also Whitehead, *Christian Progress,* pp. 368–69, 495.

94 *H.M.C., Beaufort MSS,* "Diary of Parliament," p. 104; Morrice MSS, P, 288. Grey gives no account of this or later debates on this Bill. It moved rapidly through the first stages of passage, receiving its first reading January 3 and the second reading January 6. The committee to draw up the Bill did not include any Presbyterians, but it was committed to one which included Boscawen, Philip Foley, Hampden, Ellis, Papillon, White, Love, and Henley. *C.J.,* IX, 692, 696, 700–701.

95 Grey, VII, 387–88.

96 Foley, Trenchard, Hartopp, Love, Harley, Barnardiston, Henry Henley, and Hampden were appointed. *C.J.,* IX, 661; Grey, VIII, 67, 69, 71.

97 *Ibid.,* 205–206. Citing recent cases of Francis Smith and Benjamin Harris among others, the Committee also presented evidence that punishment had not been imposed according to the nature of the offense and the ability of the person to pay, and that bail had not been accepted when tendered for crimes legally bailable. *C.J.,* IX, 692.

98 Grey, VIII, 186–88, 196–97; *H.M.C., Beaufort MSS,* "Diary of Parliament," pp. 99–100; *C.J.,* IX, 682.

99 Appointed to the single committee of twenty-five members to bring in these bills were Hampden, Paul Foley, Barnardiston, Reynell and Love. *Ibid.,* 682–83; Morrice MSS, P, 286; Carte MSS, 81, fol. 24. No further action concerning these two measures appears to have been taken by the House.

100 Boscawen, Harley, Hampden, Maynard, White, Love, Barnar-

diston, Young, Ellis, and Thomas Foley were also members of the committee. Grey, VIII, 226–29; *C.J.*, IX, 696.

101 Sir Edward Harley was prominent in the committee work for these bills, reporting amendments to the House as well as other matters. Serving with him were Hartopp, Strode, one of the Foleys, Boscawen, Hampden, White, Braman, Henry Henley, Barnardiston, and Maynard. *H.M.C.*, *Beaufort MSS*, "Diary of Parliament," p. 106; *C.J.*, IX, 639, 649, 659, 697.

102 For their earlier efforts during this Parliament see their speeches in the debates of November 27 and December 20 concerning the Commons answers to two of the King's earlier messages; in both cases Hampden made the leading speech in the debate, and in the first instance he brought in the committee report. Grey, VIII, 99–100, 103–104, 186–88, 196–97; *H.M.C.*, *Ormonde MSS*, N.S., V, 506. Also speaking in these debates were Philip Foley and Reynell. Grey, VIII, 235–36, 266–67, 273, 280, 284–85; *H.M.C.*, *Beaufort MSS*, "Diary of Parliament," pp. 110–13. Parliament was prorogued to January 20, but on January 18 it was dissolved. *C.J.*, IX, 704; *L.J.*, XIII, 742–43.

103 Rawl. Ltrs., 53, fol. 104; Heywood, II, 216–17; III, 309; Jolly, p. 44.

104 Even "Capt. Meade with several other Quakers were of the cavalcade" that accompanied the London M.P.s out of the City. Claydon House, Verney MSS, John to Sir Ralph Verney, March 21, 1680/81. See also Morrice MSS, P, 296, 297–98, 300; and for the discouragement of Court supporters, Tanner MSS, 38, fol. 121. For the forty-six known Presbyterians and Congregationalists elected see Appendix III.

105 *Smith's Protestant Intelligence*, No. 14 (March 14), and No. 15 (March 21); Rawl. Ltrs., 53, fol. 101. See also *supra*, pp. 115–16.

106 See also John Locke's letters, Christie, II, 392–99. At first Locke agreed to Gilbert's plans, but in the end Shaftesbury was lodged in Balliol College.

107 *The Debates in the House of Commons Assembled at Oxford the Twenty-first of March 1680* [O.S.] (1681), pp. 4–5; Grey, VIII, 295. The text in the *Debates in the House of Commons Assembled at Oxford* is the same as Grey's except for some slight differences in which case one of the other accounts may include a clarifying word or phrase. In this instance, for example, Grey has Hampden refusing the charge that the Presbyterians were "publicans," while the *Debates* correctly makes the word "republicans."

108 Grey, VIII, 300, 302. On the committee to prepare the subject matter for this conference were Hampden, Boscawen, Papillon,

Love, Philip Foley, Maynard, and Hewley. *C.J.*, IX, 708. As could be expected, there were no Presbyterians on the House of Lords committee to consider the failure to present the repeal Bill. *L.J.*, XIII, 755.

109  *A Letter from a Person of Quality to His Friend* (n.p., [1681]), p. 8; *H.M.C., Buckinghamshire, Lindsey MSS*, p. 431; *C.J.*, IX, 708, 711; *L.J.*, XIII, 755; *H.M.C., Buckinghamshire, Lindsey MSS*, p. 430; *Letter from a Person of Quality*, p. 3.

110  *L.J.*, XIII, 755; Grey, VIII, 337. The protesting lords held that the House could not reject an impeachment of the Commons because it was at the suit of the people and could be determined nowhere else, while indictment in the King's Bench was at the suit of the King.

111  Grey, VIII, 312–15, 331–32; *Debates in the House of Commons Assembled at Oxford*, pp. 9, 16–17; *H.M.C., Ormonde MSS*, N.S., VI, 7–8. Hampden, Philip Foley, Boscawen, and Trenchard, were on the drafting committee. *C.J.*, IX, 711.

112  Dalrymple, II, 301; Christie, *Shaftesbury*, II, 402–403; Grose, *J.M.H.*, I, 200–201.

113  Grey, IX, 340. Sir Edward Harley writing to his wife on March 26, stated that it was "confidently thought the Parliament will be prorogued on Monday," but dissolution came as a complete surprise. *H.M.C., Portland MSS*, III, 369.

NOTES FOR CHAPTER VIII

1  Add. MSS, 18,730, fols. 82–83; *C.S.P.D., 1682*, pp. 290–92, 424–26.

2  On his way to see the King at Windsor Anglesey stopped at Lord Wharton's where Richard Hampden, Dr. John Owen, and Lord Lovelace had already gathered. Sir Walter Yonge was in touch with Lord Russell who was often "locked up" with the Prince of Orange. Add. MSS, 18,730, fols. 85–86; *Letters of Rachel, Lady Russell*, II, 86. For other political activity, see *H.M.C., Ormonde MSS*, N.S., VI, 118; *C.S.P.D., 1680–1681*, p. 473; Dalrymple, App. Pt. I, p. 8.

3  In a letter to Ormonde of October 9, the Earl of Longford states that it was the Presbyterian party which sought this capitulation, but as Luttrell suggests, feeling had grown so high by September, 1681, that terms such as *Presbyterian* were more epithetical than descriptive when used by Tory partisans. It is not known what leaders were involved in this move. *H.M.C., Ormonde MSS*, N.S., VI, 184; Luttrell, *Brief Relations*, I, 124.

4  Lord Crewe to Swynfen, Dec. 15, 1681, W.S.L.49/83/44, Swynfen Ltrs.; Jolly, p. 47; William Waller to Shaftesbury, Dec. 10, 1681, P.R.O.30/24/6A, fol. 371. For an example of cases in which juries found indictments against Dissenters "Ignoramuses," see Morrice MSS, P, 322.

5  Burnet, II, 335.

6  Arthur G. Smith, "London and the Crown, 1681–1685" (Unpublished Ph.D. dissertation, University of Wisconsin, 1967), pp. 208–11, and Appendix A; *C.S.P.D., 1680–1681*, p. 638.

7  Tanner MSS, 36, fol. 91.

8  P.C.2/69/351, 386, 417 and *passim;* Tanner MSS, 35, fols. 107, 118; 36, fols. 196, 251, 257; Luttrell, *Brief Relations*, I, 125 and *passim; H.M.C., Ormonde MSS*, N.S., VI, 264, 274; *C.S.P.D., 1682*, pp. 20, 25, 26, 137–38, 192–93. Arthur G. Smith has made a thorough study of the prosecution of Dissenters in London during the four years following the Oxford Parliament, and he has demonstrated that in the metropolitan area the efforts of Government and Church officials met with only "modest success" during 1682. "London and the Crown, 1681–1685," pp. 256–69.

9  Friends MSS, Bristol MSS, V, 142; Friends MSS, Meeting for Sufferings Minutes, II (1680–1683), 158; *An Account of the Convincement . . . and Travels of . . . Richard Davis*, p. 222. See Thomas Delaune's defense of the Dissenters' activity in elections in his *Plea for the Nonconformists* (1684), p. 71.

10  *C.S.P.D., 1682*, pp. 192–93. The specific charge upon which Sherwin was indicted was public defamation and reviling of one of the magistrates.

11  *H.M.C., Ormonde MSS*, N.S., VI, 155, 274; *C.S.P.D., 1682*, pp. 20, 608–609.

12  For indications of the activity of both the Dissenters' political leaders and their ministers, see Morrice MSS, P, 333; *C.S.P.D., 1682*, p. 245; P.R.O.30/24/6A, fol. 379.

13  *C.S.P.D., 1682*, pp. 453, 487; Burnet, II, 338; Rawl. Ltrs., 51, fol. 125.

14  Burnet states that lawyers differed sharply as to whether excommunication would render a man incapable of voting; however, he noted that "it gave at least a color to deny them votes." Much to the King's displeasure, some Church officials thought he was going too far. Burnet, II, 339; *C.S.P.D., 1682*, p. 571. For a successful use of excommunication in a parliamentary election, see *supra* p. 111, and Chapter VII, n. 58.

15  Morrice MSS, P, 366; Tanner MSS, 35, fol. 163; Luttrell, *Brief Relations*, I, 251.

16  Holdsworth, *History of English Law*, VI, 210–12; E. and A. Porritt, *Unreformed House of Commons*, I, 393–95.

17  Anglesey's memorandum was dated April 27, but it was not published until 1694. It does not seem very likely that Anglesey showed the King his memorandum at the time he wrote it, for he makes no mention of doing so in his diary and he customarily made full entries concerning any audiences with the King. However, when Charles called Anglesey into his closet on April 11, and they "had long discourse," it is possible that he detected the general attitude of his Privy Seal. In late March Anglesey had dined at Lord Shaftesbury's, and a few days later he entertained Monmouth and Lord Herbert. It was perhaps knowledge of these and other close connections with such extreme Whigs which led the King to give Anglesey the warning during their April 11 discourse that his enemies in Parliament were still against him. Although Anglesey felt that the King had showed kindness to him in giving this warning, he must have realized that generally speaking his enemies had the King's confidence while he did not. Add. MSS, 18,730, fols. 95–96.

18  *Ibid.*, fol. 98; P.C.2/69/521, 525, 531, 537; *C.S.P.D., 1682*, pp. 333, 362, 532; *H.M.C., Somerset MSS*, pp. 108–109.

19  Henry, p. 316. Within the same week Dr. Owen took steps to see Lord Wharton. Rawl. Ltrs., 51, fol. 121.

20  Tanner MSS, 35, fols. 31–32.

21  Morrice MSS, P, 360.

22  Sharpe, II, 503–505. Beginning in 1683 the King also launched a most vigorous attack upon London Dissenters. See Smith, "London and the Crown, 1681–1685," pp. 269–74.

23  *The Citizens Loss, When the Charter of London is Forfeited, Or Given Up* (1683), pp. 3–4; George Sitwell, *The First Whig. An Account of the Parliamentary Career of William Sacheverell* (Scarborough, 1894), Appendix, p. 201.

24  Sharpe, II, 504, 505.

25  Friends MSS, Book of Cases, I (1661–1695), 98 (Nov. 3, 1681); Friends MSS, Bristol MSS, V, 142; Whitehead, *Christian Progress*, p. 534.

26  N.N., *Vox Clamantis; or, a Cry to Protestant Dissenters, Calling Them from Some Unwarrantable Ways* (1683), pp. 13–14, 16–17, 19–20, 80.

27  "The Form of an Address, Expressing the True Sense of the Dissenting Protestants of England" (1682), in *A Collection of Scare and Valuable Tracts* [Somers]. I, 176.

28 *C.S.P.D., 1682*, pp. 608–609; *1683 (July–Sept.)*, p. 362. For evidence of the increasing prevalence of occasional conformity see *ibid., 1682*, p. 362; Luttrell, *Brief Relations*, I, 250; Thoresby, *Diary*, I, 170–71; Edmund Calamy, *An Historical Account of My Own Life* (1671–1731), ed. John T. Rutt (2 vols.; 1830), I, 89.

29 Morrice MSS, P, 430.

30 Henry, p. 316.

31 Doreen J. Milne, "The Results of the Rye House Plot and Their Influence upon the Revolution of 1688," *R.H.S.T.*, 5th Ser., Vol. I (1951), 92; and also Milne's "The Rye House Plot, With Special Reference to Its Place in the Exclusion Contest and Its Consequences Until 1685" (Unpublished Ph.D. dissertation, Institute of Historical Research, University of London, June, 1949), pp. 59–62, 75, 77–79, 104.

32 Those who travelled to Chester were Swynfen, Lords Paget and Delamer, and Sir Thomas Wilbraham, *C.S.P.D., 1682*, pp. 362, 383, 390; *H.M.C., 7th Rept., Frere MSS*, p. 533.

33 Add. MSS, 18,730, fols. 100–102, 104 (entries of Oct. 10, Nov. 22, 27, Dec. 9, May 2, 24). "An Historical Account of . . . James, Duke of Monmouth," in Smeeton, *Historical and Biographical Tracts*, II, 44; *C.S.P.D., 1683 (July–Sept.)*, p. 17; Morrice MSS, P, 414. Anglesey's Privy Council hearing took place on January 17 according to Morrice's report of two days later. Since there is no report in the Privy Council Register of a meeting on that date, it seems probable that he was heard at the meeting on the preceding day even though there is no mention of Anglesey in the minutes of that day either, for there was no action taken in Anglesey's case and the Register is primarily a record of actions taken and petitions heard. See P.C.2/70/102–103. Anglesey was never mentioned by the informers according to Milne, "The Rye House Plot," p. 76.

34 Hampden had no connections with the group until after his return to England in September, 1682. See *ibid.*, pp. 59, 65, 81. On Trenchard see *C.S.P.D., 1683 (July–Sept.)*, pp. 77, 192.

35 Rawl. Ltrs., 109, fol. 106; Gladys Scott Thomson, *Life in a Noble Household, 1641–1700* ([1937]), p. 76, and *The Russells in Bloomsbury, 1669–1771* ([1940]), p. 67; *C.S.P.D., 1683 (July–Sept.)*, p. 83; Burnet, II, 302 n., 383; Lord John Russell, *Life of Lord William Russell* (2 vols.; 1820), App. VIII, pp. 262–79.

36 On the religious affiliations of Walcott, Rumbold, and also Abraham Holmes, another Cromwellian officer involved who was a Baptist, see Underwood, pp. 107–108; and Whitley, p. 148. There seems little doubt that Keeling was bribed by the Government,

but there is no evidence that the authorities expected to hear what they did. Milne, "The Rye House Plot," pp. 344–45.

37  Hatton, *Corres.*, II, 22; *H.M.C., Ormonde MSS, N.S.*, VII, 90–91; *H.M.C., 5th Rept.*, p. 589; Luttrell, *Brief Relations*, I, 278, 279; *C.S.P.D., 1683 (July–Sept.)*, pp. 215–16.

38  Milne, "The Rye House Plot," pp. 89–90, 102–103, 216; and Milne, *R.H.S.T.*, 5th Ser., Vol. I, 91.

39  See Milne, "The Rye House Plot," pp. 7, 79, 89, 91–93.

40  *C.S.P.D., 1683*, pp. 362–63. On Strode see also Morrice MSS, P, 32.

41  *C.S.P.D., 1683*, pp. 216, 301, 362; *1683 (July–Sept.)*, pp. 168–70, 180, 218, 227, 332, 339, 369; *H.M.C., Various MSS*, II, 174. See Appendix II for the religious position of each man.

42  *C.S.P.D., 1683*, pp. 265, 273, 301, 362; *1683 (July–Sept.)*, p. 180; *C.S.P.D., 1683–1684*, p. 216. See Appendix II on Ellis.

43  *H.M.C., Various MSS*, II, 174.

44  *C.S.P.D., 1683 (July–Sept.)*, pp. 53, 55, 80. See Appendix II on Yonge and Rich.

45  Morrice MSS, P, 385. (The date and names are in untranscribed shorthand.)

46  See Milne, "The Rye House Plot," pp. 197–205. This authority points out that the evidence upon which Hampden was convicted in 1684 was from two sources: (1) the account of Lord Howard of Escrick who had become "greatly discredited" as a result of his statements and appearance at Henry Sidney's trial, and (2) from "circumstances which the course of events after the indictment had produced."

47  Morrice MSS, P, 400, 421, 431, 432; *C.S.P.D., 1683–1684*, pp. 139, 142, 146–47; *A Complete Collection of State Trials*, comp. T. B. Howell (33 vols.; 1816–1826), IX, 1344–46.

48  Morrice MSS, P, 434. See Appendix II.

49  For a very good brief account of the whole problem of Nonconformist ministers' involvement in the Plot, see Milne, "The Rye House Plot," pp. 158–64.

50  Jolly, pp. 54–55; Newcome, *Autobiog.*, I, 249, 250. Newcome did not tell anyone of Ferguson's visit until after William of Orange was crowned.

51  Sewel, *History of the . . . Quakers*, II, 402–404.

52  Jolly, p. 55; Delaune, *Plea*, p. 70; Newcome, *Autobiog.*, II, 249.

53  "Mather Papers," p. 620. (Letter of Aug. 12, 1683.)

54  *C.S.P.D., 1683–1684*, pp. 89–90.

55  On the intensity of prosecution in the autumn of 1684, see Braithwaite, *Second Period*, pp. 99–113; "Thirnbeck Manuscripts,"

*J.F.H.S.*, IX (1912), pp. 143–44; *C.S.P.D., 1684–1685*, p. 187. Particularly indicative was the case of the Presbyterian minister Thomas Rosewell. He was sentenced to death by Chief Justice Jeffreys after being convicted of speaking treason in the pulpit on the highly questionable testimony of three women, two of whom were well-known informers. The King recognized the character of the trial when he granted Rosewell pardon for giving bail of £200 and finding sureties for £2000. *Ibid.*, pp. 171, 184, 187, 221–24, 226, 297; Howell, *State Trials*, X, 147–308. Before his death in February it appears Charles was ready to relax the prosecutions somewhat, for he approved a dispensation to Dissenters who could prove that they or their nearest relatives had suffered for the King's cause between 1642 and 1660. James put this dispensation into effect, but only a few Dissenters applied before the Monmouth Rebellion. *C.S.P.D., 1685*, pp. 131, 132.

56 *C.S.P.D., 1684–1685*, pp. 187–88.
57 See Milne, "The Rye House Plot," pp. 322–23, 334. Halifax's pamphlet first appeared in manuscript in November, 1684.
58 Jolly, p. 68.
59 Charles II was responsible for changing fifty-eight and James II added thirty-one more between February 13 and March 13, 1685. As a result Dissenters and Exclusionists suffered major losses in areas such as London and Cornwall. Milne, "The Rye House Plot," pp. 295–96; *C.S.P.D., Feb.–Dec. 1685*, pp. 15 and *passim*; Evelyn, *Diary*, IV, 419; R. H. George, "Parliamentary Elections and Electioneering in 1685," *R.H.S.T.*, 4th Ser., XIX (1936), 176.
60 For evidence of the part played by the King and Sunderland see their extensive correspondence with those of position and influence in the counties and boroughs. It contained most specific directions concerning the candidates to be supported and the actions to be taken. *C.S.P.D., Feb.–Dec. 1685*, pp. 21 and *passim*. The Bishop of Chichester is an example of a Church official who contributed to the Court's electoral success. Tanner MSS, 31, fol. 4. On the election activity of the clergy, see also [William Penn], *Advice to Freeholders and other Electors of Members to Serve in Parliament* (1687), p. 7.
61 B. M. Loan 29/140, Portland MSS, Letter #28; S.P./31/1/1, #49.
62 Morrice MSS, P, 457, entry of March 12, 1685. See also *Memoirs of Thomas, Earl of Ailesbury* (2 vols.; Westminster, 1890), I, 100. T. B. Macaulay, *History of England*, ed. C. H. Firth (6 vols.;

1913–1915), I, 473; George, *R.H.S.T.*, 4th Ser., XIX, 174. Concerning the new Tavistock charter see *H.M.C., Somerset MSS*, p. 108.

63  *S.P./*31/1/2, #82; George, *R.H.S.T.*, 4th Ser., XIX, 186–88.

64  *C.S.P.D., Feb.–Dec., 1685*, p. 23; *O.R.*, I, 556.

65  Of all the defeated Presbyterian or Congregationalist candidates John Trenchard appears to have been the only one who did not petition to be seated. See *C.J.*, IX, 715 and *passim*. In addition to the activity of these leaders there were some reports of Nonconformist activity here and there, as at Derby, Taunton, and Harwich. *H.M.C., Rutland MSS*, II, 86–87; *S.P./*31/1/2, #44, #73.

66  See Appendix II on Thompson.

67  R. H. George believes that James may well have indulged in this remark; he did write the Prince of Orange on April 13 that "most of the Parliament men are chose, and not many exclusioners [are] amongst them. . . ." *R.H.S.T.*, 4th Ser., XIX, 194; *C.S.P.D., Feb.–Dec., 1685*, p. 129. Feiling, p. 205, concurs that there were "some forty" whom the King was unable to approve. Also to the point is de Beer's analysis, Evelyn, *Diary*, IV, 444 n.4.

68  *L.J.*, XIV, pp. 3 and *passim*. In early August Wharton obtained a pass to go overseas, and by October 12 he had left with John Howe. *C.S.P.D., Feb.–Dec., 1685*, p. 441; Morrice MSS, P, 481.

69  *L.J.*, XIV, 11–12, 29–30, 42; Burnet, III, 46; Add. MSS, 34,508 (II), fol. 54 (van Citters report of June 26, 1685 N.S.). Anglesey's concern for Monmouth extended back to 1679, if not before. *Ibid.*, 18,730, fol. 63.

70  Burnet, III, 42; John, Lord Viscount Lonsdale, *Memoir of the Reign of James II* (York, 1808), pp. 8–9; Add. MSS, 34,508, II, fol. 59 (van Citters report of July 6, 1685 N.S.); Roberts, *Monmouth*, I, 281–82; Howell, *State Trials*, XI, 1043–48; *L.J.*, XIV, 68.

71  *The Several Debates of the House of Commons Pro and Contra; Relating to the Establishment of the Militia, Disbanding the New Raised Forces, and Raising a Present Supply for His Majesty* [Nov. 9–20, 1685] (1689), pp. 4–5, 8–9, 12; Morrice MSS, P, 494; *C.J.*, IX, 757.

72  Lansdowne MSS, 1152, fols. 256–61; Roberts, *Monmouth*, I, pp. 232, 235–50.

73  *Ibid.*, p. 242.

74  There is some question as to whether Cragg was to see Richard Hampden or John Hampden. In his examination before William III in 1689 Cragg stated that the Hampden he tried to see was walking in the King's Bench Garden with another person when he made the attempt, which would seem to indicate that it was

John Hampden because he was imprisoned in the King's Bench Prison at the time. When Cragg was questioned in 1685 there is no record that he gave these details, and a query was raised at the end of the interrogation as to which Hampden was meant. Nathaniel Wade stated in his Confession that it was the Hampden who "is or was" in prison who was the abettor of the Rebellion. In any event the Hampden whom Cragg attempted to approach would not speak with him according to his testimony both in 1685 and 1689. Lansdowne MSS, 1152, fols. 266, 306; *H.M.C., Stopford Sackville MSS,* I, 23; *H.M.C., H. of L. MSS, 12th Rept.,* Pt. VI, 394–95; Luttrell, *Brief Relation,* I, 292, 298, 301, 360.

75 See Appendix II on John Manley; Examination of John Madder, Lansdowne MSS, 1152, fol. 240; Morrice MSS, P, 468; *C.S.P.D., James II,* I, 178.

76 *Ibid.,* pp. 157, 166, 168, 176.

77 The known informer was Malachy Mallack (or Mallock), and the unknown may have been James Burton, and less possibly Richard Goodenough or Nathaniel Wade since there is nothing in existing records of their testimony regarding Prideaux. All four were set free at the same time. *Ibid.,* pp. 328, 329, 349; Seymour Schofield, *Jeffreys of "the Bloody Assizes"* (1937), pp. 203–204.

78 *C.S.P.D., James II,* I, 412, 416, 417.

79 A large number of other Presbyterians and Congregationalists who had been members of Parliament were apprehended and investigated within a month or so after Monmouth's landing, including Hugh Boscawen, John Swynfen, Thomas Foley, Paul Foley, Sir Edward Harley, Sir John Gell, Sir Richard Ingoldsby and Sir Walter Yonge; but in no instance were there any charges and all were eventually discharged. Morrice MSS, P, 470–73, 476, 477, 501; Luttrell, I, 342. A warrant was also issued for the arrest of John Braman on June 9, Warrant Book, 336/122, cited by Milne, p. 300.

80 Matthews, pp. 193–94; James Ferguson, *Robert Ferguson the Plotter* (Edinburgh, 1887), pp. 3–4.

81 The pamphlet's title was *A Letter to a Person of Honour Concerning the King's Disavowing His Having Been Married to the Duke of Monmouth's Mother* (1680). The most balanced account of Ferguson's role during the spring and the devious tactics he used is given by W. R. Emerson, *Monmouth's Rebellion* (New Haven, 1951), pp. 10 ff. On the authorship of the Declaration see the examination of Richard Goodenough, one of those who was with Monmouth when Ferguson presented it to the Duke

for approval prior to leaving Amsterdam. Lansdowne MSS, 1152, fol. 242.

82  Matthews, pp. lix, 48, 260. Another Presbyterian minister, Ames Short, was arrested in 1685 and was in Dorchester jail five months, but upon Monmouth's landing at Lyme he and others went to Portsmouth, and he does not seem to have been implicated as Murch concluded. *Ibid.*, pp. 440–41; cf. Jerome Murch, *History of Presbyterian and General Baptist Churches in the West of England* (1835), pp. 333–34.

83  "The Congregational Church at Axminster," *C.H.S.T.*, IV (1909), p. 108.

84  Entries of June 18 and 25, Morrice MSS, P, 468, 469.

85  Henry, p. 326. This section was not written at the time or by Philip Henry, but later and possibly by his son Matthew Henry.

86  Jolly, 71. Representative of Presbyterian laymen participating were John Hucker, a serge maker of Taunton who had a licensed Presbyterian meeting in his home in 1672, and William Jenkyn, son of a well-known ejected Presbyterian minister. Richard Locke, *The Western Rebellion* (Taunton, 1782), pp. 1–2; Turner, II, 969, 971, 1097–98.

87  Friends MSS, Bristol MSS, II, fol. 48.

88  The evidence concerning the Quakers' lack of participation is extensive. Letters were obtained from local magistrates and Anglican church officials in Bristol and eighteen or more towns certifying that no Quakers were involved, and these were later presented to the King. Friends MSS, Meeting for Sufferings Minutes, IV (1684–1685), 96–97, 101, 110–13, 120, 121, 124, 125. In addition local Friends Meetings reported on their members, including those who were implicated, of which there were three or four who were in good standing; but since they had not followed the Society's policy and refrained from participation, Whitehead explained that they had "*ipso facto* gone from the truth . . . ceasing by the same fact to be of us or in society with us." Friends MSS, Bristol MSS, II, fol. 49; Friends MSS, Meeting for Sufferings Minutes, IV (1684–1685), 103; "Two West Country Friends and the Monmouth Rebellion," *J.F.H.S.*, XII (1915), 35–36; John Whiting, *Persecution Exposed* (1715), pp. 141–42; "The Western Rebellion," *J.F.H.S.*, XVI (1919), 134; Braithwaite, *Second Period*, pp. 121–23. Lansdowne MSS, 1152, fol. 243 (examination of July 20, 1685).

89  Examination of John Madder, July 20, *ibid.*, fol. 240; Underwood, *English Baptists*, p. 109n.; Roberts, *Monmouth*, I, 259; Murch, *Presbyterian and Baptist Churches in the West*, pp. 333–34.

90  Underwood, *English Baptists*, p. 108.
91  "The Bloody Assizes, 1685," *The Baptist Quarterly*, N.S., V
    (1930–1931), pp. 25–27; Murch, *Presbyterian and Baptist
    Churches in the West*, p. 267n.; Underwood, *English Baptists*,
    p. 109.
92  See Iris Morley, *A Thousand Lives: An Account of the English
    Revolutionary Movement, 1660–1685* (1954), pp. 189–90; David
    Ogg, *England in the Reign of James II* (Oxford, 1955), pp. 148–
    49.
93  Quoted by Roberts, I, 231–32. See also John Coad, *A Memo-
    randum of the Wonderful Providences of God to a Poor Un-
    worthy Creature During the Time of the Duke of Monmouth's
    Rebellion and to the Revolution in 1688* (Reprinted, 1849), pp.
    2–4. Although John Tuchin's *The Bloody Assizes*, ed. J. G. Mud-
    diman (Edinburgh and London, 1929) is unreliable, it probably
    reflects the motives of those who were involved. For examples of
    concern with the religious question see the statements ascribed
    to William Jenkyn, Abraham Holmes, Captain Ansley, and
    Joseph Speed; and for instances in which the political issues were
    equally or more important, see the opinions ascribed to Benjamin
    Hewling, John Hicks and John Hucker. Tuchin, pp. 55, 75, 84,
    105, 117, 127; Roberts, *Monmouth*, II, 202; Kiffen, *Remarkable
    Passages*, pp. 53–56.
94  Ogg, *England . . . James II*, pp. 150–55; E. S. de Beer, "Execu-
    tions Following the Bloody Assize," *B.I.H.R.*, IV (June, 1926),
    36–39; R. G. H. Whitty, "The History of Taunton under the
    Tudors and Stuarts" (unpublished Ph.D. dissertation, Institute of
    Historical Research, University of London, 1938), pp. 204–205.
95  Jolly, p. 71; B. M. Loan 29/140, Portland MSS [Letters #51–53].
    *C.S.P.D., 1685*, p. 300. See also *supra*, Chapter VIII, note 55.

NOTES FOR CHAPTER IX

1  Steele, *Proclamations*, I, 463. About 1200 Quakers were freed by
   royal warrants during the following months, as well as some laymen and possibly thirty ministers of other Nonconformist persuasions. Braithwaite, *Second Period*, 125; Morrice MSS, P, 563,
   564.
2  Add. MSS, 34,508, II, fol. 110; Davies, *An Account*, pp. 237–40;
   Morrice MSS, P, 563.
3  Add. MSS, 34,512, fol. 36.
4  Morrice was closely in touch with the Bishop's case, for both
   his friend Dr. Fowler and the Bishop consulted with his old

patron Sir John Maynard, and he describes these and other consultations from reports that he received from either Fowler or
Maynard or both of them. He regarded the Bishop's case "the
greatest I have known in my time." Morrice MSS, P, 593–94,
601–603, 611, 613 (key sections in shorthand).

5  *Ibid.,* pp. 569, 573–74, 578, 581, 584, 634.
6  *Ibid.,* p. 594.
7  *Ibid.* (Morrice's transcript is not used for the last quotation since
it varies some from the shorthand.)
8  *Ibid.,* pp. 563, 568, 572, 584.
9  *Ibid.,* p. 615.
10  *Ibid.,* p. 611. Although Morrice is not specific, it is probable that
his reference to the penal laws was meant to include the Test
Act of 1673 and possibly that of 1678, for he had just been speaking of the royal project of "taking off the laws from the Papists,"
and previously he used the term penal laws loosely, stating that
the removal of these laws would allow Catholics to hold all
offices in church and state. *Ibid.,* p. 486.
11  *Ibid.,* p. 623.
12  *Ibid.,* pp. 615, 618, 621, 625, 634.
13  Report of van Citters in Letter of November 15, 1686, Add. MSS,
34,508, II, fol. 134; Morrice MSS, P, 642; Q, 20, 28, 49, 52.
14  *Ibid.,* P, 628; Q, 15, 17, 30, 74; W[illiam] T[ong], *An Account of
the Life and Death of Matthew Henry* (1716), p. 46; Richard
Lobb to Increase Mather, March 7, 1686/87, "Mather Papers,"
p. 650.
15  The Declaration specifically refers to the Tests contained in both
the Acts of 1673 and 1678, yet the phraseology used thereafter
refers to those "employed in any office or place of trust civil or
military under us or in our government." Since there was no
specific mention of those sitting in Parliament, it was questionable what effect the Indulgence had upon the Second Test Act.
*Documentary Annals of the Reformed Church of England,* II,
308–12.
16  Calamy, *Acct.,* II, 200, 678, 683; Matthews, p. 48; Morrice MSS,
Q, 112, 161–62; Newcome, *Diary,* p. xxxvi; William Kiffen, *Some
Remarkable Passages in the Life of William Kiffen,* ed. William
Orme (1823), p. 84. Just as in 1672, Baxter and the Presbyterian
Dons were supporters of comprehension rather than indulgence,
and this religious goal was far too important, particularly to
Baxter, to jeopardize by an address that would in effect repudiate
comprehension and that would displease the moderate Anglicans
and thus endanger its realization. Thomas, "Comprehension and

Indulgence," *From Uniformity to Unity*, pp. 236–37; Baxter to Sir John Baber, Baxter MSS, Letters, V, f. 40; Morrice MSS, P, 161, 176 (Baxter's and Baber's names are in shorthand).

17 *The Humble Address of the Presbyterians, Presented to the King* (1687); London *Gazette* No. 2238, April 28–May 2, 1687.

18 This was the phrasing of the address of the Baptist representatives from sixteen counties meeting in London. The Friends hoped for legislation which would secure the liberty for posterity. *Ibid.*, Nos. 2234, 2238, 2245, 2255.

19 Of the addresses which were published in the London *Gazette* from the issue of April 14–18, 1687 to that of February 2, 1688 there were approximately eighty which appear to have come from Nonconformist sources. Of these approximately thirty specifically refer to the statement about Parliamentary concurrence.

20 Morrice MSS, Q, 120, 132, 149.

21 For a contemporary opinion see Halifax's anonymous *Letter to a Dissenter Upon Occasion of His Majesties Late Gracious Declaration of Indulgence* ([1687]), p. 3. E. S. de Beer estimates that of the thirty-three addresses from all England during the period of August 16 to September 17 when the King made his progress to Bath, eighteen of these were the result of the pressures as a result of the progress; and authorities believe that the addresses from Wales were not spontaneous but engineered by the King's agents working on the fears of Nonconformists. Evelyn, *Diary*, IV, 560 n.1; J. M. J[ones], "The Indulgence of 1687 in Wales," *Baptist Quar.*, N.S., III (1926–1927), pp. 45–48. For evidence of the reluctance with which some individual ministers did address and the care they used in expressing thanks only for the liberty they had been given, see Henry, p. 327; Gordon, p. 265; Matthews, p. 200.

22 Thoresby, *Diary*, I, 186. The Biblical text is Psalms lxviii: 28. Other statements indicating full awareness of Catholic designs are numerous. For examples see Heywood, IV, 133; Calamy, *Abridg.*, II, 707; Morrice MSS, Q, 88; letters to Increase Mather and John Bailey of March, 1687, "Mather Papers," pp. 650, 666, 668.

23 In some instances those oblivious to the Catholic and constitutional issues were facing prosecution, either of themselves or members of their families. Thomas Jolly and Vincent Alsop were good examples. Jolly, p. 85; Calamy, *Abridg.*, II, 488; Gordon, p. 199.

24 For evidence of the Quakers' previous opinion of James and their appeals to him, see Fox, *Journal*, I, 386, 469; Friends MSS, Meet-

     ing of Suffering Minutes, I (1675–1680), 6; Friends MSS, Book of Cases (1661–1695), I, 11.

25   Morrice's entry concerning Penn's success in forestalling the *Quo warranto* writ is dated June 19, MSS, P, 551. For the details of this matter, including a discussion of the letter from Sunderland to the Attorney General of June 6 ordering the latter to suspend proceedings against Pennsylvania, see Joseph E. Illick III, *William Penn the Politician, His Relations with the English Government* (Ithaca, 1965), pp. 83–85. Sunderland's letter is found in the Albert Cook Myers Collection of William Penn Papers, LXVIIA, 93.

26   The most balanced and realistic discussions of Penn's motivations and involvement are presented by Illick and Dunn, and they serve as correctives to other accounts. Illick, *Penn*, pp. 79–85; Dunn, *Penn*, pp. viii–ix, 112–15, 120–21, 136 *passim*.

27   Whitehead, *Christian Progress*, pp. 575–80; [William Penn], *A Perswasive to Moderation to Church-Dissenters* ([1686]), pp. 22 ff.; Burnet, III, 140.

28   Morrice corroborates Penn's own statement made at the time that he had "great entrance and interest with the King," MSS, Q, 86. See also Vincent Buranelli, *The King and the Quaker* (Philadelphia, 1962), pp. 102–103.

29   [William Penn], *Good Advice to the Church of England, Roman Catholicks and Protestant Dissenters* (1687), pp. 56–58, 61; *Som[e] Free Reflections upon Occasion of the Public Discourse about Liberty of Conscience* (1687), pp. 12, 20–21.

30   Whitehead, *Christian Progress*, p. 629.

31   [Howe], *The Case of the Protestant Dissenters*, p. 2.

32   Humfrey, *The Authority of the Magistrate*, p. 28.

33   Morrice MSS, Q, 149.

34   Letter of M. d'Adda, the Nuncio, reporting conversations with Sunderland, July 28/August 7, 1687, quoted by Sir James Mackintosh, *History of the Revolution in England in 1688, Comprising a View of the Reign of James II* (1834), pp. 194–95. For Sunderland's estimate that most Dissenters belonged to the first group, see the full text of the letter which Mackintosh reprints, App. pp. 644–45.

35   This is the judgment of J. P. Kenyon based upon the diplomatic reports of d'Adda and French Ambassador Bonrepos, *Robert Spencer, Earl of Sunderland, 1641–1702* (1958), pp. 160–61.

36   The name of the person making these observations is not given. Morrice MSS, P, 628 (entry of September 26, 1686).

37  Morrice is the only known contemporary Nonconformist source concerning Dykveld's mission; MSS, Q, 124–25, 132.

38  *Ibid.*, Q, 132, 134. Dykveld was instructed to assure the Dissenters of a "full toleration; and likewise a comprehension, if possible, whensoever the crown should devolve on the Princess." Burnet, III, 174.

39  Entry of June 4, 1687, Morrice MSS, Q, 140.

40  See for example James Muilenburg, *The Embassy of Everard van Weede, Lord of Dyckveld, to England in 1687.* (University of Nebraska Studies, XX, Nos. 3 and 4, Lincoln, Nebraska, 1920), p. 45.

41  For unfavorable Nonconformist views of William dating from 1679 to early 1687, see Sidney, *Diary,* I, 3–4; Friends MSS, Morning Meeting Book, I (1673–1692), 55; Hatton, *Corres.*, II, 5; *H.M.C., Ormonde MSS*, N.S., VI, 118. Serious misgivings as to the prospects for Dissenters if the Princess were to rule in England are also evident in the information Morrice received from an unnamed person, very probably John Howe who had returned to England on May 11 after an audience with the Prince and Princess. Although the Princess told Morrice's friend that "if ever the Crown should descend upon her she thought she should never be severe to any that were religious and Godly, but show all tenderness to them, but she knew not the power of temptations, but she hoped none would ever prevail with her to do otherwise." Conceding that Burnet praised her as "the most devout woman," Morrice's friend reported that when he asked her "how she would carry towards Dissenters and Hierarchists if she came to the throne she gave him no answer, nor loves not [*sic*] to have it put." Entries of May 21 and June 11, Morrice MSS, Q, 131, 149. Information concerning Howe's return is noted May 11, *ibid.*, 129, and by Calamy, *Howe*, 131–32.

42  Morrice MSS, Q, 84–85, 86, 120. At the time of the Dykveld mission the clergy also gave assurances that "in a better time" they would offer comprehension for those who could accept and toleration for the rest. Burnet, III, 173–74.

43  Entry of May 14, Morrice MSS, Q, 128.

44  *Ibid.*, 90.

45  *Ibid.*, 166.

46  Robert Harley to Sir Edward Harley, August 17, *H.M.C., Portland MSS*, III, 400.

47  Statements that Halifax's *Letter* had a major influence upon Dissenters are not based on Nonconformist sources. See for example Hatton, *Corres.*, II, 72; Holdsworth, *History of English Law*, VI,

193, 200; P. C. Vellacott (ed.), "Diary of a Country Gentleman in 1688"; *C.H.J.,* II (1926), pp. 50–51. For Nonconformist opinion see Calamy, *Abridg.,* I, 376, and *Historical Account,* I, 194; Morrice MSS, Q, 182, 227 (entries of Oct. 29 and Jan. 7, 1688). The only reference which has been discovered in Nonconformist sources prior to late Oct., 1687 is the comment in a letter of Sept. 28 from Sir Edward Harley to his son Robert that the "witty" *Letter to the Dissenters* would make good a saying of the Lord Cottington: "'Women and ecclesiastics though never so witty would show themselves before they had done.'" B.M. Loan 29/140, Portland MSS, Letter #75.

48 Before the King dissolved Parliament in July he had indicated to Dykveld and Penn that he intended to call a new one. Morrice MSS, Q, 140, 146; Hatton, *Corres.,* II, 68.

49 Dalrymple, App. Pt. I, 205; Robert Harley to Sir Edward Harley, August 17, September 7, and 26, *H.M.C., Portland MSS,* III, 400, 403–404; Morrice MSS, Q, 176–77.

50 *H.M.C., Portland MSS,* III, 404.

51 The Prince advised Howe that "though he and his brethren made use of the liberty granted by King James, yet to be very cautious in addressing; and not to be prevailed with upon any terms, to fall in with the measures of the Court as to taking off the penal laws and test . . . ; and to use his utmost influence in order to the restraining others. . . ." Calamy, "Memoir of the Life of Howe," *Works,* I, xxviii.

52 Letters of Oct. 7, 1687, presumably to Sir Edward Harley, B.M. Loan 29/136, Portland MSS, Section 1; Morrice MSS, Q, 176–77 (the Earl of Plymouth is referred to by his earlier title Lord Windsor); *H.M.C., Portland MSS,* III, 404. Concerning Thomas Foley's opposition to James in the spring of 1688 and his active support of William in November 1688, see Browning, III, 157–63; and Chapter X, p. 221.

53 See the entry of Oct. 22, Morrice MSS, Q, 178.

54 Johnston (or Johnstone) intelligence letters of November 17, 25, December 8, and 21, U. of Nott., Portland MSS, PwA, 2100a, 2103, 2113a, 2121b. The first of these letters was possibly to Bishop Burnet, who was Johnston's cousin and who had recommended that Johnston be Sidney's assistant. The letter of December 8, and apparently the other two as well, were to Hans William Bentinck, the most trusted adviser and aide of William of Orange who made him the first Earl of Portland after the Revolution. See Bentinck to Sidney, December 5 and to Johnston, December 9, *ibid.,* 2105, [2117]; *Correspondentie van Willem III, Kleine*

*Ser.,* ed. N. Japiske (24 vols.; The Hague, 1928), XXIV, Pt. II, 597–99; Burnet, III, 277; Mackintosh, *Revolution,* p. 143n. For information concerning the code names used in his intelligence reports and his own use of the name Joseph Rivers, see Johnston's letter to Bentinck of November 17, U. of Nott., Portland MSS, PwA 2097a–c and the lists at 2087b–2095b. On Johnston's earlier meetings and friendship with Penn and his contacts with John Hampden, and Halifax, see in addition *ibid.,* 2125a, 2126c, f–i, and 2129c–d, 2135a. (Johnston undoubtedly used the singular *test* in a collective manner to refer to both Test Acts, as did van Citters in a report which clearly referred to both the Act of 1673 and 1678 when the singular form was used. Add. MSS, 34,512, fol. 66.) In a conversation with the King at the end of October, Sir John Baber told him he was wrong to expect that the Presbyterians would do "all that is required from them," because they "desired a good understanding with the sober Churchmen," but that there were some Congregationalists, Baptists, and Quakers who would support him. Morrice MSS, Q, 181. (Baber's name is in shorthand.)

55  Penn's unpublished essay, which is found in the Dreer Collection of Penn Papers (quotation from p. 67), has recently been brought to the attention of scholars by Illick, *Penn,* pp. 90–91. My suggestion concerning its date is based on information in the Johnston letters. For Penn's position on the tests in his published pamphlets in 1687, see *Good Advice to the Church of England,* pp. 58–61. It should be noted that in this major pamphlet on the subject Penn is much less concerned with Test Act repeal, which he mentions only at the very beginning and again in "The Conclusions." At the same time Penn discusses repeal of the penal laws thoroughly and throughout this pamphlet. See particularly pp. 37–56.

56  Johnston letters of November 17, 18, and December 8, U. of Nott., Portland MSS, PwA, 2100a, 2101a, 2113a. Morrice MSS, Q, 176 (entry of October 22); Add. MSS, 34,512, fol. 66 (letter of November 22 O.S.).

57  U. of Nott., Portland MSS, PwA, 2113a.

58  Add. MSS, 34,510, fol. 64 (letter of November 28).

59  Morrice MSS, Q, 179–80 (entry of October 29).

60  *Ibid.,* 203, 211.

61  The meeting took place at the house of Dr. Stratford, Dean of St. Asaph. Afterwards Dr. Tenison and Mr. Peter Allex came in accidentally. *Ibid.,* 214. On the Court's recognition of the developing relations between Dissenters and Anglicans, see van

Citters' letter of December 16, Add. MSS, 34,510, fol. 66. When Dr. Lloyd was made Bishop in 1680 he had asked John Howe what would most promote the return of the Puritans to the Church and had attempted to carry out one suggestion. Calamy, *Howe,* p. 71–72.

62 U. of Nott., Portland MSS, PwA, 2119b.

63 Morrice MSS, Q, 215.

64 [Penn], *Advice to Freeholders,* p. 9. [Penn], *Good Advice to the Church of England,* pp. 46–47. For a development of the arguments against a Nonconformist-Anglican coalition, see the Government-inspired answer to Halifax by the Nonconformist Henry Care in *Anamadversions on a Letter,* particularly pp. 9–10, 30–31.

65 [Penn], *Good Advice to the Church of England,* pp. 46–47. Nearly two years earlier the King told Whitehead that in 1673 it was really the Presbyterians in Parliament who caused the Indulgence to be made void, and the Quaker leader agreed that "they were our adversaries to be sure. . . ." *Christian Progress,* p. 577.

66 See the reports of Johnston and van Citters in December, U. of Nott., Portland MSS, PwA, 2113a, 2121b; Add. MSS, 34,510, fols. 65–66, 34,512, fols. 65–66.

67 U. of Nott., Portland MSS, PwA, 2124 (letter of January 4, 1687/88).

68 Johnston letters of November 18, December 8, 16, and January 12, 1687/88. *Ibid.,* 2101a, 2110a, 2118b, 2126g. The important letters of January were written in French.

69 *Ibid.,* 2113b, 2118b, 2126b; Morrice MSS, Q, 207. Morrice does not mention Johnston by name, even in shorthand, but he does write at some length on November 26 of "an English gentleman not long since returned hither," who could have been Johnston judging by the description Morrice gives of the gentleman's travels to Catholic and Protestant Courts on the Continent and his observations concerning them. *Ibid.,* p. 208.

70 U. of Nott., Portland MSS, PwA, 2113.

71 On the origins of the report that William and Mary favored repeal of the Test Acts, see Burnet, III, 218–19, and Johnston's letters of December 30 and January 12, U. of Nott., Portland MSS, PwA, 2122b, 2126f. His letter of January 12 also contains details on the printing and seizure at the press and in the mails. According to Johnston there were 30,000 copies printed. *Ibid.,* 2126e and h.

72 Johnston's closest Anglican connections were with the moderates Stillingfleet and Fowler, but he also had contacts with those whom he called "la meilleure sorte des Zélés" who included the

Bishop of Ely, Dr. John Patrick, and Dr. William Sherlock. *Ibid.*, 2126c and d.

73 *Ibid.*, 2122b (letter of Dec. 30). See also the letter of February 27, *ibid.*, 2148a.

74 *Ibid.*, 2126d and e. According to Morrice, Stanley had arrived in England about the beginning of October; he appears to have left about two months later. Morrice MSS, Q, 173; U. of Nott., Portland MSS, PwA, 2099a.

75 See *supra*, note 41 and Morrice MSS, Q, 164.

76 U. of Nott., Portland MSS, PwA, 2126e and f. Even at the end of January Morrice wrote there was a report that Fagel disowned the *Letter* and that the Prince would say it was written without his knowledge. Morrice MSS, Q, 234.

77 U. of Nott., Portland MSS, PwA, 2126e.

78 Add. MSS, 34,512, fol. 69.

79 Heywood, III, 228 (entry of Jan. 13).

80 During their late night discussion reported by Johnston on January 12, Penn told the Dutch agent that it would be agreed (at Court, he was implying) that Catholics would not enter the House of Commons. Within the next week Penn also told Johnston of a meeting with Sunderland during which the Quaker apparently suggested the expedient concerning Catholics sitting in the Commons, for he stated that the Secretary "appreciated his intent, or rather his expedient concerning the test; at least, so he [Penn] says, he pretends to. . . ." (The French reads: "Mr. Price [cypher used for Penn] m'a avoué que Mr. Seatoun [Sunderland] goûta son dessein, ou plutôt expédient, touchant le test, au moins, dit il, il en fait semblant.") During Johnston's discussion with Penn on this occasion he recorded parts of what Penn said in notes made during the conversation, and on both occasions he wrote his intelligence reports immediately after their discussions. U. of Nott., Portland MSS, PwA, 2126i, 2127c and 2129c–d. Mackintosh (and Macaulay after him) stated that another part of the expedient proposed by Penn was to exclude Catholics from the Commons and to divide all public offices equally among the Anglicans, Dissenters, and Catholics. He cites a Johnston report of January 13; but it is not mentioned in the copy of the report which Mackintosh presumably had made for his use. *Ibid.*, 2131a ff.; Mackintosh, *Revolution*, 196.

81 U. of Nott., Portland MSS, PwA, 2126g, 2127b, 2127c, 2129b and d (reports of Jan. 12 and 19). Johnston's French version of Penn's statement concerning his hope to be of use reads: "je

voudrois empêcher, dit il, en risquant moi même, que le choses n'allassent aux extremités."

82   Johnston's French reads: "Mr. Price fait du bien d'une main, et du mal del'autre; cependant je crois que les choses n'iront pas si bien, quand il ne s'en mêlera plus. Il adoucit S[on] M[ajesté] il suivre les desseins des gens violens, comme ceun ci suivent les siens; c'est autant de tems gagné. La vérité est que les Papistes n'ont ni du coeur, ni des mains, sans les Dissenters." *Ibid.*, 2127c.

83   The French in the original stated that the King "a dit la vérité, en disant que les plus grands ennemis de S[on] M[ajesté] n'étoient pas en etât de lui faire un si grand mal, eu égard a ses desseins." *Ibid.*, 2126b.

84   Johnston had promised not to reveal the name of his source, but he had received permission to write the information to Burnet. *Ibid.*, 2127c.

85   Morrice MSS, Q, 232 (Jan. 28 entry). For Morrice's similar report and reaction in October, 1687, see *supra* note 60.

86   On January 4 after stating that he always consulted John Hampden when the Presbyterian leader was not too sick from many ailments including a stomach disorder, Johnston wanted to know the Dutch official's reaction to this practice. His use of Hampden later that month, and Johnston's request at the end of February for a second person to perform Hampden's services because he was so ill at the time, indicate that he was actively assisting in the Dutch efforts. U. of Nott., Portland MSS, PwA, 2125a, 2129a, 2135a, 2148b.

87   *Ibid.*, 2135a.

88   *Ibid.*, 2142.

89   On the growing crisis between James and William see Kenyon, *Sunderland*, 178–79, and Lucile Pinkham, *William III and the Respectable Revolution* (Cambridge, Mass., 1954), pp. 62–63.

90   Nothing better illustrates Penn's simultaneous efforts to attain both his immediate and his final goals than two events on February 4, 1688. This was the day he saw the King and Sunderland and was so hopeful they would let the tests stand in whole or in part, and it was also the day upon which a license was granted for the publication of his anonymous pamphlet *The Great and Popular Objection Against the Repeal of the Penal Laws and Tests Briefly Stated and Considered* (1688) which contained his latest and fullest argument for complete repeal of the Tests. Johnston's intelligence letter was written Feb. 6.

91   U. of Nott., Portland MSS, PwA, 2135a, 2142. Titus was wrongly considered to be a Presbyterian by some of his contemporaries,

notably Sir John Evelyn, and by scholars since. Prior to the Restoration he had been a prominent Presbyterian Royalist, but by the time he entered Parliament in 1670 he probably had abandoned this religious position judging by a short speech he made at the time; and he left no doubt about his shift in another parliamentary speech of March, 1673, in which he stated he was "for no man sitting here who is not Church of England." However, he did favor comprehension. Grey, I, 406; II, 90; *H.M.C.*, *Beaufort MSS*, pp. 101–102; Evelyn, *Diary*, IV, 590, and n. 4.

92 According to Morrice, who knew members of this committee, it had generally recommended "sober Churchmen, and sober Dissenters," and it had not put many Papists on the list except in a few counties. Unfortunately, he believed there were many reasons why those recommended would not actually be put into commission, and there was ample evidence that his skepticism was warranted since large numbers of Presbyterians and other moderate Dissenters who had previously been given positions were being dismissed from the Corporations because they did not live up to the Government's expectations. See van Citters comment that of 800 persons changed in London, many Presbyterians as well as several Anglicans had been dismissed. Though highly colored, Macaulay's account of the changes elsewhere is still of value. Morrice MSS, Q, 239(2), 243–44; Add. MSS, 34,512, fol. 71; Macaulay, *History*, II, 982–85. See also Newdigate Letters, #1907, Jan. 12, 1687/88.

93 Morrice MSS, Q, 238, 239(1), 239(2), 239(3).

94 *H.M.C., 5th Rept. Sutherland MSS*, p. 197.

95 For example, in Le Fleming's summary of reports to him concerning Lancaster County he states that the Presbyterians were in the negative, while the Quakers and Congregationalists supported the King, except for a few Quakers in the South where the influence of Margaret Fox was felt. In Staffordshire, according to Morrice, "Protestants of all sorts" refused to give positive answers, and the Dutch agent Johnston reported that in Yorkshire "not any Dissenter of quality" wished to eliminate the test, and it also appears that this was true in Wales. Le Fleming MSS, Ambleside, 3149 (Dec. 2), quoted by J. M. Wahlstrand, "The Elections to Parliament in the County of Lancashire, 1685–1714" (University of Manchester, M.A. Thesis, 1956), p. 101; Morrice MSS, Q, 234; U. of Nott., Portland MSS, PwA, 2122b; D. M. Elis-Williams, "The Activities of Welsh Members of Parliament, 1660 to 1688" (Wales University, M.A. Thesis, 1951–52), p. 97.

96 The counties were Wilts, Dorset, Cambridge, Norfolk, Suffolk, Somerset, and Devon. Duckett, II, 217, 219 ff.

97 Penn sent a most revealing letter February 19, 1688, probably to Robert Bridgman of Huntingdon, which was undoubtedly only one of a number of the same sort sent to other Friends in different localities. He wrote: "I desire thee forthwith to return to me an account according to this direction, who fit to be out, who in power, and who in the room of those that are fit to be turned out; for all the qualifications are set down. This is expected from me, and by good advice let me know with all speed. For when a few towns are done we may expect to hear of a Parliament to render our ease legal . . . Be speedy and private." Alfred Cook Myers Collection of Penn MSS, XXIX, 239. See also *H.M.C., Portland MSS*, II, 52; Charlwood Lawton, "A Memoir of Part of the Life of William Penn," *Pennsylvania Hist. Soc.*, III, Part II (1839), pp. 223–26.

98 The pertinent Yearly Meeting Minutes are reprinted by Braithwaite, pp. 144–45. For evidence that Quakers should be active in elections see Whitehead's account of his interview with the King in December, 1687, and the Yorkshire Quarterly Meeting's decision in September, 1688 to encourage Quakers to vote. Whitehead, *Christian Progress*, pp. 618–22; Braithwaite, *Second Period*, p. 146. The question whether to accept appointment to local offices was another matter. Although James ordered that Quakers might hold any office without taking the required oaths and although some did accept, Friends in general declined to do so. Friends MSS, Book of Cases, I, 173 contains a copy of the Royal Warrant dated Nov. 6, 1687. See also *H.M.C., Fleming MSS*, p. 207; Braithwaite, *Second Period*, p. 143; *H.M.C., 7th Rept., Verney MSS*, p. 505.

99 There is very little evidence concerning the small number of more moderate Congregationalists and Baptists on the issue of the tests at this time, but there was a good indication of their position in the request to keep the Test Act of 1673 which was sent to the King by the "old sectaries" on the committee for reorganization of the corporations and the commission of the peace in Feb. See *supra* p. 202 and note 92.

100 The Anglican candidates who in April received support from Dissenters and acceptance or recommendations from the King's agents, and who had voted for the Exclusion Bill were Edward Ashe, William Ashe, Henry Mildmay, Eliab Harvey, Nicholas Gould, Edward Partridge, Sir Symon Taylor, and Sir Philip Skippon. Of three Anglican candidates who probably received

support from Dissenters Sir Thomas Mompassen voted for the Exclusion Bill, Sir Hasewell Tynte voted against it and Sir Robert Atkins was absent. Sir James Longe, who had Nonconformist support in 1688, was also absent. The other Anglicans receiving support from the Dissenters included the following men who were members of Parliament at some time during the period 1661–1689: Sir Josiah Child, Banister Maynard, Thomas Skinner, Sir Robert Brooke, Sir James Butler, Richard Duke, John Hall, Sir Richard Crumpe, Edward, Lord Cornbury, Sir James Johnston, and Henry Baynton (the evidence of Nonconformist support of the last five being indirect). In addition the following three Anglicans who were not M.P.s in this period were supported: Dr. Richard Burthogg, William Saverey, and John Coppleston. Presbyterian and Congregationalist members of Parliament who voted for the Exclusion Bill and were accepted as "right" by the agents in April as well as supported by Nonconformists, were Michael Harvey, Sir John Eyles (the one member who was apparently a Baptist), Thomas Reynell, John Trenchard, William Trenchard, Sir Samuel Barnardiston, Sir Walter Yonge, William Strode, Edward Noseworthy, and Oliver St. John. Duckett, I, 208–209, 220–27, 313–15, 407, 409, 410, 429–32; II, 217, 221–33, 260, 267, 300; "An Exclusion Bill Division List," ed. Browning and Milne, *B.I.H.R.*, XXIII, 207–225. J. R. Jones first called attention to the Whigs who supported the King in 1688 in his brief study "James II's Whigs Collaborators," *Hist. Jour.*, III (1960), 65–73. He found sixty-seven former Whig M.P.s (who are unnamed) among those who were reported suitable to be put into the commission of the peace or to serve as parliamentary candidates, but he did not attempt to distinguish between Anglican and Presbyterian (or Congregationalist) M.P.s. In the tabulation presented above only candidates for Parliament are included and only if they had Nonconformist support as well as the acceptance of the King's agents. In addition, candidates who did not sit until 1689 are also included. The degree of support the recommended candidates actually gave the King must be given careful consideration. See discussion continuing in text.

101 There were also instances in which Anglicans and Dissenters were described as being in agreement upon candidates. These were probably cases in which the Presbyterians predominated among the Nonconformists the agents consulted in that borough or county. It is probable that the Presbyterians were in the minority among Nonconformists in a good number of the instances

where Dissenters and Anglicans supported different candidates. Duckett, I, 364, 402, 409–10; II, 225–26, 228, 237.

102  *Ibid.*, I, 374; II, 233; Morrice MSS, Q, 211; Barnes, *Memoirs,* pp. 179–80. The only reported case of a Presbyterian candidate approved by the King's agents in April who did give the King's program full support was Edward Noseworthy. See Appendix II on Noseworthy.

103  Duckett, II, 253.

104  Report of d'Adda, March 12 N.S., Mackintosh, *Revolution,* pp. 644–45; Kenyon, *Sunderland,* pp. 191–92.

105  Dalrymple, I, 220 (April 12); Add. MSS, 34,510, fol. 111 (April 13).

NOTES FOR CHAPTER X

1  *Documentary Annals of the Reformed Church of England,* II, 313–15. Van Citters letter of May 18, Add. MSS, 34,510, fols. 17–18.

2  Roger Thomas wrote the first account of these conferences with the Anglican clergy in his article "The Seven Bishops and their Petition, 18 May 1688," *J.E.H.,* XII (1961), pp. 62–63, which was based on the new information in Morrice and Johnston's letter of May 23. My brief discussion is based upon his account, as well as upon Morrice and Johnston.

3  Morrice MSS, Q, 258, 259. Some support for Morrice's contention concerning the effect upon the Anglicans is found in Johnston's report that the Dissenters' statement, which he had seen and which Dr. Fowler brought back to the Anglicans, "stopped the mouth of some of the Nobility and others who were for reading [the Declaration]." U. of Nott., Portland MSS, PwA, 2162b. The efforts of Sir Edward Harley to persuade Bishop Croft in Hereford not to read the Declaration suggests that the Dissenters' leaders in London were not the only ones involved in supporting the movement to resist the Order in Council. Add. MSS, 34,515, fol. 119.

4  See R. Thomas, "Comprehension and Indulgence," *From Uniformity to Unity, 1662–1962,* pp. 238–39.

5  Morrice gives the text of the early draft under the heading "Comprehensive Sense of the Clergy" (MSS, Q, 259), and it is printed alongside the text of the Petition by R. Thomas, *J.E.H.,* XII, 64–65. U. of Nott., Portland MSS, PwA, 2161e, 2162b.

6  See van Citters' letters of May 15, 22, and 29 (O.S.) concerning the King's intent to estrange Anglicans and Dissenters. The Am-

bassador reported the Nonconformists' recognition of this intent and noted the Court's efforts to circulate reports that Dissenters were dissatisfied with the Anglican failure to read the Declaration as well as its contention that Nonconformists should therefore unite themselves with the King. Add. MSS, 34,510, fols. 118–19, 121; 34,512, fol. 82.

7 See Brother George Every's conclusions that the Petition "had nothing to say against toleration," that it was "the beginning of the comprehension scheme of 1688–9," and that it had been "resolved to seek security for the Church . . . in an accommodation between Anglicans and Presbyterians." *The High Church Party, 1688–1718* (1956), p. 20.

8 Add. MSS, 34,510, fol. 121.

9 U. of Nott., Portland MSS, PwA, 2161e and 2162b; Morrice MSS, Q, 269. Morrice undoubtedly worked through Sir John Baber.

10 *Ibid.*

11 Braithwaite, p. 144. The Quakers did not go as far as Penn desired in their Yearly Meeting, but they did make an Address of Thanks, London *Gazette*, #2354, June 7–11, 1688. This address was one of relatively few made, U. of Nott., Portland MSS, PwA, 2170.

12 Morrice gives a list of those present. Williams, Baber, and Alderman Rodbard came accidentally, he reported. Morrice MSS, Q, 263, 269; Thomas, *J.E.H.*, XII, 69.

13 In addition the Earl of Bedford, Lord Paget and an unnamed Quaker were among those ready to be the Bishops' bail. Calamy, *Howe*, pp. 135–36; Reresby, p. 500; Bishop Compton to Archbishop Sancroft, *Collectanea Curiosa; or Miscellaneous Tracts . . . Chiefly Collected from the Manuscripts of Archbishop Sancroft*, [ed. John Gutch] (2 vols.; Oxford, 1781), I, 356–57; Add. MSS, 34,510, fol. 134.

14 Calamy, *Howe*, pp. 139–40; "Life of Howe," *Works*, I, p. xxix.

15 See particularly Articles III–VII of the clearly mis-dated document found in Francis Lee's *Life of Mr. John Kettewell* (1718), pp. 393–94, which Brother Every has identified as the record of these conversations, *High Church Party*, pp. 22–24, 41–42. The only contemporary evidence that these discussions occurred is found in a newsletter of July 7 and a second letter of July 21 to John Ellis, both of which reported several consultations or conferences. Sayers' Newsletter, cited by Mackintosh, p. 286; *Ellis Correspondence*, II, 63. It would appear that only a few individuals were involved in several separate discussions and that

they were most informal. See R. Thomas, "Comprehension and Indulgence," *loc. cit.*, p. 241.

16  Gutch, *Collectanea Curiosa*, p. 286.

17  Every, *High Church Party*, pp. 22–25.

18  U. of Nott., Portland MSS, PwA, 2168d.

19  *Ibid.*, 2162b, 2174.

20  *Ibid.*, 2161e and 2162b.

21  In the undated list drawn up by Danby which contains in the main the names of men who had been members of James II's Parliament and which Professor Browning considers to have been compiled with a constitutional move of some kind in mind, there were three of the Presbyterian-Congregationalist group included: Bedford, Paget, and Edward Russell. A second undated list which Professor Browning has edited which is manifestly "the names of the men of real position and influence throughout the country who might be expected to countenance a movement against James," Bedford and Paget are again listed along with Richard Hampden, Hugh Boscawen, Sir Edward Harley, Paul Foley, Sir John Thompson, Sir John Hartopp, Sir William Ellis, Thomas Papillon, Sir Samuel Barnardiston, Sir John Fagg, and Thomas Foley. Browning, III, 152–63.

22  Kenyon, *Sunderland*, p. 200.

23  The existing evidence concerning Sir Christopher Vane, son of Sir Henry Vane the younger, has been insufficient to classify him as even a possible Dissenter in this study. In his uncontested election in 1675 to fill the place of his brother Thomas, who died before sitting for Durham County, he reportedly had the support of Dr. Nathaniel Crewe, Bishop of Durham as well as most of the gentry; and although apparently a supporter of James in 1688, he was not called a Dissenter by Morrice at the time of his appointment to the Privy Council. Sir Richard Wiseman's implication that he was a political opportunist was probably due in part to his opinion of Sir Henry's political and religious views and activity during the Civil Wars, but it seems to have had some validity, for prior to Dec., 1688, Sir Christopher joined Danby in support of William. *C.S.P.D., 1675–1676*, pp. 288, 362; Duckett [II], 283; Morrice MSS, Q, 281–82; Browning, III, 103; P.C.C. 179, Richmond. On Trevor the *D.N.B.* is revealing. For Titus see *supra*, note 92 Chapter VIII.

24  See Morrice's routine entry regarding these appointments and his rejection as "certainly false" of a report that about fifteen others would also be appointed who did have standing with moderate

Nonconformists, including the Col. Richard Norton, Lord Wharton, and Sir Edward Harley. Morrice MSS, Q, 281–82. In addition Richard Baxter was highly concerned that Sir Edward Harley was to be appointed; but Robert Harley, who was visiting Baxter, was able to reassure him. *H.M.C., Portland MSS,* III, 415.

25 Report of d'Adda, July 16, N.S., Mackintosh, Appendix, p. 663. According to this report Sunderland referred only to the old oaths ("antichi giuramenti"), but it is clear that he meant the oaths of allegiance and supremacy. In this connection, see d'Adda's report of August, 1687, *ibid.,* p. 645; see also Kenyon, *Sunderland,* pp. 200–201, 205–206. An additional indication that the King's acceptance of the "Expedient" was not published and that even if it had been it would have made no real difference is found in Morrice's entry of September 8, which states that the King had not given "any intimation . . . he would change his measures, or be satisfied with anything less than bringing in Popery, which the Kingdom will never concur to." Morrice MSS, Q, 291.

26 *H.M.C., Portland MSS,* III, 416 (Aug. 4 letter).

27 Bramston, p. 318; Ashley, *Wildman,* p. 263; *H.M.C., 7th Rept. Graham MSS,* pp. 422–23. See Appendix II on Manley and Waller.

28 Morrice MSS, Q, 290 (Sept. 1 entry); Pinkham, *Respectable Revolution,* pp. 103–25.

29 Duckett, I, 56n, 102; II, 235; Kenyon, *Sunderland,* pp. 208–209; Morrice MSS, Q, 291.

30 Duckett, I, 425, 431, 432, 440; II, 232, 240, 246, 263.

31 Morrice MSS, Q, 291. Subsequent research has proved Morrice substantially accurate. See Kenyon, *Sunderland,* pp. 208–209, regarding Sunderland's serious overestimations of support, and also J. H. Plumb, "The Elections to the Convention Parliament of 1689," *C.H.J.,* V (1937), p. 238.

32 Add. MSS, 34,512, fol. 101.

33 S.P.44/56/433.

34 Heywood, IV, 133.

35 Morrice MSS, Q, 299–300 (Oct. 6 entry). Morrice contradicts the Dutch Ambassador's later report that "by artifices some have made the Nonconformists believe that the Bishops in their frequent secret conversations with the King intend to arrange matters to their prejudice. . . ." Add. MSS, 34,512, fol. 114 (Oct. 16/26 letter).

36 Newcome, *Autobiog.,* I, 268.

37 Van Citters states that Baptists and Quakers were invited, but

Morrice lists by name only Presbyterian and Congregationalist ministers, seven in all. Add. MSS, 34,512, fol. 118; Morrice MSS, Q, 309.

38  Newcome, *Autobiog.*, I, 268.

39  Burnet, III, 330; Ferguson, *Plotter,* p. 260; Murch, *Presbyterian and Baptist Churches in the West,* II, 384–85; London *Gazette,* #2399, Nov. 12–15, 1688.

40  *H.M.C., Hodgkin MSS,* p. 75; Thoresby, *Diary,* I, 188; Jolly, p. 91.

41  Newcome, *Autobiog.*, III, 267; Morrice MSS, Q, 315. At the beginning of December, Morrice was extremely elated and relieved that "this stupendous crisis" and "adorable transaction" was "likely to pass over without the effusion of blood." *Ibid.,* pp. 332, 341, 343.

42  Concerning the week William spent at Exeter before any gentlemen of the area came to him, see Burnet, III, 331. See also Morrice's reports, MSS, Q, 316, 321.

43  Add. MSS, 34,515, fols. 121–22; Morrice MSS, Q, 333, 371; *Records of the Borough of New Lymington in the County of Southampton,* ed. Charles St. Barbe ([1849?]), p. 18; Whitty, "The History of Taunton under the Tudors and Stuarts," p. 180; *The Correspondence of Henry Hyde, Earl of Clarendon and of his Brother Laurence Hyde, Earl of Rochester; with the Diary of Lord Clarendon from 1687 to 1690,* ed. S. W. Singer (2 vols.; 1828), II, 219; Gordon, pp. 6–7, 336; Matthews, p. 73; G.E.C., *Bart.,* Index and App., p. 85.

44  Morrice MSS, Q, 333, 343, 344, 370; *H.M.C., Buckinghamshire, Lindsay MSS,* p. 449; *H.M.C., Portland MSS,* III, 421; Rawl. Ltrs., 109, fol. 115; Add. MSS, 34,510, fol. 118; 34,515, fol. 123; Luttrell, I, 475; *C. Treas. Bks.,* IX, Pt. II, p. 307–308.

45  Morrice MSS, Q, 333, 391 (Dec. 1 and 29 entries).

46  Neither John Swynfen nor Lord Wharton could have been expected to take an active part in raising forces because of their age; and on December 1 Morrice reported that Hugh Boscawen had "not come in yet for his wife died about the time that the Prince landed," but this was about the time he began taking action in Cornwall according to Morrice's report a week later. *H.M.C., Portland MSS,* III, 400; Duckett, II, 253; Morrice MSS, Q, 391, 333, 344.

47  *Ibid.,* pp. 337, 380, 384, 388, 392.

48  Reresby, p. 541. See also, *H.M.C., 7th Rept., Graham MSS,* p. 423, and Morrice MSS, Q, 376 for other evidence of such concern. In addition Morrice reports Anglican efforts to discredit Sir William Waller and Robert Ferguson. *Ibid.,* pp. 337, 380.

49 Morrice, who was almost certainly involved, gives details concerning the negotiations, the address, and the formal thanks
which the Nonconformists gave to the Bishop. *Ibid.*, pp. 364,
383–84; Calamy, *Acct.*, II, 387. The address (misdated Sept. 21)
is found in the *Compleat Collection of Papers Relating to the
Present Juncture of Affairs in England* (1689), *Sixth Collection*,
pp. 17–19.

50 Morrice reported that the address would have been made at the
time of the Anglicans' address had there been adequate notice, so
that there could have been a more general attendance of the two
Nonconformist groups. They obviously wished to match the
Anglican attendance, claiming just under 100 were present; Luttrell credits them with fifty ministers present, while a disparag-
ing newsletter which was Anglican in tone stated that only
twenty were there. Morrice MSS, Q, 411–12; Calamy, *Acct.*, I,
387–88, 423–25; Luttrell, *Brief Relations*, I, 493; Rawl. Ltrs., 109,
fol. 112.

51 Morrice MSS, Q, 347, 350, 366; *Compleat Collection of Papers,
Fourth Collection*, pp. 23–24; Ellis, *Corres.*, II, 349.

52 Morrice, who was Maynard's old chaplain, may have received
reports both from his former patron and also from the secretaries
of the House of Lords, Mr. Richard Coleing and a Mr. Wynn,
whom he knew. Clarendon was not positive that it was Paget
who made this proposal, but Morrice states it was. Morrice MSS,
Q, 350, 384–85, 392–93, 395; Clarendon, *Corres.*, II, 234–35.

53 Morrice MSS, Q, 397–98 (Dec. 29 entry).

54 *C.J.*, X, 6; Grey, IX, 1–2. The Journal does not indicate which
Hampden was Chairman but Morrice states it was John. Sir John
Maynard was also a member. Morrice MSS, Q, 409.

55 London *Gazette*, #2418, January 7–10, 1688–89; Morrice MSS,
Q, 557; Guildhall, Corporation of London Records Office, Cham-
ber Accounts 40/35 (Loan 1688/89 Posting Book), fols. 5, 6, 33.
Of many known Nonconformists who subscribed, the following
are a few of the better known names: William Kiffen and Henry
Cornish £500 each; a Thomas Langham was recorded twice,
once for £200 and another time for £300; Thomas Hartopp,
Francis Gell, and Robert Lidell £200 each; Thomas Firmin, and
Daniel Williams (perhaps not Dr. Williams) £100 each. *Ibid.*,
fols. 5, 6, 16, 17, 21, 28, 32.

56 Morrice MSS, Q, 436. Henry Capel expressed the same opinion
at the opening session of the Convention and January 22. Grey,
IX, 4. For a complete study of the election, see J. H. Plumb,
*C.H.J.*, V, 235–54.

57  Jolly, p. 92. For the names of the thirty men elected at the out-
    set, see Appendix III. The three additional members were Rob-
    ert Harley, seated April 9 in the place of Charles Boscawen,
    John White, seated on May 14, and Sir John Trenchard on June
    20. Charles Boscawen was the brother of Hugh, and he may well
    have been a Presbyterian; but, as with many members of this
    Parliament who seem likely Dissenters, it has not been possible
    to find sufficient evidence of his religious views. Other changes
    came when Sir John Gell died at the outset of the first session
    and was replaced by his son Sir Philip Gell, and in April when
    the veteran William Love died and was replaced by Sir William
    Ashurst. See Appendix II for each man.

58  Morrice MSS, Q, 458. The beginning words are in shorthand.

59  *Ibid.,* pp. 423–24. For a discussion of some of the particulars
    sought, see R. Thomas "Comprehension and Indulgence," *From
    Uniformity to Unity,* p. 244.

60  Morrice MSS, Q, 424. For Morrice's reports of meetings of the
    Bishops at Lambeth Palace and other places, as well as of the
    views of other Anglican clergymen, see also pp. 426, 430–31.
    Since Sancroft was unwilling to take any step which would imply
    recognition of William and Mary, and since he therefore wanted
    Convocation to deal with the problem, leadership in the actual
    work toward comprehension fell to a group of leaders who
    favored a religious settlement enacted by Parliament and who
    endeavored to carry out the commitments made to Dissenters to
    seek comprehension and toleration. Thomas "Comprehension and
    Indulgence," *From Uniformity to Unity,* pp. 243, 245; Sykes, pp.
    85–86; Every, *High Church Party,* pp. 27–29.

61  Morrice MSS, Q, 401, 435.

62  Other items in these proposals were that the Chancery, Treasury,
    and Admiralty be managed by commissioners, that no king or
    queen be present in the House of Lords during debates, that the
    election books of freeholders be settled each year and that a free-
    hold of £20 or a copyhold of £30 be required, and in addition
    that only freeholders be allowed to serve on juries or in the
    militia. Carte MSS, 81, fol. 766. The index of this volume wrongly
    dates the document as belonging to the beginning of James II's
    reign, which is in error as is indicated by internal evidence.

63  Humfrey's brief pamphlet of four pages appeared before March
    25; it is Calamy who states that he wrote it at the time and put
    it into the hands of the members, *Abridg.,* II, 621.

64  [Humfrey], *Advice,* pp. 3–4.

65  *Ibid.,* p. 4.

66  Morrice MSS, Q, 444.

67  *C.J.*, X, 9–11, 14; *L.J.*, XIV, 102; Hampden was chairman of the Committee of the Whole which proposed the Commons Resolution of January 28 that King James had subverted the constitution by breaking the contract between king and people and had abdicated the throne. In addition he was Chairman of the Committee to propose reasons why the Commons would not accept the Lords' substitution of *deserted* for *abdicated* and their deletion of *vacant. C.J.*, X, 14, 18–20; *The Debate at Large, Between the House of Lords and House of Commons, at the Free Conference . . . Relating to the Word, Abdicated and the Vacancy of the Throne, In the Commons Vote* (1695), pp. 19–21; Evelyn, IV, 619. His continued role as a major leader is partially evident in the fact that he gave more than eighty speeches and served on nearly eighty committees of the Convention Parliament. L. G. R. Naylor, MS biography of Richard Hampden, prepared for *The History of Parliament, 1660–1690,* ed. B. D. Henning.

68  *Debate at Large*, pp. 37–38, 107, 110, 157; Torbuck, *Collection,* II, 197–98, 225, 226–28, 249.

69  Grey, IX, 11, 23, 63, 64; *Debate at Large*, pp. 172–73; Torbuck, *Collection,* I, 256. Presbyterian and Congregationalist members of Parliament were supported by such prominent Nonconformist ministers as Richard Baxter, who held that James had abdicated and that "the Prince of Orange found the land without a King," in an unpublished pamphlet entitled "King James His Abdication of the Crown Plainly Proved, October 1, 1691," which has been edited and published by Richard Schlatter in *Richard Baxter and Puritan Politics* (New Brunswick, 1957), pp. 157–78. Evidence of Baxter's support of the Revolution in 1689 is found in the fact that he loaned William £100. *Ibid.*, p. 21.

70  Danby's notes on the Lords' Debate of January 29, Egerton MSS 3345, Bundle 3; *L.J.*, XIV, 112–13, 116.

71  Morrice MSS, Q, 446, 453–54, 459, 462.

72  Maynard also spoke, while others who were not of the Presbyterian-Congregationalist group, particularly Sir William Williams and Sir Richard Temple, gave speeches of broad scope and fundamental importance in favor of additional specific items such as the tenure of judges, the maintenance of standing armies, and the Coronation Oath. Grey, IX, 26–32, 36; Morrice MSS, Q, 445, 447.

73  Committee members included Hugh Boscawen, Thomas Foley, Richard Hampden, Henry Hobart, John Hampden, Sir William Waller, Paul Foley, and Sir William Ellis. Its first report was

made February 2 and debate was resumed February 7. *C.J.*, X, 15, 17, 21; Grey, IX, 70–71. For an indication of Nonconformist concern see Morrice who records the twenty-eight heads originally proposed by the Committee on February 2 and describes efforts to influence William's attitude before the completed Declaration was formally presented. Morrice MSS, Q, 457–58, 463–65.

74   Grey, IX, 70–71; *C.J.*, X, 22–23.

75   Grey, IX, 79–81.

76   *C.J.*, X, 22.

77   *H.M.C.*, *Portland MSS*, III, 427–28; B. M. Loan 29/140, Portland MSS, Letter #93 (Feb. 7, 1689). See also Thomas Foley to Robert Harley, April 13, 1689; *ibid.*, 29/136, Section 1.

78   P.C.2/73/1. Morrice also lists Edward Russell as a member. Although the Privy Council Register does not include his name among the original appointees on February 14, a "Mr. Russell," presumably the Earl of Bedford's Presbyterian son (see Appendix II) rather than his nephew Admiral Edward Russell, was listed among the Privy Councillors present at the next meeting on February 16. *Ibid.*, p. 4; Morrice MSS, Q, 468. Wharton's position was also recognized when the King visited Woburn Abbey. Dale, *The Good Lord Wharton*, p. 50.

79   Reresby, p. 557. See also Clarendon, *Corres.*, II, 238; Evelyn, *Diary*, IV, 635.

80   Shorthand passage, entry of February 23, Morrice MSS, Q, 470. See also Edward Harley, Jr. to Robert Harley, *H.M.C.*, *Portland MSS*, III, 432.

81   Shorthand entries of March 9 and 16, Morrice MSS, Q, 494, 495, 501. Morrice was already concerned over the number of Tories in the Navy and Army, and according to his estimate, Tories predominated in the proposed appointments to the commission of peace in many counties by four to one, while in some the ratio was six to one. Only in London were they in the minority.

82   *Ibid.*, 494, 503, 507–508. Because of his opposition to the Government, Nottingham's appointment was considered to be indicative of the "great fear and impotency in the government," Morrice reported. *Ibid.*, p. 495 (shorthand). On the implications of the appointment see Henry Horwitz, *Revolution Politicks, The Career of Daniel Finch Second Earl of Nottingham, 1647–1730* (Cambridge), pp. 83–85; Gilbert Burnet, *A Supplement to Burnet's History of My Own Time*, ed., H. C. Foxcroft (Oxford, 1902), p. 314.

83   Carte MSS, 81, fols. 752–53.

84 Burnet, IV, 12–13; *Supplement,* p. 316; *L.J.,* XIV, 150. Halifax corroborates Burnet's accounts in the entry under "Hampden Sen." among the memoranda he kept in what is now known as the Devonshire House Notebook, stating that Hampden told him "he made the speech for admitting Dissenters into places." Chatsworth MS, Notebook of George Savile, Marquis of Halifax, entry under *H.* ( I am indebted to Henry Horwitz for permitting me to use his copy of this MS.)

85 Morrice MSS, Q, 505.

86 Burnet, *Supplement,* p. 316. Edward Harley wrote his brother Robert on March 19 that "great distaste is taken at the King's last speech by the sons of the Church, who resolve to unite in her defense to keep off anything that may eclipse her dominion and grandeur." *H.M.C., Portland MSS,* III, 434.

87 *H.M.C., 12th Rept., Pt. VI, H. of L. MSS,* pp. 52–55; *L.J.,* XIV, 148, 153–54, 156–59; Horwitz, *Revolution Politicks,* pp. 88–90.

88 Morrice MSS, Q, 516; Reresby, p. 567. For the intensity of feeling see also the wording of the protest to the Lords' action of March 23 signed by Wharton and Paget. *L.J.,* XIV, 158–59. The Commons committee to which the Lords Bill was committed included Paul Foley, both Hampdens, Hugh Boscawen, Sir William Ashurst, Thomas Foley, and Sir William Ellis among its forty-three members; later during conferences between the two Houses over amendments Boscawen, both Foleys, and both Hampdens served on a committee of twenty-three to prepare reasons for the Commons position. *C.J.,* X, 69–70, 93.

89 Grey, IX, 190–97; *C.J.,* X, 64–67, 69.

90 Reresby, pp. 567, 569; Morrice MSS, Q, 514, 516 (March 30 entry). See also Evelyn's March 29 entry, which clearly refers to this bill and not the earlier one also suggested by his editor, *Diary,* IV, 631.

91 Letters of Edward Harley and Sir Edward Harley to Robert Harley, March 26, 30, April 13, and 16, *H.M.C., Portland MSS,* III, 435–36; Thomas Foley to his son-in-law Robert Harley, April 13, B. M. Loan 29/136, Portland MSS, Section 1. See also the complaint of another member of the Foley family which grew out of unsuccessful efforts in a by-election. *Ibid.,* 29/75 Portland MSS, Folder 8, Letter #1.

92 The differences between the Bills of 1680 and 1689 were depressing to Morrice, who had a friend speak to the Earl of Nottingham "to know the reason why he deserted . . . his own former Bill and directed one far more narrow than it, but to that he gave no direct nor plain answer, but said they would offer such a Bill as

was fit and convenient." Presbyterian ministers would have been particularly disturbed by two differences; the first being the declaration approving the doctrine, worship, and government of the Church of England instead of the 1680 provision for outright repeal of the Act of Uniformity clause requiring assent and consent to all things in the Book of Common Prayer. Secondly, they would have been deeply disturbed because a provision recognizing Presbyterian ordinations prior to 1660 had been dropped, and one calling for supplemental reordination had been adopted. Morrice MSS, Q, 488, 493, 501; *L.J.*, XIV, 145, 147, 163, 167, 168, 171; *H.M.C., 12th Rept., Pt. VI, H. of L. MSS*, pp. 49–52; Reresby, p. 570; Thomas, "Indulgence and Comprehension," *From Uniformity to Unity*, pp. 245–49; Horwitz, *Revolution Politicks*, pp. 87–91, 94–95; Every, *High Church Party*, pp. 32–35.

93  Morrice MSS, Q, 527; *C.J.*, X, 74–75, 84; Sir Edward Harley to Robert Harley, April 2, B. M. Loan 29/140, Portland MSS [Letter #96]; Hatton, *Corres.*, II, 128. On Anglican alarm at the possibility of infiltration by ministers of the Dutch and French Reformed Churches, see Every, 33–36. Thomas discusses the provisions of the Bill, "Comprehension and Indulgence," *loc. cit.*, pp. 249–50; Horwitz discovered a version even more favorable to the Presbyterians in the Kenyon MSS (Lancashire Record Office), Box 6, No. 32, cited in *Revolution Politicks*, p. 92, n.1. Serving on John Hampden's committee of twenty-eight members were Hugh Boscawen, Paul Foley, Sir Edward Harley, and Thomas Foley. *C.J.*, X, 74–75.

94  Morrice stated after passage of the Bill that it was certain the Devil Tavern Club "did call for it and promote it," and he thus offers evidence not only of the existence but also of the effectiveness of the political bargain which Sir Keith Feiling first noted. Morrice MSS, Q, 558; Feiling, *Tory Party*, pp. 265–66. For other details and new information see Horwitz, *Revolution Politicks*, pp. 93–94. See also Every, p. 35; R. Thomas, "Indulgence and Comprehension," *loc. cit.*, p. 250; Burnet, *Supplement*, p. 318.

95  Bishop Compton of London and Dean Tillotson were particularly active in support of the Comprehension Bill, while Lloyd, Patrick, Sharp, and Tenison also contributed their efforts. Even some nonjurors such as Bishop White of Peterborough and Bishop Turner of Ely spoke for the Bill in committee. Compton to Sancroft, Tanner MSS, 27, fol. 50; Morrice MSS, Q, 507; Every, *High Church Party*, p. 33; Sykes, pp. 86–87. On the other hand there was still very strong resentment and opposition among Anglican clergymen which was reported by Morrice and Halifax, the latter

telling Burnet and Reresby that the "Church people . . . had rather turn Papist than receive the Presbyterians among them." Morrice MSS, Q, 466; Reresby, p. 572. For the Nonconformist reaction see [John Howe], *The Case of the Protestant Dissenters Represented and Argued* [1689], p. 2; Calamy, *Howe*, p. 146.

96 Feiling, pp. 264–66; Every, *High Church Party*, pp. 33–35; Grey, IX, 197–98; Horwitz, *Revolution Politicks*, pp. 88–89 (for a modification and a correction of the evidence and conclusions presented by Every and Feiling regarding Nottingham).

97 Morrice MSS, Q, 534; Burnet, IV, 19–20; *Supplement*, p. 317.

98 Reresby, p. 572; Foxcroft, *Halifax*, p. 72. Halifax believed that the Nonconformists shared in the responsibility for the defeat. Although the political bargain had relegated consideration of comprehension to a Convocation, two months later, after the Toleration Act had been passed, the King told John Howe that "he wished the Comprehension Act might also pass." This contributed to some reconsideration of the Bill, Morrice reporting that "the Bishops seem to have intrusted the Bp. of St. Asaph and the Bp. of Salisbury," and that "John Hampden manages it together with them." These efforts were fruitless, and judging by his comments four years later they left Hampden with much the same conviction that Morrice had in April, namely that some Churchmen who apparently sought comprehension did not actually desire it. Indeed, he believed it was plain that their design "was only to destroy obliquely, and by a side-wind, what had been gained at a favorable time, in the Act of Toleration, which they dare not directly attempt to overthrow." Morrice MSS, Q, 574–75, 578; B. M., Stowe MSS, 747, fol. 16 (Hampden to the Rev. Richard Tallents, May, 1693).

99 Sykes believes that the failure in Convocation was not so much a foregone conclusion as it was the result of the subsequent development of the schism caused by the withdrawal of Archbishops Sancroft and Lamplugh and the other nonjuring Bishops, and particularly the absence of Sancroft's influence in the Royal Commission appointed to prepare a comprehension scheme for the consideration of Convocation. *Sheldon to Secker*, pp. 87–89.

100 John Hampden was clearly the most active Presbyterian, while Lord Wharton, Richard Hampden, Paul Foley, Thomas Foley and others also assisted. *L.J.*, XIV, 134, 178, 215; *C.J.*, X, 133, 137, 143; Grey, IX, 252–53, 258–62; *H.M.C.*, *12th Rept.*, *Pt. VI*, *H. of L. MSS*, pp. 35, 52. On the role of Nottingham in drafting the Bill, see Horwitz, *Revolution Politicks*, p. 87.

101 In Morrice's estimate this was "but a very little sum for the

Dissenters to lend, and it may be very easily and speedily borrowed if it be discretely managed." Morrice MSS, Q, 557 (May 18 entry). On May 16 it was reported to the auditor of the receipt that "several citizens of London are willing to forthwith lend the King considerable sums on the present Aid or the Poll," and a procedure to expedite the transaction was established. The loan may have been handled through Sir Peter Rich, Chamberlain of London, as were some other loans from London citizens at this time, and have been treated as part of the £300,000 loan on the first Poll. *C. Treas. Bks.*, IX, Pt. 1, pp. 81, 113, 123, 169; Pt. 5, pp. 1976–78.

102  Grey, IX, 261–62; *C.J.*, X, 137; *L.J.*, XIV, 215, 217; "An Act for Exempting their Majesties' Protestant Subjects Dissenting from the Church of England from the Penalties of Certain Laws," *Statutes,* VI, 74–76.

103  Jolly, 94; Morrice MSS, Q, 558; Burnet, *Supplement,* p. 317; Burnet, IV, 20–21. Morrice reported but discounted the belief of some that the Bishops and their followers in the House of Lords passed the Bill "with that latitude, concluding it would have been stopped in the Commons House, and the Commons would not stop it because then the imputation of persecution would have been laid upon them." Some evidence of concern over the latitude of the Bill can be found among staunch supporters of the Church in the Commons, notably in Clarges' motion to have the Bill's duration restricted to seven years and also in the debate upon it. Grey, IX, 253, 260–61; *C.J.*, X, 137.

104  Grey, IX, 258–61. Anglicans hoping for growth of the Church may actually have been looking forward to the attainment of comprehension in Convocation. Sykes has suggested that the speedy passage of the Toleration Bill might be attributed to the greater importance attached to comprehension. *Sheldon to Secker,* pp. 90–91.

105  Morrice MSS, Q, 558, 574–75. The number of Nonconformist places of worship registered in accordance with the Act's provisions in 1689–90 indicates the need which it fulfilled. According to E. D. Bebb's count, there were 927 temporary and 251 permaent places of worship registered, *Protestant Nonconformity*, App. I, p. 174. Using their lobbying experience the Quakers had been able to obtain the inclusion of the special clauses in Article 10 that provided for alternatives to the oath and declaration of faith and that satisfied their scruples. Among the Baptists, however, there were a few who opposed the requirement that their ministers subscribe to most of the Thirty-nine Articles and they

refused the freedom offered even though their ministers were exempted from the one concerning infant baptism. Friends MSS, Meeting for Sufferings Minutes, VII, 251; Whitehead, p. 634; *The Church Books of Ford or Cuddington and Amersham*, pp. 4, 7.

106 In discussing the Toleration Act both Morrice and Richard Hampden excluded themselves from those Dissenters whose religious status would be affected; and as already apparent, they along with such men as John Howe and John Hampden continued to work for the attainment of comprehension. Grey, IX, 262; Morrice MSS, Q, 558.

107 Jolly, p. 94.

108 Henry, p. 362.

109 *C.J.*, X, 74.

110 Morrice MSS, Q, 579–80; Grey, IX, 362–64; *C.J.*, X, 197. According to Morrice there were not twenty who opposed the petition passed in the Common Hall of London in its Midsummer Day session of June 24.

111 B. M. Loan 29/140, Portland MSS [Letter #98]; Morrice MSS, R, 592; *C.J.*, X, 233.

112 Morrice MSS, Q, 592.

113 *Ibid.*, p. 607. For a summary of the views of the King's confidential advisers at this time see Horwitz, *Revolution Politicks*, p. 99. On the King's growing displeasure with Parliament and his consideration of the idea that his government be based chiefly on the Church party, see *ibid.*, p. 98; and the original statement by Feiling, pp. 266–68.

114 Morrice MSS, Q, 607. Obviously this was entirely too sweeping a charge of disaffection, but insofar as it was meant to describe those local officials who did not take the new oaths, including that of fidelity to the King, until near the deadline of September 1, it was probably warranted, and it certainly described those who refused to do so at all and thus joined the ranks of the nonjurors.

115 Letter of December 24, Add. MSS, 29,594, fol. 185, quoted by Horwitz, *Revolution Politicks*, p. 104.

116 There would seem to be some contradiction between Nottingham and the anonymous Tory writer of *A Letter Concerning the Disabling Clauses Lately Offered to the House of Commons, for Regulating Corporations* (1690), for Nottingham's letter was written December 24, the day after the holiday recess began, and according to the writer of the pamphlet (p. 4) it would seem that a restoration of corporations to the status of 1675 had been

provided for by this time. However, there were grounds for each assertion. Even after the addition of the clause voiding all proceedings and seizures of charters on writs of *quo warranto* and *scire facias* issued after March 25, 1675, another clause in the Bill was still retained that nullified all other surrenders during the whole reign of Charles II. Thus there were some corporations that would have been restored to their status as far back as 1660. The existence of these two clauses caused some confusion of interpretation, and may explain the differing opinions of Nottingham and the anonymous Tory writer. However, as Nottingham's brother, Heneage Finch, pointed out in later debates on the Bill, most of the corporation charters were seized after the *quo warranto* proceedings were started, and the Bill would have allowed seizures under these writs prior to 1675 to remain valid. He and the Tory pamphleteer were therefore correct in their general conclusion that the Bill "puts corporations as they were in 1675." The Government's systematic use of such procedures began after March 11, 1663 when the Privy Council ordered the Attorney General to use *quo warranto* prosecutions against corporations which had not renewed their charters since the King's restoration. J. H. Sacret found that the number of new charters mentioned in the Calendar of Patent Rolls for about ten years after 1663 far exceeded that for any such period before, and thus Finch's estimate in 1690 has been corroborated. *H.M.C., 12th Rept., Pt. VI, H. of L. MSS*, pp. 423–24; Grey, IX, 518–19; P.C.2/56/338; Sacret, *E.H.R.*, XLV, 256–59; Horwitz, *Revolution Politicks*, p. 104.

117  Morrice MSS, R, 73 (Jan. 4, 1689/90 entry).

118  *Ibid.*, pp. 73–74; *C.J.*, IX, 322–23. The specific figure of seven years was not contained in Sacheverell's original motion, but was added later in the proceedings. Morrice's hitherto unused account of the January 2 proceedings is the only one known to exist except for a couple of motions described by the anonymous writer of the *Letter Concerning the Disabling Clauses*. There are some inaccuracies in the account given by Morrice which can be corrected by the House of Commons *Journal*.

119  *Ibid.*, p. 323; *A Letter Concerning the Disabling Clauses*, p. 17; Morrice MSS, R, 73; *C.J.*, X, 323.

120  Grey does not indicate which Hampden or which Foley spoke, but it was probably the senior in each case. Sir Walter Yonge also spoke out strongly in defense of the clause. Grey, IX, 511–18; Morrice MSS, R, 84; *C.J.*, X, 329.

121  Spencer House "Journals," Foxcroft, *Halifax*, II, 243.

122  On the Tory pressure for dissolution see Feiling, p. 270; Horwitz, *Revolution Politicks*, pp. 105–106.
123  Morrice MSS, Q, 458.

NOTE FOR CONCLUSION

1  Newcome, *Diary*, p. 24. The italics are Newcome's. In 1673 after speaking of the failure of the Bill for the Ease of Protestant Dissenters, the Congregationalist minister Lewis Stukely revealed the impact of such unrealized hopes in writing Lord Wharton that he wished to "see such an excellency in Christ and the upper world as to become indifferent about these lower transactions." Rawl. Ltrs., 51, fol. 9.

# APPENDIX I

## *The Evidences of Dissent*

There are particular difficulties in discovering the religious views and practices of Dissenters who sat in Parliament during the period between passage of the Act of Uniformity and the Act of Toleration. Both political and financial futures could be destroyed by the disclosure or the discovery of any Nonconformity. As a result only a very few openly acknowledged their position or attended public Nonconformist services. There was also apprehension about expressing opinions in letters, diaries and other written records, for the Government's practices in intercepting mail and seizing materials were well known, as were the consequences that could occur. Thus correspondence among politicians and ministers, a most fruitful source of evidence, was unquestionably less frequent and revealing than it would otherwise have been, and for this reason, personal visits among political leaders and Nonconformist ministers were especially significant. Likewise, diaries and journals have proved to be among the best sources of information, notably those of Philip Henry and Roger Morrice, but they could have been far more valuable. Henry was definitely inhibited in his record keeping after a friend's diary was taken by the authorities as he traveled to London and Henry learned the warrant was also for seizure of his diary. Large erasures were made in the text he had written and he wrote that thereafter he would "take warning and be more cautious. . . ." [1] Similar reasons explain why Morrice left so many critical passages and names in untranscribed characters that constituted a code as well as a form of shorthand, and also why he later left blanks in his journal.

Among those who desired to retain or obtain political office and positions of authority in the government there was an understandable tendency to gloss over or leave unstated the religious opinions and practices that would have denied them such positions or penalized them financially. Therefore many statements concerning religious beliefs and practices made by such men cannot be taken at face value. Another difficult and closely related problem is that changes frequently occurred in religious views and practices. There were many reasons for such variation in outlook, but major political developments, national crises, and shifts in royal policy all had their effect. In addition there were such factors as the attraction of the Established Church for those who possessed or who acquired position and wealth, as well as other more personal reasons. In general the shift was toward Anglicanism, as is well known, but this was not always the tendency. There is evidence that some men gravitated toward the Anglican Church and then later swung back to a position best described as Presbyterian, and among them were the Lords Delamer, Holles, and Anglesey.

Evidence of Puritanism, Nonconformity, or Anglicanism at one time in a man's life is therefore not sufficient. His religious views prior to 1661 are always germane, but it is always essential to establish his position after 1661 and to consider evidence of his later opinions and actions. For the reasons already suggested, much of the evidence concerning Presbyterians and Congregationalists holding public office is more indicative than it is conclusive. Of that which leaves no doubt there are several different types besides an outright acknowledgment of a person's position or a discussion of his religious opinions in which this becomes evident. If a person's name appears as a church member in the records of a Nonconformist congregation, if a license to hold services in his home was issued under the Indulgence of 1672, or if it was certified as a Nonconformist place of worship in accordance with the provisions of the Toleration Act of 1689, or finally, if there were reliable reports or other evidence that he attended public or private Nonconformist services, then that person can be considered a Dissenter. Since members of Parliament could rarely afford to be seen worshiping publicly, it is evidence of attendance at private Nonconformist services and of employment of Dissenters as domestic chaplains which is the most usual and conclusive manifestation of their Dissent.[2] In addition, a man should be considered a Dissenter if he was dismissed from a position in a municipal corporation by the commissioners established by the Corporation Act for its enforcement.

The types of evidence that should be regarded as highly indicative of Nonconformity rather than conclusive are much more numerous. For reasons already mentioned, having Nonconformist ministers as house guests, or having frequent and intimate contacts or correspondence with them were certainly indicative of Dissenting views. Also very significant were the favorable comments made by Nonconformist ministers concerning the religious views, piety, and character of a layman. Contributions to the financial support of Nonconformist ministers or their churches were important indications, and the employment of these ministers as stewards, tutors, or in other domestic capacities are other significant actions.[3] In addition, intervention with the authorities in order to aid or protect Dissenters who were facing prosecution or penalties was another indication which could be of consequence, depending upon the circumstances. Finally, the religious opinions and habits of worship of a political leader's wife should be weighed, as well as those of the families into which he married his children.

Turning to the estimates made by men who were not Dissenters, those of the agents of James II in 1687 and April, 1688, were very reliable, for they sought the most accurate and trustworthy sources of information in each community. Moreover their purpose was to seek cooperation and office holders among the Dissenters and not to castigate or prosecute. Thus a report or recommendation listing a man as a Dissenter can be considered accurate. But a recommendation that a man be added to the commission for the peace or that he be approved as a candidate for Parliament did not necessarily mean that he was a Dissenter. Nonconformists had been supporting moderate Anglicans in parliamentary elections for some two decades, and such men were frequently recommended to the royal agents by moderate Dissenters as "right" because moderates in each religious group favored repeal of the penal laws, but not of the Test Acts. By September the reports of the agents must be weighed with considerable caution because there was so much pressure from the Court to discover candidates who supported the King's policies.

Also generally reliable and sometimes containing information concerning the church attendance of political leaders and their families were the Episcopal surveys of conventicles made in 1665, 1669, and 1676, particularly the last. Not as reliable, yet valuable, were the comments made by Sir Richard Wiseman in his reports to Danby regarding members of Parliament, as were the comments and reports of many Anglican clergymen. Wiseman was naturally prone to equate political opposition with religious Nonconformity. However, he was correct in the basic assumption that no Nonconformist would support a Bill such as Danby's Non-resisting Test and that they would always support measures favorable to the Nonconformists. This suggests another important source of evidence, which is found in the position taken by members of Parliament upon such key measures as the Act of Uniformity, the Conventicle Acts, the Corporation Act, and the various bills to grant relief, comprehension, or toleration to the Dissenters. Finally, some degree of Nonconformity was often indicated by a dismissal from the commission of peace at certain times, such as in 1670 and 1676, or during the years of reaction following the Oxford Parliament.

In the end the evidence accumulated concerning the religious opinions of the members of Parliament who have been studied has very often been too insufficient to be conclusive. For this reason many members are described as probable or possible Presbyterians or Congregationalists in the summaries of evidence concerning their religious views found in Appendix II. The list that has been compiled is by no means to be regarded as complete or definitive. The purpose has been to discover the leaders among the Presbyterians and Congregationalists who sat in Parliament and as many others as possible so that their parliamentary activity could be studied and their contributions to the perpetuation of parliamentarianism could be evaluated.

[1] Henry, p. 173 and n.

[2] The primary sources of information concerning chaplains are Edmund Calamy's well-known accounts of the ministers who were ejected in 1662, which were based upon the work of Baxter, William Taylor, Roger Morrice, Sir Edward Harley and many other contemporaries. On their contributions to Calamy's work see, *Acct.*, II, v. A. G. Matthews in his *Calamy Revised* gives a very large amount of additional evidence about the ejected ministers which was not available to Calamy. For a full discussion of Calamy's work, see his Introduction pp. xvi–xlix.

[3] The employment of Nonconformist ministers as tutors and the enrollment of children in schools run by Dissenters are in themselves insufficient evidences, for there were moderate Anglicans who did both, but particularly the latter, in order to obtain a sound education for their children. See Martindale, p. 193; Calamy, *Acct.*, II, 148, 679.

# APPENDIX II

*Summaries of Evidence Concerning the Religious*
*Views of the Presbyterians and Congregationalists*
*Sitting in Parliament, 1661–1689*

## CONTENTS

### INTRODUCTORY NOTE

In Chapter II and in the preceding Appendix there is a full discussion of the criteria and evidence used in evaluating the religious positions of the members of Parliament whose views are described below. It should be emphasized that these members were perforce at least occasional and partial Conformists. The main criteria used has been whether there was attendance at any Nonconformist religious services or entertainment of Dissenting opinions concerning doctrines, ceremonies, or church government.

All but a small number of the members included in the list below are described as Presbyterians, the remainder being Congregationalists, except for one man who was apparently a Baptist. The term Presbyterian is being used as it was during the period after Restoration. It describes those who thought of themselves as "old Puritans" rather than Separatists, but who found their ministers excluded from the Established Church by the Act of Uniformity.

There are two asterisks preceding the name of each member who may be regarded as a Presbyterian or Congregationalist with some degree of certainty. Members for whom the evidence is either less sufficient or less reliable, and those for whom it is partially contradictory are called either probable or possible Presbyterians or Congregationalists. The names of those considered probable cases are preceded by one asterisk, while those who were only possible cases have no asterisk before the name. Finally, there were a number of members who were Presbyterians or Congregationalists for a time, but who ceased to attend such services or hold such views and became Anglicans. The names of such members are also preceded by a (*T*), indicating that the man was a temporary Presbyterian or Congregationalist.

The statement of Parliamentary service at the end of each summary of evidence includes only that in the Parliaments of 1661–1689.

A. MEMBERS OF THE HOUSE OF COMMONS

\*\* ASHTON or ASSHETON, SIR RALPH (c. 1605–1680), the second Baronet of Whalley Abbey, Lancashire. He was a member of the Long Parliament [1] until he was secluded in Pride's Purge, and was later made an elder in one of the new Lancashire presbyteries.[2] His Presbyterianism after the Restoration was fully evident in his reaction to the Resolution of the House passed May 13, 1661 that required all members to receive the Sacrament according to the rites of the Anglican Church at St. Margaret's Church, Westminster, on May 26. Sir Ralph desired permission on May 22 to state "why he could not . . . with good conscience receive the Communion as he was enjoined," and according to a report made on July 3 concerning those who were delinquent he was given "tacit dispensation" of the House from carrying out its order. However, it seems of some significance that he was unseated on February 4, 1662, and it is also revealing that he served as a teller for the *noes* in the division on the final reading of the Corporation Bill.[3] His will indicates that during the intervening two decades he had gravitated back to the Anglican Church to a considerable degree, though probably not completely.[4]

*M.P.:* 1661, until his election was voided February 4, 1662, for Clitheroe, Lancashire; March and October 1679 until his death January 30, 1680, again for Clitheroe.[5]

[1] G.E.C., *Bart.,* I, 150.       [2] Shaw, II, 393–94.
[3] *C.J.,* VIII, 247, 258, 289, 357.

[4] Thomas Dunham Whitaker, *An History of the Original Parish of Whalley, and Honor of Clitheroe,* revised and enlarged by John Gough Nichols and the Rev. Ponsonby A. Lyons (2 vols.; 4th ed.; 1872), II, opposite p. 2.

[5] *C.J.,* VIII, 357; William W. Bean, *The Parliamentary Representation of the Six Northern Counties of England* (Hull, 1890), p. 265; *O.R.,* I, 536, 542.

** ASHURST, SIR HENRY (1645–1711) was the eldest son of the well-known Presbyterian of the same name who was usually called "Alderman" Henry Ashurst (d. 1680). Both were close friends of Richard Baxter. The younger Ashurst stood by Baxter during his rigorous trial before Chief Justice Jeffrey at the Guildhall in May, 1685. Baxter dedicated one of his works to Sir Henry in 1689, urged him to work for the abolition of religious persecution in the Convention Parliament of 1689, and appointed him as one of the executors of his will.[1] In addition Ashurst had close connections with three other Nonconformist divines, Henry Newcome, Nathaniel Heywood, of whom he wrote a short biography, and Philip Henry.[2] Also indicative of his religious beliefs was his pledge of an annual contribution of £10 to the Common Fund for the benefit of Presbyterian and Congregationalist Ministers in 1690, and his appointment to be one of the managers of the Fund in 1695.[3] A more direct expression of his religious feeling is found in his reference to St. Bartholomew's Day of 1662 as "that black Doomsday, wherein so many were sentenced and struck dead in law as to any public service."[4]

Ashurst was a brother-in-law of Philip Foley and Richard Hampden (q.v.), all three having married daughters of William, 6th Lord Paget (q.v.). He also had a close connection with Sir Charles Hoghton (q.v.), who used his influence in Ashurst's behalf when the latter was an unsuccessful candidate in the parliamentary election at Liverpool in October, 1670.[5]

*M.P.:* 1681, in the last Exclusion Parliament, and 1689 for Truro, Cornwall.[6]

[1] F. F. Powicke, "The Rev. Richard Baxter and His Lancashire Friend Mr. Henry Ashurst," *Bulletin of the John Rylands Library,* XIII (July, 1929), 324–25; Calamy, *Acct.,* I, 404.

[2] Sir Henry Ashurst, *Life of Nathaniel Heywood* (1695); Newcome, *Diary,* pp. 47 n; Henry, p. 360.

[3] Gordon, pp. 164, 202.          [4] Ashurst, *Heywood,* p. 10.

[5] Henry, p. 231; *H.M.C., Westmorland MSS,* p. 117.     [6] *O.R.,* I, 546, 558.

** ASHURST, SIR WILLIAM (1661–1754) of London and a brother of Sir Henry (q.v.). Sir William was a merchant and in 1693 was Lord Mayor. Along with his father and brother he was a friend of Richard Baxter. He had two Presbyterian chaplains, Peter Finch after 1680, and a decade later John Thornley.[1] He was knighted in 1687 and was one of the aldermen appointed in 1687 by royal commission when James II replaced the Anglican aldermen. When the City charter was restored he was ejected.[2] At the time he was elected to fill the seat of William Love in May, 1689, he was a Presbyterian.

*M.P.:* From May 14, 1689 for London.[3]

[1] Gordon, pp. 202, 263, 367.
[2] Beaven, pp. 114–15; Morrice MSS, Q, 189.    [3] *O.R.*, I, 560.

** BARNARDISTON, SIR SAMUEL (1620–1707), of Brightwell Hall, Suffolk, was the son of Sir Nathaniel Barnardiston of Ketton (d. 1653) who was a Puritan member of the Long Parliament and who belonged to the Suffolk Presbytery during the Civil War.[1] Sir Samuel was also known for his Puritanism, and after the Restoration he continued to hold such views. This is evidenced primarily by his employment of the Presbyterian Robert Franklin as his chaplain after Franklin's ejection in 1662.[2] Barnardiston also indicated his religious sympathies by giving refuge to Edmund Calamy, the younger (d. 1685), during the plague in 1665, and also by taking steps in 1681 to help French Huguenots establish looms in Ipswich.[3] In parliamentary elections he had the active support of Dissenters, it being reported to Sir Joseph Williamson that they even purchased land prior to the election of February, 1673, so that they could qualify as electors.[4] According to the agents of James II in 1687, Barnardiston was considered "right, out of principle" both by Dissenters and by Anglican Churchmen, who would have been of latitudinarian views, and he was supported by both.[5] Also of significance was a casual and matter-of-fact comment made in 1671 by Sir Charles Lyttelton, Barnardiston's "next neighbor" in Suffolk, that Sir Samuel "be a Presbyter." [6]

*M.P.:* From February 24, 1673–1678; and 1679–1681, in the three Exclusion Parliaments, all for Suffolk.[7]

1 Shaw, II, 429; Keeler, pp. 96–97.
2 Gordon, p. 267; Matthews, p. 212. According to Morrice's account of ejected ministers which Calamy accepted, Robert Mercer was also a chaplain to Barnardiston, but Matthews is not certain this was the case. *Ibid.,* p. 349.
3 Calamy, *Historical Account of My Own Life,* I, 65; *C.S.P.D., 1680–1681,* p. 437.
4 *Ibid.,* 1672–1673, p. 597.         5 Duckett, II, 225–26.
6 Hatton, *Corres.,* I, 70–71.         7 *O.R.,* I, 528, 538, 544.

(*T*) BARNHAM, SIR ROBERT (d. 1685), of Boughton, Monchelsea, Kent, a member for Maidstone in the Long Parliament and almost every other parliament after 1603.[1] Sir Robert apparently opposed Cromwell and he took part in the Kentish Rising of 1648. Only one indication has been discovered that he possibly held Presbyterian views for a while after the Restoration. Along with Secretary Morrice, he was a teller for those opposed to the Commons' resolution for burning the Solemn League and Covenant by the common hangman.[2] He may be considered a possible Presbyterian until sometime in 1662.

*M.P.:* 1661, for Maidstone, Kent.[3]

1 G.E.C., *Bart.,* III, 285.
2 *C.J.,* VIII, 254. It was probably his younger brother William, Mayor of Norwich in 1652, who was called one of the chief Presbyterians of that city in a report to the Government after the Declaration of Indulgence. *C.S.P.D., 1673–1675,* p. 468.
3 *O.R.,* I, 524.

** BARRINGTON, SIR JOHN (1615–1683), of Hatfield Broadoak, Essex, was a member of a politically important and wealthy family in the County. Both his grandfather and his father, Sir Francis and Sir Thomas Barrington, were prominent Essex Parliamentarians and Puritans. His father was a lay member of the Westminster Assembly, and indicated his Presbyterian leanings in 1644, the year of his death, when he took the Covenant.[1] Sir John Barrington was elected to the Long Parliament in 1645 and sat until he was secluded in 1648 in Pride's Purge.[2] He was nominated to the Court of Justice to try Charles I, but refused to attend and withheld his signature from the death warrant; however, he maintained friendly relations with his kinsman Oliver Cromwell throughout the years of the Commonwealth.[3] During this period he installed an Independent, John Warren, as a parish minister, and was a member of the Essex Presbytery.[4]

Two significant facts are known that have a direct relation to Sir John Barrington's religious views following 1660, and although at first sight they seem to be contradictory, actually they are not. In his account books, under items for the religious education of his children at the time of the Restoration, are listed expenditures for Books of Common Prayer,[5] and this would suggest that previously his views and his children's training had been essentially if not exclusively Presbyterian in character. It likewise suggests that some change occurred at this juncture, but it should be emphasized that use of the Common Prayer did not preclude a continuing Presbyterian position.[6] It is then understandable that Barrington had James Small, an ejected Presbyterian minister, as a chaplain at Hatfield Broadoak probably from 1678 until Barrington's death in 1682.[7]

*M.P.:* 1661–1678, for Newton, Hampshire.[8]

[1] Keeler, pp. 97–98; G.E.C., *Bart.,* I, 28; F. W. Galpin, "Household Expenses of Sir John Barrington," *Essex Arch. Soc. Trans.,* N.S., XII (1913), 211–13. This study is continued in Vol. XXIII, Pt. II (1945), pp. 280–97.

[2] Brunton and Pennington, p. 227.

[3] Galpin, *Essex Arch. Soc. Trans.,* XXIII, 282–83.

[4] Palmer, II, 201; Shaw, II, 382.     [5] Galpin, *Essex Arch. Soc. Trans.,* XXIII, 284.

[6] See positions of the Presbyterian ministers, *supra,* Chapter II.

[7] Calamy, *Cont.,* I, 474; *infra.* App. II, notice of Sir John Davie.

[8] *O.R.,* I, 528.

* BASTARD, SIR WILLIAM (?1636–1690) of Gerston, Devon, was the son of William Bastard who held local commissions throughout the Interregnum and sat in the parliament of 1654.[1] Evidence that Sir William was a probable Dissenter is found in the fact that he was twice dismissed from the position of justice of the peace, the second time specifically "for being a great fanatic and an indulger of conventicles."[2] In addition, he assented to the first two of James II's questions regarding the Test Act and

penal laws, though with the provision that the protestant religion be maintained, and also to the third as most men did.[3]

*M.P.:* 1679, in March and October, for Beeralston.[4]

[1] John S. Crossette, MS biography of Bastard prepared for *The History of Parliament, 1660–1690,* ed. B. D. Henning; *O.R.,* I, 499.
[2] *C.S.P.D., 1676,* p. 327.
[3] Duckett, I, 374.                              [4] *O.R.,* I, 535, 541.

** (*T*) BIRCH, COL. JOHN (1616–1691) the prominent Presbyterian colonel of the Parliamentary Army during the Civil War and the aggressive and outspoken debater of the Restoration Parliaments, may be considered a Presbyterian until sometime during the early 1670's. During the early years of the Restoration he had close associations with Henry Newcome, who had preached the funeral sermon for his mother in 1660, and also with another Presbyterian minister, Henry Stubbs, to whom Birch offered £5 a year while Stubbs was in need after being ejected.[1] Birch's religious position was made apparent in his efforts to obtain adoption of the amendment to the first Conventicle Bill that in effect would have given legal sanction to occasional conformity, efforts that were recognized when he was made teller for the *yeas* in the House of Commons division of June 30, 1663, on the question of adopting the amendment.[2] Another parliamentary maneuver is also revealing. During the debate on the Poll Bill, November 20, 1666, it was moved that "whosoever kept a Nonconformist minister" should be polled at £5, and according to the parliamentary diarist John Milward "this was in relation to Colonel Birch."[3] In the debates of March and April, 1668, Birch advocated abolishing the three oaths required by the Act of Uniformity and urged a policy of toleration and comprehension, while two years later he opposed the second Conventicle Bill.[4] Another three years passed, and in debates on the Bill for the Ease of Dissenters during February and March, 1673, Birch was still vigorous in his defense of a moderate policy towards Dissenters and against rigid standards of conformity, stating that he "would fain know what it is to be of the Church and what not."[5] In addition he defended those who had taken the Covenant, proudly declaring that he had done so and that he had stuck to his engagement even though his life had been threatened and he had suffered many imprisonments as a result.[6] However, both in 1668 and again in 1673 there were implications in Birch's remarks which indicated that he was gravitating away from Presbyterianism, and a year later he leaves no doubt about this change. In opening a long speech on grievances given January 12, 1674, and before speaking about religion he made a plea to be heard "without prejudice" since he had been constantly attending Confession and Absolution, and the Communion.[7] Obviously Birch felt that he had established himself as a Conformist. This would not preclude continuance of some Presbyterian views, but since there is no evidence as to whether he subsequently attended any Presbyterian services, and since he made his announcement so openly before the Commons, he is best considered a moderate Anglican from some time during the early 1670's. He was still regarded by some of the more strict Anglicans as one of those "that do not love the Church," perhaps because he continued to support measures to give relief to Dissenters and because Nonconformist ministers also kept up some contact with him.[8]

*M.P.:* 1661 for Penryn, Cornwall.[9]

[1] John Booker, *A History of the Ancient Chapel of Birch, in Manchester Parish* (Chetham Soc. Pub., Vol. XLVII; Manchester 1859), p. 106; Newcome, *Autobiog.*, I, 203–204; *C.S.P.D., 1661–1662*, p. 565, intercepted letter of November, 1662, from Birch to Stubbs.
[2] *C.J.*, VIII, 513.     [3] Milward, p. 50.
[4] *Ibid.*, pp. 216–17, 248; Grey, I, 127, 221–222, 228; II, 42; *H.M.C., Kenyon MSS*, p. 84.
[5] Grey, II, 89, 95, 172–73.     [6] *Ibid.*, pp. 46–47.     [7] *Ibid.*, p. 228.
[8] *C.S.P.D., 1675–1676*, pp. 460–61; *C.J.*, IX, 506; Newcome, *Autobiog.*, I, 221; W[illiam] T[ong], *An Account of the Life and Death of Matthew Henry* (1716), p. 34; Whitehead, *Christian Progress*, p. 495.
[9] *O.R.*, pp. 520, 535, 542, 547.

\* BOSCAWEN, EDWARD (d. Oct. 28, 1685) [1] was a member of the prominent Puritan and Presbyterian family of Tregothnan, Cornwall, and was known as a rich Turkey merchant of London.[2] Evidence that he was probably a Presbyterian is found in his activities and in his Presbyterian associates at the time of the

Restoration, and there are a number of indications that he continued to hold these religious views. Roger Morrice was shocked by the news of Boscawen's sudden death in 1685, and wrote that he "was a very useful man to those that knew him well, and my particular acquaintance."[3] Danby's political associate, Sir Richard Wiseman, included Edward Boscawen in a list of Cornishmen thought to be Presbyterians; and there is some possibility that it was Edward Boscawen to whom Bishop Ward had reference in his letters of 1665 when he complained to Archbishop Sheldon that a Boscawen of the House of Commons was one of three principal supporters of Presbyterianism in Cornwall.[4]

Unfortunately there is frequent confusion of Edward with his brother Hugh, also a member of the House of Commons during this period, because contemporary references usually fail to distinguish between them. Judging by the usage in the *Journals of the House of Commons,* a reference to "Mr. Boscawen" appears to mean Hugh Boscawen; for on occasions when both are assigned to a committee, Edward is identified by his full name while Hugh is listed as "Mr. Boscawen."[5] No instance has been discovered in which this usage was reversed, although there are a few in which both have their full name used.[6] Undoubtedly, reference to Hugh as "Mr. Boscawen" is explained by the fact that he was first selected to the House in 1646,[7] fourteen years earlier than Edward's election in 1660, and it was felt that the senior member needed no specific identification. Compounding the confusion is evidence that speeches recorded by Anchitell Grey as given by "Mr. Boscawen" could have been given by either Edward or Hugh, for in a speech of March 3, 1676/77, "Mr. Boscawen" refers to his having been in the House sixteen years, a clear indication that in this instance it was Edward who was speaking.[8] On the other hand a speech Grey reports as given by "Mr. Boscawen" at the Oxford Parliament of 1681 is ascribed to "H.B." in the *Debates of the House of Commons Assembled at Oxford.*[9] The parliamentary diarists Milward and Dering likewise merely record speeches by "Mr. Boscawen" and fail to distinguish between the two; however, Milward's editor states that it is Edward to whom Milward refers when he records that on March 11, 1668, "Mr. Boscawen and the Dissenters earnestly pressed" for sending a discourse on toleration to the King.[10] Although it appears that most of "Mr. Boscawen's" speeches recorded by Grey, Milward, and Dering were undoubtedly given by Hugh Boscawen, it is possible that some of them, including some of those reflecting a Nonconformist point of view, should be ascribed to Edward Boscawen.[11]

*M.P.:* 1661–1678, and 1679–1681, in the three Exclusion Parliaments, for Truro, Cornwall.[12]

[1] Morrice MSS, P, 487.

[2] *Buller Papers,* pp. 115–16; Walter H. Tregallas, *Cornish Worthies: Sketches of Some Eminent Cornish Men and Families* (1884), I, 196–97; Coate, p. 327.

[3] *Buller Papers,* pp. 115–16; Coate, pp. 310n., 326–27.

[4] "Some Letters from Bishop Ward of Exeter, 1663–1667," ed. J. Simmons, *D.C.N.Q.,* XXI (July, 1941), 330–32. It is more probable that Ward was speaking of Hugh Boscawen.

[5] *C.J.,* IX, 21, 297.                           [6] *Ibid.,* VIII, 246; IX, 272.

[7] *O.R.,* I, 486, 513.                 [8] Grey, IV, 178.                 [9] P. 2.

[10] Milward, pp. xlix, 220–21. For speeches noted by Dering see pp. 25, 40, 45, 60, 159. B. D. Henning, Dering's editor, indexes these speeches as having been given by either Edward or Hugh.

[11] See for example an earlier speech of March 4 on the same matter, Grey, I, 106; one of March, 1678, favored a motion for a committee to consider some way of distinguishing between Quakers and Catholics, Grey, V, 255; and a third speech supported a Bill to unite Protestants, December 21, 1680, *H.M.C., Beaufort MSS,* pp. 101–102. There were other Boscawens sitting in Parliament during this period, but it is very unlikely that they made any of the recorded speeches, for they made very minor if any contributions in the House, judging by the lack of references to them in the *Journal.*

[12] *O.R.,* I, 521, 524, 541, 546.

\*\* BOSCAWEN, HUGH (1625–1701),[1] of Tregothnan, Cornwall. He was Knight of the Shire in the Long Parliament until he was secluded in Pride's Purge.[2] Evidence of his continuing Presbyterianism is found on every hand, but most striking is Roger Morrice's tribute to him in December, 1688, as "the great pillar of the Presbyterians."[3] Boscawen had Nonconformist chaplains, notably Mr. John Cowbridge, who according to Calamy was with Boscawen for some years.[4] In addition Calamy states that at the request of Boscawen and his wife, the Presbyterian Joseph Halsey, who had formerly been their chaplain, moved nearer to Tregothnan after his ejection and on Saturday evenings and Sunday mornings preached in Boscawen's house "as long as he lived."[5] Another Nonconformist divine, Joseph Allen, received most of his subsistence from Boscawen.[6]

Authorities in both the Anglican Church and the Government

also reported that Hugh Boscawen was a Presbyterian. Since he was a more prominent Presbyterian than his brother Edward, it was probably he rather than Edward to whom Bishop Ward was referring when complaining about the power of the Presbyterians in the County.[7] In 1676 Sir Richard Wiseman was certainly correct in considering Hugh Boscawen one of the Presbyterians, and in 1687 he was again described as a Dissenter in the Lord Lieutenant's report to James II.[8]

There may have been some change in his position in January, 1688, for he was reported to have "not only discharged some Nonconformist ministers who have been a long time very dependable to him and his table, but also forbid them his house, telling them they had deceived him in their constant opinions of the Bishops and clergy of the Church of England who he now sees acted more like Protestants than [the] Dissenters, and the next Lords Day [he] took the Sacrament at his Parish Church." [9] However, this was the point at which moderate Presbyterians were much estranged from the more rigid Nonconformists over repeal of the Test Acts and cooperation with James. In addition it should not be overlooked that Joseph Halsey continued to preach in Boscawen's house until 1701 according to Calamy, and it was twelve months later that Morrice called him "the great pillar of the Presbyterians." As for receiving the Sacrament, he had been an occasional conformist ever since 1661.

*M.P.:* 1661–1678, and 1679–1681, in the three Exclusion Parliaments, for Tregony, Cornwall; 1689 for Cornwall.[10]

[1] *The Visitations of Cornwall, Comprising the Heralds Visitations of 1530, 1573, and 1620,* ed. J. L. Vivian (Exeter, 1887), p. 47.

[2] *O.R.,* I, 486; Brunton and Pennington, p. 227; Coate, p. 246.

[3] Morrice MSS, Q, 333.

[4] Calamy, *Acct.,* II, 148; Gordon, p. 243; Matthews, p. 139.

[5] This is a reference to Boscawen's death; Halsey did not die until 1711. His views and practice were "very like Mr. Baxter's." Calamy, *Acct.,* II, 148–49; Gordon, p. 277; Matthews, p. 244. See also Boscawen's letter to the ejected minister Francis Tallents in 1693. Add. MSS, 15,857, fol. 67.

[6] Calamy, *Cont.,* I, 216; Matthews, p. 6.

[7] "Some Letters from Bishop Ward of Exeter, 1663–1667," *D.C.N.Q.,* XXI, 330–32.

[8] Browning, III, 101–102; Duckett, I, 379.

[9] Newdigate Newsletter #1906, Jan. 10, 1688.

[10] *O.R.,* I, 521, 534, 541, 546, 558.

* BRAMAN, JOHN (c. 1625–1703) of Chichester and Lewes, Sussex, was an Independent and a republican who served in the Parliamentary Army and opposed the Restoration.[1] Although conclusive evidence has not been discovered, it is most probable that he retained his Nonconformist views thereafter. When he was elected to the first Exclusion Parliament he was "reputed to be a great fanatic," and in September, 1681, Secretary Jenkins received a report that the Dissenting party were resolved to choose him for the next Parliament.[2] Both at this time and again in 1683 he was regarded with suspicion by the Government, but the cause was much more political than religious, particularly in 1683 when he was actively engaged in welcoming the Duke of Monmouth to Chichester and suspected of involvement in the Rye House Plot.[3]

His religious position was most clearly implied by the freedom with which a correspondent wrote him in 1678 asking for God's blessing on "poor Protestant Dissenters" and attacking bishops.[4] Likewise highly indicative, he was considered to be a fanatic by Roger Morrice in December, 1686. Although the Presbyterian journalist may merely have been accepting the description of Braman then current in persistent reports that he had been put into the commission of the peace, Morrice was using the term in its religious sense and he was not prone to use it indiscriminately. Moreover, he had a reliable informant, and he therefore consistently and correctly rejected the reports of the appointment. Also significant was the alarm with which leaders of the Church reacted to news of the appointment that they believed had been made.[5]

Finally, Braman received favorable consideration from James II and his agents during the period when the King sought Nonconformist support. In December, 1687, he was appointed to a Commission of Enquiry of about ten members, including William Penn, which was charged with checking into the fines levied on Dissenters and Recusants from 1677 for which the sheriffs had not given account to Charles II or James II.[6] In addition he was proposed as a justice of the peace by the Lord Lieutenant, and apparently by the royal agents as well, and he was appointed to this position in May, 1688. Moreover, the agents imply that Braman had the approval of Chichester Dissenters as a candidate for Parliament in September, 1688. Since at this same time he talked persuasively to Colonel Richard Norton (q.v.) and as a result was able to report him "thoroughly right" as a candidate for Parliament, it appeared that Braman was actively engaged in support of the King's policies.[7] However, it is unlikely that either he or Norton favored repeal of the Test Acts, particularly at this juncture, and consistent with these contentions was the fact that he joined the forces of William of Orange before November 30.[8] Although it is most probable that Braman continued to hold Congregationalist views, it is also likely that he had become an occasional conformist by the time he was first elected to Parliament in 1679, a practice which he unquestionably had adopted by the time he was appointed Deputy Governor of the Isle of Wight in 1692.

*M.P.:* 1679–1681 in the three Exclusion Parliaments for Chichester.[9]

[1] B. D. Henning, MS biography of Braman prepared for *The History of Parliament 1660–1690.*

[2] *H.M.C., Fitzherbert MSS,* p. 13; *C.S.P.D., 1680–1681,* p. 473.

[3] *Ibid., 1681,* p. 585; *1683,* pp. 58, 70, 358, 375–76.

[4] *Ibid., 1678,* p. 246.          [5] Morrice MSS, Q, 20, 28, 49, 52.

[6] *Cal. Treas. Books,* VIII, Pt. III, 1685–1689, pp. 1695–1696.

[7] Duckett, I, 189, 432, 441; II, 261.

[8] Add. MSS, 34,510, fol. 118, Van Citter's report November 30, 1688; Rawl. Ltrs., fols. 109, 115.

[9] *O.R.,* I, 538, 544, 550.

** BULKELEY, JOHN (1613?–1662) of Nether Burgate, Hants. He was a recruiter to the Long Parliament, took the Covenant, was a parliamentary commissioner to negotiate with the King at Newport in 1648, and was secluded in Pride's Purge. After serving in the Parliaments of 1654 and 1656 he was again elected in 1660 and worked hard for the moderate Presbyterian settlement of comprehension and for enactment of the King's Worcester House Declaration.[1] In the Cavalier Parliament he continued to be very active, serving on thirty-eight committees, including the one on the Corporation Bill.[2] In this case Lord Wharton was correct including him among his "Names of Friends, 1661."[3] He was a moderate Presbyterian.

*M.P.:* 1661–Sept. 1662, for Lymington, Hants.[4]

[1] Helms, "The Convention Parliament, 1660," pp. 516–17.
[2] Paula Watson, MS biography of Bulkeley prepared for *The History of Parliament, 1660–1690,* ed. B. D. Henning.
[3] Carte MSS, 81, fol. 82.                    [4] *O.R.,* I, 528.

\* BULLER, FRANCIS JR. (1631–1694), of Shillingham, Cornwall and Isleham, Cambridge Co., was a member of a politically prominent Cornish family. His father was a Puritan and parliamentarian who served in various parliaments from 1624 until 1648 when he was secluded.[1] Francis Buller, Jr. followed in these traditions, and in March, 1660, served on the new country committee of militia that consisted primarily of Presbyterian gentry, and was formed under the New Militia Act passed by the restored Long Parliament in order to disband the local levies previously established by the Rump.[2] In 1665 he was regarded by Bishop Ward of Exeter as one of the three most powerful Presbyterians in the country,[3] and in 1676 Sir Richard Wiseman included him in a list of those whom he considered to be Presbyterians.[4] When the Charter of Saltash was to be renewed in 1677, the King took steps to prevent him from retaining the recordership, an action which could have been based upon religious as well as political grounds, but it could also have been a matter of health since the position was given to Buller's son.[5]

*M.P.:* 1661–1678 for Saltash, Cornwall.[6]

[1] *Buller Papers,* pp. vi–vii; Keeler, pp. 120–22; Coate, pp. 326–27; Vivian, *Visitations of Cornwall . . . ,* p. 65.
[2] Coate, p. 310.
[3] "Some Letters from Bishop Ward of Exeter, 1663–1667," *D.C.N.Q.,* XXI, 331–32.
[4] Browning, III, 101.                    [5] *C.S.P.D., 1677–1678,* pp. 193, 200.
[6] *O.R.,* I, 521.

\* BULLER, JOHN (1632–1716), of Morval, Cornwall, was a brother of Francis Buller, a probable Presbyterian of this period.[1] He sat in the 1656 Parliament.[2] In the spring of 1660 he too was one of those who served on the county committee of militia, consisting primarily of Presbyterians, which was established by the restored Long Parliament to take the place of the disbanded militia that the Rump had raised.[3] Evidence concerning his religious position after the Restoration is fragmentary. However, his resignation as Recorder of Saltash on August 4, 1662 was of import, and in 1676 Sir Richard Wiseman included him in his list of men whom he considered to be Presbyterians.[4] More reliable was the report of the Lord Lieutenant to James II that he was one of the Dissenters of the county, and on the strength of this report and his action in 1662 he may be considered a probable Presbyterian.[5] However, by the time of his death in 1716 he appears to have become a devoted Anglican.[6]

*M.P.:* 1661–1678, for Saltash; 1679–1681, in the three Exclusion Parliaments and 1689 for Liskeard, Cornwall.[7]

[1] *Buller Papers*, p. vi; Coate, pp. 294–95, 326–27; Pink, MSS 298/658.
[2] *Buller Papers*, pp. vi, 97.　　　　　　　　[3] Coate, p. 310n.
[4] Carew-Pole MSS, BO/21/18; Browning, III, 101–102.
[5] Duckett, I, 379.
[6] In his will drawn in 1714 he left £8 annually to pay a person "well asserted to the Church of England" to teach the poor of his parish the catechism of the Church, P.C.C. 131 Fox.
[7] *O.R.,* I, 521, 534, 540, 546, 558.

* COURTENAY, SIR WILLIAM (1628–1702), of Powderham Castle, and Forde House, Newton Abbot, Devon. In 1643 he married the daughter of Sir William Waller and came under the influence of that family's Presbyterianism. Like his father-in-law he remained a supporter of the monarchy during the Interregnum, and in 1659 became involved in efforts to restore the King.[1] Although he maintained the Dean of Exeter in his house after the Dean was turned out for loyalty to the King, he also presented the Presbyterian Francis Soreton to Honiton Parish in 1652, the position from which he was ejected in 1662. Three years later when Soreton was imprisoned for violation of the Five Mile Act, Courtenay "being then High-Sheriff of the County, got him released and conveyed him, in his own coach, to his own house where he continued until he died [in 1693]."[2] Since Soreton married an aunt of Courtenay's and since Morrice, who emphasized this connection, and Calamy both refrained from calling him a chaplain to Courtenay, there is question how much his presence at Powderham indicated concerning Sir William's religious views and prac-

tices.³ Soreton was licensed in 1672, but his benefactor did not license Powderham, perhaps because this was not needed for family services.⁴ In his will Soreton himself was noncommittal about Courtenay's religious views in expressing his gratitude to Sir William and his wife, writing that "their Honors have been the great instruments of the providence of God towards us." ⁵

He appears to have been instrumental in the election of Sir Walter Young (q.v.) to Parliament in 1667 by failing to support Joseph Williamson, and in 1677 he supported Thomas Reynell (q.v.). About 1680 he was removed from the lieutenancy, and he was implicated in the Rye House Plot. In 1688 he was restored to local office, and the King's agents reported him as "supposed to be right" in 1688.⁶

It seems likely that Courtenay attended private services conducted by Soreton. Yet neither Morrice nor Calamy considered him a chaplain, and the family relationship between minister and benefactor cannot be overlooked. For these reasons Courtenay should be considered only a probable Presbyterian.

*M.P.:* 1679–1681 in the three Exclusion Parliaments, for Devon.⁷

¹ G.E.C., *Bart.,* II, 241; E. Cleaveland, *Geneological History of the Noble Family of Courtenay* (Exon, 1735), p. 303.
² Calamy, *Acct.,* II, 241, 254; Matthews, p. 452.
³ *Ibid.,* Morrice MSS, Q, 230.        ⁴ Turner, III, 688.
⁵ Matthews, p. 452.
⁶ J. P. Ferris, MS biography of Courtenay prepared for *The History of Parliament, 1660–1690,* ed. B. D. Henning.
⁷ *O.R.,* I, 535, 541, 547.

\*\* DAVIE, SIR JOHN (1612–1678) was the second baronet, of Creedy, in Sampford, and near Crediton, Devon.¹ In 1663 Bishop Ward reported to Archbishop Sheldon that Sir John Davie headed the list of the fourteen or more justices of the peace in Devon who were "arrant Presbyterians," and stated that Davie's mansion at Creedy was their "chief place of resort." ² He had the Presbyterian James Small as his chaplain after Small was silenced in 1660, and in 1672 this minister was licensed as a Presbyterian to preach at Creedy.³ When the House divided upon the question of his contested seat, the Presbyterian Sir Ralph Ashton was one of the tellers for the side favoring Davie.[4] Small was again his chaplain at the time he made his will in January, 1678.[5]

*M.P.:* May to December 17, 1661, for Tavistock, Devon.[6]

[1] G.E.C., *Bart.,* II, 143–44.
[2] "Some Letters from Bishop Ward of Exeter, 1663–1667," *D.C.N.Q.,* XXI, 226, 284.
[3] Calamy, *Cont.,* I, 474; Turner, II, 1155; Matthews, p. 445.
[4] *C.J.,* VIII, 334. He was unseated by a vote of 108 to 85.
[5] P.C.C. 3 Reeve.          [6] *C.J.,* VIII, 334; G.E.C., *Bart.,* II, 144.

DUKE, RICHARD JR. (1652–1733) was of Otterton, Devon. His father took arms for Parliament in the Civil War and was known as a busy fanatic who insisted on reading prayers himself in a Presbyterian manner.[1] Although there is no conclusive evidence concerning the younger Duke's religious position, it appears he was a possible Dissenter, since James II's agents were assured in April, 1688 (and also in September) that he along with Thomas Reynell (q.v.) were "right men." [2]

*M.P.:* Ashburton, Devon, 1679 in the second Exclusion Parliament.[3]

[1] J. P. Ferris, MS biography of Duke prepared for *The History of Parliament, 1660–1690,* ed. B. D. Henning.
[2] Duckett, II, 233, 241.          [3] *O.R.,* I, 541.

** ELDRED, JOHN (1629–1717) of Stanway, Essex. He was of Caius College, Cambridge and was admitted to Lincoln's Inn in May, 1648.[1] Although nothing has been discovered concerning him in Nonconformist sources, in April, 1688 James II's agents were positive in stating that he was a Dissenter and such explicit statements made by the agents at that time are reliable.[2]

*M.P.:* 1689 for Harwich, Essex.[3]

[1] *Al. Cant.,* II, 93.          [2] Duckett, I, 410.          [3] *O.R.,* II, 559.

ELLIS, SIR WILLIAM (1654–1727) was of Wyham, and after the death of his great-uncle, Judge William Ellis in 1680,[1] also of

Nocton, Lincolnshire.[2] As a young man he had close associations with Presbyterian ministers and political leaders such as the ejected ministers Samuel Birch, Lord Wharton, and Richard Hampden.[3] According to a report the Earl of Lindsey sent Secretary Jenkins in 1683, Ellis was "the head of all the Presbyterians in the County. . . ."[4] It is evident from the Earl's letter that one of the reasons for this reputation was the fact that Ellis had married Isabella Hampden, daughter of Richard Hampden.[5] Also lending some substance to this contention was the fact that Sir William sent his eldest son to the school kept by the Nonconformist divine Samuel Cradock at Geesings, Suffolk.[6] In the 1680's it appears that he was one of those who came closer to the Established Church in habits of worship. From 1683 to 1692 his chaplain was Joseph Farrow, who could not accept the conditions of conformity, even though he had been Episcopally ordained. Although he had previously served as a curate to an Anglican clergyman, he did not have an Anglican license or living.[7] Farrow's Dissent was marginal, but it would seem to indicate that Ellis was a possible Presbyterian from 1683 to 1692.

*M.P.:* 1679–1681, in the three Exclusion Parliaments, and 1689 for Grantham, Lincolnshire.[8]

[1] Judge of the Common Pleas, 1673–1676, 1679–1680, and prominent member of the opposition, March to May, 1679; Hatton, *Corres.,* I, 133; *O.R.,* I, 536; *C.J.,* IX, 613.

[2] G.E.C., *Bart.,* III, 71.

[3] Rawl. Ltrs., H 50, fol. 17 (letter of Samuel Birch to Lord Wharton, Dec., 1668).

[4] *C.S.P.D., 1683* (July–Sept.), p. 180.

[5] G.E.C., *Bart.,* III, 71. Roger Morrice, who appears to have known the family well, recorded that Isabella Ellis died in childbirth on Jan. 16, 1686. Morrice MSS, P, 510.

[6] Calamy, *Historical Account,* II, 134.

[7] Calamy, *Acct.,* II, 459; Palmer, II, 443.     [8] *O.R.,* I, 536, 542, 548, 560.

** EYLES, SIR JOHN (d. 1703), of South Brome (or Broom) and Devizes, Wiltshire, was a London merchant who came into prominence as a result of James II's policy of favoring Nonconformists as office holders.[1] In the Lord Lieutenant's report Eyles was listed as a Dissenter who was "very honest and fit" to be a deputy lieutenant or a justice.[2] Just after the strong Anglican aldermen of London were ejected from office (August 2–6, 1687), Eyles was made an alderman by Royal Commission on August 12, and three days later he was knighted.[3] The following year when Sir John Shorter, the Nonconformist Lord Mayor,[4] died in office, Eyles was appointed to this position and served a few weeks until James was compelled to restore the London Charter in early October.[5] At this time Roger Morrice referred to Eyles as an Anabaptist "of good parts" and "especially of temper." [6]

*M.P.:* October, 1679, in the second Exclusion Parliament, for Devizes, Wiltshire.[7]

[1] *C.S.P.D., Oct. 1683–Apr. 1684,* p. 193; C.E.C., *Bart.,* V, 22; Beaven, II, 114–15.

[2] Duckett, I, 210, 220, 228; II, 268.      [3] Beaven, I, 77; II, 114.

[4] According to Morrice, Shorter was an Independent and was a member of Mr. Richard Wavell's congregation. In Dec., 1682, he was removed as an alderman by order of Charles II because of his nonconformity. He died in early Sept., 1688. Morrice MSS, Q, 189; Sharpe, II, 524; Beaven, II, 107.

[5] *Ibid.,* pp. xxv, 114–15.

[6] Morrice MSS, Q, 174, 189. Sir John Bramston also referred to Eyles as an Anabaptist a month earlier. It is possible that each was merely echoing the current newsletters' terminology, although Morrice's additional comments would seem to indicate that he either had other sources of information or was acquainted with Eyles. Bramston, p. 315. See also Ellis, *Corres.,* II, 150.

[7] *O.R.,* I, 544. Eyles stood for election in 1681, but the contested election that resulted was never resolved because of the quick dissolution. Beaven, II, 114.

\*\* FAGG, SIR JOHN (d. 1701) was of Wiston, Sussex. He was appointed a commissioner to try Charles I and sat in the Rump Parliament. The best evidence of his religious views after the Restoration is that he both lodged and supported the Presbyterian minister Sampson Herne at his house from the time of Herne's ejection in 1662 until his death in 1677, and that during this time Herne preached for him, though not regularly.[1] He also received John Beaton into his family after this Presbyterian minister was ejected, and he left Beaton's widow a bequest of £10 a year in his will.[2] Other evidence of Fagg's religious views may be found in the fact that he sent his two sons to a school run by the Nonconformist William Corderoy in Steyning, Sussex.[3] In addition he was one of those whom the Dissenters had resolved to choose for Sussex in the elections of 1681.[4] Another indication is perhaps to be found in the fact that William Penn sought out

Fagg and dined with him at the time he was working for the election of Algernon Sidney.[5] Of importance in 1688 was the approval given him by the Lord Lieutenant and by the agents of James II as a candidate for a deputy lieutenant, and also his later opposition to James II on the eve of the Revolution.[6] Sir John married Mary Morley, member of the Presbyterian family of Glynde, Sussex.[7]

*M.P.:* 1661–1689 in all Parliaments, for Steyning, Sussex.[8]

[1] Calamy, *Acct.*, II, 381; Matthews, p. 255.

[2] Beaton was at Wiston in 1669, for he was prosecuted under the Five Mile Act in that year, and also in 1672, when he received a license as a Presbyterian teacher; but this does not necessarily mean that he was still with Sir John Fagg. Calamy, *Acct.*, II, 685; Matthews, p. 42; Turner, I, 417; II, 1023; P.C.C., 88 Dyor.

[3] Calamy, *Cont.*, II, 818–19.

[4] *C.S.P.D., 1680–1681*, p. 473. Fagg was chosen to represent both Steyning and the County, but preferred to represent the latter.

[5] Meadley, *Memoirs of Algernon Sydney*, App. XII, pp. 336–37, letter of Penn, July 29, 1679.

[6] Duckett, I, 188, 441; II, 260; Browning, III, 162.

[7] *Visitation of Sussex, 1662*, ed. A. W. Hughes Clark (Harleian Soc. Pub., No. 89; 1937), p. 43; Calamy, *Acct.*, II, 691. For the Morley family, see *infra*, Appendix II.

[8] *O.R.*, I, 529, 538, 544, 550, 562.

FAGG, SIR ROBERT (d. 1715), of Wiston, Sussex, was the son of the prominent Presbyterian Colonel, Sir John Fagg (q.v.). He grew up in a strongly Presbyterian atmosphere which was created by his father's Presbyterian chaplain John Beaton, and by his mother, née Mary Morley whose family was also known for its Presbyterianism. He received some of his education at the boarding school kept by the ejected minister William Corderoy at Steyning, Sussex.[1] In 1681 it was reported that Sir Robert, along with his father, his brother and his brother-in-law, the Presbyterian Sir Philip Gell, were the candidates whom "the Dissenting party are resolved to choose for Sussex. . . ."[2] It is possible that he retained the Presbyterian views of his father until 1681.

*M.P.:* March, 1679, and 1681, in the first and last Exclusion Parliaments, for Shoreham, Sussex.[3]

[1] Calamy, *Cont.*, II, 818–19.  [2] *C.S.P.D., 1680–1681*, p. 473.
[3] *O.R.*, I, 538, 550.

\* FAIRFAX, HENRY (1631–1688), of Denton, Yorkshire, was fourth Baron of Cameron of the Scottish Peerage. He was son of the Puritan clergyman Henry Fairfax and cousin of the famous Parliamentary General, Thomas, Lord Fairfax (the third Baron of Cameron). Evidence concerning young Henry Fairfax's religious views is found primarily in the diary of his well-known antiquarian and Presbyterian friend, Ralph Thoresby. Upon one of the diarist's visits with Fairfax at Denton he wrote that he was "mightily pleased with the religious order of the family." [1] Thoresby also writes of supporting his "kind friend" in the two Yorkshire elections of March and September, 1679, when Fairfax stood for Knight of the Shire and was elected.[2] Thomas Heywood likewise attested to the Nonconformist support given to Fairfax in these elections; and another Yorkshire diarist, Sir John Reresby, complained bitterly in 1679 of the "sectarys and fanatics" who supported Fairfax, particularly of the cutlers near Sheffield for whom Reresby had successfully intervened in 1675–1676 after the collectors of chimney money had levied this duty on their furnaces.[3] In view of such Nonconformist support for Fairfax in these elections, it is not surprising to find that he was one of the members of Parliament to whom the Quakers made appeals for help in 1680.[4] In 1683 Reresby tells of Fairfax's visit to him and calls him a great leader of the Presbyterian party in Yorkshire.[5] Fairfax was a member of the Privy Council under James II and also served as the Lord Lieutenant of the North Riding in 1687–1688,[6] when the King was pursuing his policy of cooperation with the Dissenters in order to obtain religious toleration.

*M.P.:* 1679–1681, in the three Exclusion Parliaments, for Yorkshire.[7]

[1] Thoresby, I, 176. This entry was made in June, 1684, six months after Thoresby was indicted at quarter sessions under the Conventicle Act, having been apprehended as a result of his most faithful attendance at Nonconformist meetings. After his acquittal he began attending both an Anglican and a Nonconformist service on Sundays. However, there can be no real question of whether he was considering Fairfax's religious practices in the light of his own Presbyterian religious beliefs, which had not changed. He continued to call himself a Dissenter and was so regarded by the authorities. *Ibid.,* pp. 169–78, 181, 186–87.

[2] *Ibid.,* pp. 28, 31, 50.

[3] Heywood, I, 348–49; II, 104; Reresby, pp. 104–105, 185, 186–87.

[4] Friends' MSS, Meeting for Sufferings Minutes, II (1680–1683), 34.

⁵ Reresby, pp. 312–13. See also the report from Sir Joseph Williamson's correspondents in Dec., 1678, *C.S.P.D., 1678*, pp. 562–63.

⁶ A[rthur] Gooder, *Parliamentary Representation of the County of York, 1258–1832* (2 vols.; Yorks. Arch. Soc. Record Ser. Vols. 91, 96; [Wakefield], 1935, 1937), II, 93.

⁷ *Ibid.*, pp. 92–93; *O.R.*, I, 539, 545, 550.

FARRINGTON, RICHARD (c. 1650–1719) of Chichester, Bart. from December, 1697,¹ was the second son of John Farrington who sat in the second Exclusion Parliament for Chichester until his death in December, 1680, whereupon his son Richard was elected to his seat.² There are several indications that Richard Farrington may have been a Dissenter, one of the most significant being that Morrice called him a fanatic, along with Major John Braman (q.v.), when reports were consistently circulated in 1686 that these two men had been put into the commission of peace. Also indicative of his religious views was the alarm of the Church leaders who believed that these appointments had been made.³

In September, 1681, there was an unreliable report that arms were stored in a house that he owned, but the assertion that the "fanatic party" formerly met there may have had more validity, though this informant probably used the phrase in more of a political than a religious sense. At the same time, Secretary Jenkins received a reliable report that the "Dissenting party" were resolved to choose Farrington and Braman to sit for Sussex in the next Parliament.⁴ Farrington was again under suspicion in 1683 for reported activity in welcoming the Duke of Monmouth to Chichester, and the King ordered his house searched.⁵ However, more indicative of his religious views was the favor with which he was regarded by James II when the King sought Nonconformist support. Along with William Penn and Braman, he was appointed to the Commission of Enquiry directed to check upon the fines levied on Dissenters and Recusants after 1677 and for which the sheriffs had not given accounts to the King.⁶ Secondly the Lord Lieutenant, and apparently the King's agents as well, proposed Farrington for a justice of the peace. Finally, the King's agents implied that Farrington had the approval of the Dissenters of Chichester as a candidate for Parliament in September, 1688.⁷ Such evidence suggests that he was a Dissenter.

*M.P.:* From January 4, 1681 and March, 1681, in the last two Exclusion Parliaments, for Chichester, Sussex.⁸

[1] G.E.C., *Bart.*, IV, 172.  [2] *O.R.*, I, 544.
[3] Morrice MSS, Q, 20, 28, 49, 52.
[4] *C.S.P.D., 1680–1681*, pp. 472, 473, 585.
[5] *Ibid., 1683*, pp. 58, 70, 358, 375–76.
[6] *Cal. Treas. Books*, VIII, Pt. III, 1685–1689, pp. 1695–96.
[7] Duckett, I, 189, 441; II, 261.  [8] *O.R.*, I, 544, 550.

FOLEY, PAUL (1645?–1699), of Stoke Edith, Herefordshire, was the second son of the well-known, wealthy Nonconformist iron manufacturer Thomas Foley (d. 1677) of Witley Court, Worcestershire. Ultimately Paul Foley became a Tory and served as Speaker of the House of Commons from 1695–1698. He was brought up in a Puritan atmosphere in which the influence of his father's close friend Richard Baxter was particularly pervasive,[1] and it is likely that he was still of much the same religious point of view when he served in the Parliaments of 1679–1689. Indicative of his views was his engagement of Presbyterian ministers as tutors for his children, his reputedly intimate acquaintance with the ejected minister Edward Rogers, and his close friendship with Sir Edward Harley and their correspondence concerning religious topics and problems during these years.[2] For these reasons he may be regarded as a possible Presbyterian at this time in his life.

*M.P.:* 1679–1681, in the three Exclusion Parliaments, and 1689, for Hereford City.[3]

[1] See Baxter, Pt. III, p. 148.
[2] Gordon, p. 322; William Urwich, *Nonconformity in Worcester* (1897), pp. 91n., 93; *C.S.P.D., 1683* (*July–Sept.*), pp. 133–34; Calamy, *Acct.*, II, 221; B.M. Loan 29/75, Portland MSS, Folder 9, a series of eighteen letters from 1684–1690; also *H.M.C., Portland MSS*, III, 367, 372.
[3] *O.R.*, I, 535, 542, 547, 559.

\*\* FOLEY, PHILIP (1653–1716), of Prestwood Hall, Staffordshire, was the youngest of three politically prominent sons of the wealthy Nonconformist iron manufacturer Thomas Foley of Witley Court, Worcestershire. Philip Foley maintained a considerable number of Nonconformist ministers as his chaplains or stewards, and in addition he also had close contacts with others not in his employment, notably Philip Henry. He visited the Foleys sometimes for as much as a fortnight, particularly upon important occasions such as the birth of children. Although it seemed that his ministrations were especially sought by Mrs. Foley, who was a daughter of William, the 6th Lord Paget, Henry found the Foleys "a good and great family" which was "well ordered," and he added rather plaintively, "would there were more such." [1]

Of the numerous Nonconformist ministers whom Foley had as chaplains, Richard Hilton appears to have served during the 1660's,[2] and during the late 1670's he appears to have had several other chaplains, some of them at the same time, including George Fowler, Richard Cook, and John Warren.[3] For a few years, presumably about 1678, James Illingworth served him in this capacity, and later chaplains were Mr. Willets, who was in his service in 1691, John Reynolds, who was with him from 1699–1706, and George Fowler whose dates of service are not known.[4] In his employment as steward was the Nonconformist minister, Edward Pasten who was with him for some time.[5] In addition there is evidence that Foley helped other Nonconformists find places of employment.[6]

Also very conclusive was Foley's subscription of an annual contribution of £10 to the Common Fund for the Benefit of Presbyterian and Congregational Ministers in 1690.[7]

M.P.: From November 7, 1673 until voided March 10, 1677; 1679–1681, in the three Exclusion Parliaments, for Bewdley Worcestershire; [8] and 1689 for Stafford.

---

[1] Henry, *Diaries*, pp. 231, 243, 292, 314.

[2] Calamy, *Acct.*, II, 628; "Ebenezer Church, West Bromwich," *C.H.S.T.*, III (May, 1907), 105.

[3] Turner, III, 526; Calamy, *Acct.*, II, 777; *Cont.*, II, 896.

[4] Gordon, p. 230; Matthews, p. 287; "Early Nonconformist Academies," *C.H.S.T.*, VI (Oct., 1914), 377; Gordon, *Cheshire Classic Minutes, 1691–1745*, p. 200; Urwick, *Nonconformity in Worcester*, p. 91n.

[5] Calamy, *Acct.*, II, 565; Calamy, *Cont.*, II, 724; Matthews, p. 383.

[6] Arthur S. Langley, "Correspondence of Sir Edward Harley, K.B. and Rev. Francis Tallents," *C.H.S.T.*, VIII (Oct., 1923), 309.

[7] Gordon, p. 165.

[8] Wedgwood, Vol. II, Pt. 1, p. 167; *C.J.*, IX, 397; *O.R.*, I, 531, n.4, 539, 545, 550, 561.

* FOLEY, THOMAS (d. 1701), of Witley Court, Worcestershire, was the eldest son of the wealthy iron manufacturer of the same name and place. His marriage showed the influence of the

religious atmosphere of the Foley family, for his wife was a daughter of Edward Ashe (d. 1656), a prominent Puritan draper who played an active role in the Long Parliament.[1] It appears that he may have had either the Presbyterian Joshua or John Old-field as a chaplain for a short time, for in 1687 he wrote his son-in-law Robert Harley that "Mr. Olfield [*sic*] is more and more a comfort to us and much improves."[2] Like many well-to-do Presbyterians, Foley had the presentation of an Anglican living, but he was so indifferent to the Church of England's requirements that when he chose a minister in 1685 he again confided in Robert Harley: "I suppose he must be ordained if he is not, before he can have the living." Moreover, the minister, who had not been or-dained, did not qualify in the bishop's judgment, and he had to go to Dr. Thomas Turner in London for ordaining.[3] Foley also had a son placed with a Nonconformist minister for schooling.[4]

He seems to have been considered a Dissenter by James II's agents, and was approved to be a new justice of the peace for Worcestershire.[5] It appears that he was probably more acquies-cent to, than in agreement with James II and his policy. Roger Morrice reports that at a meeting of Worcestershire Catholics to which a few Nonconformist leaders were invited, the Earl of Plymouth (one of James II's privy councilors) questioned whether Foley would be acceptable to the King as a candidate for the House of Commons. Although his brother Philip Foley, who was present, held that "there was no reason to doubt but that he stood well in his Majesty's opinion," it is obvious that there were both political and personal reasons for this defense.[6] Consistent with Plymouth's view is another report that Foley was one of the eminent commoners throughout the country who were opposed to James II,[7] and also Morrice's report that he went to the support of the Prince of Orange in early December, 1688. For these reasons it is understandable that Morrice seems to write of Foley as though he considered him to have the same religious and political point of view as his own.[8]

*M.P.:* 1679–1681, in the three Exclusion Parliaments, and 1689 for Worcestershire.[9]

---

[1] Williams, *Parliamentary History of the County of Worcester*, p. 53; Keeler, pp. 90–91. Morrice noted Elizabeth Ashe Foley's death which occurred on Jan. 6, 1686. Morrice MSS, P, 510.

[2] B.M. Loan 29/136, Portland MSS, Section 1, letter of Nov. [?] 10, 1687. Joshua Oldfield had served as a tutor to a son of Paul Foley, thus it was more likely that it was he of whom Foley wrote rather than his father named John, also a Presbyterian, or his brother likewise named John who was ordained a Presbyterian in 1681, but who later in life took Anglican orders. Gordon, p. 322; Matthews, 373; *Al. Cant.*, III, Pt. I, 278. See also notice of Sir Philip Gell, *infra*, App. II.

[3] B.M. Loan 29/136, Portland MSS, Section 1, letter of Nov. 7, 1685; 29/75, Folder 12 [Letters #3 and #4 to Edward Harley].

[4] *Ibid.*, 29/136, Section 1, letter to Edward Harley, Dec. 17, 1687.

[5] Duckett, I, 241n., 241; II, 255.

[6] Morrice MSS, Q, 176–77 (Morrice refers to Thomas Hickman, the first Earl of Plymouth by his former title of Lord Windsor).

[7] Browning, III, 162.

[8] Morrice, MSS, Q, 343, 347, entries of Dec. 8 and 15, 1688.

[9] Williams, *Parliamentary History of the County of Worcester*, p. 53; *O.R.*, I, 539, 545, 550, 562.


** FOWKE, JOHN (d. April 22, 1662) was a prominent Presbyterian merchant and former Lord Mayor of London (1652–1653) who was one of the four Nonconformist members returned to the House of Commons by London in 1661.[1] Fowke had a long record as an aggressive opponent of royal policy prior to the Civil War, and he was named one of Charles I's judges, but refused to attend the trial.[2] At the time of his election to the Commons in March, 1661, he and the other three London members were considered to be Nonconformists by Englishmen of a wide variety of religious and political viewpoints.[3] In March, 1662, a month before his death, Fowke demonstrated in a Commons debate that he was still a courageous opponent of the Court when he presented the point of view of London Nonconformists concerning the Militia Bill and was thereupon reprehended at the Bar of the House.[4]

*M.P.*: 1661 until his death on April 22, 1662, for London.[5]

[1] Beaven, I, 149, 291; II, 66.          [2] *Ibid.*, II, 181.
[3] *H.M.C.*, *Finch MSS*, I, 120; *C.S.P.D.*, *1660–1661*, pp. 535 *passim.; 1670* (*Addenda 1660–70*), p. 660.
[4] *C.J.*, VIII, 386.          [5] *O.R.*, I, 525; Beaven, I, 277.


* FREDERICK, JOHN (1601–1685) of the Old Jewry, London, was very prominent because of his business and political activities. He sat for Dartmouth in the Restoration Convention

Parliament, and he was elected Lord Mayor of London in November, 1661 before the Royalist tide of feeling had overcome the strength of Puritanism in the City.[1] In March, 1663 he was elected to fill the Commons vacancy left by the death of the Presbyterian merchant John Fowke (q.v.). Frederick may be regarded a probable Presbyterian, for in 1678 a correspondent in Scotland wrote that he could not be persuaded from his "manifold errors, among which I esteem this the greatest, that you will always maintain the Presbyterian principles and justify their practices."[2] In addition there were several indications that he was concerned for Nonconformists as a member of the commission of peace.[3]

*M.P.:* From March 10, 1663 to 1678 for London.[4]

[1] M. W. Helms and J. P. Ferris, MS biography of Frederick prepared for *The History of Parliament, 1660–1690,* ed. B. D. Henning.

[2] *C.S.P.D., 1678,* p. 353.

[3] Helms and Ferris, MS biography.      [4] *O.R.,* I, 525.


** GELL, SIR JOHN (1612–1689), second Bart. of Hopton, Derby.[1] He had two Presbyterian ministers who apparently served as chaplains. In 1669 the Episcopal returns reported that Francis Tallents held a meeting in the house of John Gell "who comes to Church to divine service and sermon constantly and his family; but no other conventicle in the county observes this decorum."[2] Subsequently Benjamin Robinson began his ministry as chaplain to Gell.[3] In addition Gell assisted Presbyterian ministers who were in difficulties or who needed assistance in their education.[4] In 1688 the Lord Lieutenant proposed him both for an M.P. and a justice of the peace, while the Regulators listed him for a deputy lieutenant. In Gell's case the King's agents were right in September in reporting that those whom they consulted considered him as "very right."[5]

*M.P.:* 1689, until about February 9, for Derby County.[6]

[1] W. A. H. Schilling, "The Parliamentary Diary of Sir John Gell, 5 Feb.–21 March 1659" (Unpublished M.A. Thesis, Vanderbilt Univ., 1961), p. v.

[2] Turner, I, 54; II, 603.      [3] Gordon, p. 34.

[4] *Ibid.,* p. 329; Calamy, *Acct.,* II, 197.

[5] Duckett, I, 168, 440; II, 293.

[6] On his way to Westminster, where he arrived Feb. 11, his son Philip heard of his father's death. *H.M.C., 9th Rept., Poll-Gell MSS,* 398; *O.R.,* I, 558.

** (*T*) GELL, SIR PHILIP (1651–1719) [1] third Bart., and son of Sir John (q.v.). Raised in a family which had Presbyterian chaplains, Sir Philip continued this tradition for a time by engaging Joshua Oldfield, presumably before 1682.[2] Gell was listed by the Regulators in February, 1688, as suitable for a justice of the peace, but nothing more has been discovered which would indicate his religious views until 1701 when he had an Anglican chaplain.[3] Although certainly a Presbyterian when he was finally seated with his father-in-law Sir John Fagg (q.v.) for about ten days in January, 1681, he should be considered only a probable Presbyterian in 1689.

*M.P.:* 1679 in the second Exclusion Parliament from Jan. 3, 1680 until the prorogation on Jan. 10, for Steyning, Sussex and from April 18, 1689 for Derbyshire.[4]

[1] Schilling, "Parliamentary Diary of Sir John Gell," p. v.
[2] Gordon, p. 322.
[3] Duckett, II, 294; *H.M.C., 9th Rept. Poll-Gell MSS*, p. 399; *Al. Cant.*, I, 181.
[4] *O.R.*, I, 544, 558; *C.J.*, IX, 697.

GOULD, WILLIAM (1640–1671) of Downes, Crediton, Devon. He was the son of a Parliamentarian and the grandson of a Rumper and Independent. He probably came under his grandfather's care when he was orphaned at the age of four. It would seem that Gould retained some of his family's religious views, and that this would explain his removal from the commission of peace in 1670, just a year after he was appointed. He may be considered a possible Dissenter when he was elected to Parliament some months later on the interest of his cousin John Upton (q.v.).[1]

*M.P.:* From December 22, 1670 to October 24, 1671, for Dartmouth, Devon.[2]

[1] J. P. Ferris, MS biography of Gould prepared for *The History of Parliament, 1660–1690*, ed. B. D. Henning.
[2] *O.R.*, I, 521.

** HAMPDEN, JOHN (1653–1696) of Great Hampden, Bucks, was a grandson of the famous John Hampden and second son of

Richard Hampden (q.v.). He was raised in the religious and political traditions of his family and was tutored by the Presbyterian
Francis Tallents. In November, 1680, Hampden and his wife, the
sister of Paul, Philip, and Thomas Foley (q.v.), had Tallents accompany them to Europe.[1] The other main evidence of Hampden's Presbyterianism is that at some time he had Josiah Hort as
a chaplain.[2] It is well known that he became a kind of religious
"free thinker" during the 1680's, the change starting while he was
in France where he came under the influence of Father Richard
Simon, and perhaps continuing under the influence of friends
who visited him while he was imprisoned from 1684–1686 for
alleged complicity in the Rye House Plot; however, in April,
1688, he confessed that he had adopted views which questioned
the "truth and authority of the Holy Scriptures" and that he
recanted, stating that his arguments to support his "libertine
opinions" had been weak.[3] Consistent with his Presbyterianism he
played a major role in the attempt to obtain comprehension in
the Convention Parliament in the spring of 1689, for he was given
the responsibility "to bring in the Act for Comprehension." [4]

James II made "great offers" to Hampden in an effort to engage
him, but he refused and from December, 1687, worked with the
Dutch secret agent James Johnston, thus becoming one of the
very earliest of all Englishmen to give active support to William's
interest during the year prior to the Revolution.[5] The nation's
critical time from November, 1687 to June, 1688, was also a period of intense emotional experience for Hampden. His wife,
known for her eminent "piety and prudence," died after childbirth on November 5. Johnston started consulting him in December, but he was afflicted with "les vapeurs" and "a thousand ailments" so that on one occasion Johnston found him "in a great
state of confusion: all his insides and his stomach are hard as
marble." Johnston's doctor thought Hampden would get over this
trouble, but late in February the Dutch agent had to request
authority to obtain another person to assist in dealing with Nonconformist leaders who seemed to be, or who were cooperating
with James II.[6] The emotional and religious tension which Hampden had been experiencing was in part resolved in April when he
wrote his so-called religious confession and circulated it to friends
so that any whom he had influenced would also see their errors.
Finally in June his political judgment and views were fully evi-

dent when he advised Johnston that the time had come for William to prepare for an invasion of England.[7]

Hampden's alleged madness and his suicide in 1696 were probably much more the result of poor health than heretofore believed. In 1693 he wrote Rev. Richard Tallents: "I have been reported a Papist, an atheist, a Socinian, a republican, a madman; and yet I would not go over the threshold to disprove any of these false reports. Truth is the daughter of time. . . ."[8]

*M.P.:* 1679–1681, in the three Exclusion Parliaments, and 1689, the first two for Buckinghamshire and the last two for Wendover.[9]

[1] Calamy, *Acct.*, II, 550; Gordon, p. 364; Matthews, p. 474; *C.S.P.D., 1680–1681*, p. 86; Stowe MSS, 747, fol. 16.

[2] Gordon, p. 287.

[3] Sloane MSS, 3299, fols. 185–86. Morrice noted that certain visitors were very often with Hampden and states that "what influence they may have [had] upon him of changing his religion we know not"; however, it appears from Hampden's confession that he was influencing those who visited as much if not more than they were him. Morrice MSS, P, 509, shorthand entry of Jan. 9, 1686.

[4] B.M. Loan 29/140, [Letter #96], Sir Edward to Robert Harley, April 2, 1689.

[5] U. of Nott., Portland MSS, PwA 2124b, Jan. 4, 1688.

[6] Morrice MSS, Q, 196; U. of Nott., Portland MSS, PwA 2124b and 2148b, Jan. 4, and Feb. 27, 1688.

[7] See *supra*, pp. 213–14.

[8] Stowe MSS, 747, fol. 16.

[9] *O.R.*, I, 534, 540, 546, 557. Hampden appears to have returned to England to sit in the Oxford Parliament of 1681; at least he did not remain in France from 1680–1682, for he was granted a second pass to travel to the Continent in Sept., 1681. *C.S.P.D., 1680–1681*, p. 685.

** HAMPDEN, RICHARD (1631–1695), of Great Hampden, Buckinghamshire, was the eldest son of the famous John Hampden (d. 1643). As Richard Baxter wrote, he was "the true heir of his famous father's sincerity, piety and devotedness to God";[1] and as his career in the House of Commons indicates, he was also the heir of his father's political principles. He is known to have had three Presbyterian chaplains between 1662 and his death. George Swinnock was in his service after his ejection in 1662 and apparently until 1672. During the last six or seven years that Swinnock was with Hampden, the ejected minister John Nott also became one of Hampden's chaplains and served him the longest of all, from 1665 or 1666 until 1689. Thereafter a Mr. Barton held this position with Hampden.[2] Hampden's religious Nonconformity is also evident in a Commons debate of April 8, 1668, on uniting the King's Protestant subjects, for he not only supported the efforts to obtain comprehension but also identified himself with the Nonconformists.[3] Consistent with this evidence, he was reported in attendance at Dr. Manton's meeting, along with Lord Wharton, on March 20, 1670.[4]

Additional evidence concerning his friendships with Baxter and with other Nonconformists is also significant. On two occasions Hampden came to Baxter's assistance, once during the plague in 1665 when he gave him shelter at his home in Buckinghamshire, and again in 1675 when he contributed £8 to the church being built for Baxter in London.[5] It is no wonder that Baxter called Hampden his "dearly beloved and honored friend," and that in 1669 he dedicated a sermon to Hampden and his wife.[6] The Hampdens were also on very friendly terms with Dr. Owen and his wife and with the other major Presbyterian political leaders—John Swynfen, Lord Wharton, and the Earl of Anglesey.[7]

In the Lord Lieutenant's 1687 report to James II, Hampden was included in a list of persons "supposed to be Dissenters," and he was supported as a candidate for deputy lieutenant. However, he opposed James II's policies, for he did not respond to the King's "great offers" to him in January, 1688, and he was listed among the eminent commoners throughout the country who were opposed to James.[8] He became the major Presbyterian political leader in the Convention Parliament of 1689.

Hampden married Letitia Paget, the second daughter of William, 6th Lord Paget, and was therefore the brother-in-law of Sir Henry Ashurst and Philip Foley, two other Presbyterian politicians of the period.

*M.P.:* 1661–1678, and March and October, 1679, in the first two Exclusion Parliaments for Wendover, Buckinghamshire; 1681, in the third Exclusion Parliament for Buckinghamshire; and 1685 and 1689 for Wendover.[9]

[1] Baxter, Pt. I, Sec. 2, p. 448.

[2] Calamy, *Acct.*, II, 104, 628; Gordon, pp. 1, 10, 320; Matthews, p. 473; Add. MSS, 29,910, fols. 84–85.

[3] Grey, I, 130.

[4] Add. MSS, 36,916, Aston News Letters, March 26, 1670.

[5] Baxter, Pt. I, Sec. 2, p. 448; Pt. II, pp. 171–72. The ejected minister George Crosse also stayed with Hampden during part of the plague. Calamy, *Acct.*, II, 631.

⁶ In the "Epistle Dedicatory" to the sermon "Life of Faith" Baxter also wrote that he made this dedication in order "to tell the present and future ages, how much I love and honor your piety, sobriety, integrity and moderation, in an age when such virtues grow into contempt . . ." Richard Baxter, *The Practical Works,* ed. Rev. William Orme (23 vols.; 1830), XII, iii.

⁷ Add. MSS., 18,730, fols. 85–86; 29,910, fols. 50–51, 84–85, 137, 226; 30,013, fols. 58–59, 260, 290; W.S.L. MSS., 254, Swynfen Ltrs., No. 28.

⁸ Duckett, II, 149, 154; U. of Nott., Portland MSS, PwA 2124b ff.; Browning, III, 158.

⁹ *O.R.,* I, 519, 534, 540, 546, 557; George, *R.H.S.T.,* 4th Ser., XIX, 186.

\*\* **HARCOURT, SIR PHILIP** (d. 1688), of Stanton Harcourt, Oxford was the son of Sir Simon Harcourt (d. 1642) and Anne, daughter of William, the 5th Lord Paget. Sir Philip's Presbyterianism is clearly indicated by the chaplains whom he had. Henry Cornish appears to have served him in the 1660's and probably in the early 1670's, for in 1672 when Cornish was licensed as a Presbyterian he was "dwelling at Stanton Harcourt in Oxon." ¹ Serving Harcourt as chaplain from 1675 until 1680 or later was Thomas Clark, whose daughter secretly married Simon Harcourt, Sir Philip's only son.² Other Nonconformist ministers, such as Thomas Gilbert, wrote of going to Stanton Harcourt for visits with Sir Philip and his chaplains.³ Both his religious and political outlook reflected the Puritan and parliamentarian traditions of his father, and more especially of his mother and his stepfather, Sir William Waller (the parliamentary general) who was also Sir Philip's father-in-law since he married his step-sister Anne Waller. An account of the members of the House of Commons which Sir Richard Wiseman drew up for Danby in 1676 described Harcourt along with Sir Anthony Irby as "gentlemen I have little hopes of." ⁴ In a similar vein Anthony Wood wrote that Harcourt was "a gentleman but a Presbyterian." ⁵

*M.P.:* October 26, 1666 to 1678, for Boston, Lincolnshire; and 1681, for Oxfordshire.⁶

¹ Calamy, *Acct.,* II, 67; Gordon, p. 242; Turner, III, 770–71.

² Gordon, p. 238; Matthews, p. 120.

³ Rawl. Ltrs., H53, fol. 13.  ⁴ Browning, III, 110.

⁵ *The Life and Times of Anthony Wood, Antiquary, of Oxford, 1632–1695, Described by Himself,* ed. Andrew Clark (5 vols.; Oxford, 1891–1900), II, 519; see also pp. 525–26.

⁶ *O.R.,* I, 524, 549.

** HARLEY, SIR EDWARD (1624–1700) was of a well-known Herefordshire Puritan family. He was secluded at Pride's Purge. In the last months of the Long Parliament's existence, February and March, 1660, he took a leading part in the efforts of the majority in the House of Commons to establish Presbyterianism, and at the Restoration he was regarded by Presbyterian ministers of Hereford Cathedral as their "chief patron."[1] Harley's Presbyterianism brought reports to Clarendon that he was "not well affected, neither to the Church nor State, and that he countenanced factious persons."[2] Informed of these reports by the Bishop of Hereford, Harley wrote a letter to Clarendon in December, 1665, in which he professed his doctrinal orthodoxy in general terms and stated that in an endeavor to clear himself of "all suspicion of schism" he had always been a "constant and reverend" attender of Church services.[3] The tone of the letter makes it evident that Harley was very much concerned about the effect these reports might have upon his public life,[4] and therefore his statements concerning his religious beliefs and practices at this juncture need to considered in the light of other evidence. In 1681 when discussing the requirements that ministers had to satisfy in order to become Anglican clergymen, Harley appears to have revealed his own views, for he was strongly in favor of the stipulations which existed prior to the Act of Uniformity when "the only condition of Communion enjoined by law was subscription and assent, not to a uniformity in rites and ceremonies, but to all the articles of religion, which only concern the confession of the true Christian faith, and the doctrine of the Sacraments."[5]

Such views and the practice of attending Anglican services and receiving the Sacrament were in consonance with those of Harley's close friend Richard Baxter. Most important, during the coming years Harley sometimes went to the meetings conducted by Baxter and other ejected ministers in London, and he was thus one of the few Presbyterian political leaders known to attend public Nonconformist services. Although he maintained a close relationship with various Presbyterian ministers, it was Baxter who most influenced the Harley family. The correspondence between Harley and his children contain frequent references to occasions when they had been with Baxter or attended his services.[6] Twice in 1680, for example, Harley wrote to his son Robert (q.v.), telling him that when he heard Mr. Baxter preach on Sundays he should also see him when he could; and again at the end of the year he reminded Robert of some religious advice given to him by the "good Mr. Baxter (who still inquires after you with great affection)." [7] The approval with which Harley and his children regarded the religious position of Baxter and others of similar views is also reflected in a letter of Harley's son Edward, who wrote to his father in 1688 that he had been to Mr. Daniel Burgess's Presbyterian meeting house, and since Baxter and Burgess both believed the Sabbath was not complete without the Sacrament, he "was put upon the thought of more fully partaking of that ordinance and that it ought to be received every Lord's Day." [8] Through his daughter Abigail, who also made calls upon Baxter, the latter sent a request to have a copy of the catalogue of ejected ministers that Harley had compiled and that was undoubtedly used by Baxter in compiling his own authoritative catalogue, later worked upon and revised by Calamy.[9] In addition to his friendship with Baxter, Harley was also a friend of such Nonconformist ministers as Francis Tallents, Ralph Strettell, Joshue Barnett, Richard Sadler and others, as is evidenced by his correspondence with them or the help which he gave them.[10]

As was often the case with men of moderate Nonconformist views, Harley did not confine his ministerial friendships to Nonconformists. Moderate Anglican clergymen were also appealing to him, and it is therefore not surprising to find that the letters written to him by Bishop Burnet indicate that the two were congenial friends.[11] It is significant that this appears to be the only relationship of the sort that he is known to have had with an Anglican clergyman, and that others of the Church considered "Harley to be one of those that do not love the Church," and that he was "not for the Church." [12] Although evidence already presented would explain this opinion, it is more understandable when consideration is given to Harley's opposition to the repressive legislation against Dissenters and his support of bills to relieve them.[13] He also appears to have actively sought the intervention of government officials in cases of Dissenters who were facing legal action.[14] Finally, he was one of the original trustees of Lord Wharton's Bible Trust.[15]

Such actions and views as have been described explain why Calamy described Harley as "that ornament, and support of religion." [16]

*M.P.*: 1661–1678, and March, 1679, for Radnor Borough; October 1679, 1681, and 1689, for Herefordshire.[17]

---

[1] *C.J.*, VIII, 858, 862; *H.M.C.*, *Portland MSS*, III, 219; "Welbeck, Abbey MSS," *C.H.S.T.*, XIV (May, 1944), 219–20.

[2] *Letters of the Lady Brilliana Harley, Wife of Sir Robert Harley*, ed. T. Lewis (Camden Soc. Pub.), No. 58; (1854), p. 240.

[3] *Ibid.*, p. 241.

[4] Clarendon, recognizing Harley's excessive concern, wrote in answer: "I was in some amazement when I read your letter. You will give better reason to be ill thought of, than you have yet done, if you are much troubled with the license men take of talking, of whom they please, and what they please." This answer was reassuring, but it was not until 1668 that the King ordered that Harley be given command of the regiment of foot in Herefordshire even though "there was *some* or *one* . . . that were against it" because he was a Presbyterian. *Ibid.*, p. 243; *H.M.C.*, *Portland MSS*, III, 306.

[5] [Harley], *Humble Essay*, pp. 24–25.

[6] Add. MSS, 34,515, fol. 119. In 1675 Harley contributed £10 to the fund for the church being built for Baxter. Baxter, III, 161–62.

[7] B.M. Loan 29/140, Portland MSS [Letters #3 and #18]; "Welbeck Abbey MSS," *C.H.S.T.*, XIV, 230.

[8] *H.M.C.*, *Portland MSS*, III, 407; B.M. Loan 29/140, Portland MSS [Letters #2, #8, #97]; Matthews, p. 88.

[9] Letter of Abigail to her father, Sept. 14, 1689, *H.M.C.*, *Portland MSS*, III, 440; B.M. Loan 29/87, Portland MSS, Misc. #59.

[10] Arthur S. Langley, "Correspondence of Sir Edward Harley K.B., and Rev. Francis Tallents," *C.H.S.T.*, VIII, 267–77, 306–17; for the correspondence of Strettell with Harley see, "Welbeck Abbey MSS," *ibid.*, XIV, 221–32; for his correspondence or relations with other ministers see *H.M.C.*, *Portland MSS*, III, 310, 313, 348, 349; Matthews, p. 30.

[11] Harley had known Burnet as early as 1662, but the letters now known to exist are the eleven written by Burnet to Harley between 1683 and 1685; *H.M.C.*, *Bath MSS*, I, 44–50.

[12] *C.S.P.D.*, *1675–1676*, pp. 460–61; *H.M.C.*, *Portland MSS*, III, 428.

[13] Add. MSS, 34,515, fol. 119; *H.M.C.*, *Portland MSS*, III, 313, 334–36; Baxter, App. IX.

[14] Nehemiah Lyde states that Harley even attended the King concerning the prosecution of some Herefordshire Dissenters, including his father Richard Lyde; Turner, III, 547–48.

[15] Dale, *Good Lord Wharton*, p. 71.

[16] Calamy, *Acct.*, II, 354. See also other Nonconformist opinions of the same sort; *ibid.*, pp. 352–53; *The Nonconformist Register of Baptisms, Marriages, and*

\* HARLEY, ROBERT (1661–1724), son of Sir Edward Harley (q.v.). As has long been known, the future first Earl of Oxford and Lord Treasurer of Queen Anne's reign was by birth and education a Presbyterian, and it is very probable he continued to hold these views while sitting in the Convention Parliament of 1689. It is known that he attended the services of Richard Baxter in 1680,[1] but the royalist reaction after 1681 brought an end to such meetings. From 1687–1689 he was very much a part of the group of Presbyterian political leaders to which his father and father-in-law, Thomas Foley, belonged. At least twice in 1687 he called on John Swynfen and relayed to his father that leader's conviction that Churchmen were not to be trusted, and other related information; and in July, 1688, he visited Richard Baxter and discussed issues critical to the Dissenters. Most revealing, however, was Hugh Boscawen's quickness in accepting young Harley as a candidate to fill the place of his brother Charles Boscawen, M.P. for Tregony, who died in March, 1689, just as it first became obvious that the Tory Churchmen were in sufficient control to jeopardize seriously the prospects of obtaining comprehension and other Presbyterian aims.[2] Another indication of young Harley's religious position is found in a letter from Sir Edward during a parliamentary crisis in August, 1689, which involved the interests of the "Reformed Churches."[3] In addition Dissenters in legal difficulty appealed to young Harley during this parliament.[4]

*M.P.:* From April 6, 1689 for Tregony, Cornwall.[5]

    [1] Notice of Sir Edward Harley, n.7, *supra.*
    [2] *H.M.C., Portland MSS,* III, 415, 435, 436; B.M. Loan 29/136, Portland MSS, Thomas Foley to Robert Harley, April 13, 1689.
    [3] *Ibid.,* 29/140, [Letter #106].
    [4] "Welbeck Abbey MSS," *C.H.S.T.,* XIV, 225.     [5] *O.R.,* I, 558.

\*\* HARTOPP, SIR JOHN (1636–1722), of Freeby, Leicestershire, and Stoke Newington, Middlesex, the latter home being inherited from his father-in-law, the famous Charles Fleetwood. Hartopp and his wife began attending the services of William Jenkyn in February, 1661.[1] They also became members of Dr. John Owen's church, being listed as such at the time of its union with that of Joseph Caryll in June, 1673, as well as nearly thirty years later when Isaac Watts was chosen minister in January, 1702.[2] Hartopp's Nonconformity did not prevent his serving as high sheriff of Hertfordshire,[3] and it probably explains the fact that he was recommended and served as a new justice of the peace for the county in 1688. In spite of this, however, there is evidence that he did not actually favor James II's policies, for he gave negative replies to the questions on repeal of the test and penal laws and his name is among those contained in the list of eminent commoners opposed to James II.[4]

*M.P.:* April 24, 1679–1681 in the three Exclusion Parliaments, for Leicestershire.[5]

[1] Entry in book of sermon notes kept by Hartopp and his wife. Prior to this they had attended Benjamin Cox' meeting. "Benjamin Cox," *B.H.S.T.*, VI (1918), 56.

[2] T. G. Crippen "Dr. Watts' Church-Book," *C.H.S.T.*, I (April, 1901), 26–27.

[3] *C.S.P.D., 1670*, p. 544.      [4] Duckett, II, 105, 195; Browning, III, 160.

[5] *O.R.*, I, 536, 542, 548.

\*\* HARVEY, MICHAEL (c. 1635–1712) was of Clifton, Dorset.[1] In the Episcopal Returns of 1669 concerning Nonconformists, Harvey was reported to have a conventicle of sixty or eighty at his house, and in addition he was reported to be a justice of the peace.[2] When he was standing for re-election at Weymouth in February, 1679, Samuel Hieron described him to Lord Wharton as "a fanatic," [3] which would imply that he was more sectarian than the Presbyterian Hieron. The reports to James II in 1687 stated that he "has been accounted a Dissenter," that in an election he would be "set up by the Dissenters who are numerous," and in addition that he was considered qualified to serve as a deputy lieutenant.[4] Also significant was the fact that in August, 1680, when Monmouth made his trip into Western England, he dined at Harvey's; [5] and perhaps not unrelated was the report recorded by Roger Morrice in April, 1684, that Harvey was one of "several persons of great quality presented by the grand jury as disaffected to the government," and that it was said he refused to put up security for good behavior and therefore would probably be committed to prison.[6]

*M.P.:* 1679–1681, in the three Exclusion Parliaments, and 1689 for Weymouth, Dorset.[7]

[1] John Hutchins, *The History and Antiquities of the County of Dorset* (4 vols.; 3rd ed.; Westminster, 1861–1870), IV, 123, 430n.

[2] Turner, I, 124; II, 123, 1134.

[3] Rawl. Ltrs., H 51, fol. 89.

[4] Duckett, II, 38–39, 221, 242, 264.

[5] "An Historical Account of . . . Monmouth," in Smeeton, *Historical and Biographical Tracts*, II, 32.

[6] Morrice MSS, P, 434.

[7] *O.R.*, I, 535, 541, 547, 559. In Feb., 1667, Harvey was returned for Weymouth on a double return, but Sir John Coventry was seated by the House. *C.J.*, VIII, 691–92; IX, 3, 23.

\*\* HENLEY (or HENLY), HENRY (c. 1605–1697), of Colway, near Lyme Regis, Dorset, was apparently the son of Henry Henley of Leigh and Colway. The younger Henley was a colonel in the Parliamentary Army and the sheriff of Dorset in 1648.[1] His religious position first became evident when he was slow to comply with the order of the House of Commons of May, 1661, requiring the members to receive the Sacrament together at St. Margaret's Church.[2] According to Calamy, John Hodder usually preached at Mr. Henley's at Colway House, after his ejection, and it is probable that it was this "Henry Henly Esq." who was co-owner of a house in nearby Marchwood, Dorset, for which a license as a Presbyterian meeting place was sought in 1672.[3] However, there is no doubt that it was this "Mr. Henly a parliament man" who contributed £5 to the fund for Richard Baxter's new church in 1675,[4] and that he was also the Mr. Henly, then in Parliament, who had some connections with the Presbyterian minister Samuel Hieron.[5] Henley's name also appeared in three other places of religious and political import during this period. He opposed the Conventicle Bill and on December 7, 1669, he and Andrew Marvell were tellers for those in the House of Commons who favored seating Sir Francis Rolle, a possible Dissenter, in a disputed election.[6] Secondly, it was alleged that he sent £300 to the Duke of Monmouth in 1685.[7] Finally, it was probably he rather than his son who was among those listed by James II's agents as a suitable justice of the peace for Dorset.[8]

*M.P.:* 1661–1678, and 1679–1681, in the three Exclusion Parliaments, for Lyme Regis, Dorset.[9]

[1] Pink MSS, 303/282; Hutchins, III, 742.　　[2] *C.J.,* VIII, 289.

[3] Calamy, *Cont.,* I, 420; Turner, II, 1136. The application stated that "John Goddard" and others were to preach there; this could have been a mistake for John Hodder.

[4] Baxter, Pt. III, p. 172.　　　　　　[5] Rawl. Ltrs., H 51, fol. 83.

[6] *C.J.,* IX, 90, 119.

[7] Lansdowne MSS, 1152 fol. [240] Testimony of John Madder, July 20, 1685.

[8] Henry Henley, III sat in the House apparently for the first time in 1695, while it was his father who was still M.P. for Lyme Regis in 1689–1690. *O.R.,* I, 565, 573; Duckett, II, 263.

[9] *O.R.,* I, 522, 535, 541, 547.

\* HERLE (or HEARLE), EDWARD (c. 1617–1695), of Prideaux, in Luxulyan Cornwall, was a leading gentleman of the County who supported Parliament in the Civil Wars, and had risen to the rank of colonel by 1646. He sat in the Parliament of 1659 and the Convention Parliament of 1660. He was a justice of the peace at that time, but he was removed from the commission and not replaced on it in 1662, an action which could have been the result of both religious and political considerations.[1] Somewhat more positive evidence concerning his religious position appeared in 1683, for he was listed among the Roman Catholics and Dissenters of the County formerly out of position and recommended by the Regulators for appointment as deputy lieutenants.[2] He should be considered a probable Dissenter when he sat in the Convention Parliament of 1689.

*M.P.:* 1689 for Grampound, Cornwall.[3]

[1] Helms, "Convention Parliament of 1660," p. 730.

[2] Duckett, I, 371, 379.　　　　　　[3] *O.R.,* I, 438.

\*\* HEWLEY, SIR JOHN (1619–1697) was of York. He and his wife Lady Sarah Hewley were well-known Nonconformists. Sir John had the Congregationalist Ralph Ward as his chaplain from 1662 to 1666, and Timothy Hodgson became his chaplain in 1671 and remained with the Hewley's the greater part of his life.[1] In addition the Presbyterian Oliver Heywood was a frequent visitor and an intimate friend of the Hewleys. He also conducted services for the family on his visits, recording in his diary on September 18, 1679, for example: "I preached in Sir John Hewley's chamber, God helped in duties with the family, none besides."[2] Hewley was regarded by his fellow Yorkshireman Sir John Reresby as one of the factious party of York who were not Churchmen, and the evidence indicated that in regard to Hewley's religious opinion, Reresby was correct.[3]

*M.P.:* 1679–1681, in the three Exclusion Parliaments, for York City.[4]

[1] Calamy, *Acct.*, II, 507; Hunter, p. 218; Heywood, I, 278.

[2] Heywood, I, 298; II, 44, 104; IV, 92; Hunter, pp. 331 *passim*.

[3] Reresby, pp. 579–80.

[4] *O.R.*, I, 539, 545, 550. Hewley also stood for election at York in Nov., 1673. He failed to be elected and then was unsuccessful in his petition to be seated. *C.S.P.D., 1675–1676*, p. 122; Marvell, II, 313–18.

** HOBART, SIR HENRY (c. 1658–1698), of Blickling Hall, Norfolk, he came from a family with a Presbyterian and Puritan tradition and had the same Presbyterian chaplain, Dr. John Collins, who served his grandfather.[1] Both Hobart and his chaplain were active in Norwich, and Norfolk County politics. In April, 1688, the King's agents reported that Hobart was "right by inclination" and that Dr. Collins had "engaged for him," and Sir Henry was also on the Regulators' list of approved candidates for the commission of peace.[2] However, he was a strenuous supporter of the Revolution. He married Sir John Maynard's granddaughter.[3]

*M.P.:* 1689 for Norfolk.[4]

[1] Duckett, I, 313; Matthews, p. 128 (under Collinges).

[2] *C.S.P.D., 1682*, p. 54; Duckett, I, 313–14; II, 279.

[3] G.E.C., *Bart.*, I, 13.                    [4] *O.R.*, I, 560.

** HOGHTON, SIR CHARLES (1651–1710), of Hoghton Tower, Lancaster, was the son of the Presbyterian Sir Richard

Hoghton (d. 1678). Sir Richard had the Presbyterian Josiah Holdsworth as his chaplain, and in addition there were several other Nonconformists who conducted services for the family during the years that Charles was a boy and young man.[1] In 1664 the Presbyterian Adam Martindale became the tutor to the Hoghton children.[2] These early influences set the pattern for Sir Charles' later religious friendships and views. He developed close connections of his own with notable Nonconformist ministers. For example, John Howe preached the funeral sermon for Sir Charles's eldest son.[3] Two more of his Nonconformist friends were Thomas Jolly and Henry Newcome, both of whom visited Hoghton Towers and conducted services. On one occasion Jolly returned thanks with Sir Charles for Lady Hoghton's safe delivery, and on another he commended "that worthy patriot to the Lord" before he went to London to sit in Parliament.[4] On one occasion Newcome appears to have stayed at Hoghton Towers for a month, and as he wrote on another visit in 1691, he was "in much content and freedom with our old friend Sir Charles . . ."[5] The most conclusive evidence of Sir Charles's Nonconformity, however, is that in 1703 Hoghton Tower was certified as a Nonconformist place of worship in accordance with the provisions of the Toleration Act of 1689.[6]

It is understandable that Sir Charles had the support of Dissenters in elections and that he had friendships and connections with other Nonconformist politicians. Notable among these was Henry Ashurst, whom he described as his friend in a letter he wrote to Edward Moore, an important citizen of Liverpool, in an endeavor to gain support for Ashurst when the latter was standing for burgess in the Liverpool election of October, 1670.[7]

As in a good number of other instances in which Presbyterians were of the gentry or aristocracy, Hoghton was the patron of an Anglican Church, in this case the one of Preston in Lancashire. His presentation in 1682 of Thomas Birch to be vicar of this Church is revealing. Thomas Birch was the brother of Colonel John Birch, the famous parliamentary debater who had been a Presbyterian, and it appears that he as well as the Colonel was of a Puritan disposition,[8] for among other complaints he was reported not to christen according to the custom and tradition of the Church. Oliver Heywood considered Hoghton to be a "favorer of good things, though no great zealot," [9] and this is an apt description of Hoghton's moderate Presbyterianism.

*M.P.*: 1679–1681, in the last two Exclusion Parliaments, and in 1689 for Lancashire.[10]

[1] Calamy, *Acct.*, II, 822; Hunter, p. 106n.     [2] Martindale, p. 177.

[3] "A Discourse Concerning the Redeemer's Dominion over the Invisible World, and the Entrance thereinto by Death," John Howe; *The Whole Works* (7 vols.; 1810), I, 1–75.

[4] Jolly, pp. 89, 97. In addition Hoghton corresponded with Thomas Heywood. Hunter, p. 106n.

[5] Newcome, *Autobiog.*, [II], 242, 273.

[6] Somerset House, Return made by the Clerk of the Peace of the County Palatine of Lancaster . . . of all Places of Public Religious Worship which have been certified . . . from the year 1688 . . . No. 285.

[7] Jolly, p. 92; *H.M.C., Westmorland MSS*, p. 117.

[8] *C.S.P.D., 1683, July–Sept.*, pp. 187, 234; Booker, *History of the . . . Chapel of Birch*, p. 120 (facing genealogical table). The Hoghton heirs receive the position of Lay Rector which after 1607 gave them the right of appointing the vicars as well as the responsibility for the upkeep of the Chancel. A reference to Charles Hoghton as the "patron and parson" of the Church in a deed of 1683 probably refers to his position as the Lay Rector. I am grateful to J. Mary Wahlstrand Chivers for this information and opinion. See also J. M. Wahlstrand, "The Elections to Parliament in the County of Lancashire, 1685–1714" (Unpublished M.S. Thesis, Univ. of Manchester, 1956), pp. 173, 244.

[9] *C.S.P.D., 1683, July–Sept.*, p. 187.

[10] *O.R.*, I, 542, 548, 559; Bean, p. 180, 208.

** INGOLDSBY, SIR RICHARD (d. 1685) was the well-known regicide of Lenthenborough, Buckinghamshire. However, having worked for the Restoration of Charles II, Ingoldsby was able to win a pardon and hold his lands.[1] It appears that he retained his former religious views for some years after the Restoration. He had the Nonconformist John Wilson as his chaplain for an unknown period after this minister had served Sir Thomas Lee following his ejection. Calamy states that Wilson subsequently "betook himself to the practice of physic," and presumably he had done this by 1672, for he did not take out a license to preach under the Declaration of Indulgence.[2] During the 1660's Ingoldsby had the reputation of being a Presbyterian.[3] In 1680 he lost his position as deputy lieutenant of Buckinghamshire at the King's instigation, and in 1685 he was seized at the time of the Monmouth Rebellion for "dangerous and seditious practices." [4]

However, these actions were undoubtedly more the result of his past reputation than his more recent actions. The lack of evidence of a continuing Presbyterianism during the 1670's, and the fact that in September, 1685, he was buried in the Parish Church at Hartwell,[5] may indicate some gravitation back to the Established Church; however, many known Presbyterians were buried among their ancestors in Parish Church grounds. Any change in his religious practice could have occurred during the years of reaction following the Oxford Parliament of 1681, when many Presbyterians became more regular communicants. It is of some importance that two of the trustees Ingoldsby selected were the Presbyterians Sir Philip Harcourt and Sir Henry Hobart.[6] Nevertheless, from about 1672 to 1681, Ingoldsby should be considered no more than a probable Presbyterian.

*M.P.:* 1661–1678, and 1679–1681, in the three Exclusion Parliaments, for Aylesbury, Buckinghamshire.[7]

[1] Carte, *Ormonde Letters,* II, 332–34; *C.S.P.D., 1663–1664,* pp. 98, 108, 117.
[2] Calamy, *Acct.,* II, 109.　　　　　　　　[3] Pepys, VI, 364.
[4] *C.S.P.D., 1679–1680,* pp. 438–39; Luttrell, *Brief Relations,* I, 342.
[5] George Lipscombe, *The History and Antiquities of the County of Buckingham* (4 vols.; 1847), II, 320.
[6] PCC, 2 Cann, fol. 102.　　　　　　　　[7] *O.R.,* I, 519, 534, 540, 546.


** IRBY, SIR ANTHONY (1605–1682), of Quaplode and Boston, Lincolnshire, was a prominent and wealthy leader in his county during the Civil Wars and Interregnum, serving in the Short Parliament and again in the Long Parliament until he was secluded in 1648, as well as again in 1656 and 1659.[1] After the Restoration he had three Presbyterian chaplains, Thomas Cawton from 1662 to 1665, Thomas Clark from 1665 to 1675, and William Bruce after 1675.[2] Although he was perforce an occasional conformist, there is some indication that he may have taken this step with reluctance. Just after the House order was passed in May, 1661, that members were to go together to receive the Sacrament at St. Margaret's Church on a specific Sunday, Irby obtained leave to go into the country for "special occasions requiring his speedy repair in the country," and this may have been a step taken in order to delay compliance or in order to obtain a certificate of having received the Sacrament in a Church still served by a Presbyterian or Puritan minister.³ In 1676 Sir Richard Wiseman was correct when in a report on the members of the House made to Danby he linked Irby with Sir Philip Harcourt, his Presbyterian colleague from Lincolnshire, stating that they were "two gentlemen I have little hopes of." ⁴

*M.P.:* 1661–1678, and 1679–1681, in the three Exclusion Parliaments, for Boston, Lincolnshire.⁵

¹ *LeNeve's Pedigrees of the Knights Made by King Charles II, King James II, King William III and . . . Queen Anne,* ed. George W. Marshall (Harleian Soc. Pub., vol. VIII; 1873), p. 488; Keeler, pp. 230–31.
² Calamy, *Acct.,* II, 73, 346; *Cont.,* I, 76; Matthews, p. 82.
³ *C.J.,* VIII, 254.                                                ⁴ Browning, III, 110.
⁵ *O.R.,* I, 524, 536, 542, 548; *C.J.,* VIII, 484.


\*\* JONES, JOHN (fl. 1656–1678), sometimes termed Captain Jones, was one of the four Presbyterian or Congregationalist members elected to serve of London in 1661, after having sat for the City in 1656 and 1659.¹ Although the evidence that he was of one of these two persuasions rests primarily upon letters written by Londoners and intercepted by the government at the time, it should be remembered that many of these were written by Nonconformists.² An additional indication of his religious position is found in his opposition to the Second Conventicle Act.³ Although he was still speaking in the debates of the early and middle 1670's, he was primarily concerned with economic grievances and is not reported as speaking again on the religious issues that concerned Nonconformists during these years.⁴ This could indicate some shift in his religious position, but since he spoke on such matters only once so far as known, and since there is no other indication that he changed, such a shift should be considered only a possibility.

*M.P.:* 1661–1678, for London.⁵

¹ Beaven, I, 277.
² *C.S.P.D., 1660–1661,* pp. 535–43; *1670 (Addenda 1660–1670),* p. 660; *H.M.C., Finch MSS,* I, 120.
³ Milward, p. 225. The speeches on the Conventicle Bill, City affairs, and trade reported by Milward as given on February 20, March 6, and 13, 1668, should be ascribed to John Jones of London and not Thomas Jones of Shrewsbury, later Chief Justice of the Common Pleas. The latter was known as a trimmer on religion,

while Jones of London was a Presbyterian who is known to have given other speeches concerning London affairs and trade, among other matters. See Grey, I, 216, 415; II, 234; Dering, pp. 45, 49, 83, 93; Milward, pp. 192, 210.

⁴ See speech in debate on grievances, Jan. 12, 1674, Grey, II, 234.

⁵ *O.R.*, I, 525.

** KEATE, SIR JONATHAN (c. 1633–1700) a London merchant, was of the Hoo, Hertfordshire, and was of sufficient prominence in this county to serve as sheriff in 1665–1666.¹ He is known to have had two chaplains. The ejected Presbyterian minister John Peachy served him at an unknown period, while Joseph Hussey preached for him constantly from 1683, if not earlier, until May, 1688.² In 1686 Roger Morrice implied that Sir Jonathan had non-Anglican affections and interests in the confidence of a shorthand passage, and it should be added that Morrice may have been acquainted with Keate.³ His will, drawn in 1698, provided that his daughter be given Baxter's, *Christian Directory,* and Foxe's, *Book of Martyrs.*⁴

*M.P.:* October, 1679, in the second Exclusion Parliament, for Hertfordshire.⁵

¹ G.E.C., *Bart.*, III, 36.

² Matthews, p. 384; Gordon, p. 289; Walter Wilson, *History and Antiquities of Dissenting Churches and Meeting Houses in London, Westminster, and Southward, Including the Lives of their Ministers* (4 vols.; 1808–[1814]), IV, 411.

³ Morrice MSS, P, 579.    ⁴ P.C.C., 154 Noel.    ⁵ *O.R.*, I, 542.

** LANGHAM, SIR JAMES (c. 1620–1699), of Cottesbrooke Park, Northamptonshire, was the son of Sir John Langham (d. 1671), who was also a Nonconformist political figure.¹ Sir James was prominent in county politics, sitting as knight of the shire in 1656, and for Northampton Borough in 1659, as well as serving as high sheriff in 1664–1665 and 1671–1672.² He attended Richard Baxter's church in 1676 and contributed £20 to the fund for its construction in 1675 upon the first solicitation.³

*M.P.:* May 22 to June 13, 1661; and February 21 to April 26, 1662, for Northampton Borough.⁴

¹ Sir John, who had Nonconformist chaplains after 1662, had been prominent in London and Southwark politics, sitting in the House of Commons for London

in 1654 and Southwark in 1660, but he was defeated there in 1661. He petitioned against the returns made, and it appears that he was not seated; the House ruled that the demand for a poll that had been made for Langham at the election, had been made too late and that his opponents were duly elected. *C.J.*, VIII, 280; *A General Index to the Eighth, Ninth, Tenth, and Eleventh Volumes of the Journals of the House of Commons*, compiled by Roger Flexman (1780), p. 342; *O.R.*, I, 500, 516; Beaven, I, 301; II, 66; G.E.C., *Bart.*, III, 31; Calamy, *Acct.*, II, 496; Matthews, p. 346.

² *O.R.*, I, 509; G.E.C., *Bart.*, III, 30–31; *C.S.P.D.*, *1664–1665*, p. 105; *1671–1672*, p. 49.

³ *H.M.C., Leeds MSS*, p. 15; Baxter, Pt. III, pp. 171–72.

⁴ There was a double return in April, 1661, with Langham being on each. He was seated on May 22 pending the outcome of the disputed election, and on June 13 the whole election was voided. He was not returned in the following election, but the next year he was successful in a by-election, and he began taking an active part in the work of the House. Two months later on April 2 his election was voided as a result of a petition presented on behalf of Sir William Dudley, which the House voted to accept even though it was not presented within the time stipulated by the rule of House. *C.J.*, VIII, 257, 269–70, 376, 379, 386, 394.


\* (*T*) LEE, SIR THOMAS (c. 1635–1691), of Hartwell, Buckinghamshire, was an articulate leader of opposition forces in the House of Commons' debates during the parliaments of Charles II and from 1688 until 1691. He had John Wilson as a chaplain after his ejection and before Wilson took the same position with Sir Richard Ingoldsby, who was Lee's step-father as well as his father-in-law.¹ In the debates of March and April, 1668, on the King's speech for uniting his Protestant subjects Lee supported the efforts to remove the oaths required by the Act of Uniformity; however, he implied that he considered himself an Anglican.² By 1673 he left no doubt that this was how he felt, but he was not one who believed that Episcopal church government was essential, for he favored the Bill to Ease Tender Consciences that would have allowed comprehension of those who would subscribe to all of the doctrinal articles of the Thirty-nine Articles.³ At the same time he also opposed a move to provide for a test that would have made Dissenters incapable of sitting in the House, arguing that it would make the "Church of England so mean that you should have none [in the country] but Dissenters." ⁴ However, by this time there were powerful political reasons to support such measures; and in view of Lee's own political astuteness, and his association with Shaftesbury and Sacheverell which began shortly,⁵ it would appear that his motivation was probably more political than religious. For these reasons and the fact that he had a Nonconformist chaplain for only a short time right after that minister's ejection, Lee should be considered as a probable Presbyterian during only the first few years of the Restoration period, and thereafter as a moderate Anglican.

*M.P.:* 1661, for Aylesbury, Buckinghamshire.[6]

[1] Calamy, *Acct.*, II, 109; Matthews, p. 536.  [2] Grey, I, 130.
[3] Dering, p. 123; Grey, II, 30, 40, 41.  [4] *Ibid.*, pp. 95–96.
[5] Brown, *Shaftesbury*, pp. 221, 224.
[6] *O.R.*, I, 519, 534, 540, 546.

\*\* LOVE, WILLIAM (c. 1620–1689) [1] was a wealthy London merchant and among the four Nonconformists elected to sit for the City in 1661. After the House ordered its members to receive the Sacrament at St. Margaret's Church on May 26, Love proved to be the most intractable of the Dissenters in the Commons; and as a result of his continuing refusal to comply and his unsatisfactory explanations, he was suspended in July, 1661, and he was again in trouble in the spring of 1662 concerning the same matter.[2] Another action taken against him at this time because of his Nonconformity was that of the Commissioners for Regulating the Corporations, who displaced him as an alderman of London in accordance with the Corporation Act in May, 1662.[3] In 1665 Love briefly described his religious position as being that of a Nonconformist if "by that term they mean one who concurs not in every point of church government"; as for his position upon doctrines, however, there is some indication he accepted those of the Thirty-nine Articles.[4] There is also conclusive evidence of his continuing Nonconformity. In the debate on the content of a bill to ease Protestant Dissenters of February 20, 1673, he demonstrated both courage and candor in referring to his religious beliefs, stating that "some men may possibly think what principles he is of, which he is not ashamed to own and justify." [5] In 1678 an informer reported that Love was one of those who came in coaches to a great Presbyterian meeting in Cutlers Hall, Cloak Lane; and in the spring of 1689, a month or so before his death, Roger Morrice recorded that Tory members of the Commons meeting in the Devils Tavern on March 19 would make a motion in the House to remove Love and all other members who did not conform.[6] He was buried privately at St. Andrew Undershaft, May 1, 1689.[7]

*M.P.:* 1661–1678, 1679–1681, in the three Exclusion Parliaments, and to late April, 1689, for London.[8]

[1] J. B. Whitmore and H. W. Hughes, *London Visitation Pedigrees, 1664* (Harleian Soc. Pub., Vol. 92; 1940), p. 92.

[2] He was one of about a half dozen Presbyterians and Congregationalists who had not yet received the Sacrament by early July, and he with others of this group offered their excuses on July 3. The others were given a few days to bring in certificates, but an exception was made in the case of Love because the House was "much unsatisfied both with the matter and manner of his excuse." As a result he was suspended from sitting until he brought evidence of having complied. The record is incomplete, but he was laggard again over the same matter at the beginning of the next session in March, 1662. *C.J.*, VIII, 289, 444.

[3] Beaven, I, 184; II, 186.       [4] *H.M.C., Finch MSS*, I, 356–57; Grey, I, 228.

[5] *Ibid.*, II, 47–48.       [6] *C.S.P.D., 1678*, p. 246; Morrice MSS, Q, 505.

[7] Whitmore and Hughes, *London . . . Pedigrees, 1664*, p. 92; P.C.C., 2 Ent 395, fol. 67.

[8] *O.R.*, I, 525, 536, 542, 548, 560.

\* \* MANLEY, JOHN (c. 1625–1699) of Wrexham, Denigh Co., a captain in the Parliamentary Army and under Monmouth in 1685 a major. About 1643 he stated publicly that infant baptism was unlawful and that ministers of the Anglican Church were unchristian.[1] In 1659 he was elected to Parliament. He opposed the Restoration and in 1663 was presented for Nonconformity at the sessions, but this did not stop him and in 1665 a conventicle of 80 or 100 persons meeting in his house was interrupted and prosecutions were obtained.[2] Thereafter there is a lack of definite evidence concerning his religious views. He did not apply for a license in 1672. However, his political activities and associations strongly indicate that he remained a Dissenter. Before 1685 he joined Monmouth on the Continent and became a major in his invasion force. He had been sent to London before the battle of Sedgemoor, and when news of Monmouth's defeat came he escaped to Holland with John Wildman.[3] Three years later he accompanied William of Orange to England.[4] After his election to the Convention Parliament, George Fox and the Quakers conculted him on one occasion in a coffee house near the Parliament House.[5] He was very active in the Convention during the period that the Dissenters' opportunities seemed the best, the first two months and the last. He was named to 50 committees, helped draft the corporation oath, the oath of allegiance, the Bill of Rights and the Mutiny Bill.[6]

*M.P.:* 1689 for Bridport.[7]

[1] *H.M.C., 4th Rept. Denbigh MSS*, p. 271.

[2] A. N. Palmer, *A History of the Older Nonconformity of Wrexham* (Wrexham, [1888]), p. 5; *C.S.P.D., 1663–1665*, pp. 205–206.

[3] *H.M.C., Stopford-Sackville MSS*, I, 24; Ford Lord Grey, *The Secret History of the Rye House Plot: and of the Monmouth Rebellion* (2nd ed., 1754), pp. 131–32. Ashley, *Wildman*, p. 263.

[4] Bramston, p. 318.     [5] Fox, *Short Jour.*, pp. 190, 191.

[6] J. P. Ferris, MS biography of Manley prepared for *The History of Parliament, 1660–1690*, ed. B. D. Henning.

[7] *O.R.*, I, 559.

(*T?*) MASSEY, SIR EDWARD (1619?–1674), the son of John Massey of Coddington, Cheshire, was a well-known Civil War military leader who became known as a strong Presbyterian. He was secluded in Pride's Purge, and escaped to Holland, where he worked vigorously for the return of Charles to the throne.[1] At the Restoration he was rewarded with a knighthood.[2] There is little evidence concerning his religious beliefs following the Restoration, but the fact that he was a teller for those opposed to the Corporation Act on its second reading is a clear indication that he was working with the Presbyterian-Congregationalist group in the House.[3] In January, 1666, the officials in London received a report from an informant in Dover who stated that most of the magistrates acted as though they were Presbyterians and did not execute justice against the Nonconformists, and he hoped that authority "might be given to Sir Edward Massey, an honest active soldier, and much loved by the people." [4] This certainly suggests that Massey was no longer the strong Presbyterian that he had been. On the other hand he supported the same parliamentary proposal that "Mr. Boscawen and the Dissenters" did in the Commons' debate of March 11, 1668, on the King's speech for uniting Protestant subjects.[5]

Because of his earlier strong Presbyterianism and his stand on the Corporation Bill he may be considered a possible Presbyterian during the first few years of the Restoration period, but the conflicting character of the later evidence which has been discovered raises much doubt as to his position after 1665.

*M.P.:* 1661, until his death in late 1674 or early 1675, for Gloucester City.[6]

[1] W. R. J. Williams, *The Parliamentary History of the County of Gloucester, Including the Cities of Bristol and Gloucester* (*1213–1898*), (Hereford, 1898), pp. 199–200; Brunton and Pennington, p. 237; Carte, *Ormonde Letters,* II, 242; *H.M.C., Bath MSS,* II, 139; *C.S.P.D., 1659–1660,* p. 280, 305; Guizot, *R. Cromwell,* II, 404–405.

[2] LeNeve, p. 51.                    [3] *C.J.,* VIII, 276.
[4] *C.S.P.D., 1665–1666,* p. 225.          [5] Milward, pp. 220–21.
[6] Williams, *Parliamentary History . . . Gloucester,* pp. 199–200; *O.R.,* I, 523.

** MAYNARD, SIR JOHN (1604–1690),[1] of Tavistock, Devonshire and of London, was a prominent and strong Presbyterian in the Long Parliament. At an unknown time, but most probably sometime after the Restoration, Maynard had the ejected minister Roger Morrice as his chaplain,[2] and it is from the Morrice manuscripts as well as Calamy that knowledge of Maynard's religious views after 1660 are chiefly derived. Calamy reports that Maynard had Richard Whiteway as his domestic chaplain in Devon for some weeks just after his ejection from a fellowship in Exeter College, Oxford, in September, 1662, for non-subscription to the Anglican liturgy.[3] After Whiteway's death while he was with Maynard, it appears that a second university fellow, Edmund Moore, ejected from Trinity College, Cambridge, probably served Maynard as a chaplain, and he remained there until his marriage, which according to Calamy was a sufficient length of time to allow him to acquire some knowledge of the law.[4] It seems quite likely that Roger Morrice followed Moore as Maynard's chaplain sometime in the late 1660's or after. Indications of continuing Nonconformist views are found in his contribution of £40 to the church being built for Richard Baxter in 1675,[5] and also in the fact that he allowed ejected ministers to preach in Tavistock Abbey, to which he held a life lease.[6]

Maynard changed some of his Presbyterian views by 1680, as became apparent in the debate of December 21, on the Bill for Uniting Protestants. Although he favored the purpose of the Bill he did not want to let a clergyman "use what prayers he lists," holding that "we had better lose the Bill than our liturgy." In addition he did not wish to let clergymen wear what they wished when officiating, apparently favoring the surplice.[7] Significantly, these two matters of dress and liturgy were exactly the ones upon which two of his former chaplains had been remiss and for which they had been ejected. Nevertheless, Maynard does not seem to have abandoned his Presbyterianism, for he favored the other provisions of the Bill which provided that Presbyterian ordination was acceptable, eliminated the requirements of the oath of Allegiance and Supremacy and the oath against the Covenant, and which allowed any posture at communion. In addition, subscription to four of the Thirty-nine Articles that Presbyterians found objectionable was not to be required.[8] Roger Morrice continued to maintain a connection with Maynard, about whom he knew highly personal matters.[9] Morrice considered him "the greatest lawyer in England," and in June, 1687, at the time of James II's attack upon the universities, his old chaplain wrote that "the fellows of Magdalen College had taken very good counsel, i.e. Sir John Maynard, which the deputies of Cambridge did not, for they thought fit to advise with none but such as were of very known affections to the Church. . . ."[10] The implication is clear. Though Maynard had certainly ceased to be as strong a Presbyterian as he had been in prior decades, he was not considered on the other hand to be "of very known affections to the Church," and it is certainly evident that he had not lost the respect of his old Presbyterian chaplain.

*M.P.:* 1661–1678, for Beeralston; 1679–1681 in the three Exclusion Parliaments for Plymouth; 1685 for Beeralston; and 1689 for Plymouth.[11]

[1] Morrice MSS, R, 212.

[2] Calamy, *Acct.*, II, 166–67. Calamy merely states that Morrice "was sometime chaplain to my Lord Hollis, and afterwards to Sir John Maynard." For a discussion of the other reasons why it seems that Morrice probably served these two Presbyterian leaders sometime between the middle 1660's and the middle 1670's, see the summary of evidence concerning Lord Holles' religious views, *infra*, Appendix II.

[3] Calamy, *Acct.*, II, pp. 75–76.

[4] Calamy, *Cont.*, I, 123; Matthews, p. 352. Moore was ejected on Oct., 1661, refusal to wear the surplice being the particular charge against him, as well as general Nonconformity.

[5] Baxter, Pt. III, pp. 171–72.

⁶ Thomas Larkham, a zealous Puritan preached there until his death in 1669; then William Pearse preached as he had opportunity until 1688, and Henry Flammanck followed him and was there until 1692. The latter two were Presbyterians. W. G. Hoskins and H. P. R. Finberg, *Devonshire Studies* (1952), p. 387, n.2; Calamy, *Cont.*, I, 340; R. R. Hicks, "Ministers of the Abbey Chapel, Tavistock," *D.C.N.Q.*, XXIII (July, 1948), pp. 212–14.

⁷ Grey, VIII, 201; "Diary of Parliament," *H.M.C., Beaufort MSS*, pp. 101–102.

⁸ *Ibid.*; Morrice MSS, P, 288.

⁹ See for example, *ibid.*, 390, 430, 494, 594, 603, 611; Q, 147. (In several of these accounts Maynard's name is in untranscribed shorthand.)

¹⁰ *Ibid.*                           ¹¹ *O.R.*, I, 521, 535, 541, 547, 552, 558.

\*\* MOORE, THOMAS (1618–1695), often called Esquire Moore, was a wealthy Nonconformist of Spargrove, Somerset, and Hawkchurch, Dorset. Until he was secluded in 1648, he sat in the Long Parliament for Heytesbury, where he had owned the manor before 1641.[1] After the Restoration Moore had a half dozen or more Nonconformist ministers conduct services in his home for audiences up to 300, according to the report in the Episcopal Returns of 1669.[2] One minister who is not listed in this report, the Presbyterian Thomas Rowe, resided at Moore's house at Spargrove in the parish of Batcomb from 1662–1665 and he preached every week for the family.[3] Of two other ministers listed in the Episcopal Returns, Calamy reports that the Presbyterian Henry Albin preached twice Sunday in Moore's home for many years, presumably beginning in the middle or late 1660's and continuing through 1672 at least, for Moore's houses in Spargrove and Hawkchurch were both licensed as Presbyterian meeting houses in 1672, and Albin was licensed as a Presbyterian minister in Spargrove.[4] The second minister noted in both the Episcopal Returns and Calamy's account was Richard Allein, also a Presbyterian, who according to Calamy was once apprehended at Moore's house.[5] In 1675 Anthony Thorold wrote to Secretary Williamson that Moore was "the greatest upholder of illegal meetings" of any in Dorset, and he added that Shaftesbury was supporting Moore in the by-election of October, 1675, to choose a knight of the shire for Dorset.[6] Another important indication of Moore's religious, political, and social connections is that Lord Wharton and Moore engaged the same ejected minister, Anthony Withers, to tutor their sons and to take them abroad.[7] In view of Moore's wealth and well-known Nonconformity, it certainly is understandable that he was recommended for a deputy lieutenant and a justice of the peace in both Dorset and Somerset in 1687.[8]

*M.P.:* October, 1679, and 1681, in the last two Exclusion Parliaments, for Lyme Regis, Dorset.[9]

---

[1] Toulmin, *The History of Taunton in the County of Somerset,* enlarged by James Savage (New ed.; Taunton, 1822), pp. 95–96; Keeler, pp. 278–79; Brunton and Pennington, p. 237.

[2] Turner, I, 12.                      [3] Calamy, *Acct.,* II, 271.

[4] *Ibid.,* p. 600; Matthews, p. 4; *C.S.P.D., 1672,* p. 578; Turner, II, 1088; III, 332, 333.

[5] According to Calamy, Moore wanted to pay Allein's fine of £5, while he went to prison for his own fine. *Acct.,* II, 580.

[6] *C.S.P.D., 1675–1676,* p. 245. In the electioneering Shaftesbury appeared with Moore at Weymouth among other places. The Dissenters in the County were reported to be "very confident of their strength" for Mr. Moore, and therefore when he polled only 520 to Lord Digby's 1000 they had much to trouble them. *Ibid.,* pp. 331, 355.

[7] *C.S.P.D., 1684–1685,* p. 46; Matthews, p. 540.

[8] Duckett, II, 262, 292.                      [9] *O.R.,* I, 541, 547.

MORICE, SIR WILLIAM (1602–1676) was primarily of Warrington, Devon, but he had interests in Carnarvon, where he was born, and also in Cornwall. He was a kinsman of General Monck's, and came into prominence at the Restoration because of this connection and also because of his later appointment as a principal Secretary of State. He was first elected to Parliament in 1648 and was secluded in Pride's Purge.[1] Morice's Presbyterian opinions were involved in this expulsion, and ten years later he remained a Presbyterian as he worked first with those who planned a Presbyterian-Royalist uprising in the West of England during the summer of 1659, and later he joined General Monck as a counselor.[2] It appears possible that Morice continued to hold Presbyterian views after the Restoration as well. In May, 1661, when the House of Commons was considering a motion to thank the Anglican clergyman who had delivered the sermon on the Sunday that the members took Communion together at St. Margaret's Church, Morice joined William Prynne in opposition and stated that it had been a "scandalous sermon."[3] He was very friendly toward Puritan and later Nonconformist ministers, and gave a yearly pension to William Oliver after his ejection.[4] Reflecting such feeling, Dr. John Owen dedicated to Morice the first volume of his well-known treatise, *Exposition of the Epistle to the He-brews* which was published in 1668. Thanking Morice for his "candid esteem of some former endeavors of this kind," and for his influence which allowed this and other treatises "to pass freely into the world," Owen wrote that he "highly and singularly esteemed" Morice.[5] In addition the Secretary of State took some surprising actions in the House of Commons in view of his position. For example he opposed the motion to have the Solemn League and Covenant burned by the common hangman and served as a teller for the opposition in a division on this proposal.[6] Finally, his discontent with Royal policy led him to resign from his position in 1668, and one of the major reasons for taking this step was his bitterness that Charles had not kept his promises.

*M.P.:* 1661 until his death December 12, 1676, for Plymouth.[7]

[1] Brunton and Pennington, p. 237.

[2] Coate, "William Morice and the Restoration of Charles II," *E.H.R.*, XXXIII, 367; Coate, *Cornwall*, pp. 308–309.

[3] *H.M.C., 5th Rept., Sutherland MSS*, p. 160.

[4] Calamy, *Acct.*, II, 147; Matthews, p. 373; *Yorkshire Diaries and Autobiographies in the 17th and 18th Centuries* (Pub. of the Surtees Soc., Vol. LXV; Durham, London, and Edinburgh, 1877), "The Life of Master John Shaw [written by Himself]," p. 155.

[5] Owen, *Works*, XXII, vi–viii.          [6] *C.J.*, VIII, 254.

[7] *O.R.*, I, 522.

** MORLEY, COL. HERBERT (1616–1667), of Glynde, Sussex, was a well-known and influential officer in the Parliamentary Army and a member of the Long Parliament for Lewes.[1] While serving as the chief agent for raising troops, levying money and sequestrating estates in Sussex, he became notorious for his rough treatment of the clergy. Twenty years later his religious views were much the same it appears, for he took Nehemiah Beaton into his family after that minister's ejection.[2] He was a brother-in-law of Sir John Fagg, the Presbyterian member for Steyning, Sussex in 1661 and later parliaments.[3] In his will he made a bequest to the ejected minister who later became chaplain to his brother William.[4]

*M.P.:* 1661, until his death in September, 1667, for Rye.[5]

[1] Keeler, p. 280.

[2] Calamy, *Acct.*, II, 686. Beaton died in January, 1663.

³ *Supra,* Appendix II, summary of evidence for Sir John Fagg.

⁴ P.C.C., 141 Carr; Calamy, *Acct.,* II, 690–91; William Berry, *County Genealogies: Pedigrees of the Families of Sussex* (1830), p. 175.

⁵ *O.R.,* I, 532. Morley's *D.N.B.* biographer states that Morley probably did not sit, but the *C.S.P.D.* source cited in this connection says nothing to this effect. Although Morley was not able to attend the election because of "an indisposition of health," he wrote the mayor, jurats, and freemen of Rye prior to the election in March, 1661, that if they elected him he would "endeavor to be diligent and faithful" in their service, and after the election he wrote a note of thanks to them for electing him. *H.M.C., Rye and Hereford MSS,* pp. 236–39; *C.S.P.D., 1667,* p. 543.

\*\* NORTON, COL. RICHARD (c. 1615–1691), of Southwick, Southampton, was the neighbor and friend of Oliver Cromwell, whom the latter called "Idle Dick." ¹ The Colonel was a member of a prominent Hampshire parliamentary family, was elected to the Long Parliament in 1645, and was purged by Pride.² In February and March of 1660 he was active in the Presbyterian maneuvers to take control of the local militias.³ Evidence concerning his religious position after the Restoration indicates that he probably retained Nonconformist views. He was one of five members of the House of Commons who had no reason to offer for not receiving the Sacrament together with the other members at St. Margaret's Church, Westminster, on May 26, as ordered by the House. Nor was he present on July 3 to offer an excuse, but presumably he did present a certificate for having received the Sacrament at a later date.⁴ After the Act of Uniformity Urian Oakes became Norton's chaplain until "the heat of the persecution was a little abated," and a few years later he befriended the Congregational minister Giles Say, who according to a family report appears to have had a connection with the Norton family as a teacher and chaplain, possibly from about 1669 until 1676 or after.⁵ There are indications in family papers that Say was most respected in the family during the life of Norton's wife, which suggests that he was less staunch in maintaining his old views than she. In 1662 he was unsuccessful in an attempt to persuade Say to accept the living at Wellow, which was Norton's for presentation.⁶ Say's reported service as a chaplain to the family after his refusal to conform would appear to indicate that Norton had not rejected his old religious opinions. Another very good indication is found in his answers to James II's three questions of 1687, for he stated that he approved of repealing the penal laws but not the test.

Apparently because he originally refused to go along with the more Catholic part of James II's policy he was left out of the recommendations for the commission of peace, though in September the King's agents reported that Major Braman (q.v.) had found him "thoroughly right." [7] Among political leaders he was still considered a Presbyterian at the time of the elections to the Convention Parliament of 1689.[8]

*M.P.:* 1661–1678 for Portsmouth, and 1679 in the first Exclusion Parliament for Hampshire; 1679 and 1681 in the last two Exclusion Parliaments, and in 1689, for Portsmouth.[9]

[1] He negotiated Richard Cromwell's marriage. *The Letters and Speeches of Oliver Cromwell with Elucidations by Thomas Carlyle,* ed., S. C. Lomas, with an Introduction by  C. H. Firth (3 vols.; 1904), I, 292, 293, 298, 300; III, 471–72; Mark Noble, Memoirs of the Protectorate: House of Cromwell (Birmingham, 1784), pp. 421–26.

[2] *O.R.,* I, 493; Brunton and Pennington, pp. 31, 238; Cromwell, *Letters and Speeches,* I, 299.

[3] J. Silvester Davies, *A History of Southampton* (1883), p. 492.

[4] *C.J.,* VIII, 247, 289. The others who were delinquent were all Presbyterians or Congregationalists or probably so, and included Richard Hampden, Henry Henley, John Ratcliffe, and William Love.

[5] Cotton Mather, *Magnalis Christi Americana* (2 vols.; Hartford, 1853–1855), II, 97; Samuel Say Toms, "Memoir of Mr. Gyles Say, Father of Mr. Samuel Say, Drawn Up from the 'Say Papers,'" *Monthly Repository of Theology and General Literature,* IV (Sept., 1809), 477–79.

[6] *Ibid.,* p. 477.

[7] Duckett, I, 425, 431, 432.

[8] *H.M.C., Dartmouth MSS,* p. 142.

[9] *O.R.,* I, 528, 537, 543, 549, 561. He was elected Knight of the Shire in 1690, and died in May, 1691. *Ibid.,* p. 568; Luttrell, *Brief Relations,* II, 238.

\* NOSWORTHY, EDWARD, SR. (d. 1690?),[1] of Ince Castle, Cornwall, was a merchant who first came into prominence when he was appointed from Cornwall to assist Major-General John Desborough, one of the ten of that rank who had been commissioned in 1655 to maintain a military and godly administration.[2] In March of 1660 Nosworthy was of the committee of militia in Cornwall which was primarily Presbyterian in membership and was formed under the New Militia Act.[3] It would appear that Nosworthy was not in favor of the constitutional and religious status quo after the Restoration; for late in 1661 when he petitioned through the Bishop of Exeter to contract for a lease that he had purchased "during the late times," the King refused on the grounds that "his actions have not been such as to merit favor." [4] During the six weeks before this refusal, he was also twice defeated in the House of Commons in his efforts to be seated for St. Ives.[5] Finally he was elected and seated on January 19, 1664. Danby's parliamentary manager, Sir Richard Wiseman, included Nosworthy in a list of members, most of whom he felt were Presbyterians. Also indicative of his religious position is that fact that he was struck off the commission of peace for Cornwall in 1680, and in addition his son was considered a Dissenter.[6]

*M.P.:* May to December 18, 1661; again from January, 1665, to 1678; and 1679, in the first two Exclusion Parliaments, all for St. Ives, Cornwall.[7]

[1] His will was first proved May 23, 1690, P.C.C., 77 Dyke.
[2] Coate, pp. 291–93.
[3] *Ibid.*, pp. 310–11.    [4] *C.S.P.D., 1661–1662*, p. 260.
[5] He was returned on March 27, 1661, for St. Ives, but on Dec. 17, 1661, this return was ordered taken off the file. He was returned again in an indenture of Jan. 10, 1662, but this time there was a double return and his opponent was seated. *O.R.*, 521 nn.1 and 2; *C.J.*, VIII, 336; *C.S.P.D., 1670 (Addenda to 1660–1670)*, p. 663.
[6] Browning, III, 101–102. There was a Nonconformist minister named John Nosworthy to whom he may have been related. "Some Vicars or Ministers of Seaton," *D.C.N.Q.*, IV (Jan., 1906–Oct., 1907), 264; Matthews, p. 368; Turner, I, 189; II, 1162.
[7] *O.R.*, I, 521, 534, 541; *C.J.*, VIII, 336.

\*\* NOSWORTHY, EDWARD, JR. (1637–1701),[1] also of Ince Castle, Cornwall, he was considered to be a Nonconformist by his contemporaries. In 1687 he was listed as a Dissenter in the reports to James II, and he was recommended as a justice of the peace by the King's agents not only in a regular report but also in a special one stating their desires. In addition the Earl of Bath's report stated that "Mr. Nosworthy [will] undertake to choose who the King pleases." [2] In 1683 it was reported to government authorities that he had been successful in gaining control of the St. Ives borough government and in eliminating "loyal magistrates," and in October, 1688 the Earl of Bath singled out Nosworthy when complaining that the Regulators of Corporations had similarly purged the Exeter chamber and that thereafter it was made up of Dissenters, while the Mayor went in state to a conventicle every Sunday.[3] Nosworthy married one of Sir John Maynard's daughters.

*M.P.:* 1679–1681, in the three Exclusion Parliaments, for St. Ives, Cornwall.[4]

[1] *Register of St. Mary's Truro, 1597–1837* [Exeter, 1919], pp. 101, 162; Davies Gilbert, *The Parochial History of Cornwall, Founded on the Manuscript Histories of Mr. Hals and Mr. Tonkin* (4 vols.; 1838), II, 55.
[2] Duckett, I, 371; II, 217, 270, 300.
[3] *C.S.P.D., 1683–1684*, pp. 78–79; S.P.D., 31/3/2, fols. 104–105.
[4] *O.R.,* I, 534, 541, 546.

ONSLOW, SIR RICHARD (1601–1664), of Knoll in Crawley, Surrey, was a member for Surrey in both the Short and Long Parliaments until his seclusion in 1648. He was a generous supporter of the parliamentarian cause, and he was known for his Presbyterian views after 1640.[1] He sat in Cromwell's two Parliaments of 1654 and 1656, was one of the committee which urged the Protector to take the Crown, and also one of those called to sit in Cromwell's House of Peers. By 1660 he favored the Restoration and served on the Council of State established in February, 1660, when the Presbyterians were once again powerful. In 1661 he assisted Lord Wharton in drawing up a list of "Friends." [2] However, after the Corporation Act was passed he obtained a position as one of the Commissioners for Regulating Corporations. This creates definite doubt concerning his religious position during the last two years of his life even though he is supposed to have done this "for the sake of his friends," which could be construed to mean that he did so in order to protect the moderate Presbyterian royalists from the Anglican royalists.[3] But a pamphlet defending his actions just after the Restoration proves "not so much the political integrity of Onslow as the constancy with which he protected his friends, regardless of party," [4] and he was able to "hinder his enemies from ruining his interest in that town. . . ." [5] His instinct for political survival was obviously stronger than his religious conviction, and therefore he can be regarded as no more than a possible Presbyterian during the three years that he sat in the Cavalier Parliament.

*M.P.:* 1661, until his death on May 19, 1664, for Guildford, Surrey.[6]

¹ Keeler, p. 290.                                    ² Carte MSS, 81, fol. 81.
³ *H.M.C., Buckinghamshire, Lindsey* . . . *MSS*, p. 483.
⁴ C. E. Vulliany, *The Onslow Family 1528–1874* (1953), pp. 20–21.
⁵ *H.M.C., Buckinghamshire, Lindsey* . . . *MSS*, p. 483.
⁶ *O.R.*, I, 529.

\* OWEN, THOMAS (fl. 1679–1702) was either of Comeog, Pembroke, or Motheway, Carmarthen, and also of Gray's Inn.¹ He did not become prominent until September, 1679, when he was elected to the House of Commons from Haverfordwest. As a result of his zeal during that parliament in supporting measures to relieve the Dissenters, the Quaker leaders in London directed that Friends in Haverfordwest were to support Owen in the election of 1681.² Morrice reported a Commons debate of December 7, 1689 in which it was noted that Owen "was for toleration in King James's time," but that he had been of "great service" to King William, and Sir Edward Harley told his son Robert that he was to judge Owen's election return in November 1690 to be satisfactory.³ It is very likely that this Thomas Owen was the same counsellor at law who served as a Manager of the Common Fund for the Benefit of Presbyterian and Congregational Ministers, established in 1690; and it may also have been he who was a member of Stephen Lobb's congregation.⁴ Because of the lack of positive identity between the Thomas Owen M.P., and the Thomas Owen of the Common Fund or Lobb's congregation, he can be considered only a probable Dissenter.

*M.P.:* October, 1679, in the second Exclusion Parliament, for Haverfordwest, Pembroke.⁵

¹ Williams, *Parliamentary History of Wales*, p. 168; Joseph Foster, *The Register of Admissions to Gray's Inn, 1521–1889* (1889), pp. 205, 295.
² Friends' MSS, Book of Cases, I (1661–1695), 83–84.
³ Morrice MSS, Q, 26; B.M. Loan 29/140, Portland MSS, Letter #110.
⁴ Gordon, p. 324.                                    ⁵ *O.R.*, I, 545.

\* PAPILLON, THOMAS (1623–1702), of London and Dover, was a well-known merchant and political leader. He was a deacon of the French Protestant Church in London prior to the Restoration, and he continued his connection after 1660, serving as the sponsor of two of his children when they became members in

1676 and 1681.[1] Evidence of his religious views after the Restoration is found primarily in his letters and other of his writings. In these he reveals his strong Calvinistic theological views,[2] and he also reveals his desire for a religious comprehension in England that would include those who promote true religion and piety.[3] He was very strict and puritanical in his opinions concerning the observation of the Sabbath.[4] More specific concerning his position was the report that Roger Morrice accepted and recorded in March, 1689, to the effect that Tory members of the House would make a motion to remove Papillon, Love, and all other members of the House who would not conform.[5] Actually he attended the Parish Church of St. Katherine Coleman, London, but he remained loyal to the French Church and also had sermons given for him at home by a Mr. Calandrine who could have been the ejected Presbyterian minister Lewis Calandrine, but was more likely a son of this man.[6] In addition there was a report in 1673 indicating that Papillon had the support of the Nonconformists at Dover.[7]

*M.P.:* From January 16, 1675, to 1678; and 1679–1681, in the three Exclusion Parliaments, and 1689 all for Dover.[8]

---

[1] *Livre des Tesmoignages de L'Eglise de Threadneedle Street, 1669–1789*, ed. William Minet (Pubs. of the Huguenot Soc., Vol. XXI; 1909), p. 211; A. F. W. Papillon, *Memoirs of Thomas Papillon, of London, Merchant, 1623–1702* (Reading, 1887), p. 48.

[2] *Ibid.*, 110–11; 309–24 (Address to His Children).

[3] "Memorandum" written by Papillon, *ibid.*, pp. 375–76.

[4] See Papillon's "Sanctity of the Sabbath," *ibid.*, pp. 282–305.

[5] Morrice MSS, Q, 505.

[6] "An Account of Thomas Papillon, Esquire, His Illness Beginning the 30th January, 1700/1," kept by one of the family, Papillon, pp. 378–79. Both Papillon and the Calandrines had connections with the Dutch Reform Church. *Ibid.*, p. 50; Matthews, p. 98. In his will Papillon left £50 to the poor of the Parish of St. Katherine Coleman and £100 to the poor of the French Church as well as £25 for the ministers of each. *Ibid.*, p. 382.

[7] *C.S.P.D., 1672–1673*, pp. 510, 522.

[8] *C.J.*, IX, 294; *O.R.*, I, 532, n.6; 539, 545, 551, 563.

POPHAM, COL. ALEXANDER (1605–1669), of Littlecote and Wellington, Wiltshire. He served in both the Short and the Long Parliaments.[1] He was a Presbyterian elder, but was not secluded by Pride and continued to sit with the Independents until 1653, and afterwards he became one of Cromwell's peers.[2] In 1661 he and William Prynne were elected in spite of the vigorous efforts of Anglican Royalists to defeat them,[3] and it is likely that he was of similar religious views except that he would have been more Congregationalist than Prynne. Since no other evidence between this date and his death in 1669 has been discovered, he should be considered only a possible Presbyterian or Congregationalist.

*M.P.:* 1661, until the autumn of 1669, for Bath, Somerset.[4]

[1] Keeler, p. 310; Brunton and Pennington, p. 239.
[2] J. H. Hexter, "The Problem of the Presbyterian Independents," *A.H.R.*, XLIV (Oct., 1938), p. 31, n.32; Yule, p. 113.
[3] *C.S.P.D., 1660–1661*, p. 544.     [4] *O.R.*, I, 527.

** PRIDEAUX, EDMUND (c. 1634–1702) was of Ford Abbey at Thornecombe, Devonshire, and had connections or property in Dorset, Somerset and Cornwall as well. He was the son of the very wealthy Sir Edmund Prideaux (d. 1659) who sat for Lyme Regis in the Long Parliament, served as an elder in his Presbytery, and was later Cromwell's Attorney General.[1] In the Episcopal Returns of 1669 it was reported that a Presbyterian congregation of about 100 persons met at the younger Prideaux's house in Thornecombe, Devon.[2] According to Calamy, Henry Backaller (or Baccaller) was sometime chaplain to the younger Edmund, and he also states that the ejected minister John Turner preached "often in a cellar of Prideaux," adding that being a member of Parliament, Prideaux "usually engaged Mr. Turner to spend a day in prayer with him at the beginning of each session and another at the end."[3] In view of this information, the reports of two government informants after 1680 become highly credible. In June, 1682, a Captain Gregory Alford, one of Secretary Jenkins' correspondents, wrote from Lyme that Prideaux had in his house, which was formerly an abbey, "a chapel wherein preaches a Nonconformist," and in 1684, there was another, though not reliable report made by James Harris, then confined to Fleet Prison, that Prideaux was a Dissenter.[4] Consistent with his religious and political background, Prideaux became one of those who backed the Duke of Monmouth, entertaining him overnight during his Western trip in August, 1680, and according to traditional accounts,

engaging in the Rebellion in 1685, though he escaped the consequences by paying a heavy fine or bribe to Jeffreys.[5] It is also
significant that James II's agents reported that the Dissenters at
Honiton, Devonshire were considering him along with two others
as a candidate for one of their burgesses.[6]

*M.P.:* October, 1679, and 1681, in the last two Exclusion Parliaments, for Taunton, Somerset.[7]

[1] Hexter, *A.H.R.,* XLIV, 31, n.32; Keeler, pp. 315–16; Coate, pp. 307–308, 310–
11. The younger Edmund succeeded to the baronetage in 1659, but in May, 1660,
it was voided. G.E.C., *Bart.,* III, 6.

[2] Turner, I, 44; II, 1145.

[3] Calamy, *Cont.,* II, 752, 754–55; Matthews, p. 497.

[4] *C.S.P.D., 1682,* p. 26; *1683–1684,* p. 362.

[5] "An Historical Account of . . . James, Duke of Monmouth," in *Historical
and Biographical Tracts,* II, 31.

[6] Duckett, II, 232.

[7] *O.R.,* I, 543, 549.

** PRYNNE, WILLIAM (1600–1669) was of Bath, Somerset.
This famous protagonist continued to hold Presbyterian views
for at least several years after the Restoration. In a pamphlet of
1661, he called for a revision of the Prayer Book and stated some
of his religious opinions at a time when there was hope for comprehension within the Established Church, and his position was
one held by many of the moderate Presbyterians. He wrote that
although he "was never . . . [a] separatist from the Book of
Common-Prayer, and administration of the Sacrament, established
in the Church of England," to which he had "constantly resorted,"
yet there were many matters concerning the liturgy and ceremonies that he wanted to have changed. He felt that there should
not be one unalterable and set form of prayer and that there
ought to be extemporaneous prayers. He also maintained that
reading prayers was not the principal part of a minister's duty,
but that it was "constant, frequent preaching of the Gospel and
administration of the Sacraments. . . ." He could find no command in the Scriptures for standing at the Common Prayer, kneeling at the Sacrament, or for using the cross in baptism, or the
ring in marriage.[1] After stating that no particular kind of garment
was instituted by God, and following this with 100 pages of his
inimitable marshalling of evidence, he concludes that surplices

and other garments are "not to be used or worn by bishops, ministers, deacons, or clergy-men alone, as a badge of their distinction from and elevation above lay Christians." [2]

Consistent with a part of what he had written was Prynne's well known refusal to kneel when the members of the House of Commons were receiving the Sacrament together at St. Margaret's Church in Westminster on May 26, 1661.[3] Also indicating his religious views to some degree was his vigorous leadership of the opposition to the Corporation Act and his earlier attack upon the Bishops and the Bill restoring them to the House of Lords, which was reportedly introduced earlier than planned as a result of Prynne's activity.[4] He met defeat upon all of these matters and even begged the pardon of the House "very submissively" for his pamphlet attacking the Corporation Bill.[5]

On at least one other occasion, a reading at Gray's Inn given February 17, 1662, Prynne again attacked the right of Bishops to sit in Parliament except "by reason of their temporal Baronies." [6] Nevertheless, there was a definite change in Prynne's activity in the Commons after he lost his Corporation Bill battle and submissively expressed his *mea culpa* to the House. The old spirit left him, and he ceased to be the protagonist he had been in both political and religious controversies. In addition there was some shift in his views. In 1663 he abandoned his parliamentarian colleagues and favored the New Triennial Bill.[7] There were also indications which raise the question whether he continued to be a moderate Presbyterian during the last several years of his life. However, the evidence is indirect and inconclusive, and should be considered in reference to the position of other moderate Presbyterians of the day as well as in comparison to Prynne's views prior to 1661. After the Restoration, theology was far less an issue between those in the Church and the moderate Presbyterians than it had been between Anglicans and Puritans earlier in the century. Thus when the question of Calvinism was raised in the debate of March 11, 1668, on uniting Protestants, and Prynne avoided the issue rather than taking a strong pro-Calvinist position as he had in pre-Restoration years, it was not as indicative of a shift toward Anglicanism as it might at first seem.[8] Moreover, in the same speech he expressed the hope that the causes of separation would be taken away and that "painful ministers" would be put in vacant Anglican churches. The hope that comprehension could be attained and that ministers of their own kind could be given positions within the Church was a predominant one among moderate Presbyterians of that time.[9] He therefore should be considered at least a possible Presbyterian during the last few years of his life.

*M.P.:* 1661, until October 24, 1669, for Bath, Somerset.[10]

[1] *A Short Sober Pacific Examination of Some Exuberances in, and Ceremonial Appurtenances to, the Common Prayer* (1661), pp. 1–3, 7. In addition he objected to the frequent repetition of "Glory be to the Father" at the end of every Psalm, and in or at the end of prayers, canticles, songs and scriptures; and he wanted no standing every time there was a "Glory be to the Father" or when the Gospel and the three Creeds were read. *Ibid.,* pp. 8–18.

[2] *Ibid.,* pp. 30–136.

[3] Egerton MSS, 2043, fol. 9; Pepys, II, 42–43; *H.M.C., 5th Rept., Sutherland MSS,* pp. 160, 171.

[4] Pepys, II, 46.

[5] *H.M.C., Beaufort MSS,* pp. 50–51; *C.J.,* VIII, 302.

[6] Inner Temple MSS, 538.32, fol. 11. (The Reading of William Prynne at Gray's Inn, February 17, 1662, on the Petition of Right; and Observations on the Right of Bishops to Sit in Parliament.)

[7] *H.M.C., 7th Rept. Verney MSS,* p. 484; Pepys, IV, 87–88; *C.J.,* VIII, 537.

[8] W. M. Lamont has presented the case that Prynne had become a Latitudinarian Anglican. It should be noted, however, that Prynne's decline in anti-episcopal zeal and his failure to rise to the defense of Calvinism in the debates of 1668 constituted essentially negative evidence, and these actions were consistent with Prynne's much subdued activity on issues which came before the House after 1661. In addition, serving on committees against profanity and swearing, and Popish Recusancy, and on a third misconstrued to have been concerned with "neglect of the Sacrament" by House members did not necessarily constitute evidence of Prynne's "cooperation with the Established Church in 1666." Presbyterian M.P.s had not lost their concern about the matters charged to the first two of these committees. The third committee was concerned with absenteeism of the members from the Commons and not with their failure to receive the Sacrament. *Marginal Prynne,* pp. 216–19; *C.J.,* VIII, 630, 638, 663; E. and A. Porritt, *Unreformed House of Commons,* I, 428.

[9] Milward, p. 222; *supra,* pp. 56–57.     [10] *O.R.,* I, 527.

** PYNSENT (or PINCENT), SIR WILLIAM (1650?–1719) of Urchfont (or Erchfont), Wiltshire, was admitted to Lincoln's Inn in 1667, and became prominent in James II's reign.[1] Evidence of his Nonconformity is found in the report of the King's agents where he is listed among the "Dissenters that are fit" for a deputy lieutenant or justice of the peace. But more important honors were to be granted to him. The King created him a baronet in September, 1687, and in 1688 he was made sheriff of Wiltshire. These appointments and the approval of the Board of Regulators that he be appointed to the commission of the peace give substantial corroboration to the royal agents' report that Pynsent was a Dissenter.[2]

*M.P.:* 1689 for Devizes, Wiltshire.[3]

[1] P.C.C., 193 Browning; G.E.C., *Bart.*, IV, 145–46.
[2] Duckett, I, 220; II, 268.          [3] *O.R.*, I, 562.

** RATCLIFFE, JOHN (d. January 13, 1673), of Chester, was a Recruiter in the Long Parliament for that City and was secluded in Pride's Purge.[1] He was elected burgess for the City again in 1661, and his name was given to Lord Wharton as a "Friend." This was a correct estimate, for in 1661 Ratcliffe had not received the Sacrament in a year, and in August, 1662, he was ejected as alderman and recorder of Chester for refusing the oaths required by the Corporation Act.[2] In 1667, when a recorder for the City was to be elected, Sir Geoffry Shakerly, Governor of Chester Castle, wrote Secretary Williamson of his "fears that Mr. Ratcliffe, formerly recorder, and burgess of the city in the present Parliament may be chosen; but he is a Presbyterian and a great favorer of Nonconformity." Shakerly hoped that the King would "help them to an able careful man," and later he reported that Chester chose another person who was "a true son of the Church."[3] In Parliament he urged that the Act of Uniformity be revised and that "an eye may be had to tender consciences."[4] Also of weight is the opinion of the Presbyterian minister Philip Henry, who commented upon the "worthy Mr. Ratcliff" when writing in his diary about the by-election to fill his place after his death.[5]

*M.P.:* 1661, until January 13, 1673, for Chester City.[6]

[1] *O.R.*, I, 486 (elected in 1646); Brunton and Pennington, p. 210.
[2] Carte MSS, 81, fol. 81; Pink MSS, 320; George Ormonde, *The History of the County Palatine and City of Chester* (3 vols.; 1819), I, 187–88.
[3] *C.S.P.D., 1667*, p. 14, 25.
[4] Milward, p. 58; Grey, I, 111.          [5] Henry, pp. 258–59.
[6] *O.R.*, I, 520.

REYNELL, THOMAS (1625–1698), of West Ogwell, was the eldest son of Sir Richard Reynell. He served as a justice of the peace in 1647 and 1654, and sat in the House of Commons for Devon in 1654 and Ashburton in 1659.[1] In 1664 Bishop Ward of Exeter listed him as one of the fourteen justices in Devon who were "arrant Presbyterians," and added in Reynell's case that he was a "very dangerous Common wealthsman." [2] Also indicative of his religious views was his removal as justice of peace in 1676, and although he was selected as sheriff the following year,[3] it was not unknown for Dissenters to serve as such in Dorset at this time. In the debates of 1680 Reynell spoke strongly for the move to repeal the Corporation Act.[4] Finally, he gave conditional consent to the policy of James II in 1687–1688, and in April he was considered "right" for election to the House by the King's agents, who reported that in Ashburton "the interest of the town is in the Dissenters [and] . . . they propose to chose Mr. Reynell. . . ." [5] He may be considered a possible Presbyterian.

*M.P.:* 1679–1681, in the three Exclusion Parliaments, and 1689 for Ashburton, Devon.[6]

[1] Add. MSS, 34,551, fol. 24; J. J. Alexander, "Devon County Members of Parliament, Part V, The Stuart Period (1603–1688)," *Trans. Devon. Assoc.,* XLVIII (1916), 335.

[2] "Some Letters from Bishop Ward of Exeter, 1663–1667," *D.C.N.Q.,* XXI (April, 1941), 226, 284.

[3] *H.M.C., Finch MSS,* II, 43; J. J. Alexander, *Trans. Devon. Assoc.,* XLVIII, 335.

[4] *H.M.C., Beaufort MSS,* p. 104.

[5] Duckett, I, 374; II, 233; Morrice MSS, Q, 211.

[6] *O.R.,* I, 535, 541, 547, 558; J. J. Alexander, *Trans. Devon. Assoc.,* XLVIII, 335.

\*\* RICH, SIR ROBERT (1648–1699), of Roos Hall in Beccles, Suffolk. He was a leading member of a Presbyterian congregation and from May, 1689, his chaplain was Thomas Emlyn, who became known as the first Unitarian minister.[1] In April, 1688, the King's agents reported that those whom they had consulted at Dunwich would elect Rich, and in September they added that he was "ready to serve his Majesty in the meanest capacity." [2] He and his wife were friends of the Presbyterian minister and plotter

Robert Ferguson and his wife as early as 1679, and in 1683 Mrs. Ferguson stayed at the Rich home while she was sick. During this time Ferguson visited twice, and as a result Rich was questioned by the Privy Council but was able to clear himself.[3] He is best known as one of the Admiralty Commissioners under William III.

*M.P.:* 1689 for Dunwich Suffolk.[4]

[1] Gordon, *Cheshire Classis,* p. 171; also Gordon's biography of Thomas Emlyn in the *D.N.B.*
[2] Duckett, II, 227, 246.
[3] *C.S.P.D., 1679–1680,* p. 541; *1683,* 196, 234, 256, 263, 277; *1683 July–Sept.,* pp. 53, 55.
[4] *O.R.,* I, 561.

ROLLE, SIR FRANCIS (d. 1686)[1] was of East Tytterly, Hants.[2] He first came to parliamentary notice in 1669 as a result of the disputed by-election in Bridgewater, Somerset. It was contended that among the burgesses voting for Rolle there were some who were "not qualified according to the Act for Corporations; and being all persons holding Conventicles in their houses, and resorting to them in others; and refusing to conform or resort to the service of the Church, or receive the Sacrament as the Act does enjoin, and one of them being, at the time of his being elected burgess actually excommunicated. . . ." In the division which went for Rolle's rival 167 to 80, one of the tellers favoring Rolle was the Presbyterian Henry Henley.[3] Also suggestive of Rolle's religious views was the fact that he reportedly had his son tutored by a "Nonconformist parson." [4] Another report to London authorities from the Mayor of Bridgewater in 1685 charged that when there was news that there would be a Parliament, one of Rolle's servants who was a "fanatic . . . made it his business to run up and down to the grand fanatics in their houses. . . ." [5] Of some significance is the comment made by Roger Morrice when Rolle died in the autumn of 1686, that his death was "a public loss to that country, and other places." [6] This evidence suggests that he may have been a Presbyterian.

*M.P.:* From November 3–December 7, 1669 for Bridgewater; from April 26, 1675 in the Cavalier Parliament and again in October,

1679, and 1681 in the last two Exclusion Parliaments for Hampshire.[7]

---

[1] Morrice MSS, P, 631. Oct. 9, 1686: "Sir Francis Rolle is lately dead. . . ."
[2] *O.R.*, I, 527.                                [3] *C.J.*, IX, 118.
[4] *H.M.C., 7th Rept., Verney MSS*, p. 468.
[5] P.R.O., S.P.30/I/1/55.
[6] Morrice MSS, P, 631.
[7] *O.R.*, I, 527, 543, 549. In March, 1679, Rolle was one of those on a double return for Bridgewater, Somerset. No decision had been reached before the Parliament was dissolved. *C.J.*, IX, 571, 578, 579, 580–81.

RUSHWORTH, JOHN (1612?–1690) was of Berwick-on-Tweed, Northumberland. In 1643 this well-known historian took the Covenant. His first post of importance was that of Secretary to General Fairfax and the Council of War when the New Model Army was formed. After Fairfax resigned rather than invade Scotland, Rushworth continued as Cromwell's secretary for only a few months. Just before the Restoration he was considered the "darling agent" of the members of the Commons who had been secluded in Pride's Purge, and when they were restored in February, 1660, he was made Secretary to the new Council of State. Later that year he sat in the Convention Parliament.[1] There are some indications that Rushworth may have retained his Presbyterian views during the Restoration Period. In an intercepted letter which he wrote on June 15, 1667, he was bitter against the "Bishops and Papists, and all those who cozened and cheated the King. . . ."[2] He was intimate with the Presbyterian Sir John Hewley and his wife and gave him political advice and support.[3] In 1676 he stood for election in the by-election at Berwick-on-Tweed, the borough he had represented as an agent for three decades and as a member of the House three times before.[4] Unfortunately he was opposed by Danby's son, Peregrine (Lord Viscount of Dunblaine) and thus by Danby, the Earl of Newcastle, and the sheriff, Sir Richard Stote. Stote's tactic was to disallow most of Rushworth's votes, and after the election he reported to Danby that "after a troublesome contest with an unreasonable party . . . we found many of them stood excommunicate for not reparing to divine service and not receiving the Sacrament. . . ."[5] Stote frankly admitted that this was a "game," and there is no doubt that the Dissenters favored Rushworth. For these reasons he may be regarded as a possible Presbyterian.

*M.P.:* 1679–1681, in the three Exclusion Parliaments, for Berwick-on-Tweed, Northumberland.[6]

[1] Bean, pp. 504–505, 534; *Clar. S.P.*, III, 694.

[2] *C.S.P.D., 1667*, p. 188. See also the report to Williamson in July that Rushworth "often writes seditious letters." *Ibid.*, p. 290.

[3] Marvell, II, 313–18.

[4] 1657, 1659, and 1660. Bean, pp. 504–505.

[5] Browning, I, 206 and n.5. Lord Dunblaine was under age when elected. Rushworth petitioned against this return in 1676 and again in 1678, but there is no record of any action, Danby undoubtedly having blocked it. *C.J.*, IX, 400, 485.

[6] *O.R.*, I, 537, 543, 548; Bean, pp. 504–505.


** RUSSELL, EDWARD (1643–1714), commonly called Lord Edward Russell, the fourth son of the Earl, later Duke, of Bedford. He grew up in a Presbyterian atmosphere and remained Presbyterian in position, having the ejected minister Phineas Flavell as a chaplain in his family.[1] Also indicative of his religious views was his marriage, which was proposed and negotiated by John Howe.[2] Although Russell was recommended to be a justice by the Lord Lieutenant in November, 1687, Danby was more correct in the spring of 1688 when he included Russell on the list of those members of Parliament whom he thought might give support to some kind of a constitutional move against James.[3] Russell did become one of the earlier supporters of William.[4]

*M.P.:* 1679–1681 in the three Exclusion Parliaments for Tavistock, and in 1689 for Bedfordshire.[5]

[1] Calamy, *Cont.*, p. 501; Matthews, p. 201.

[2] Rogers, *Life of Howe*, p. 337.

[3] *Supra*, Chap. X, n.23.   [4] Duckett, II, 57.   [5] *O.R.*, I, 535, 541, 547, 557.


ST. JOHN, OLIVER (c. 1644–1689), of Farley, Hants. Son of the parliamentarian Chief Justice and related through his mother to Oliver Cromwell.[1] There is a good indication that he was possibly a Dissenter when he sat in the Exclusion and Convention Parliaments. James II received a confidential report that St. John had "promised to comply" on penal laws and Test Acts repeal.[2]

The lack of other evidence about his religious position is matched by a similar lack regarding his political activities. Yet judging by a report in Benjamin Harris' *Domestick Intelligence* in 1679, St. John had the support of Dissenters.[3]

*M.P.:* 1679–1681 and 1689 to about September, for Stockbridge, Hants.[4]

[1] Noble, *Memoirs of the Protectorate,* II, 26–31.
[2] Duckett, I, 430.           [3] *C.S.P.D., 1679–1680,* p. 234.
[4] *O.R.,* I, 537, 549, 561.

* STAPELY, SIR JOHN (1628–1701), of Patcham, Sussex, was the son of the regicide Anthony Stapely. By 1657 he had abandoned the political views of his father, for he became involved in a plot to restore Charles Stuart.[1] In 1672 a house of his at Hove, Sussex was licensed as a Presbyterian meeting place and William Wallis, a Presbyterian minister, was licensed to be the preacher.[2] Between 1675 and 1678 Stapely may have given some support to Danby, but at best it was unreliable.[3] However, in 1688 he favored repeal of both the penal laws and the Test Acts and was recommended for addition to the commission of peace.[4] This evidence indicates he was probably a Dissenter.

*M.P.:* 1661–1678, for Lewes, Sussex.[5]

[1] Mark Noble, *The Lives of the English Regicides* (2 vols.; 1798), II, 242–46.
[2] Turner, I, 466; II, 1023; III, 788–89.
[3] Unreliability seems to have been a characteristic, for he was frequently absent from the House, being cited once as a defaulter and on a second occasion for departing the service of the House without leave. *C.J.,* VIII, 663; IX, 556. Wiseman also reported him wanting in attendance, Browning, III, 84–86. Stapely was given a £1000 customs post at the Restoration and was thus under pressure from the Government to give support. G.E.C., *Bart.,* III, 97.
[4] Duckett, I, 188–89, 193.
[5] *O.R.,* I, 529.

* STRODE, WILLIAM (d. 1695), of Barrington, near Ilchester, Somerset. He was the son of William Strode, a well-to-do and prominent Colonel in the Parliamentary Army and a strong Presbyterian Recruiter in the Long Parliament for Ilchester. He was secluded in Pride's Purge.[1] About a year before the elder Strode's

death in December, 1666, he appears to have engaged the ejected Presbyterian minister Humphrey Philips to accompany his son William on a visit to Holland.[2] It is possible that the younger William Strode was "Stroud" who gave the Presbyterian minister John Turner two small "parishes" in Somerset late in the reign of Charles II.[3] However, there is no question that it was William Strode of Barrington who entertained Monmouth in 1680 and in 1688 was listed in the Lord Lieutenant's report to James II among the "Catholics and Dissenters proposed to be added to the Commission of Peace . . . in Somerset."[4] Strode was considered one of the leaders of the "fanatic party" in Somerset and was criticized by Royalists in October, 1681, for "his great treats in town and large invitations of his party to his house in Barrington. . . ."[5] His religious and political views and activity led to a charge of disaffection in April, 1684, according to Morrice.[6] It is also significant that James II's agents approved him as a candidate in April, 1688, and reported that he was being considered for knight of the shire or as a possible burgess for Milborne Port of Ilchester if not elected for the County.[7]

*M.P.:* March, 1679, and October, 1679–1680, in the first two Exclusion Parliaments for Ilchester, Somerset.[8]

[1] Pink MSS, 320.  [2] Matthews, p. 388; Calamy, *Acct.*, II, 260.
[3] Calamy, *Cont.*, II, 755.
[4] "An Historical Account of . . . James Duke of Monmouth," in *Historical and Biographical Tracts,* II, 31; Duckett, II, 15.
[5] *C.S.P.D., 1680–1681,* p. 514.  [6] Morrice MSS, P, 434.
[7] Duckett, II, 228, 230, 244.  [8] *O.R.,* I, 537, 543.

** SWYNFEN, JOHN (1613–1694) was of Swynfen, Staffordshire. He first gained prominence as a parliamentarian following his election to the Long Parliament in October, 1645. As a member of the House he subscribed to the Solemn League and Covenant in January, 1646, and subsequently opposed the Independents and Army leaders. As a result he was secluded in Pride's Purge in December, 1648, and took no part in politics again until 1659 when he was elected for Tamworth.[1] At this juncture Richard Baxter looked to him to work for regulations of parliamentary elections which would in effect have established a theocracy for they provided that "none but church members may govern and choose governors," and "let only Presbytery have a justice or offices of appointment. . . ." [2]

Baxter would have agreed with the compiler of a survey of Staffordshire gentry in 1663, for Swynfen was described as a "rigid Presbyterian" and also a "very prudent and able man." [3] However, he was most probably more moderate than reported, and if not he became so within the next five years. Judging by his speeches in the Commons, particularly in the debates of March and April, 1668, on the part of the King's speech concerning the uniting of his Protestant subjects, it appears that he was in doctrinal agreement with the Anglican Church, but that this was not the case concerning matters of ceremony. In urging that concessions be made he pointed out "that by reason of the late wars there has been a long and great separation from the Church, in which time many have been brought up in a form of worship, and knowing no other, it will be hard and not easy upon the sudden to reduce their conscience to that discipline they were never acquainted with." As Grey reported his views, he wanted to "indulge tender consciences that dissent only in ceremonies." [4] A later speech of the debate is most significant, for he makes his underlying Dissent most apparent at the very moment that he also reveals his feeling that he and those who dissented upon matters of ceremony were actually of the Church. "It was never thought," he stated, "that the law for Conventicles extended to any other persons than such as were out of all communion with us in doctrine, and hold no salvation in our Church, . . . the Dissenters being a people in communion with us in doctrine, though different in ceremonies." [5] It appears from this novel and Nonconformist interpretation that Swynfen believed those who were in doctrinal agreement were in real communion and should be comprehended legally as well. However, the very fact that a statute was needed to accomplish this end is in itself evidence that both legally and actually those who dissented in ceremonies were not of the Anglican Church as established by the Act of Uniformity and the Common Prayer Book appended to it.

Swynfen's statements certainly seem to contain overtones of personal experience and rationalization. It appears that only by such a line of reasoning and by overlooking any dissent upon matters of ceremony was he able to identify himself with the

Church. Actually he was an excellent example of an "old Puritan" who is best described as a Presbyterian during the Restoration period, and this is evident in the judgment of his contemporaries, both Nonconformist and Anglican, as well as in his own correspondence. As would be expected, those who were supporters of the Court and the Church in the House of Commons considered him to be among the Dissenters in the House, as they did in this very debate of March–April, 1668.[6] Even those of more moderate political and religious views, such as Sir Thomas Clarges, considered him to be no supporter of the Church and regarded him as a member of the Presbyterian wing of the opposition. Certainly this is the import of a retort made to a speech which Swynfen gave eleven years later in which Clarges dramatically charged: "Geneva, Geneva itself could not more reflect upon the Holy Hierarchy than this gentleman."[7]

Throughout the period between the Restoration and his death in 1694, Swynfen had continuing close friendships with several Nonconformist ministers and contacts with numerous others. Of these friendships the most significant from a religious standpoint was the one with the famous Presbyterian John Howe. Highly revealing is a draft of an answer Swynfen wrote Howe in September, 1687, after the latter and Richard Hampden had come to visit Swynfen and his wife at his seat in Staffordshire. Referring to himself as an "old friend," he wrote Howe with "much thankfulness" for the "extraordinary favor of the tedious (but kind) journey which you undertook with my dear friend [Hampden] to bestow your estimable [?] company. . . ." He continued in the same vein at some length, saying among other things that he and his wife "enjoy yet much these . . . hours in which you served [?] us," for which, he added, "I bless God."[8] That such feelings were mutual is evident in Howe's letter which was written in a spirit of "much obligation and affection" and in which he said: "I pray God the residue of your life may be proportionately serviceable to Him, as the present state of things requires, and as your former life has been."[9] The two men had been in particularly close contact in early 1676 when Howe was in the process of giving up his position as domestic chaplain to John, Second Viscount Massereene of Antrim Castle in Ireland, and of accepting a position as co-pastor of the Presbyterian Congregation meeting at

Haberdasher's Hall in London. Massereene was much disturbed to lose Howe, of whom he said "no man can be better fitted to steer between the two extremes" of Conformity and Nonconformity, and as a result he as well as Howe turned to Swynfen, for as he wrote Swynfen, "you found so good success in the choice of the last," and "no man can better discern than you, with Mr. Howe's help. . . ." [10]

Swynfen and Roger Morrice also had a close relationship which was of both religious and political significance, for Morrice served Swynfen as an informant concerning developments in these fields, and at the same time he undoubtedly received information for his "Ent'ring Book." [11] In addition many Presbyterian ministers admired him and sought his counsel. Calamy called him "pious and judicious," and Philip Henry left a sick wife in order to go "discourse Lord Paget and Mr. Swinfen concerning public affairs" during the summer of 1682 when the Dissenters were facing increasing prosecution. [12]

Also revealing were statements which he made to his close friends and associates who sought his advice in the late summer and early fall of 1687 "that the Churchmen must not be trusted" in the offers they were making to counter the effect of James II's policies of favoring the Dissenters. [13] Undoubtedly he was moved to give this advice partly because of such Anglican support then being proffered him as that which reportedly came from Thomas, Lord Weymouth, and also by such decisions as the one of the Dean and Chapter, and the Church of Lichfield that "Mr. Swynfen is the fittest man to serve them for they now see they were mistaken in him, and understand by information . . . that he was always against the King's death, that he has carried in all Parliaments with great moderation and temper. . . ." [14] It is understandable that after facing Anglican opposition based upon such grounds over the years, Swynfen would be skeptical that an enduring change of attitude had occurred. In view of this response to Anglican approaches and his religious position in the past, it was to be expected that his name was on James II's list of approved candidates for Parliament and that he was also considered fit to be a justice of the peace. [15] However, it is clear that he felt even more wary of James II's policies. To John Howe, Richard Hampden, Philip Foley, and Robert Harley he stated his conviction that "those that can should get into the House," but he added

the warning that "none but staunch men are to be trusted." [16]
He had described himself, all would have agreed.

*M.P.:* 1661–1678; March, 1679, and 1681, in the first and last Exclusion Parliaments, all for Tamworth, Staffordshire.[17]

[1] Wedgewood, II, 76–78; Brunton and Pennington, pp. 210, 242.

[2] Schlatter, *Baxter,* p. 64. In May, 1660, the House of Commons delegated Swynfen to thank Baxter for his sermon at St. Margaret's Church for the House. *C.J.,* VII, 7.

[3] Col. Edward Vernon was apparently the compiler. "The Gentry of Staffordshire, 1662–3," MS 100/1, Stafford Co. Record Office, ed. Ruth M. Kidson, *Collections for a History of Staffordshire* (Stafford Co. Record Office, 4th Ser., Shrewsbury, 1958), II, 29.

[4] Milward, p. 217; Grey, I, 104.     [5] *Ibid.,* p. 131.

[6] Milward, pp. 214, 216. For a bishop's opinion of Swynfen in 1669 see Tanner MSS, 45, fol. 121.

[7] In his entry of April 19, 1679, Morrice reports that this taunt was made in the debate on the Bill of Disarming Catholics, after Swynfen suggested that the Bishops, though pious, did not execute the laws against Papists in the Ecclesiastical Courts as they should. The debate he refers to was apparently held April 16 (he thought it occurred the following day) and was on the second reading of the Bill for Securing the King and Kingdom against the Growth and Danger of Popery. Clarges was made chairman of the Committee on the Bill, and Swynfen was the fifth appointed. Morrice MSS, P, 164; *C.J.,* IX, 597, 598.

Clarges had served Richard Cromwell, and came into prominence as the agent of General Monck, his brother-in-law, in the negotiations leading to the Restoration. For a while he had his son tutored by Thomas Lisle, an ejected minister. In 1679 he was a member of the opposition ranks. S. R. J. Williams, *The Parliamentary History of the County of Oxford* (Brecknock, 1899), pp. 157–58; Calamy, *Cont.,* I, 363.

[8] Add. MSS, 29,910, fol. 226.

[9] *Ibid.*

[10] W.S.L. MSS, 254, Swynfen Ltrs., No. 24, pp. 1–2.

[11] Add. MSS, 29,910, fols. 108, 119–20; 30,013, fols. 35, 36; Morrice MSS, Q, 239 (third page so numbered).

[12] Calamy, *Cont.,* II, 770; Henry, p. 316. Two years before Henry had spent a fortnight at Lord Paget's estate, Boreatton, while Swynfen and Philip Foley (Paget's son-in-law) were there, and judging from his diary entry he conducted services and performed other ministerial duties. *Ibid.,* p. 292. Among the ministers to whom Swynfen gave assistance were John Chester, John Butler, Richard Chantrye, and Richard Hilton, all of whom were silenced in 1660 or ejected in 1662. Matthews, pp. 94, 109, 113–14, 267; Add. MSS, 30,013, fol. 31.

[13] *H.M.C., Portland MSS,* III, pp. 400, 404.

[14] Morrice MSS, Q, 215.

[15] His name was later dropped from the list of candidates for the House since he was considered "super annuated." Duckett, II, 253, 290.

[16] *H.M.C., Portland MSS,* III, 400,404 (Letters of Robert Harley to his father Sir Edward Harley).

[17] *O.R.,* I, 528, 538, 549; Gooder, II, 76–78. In the autumn of 1679 he stood for election but lost by one vote.

** THOMPSON, SIR JOHN (1647–1610), of Haversham, Bucks, was created a baronet in 1673 and Baron Haversham in 1696. His father, Morris Thompson was prominent in Cromwell's government. Sir John reportedly became closely associated with Lord Wharton and through him "grew into the esteem" of the Earl of Anglesey. He eventually married Anglesey's daughter, who like her mother was a member of Dr. John Owen's congregation.[1] His own religious position is evident in his close friendship with John Howe and his statement that he went sometimes to Church and sometimes to Nonconformist meetings, a practice which he still continued in 1705.[2] Morrice noted that he defended Dissenters in parliamentary debates during the Convention.[3]

*M.P.:* 1685 and 1689 for Gatton, Surrey.[4]

[1] *Memoirs of Lord Haversham,* pp. i–ii; "Dr. Watts Church Book," *C.H.S.T.,* I, 27.
[2] *Memoirs of Lord Haversham,* pp. iii.    [3] Morrice MSS, Q, 639.
[4] *O.R.,* I, 555, 562.

** THOMPSON, SIR WILLIAM (d. 1681), of London, was a merchant and politician. He served as an alderman in 1653, sheriff in 1655–1656, member of Parliament in 1659, and in 1660 he was knighted.[1] In 1661 he was one of the four Presbyterians or Congregationalists who were elected to sit for London.[2] On only one occasion did Thompson speak in the debates on religious matters so far as the incomplete records indicate. In March, 1668, he favored toleration "because those that desired it were true worshippers of God, and . . . a restraint would prove destructive to trade. . . ."[3] From 1671 to 1675 Thompson was a commissioner of the customs,[4] and as a result he was subject to some pressure to support the Government, particularly in 1675, but Wiseman considered him unreliable, and Danby did not even consider him a possible supporter.[5] There seems to be no question that Thompson was a Presbyterian or Congregationalist when he was elected in 1661, but the lack of any very substantial evidence between then and 1668, and the complete absence of evidence after that year indicate that within a year or two after 1661 he should be considered a probable Presbyterian or Congregationalist, and after 1668 only a possible one.

*M.P.:* 1661–1678, for London.[6]

[1] Beaven, II, 82, 184; LeNeve, p. 45.

[2] One of the many letters written at the time described him as a Congregationalist, while another stated he was a Presbyterian; in addition there were those who wrote that there were two Congregationalists and two Presbyterians among the four, and others who thought all four were Presbyterians. *C.S.P.D., 1660–1661,* pp. 535–43; *1670 (Addenda 1660–1670),* p. 660; *H.M.C., Finch MSS,* I, 120.

[3] Milward, p. 216.

[4] Beaven, II, 82; *H.M.C., Fitzherbert MSS,* p. 6.

[5] Browning, III, 61–63.

[6] *O.R.,* I, 525.

\* THURBARNE, JAMES (c. 1607–1688), of Sandwich.[1] Although not active in the Civil Wars, Thurbarne favored the parliamentary cause. He was a member of the Convention Parliament of 1660, but not sufficiently active to reveal his religious position. However, in 1662 he was ejected from his position as jurat and town clerk, and in the Episcopal Returns of 1669 he was listed as either a principal member or an abettor of a Presbyterian-Congregationalist Conventicle.[2] It therefore appears that he was a probable Dissenter. In the Cavalier Parliament he was neither active nor apparently regular in attendance.[3]

*M.P.:* 1661 for Sandwich.

[1] Unless otherwise attributed, information in this notice comes from B. D. Henning, MS biography of Thurbarne, prepared for *The History of Parliament, 1660–1690,* ed. B. D. Henning.

[2] Turner, I, 14.

[3] *O.R.,* I, 532.

TRENCHARD, SIR JOHN (1649–1695), of Taunton, Somerset, was the outspoken and aggressive Whig partisan during the Popish Plot, the Exclusion Crisis, and the Rye House Plot, who under William III became a Secretary of State (1692–1695). He was the son of Thomas Trenchard of Wolverton (d. 1658) and was brought up in a Puritan and Nonconformist atmosphere,[1] for apparently his mother was the "Madame Trenchard" for whom the ejected minister Thomas Rowe used to preach twice every Sunday in 1665–66.[2] It is less certain that the Nonconforming minister Samuel Hardy served her or her son Thomas, the heir, but according to Calamy he was a "sort of chaplain to the family" both before and after Bartholomew and had the opportunity to form the mind of young John.[3] Calamy states that when a by-election was held at Poole in March, 1673, to fill the place of John's brother, Thomas (d. 1671) Hardy brought in John Trenchard as a "fitter man" than Shaftesbury's son, whom the Earl naturally "was very earnest to have . . . chosen," but this does not appear to be correct.[4] In any event, Trenchard's entry into the House was not to come until March, 1679. When the mayor of Taunton reported in January, 1684, that he had taken Mr. Trenchard's wife at a conventicle, Secretary Jenkins not only replied that special attention had been given to the report by the King in Council, but that it was well known that Trenchard and another man convicted for attending conventicles had "appeared there to give countenance to their party."[5] Trenchard was called a Dissenter by the informer James Harris in the same year. Although this could have been a charge growing out of Trenchard's involvement in the Rye House Plot rather than from any specific knowledge of his beliefs, and although Harris cannot be considered reliable, nevertheless this informer called Edmund Prideaux (q.v.) a Dissenter at the same time and other evidence shows that he was correct.[6] There is no question about the strong support given to Trenchard by the Dissenters of Taunton in the elections between 1679 and 1689, and as the agents of James II reported in April, 1688, the "greatest part of the town are Dissenters. . . ."[7] For these reasons Trenchard may be considered as a possible Presbyterian.

*M.P.:* 1679–1681, in the three Exclusion Parliaments, for Taunton, Somerset, and from June 20, 1689 for Thetford, Norfolk.[8]

[1] J. P. Ferris, "Sir John Trenchard and His Family," *Notes and Queries for Somerset and Dorset*, XXVIII (Sept., 1966), 285–87.

[2] Calamy, *Acct.*, II, 270; Matthews, p. 419.

[3] Hardy was the minister at Charminster Church, which as Calamy states was "a *Peculiar* belonging to the family of the Trenchards, within a little mile of Dorchester, and out of any Episcopal inspection or jurisdiction. The minister there, is a sort of a chaplain to that family, but neither parson nor vicar; nor does he

take any institution or induction." Hardy continued to hold the position after the Act of Uniformity went into effect, being protected from the Bishop's Court and the justices of the peace by the Trenchards. In 1669 he went to the Church at Poole on the same terms, for it was also a "Peculiar" over which ecclesiastical authorities were much disturbed. Eventually they obtain Hardy's removal on August 3, 1682, after he had conducted an "appointed" or trial service in which he went into the pulpit without using the Common Prayer. Calamy, *Acct.*, II, 281–83; Matthews, p. 248.

⁴ I am indebted to J. P. Ferris for questioning Calamy's accuracy and for the suggestion that he has confused the by-election of 1673 with that of 1670 when Thomas Trenchard was returned and the then Lord Ashley was displeased. In 1673 John Trenchard does not appear to have been a candidate. *C.S.P.D., 1671,* p. 586; *1671–1672,* p. 83; *1672–1673,* pp. 510–11, 572.

⁵ *Ibid., 1683–1684,* pp. 229–30, 246.

⁶ Trenchard was arrested on suspicion of involvement in the Rye House Plot in June, 1683. *Ibid., 1683,* p. 16. Milne concluded that Trenchard played a part of "considerable importance." "The Rye House Plot," pp. 187–88.

⁷ More specifically the agents reported that the suffrage at Taunton was "popular" and consisted of about 700 voters. *C.S.P.D., 1680–1681,* pp. 211, 514–15; *1683–1684,* pp. 229–30; Duckett, II, 229; [Benjamin Harris], *Protestant (Domestick) Intelligence,* March 15, 1681.

⁸ *O.R.,* I, 537, 543, 549, 560.

** TRENCHARD, THOMAS (1640–1671), of Wolverton, Dorset, was the son of Thomas Trenchard (bur. 1658) and the brother of Sir John Trenchard who has just been noted.¹ The religious views of Thomas Trenchard after the Restoration are clearly evident in his relationship to the Nonconformist minister Samuel Hardy. It appears that it was actually he who was responsible for protecting Hardy from the authorities and for retaining him in his post at Charminster Church and as a family chaplain in spite of his failure to conform.² Calamy reports that when Dr. Ralph Rideoake, later Bishop of Chichester came to see Thomas Trenchard regarding Hardy's Nonconformity and "began to persuade that he might be instituted and inducted," Trenchard "vehemently opposed, saying that he would turn [Hardy] out, if he listened to any such motion." ³

*M.P.:* November 7, 1670, until his death in 1671, for Poole.⁴

¹ Ferris, *Notes and Queries for Somerset and Dorset,* XXVIII, 285–87.

² A full description of Hardy's position and religious views is given under Sir John Trenchard's notice, *supra.,* n.3.

³ Calamy, *Acct.,* II, 282.

⁴ Since Trenchard was buried on Dec. 1, 1671 he would have sat in all of the remainder of the session which was underway at the time of his election, and

which ended April 22, 1671. The next session did not begin until Feb. 4, 1673, *O.R.,* I, 522; Ferris, *Notes and Queries for Somerset and Dorset,* XXVIII, 285–87.

\*\* TRENCHARD, WILLIAM (1640–1710), of Cutteridge, between Westbury and Trowbridge, Wiltshire, was a distant relation of the Secretary of State, Sir John Trenchard, and father of the well-known eighteenth century political writer John Trenchard. The evidence that he was a Nonconformist is found in the reports of both the Lord Lieutenant of Wiltshire and James II's agents, who with complete assurance listed Trenchard as a Dissenter and stated that he was "undoubtedly right and hath so declared himself." He was therefore recommended to be a deputy lieutenant and was backed as a possible member of the Lower House.[1]

*M.P.:* 1679–1681, in the three Exclusion Parliaments, for Westbury, Wiltshire.[2]

[1] P.C.C., 283 Leeds; Duckett, I, 221, 225.
[2] *O.R.,* I, 538, 545, 550.

\*\* UPTON, JOHN (1639–1687) of Lupton, Devon. His immediate family background was both Parliamentarian and Puritan. His father supported the Parliamentarian cause in the Civil War and sat for Devonshire in 1654 and 1656, while considerably later in 1672 a house belonging to his mother was licensed for Presbyterian worship.[1] Upton continued in the Puritan tradition of his parents, for he was the patron of the well-known Congregationalist minister John Flavel. One of this minister's most famous sermons was delivered for his patron's funeral, and Upton therefore may be considered a Dissenter of Congregationalist leanings.[2]

*M.P.:* In March and October 1679 and 1681, in the three Exclusion Parliaments for Dartmouth, Devon.[3]

[1] J. P. Ferris, MS biography of Upton prepared for *The History of Parliament, 1660–1690,* ed. B. D. Henning; Turner, II, 1165.
[2] John Flavel "The Balm of the Covenant," *Whole Works* (1716), pp. 546–53; P. Varwell, "Notes on the Ancient Parish of Brixham, Devon . . ." *Trans. Devon. Assoc.,* XVIII (July, 1886), 197–214.
[3] *O.R.,* I, 535, 541, 547.

\* VAUGHAN, EDWARD (d. 1661) was of Lloydiarth, Montgomery. He was a captain in the Parliamentary Army, and a Recruiter in the Long Parliament, sitting as knight of the shire for Montgomery. In 1648 he was secluded in Pride's Purge, and he did not sit again until the Parliament of 1659.[1] In 1661 he remained a strong believer in limited monarchy and expressed the opinions that the King and Council could not raise either men and arms or money without the consent of Parliament.[2] His record in the 1640's indicates that he was probably of Presbyterian persuasion, and it is likely he remained so during the half year that he sat in the Cavalier House of Commons.

*M.P.:* From May until his death October 25, 1661, for the county of Montgomery.[3]

[1] Williams, *Parliamentary History of Wales*, pp. 143–44; Brunton and Pennington, p. 243.
[2] *C.S.P.D., 1660–1661*, pp. 582, 594–95.
[3] Williams, *Parliamentary History of Wales*, p. 143; *O.R.*, I, 533 and n.1.

WALLER, EDMUND JR. (?–1699), of Hallbarne, Beaconsfield, Bucks. In 1688 he was included in a list sent to James that was considered to be mostly made up of supposed Dissenters, and he was recommended by the Regulators for a deputy lieutenant.[1] Before he became a Quaker in 1698 he had been in touch with various Friends, and he then commenced attending meetings.[2] This evidence is insufficient to be at all conclusive, but it indicates that he was possibly a Dissenter at the time of the Convention Parliament.

*M.P.:* 1688 for Agmondesham, Bucks.[3]

[1] Duckett, II, 151, 296.
[2] Evelyn Roberts "Notes on the Life of Edmund Waller," *J.F.H.S.*, VIII, 129–33; *A Quaker Post-Bag*, ed. Mrs. Godfrey Lampson (1910), p. 66.
[3] *O.R.*, I, 557.

WALLER, SIR WILLIAM (d. 1699) of Westminster, Middlesex, was the son of the famous Parliamentary general of the same name. He grew up in an atmosphere of Puritanism and Nonconformity,[1] and at the time of the religious census of the Province of Canterbury in 1676 it was reported in the "Particulars of Conventicles in London and Westminster" that "Sir William Waller frequents [a] conventicle in Westminster in the Great Almry where Mr. Cotton alias Turner a silenced Presbyterian preached."[2] A dozen years later Roger Morrice likewise considered him a Dissenter, his estimate being necessarily based on Waller's views prior to his flight to Amsterdam at the time of the Rye House Plot.[3] However, since the minister named Cotton or Turner cannot be identified with certainty, and since Morrice is in this instance probably basing his estimate more upon Waller's general reputation in the past than upon specific knowledge, these sources cannot be considered quite as reliable as usual; but together with other evidence, they indicate that until 1681 he was probably a Presbyterian. He maintained a relationship with Lord Wharton.[4] In addition it was reported that he helped Sir John Trenchard electioneer effectively among the Dissenters of Taunton.[5] Finally, when he was in the House he pressed for measures such as the repeal of the Corporation Act.[6] He was best known for his rigorous prosecution of the Popish Plot.

*M.P.:* October, 1679, and 1681, in the last two Exclusion Parliaments, for Westminster.[7]

[1] Calamy, *Acct.*, II, 57, 75.

[2] *H.M.C., Leeds MSS*, p. 15. There is no known ejected minister named Cotton, though there are several named Turner. John Turner, ejected vicar of Sunbury, Middlesex was known to have been preaching in London at this time, but his regular meeting was in New Street, St. Dunstans in the West. Matthews, p. 497.

[3] Morrice MSS, Q, 392 (Dec. 1, 1688); see also p. 337.

[4] Carte MSS, 79, fol. 175.

[5] *C.S.P.D., 1680–1681*, pp. 514–15.

[6] *H.M.C., Beaufort MSS*, p. 104.          [7] *O.R.*, I, 542, 548.

** WHITE, JOHN (1634–1713), of Cotgrave, Nottingham, was of an old and well-established family in the county.[1] His religious views are evident in the fact that he had a leading Presbyterian divine, Matthew Sylvester, as his chaplain between Sylvester's ejection and the Declaration of Indulgence in 1672.[2] It may well have been largely because of his religious views that his house was searched for arms at the time of the Rye House

Plot,[3] and it was undoubtedly for the same reason that he was recommended for a position as justice of the peace by the Lord Lieutenant and the King's agents in 1687–1688.[4] He was also one of the original trustees of Lord Wharton's Bible Trust.[5]

*M.P.:* 1679–1681, in the three Exclusion Parliaments, and from May 14, 1689 for Nottingham County.[6]

[1] A. C. Wood, *A History of Nottinghamshire* (Nottingham, 1947), p. 208.
[2] Calamy, *Acct.,* II, 449; Baxter MSS, Letters, IV, fol. 24.
[3] *C.S.P.D., 1683,* p. 301; *1683–1684,* p. 216.
[4] Duckett, II, 121, 289.
[5] Dale, *Good Lord Wharton,* p. 72.
[6] *O.R.,* I, 537, 543, 548, 560.

\* WIDDRINGTON, SIR THOMAS (c. 1600–1664) was of Cheesebourne Grange in Stamfordham, Northumberland. He was a prominent lawyer and a man of wealth who served in both the Short and Long Parliaments.[1] He reputedly took the Covenant, but he was not secluded in Pride's Purge. Although he "had no mind to sit in the House" for some weeks thereafter, he did return to sit in the Rump. Subsequently he held several important positions in the House and the Government, including membership on the committee for ejecting scandalous ministers. In the spring of 1660 when the Presbyterians were again powerful, he was a Commissioner of the Great Seal, and in February, 1660, a member of the Council of State.[2] He sat for York in the Convention Parliament, and worked with Lord Wharton in compiling a list of members who would supposedly support or oppose their policies.[3] After the passage of the Corporation Act in the next parliament he surrendered his position as Recorder of York,[4] quite probably because of his Nonconformist views. Although there is no other evidence concerning his religious position during the next and last two years of his life, it seems probable that he retained his previous Presbyterian or Congregationalist views.

*M.P.:* 1661 until his death on May 13, 1664, for Berwick-on-Tweed, Northumberland.[5]

[1] Keeler, pp. 393–94.
[2] Brunton and Pennington, p. 245; Clements R. Markham, *Life of the Great Lord Fairfax Commander in Chief of the Army of the Parliament of England*

(London and New York, 1870), p. 390n.; Bean, *Parliamentary Representation,*
pp. 501–502.
    [3] Carte MSS, 81, fols. 74–77 (see 75 *verso*).
    [4] *C.S.P.D., 1661–1662,* p. 612.
    [5] *O.R.,* I, 526.


WILBRAHAM, SIR THOMAS (1630–1692) was of Weston-
under Lizard, Staffordshire, and also of Woodhey Hall, Acton,
Cheshire. He was prominent in both counties, having served as
sheriff of Staffordshire in 1654–1655 and of Cheshire in 1663–
1664.[1] Calamy reports several ejected ministers were associated
with the Wilbrahams as chaplains, but it is clear that it was Lady
Wilbraham who was primarily responsible. After his ejection
John Cartwright served as her chaplain at Woodhey for an unknown period of time.[2] Samuel Edgley was chaplain to the Wilbrahams sometime before the spring of 1675. Edgley became
Vicar of Acton, of which Wilbraham was the patron, in September, 1675, and presumably it is for this reason that Calamy lists
him as an "afterconformist." [3] In May, 1683, Wilbraham was seeking a minister through Sir Edward Harley, who wrote Dr. Gilbert
Burnet for a recommendation. Burnet replied that he would take
care that the person he suggested would have the qualifications
Lady Wilbraham desired. He apparently had a Scotsman in mind,[4]
and in view of the other chaplains whom she had, it would seem
that she was seeking a moderate Presbyterian. The last chaplain
to serve her was James Illingworth, an ejected minister who was
licensed as a Presbyterian in 1672, and he was with her from
sometime after he left the same position with Philip Foley (probably after 1678) until his death in 1693, one year after Sir Thomas
died.[5]
    This evidence is obviously much more conclusive concerning
the religious beliefs of Lady Wilbraham than those of her husband. However, Newcome specifically states that Edgley was Sir
Thomas' chaplain. In addition he seems to have been most cooperative in efforts to obtain suitable chaplains for his wife. Until
the middle 1670's it seems that he should be considered a probable Presbyterian, but after that there is more doubt as to his
position. During the time he sat in Parliament he can be considered only a possible Presbyterian.

*M.P.:* October, 1679, in the second Exclusion Parliament, for Stafford Borough.[6]

¹ G.E.C., *Bart.*, I, 164; Wedgwood, *Staffs. Parl. Hist.*, Vol. II, Pt. I, pp. 145–46.
² Calamy, *Acct.*, II, 125; Matthews, pp. 102–103.
³ Newcome, *Autobiog.*, I, 212; Matthews, pp. 179–80.
⁴ *H.M.C., Bath MSS*, I, 45, 46, 48.
⁵ Calamy, *Cont.*, I, 116–17; Matthews, p. 288.
⁶ *O.R.*, I, 544.

WINWOOD, RICHARD (1609–1688), of Denham and Ditton, Buckinghamshire, was the son of Sir Ralph Winwood, the diplomat and Secretary of State (d. 1617) who sympathized with the political and religious principles of the Dutch Republic and who was granted a pension by the Republic which was paid to him and his son for life. Richard Winwood served in the Long Parliament and was secluded in 1648; he was also elected to the Convention Parliament in 1660.[1] Little information concerning his religious views after the Restoration has been discovered, but such as there is suggests that he may have continued to hold Presbyterian views. Not long before he sat in the House once again in 1679, he wrote the Baron of Montagu that he was happy the latter had taken into his family Dr. Robert Wild, the ejected Presbyterian minister and well-known Nonconformist poet, for he was the son of his "old and very good friend. . . ."[2] In 1688 the Lord Lieutenant's report to James II from Buckinghamshire had his name in a list headed "most of them supposed to be Dissenters," and he was recommended to be a deputy lieutenant by both the Lord Lieutenant and the King's agents.[3]

M.P.: 1679–1681, in the three Exclusion Parliaments, for New Windsor, Berkshire.[4]

¹ Keeler, pp. 397–98; Brunton and Pennington, p. 245.
² *H.M.C., Montagu MSS*, p. 186; Matthews, p. 529.
³ Duckett, II, 151 and n., 154, 296. He had previously been a deputy lieutenant, but in April, 1680, the King had him removed at the same time as Sir Richard Ingoldsby was. *C.S.P.D., 1679–1680*, pp. 438–39.
⁴ *O.R.*, I, 534, 540, 546.

\* YONGE, SIR WALTER (c. 1625–1670), of Colyton, Devon, was the grandson of the well-known Puritan diarist and member of Parliament who had the same name, and a son of Sir John Yonge. Sir Walter, the second baronet, was admitted to the Inner Temple in 1645; in 1659 and 1660 he was a member of Parliament.[1] After the Restoration he remained active in local politics. Although he was a commissioner for corporations, in January, 1664, Bishop Ward wrote Archbishop Shelden that Yonge was one of the fourteen justices of the peace in Devon who were "arrant Presbyterians."[2] Nevertheless, in May, 1666, the King recommended to the Dean and Chapter of Exeter that the lease of the parsonage of Sidbury, which the Yonge family had held in the past, be granted for three lives as Sir Walter requested instead of twenty-one years as had been recommended by "one of the two late Kings."[3] When handling this matter, Bishop Ward again wrote Shelden that Yonge was "*able* to do good service if his inclinations *shall turn* that way."[4] This seems to indicate that there had been little if any change in Yonge, and it suggests that the King's action was the result of influence Yonge had at Court, probably in the person of Secretary Morice. In any event it was the Secretary who "highly recommended" Yonge when he stood against Sir Joseph Williamson and another candidate in the by-election at Dartmouth the following January, and according to reports this support was very influential. Yonge was successful "by many votes carried by the fanatic party."[5]

In the House, Yonge soon became a participant in the debates and showed where his religious sympathies lay. In March, 1668, he spoke against a motion to have the King issue a proclamation for execution of the penal laws. The following month he "spoke much for an indulgence" during the debate on the King's speech for uniting Protestant subjects, and later in the same debate he supported the move to repeal the requirement in the Act of Uniformity that ministers must declare their unfeigned assent and consent to the Book of Common Prayer and the Thirty-nine Articles.[6] This would appear to indicate that upon matters of liturgy and church discipline he was probably Presbyterian in his views.

*M.P.:* From January 22, 1667, until his death in 1670, for Clifton Dartmouth Hardness, Devon.[7]

[1] G.E.C., *Bart.*, III, 232; *O.R.*, I, 508, 514.
[2] *C.J.*, VIII, 287; "Some Letters from Bishop Ward of Exeter," *D.C.N.Q.*, XXI, 226, 284.
[3] *C.S.P.D.*, *1665–1666*, p. 415.
[4] "Some Letters from Bishop Ward of Exeter," *D.C.N.Q.*, XXI, 366.
[5] *C.S.P.D.*, *1666–1667*, pp. 445–46, 470.

[6] Grey, I, 106, 127; Milward, p. 218.

[7] *O.R.,* I, 521. The member elected to fill Yonge's place was returned Dec. 22, 1670.

YONGE, SIR WALTER (c. 1653–1731) of Colyton, Devon, was the son of the Sir Walter already noted as a probable Presbyterian. The younger Sir Walter had the active support of the Nonconformist minister Samuel Hieron in the election of March, 1679, Hieron even stating in a letter to Lord Wharton that he had been "instrumental in [Yonge's] election." [1] Before giving this support, Hieron had written Wharton that Yonge's "conversation [is] sober, and by the other party [he is] counted a fanatic. His family [is] well ordered, himself praying in it morning and evening. . . . " It appears possible that Yonge may have held moderate Presbyterian views similar to those of Hieron. Also indicative was Hieron's report after the election that Yonge "did seem to speak of the Young Mr. [John] Hampden as his intimate acquaintance, when I told him of the said Mr. H's being chosen." [2] Yonge's election to serve for Honiton three times between 1679 and 1681 is likewise significant, for James II's agents reported, in April, 1688, the election was "popular" consisting of about 300, and "the majority of the town are Dissenters." Then, as before, they proposed to choose Yonge. He was also recommended to be chosen for a deputy lieutenant or justice of the peace. [3]

*M.P.:* 1679–1681, in the three Exclusion Parliaments, for Honiton, Devon, and 1689 for Ashburton, Devon. [4]

[1] Rawl. Ltrs., H 51, fols. 89, 98.

[2] *Ibid.,* fols. 83, 98.

[3] Duckett, II, 232, 263, 298.

[4] *O.R.,* I, 535, 541, 547, 558. He also stood in the by-election at Newport, Cornwall in Feb., 1678, and petitioned twice against the return of the successful candidate, but there is no record of any committee report to the House concerning his petition. *C.J.,* IX, 444, 483, 521.

## B. MEMBERS OF THE HOUSE OF LORDS

\*\*ANGLESEY, ARTHUR ANNESLEY, FIRST EARL (1614–1686) was of Blechington, Oxford, and Newport Pagnel, Buckinghamshire. He held Presbyterian views and except for two

or three years he was privately a Nonconformist and publicly
a Conformist in his worship from 1661 until 1684 or later. Because
of the diary which he kept more is known concerning Anglesey's
habits of worship than of any other prominent Presbyterian leader
during this period. Although he attended Anglican services nearly
every Sunday, he was also punctilious about having private services conducted on Sunday afternoons by his Nonconformist chaplains in his own chapel.[1] During this period he had three such
chaplains, each of whom served him for a number of years. After
the well-known ejected clergyman Edward Bagshaw the younger,
who was his chaplain in the early 1660's, Anglesey had Benjamin
Agas serve him in this capacity from sometime before August,
1665, until July, 1673. After a three-year period during which he
appears to have had an Anglican chaplain, the Nonconformist
minister Henry Hurst became his regular chaplain in June, 1677;
although his preaching for Anglesey was intermittent from 1679–
1682, it again became regular and Hurst still held his position in
August, 1684.[2]

Although these Nonconformist chaplains were Presbyterians,
Anglesey had connections with Congregationalists, particularly
with Dr. John Owen; the two visited each other on a good number of occasions, usually for dinner at the Angleseys, accompanied by their wives. The Countess of Anglesey was a member
of Dr. Owen's congregation during this period. She was even
bold enough to continue her attendance during the time of the
Government's rigorous enforcement of the statutes against Nonconformity in 1683–1684, and as a result she was one of nineteen
persons seized in January, 1684, at a meeting led by Dr. Owen.[3]
Other Nonconformist ministers and leaders from whom Anglesey
received visits or with whom he had connections were Philip Nye,
Sir Charles Wolesley, and Richard Baxter.[4]

Although Anglesey's diary entries are almost entirely brief accounts of his actions during the day, he occasionally records some
reflections concerning religious matters which indicate his Puritanical and Presbyterian feelings. A major reason for keeping the
diary is revealed in his first entry on May 26, 1671, in which he
stated that he had "begun the Bible again," and then adds:

This morning considering the great decay of piety and increase of profane-
ness and atheism, and particularly my own standing at a stay if not declin-

ing in grace, I fixed a resolution to renew the course I had in former times held of watching over my ways and recording the actions and passages of my life, both to quicken me in good ways and to leave a memorial thereof to my posterity for imitation and to give God the glory of his guidance and mercy towards me and mine. . . .[5]

In other entries he notes that he had resolved "to make a collection of the works of the Nonconformists," and to compile "a diurnal chronicle of Nonconformity . . . from the beginning of the Reformation." He felt that it was "the wickedness of the times" that had driven the Dissenters out of the Church.

The best indication of the position of compromise to which he adhered in his religious views is found in his contention that both "set and sudden prayer . . . are lawful and useful," and his observation that "good men" are Nonconformists "though agreeing in foundations," and that therefore both Nonconformists and Conformists should mutually work for peace.[6] Likewise indicating his views is an anonymous pamphlet ascribed to him in which it becomes evident that his theological views were strongly Calvinistic, and in which he contended that "an Episcopal Calvinist is the rightest son or father of the Church of England. . . ."[7]

Other evidence of Anglesey's Nonconformist outlook is to be found in his defense of individual Dissenters and of Nonconformist interests in general. Among the half dozen Nonconformists who are known to have looked to Anglesey when in legal difficulties, or in whose behalf he intervened on various occasions, were the well-known Baptist printer Francis Smith in 1661, Ralph Button, a Congregationalist accused of regicide in 1675, and another Congregationalist who had been excommunicated in 1678.[8] On several occasions Anglesey is known to have spoken out vigorously or taken action in the Privy Council in order to defend Dissenters and their interests. Of particular significance were his efforts in the Council to protect Dissenters during the period just after Charles II revoked the Declaration of Indulgence, for he took a position contrary to that of the Court and the Council; and again in March, 1682, he "spoke strongly" in the Council for granting relief to Dissenters in danger of death because of overcrowding in Bristol prison, while the other Counsellors were "much against them."[9]

There are indications that because of his well-known eagerness to obtain offices and recognition, Anglesey allowed social and political pressures to make him a more apparent Conformist than he would otherwise have been, particularly during the mid-1670's. It was during this period of Danby's ascendancy and the King's pro-Anglican policy while Anglesey was Lord Privy Seal that he did not have a Nonconformist chaplain, and this was undoubtedly the result of official pressure.[10] Certainly it is significant that he employed a Nonconformist chaplain again in June, 1677, the very month in which Danby received a decisive parliamentary defeat,[11] and that the last time his former Anglican chaplain preached for him privately was in November of that year.

Except for this brief period Anglesey had a lifelong record of Puritan views and of private Nonconformity. Nevertheless, it was reported that on his deathbed he told Dr. John Sharp that he was "ever of the Church of England, and would die so. . . ."[12] The very fact that Anglesey felt that he needed to make such a statement, and that it was considered newsworthy by his contemporaries is most revealing. Although he may have changed in feeling in 1686, it is clear that except for the years 1674–1677 he was a Nonconformist in his private worship from 1661 until August, 1684, if not longer. Moreover, it would seem that private worship must be considered a more true reflection of a man's beliefs than his public worship, particularly when the public observances were necessary to retain public office and the man was known to be especially ambitious.

*House of Lords:* From April, 1661, to 1686.[13]

---

[1] See for example his first diary entries for the Sundays of May and June, 1671. Add. MSS, 40,860, fols. 5–7.

[2] Baxter, Pt. I, p. 378; *Bulstrode Papers*, I, 3; [Francis Chandler], "The Diary of an Ejected Minister," *C.H.S.T.*, VII (Oct., 1918), 380; Add. MSS, 40,860, fols. 43, 52, 59, 60 ff.; 18,730, fols. 23, 26 ff.; Matthews, pp. 3, 22, 286. From Nov., 1673, until Nov., 1675, Anglesey had a Dr. Squibb as a chaplain who preached for him regularly until Nov., 1677. Positive identity of this clergyman has not been made, but Anglesey notes that he preached at Kensington and Blechington Churches, indicating that he was an Anglican. It may have been Laurence Squibb, who in 1679 became Rector of Stanton St. John, Oxford. Add. MSS, 40,860, fols. 60 *passim.*; 18,730, fol. 42; *Al. Oxon.*, IV, 1403.

[3] Add. MSS, 40,860, fols. 6, 9, 28, 77; 18,730, fols. 20, 36. More than a dozen of Owen's treatises and sermons were in Anglesey's library. *Bibliotheca Anglesiana, Sive Catalogus Variorum Librorum in Quavis Lingua, [et] Facultate Insignium* (n.p., 1686), [Pt. II], pp. 3, 8, 10, 13, 19, 23. [Francis Chandler], "The Diary of an Ejected Minister," *C.H.S.T.*, VII (Oct., 1918), 374; Morrice MSS, P, 415, 424.

⁴ Add. MSS, 40,860, fols. 6, 28; *C.S.P.D., 1679–1680*, p. 315. About two dozen of Baxter's sermons and other works were in his library. Prior to the sale of the library following Anglesey's death, Roger Morrice reports that a Mr. Millington, who was the auctioneer, went to one of the Secretaries of State and Sir Roger L'Estrange, being much concerned because Anglesey "by his place as a Privy Councillor might read such books as others might not, [and] that he knew not what were fit to be sold and what were not, and therefore he had submitted the catalogue to them." Among the books L'Estrange did not allow to be sold were "all Mr. Baxter's works and Milton's *Iconoclastes* in French." Morrice MSS, P, 646; Q, 14–15. *Bibliotheca Anglesiana* [Pt. II], pp. 5, 14, 18, 19, 22.

⁵ Add. MSS, 40,860, fol. 5.

⁶ *Ibid.*, 18,730, fol. 1.

⁷ *The Truth Unvailed, in Behalf of the Church of England* (1676), pp. 28, 33–39.

⁸ *C.S.P.D., 1661–1662*, p. 109; *1678*, p. 577; Matthews, pp. 95, 437; Calamy, *Acct.*, II, 86. In addition he was an eager and vigorous supporter of the royal policy of clemency toward Dissenters which was adopted in the summer of 1680, even going so far as to write a letter of admonishment to the Mayor of Gloucester for enforcing the Five Mile Act instead of imitating the King's new clemency. *C.S.P.D., 1680–1681*, pp. 45–46.

⁹ Add. MSS, 40,860, fol. 25; *Letters Addressed from London to Sir Joseph Williamson While Plenipotentiary at the Congress of Cologne, 1673–1674*, ed. W. D. Christie (2 vols.; Camden Soc. Pub., Nos. 8 and 9; 1874), II, 59; *C.S.P.D., 1673–1675*, p. 152; Morrice MSS, P, 330, 332.

¹⁰ *C.S.P.D., 1676–1677*, p. 188. He was appointed Privy Seal April 22, 1673.

¹¹ *C.J.*, IX, 499–500; Browning, I, 282.

¹² *H.M.C., Montagu MSS*, pp. 192, 193.

¹³ G.E.C., *Peerage*, I, 133.

\*\* BEDFORD, WILLIAM RUSSELL, FIFTH EARL AND FIRST DUKE (1613–1700) of Woburn Abbey, Devonshire, and London, was head of the well-known Puritan and Whig Russell family during the last half of the seventeenth century. According to his neighbor the Earl of Ailesbury, Bedford went to the Parish [Church] on Sunday morning; but in his own chapel he had a Presbyterian chaplain, and there was no Common Prayer.¹ This minister was John Thornton, who until 1700 served both as chaplain and as tutor to Bedford's children, and his service at Woburn constitutes the chief evidence that Bedford continued to hold Presbyterian views during this period.² Bedford was also a benefactor to Nonconformist ministers, and he was most respected by their leaders. Among the known donations made by Bedford to ministers were those of 1661 and 1664 when he gave £50 in three gifts which were to be distributed by Thomas Manton; in 1684 Richard Baxter was given £40 for the same purpose, part of which Roger Morrice was charged with distributing. When reporting on the distribution that had been made, Baxter wrote a letter that reflects his respect and admiration for Bedford, and that was clearly designed to give the Duke spiritual encouragement during his long sorrow following the execution of his son William, Lord Russell, for his activity in the Rye House Plot, though he states that it was only the Countess of Bedford whom he knew.[3] Another indication of the feeling which Nonconformist ministers had for the Duke and his family is seen in William Bates' letter to Thornton, stating that before publishing fourteen sermons he has sent copies for the Duke and various members of the family, the one for the Duke being dedicated to him it appears.[4] There were other indications of the mutual esteem Bates and Bedford had for each other, which John Howe recognized when he dedicated to the Earl of Bedford the funeral sermon he gave for Bates.[5]

Like Anglesey, Bedford apparently did not attend public Nonconformist services during the Restoration period, but he maintained a cordial friendship with his former Puritan minister, Thomas Manton just as Anglesey did with Dr. John Owen. Moreover, Lady Bedford continued to attend Manton's meetings just as Lady Anglesey attended Owen's, and like Lady Anglesey, Lady Bedford was apprehended while worshipping at one of these meetings.[6]

*House of Lords:* 1660–1700.[7]

[1] *Memoirs of Thomas, Earl of Ailesbury* (2 vols.; Westminster, 1890), I, 182 (written about 1688).

[2] Rawl. Ltrs., H 109, fols. 12, 33, 100, 109; Calamy, *Acct.*, II, 94–95; Thomson, *Life in a Noble Household*, pp. 72–73, 386; Matthews, p. 484; Woburn Abbey MSS, L, IV, No. 43.

[3] Rawl. Ltrs., H 109, fols. 8, 33; "Woburn Abbey MSS," *C.H.S.T.*, XIV (May, 1944), 233.

[4] Rawl. Ltrs., H 109, fol. 4. See also his letter of condolence, *ibid.*, fol. 6. Thomas Heywood considered him a "godly man." Heywood and Dickenson, *Nonconformist Register*, Pt. I, p. 102.

[5] William Bates, *Works* (1742), p. 947.

[6] This occurred in 1675. Calamy, *Acct.*, II, 43; Palmer, I, 426–31; *H.M.C.*, *Leeds MSS*, p. 15; Baxter, Pt. III, p. 156.

[7] G.E.C., *Peerage*, II, 79–80.

** DELAMER, GEORGE BOOTH, FIRST BARON (1622–1684) was of Dunham Massey, Cheshire. Elected to the Long

Parliament in 1645 and secluded by Pride's Purge in 1648, he was a well-known parliamentarian and Presbyterian during the Civil Wars.[1] In 1659 he was one of the committee of fourteen secluded members who sought admittance to the restored Rump following Richard Cromwell's death, and then he became a key figure in the Presbyterian-royalist plot of August to restore Charles Stuart, an attempt that is known as Booth's Rising. Although the effort failed after temporary success in the area he commanded (Cheshire, Lancashire, and North Wales), it did contribute to the royalist movement. As a result he was rewarded by a barony, a parliamentary grant of £10,000 and appointment as Custos Rotulorum of Cheshire, a position which he held until 1673.[2]

There is considerable evidence that Delamer continued to retain Presbyterian views after the Restoration. He continued to keep Presbyterian chaplains in his service, Robert Eaton holding this position after his ejection and for some time thereafter, and from September 30, 1671 to Delamer's death in 1684 Adam Martindale was his chaplain.[3] In his autobiography, Martindale stated that during the years 1672–1680 he "attended at Dunham usually from May, when my Lord came down, till October or November, [that] he went up again to London." He also states that after the withdrawal of the licenses which had been issued under the Declaration of Indulgence, "it was not thought convenient that my Lord or Lady should give way to my preaching publicly," and it is evident that he felt the Delamers were less zealous than they had been in the past. However, a part of his discouragement was obviously the result of the much diminished size of his audience and the cut in his salary from £40 to £20 or less because the family was away about half the year.[4]

Since Delamer had gained such a reputation among Presbyterian leaders prior to the Restoration and had acquired positions of authority afterwards, it was understandable that Presbyterian ministers would look to him for complete support and that any conformity or compromise with the Established Church would be frowned upon. Thus at the time the Act of Uniformity went into effect he was subject to criticism,[5] and it is implied again in Martindale's comments a decade later. Nevertheless, Delamer did continue to retain his Presbyterian chaplain and attend his services even during the years of strict enforcement of the laws against Nonconformity under Danby and the extreme reaction following the Oxford Parliament of 1681. In addition he was a vigorous opponent of Danby and his policies in the House, particularly the Non-resisting Test (1675), and a faithful member of the group of Presbyterian lords.

*House of Lords:* From April, 1661, to 1684.[6]

---

[1] Brunton and Pennington, p. 227.  [2] G.E.C., *Peerage*, IV, 135.

[3] Calamy, *Acct.*, II, 407; Martindale, p. 197. Martindale also did some tutoring in the family.

[4] *Ibid.*, p. 202–203.

[5] An unknown minister who signed his name "J O" wrote to John Thornton shortly after the Act of Uniformity went into effect: "the Lord Booth is ragingly distrusted, the Lord remember him for good." Rawl. Ltrs., H 109, fol. 87. Clarendon and the King may have made some use of Delamer in their efforts just before St. Bartholomew Sunday in 1662 during which they suggested that some of the Presbyterian ministers petition for the grant of a royal indulgence. Since they did petition, and as "J O" puts it, since they were then not only "put off with the flop of a fox tail" but were also possibly going to be called before the House of Commons for petitioning against an Act of Parliament, the writer was understandably bitter.

[6] G.E.C., *Peerage*, IV, 135–36.

---

** HOLLES OF IFIELD, DENZIL, FIRST BARON (1599–1680), of Dorchester and Damerham South, Wiltshire, was a famous parliamentarian and Presbyterian leader during the Civil War period.[1] He was a member of the Long Parliament and was arrested by the Army and impeached in 1647. Reseated in 1648, he became one of the ten commissioners whom the members of the House of Commons appointed to represent them at the Treaty of Newport on the Isle of Wight. Threatened by the Army's demand for his arrest in December, 1648, he escaped to France; and when he later returned to England he remained staunchly opposed to Cromwell.[2] When the secluded members were readmitted to the House on February 21, 1660, Holles also took his seat, and appears to have favored efforts of the moderate Presbyterian political leaders to effect a restoration on terms satisfactory to them.[3] But during May he became one of the leaders in welcoming the King back to England.[4] As a result he was rewarded at the Restoration, being appointed to the Privy Council and on April 20, 1661, being created Baron Holles of Ifield.[5]

Holles is known to have retained Presbyterian views after the Restoration, but he was very moderate and was not only friendly with an Anglican clergyman such as Burnet, but like Anglesey he had an Anglican chaplain for a short time.[6] Nevertheless, Burnet who states that Holles used him with great freedom from 1664 until his death, wrote that he "was for many years counted the head of the Presbyterian party," and added that "he was faithful and firm to his side, and never changed through the whole course of his life."[7] The most important Presbyterian in Holles' service was Roger Morrice, who was his chaplain. Unfortunately there is no indication in Calamy, who reports this fact, or in Morrice's later manuscripts as to the dates of his employment, but there seems little question that it occurred after the Restoration, most probably sometime after the spring of 1666 when Holles returned from his position as Ambassador to France and before 1677 when Morrice began his "Ent'ring Book."[8] Regardless of the dates of his service, Morrice obviously remained an intimate and trusted confidant of Lord Holles until Holles' death. The Presbyterian minister was kept informed of the negotiations between Holles and Danby regarding the termination of the Cavalier Parliament, and he was trusted with other highly significant political information concerning Privy Council meetings and the like.[9] In fact it is very probable that a considerable amount of the important political information in Morrice's manuscript journal prior to Holles' death in 1680 was derived from this source.

Likewise in the service of Holles were two other ejected ministers. Edward Damer was his steward "sometime after his ejectment," and John Hodges was reported by Baxter in 1679 to have been lately living with Holles, but in what capacity it is not known.[10] His physician was Nicholas Cary, another ejected minister, and Cary was also the man who took charge of publishing Holles' anonymous pamphlet "The Grand Question Concerning the Prorogation of this Parliament" in 1676.[11] Other evidence of his contacts with Presbyterian ministers is found in his activity as an agent to procure licenses for them under the Declaration of Indulgence of 1672.[12]

Holles' third wife Esther, daughter of Gideon le Lou of Colombiers, France, whom he married in September, 1666, shared her husband's religious views. In 1675 she contributed £5 to the Church being built for Dr. Baxter, and in 1676 she, as well as the Countess of Bedford, was reported to attend Dr. Baxter's conventicle in Great Russell Street.[13]

Finally there is evidence that Holles, John Swynfen, Sir Edward Harley, John Howe and others consulted and worked together in personal affairs as well as in matters of public policy which concerned those of his religious position.[14]

Holles died in his house at Covent Garden on February 17, 1680, but the "invaulting" service in Dorchester, was not held until April. Morrice, who faithfully made the trip from London, wrote that "as great respects and honor [were] paid to his memory by the town and country as hath ever been known, and more coaches and horsemen attended his corpse out of the City then (as its said) has ever been seen." [15]

*House of Lords:* From April, 1661, to February 17, 1680.[16]

[1] Brunton and Pennington, pp. 155–59, 163–64, 168; Keeler, p. 220.

[2] Burnet, I, 175.    [3] *Supra*, pp. 9–10.

[4] *C.J.*, VIII, 4, 20.    [5] G.E.C., *Peerage*, VI, 546.

[6] In March, 1663, it is known that Richard Russell, Rector of Brixton, and of Frome Billet and West Stafford, Dorset, was his chaplain. *C.S.P.D., 1663–1664*, p. 67.

[7] Burnet, I, 175.

[8] Calamy, *Acct.*, II, 166–67. Calamy merely states that Morrice "was sometime chaplain to my Lord Hollis, and afterwards to Sir John Maynard." Although he might possibly have held these posts in the very late 1650's, it does not seem likely. Morrice received his B.A. from St. Catherine's, Cambridge in 1656 and his M.A. in 1659. From 1658 until his ejection in August, 1662, he was Vicar of Duffield, Derbyshire. This living in Derbyshire would seem to preclude positions as a chaplain with either Holles or Maynard who were of London, Devon, and Dorset during the years 1658–1662. Morrice could have served Holles between August, 1662, and July, 1663, when he became Ambassador to France; but this does not seem likely since Holles apparently had Richard Russell as a chaplain at this time, and also since Calamy customarily mentions the fact when a minister became a chaplain directly after his ejection. For biographical data concerning Morrice see Matthews, p. 355.

[9] The most important instances are considered in the text of this study. Morrice also may have handled some personal matters for Holles. See Morrice MSS, P, 226.

[10] Calamy, *Cont.*, I, 422; Baxter, Pt. I, p. 96.

[11] *H.M.C., 9th Rept., H. of L. MSS*, pp. 71–72.

[12] He procured a dozen or more, all for Presbyterian ministers. *C.S.P.D., 1671–1672*, pp. 588–89; Turner, III, 435–36.

[13] *H.M.C., Leeds MSS*, p. 15; Baxter, Pt. III, pp. 171–72. She is listed here as Eleanor, but this is evidently a mistake. There was no other Lady Holles at this time. Cokayne, *Peerage*, VI, 546.

[14] W.S.L. MSS, 454, Swynfen Ltrs., No. 33, p. 3; *H.M.C., Portland MSS*, III, 353; Turner, III, 548.

[15] Morrice MSS, P, 251, 256. Since he was returned to the family parish church for burial, a tradition to which most moderate Presbyterians adhered, particularly those of public life, it was necessary to have an Anglican clergyman deliver the funeral sermon. The man who was chosen, Samuel Reyner, had been ejected for Nonconformity after the Act of Uniformity went into effect, and he became an

Anglican by 1670. Reyner paid sincere tribute to Holles as "one who stuck close to the reformed religion, understood its principles, well and thoroughly," and who "practised them conscientiously. . . ." *Life and Times of Anthony Wood*, II, 480; Calamy, *Acct.*, II, 103; Matthews, p. 408; Samuel Reyner, *A Sermon Preached at the Funeral of the Right Honourable Denzell Lord Holles* (1680), pp. 18, 24.
    16 G.E.C., *Peerage*, VI, 546.


*(T) PAGET, WILLIAM, SIXTH BARON (1609–1678), of Boreatton, North Salop, who also held manors in Staffordshire. In 1645 Paget took the Covenant, and for about fifteen years after the Restoration he appears to have remained a Presbyterian. In a survey of Staffordshire leaders made in 1662–63 he was described as a Presbyterian.[1] John Swynfen, who was also described as a Presbyterian in this same survey, was in Paget's service, presumably in a legal capacity, for in 1660 he received £100 as his yearly "allowance." But the two men were also friends and political allies, and when Parliament was in session Swynfen lodged with the Pagets in the Old Palace Yard, Westminster, throughout Paget's life.[2] Presumably he remained Presbyterian until near his death. He was a friend of Richard Baxter, and in 1675 John Howe dedicated his chief work to him, *The Living Temple*.[3] In addition Paget's daughters were married to leading Presbyterian political leaders, one to Philip Foley (q.v.) in 1670, a second to Richard Hampden (q.v.), and a third to Sir Henry Ashurst (q.v.).[4] However, sometime before May, 1677, Paget is known to have had Jonathan Jenner, an Anglican, as a chaplain. During the last year or so of his life Paget must therefore be considered a moderate Anglican.

*House of Lords:* From 1639 to 1678.[5]

    1 G.E.C., *Peerage*, X, 284–85. *L.J.*, VI, 711; "The Gentry of Staffordshire, 1662–1663," *Collections for a History of Staffordshire*, 4th Ser., II, 40.
    2 *Ibid.*, 29, 40; Add. MSS, 29,910, fols. 12, 20, 62–63, 67; 30,013, fols. 20, 259.
    3 Powicke, *John Rylands Library*, Bul., XIII, 325; Howe, *Works*, I, 77.
    4 Henry, 231.                                5 G.E.C., *Peerage*, X, 284–85.


PAGET, WILLIAM, SEVENTH BARON (1637–1713) was of Boreatton, North Salop. The main evidence that he may have been Presbyterian in views was that Philip Henry was on intimate terms with him, and when Henry visited Boreatton, as he did occasionally, he apparently conducted religious services for the family and other guests. In August, 1680, Henry wrote of such a visit at Paget's seat, "where Lord Paget then was and his Lady, Mr. [Philip] Foley and his Lady [who was Paget's sister] and Mr. Swinfen; I stayed with them there [from August 13] until August 24 and unprofitable servant, obliged to do good but falling short." [1] It also appears that Roger Morrice continued to have frequent occasion to visit the Paget home in London, possibly for both political and religious reasons. [2]

It is clear that the young Lord Paget was also very intimate and closely associated with John Swynfen, as his father had been. After the latter's death in 1678, and again in 1679, he wrote Swynfen that he was to come up to his "old lodgings" in the Paget home in the Old Palace Yard "where you shall always be very welcome," and just as in the past, Swynfen continued to stay there when Parliament was in session. [3] Moreover, Paget consulted him on such matters as the education of his sons, and in 1677 he wanted to move one strong-willed son from a tutor, who was a lenient ejected minister and who later conformed, to the Presbyterian Francis Tallents. [4]

Paget's first wife was the daughter of Francis Pierrepoint of Nottingham, who with his brother William was known for his Presbyterian views; and his second wife was his cousin and the daughter of the Presbyterian Sir Anthony Irby. [5]

Although Paget's religious opinions may have changed by 1689 when he became Ambassador to Vienna, during this earlier period of his public life the evidence indicates that he may have held Presbyterian views.

*House of Lords:* From November 25, 1678 to 1713. [6]

---

[1] Henry, p. 292. See also his notice of visiting Paget and Swynfen at Boreatton in July, 1682, to discuss "public affairs." *Ibid.*, p. 316.

[2] Add. MSS, 29,910, fols. 108, 119–20.

[3] *Ibid.*, fols. 93, 99, 106. *Ibid.*, fols. 84–85, 130; 30,013, fols. 27, 250.

[4] *Ibid.*, fols. 24–25.

[5] Calamy, *Acct.*, II, 80; Keeler, p. 306.

[6] *L.J.*, XIII, 375.

(*T*) ROBARTES OF TRURO, JOHN, SECOND BARON [1] (1606–1685) was of Botreux Castle, Lanhydrock, Cornwall. He was well known for his strong Presbyterianism during the Civil

Wars and afterwards.[2] After the execution of Charles I he withdrew from public affairs, and although there were reports that he was ready to support Presbyterian-royalist plots in 1654 and 1657, it was apparently not until the spring of 1660 that he again became active in politics.[3] As a result of Monck's support he was admitted to the Privy Council on June 1, 1661, and shortly thereafter he was being considered for the post of Lord Deputy of Ireland under Monck, who did not intend to go to Ireland. It was at this juncture that Robartes' Presbyterianism came under scrutiny. When Clarendon and the Lord Treasurer went to Robartes to tell him that the King had "good esteem of him, and of his abilities to serve him if he would give his word whether or not he was a Presbyterian," Robartes answered: "'that no Presbyterian thought him to be a Presbyterian, or that he loved their party. He knew them too well. That there could be no reason to suspect him to be such, but . . . that he went constantly to Church as well in the afternoons as forenoons on the Sundays, and on those days forbore to use those exercises and recreations, which he used to do all the week besides.' He desired them 'to assure the King, that he was so far from a Presbyterian, that he believed Episcopacy to be the best government the Church could be subject to.'"[4]

At first this statement seems to be a complete disavowal of Presbyterian views. However, several matters must be considered. First, Robartes was obviously in a position where he would gloss over any Presbyterian views, because he was a very ambitious man and he was clearly anticipating a major appointment. This was evident when Clarendon told Robartes after his statement about his religious views that the King offered him the post of deputy lieutenant for Ireland, for he then showed "great mortification" that he would not be in the superior position.[5] The second matter which must be considered is that he made no statements to Clarendon concerning his views about ceremonies and doctrines and spoke only of church government. Thirdly, he acknowledged that he attended afternoon services as well as morning ones, a custom which was characteristic of the Presbyterians as he implied. Finally, he had been more of a Presbyterian than he admitted, and there is some evidence that he continued to hold Presbyterian views for at least another few years. Not to be overlooked is that in 1683 Robartes backed the King's plans and introduced a bill which would have given the king power to grant dispensation to Protestants from the provisions of that Act and any other laws requiring oaths or subscriptions to the "order, discipline, and worship established. . . ." [6] In addition he kept up close contacts with at least two ejected ministers. According to Calamy, Thomas Travers was "much favored by the noble Lord Roberts" after his ejection, in part probably because he was related to Lady Robartes, and he also states that Robartes had a "great respect" for the Presbyterian Nathaniel Ranew, and "admitted him to an intimate acquaintance with him." [7]

During the first few years of the Restoration period Robartes may be considered a possible Presbyterian.[8]

*House of Lords:* From 1634 to 1685.[9]

[1] On July 23, 1679 he was made Viscount Bodmin and the First Earl of Radnor. G.E.C., *Peerage,* X, 712–14.

[2] Coate, pp. 247, 327; Palmer, II, 209.

[3] *Ibid.,* pp. 285, 296–97, 310–11. Along with other Presbyterians he served on the county committee of militia established by the restored Long Parliament in order to eliminate the forces raised previously by the Rump.

[4] *The Life of Edward Earl of Clarendon, Written by Himself* (2 vols.; Oxford, 1857), I, 396–97.

[5] *Ibid.,* pp. 397–98.

[6] *H.M.C., 7th Rept., H. of L. MSS,* pp. 167–68; Lister, II, 209–10.

[7] Palmer, I, 349; Calamy, *Acct.,* II, 145, 300.

[8] Later statements that he was an avowed Presbyterian were undoubtedly based more upon his prior reputation, his support of toleration and his assistance to the Quakers than upon any real evidence. In 1679 he supported the Bishops and the Government, and 1683 it is known that he had an Anglican chaplain. See *supra,* p. 309, n. 39; Browning, III, 137–39; *C.S.P.D., July–Sept.,* p. 26.

[9] G.E.C., *Peerage,* X, 712–14.

** SAYE AND SELE, WILLIAM FIENNES, FIRST VISCOUNT (1582–April 14, 1662) was of Broughton Castle, Oxfordshire. He was well known for his long and vigorous leadership against the policies of James I and Charles I, as well as for his position of great authority in the House of Lords and for his support of the parliamentary cause in the First Civil War. He was considered the only Independent in the House, and at first sided with the Army in the struggle between it and Parliament. However, in the summer of 1648 he began to change his policy, joined those who sought a peace with the King, and served as one of the commissioners at the Treaty of Newport on the Isle of Wight.

From the King's death he took no part in politics, refusing to sit in Cromwell's Upper House.[1] In 1658 he was reported to favor the restoration of Charles Stuart, but only on the terms of the Treaty of Newport Articles.[2] Taking his seat in the Lords at the opening of the Convention Parliament, he worked with Wharton, Manchester, and Northumberland to obtain limitations upon royal power.[3] His religious views between the time of the King's return and his death a year later are revealed by the fact that he had the ejected minister Ambrose Moston as his chaplain.[4]

*House of Lords:* From 1625 to April 14, 1662.[5]

[1] G.E.C., *Peerage*, XI, 486–87.   [2] *Clar. S.P.*, III, 392.
[3] Lister, III, 99–100 (Letter of Mordaunt to Hyde, May 4, 1660).
[4] Calamy, *Acct.*, II, 714; Palmer, III, 479–80.   [5] G.E.C., *Peerage*, XI, 486–88.

** WHARTON, PHILIP, FOURTH BARON (1613–1696) was of Wooburn, Buckinghamshire, and Wharton Hall, near Raven-stonedale, Westmorland.[1] He was a lay member of the Westminster Assembly and acted with the Independents against the Presbyterians.[2] During the Civil Wars he was a strong supporter of the parliamentary cause. Afterwards he veered away from the political course of the Independents, disapproving of both Pride's Purge and the execution of Charles I. Though he was intimate with Cromwell he would not take part in his government or sit in the House of Peers. After taking his seat in the Convention Parliament he worked with the Presbyterian leaders for limitations upon the royal prerogative.

Wharton is one of a very few members of either House known to have attended public Nonconformist services during the three decades after the Restoration. On one occasion he was apprehended at a meeting being conducted by the Presbyterian Dr. Manton, while on another occasion he was reported present at one which Dr. Manton and Dr. Bates were conducting. He and Manton were cordial friends, and he also had a close friendship with John Howe, with whom he crossed to Holland in 1685.[3] It therefore would seem that following the Restoration he became somewhat more Presbyterian. But at the same time he continued to maintain many Congregationalist connections, notably his close friendship with Dr. John Owen, whom Anglesey found at Wooburn on occasions.[4]

A considerable number of ejected ministers and their sons served him as chaplains and tutors, and they seem somewhat more Presbyterian than Congregationalist in disposition. From the time he was silenced and until his death in September, 1673, Rowland Stedman served Wharton in this capacity, and during part of this time Samuel Birch was also a chaplain.[5] Other chaplains were Samuel Clark and William Taylor, who was the son of an ejected minister and who remained with Wharton as a chaplain for twenty years.[6] The ejected ministers whom Wharton had as tutors included Thomas Elford, Theophilus Gale, and Abraham Clifford.[7] In addition he employed ejected ministers in other capacities,[8] and he gave still others and their projects financial support.[9]

Just as in the case of other prominent Dissenters, Wharton had the presentation of several Anglican livings, and as could be expected he sought to give these positions to moderate ministers. For example, in 1673 he gave the curacy at Ravenstonedale Church to Anthony Proctor, who had been a Nonconformist since 1662, and who had been licensed as a Presbyterian to preach in his own house in 1672. He apparently conformed to some degree upon accepting the living, but he retained a reputation as "a kind of Non-conformist," probably because the Dissenters were called into the church services at the appropriate time in the services on Sundays in order to hear his sermons, which they found satisfactory.[10]

There were many other Nonconformist ministers who consulted and corresponded with Wharton regarding matters of politics and religion, as has been made evident throughout this study, three of those whose letters have been most pertinent being the Presbyterian Samuel Hieron, and the Congregationalists Lewis Stukely and Thomas Gilbert.

Certainly no other peer of the Restoration period had such intimate connections with as many Presbyterian and Congregationalist ministers or was as much esteemed both by them and the political leaders who held these religious views.

*House of Lords:* From 1640 to 1696.[11]

---

[1] In addition he held the manors of Nateby in Kirkby Stephen, Westmorland, and of Healaugh in York. G.E.C., *Peerage,* XII, Pt. 2, 602–606.

[2] Dale, *The Good Lord Wharton,* p. 67.

[3] Add. MSS, 36,916, fol. 916 (Mar., 1670); Dale, *The Good Lord Wharton,* pp. 45–46; Baxter, Pt. III, pp. 156–57; *H.M.C., Leeds MSS,* p. 15; Calamy, *Acct.,* II, 43; Matthews, pp. 279–80; Carte MSS, 228, fol. 167.

[4] Add. MSS, 18,730, fols. 85–86; Rawl. Ltrs., H 51, fol. 121.

[5] Calamy, *Acct.,* II [99]; *Cont.,* II, 710. Birch seems to have been with Wharton at least in 1665 and 1666.

[6] Gordon, p. 237; Rawl. Ltrs., H 51, fol. 121; H 53, fol. 105; Matthews, p. 479.

[7] Matthews, pp. 182, 216; Matthews, "The Wharton Correspondence," *C.H.S.T.,* X (Sept., 1927), 56.

[8] Calamy, *Acct.,* II, 820; Thoresby, *Diary,* I, 151n.; Matthews, 47.

[9] Calamy, *Acct.,* II, 720, 811; Bryan Dale and T. G. Crippen, "The Ancient Meeting-house at Ravenstonedale," *C.H.S.T.,* III (May, 1907), 93.

[10] *Ibid.,* p. 92; Matthews, p. 400; Rawl. Ltrs., H 51, fol. 77; J. Hay Colligan, "Nonconformity in Cumberland and Westmorland," *C.H.S.T.,* III (Feb., 1908), 217; Nightingale, *The Ejected of 1662 in Cumberland and Westmorland,* II, 1107–1109.

[11] G.E.C., *Peerage,* XII, 603.

# APPENDIX III

*Tabulation by Year of the Presbyterians and Congregationalists Sitting in the House of Commons, 1661–1689*

*Legend:*

—   Presbyterian or Congregationalist

······   Probable Presbyterian or Congregationalist

- - -   Possible Presbyterian or Congregationalist

V   Election voided

D   Died

T   Temporary Presbyterian or Congregationalist

*Note:* For purposes of this tabulation the durations of the three Exclusion Parliaments are considered to have been coincident with the years 1679, 1680, and 1681 respectively.

| | 1661 | 1662 | 1663 | 1664 | 1665 | 1666 | 1667 | 1668 | 1669 | 1670 | 1671 | 1672 | 1673 | 1674 | 1675 | 1676 | 1677 | 1678 | 1679 | 1680 | 1681 | 1685 | 1689 |
|---|---|---|---|---|---|---|---|---|---|---|---|---|---|---|---|---|---|---|---|---|---|---|---|
| Ashton, R. | | V | | | | | | | | | | | | | | | | | | D | | | |
| Ashurst, H. | | | | | | | | | | | | | | | | | | | | | | | |
| Ashurst, W. | | | | | | | | | | | | | | | | | | | | | | | |
| Barnardiston, S. | | T | | | | | | | | | | | | | | | | | | | | | |
| Barnham, R. | | | | | | | | | | | | | | | | | | | | | | | |
| Barrington, J. | | | | | | | | | | | | | | | | | | | | | | | |
| Bastard, W. | | | | | | | | | | | | | | T | | | | | | | | | |
| Birch, J. | | | | | | | | | | | | | | | | | | | | | | | |
| Boscawen, E. | | | | | | | | | | | | | | | | | | | | | | | |
| Boscawen, H. | | | | | | | | | | | | | | | | | | | | | | | |
| Braman, J. | | | | | | | | | | | | | | | | | | | | | | | |
| Bulkeley, J. | | | | | | | | | | | | | | | | | | | | | | | |

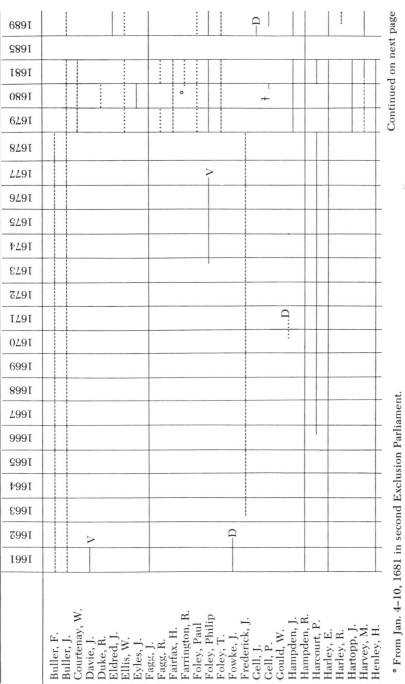

Continued on next page

° From Jan. 4–10, 1681 in second Exclusion Parliament.
† From Jan. 3–10 in second Exclusion Parliament.

Appendix III (Continued)

| | 1661 | 1662 | 1663 | 1664 | 1665 | 1666 | 1667 | 1668 | 1669 | 1670 | 1671 | 1672 | 1673 | 1674 | 1675 | 1676 | 1677 | 1678 | 1679 | 1680 | 1681 | 1685 | 1689 |
|---|---|---|---|---|---|---|---|---|---|---|---|---|---|---|---|---|---|---|---|---|---|---|---|
| Herle, E. | | | | | | | | | | | | | | | | | | | | | | | |
| Hewley, J. | | | | | | | | | | | | | | | | | | | | | | | |
| Hobart, H. | | | | | | | | | | | | | | | | | | | | | | | |
| Hoghton, C. | | | | | | | | | | | | | | | | | | | | | | | |
| Ingoldsby, R. | | | | | | | | | | | | | | | | | | | | | | | |
| Irby, A. | | | | | | | | | | | | | | | | | | | | | | | |
| Jones, J. | | | | | | | | | | | | | | | | | | | | | | | |
| Keate, J. | | | | | | | | | | | | | | | | | | | | | | | |
| Langham, J. | V | —V | | | | T | | | | | | | | | | | | | | | | | |
| Lee, T. | | | | | | | | | | | | | | | | | | | | | | | |
| Love, W. | | | | | T | | | | | | | | | | | | | | | | | | |
| Manley, J. | | | | | | | | | | | | | | | | | | | | | | | |
| Massey, E. | | | | | | | | | | | | | | | | | | | | | | | |
| Maynard, J. | | | | | | | | | | | | | | | | | D | | | | | | |
| Moore, T. | | | | | | | | | | | | | | | | | | | | | | | |
| Morice, W. | | | | | | | | D | | | | | | | | | | | | | | | |
| Morley, H. | | | | | | | | | | | | | | | | | | | | | | | |
| Norton, R. | | | | | | | | | | | | | | | | | | | | | | | |
| Nosworthy, E. | | V | | | | | | | | | | | | | | | | | | | | | |
| Nosworthy, E., Jr. | | | | D | | | | | | | | | | | | | | | | | | | |
| Onslow, R. | | | | | | | | | | | | | | | | | | | | | | | |
| Owen, T. | | | | | | | | | | | | | | | | | | | | | | | |
| Papillon, T. | | | | | | | | D | | | | | | | | | | | | | | | |
| Popham, A. | | | | | | | | D | | | | | | | | | | | | | | | |
| Prideaux, E. | | | | | | | | | | | | | | | | | | | | | | | |
| Prynne, W. | | | | | | | | | | | | | | | | | | | | | | | |
| Pynsent, W. | | | | | | | | | | | | | | | | | | | | | | | |
| Ratcliffe, J. | | | | | | | | | | | | | | | | | | | | | | | |
| Reynel, T. | | | | | | | | | | | | | | | | | | | | | | | |
| Rich, P. | | | | | | | | | | | | | D | | | | | | | | | | —D |
| Rolle, F. | | | | | | | | | | V | | | | | | | | | | | | | |

| | 1661 | 1662 | 1663 | 1664 | 1665 | 1666 | 1667 | 1668 | 1669 | 1670 | 1671 | 1672 | 1673 | 1674 | 1675 | 1676 | 1677 | 1678 | 1679 | 1680 | 1681 | 1685 | 1689 |
|---|---|---|---|---|---|---|---|---|---|---|---|---|---|---|---|---|---|---|---|---|---|---|---|
| Rushworth, J. | | | | | | | | | | | | | | | | | | | | | | | |
| Russell, E. | | | | | | | | | | | | | | | | | | | | | | | |
| St. John, O. | | | | | | | | | | | | | | | | | | | | | | | D |
| Stapely, J. | | | | | | | | | | | | | | | | | | | | | | | |
| Strode, W. | | | | | | | | | | | | | | | | | | | | | | | |
| Swynfen, J. | | | | | | | | | | | | | | | | | | | | | | | |
| Thompson, J. | | | | | | | | | | | | | | | | | | | | | | | |
| Thompson, W. | | | | | | | | | | | | | | | | | | | | | | | |
| Thurbarne | | | | | | | | | | | | | | | | | | | | | | | |
| Trenchard, J. | | | | | | | | | | | | | | | | | | | | | | | |
| Trenchard, T. | | | | | | | | | | D | | | | | | | | | | | | | |
| Trenchard, W. | | | | | | | | | | | | | | | | | | | | | | | |
| Upton, J. | | | | | | | | | | | | | | | | | | | | | | | |
| Vaughan, E. | | | | | | | | | | | | | | | | | | | | | | | |
| Waller, E. | | | | | | | | | | | | | | | | | | | | | | | |
| Waller, W. | | | | D | | | | | | | | | | | | | | | | | | | |
| White, J. | | | | | | | | | | | | | | | | | | | | | | | |
| Widdrington, T. | | | | | | | | | | | | | | | | | | | | | | | |
| Wilbraham, T. | | | | | | | | | | | | | | | | | | | | | | | |
| Winwood, R. | D | | | | | | | | | D | | | | | | | | | | | | | |
| Yonge, W., II | | | | | | | | | | | | | | | | | | | | | | | |
| Yonge, W., III | | | | | | | | | | | | | | | | | | | | | | | |
| **TOTALS** | 37 | 34 | 30 | 30 | 29 | 29 | 29 | 28 | 27 | 28 | 27 | 25 | 26 | 25 | 27 | 27 | 26 | 25 | 42 | 52 | 46 | 4 | 35‡ |

‡ See Chapter X, note 57. No more than thirty-three sat at any one time.

*Note:* This list of Presbyterians and Congregationalists sitting in the House of Commons is not complete and definitive. The totals are given so that the general trend throughout the approximately thirty-year period can be seen.

## Bibliographical Note on Manuscript Sources

The major manuscript sources for the politico-religious activities
of Dissenters who were involved in parliamentary politics are relatively few in number. The papers of Lord Wharton in the Carte
and Rawlinson Collections of the Bodleian Library are the best
known of these sources, but Roger Morrice's "Entr'ing Book" (MSS
P, Q, and R) in the Dr. Williams's Library is another of the rich-
est collections of material, particularly some of the sections that
were left in untranscribed shorthand. The correspondence of John
Swynfen now in the Staffordshire Record Office and the British
Museum Additional Manuscripts, along with the papers of Sir
Edward Harley in the Portland Manuscripts now on loan to the
British Museum are of less scope and volume; but they reveal the
close political and religious connections that existed among the
Hampdens, the Foleys, and the Harleys and Swynfen, as well as
the intermarriages and close relationships that continued thereafter among the first three of these families. In addition, these
collections contain information concerning some of the connections these leaders had with others among the Presbyterian-Congregationalist group in Parliament and with ministers of these
two persuasions. Although more personal, the diary of the Earl of
Anglesey in the British Museum Additional Manuscripts contains
similar information, as well as a revealing account of his own
religious life and the problems of the only moderate Presbyterian
who held high office under Charles II.

In another category of valuable manuscript sources are the reports of ambassadors at the Court of St. James's, notably those of
the French ambassadors throughout the three decades. They are
most conveniently used in the Bashet Transcripts at the Public
Record Office, but on occasion they need to be supplemented by

dispatches from the French Court which for most of the period are found only in the Archives des Affaires Étrangères, Quai d'Orsay. Also valuable for the critical years 1685–1688 are the reports of Dutch Ambassadors and official envoys, transcripts of which are found in the British Museum Additional Manuscripts (Mackintosh Collection). The intelligence letters of James Johnston, secret agent of the United Provinces and assistant to Henry Sidney from late 1687 to the summer of 1688, are particularly rich and describe Johnston's efforts to win over Nonconformists who were supporting James II, particularly William Penn, and also his use of John Hampden who supported the cause of William from December, 1688. The complete file of originals and deciphered transcripts of these reports are in the Portland Manuscripts on loan to the University of Nottingham.

Of the four major Nonconformist Church organizations only the Society of Friends consistently kept records, and the extensive manuscript collection in the Library at Friends House, London, contains valuable information, notably the Book of Cases and the minutes of the London Meeting for Sufferings.

The final category of major manuscript sources is of an official nature. Government sources of most importance are the State Papers Domestic of the three reigns from 1661 through 1689, and also the Privy Council Register, at the Public Record Office. In addition the correspondence of the Archbishop of Canterbury and the bishops in the Tanner Manuscripts, Bodleian Library, has valuable information regarding the Dissenters' political activities upon important occasions.

MANUSCRIPTS CITED

I. Dr. Williams's Library
    Roger Morrice Collection
        MSS P, Q, and R, "The Entr'ing Book, Being an Historical Register of Occurrences from April, Anno 1677, to April, 1691"
        MS U, "Outline of First Sketch for the Politico-Ecclesiastical History of England"
    Richard Baxter's Manuscripts, Letters
    Harmer MSS, Church Records transcribed by Joseph Davey, 1846–1848

The Church Book Belonging to a Society of Christians
. . . at the Old Meeting in Norwich. MS No. 1
The Entire Records of the Congregational Church at
Great Yarmouth. (1642–1813) MS No. 2
A Register or Church Book . . . Church of Christ . . .
in and about Guestwick. MS No. 6

II. The Library at Friends' House, London
The Book of Cases, Vol. I, 1661–1695
Meeting for Sufferings Minutes, Vols. I–VII, 1675–1690
Morning Meeting Minutes, Vol. I, 1673–1692
Six Weeks Meeting Minutes, Vols. I, II, 1671–1692
Yearly Meeting Minutes, Vol. I, 1668–1693
Original Records of Sufferings
Penn MSS, Portfolios 1–41
Bristol MSS, Vols. I–V, Letters and Papers of George Fox
and Other Early Friends

III. Bodleian Library
Carte MSS, Vols. 66, 72, 77, 79–81, 228. Correspondence
and Parliamentary Papers of Philip, Lord Wharton
Clarendon MSS, Vol. 72. Correspondence of Edward
Hyde, Earl of Clarendon, April 21–30, 1660
Rawlinson Letters, Vols. 49–54, 104, 109, 110. Correspondence between Philip, Lord Wharton and Nonconformist ministers; and letters of John Thornton,
chaplain to the Earl of Bedford
Tanner MSS, Vols. 27–45. Correspondence of the Archbishop of Canterbury

IV. British Museum
Additional MSS
18,730 } Diary of Arthur Annesley, { 1667–1675
40,860 } Earl of Anglesey          { 1675–1684
29,910 } Correspondence and Papers of John Swynfen
30,013 }
34,508 } Dutch Political Correspondence Relating to
34,510 }   England, from 1685–1688, from the Mackin-
34,512 }   tosh Collection of Transcripts
15,857 }
32,675 } Miscellaneous letters and papers
35,865 }

34,546 ⎫
34,522 ⎬ Vivian Collection (Abstracts of Devon and
34,810 ⎭ Cornwall wills)

36,709 Bradburn and Sevenoaks Church Book, 1671–
1802

Egerton MSS

2043 Diary of Col. Bullen Reames, 1661–1662

2050 Barrington Papers

3345 Leeds MSS (Danby's notes of Jan. 29, 1689 debate)

3346 Leeds MSS (Boscawen's statement in April 11, 1677 debate)

Lansdowne MSS, 1152 (Material on Monmouth Rebellion)

Loan 29 Portland Manuscripts (The papers of Robert Harley, Earl of Oxford, on loan from the Duke of Portland)

Sloane MSS, 3299 and 4107

Stowe MSS, 185, 304, and 747

V. Public Record Office

P.C.2, Privy Council Register, vols. 54–73

P.R.O.30/24, Papers of the Earl of Shaftesbury

P.R.O.31/3, Bashet Transcripts of Correspondence Politique, Angleterre, Archives des Affaires Étrangères, Quai d'Orsay. Vols. 106–174

S.P. 29, 30, 31, State Papers Domestic, Charles II, James II, and William and Mary

VI. House of Lords Record Office

Main Papers, 1661–1690

Manuscript Minutes of Committees, 1661–1690

VII. Somerset House

Returns of Certificates Issued under the Toleration Act, 1689–1852

Wills Proved in the Prerogative Court of Canterbury

VIII. Guildhall Library, London

Corporation of London Records Office, Chamber Accounts 40/35 (Loan of 1688/89 Posting Book)

MS 592, White's Alley Church Book

IX. Other Libraries and Archives

Archives des Affaires Étrangères, Quai d'Orsay

Correspondence Politique, Angleterre, 1677–1681.
Tomes 122–142
Folger Shakespeare Library
Newdigate Newsletters
Inner Temple Library
MS 538–32, The Reading of William Prynne at Gray's
Inn, Feb. 17, 1661/62
Leicestershire Record Office
Finch Manuscripts, Political Papers
Library of Congress
Claydon House, Verney MSS (Microfilm copy)
National Register of Archives: Cornwall
Carew-Pole MSS, Antony, Cornwall, Vol. II. The Buller
Family Records
University of Nottingham
Portland Manuscripts, Letters of James Johnston, 1687–
1688
John Rylands Library
Pink MSS
Staffordshire Record Office
Swynfen Correspondence, formerly in the William Salt
Library
Yale University
Aiken transcripts of Finch Manuscripts
X. Personally Owned Manuscripts
Duke of Devonshire
Notebook of George Saville, first Marquess of Halifax,
known as "Devonshire House Notebook"
Doreen, Lady Brabourne
Parliamentary Diary of Sir Edward Dering
Albert Cook Myers Collection of William Penn Papers
In the custody of the Chester County Historical Soci-
ety, West Chester, Pennsylvania

# Index

Morrice, Roger (cont.)
   sacramental test, 233–34; on the
   Sharp case, 177, 339n4; on
   Strode, 443; Test Acts repeal is-
   sue and, 192, 199, 218, 355n25;
   on Thompson, 448; Toleration
   Act and, 237, 365n106; on Tri-
   ennial Act, 39; on Waller, 454;
   on William of Orange, 186, 187,
   217, 220, 221–22, 347n76, 356–
   nn41–48, 397
Morval, Cornwall, 386
Moston, Ambrose, 473
Motheway, Carmarthen, 431
Musgrave, Sir Christopher, 233
Musgrave, Sir Philip, 298n47
Mutiny Bill, 421

Nether Burgate, Hampshire, 385
Neutralism, *see* Quietism
Newcastle, John Holles, first Duke
   of, 160, 274n57; quoted, 27
Newcastle-under-Lyme, Stafford-
   shire, 306n12
Newcome, Henry, 273n43, 287n48,
   375, 379; cited, 284nn16, 18–19,
   305n5, 334n50, 367n1; quoted,
   19, 34, 51, 66, 162–63, 219, 220,
   221, 247, 413
Newport Treaty (1648), *see* Isle of
   Wight Proposals
Newport Pagnel, Buckinghamshire,
   459
Newton, Hampshire, 378
Newton Abbot, Devon, 387
New Windsor, Berkshire, 457
Nicholson, Francis, 274n54
Nineteen Propositions (1642), *xiii*,
   127, 252
Nocton, Lincolnshire, 110, 390
Nonconformists, *xii, xv*, 15–28, 100,
   269nn43; number of clergy resist-
   ing the oaths, 55; Declaration of
   Indulgence (1672), reception by,
   65–70, 73, 248; evidence of, 369–
   72; James II and, *xiv*, 150, 175–

208, 209–15, 249–50, 376, 384;
   Monmouth and, 170–74, 214,
   249; Rye House Plot and, *xiv*,
   150, 159, 160, 162, 249, 334n49;
   William of Orange invasion and,
   219–23, 250. *See also* Baptists;
   Congregationalists; Presbyterians;
   Quakers; Act of Uniformity; Con-
   venticle Acts; St. Bartholomew's
   Day
Non-resisting or Anglican Test Bill,
   72, 76, 77–78, 372
Norfolk County, 104, 110, 350n96,
   412, 450
North, Francis, Chief Justice, 145
Northallerton, Yorkshire, 113, 114
Northamptonshire, 417
Northern Plot, 38, 279n43
Northumberland, Algernon Percy,
   Earl of, 7, 9, 265n20, 266n23,
   473
Northumberland, 440, 441, 455
*Norton, Col. Richard*, 44, 218, 277–
   n15, 321n41, 354n24, 385, 427–
   28
Norwich, Norfolk, 377n2, 412
Norwich, Bishop of, *see* Reynolds,
   Edward, bishop of Norwich
*Nosworthy, Edward, Sr.*, 279n41,
   350n100, 352n102, 428–29
Nosworthy, Edward, Jr., 429–30
Nosworthy, John, 429n6
Nott, John, 402
Nottingham, Daniel Finch, second
   Earl of, 232, 234, 235, 236, 294–
   n15, 322n53, 360n82, 361n92;
   on Bill for Restoring the Corpora-
   tions (1689), 240–41, 365n116;
   quoted, 83, 304n119
Nottingham, Nottinghamshire, 152
Nottinghamshire, 160, 454; Dis-
   senter M. P., 455
Nye, Henry: cited, 271n16, 290n84;
   quoted, 17
Nye, Philip, 20, 274n54, 460; cited,
   17, 27, 263n4, 271nn14–15, 305–